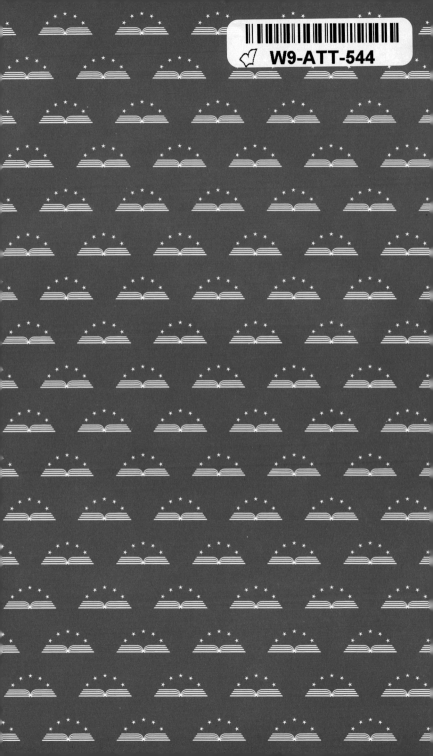

ABRAHAM LINCOLN

ABRAHAM LINCOLN

SPEECHES AND WRITINGS
1832–1858

Speeches, Letters, and Miscellaneous Writings
The Lincoln-Douglas Debates

THE LIBRARY OF AMERICA

The texts in this volume are from THE COLLECTED WORKS OF
ABRAHAM LINCOLN, edited by Roy P. Basler, copyright © 1953
by the Abraham Lincoln Association, and THE COLLECTED WORKS
OF ABRAHAM LINCOLN SUPPLEMENT 1832–1865, copyright © 1974
by Roy P Basler. Reprinted by permission of
Rutgers University Press.

The paper used in this publication meets the
minimum requirements of the American National Standard for
Information Sciences—Permanence of Paper for Printed
Library Materials, ANSI Z39.48–1984.

Distributed to the trade in the United States
by Penguin Putnam Inc. and
in Canada by Penguin Books Canada Ltd.

Library of Congress Catalog Card Number: 89–2362
For cataloging information, see end of Index.
ISBN 978–0–940450–43–1
ISBN 0–940450–43–7

Thirteenth Printing
The Library of America—45

Manufactured in the United States of America

DON E. FEHRENBACHER
WROTE THE NOTES AND SELECTED
THE CONTENTS FOR THIS VOLUME

The publishers wish to thank the Illinois State Historical Library, the Lincoln Legals Project of the Illinois Historic Preservation Agency, and the Illinois State Historical Society for the use of Abraham Lincoln materials.

Contents

To the People of Sangamo County

To the People of Sangamo County

FELLOW-CITIZENS: Having become a candidate for the honorable office of one of your representatives in the next General Assembly of this state, in accordance with an established custom, and the principles of true republicanism, it becomes my duty to make known to you—the people whom I propose to represent—my sentiments with regard to local affairs.

Time and experience have verified to a demonstration, the public utility of internal improvements. That the poorest and most thinly populated countries would be greatly benefitted by the opening of good roads, and in the clearing of navigable streams within their limits, is what no person will deny. But yet it is folly to undertake works of this or any other kind, without first knowing that we are able to finish them—as half finished work generally proves to be labor lost. There cannot justly be any objection to having rail roads and canals, any more than to other good things, provided they cost nothing. The only objection is to paying for them; and the objection to paying arises from the want of ability to pay.

With respect to the county of Sangamo, some more easy means of communication than we now possess, for the purpose of facilitating the task of exporting the surplus products of its fertile soil, and importing necessary articles from abroad, are indispensably necessary. A meeting has been held of the citizens of Jacksonville, and the adjacent country, for the purpose of deliberating and enquiring into the expediency of constructing a rail road from some eligible point on the Illinois river, through the town of Jacksonville, in Morgan county, to the town of Springfield, in Sangamo county. This is, indeed, a very desirable object. No other improvement that reason will justify us in hoping for, can equal in utility the rail road. It is a never failing source of communication, between places of business remotely situated from each other. Upon the rail road the regular progress of commercial intercourse is not interrupted by either high or low water, or freezing weather, which are the principal difficulties that render our future hopes of water communication precarious and un-

certain. Yet, however desirable an object the construction of a
rail road through our country may be; however high our
imaginations may be heated at thoughts of it—there is always
a heart appalling shock accompanying the account of its cost,
which forces us to shrink from our pleasing anticipations. The
probable cost of this contemplated rail road is estimated at
$290,000;—the bare statement of which, in my opinion, is
sufficient to justify the belief, that the improvement of Sangamo river is an object much better suited to our infant
resources.

Respecting this view, I think I may say, without the fear of
being contradicted, that its navigation may be rendered completely practicable, as high as the mouth of the South Fork, or
probably higher, to vessels of from 25 to 30 tons burthen, for
at least one half of all common years, and to vessels of much
greater burthen a part of that time. From my peculiar circumstances, it is probable that for the last twelve months I have
given as particular attention to the stage of the water in this
river, as any other person in the country. In the month of
March, 1831, in company with others, I commenced the building of a flat boat on the Sangamo, and finished and took her
out in the course of the spring. Since that time, I have been
concerned in the mill at New Salem. These circumstances are
sufficient evidence, that I have not been very inattentive to the
stages of the water. The time at which we crossed the mill
dam, being in the last days of April, the water was lower than
it had been since the breaking of winter in February, or than
it was for several weeks after. The principal difficulties we
encountered in descending the river, were from the drifted
timber, which obstructions all know is not difficult to be removed. Knowing almost precisely the height of water at that
time, I believe I am safe in saying that it has as often been
higher as lower since.

From this view of the subject, it appears that my calculations with regard to the navigation of the Sangamo, cannot
be unfounded in reason; but whatever may be its natural advantages, certain it is, that it never can be practically useful
to any great extent, without being greatly improved by art.
The drifted timber, as I have before mentioned, is the most
formidable barrier to this object. Of all parts of this river,

none will require so much labor in proportion, to make it navigable, as the last thirty or thirty-five miles; and going with the meanderings of the channel, when we are this distance above its mouth, we are only between twelve and eighteen miles above Beardstown, in something near a straight direction; and this route is upon such low ground as to retain water in many places during the season, and in all parts such as to draw two-thirds or three-fourths of the river water at all high stages.

This route is upon prairie land the whole distance; — so that it appears to me, by removing the turf, a sufficient width and damming up the old channel, the whole river in a short time would wash its way through, thereby curtailing the distance, and increasing the velocity of the current very considerably, while there would be no timber upon the banks to obstruct its navigation in future; and being nearly straight, the timber which might float in at the head, would be apt to go clear through. There are also many places above this where the river, in its zig zag course, forms such complete peninsulas, as to be easier cut through at the necks than to remove the obstructions from the bends — which if done, would also lessen the distance.

What the cost of this work would be, I am unable to say. It is probable, however, it would not be greater than is common to streams of the same length. Finally, I believe the improvement of the Sangamo river, to be vastly important and highly desirable to the people of this county; and if elected, any measure in the legislature having this for its object, which may appear judicious, will meet my approbation, and shall receive my support.

It appears that the practice of loaning money at exorbitant rates of interest, has already been opened as a field for discussion; so I suppose I may enter upon it without claiming the honor, or risking the danger, which may await its first explorer. It seems as though we are never to have an end to this baneful and corroding system, acting almost as prejudicial to the general interests of the community as a direct tax of several thousand dollars annually laid on each county, for the benefit of a few individuals only, unless there be a law made setting a limit to the rates of usury. A law for this purpose, I am of opinion, may be made, without materially injuring any class of people. In cases of extreme necessity there could always be means found to cheat the law, while in all other cases it would have its intended effect. I would not favor the passage of a law upon this subject, which might be very easily evaded. Let it be such that the labor and difficulty of evading it, could only be justified in cases of the greatest necessity.

Upon the subject of education, not presuming to dictate any plan or system respecting it, I can only say that I view it as the most important subject which we as a people can be engaged in. That every man may receive at least, a moderate education, and thereby be enabled to read the histories of his own and other countries, by which he may duly appreciate the value of our free institutions, appears to be an object of vital importance, even on this account alone, to say nothing of the advantages and satisfaction to be derived from all being able to read the scriptures and other works, both of a religious and moral nature, for themselves. For my part, I desire to see the time when education, and by its means, morality, sobriety, enterprise and industry, shall become much more general than at present, and should be gratified to have it in my power to contribute something to the advancement of any measure which might have a tendency to accelerate the happy period.

With regard to existing laws, some alterations are thought to be necessary. Many respectable men have suggested that our estray laws—the law respecting the issuing of executions, the road law, and some others, are deficient in their present form, and require alterations. But considering the great probability that the framers of those laws were wiser than myself, I should prefer not meddling with them, unless they were first attacked by others, in which case I should feel it both a privilege and a duty to take that stand, which in my view, might tend most to the advancement of justice.

But, Fellow-Citizens, I shall conclude. Considering the great degree of modesty which should always attend youth, it is probable I have already been more presuming than becomes me. However, upon the subjects of which I have treated, I have spoken as I thought. I may be wrong in regard to any or all of them; but holding it a sound maxim, that it is better to be only sometimes right, than at all times wrong, so soon as I discover my opinions to be erroneous, I shall be ready to renounce them.

Every man is said to have his peculiar ambition. Whether it be true or not, I can say for one that I have no other so great as that of being truly esteemed of my fellow men, by rendering myself worthy of their esteem. How far I shall succeed in gratifying this ambition, is yet to be developed. I am young and unknown to many of you. I was born and have ever remained in the most humble walks of life. I have no wealthy or popular relations to recommend me. My case is thrown exclusively upon the independent voters of this county, and if elected they will have conferred a favor upon me, for which I shall be unremitting in my labors to compensate. But if the good people in their wisdom shall see fit to keep me in the background, I have been too familiar with disappointments to be very much chagrined. Your friend and fellow-citizen,

New Salem, March 9, 1832.

To the Editor of the Sangamo Journal

To the Editor of the Journal: New Salem, June 13, 1836.

In your paper of last Saturday, I see a communication over the signature of "Many Voters," in which the candidates who are announced in the Journal, are called upon to "show their hands." Agreed. Here's mine!

I go for all sharing the privileges of the government, who assist in bearing its burthens. Consequently I go for admitting all whites to the right of suffrage, who pay taxes or bear arms, (by no means excluding females.)

If elected, I shall consider the whole people of Sangamon my constituents, as well those that oppose, as those that support me.

While acting as their representative, I shall be governed by their will, on all subjects upon which I have the means of knowing what their will is; and upon all others, I shall do what my own judgment teaches me will best advance their interests. Whether elected or not, I go for distributing the proceeds of the sales of the public lands to the several states, to enable our state, in common with others, to dig canals and construct rail roads, without borrowing money and paying interest on it.

If alive on the first Monday in November, I shall vote for Hugh L. White for President. Very respectfully,

To Robert Allen

Dear Col.   New Salem, June 21. 1836

I am told that during my absence last week, you passed through this place, and stated publicly, that you were in possession of a fact or facts, which, if known to the public, would entirely destroy the prospects of N. W. Edwards and myself at the ensuing election; but that, through favour to us, you should forbear to divulge them.

No one has needed favours more than I, and generally, few have been less unwilling to accept them; but in this case, favour to me, would be injustice to the public, and therefore I must beg your pardon for declining it. That I once had the confidence of the people of Sangamon, is sufficiently evident, and if I have since done any thing, either by design or misadventure, which if known, would subject me to a forfeiture of that confidence, he that knows of that thing, and conceals it, is a traitor to his country's interest.

I find myself wholly unable to form any conjecture of what fact or facts, real or supposed, you spoke; but my opinion of your veracity, will not permit me, for a moment, to doubt, that you at least believed what you said.

I am flattered with the personal regard you manifested for me, but I do hope that, on more mature reflection, you will view the public interest as a paramount consideration, and, therefore, determine to let the worst come.

I here assure you, that the candid statement of facts, on your part, however low it may sink me, shall never break the tie of personal friendship between us.

I wish an answer to this, and you are at liberty to publish both if you choose   Verry Respectfully,

To Mary S. Owens

Mary   Vandalia, Decr. 13 1836

I have been sick ever since my arrival here, or I should have written sooner. It is but little difference, however, as I have verry little even yet to write. And more, the longer I can avoid the mortification of looking in the Post Office for your letter and not finding it, the better. You see I am mad about that *old letter* yet. I dont like verry well to risk you again. I'll try you once more any how.

The new State House is not yet finished, and consequently the legislature is doing little or nothing. The Governor delivered an inflamitory political Message, and it is expected there will be some sparring between the parties about it as soon as the two Houses get to business. Taylor delivered up his petitions for the *New County* to one of our members this morning. I am told that he dispairs of its success on account of all the members from Morgan County opposing it. There are names enough on the petitions, I think, to justify the members from our county in going for it; but if the members from Morgan oppose it, which they say they will, the chance will be bad.

Our chance to take the seat of Government to Springfield is better than I expected. An Internal Improvement Convention was held here since we met, which recommended a loan of several millions of dollars on the faith of the State to construct Rail Roads. Some of the legislature are for it, and some against it; which has the majority I can not tell. There is great strife and struggling for the office of U.S. Senator here at this time. It is probable we shall ease their pains in a few days. The opposition men have no candidate of their own, and consequently they smile as complacently at the angry snarls of the contending Van Buren candidates and their respective friends, as the christian does at Satan's rage. You recollect I mentioned in the outset of this letter that I had been unwell. That is the fact, though I believe I am about well now; but that, with other things I can not account for, have conspired and have gotten my spirits so low, that I feel that I would rather be any place in the world than here. I really can not endure the thought of staying here ten weeks. Write back as soon as you get this, and if possible say something that will please me, for really I have not been pleased since I left you. This letter is so dry and stupid that I am ashamed to send it, but with my present feelings I can not do any better. Give my respects to Mr. and Mrs. Abell and family. Your friend

Speech in the Illinois Legislature
on the State Bank

REMARKS OF MR. LINCOLN,

In the House of Representatives, upon the resolution offered
by Mr. Linder, to institute an enquiry into the management
of the affairs of the State Bank.

MR. CHAIRMAN: Lest I should fall into the too common
error, of being mistaken in regard to which side I design to be
upon, I shall make it my first care to remove all doubt on that
point, by declaring that I am opposed to the resolution under
consideration, in toto. Before I proceed to the body of the
subject, I will further remark, that it is not without a considerable degree of apprehension, that I venture to cross the
track of the gentleman from Coles (Mr. Linder). Indeed, I do
not believe I could muster a sufficiency of courage to come in
contact with that gentleman, were it not for the fact, that he,
some days since, most graciously condescended to assure us
that he would never be found wasting ammunition on *small
game*. On the same fortunate occasion, he further gave us to
understand, that he regarded *himself* as being decidedly the
superior of our common friend from Randolph (Mr. Shields);
and feeling, as I really do, that I, to say the most of myself,
am nothing more than the peer of our friend from Randolph,
I shall regard the gentleman from Coles as decidedly my superior also, and consequently, in the course of what I shall have
to say, whenever I shall have occasion to allude to that gentleman, I shall endeavor to adopt that kind of court language
which I understand to be due to *decided superiority*. In one
faculty, at least, there can be no dispute of the gentleman's
superiority over me, and most other men; and that is, the
faculty of entangling a subject, so that neither himself, or any
other man, can find head or tail to it. Here he has introduced
a resolution, embracing ninety-nine printed lines across common writing paper, and yet more than one half of his opening
speech has been made upon subjects about which there is not
one word said in his resolution.

Though his resolution embraces nothing in regard to the
constitutionality of the Bank, much of what he has said has

been with a view to make the impression that it was unconstitutional in its inception. Now, although I am satisfied that an ample field may be found within the pale of the resolution, at least for small game, yet as the gentleman has travelled out of it, I feel that I may, with all due humility, venture to follow him. The gentleman has discovered that some gentleman at Washington city has been upon the very eve of deciding our Bank unconstitutional, and that he would probably have completed his very authentic decision, had not some one of the Bank officers placed his hand upon his mouth, and begged him to withhold it. The fact that the individuals composing our Supreme Court have, in an official capacity, decided in favor of the constitutionality of the Bank, would, in my mind, seem a sufficient answer to this. It is a fact known to all, that the members of the Supreme Court, together with the Governor, form a Council of Revision, and that this Council approved this Bank Charter. I ask, then, if the extra judicial decision—not quite, but only almost made, by the gentleman at Washington, before whom, by the way, the question of the constitutionality of our Bank never has, nor never can come—is to be taken as paramount to a decision officially made by that tribunal, by which and which alone, the constitutionality of the Bank can ever be settled? But aside from this view of the subject, I would ask, if the committee which this resolution proposes to appoint, are to examine into the constitutionality of the Bank? Are they to be clothed with power to send for persons and papers, for this object? And after they have found the Bank to be unconstitutional, and decided it so, how are they to enforce their decision? What will their decision amount to? They cannot compel the Bank to cease operations, or to change the course of its operations. What good, then, can their labors result in? Certainly none.

The gentleman asks, if we, without an examination, shall, by giving the State deposites to the bank, and by taking the stock reserved for the State, legalize its former misconduct? Now I do not pretend to possess sufficient legal knowledge to decide, whether a legislative enactment, proposing to, and accepting from, the Bank, certain terms, would have the effect to legalize or wipe out its former errors, or not; but I can assure the gentleman, if such should be the effect, he has already got behind the settlement of accounts; for it is well known to all, that the Legislature, at its last session, passed a supplemental Bank charter, which the Bank has since accepted, and which, according to his doctrine, has legalized all the alleged violations of its original charter in the distribution of its stock.

I now proceed to the resolution. By examination it will be found that the first thirty-three lines, being precisely one third of the whole, relate exclusively to the distribution of the stock by the commissioners appointed by the State. Now, sir, it is clear that no question can arise on this portion of the resolution, except a question between capitalists in regard to the ownership of stock. Some gentlemen have the stock in their hands, while others, who have more money than they know what to do with, want it; and this, and this alone, is the question, to settle which we are called on to squander thousands of the people's money. What interest, let me ask, have the people in the settlement of this question? What difference is it to them whether the stock is owned by Judge Smith, or Sam. Wiggins? If any gentleman be entitled to stock in the Bank, which he is kept out of possession of by others, let him assert his right in the Supreme Court, and let him or his antagonist, whichever may be found in the wrong, pay the costs of suit. It is an old maxim and a very sound one, that he that dances should always pay the fiddler. Now, sir, in the present case, if any gentlemen, whose money is a burden to them, choose to lead off a dance, I am decidedly opposed to the people's money being used to pay the fiddler. No one can doubt that the examination proposed by this resolution, must cost the State some ten or twelve thousand dollars; and all this to settle a question in which the people have no interest, and about which they care nothing. These capitalists generally act harmoniously, and in concert, to fleece the people, and now, that they have got into a quarrel with themselves, we are called upon to appropriate the people's money to settle the quarrel.

I leave this part of the resolution, and proceed to the remainder. It will be found that no charge in the remaining part of the resolution, if true, amounts to the violation of the Bank Charter, except one, which I will notice in due time. It might seem quite sufficient, to say no more upon any of these charges or insinuations, than enough to show they are not violations of the charter; yet, as they are ingeniously framed and handled, with a view to deceive and mislead, I will notice in their order, all the most prominent of them. The first of these, is in relation to a connexion between our Bank and several Banking institutions in other States. Admitting this connection to exist, I should like to see the gentleman from Coles, or any other gentleman, undertake to show that there is any harm in it. What can there be in such a connexion, that the people of Illinois are willing to pay their money to get a peep into? By a reference to the tenth section of the Bank charter, any gentleman can see that the framers of the act contemplated the holding of stock in the institutions of other corporations. Why, then, is it, when neither law nor justice forbids it, that we are asked to spend our time and money, in inquiring into its truth?

The next charge, in the order of time, is, that some officer, director, clerk or servant of the Bank, has been required to take an oath of secrecy in relation to the affairs of said Bank. Now, I do not know whether this be true or false — neither do I believe any honest man cares. I know that the seventh section of the charter expressly guarantees to the Bank the right of making, under certain restrictions, such by-laws as it may think fit; and I further know that the requiring an oath of secrecy, would not transcend those restrictions. What, then, if the Bank has chosen to exercise this right? Who can it injure? Does not every merchant have his secret mark? and who is ever silly enough to complain of it? I presume if the Bank does require any such oath of secrecy, it is done through a motive of delicacy to those individuals who deal with it. Why, sir, not many days since, one gentleman upon this floor, who, by the way I have no doubt is now ready to join this hue and cry against the Bank, indulged in a philippic against one of the Bank officers, because, as he said, he had *divulged a secret*.

Immediately following this last charge, there are several insinuations in the resolution, which are too silly to require any sort of notice, were it not for the fact, that they conclude by saying, *"to the great injury of the people at large."* In answer to this I would say, that it is strange enough, that the people are suffering these "great injuries," and yet are not sensible of it! Singular indeed that the people should be writhing under oppression and injury, and yet not one among them to be found, to raise the voice of complaint. If the Bank be inflicting injury upon the people, why is it, that not a single petition is presented to this body on the subject? If the Bank really be a grievance, why is it, that no one of the real people is found to ask redress of it? The truth is, no such oppression exists. If it did, our table would groan with memorials and petitions, and we would not be permitted to rest day or night, till we had put it down. The people know their rights; and they are never slow to assert and maintain them, when they are invaded. Let them call for an investigation, and I shall ever stand ready to respond to the call. But they have made no such call. I make the assertion boldly, and without fear of contradiction, that no man, who does not hold an office, or does not aspire to one, has ever found any fault of the Bank. It has doubled the prices of the products of their farms, and filled their pockets with a sound circulating medium, and they are all well pleased with its operations. No, Sir, it is the *politician* who is the first to sound the alarm, (which, by the way, is a false one.) It is he, who, by these unholy means, is endeavoring to blow up a storm that he may ride upon and direct. It is he, and he alone, that here proposes to spend thousands of the people's public treasure, for no other advantage to them, than to make valueless in their pockets the reward of their industry. Mr. Chairman, this movement is exclusively the work of politicians; a set of men who have interests aside from the interests of the people, and who, to say the most of them, are, taken as a mass, at least one long step removed from honest men. I say this with the greater freedom because, being a politician myself, none can regard it as personal.

Again, it is charged, or rather insinuated, that officers of the Bank have loaned money at usurious rates of interest. Suppose this to be true, are we to send a committee of this House to enquire into it? Suppose the committee should find it true can they redress the injured individuals? Assuredly not. If any individual had been injured in this way, is there not an ample remedy, to be found in the laws of the land? Does the gentleman from Coles know, that there is a statute standing in full force, making it highly penal, for an individual to loan money at a higher rate of interest than twelve per cent? If he does not he is too ignorant to be placed at the head of the committee which his resolution proposes; and if he does, his neglect to mention it, shows him to be too uncandid to merit the respect or confidence of any one.

But besides all this, if the Bank were struck from existence, could not the owners of the capital still loan it usuriously, as well as now? Whatever the Bank, or its officers, may have done, I know that usurious transactions were much more frequent and enormous, before the commencement of its operations, than they have ever been since.

The next insinuation is, that the Bank has refused specie payments. This, if true, is a violation of the charter. But there is not the least probability of its truth; because, if such had been the fact, the individual to whom payment was refused, would have had an interest in making it public, by suing for the damages to which the charter entitles him. Yet no such thing has been done; and the strong presumption is, that the insinuation is false and groundless.

From this to the end of the resolution, there is nothing that merits attention—I therefore drop the particular examination of it.

By a general view of the resolution, it will be seen that a principal object of the committee is, to examine into, and ferret out, a mass of corruption, supposed to have been committed by the commissioners who apportioned the stock of the Bank. I believe it is universally understood and acknowledged, that all men will ever act correctly, unless they have a motive to do otherwise. If this be true, we can only suppose that the commissioners acted corruptly, by also supposing that they were bribed to do so. Taking this view of the subject, I would ask if the Bank is likely to find it more difficult to bribe the committee of seven, which we are about to appoint, than it may have found it to bribe the commissioners?

(Here Mr. Linder called to order. The Chair decided that Mr. Lincoln was not out of order. Mr. Linder appealed to the House; but before the question was put, withdrew his appeal, saying, he preferred to let the gentleman go on; he thought he would break his own neck. Mr. Lincoln proceeded) —

Another *gracious condescension*. I acknowledge it with gratitude. I know I was not out of order; and I know every sensible man in the House knows it. I was not saying that the gentleman from Coles could not be bribed, nor, on the other hand, will I say he could. In that particular, I leave him where I found him. I was only endeavoring to show that there was at least as great a probability of *any* seven members that could be selected from this House, being bribed to act corruptly, as there was, that the twenty-four commissioners had been so bribed. By a reference to the ninth section of the Bank charter, it will be seen that those commissioners were John Tilson, Robert K. McLaughlin, Daniel Wann, A. G. S. Wight, John C. Riley, W. H. Davidson, Edward M. Wilson, Edward L. Pierson, Robert R. Green, Ezra Baker, Aquilla Wren, John Taylor, Samuel C. Christy, Edmund Roberts, Benjamin Godfrey, Thomas Mather, A. M. Jenkins, W. Linn, W. S. Gilman, Charles Prentice, Richard J. Hamilton, A. H. Buckner, W. F. Thornton, and Edmund D. Taylor.

These are twenty-four of the most respectable men in the State. Probably no twenty-four men could be selected in the State, with whom the people are better acquainted, or in whose honor and integrity, they would more readily place confidence. And I now repeat, that there is less probability that those men have been bribed and corrupted, than that *any* seven men, or rather any *six* men, that could be selected from the members of this House, might be so bribed and corrupted; even though they were headed and led on by "decided superiority" himself.

In all seriousness, I ask every reasonable man, if an issue be joined by these twenty-four commissioners, on the one part, and *any* other seven men, on the other part, and the whole depend upon the honor and integrity of the contending parties, to which party would the greatest degree of credit be due? Again: Another consideration is, that we have no right to make the examination. What I shall say upon this head, I design exclusively for the law-loving and law-abiding part of the House. To those who claim omnipotence for the Legislature, and who in the plenitude of their assumed powers, are disposed to disregard the Constitution, law, good faith, moral right, and every thing else, I have not a word to say. But to the law-abiding part I say, examine the Bank charter, go examine the Constitution; go examine the acts that the General Assembly of this State has passed, and you will find just as much authority given in each and every of them, to compel the Bank to bring its coffers to this hall, and to pour their contents upon this floor, as to compel it to submit to this examination which this resolution proposes. Why, sir, the gentleman from Coles, the mover of this resolution, very lately denied on this floor, that the Legislature had any right to repeal, or otherwise meddle with its own acts, when those acts were made in the nature of contracts, and had been accepted and acted on by other parties. Now I ask, if this resolution does not propose, for this House alone, to do, what he, but the other day, denied the right of the whole Legislature to do? He must either abandon the position he then took, or he must now vote against his own resolution. It is no difference to me, and I presume but little to any one else, which he does.

I am by no means the special advocate of the Bank. I have long thought that it would be well for it to report its condition to the General Assembly, and that cases might occur, when it might be proper to make an examination of its affairs by a committee. Accordingly, during the last session, while a bill supplemental to the Bank charter, was pending before the House, I offered an amendment to the same, in these words: "The said corporation shall, at the next session of the General Assembly, and at each subsequent General Session, during the existence of its charter, report to the same the amount of debts due *from* said corporation; the amount of debts due *to* the same; the amount of specie in its vaults, and an account of all lands then owned by the same, and the amount for which such lands have been taken; and moreover, if said corporation shall at any time neglect or refuse to submit its books, papers, and all and every thing necessary for a full and fair examination of its affairs, to any person or persons appointed by the General Assembly, for the purpose of making such examination, the said corporation shall forfeit its charter."

This amendment was negatived by a vote of 34 to 15. Eleven of the 34 who voted against it, are now members of this

House; and though it would be out of order to call their names, I hope they will all recollect themselves, and not vote for this examination to be made without authority, inasmuch as they refused to reserve the authority when it was in their power to do so.

I have said that cases might occur, when an examination might be proper; but I do not believe any such case has now occurred; and if it has, I should still be opposed to making an examination without legal authority. I am opposed to encouraging that lawless and mobocratic spirit, whether in relation to the bank or any thing else, which is already abroad in the land; and is spreading with rapid and fearful impetuosity, to the ultimate overthrow of every institution, or even moral principle, in which persons and property have hitherto found security.

But supposing we had the authority, I would ask what good can result from the examination? Can we declare the Bank unconstitutional, and compel it to cease operations? Can we compel it to desist from the abuses of its power, provided we find such abuses to exist? Can we repair the injuries which it may have done to individuals? Most certainly we can do none of these things. Why then shall we spend the public money in such employment? O, say the examiners, we can injure the credit of the Bank, if nothing else. Please tell me, gentlemen, who will suffer most by that? You cannot injure, to any extent, the Stockholders. They are men of wealth—of large capital; and consequently, beyond the power of fortune, or even the shafts of malice. But by injuring the credit of the Bank, you will depreciate the value of its paper in the hands of the honest and unsuspecting farmer and mechanic, and that is all you can do. But suppose you could effect your whole purpose; suppose you could wipe the Bank from existence, which is the grand *ultimatum* of the project, what would be the consequence? Why, sir, we should spend several thousand dollars of the public treasure in the operation, annihilate the currency of the State; render valueless in the hands of our people that reward of their former labors; and finally, be once more under the comfortable obligation of paying the Wiggins' loan, principal and interest.

January 11, 1837

Protest in the Illinois Legislature on Slavery

The following protest was presented to the House, which was read and ordered to be spread on the journals, to wit:

"Resolutions upon the subject of domestic slavery having passed both branches of the General Assembly at its present session, the undersigned hereby protest against the passage of the same.

They believe that the institution of slavery is founded on both injustice and bad policy; but that the promulgation of abolition doctrines tends rather to increase than to abate its evils.

They believe that the Congress of the United States has no power, under the constitution, to interfere with the institution of slavery in the different States.

They believe that the Congress of the United States has the power, under the constitution, to abolish slavery in the District of Columbia; but that that power ought not to be exercised unless at the request of the people of said District.

The difference between these opinions and those contained in the said resolutions, is their reason for entering this protest."

DAN STONE,

A. LINCOLN,

Representatives from the county of Sangamon.

March 3, 1837

To Mary S. Owens

Friend Mary   Springfield, May 7. 1837

I have commenced two letters to send you before this, both of which displeased me before I got half done, and so I tore them up. The first I thought wasn't serious enough, and the second was on the other extreme. I shall send this, turn out as it may.

This thing of living in Springfield is rather a dull business after all, at least it is so to me. I am quite as lonesome here as ever was anywhere in my life. I have been spoken to by but one woman since I've been here, and should not have been by her, if she could have avoided it. I've never been to church yet, nor probably shall not be soon. I stay away because I am conscious I should not know how to behave myself.

I am often thinking about what we said of your coming to live at Springfield. I am afraid you would not be satisfied. There is a great deal of flourishing about in carriages here, which it would be your doom to see without shareing in it. You would have to be poor without the means of hiding your poverty. Do you believe you could bear that patiently? Whatever woman may cast her lot with mine, should any ever do so, it is my intention to do all in my power to make her happy and contented; and there is nothing I can immagine, that would make me more unhappy than to fail in the effort. I know I should be much happier with you than the way I am, provided I saw no signs of discontent in you. What you have said to me may have been in jest, or I may have misunderstood it. If so, then let it be forgotten; if otherwise, I much wish you would think seriously before you decide. For my part I have already decided. What I have said I will most positively abide by, provided you wish it. My opinion is that you had better not do it. You have not been accustomed to hardship, and it may be more severe than you now immagine. I know you are capable of thinking correctly on any subject; and if you deliberate maturely upon this, before you decide, then I am willing to abide your decision.

You must write me a good long letter after you get this. You have nothing else to do, and though it might not seem interesting to you, after you had written it, it would be a good deal of company to me in this "busy wilderness." Tell your sister I dont want to hear any more about selling out and moving. That gives me the hypo whenever I think of it. Yours, &c.

To Mary S. Owens

Friend Mary.   Springfield Aug. 16th 1837

You will, no doubt, think it rather strange, that I should write you a letter on the same day on which we parted; and I can only account for it by supposing, that seeing you lately makes me think of you more than usual, while at our late meeting we had but few expressions of thoughts. You must know that I can not see you, or think of you, with entire indifference; and yet it may be, that you, are mistaken in regard to what my real feelings towards you are. If I knew you were not, I should not trouble you with this letter. Perhaps any other man would know enough without further information; but I consider it *my* peculiar right to plead ignorance, and your bounden duty to allow the plea. I want in all cases to do right, and most particularly so, in all cases with women. I want, at this particular time, more than any thing else, to do right with you, and if I *knew* it would be doing right, as I rather suspect it would, to let you alone, I would do it. And for the purpose of making the matter as plain as possible, I now say, that you can now drop the subject, dismiss your thoughts (if you ever had any) from me forever, and leave this letter unanswered, without calling forth one accusing murmer from me. And I will even go further, and say, that if it will add any thing to your comfort, or peace of mind, to do so, it is my sincere wish that you should. Do not understand by this, that I wish to cut your acquaintance. I mean no such thing. What I do wish is, that our further acquaintance shall depend upon yourself. If such further acquaintance would contribute nothing to your happiness, I am sure it would not to mine. If you feel yourself in any degree bound to me, I am now willing to release you, provided you wish it; while, on the other hand, I am willing, and even anxious to bind you faster, if I can be convinced that it will, in any considerable degree, add to your happiness. This, indeed, is the whole question with me. Nothing would make me more miserable than to believe you miserable—nothing more happy, than to know you were so.

In what I have now said, I think I can not be misunderstood; and to make myself understood, is the only object of this letter.

If it suits you best to not answer this—farewell—a long life and a merry one attend you. But if you conclude to write back, speak as plainly as I do. There can be neither harm nor danger, in saying, to me, any thing you think, just in the manner you think it.

My respects to your sister. Your friend

Second Reply to James Adams

TO THE PUBLIC.

Such is the turn which things have lately taken, that when Gen. Adams writes a book, I am expected to write a commentary on it. In the Republican of this morning he has presented the world with a new work of six columns in length; in consequence of which I must beg the room of one column in the Journal. It is obvious that a minute reply cannot be made in one column to every thing that can be said in six; and, consequently, I hope that expectation will be answered, if I reply to such parts of the General's publication as are worth replying to.

It may not be improper to remind the reader that in his publication of Sept. 6th, General Adams said that the assignment charge was manufactured *just before the election*; and that in reply I proved that statement to be false by Keyes, his own witness. Now, without attempting to explain, he furnishes me with another witness (Tinsley) by which the same thing is proved, to wit, that the assignment *was not* manufactured *just before the election*; but that it was seen *some weeks* before. Let it be borne in mind that Adams made this statement—has himself furnished two witnesses to prove its falsehood, and does not attempt to deny or explain it. Before going farther, let a pin be stuck here, labelled "one lie proved and confessed." On the 6th of Sept. he said he had before stated in a handbill that he held an assignment dated May 20th, 1828, which in reply I pronounced to be false, and referred to the hand bill for the truth of what I said. This week he forgets to make any explanation of this. Let another pin be stuck here, labelled as before. I mention these things, because, if, when I convict him in one falsehood, he is permitted to shift his ground, and pass it by in silence, there can be no end to this controversy.

The first thing that attracts my attention in the General's present production, is the information he is pleased to give to "those who are made to suffer at his (my) *hands*." Under present circumstances, this cannot apply to me, for I am not a *widow* nor an *orphan*: nor have I a wife or children who by possibility might become such. Such, however, I have no doubt, have been, and will again be made to suffer at his *hands!! Hands!* yes, they are the mischievous agents. The next thing I shall notice is his favorite expression, "knot of lawyers, doctors and others," which he is so fond of applying to all who dare expose his rascality. Now, let it be remembered that when he first came to this country, he attempted to impose himself upon the community as a *lawyer*, and actually carried the attempt so far, as to induce a man who was under a charge of murder to intrust the defence of his life in his hands, and finally took his money and got him hanged. Is this the man that is to raise a breeze in his favor by abusing lawyers? If he is not himself a lawyer, it is for the lack of sense, and not of inclination. If he is not a lawyer, he *is* a liar, for he proclaimed himself a lawyer, and got a man hanged by depending on him.

Passing over such parts of the article as have neither fact nor argument in them, I come to the question asked by Adams whether any person ever saw the assignment in his possession. This is an insult to common sense. Talbott has swore once, and repeated time and again, that he got it *out* of Adams' possession and returned it *into* the same possession. Still, as though he was addressing fools, he has assurance to ask if any person ever saw it in his possession. Next I quote a sentence "Now my son Lucian swears that when Talbott called for the deed, that he, Talbott, opened it and *pointed out the error.*" True. His son Lucian did swear as he says; and in doing so, he swore what I will prove by his own affidavit to be a falsehood. Turn to Lucian's affidavit, and you will there see, that Talbott called for the deed by which to correct an error on the *record.* Thus it appears that the error in question was on the *record*, and not in the *deed.* How then could Talbott open the deed and point out the *error?* Where a thing *is not*, it cannot be pointed out. The error *was not* in the *deed*, and of course could not be pointed out there. This does not merely prove, that the error could not be pointed out, as Lucian swore it was; but it proves, too, that the deed was not opened in his presence with a special view to the error, for if it had been, he could not have failed to see that there was no error in it. It is easy enough to see why Lucian swore this. His object was to prove that the assignment *was not* in the deed, when Talbott got it: but it was discovered he could not swear this safely, without first swearing the deed was *opened*— and if he swore it was *opened*, he must show a *motive* for opening it, and the conclusion with him and his father was, that the pointing out the error, would appear the most plausible.

For the purpose of showing that the assignment was not in the bundle when Talbott got it, is the story introduced in Lucian's affidavit, that the deeds were *counted*. It is a remarkable fact, and one that should stand as a warning to all liars and fabricators, that in this short affidavit of Lucian's, he only attempted to depart from the truth, so far as I have the means of knowing, in two points, to wit, in *the opening the deed and pointing out the error*; and the *counting of the deeds*,—and in both of these he caught himself. About the counting, he caught himself thus—After saying the bundle contained *five* deeds and a lease, he proceeds, "and I saw no other papers than the *said deed* and lease." First he has *six* papers, and then he saw none but *two*. For "my son Lucian's" benefit, let a pin be stuck here.

Adams again adduces the argument, that he could not have forged the assignment, for the reason that he could have had no *motive* for it. With those that know the facts there is no absence of motive. Admitting the paper, which he has filed in the suit to be genuine, it is clear that *it* cannot answer the purpose for which he designs it. Hence his motive for making one that he supposed would answer, is obvious. His making the date too old is also easily enough accounted for. The records were not in his hands, and then there being some considerable talk upon this particular subject, he knew he could not examine the records to ascertain the precise dates without subjecting himself to suspicion; and hence he concluded to try it by guess, and as it turned out, missed it a little. About Miller's deposition, I have a word to say. In the first place, Miller's answer to the first question shows upon its face, that he had been tampered with, and the answer dictated to him. He was asked if he knew Joel Wright and James Adams; and above three-fourths of his answer consists of what he knew about Joseph Anderson, a man about whom nothing had been asked, nor a word said in the question— a fact that can only be accounted for upon the supposition, that Adams had secretly told him what he wished him to swear to.

Another of Miller's answers I will prove both by common sense and the court of record is untrue. To one question he answers, "Anderson brought a suit against me before James Adams, then an acting Justice of the Peace in Sangamon County, before whom he obtained a judgment.

"Q. Did you *remove* the same by injunction to the Sangamon Circuit Court? Answer. I did remove it." Now mark—it is said he *removed* it by *injunction*. The word *"injunction"* in common language imports a command that some person or thing shall not *move* or be *removed*; in law it has the same meaning. An injunction issuing out of chancery to a Justice of the Peace, is a command to him to stop all proceedings in a name case till further orders. It is not an order to *remove*, but to *stop* or stay something that is already *moving*. Besides this, the records of the Sangamon Circuit Court show, that the judgement of which Miller swore was never removed into said court by injunction or otherwise.

I have now to take notice of a part of Adams' address which in the order of time should have been noticed before. It is in these words, "I have now shown, in the opinion of 2 competent judges that the hand writing of the forged assignment differed from mine, *and by one of them that it could not be mistaken for mine.*" That is false. Tinsley no doubt is the judge referred to; and by reference to his certificate it will be seen, that he did not say the hand writing of the assignment could not be mistaken for Adams'—nor did he use any other expression substantially, or any thing near substantially the same. But if Tinsley had said the hand writing could not be mistaken for Adams', it would have been equally unfortunate for Adams: for it then would have contradicted Keyes, who says, "I looked at the writing and judged it the said Adams' or a good imitation."

Adams speaks with much apparent confidence of his success on the pending law suit, and the ultimate maintainance of his title to the land in question. Without wishing to disturb the pleasure of his dream, I would say to him that it is not impossible, that he may yet be taught to sing a different song in relation to the matter.

At the end of Miller's deposition, Adams asks, "Will Mr. Lincoln *now* say that he is almost convinced my title to this ten acre tract of land is founded in fraud?" I answer, I will not. I will *now* change the phraseology so as to make it run— I am *quite* convinced, &c. I cannot pass in silence Adams' assertion that he has proved that the forged assignment was not in the deed when it came from his house by *Talbott*, the Recorder. In this, although Talbott has sworn that the assignment was in the bundle of deeds when it came from his house, Adams has the unaccountable assurance to say that he has proved the contrary by Talbott. Let him, or his friends attempt to show, wherein he proved any such thing by Talbott.

In his publication of the 6th of Sept. he *hinted* to Talbott, that *he might be mistaken.* In his present, speaking of Talbott and me, he says *"They may have been imposed upon."* Can any man of the least penetration fail to see the object of this? After he has stormed and raved till he hopes or imagines that he has got us a little scared, he wishes to softly whisper in our ears, *"If you'll quit I will."* If he could get us to say, that some unknown, undefined being had slipped the assignment into our hands without our knowledge, not a doubt remains but that he would immediately discover, that we were the purest men on earth. This is the ground he evidently wishes us to understand he is willing to compromise upon. But we ask no such charity at his hands. We are neither *mistaken* nor *imposed upon.* We have made the statements we have, because we know them to be true—and we choose to live or die by them.

Esq. Carter, who is Adams friend, personal and political, will recollect, that, on the 5th of this month, he, (Adams) with a great affectation of modesty, declared that he would never introduce his own child as a witness. Notwithstanding this affectation of modesty, he has in his present publication, introduced his child as a witness; and as if to show with how much contempt he could treat his own declaration, he has had this same Esq. Carter to administer the oath to him. And so important a witness does he consider him, and so entirely does the whole of his present production depend upon the testimony of his child, that in it he has mentioned "my son,"

"my son Lucian," "Lucian my son," and the like expressions
no less than fifteen different times. Let it be remembered
here, that I have shown the affidavit of "my darling son Lucian," to be false by the evidence apparent on its own face;
and I now ask if that affidavit be taken away, what foundation
will the fabric have left to stand upon?

General Adams' publications and out-door manoevring,
taken in connection with the editorial articles of the Republican, are not more foolish and contradictory than they are ludicrous and amusing. One week the Republican notifies the
public that Gen. Adams is preparing an *instrument* that will
tear, rend, split, rive, blow up, confound, overwhelm, annihilate, extinguish, exterminate, burst asunder, and grind to
powder all his slanderers, and particularly Talbott and Lincoln—all of which is to be done *in due time*. Then for two or
three weeks all is calm—not a word said. Again the Republican comes forth with a mere passing remark that "public
opinion has decided in favor of Gen. Adams," and intimates
that he will give himself no more trouble about the matter. In
the mean time Adams himself is prowling about, and as Burns
says of the devil, *"For prey, a' holes and corners tryin,"* and in
one instance, goes so far as to take an old acquaintance of
mine several steps from a crowd, and apparently weighed
down with the importance of his business, gravely and solemnly asks him if *"he ever heard Lincoln say he was a deist."*
Anon the Republican comes again, "We invite the attention
of the public to Gen. Adams' communication," &c, "The victory is a great one." "The triumph is overwhelming." [I really
believe the editor of the Ill. Republican is fool enough to
think General Adams is an honest man.] Then Gen. Adams
leads off. *"Authors most egregiously mistaken,"* &c. *"most wofully
shall their presumption be punished,"* &c. [Lord have mercy on
us.] *"The hour is yet to come, yes nigh at hand*—(how long first
do you reckon?)—*when the Journal and its junto shall say, I
have appeared too early."*—*"then infamy shall be laid bare to the
public gaze."* Suddenly the Gen. appears to relent at the sever-
ity with which he is treating us and he exclaims, *"The condemnation of my enemies is the inevitable result of my own defence."*
For your health's sake, dear Gen. do not permit your tender-
ness of heart to afflict you so much on our account. For some

reason (perhaps because we are killed so quickly) we shall never be sensible of our suffering.

Farewell, General. I will see you again at court, if not before—when and where we will settle the question whether you or the widow shall have the land.

Oct. 18, 1837.

Address to the Young Men's Lyceum of Springfield, Illinois

THE PERPETUATION OF OUR POLITICAL INSTITUTIONS

As a subject for the remarks of the evening, *the perpetuation of our political institutions*, is selected.

In the great journal of things happening under the sun, we, the American People, find our account running, under date of the nineteenth century of the Christian era. We find ourselves in the peaceful possession, of the fairest portion of the earth, as regards extent of territory, fertility of soil, and salubrity of climate. We find ourselves under the government of a system of political institutions, conducing more essentially to the ends of civil and religious liberty, than any of which the history of former times tells us. We, when mounting the stage of existence, found ourselves the legal inheritors of these fundamental blessings. We toiled not in the acquirement or establishment of them—they are a legacy bequeathed us, by a *once* hardy, brave, and patriotic, but *now* lamented and departed race of ancestors. Their's was the task (and nobly they performed it) to possess themselves, and through themselves, us, of this goodly land; and to uprear upon its hills and its valleys, a political edifice of liberty and equal rights; 'tis ours only, to transmit these, the former, unprofaned by the foot of an invader; the latter, undecayed by the lapse of time, and untorn by usurpation—to the latest generation that fate shall permit the world to know. This task of gratitude to our fathers, justice to ourselves, duty to posterity, and love for our species in general, all imperatively require us faithfully to perform.

How, then, shall we perform it? At what point shall we expect the approach of danger? By what means shall we fortify against it? Shall we expect some transatlantic military giant, to step the Ocean, and crush us at a blow? Never! All the armies of Europe, Asia and Africa combined, with all the treasure of the earth (our own excepted) in their military chest; with a Buonaparte for a commander, could not by force, take a drink from the Ohio, or make a track on the Blue Ridge, in a trial of a thousand years.

At what point then is the approach of danger to be expected? I answer, if it ever reach us, it must spring up amongst us. It cannot come from abroad. If destruction be our lot, we must ourselves be its author and finisher. As a nation of freemen, we must live through all time, or die by suicide.

I hope I am over wary; but if I am not, there is, even now, something of ill-omen amongst us. I mean the increasing disregard for law which pervades the country; the growing disposition to substitute the wild and furious passions, in lieu of the sober judgement of Courts; and the worse than savage mobs, for the executive ministers of justice. This disposition is awfully fearful in any community; and that it now exists in ours, though grating to our feelings to admit, it would be a violation of truth, and an insult to our intelligence, to deny. Accounts of outrages committed by mobs, form the every-day news of the times. They have pervaded the country, from New England to Louisiana;—they are neither peculiar to the eternal snows of the former, nor the burning suns of the latter;—they are not the creature of climate—neither are they confined to the slaveholding, or the non-slaveholding States. Alike, they spring up among the pleasure hunting masters of Southern slaves, and the order loving citizens of the land of steady habits. Whatever, then, their cause may be, it is common to the whole country.

It would be tedious, as well as useless, to recount the horrors of all of them. Those happening in the State of Mississippi, and at St. Louis, are, perhaps, the most dangerous in example, and revolting to humanity. In the Mississippi case, they first commenced by hanging the regular gamblers: a set of men, certainly not following for a livelihood, a very useful, or very honest occupation; but one which, so far from being forbidden by the laws, was actually licensed by an act of the Legislature, passed but a single year before. Next, negroes, suspected of conspiring to raise an insurrection, were caught up and hanged in all parts of the State: then, white men, supposed to be leagued with the negroes; and finally, strangers, from neighboring States, going thither on business, were, in many instances, subjected to the same fate. Thus went on this process of hanging, from gamblers to negroes, from negroes to white citizens, and from these to strangers; till, dead men were seen literally dangling from the boughs of trees upon every road side; and in numbers almost sufficient, to rival the native Spanish moss of the country, as a drapery of the forest.

Turn, then, to that horror-striking scene at St. Louis. A single victim was only sacrificed there. His story is very short; and is, perhaps, the most highly tragic, of any thing of its length, that has ever been witnessed in real life. A mulatto man, by the name of McIntosh, was seized in the street, dragged to the suburbs of the city, chained to a tree, and actually burned to death; and all within a single hour from the time he had been a freeman, attending to his own business, and at peace with the world.

Such are the effects of mob law; and such are the scenes, becoming more and more frequent in this land so lately famed for love of law and order; and the stories of which, have even now grown too familiar, to attract any thing more, than an idle remark.

But you are, perhaps, ready to ask, "What has this to do with the perpetuation of our political institutions?" I answer, it has much to do with it. Its direct consequences are, comparatively speaking, but a small evil; and much of its danger consists, in the proneness of our minds, to regard its direct, as its only consequences. Abstractly considered, the hanging of the gamblers at Vicksburg, was of but little consequence. They constitute a portion of population, that is worse than useless in any community; and their death, if no pernicious example be set by it, is never matter of reasonable regret with any one. If they were annually swept, from the stage of existence, by the plague or small pox, honest men would, perhaps, be much profited, by the operation. Similar too, is the correct reasoning, in regard to the burning of the negro at St. Louis. He had forfeited his life, by the perpetration of an outrageous murder, upon one of the most worthy and respectable citizens of the city; and had he not died as he did, he must have died by the sentence of the law, in a very short time afterwards. As to him alone, it was as well the way it was, as it could otherwise have been. But the example in either case, was fearful. When men take it in their heads to day, to hang gamblers, or burn murderers, they should recollect, that, in the confusion usually attending such transactions, they will be as likely to hang or burn some one, who is neither a gambler nor a murderer as one who is; and that, acting upon the example they set, the mob of to-morrow, may, and probably will, hang or burn some of them, by the very same mistake. And not only so; the innocent, those who have ever set their faces against violations of law in every shape, alike with the guilty, fall victims to the ravages of mob law; and thus it goes on, step by step, till all the walls erected for the defence of the persons and property of individuals, are trodden down, and disregarded. But all this even, is not the full extent of the evil. By such examples, by instances of the perpetrators of such acts going unpunished, the lawless in spirit, are encouraged to become lawless in practice; and having been used to no restraint, but dread of punishment, they thus become, absolutely unrestrained. Having ever regarded Government as their deadliest bane, they make a jubilee of the suspension of its operations; and pray for nothing so much, as its total annihilation. While, on the other hand, good men, men who love tranquility, who desire to abide by the laws, and enjoy their benefits, who would gladly spill their blood in the defence of their country; seeing their property destroyed; their families insulted, and their lives endangered; their persons injured; and seeing nothing in prospect that forebodes a change for the better; become tired of, and disgusted with, a Government that offers them no protection; and are not much averse to a change in which they imagine they have nothing to lose. Thus, then, by the operation of this mobocratic spirit, which all must admit, is now abroad in the land, the strongest bulwark of any Government, and particularly of those constituted like ours, may effectually be broken down and destroyed—I mean the *attachment* of the People. Whenever this effect shall be produced among us; whenever the vicious portion of population shall be permitted to gather in bands of hundreds and thousands, and burn churches, ravage and rob provision stores, throw printing presses into rivers, shoot editors, and hang and burn obnoxious persons at pleasure, and with impunity; depend on it, this Government cannot last. By such things, the feelings of the best citizens will become more or less alienated from it; and thus it will be left without friends, or with too few, and those few too weak, to make their friendship effectual. At such a time and under such circumstances, men of sufficient talent and ambition will not be wanting to seize the opportunity, strike the blow, and overturn that fair fabric, which for the last half century, has been the fondest hope, of the lovers of freedom, throughout the world.

I know the American People are *much* attached to their Government;—I know they would suffer *much* for its sake;—I know they would endure evils long and patiently, before they would ever think of exchanging it for another. Yet, notwithstanding all this, if the laws be continually despised and disregarded, if their rights to be secure in their persons and property, are held by no better tenure than the caprice of a mob, the alienation of their affections from the Government is the natural consequence; and to that, sooner or later, it must come.

Here then, is one point at which danger may be expected.

The question recurs "how shall we fortify against it?" The answer is simple. Let every American, every lover of liberty, every well wisher to his posterity, swear by the blood of the Revolution, never to violate in the least particular, the laws of the country; and never to tolerate their violation by others. As the patriots of seventy-six did to the support of the Declaration of Independence, so to the support of the Constitution and Laws, let every American pledge his life, his property, and his sacred honor;—let every man remember that to violate the law, is to trample on the blood of his father, and to tear the character of his own, and his children's liberty. Let reverence for the laws, be breathed by every American mother, to the lisping babe, that prattles on her lap—let it be taught in schools, in seminaries, and in colleges;—let it be written in Primmers, spelling books, and in Almanacs;—let it be preached from the pulpit, proclaimed in legislative halls, and enforced in courts of justice. And, in short, let it become the *political religion* of the nation; and let the old and the young, the rich and the poor, the grave and the gay, of all sexes and tongues, and colors and conditions, sacrifice unceasingly upon its altars.

While ever a state of feeling, such as this, shall universally, or even, very generally prevail throughout the nation, vain will be every effort, and fruitless every attempt, to subvert our national freedom.

When I so pressingly urge a strict observance of all the laws, let me not be understood as saying there are no bad laws, nor that grievances may not arise, for the redress of which, no legal provisions have been made. I mean to say no such thing. But I do mean to say, that, although bad laws, if they exist, should be repealed as soon as possible, still while they continue in force, for the sake of example, they should be religiously observed. So also in unprovided cases. If such arise, let proper legal provisions be made for them with the least possible delay; but, till then, let them if not too intolerable, be borne with.

There is no grievance that is a fit object of redress by mob law. In any case that arises, as for instance, the promulgation of abolitionism, one of two positions is necessarily true; that is, the thing is right within itself, and therefore deserves the protection of all law and all good citizens; or, it is wrong, and therefore proper to be prohibited by legal enactments; and in neither case, is the interposition of mob law, either necessary, justifiable, or excusable.

But, it may be asked, why suppose danger to our political institutions? Have we not preserved them for more than fifty years? And why may we not for fifty times as long?

We hope there is no *sufficient* reason. We hope all dangers may be overcome; but to conclude that no danger may ever arise, would itself be extremely dangerous. There are now, and will hereafter be, many causes, dangerous in their tendency, which have not existed heretofore; and which are not too insignificant to merit attention. That our government should have been maintained in its original form from its establishment until now, is not much to be wondered at. It had many props to support it through that period, which now are decayed, and crumbled away. Through that period, it was felt by all, to be an undecided experiment; now, it is understood to be a successful one. Then, all that sought celebrity and fame, and distinction, expected to find them in the success of that experiment. Their *all* was staked upon it: — their destiny was *inseparably* linked with it. Their ambition aspired to display before an admiring world, a practical demonstration of the truth of a proposition, which had hitherto been considered, at best no better, than problematical; namely, *the capability of a people to govern themselves*. If they succeeded, they were to be immortalized; their names were to be transferred to counties and cities, and rivers and mountains; and to be revered and sung, and toasted through all time. If they failed, they were to be called knaves and fools, and fanatics for a fleeting hour; then to sink and be forgotten. They succeeded. The experiment is successful; and thousands have won their deathless names in making it so. But the game is caught; and I believe it is true, that with the catching, end the pleasures of the chase. This field of glory is harvested, and the crop is already appropriated. But new reapers will arise, and *they*, too, will seek a field. It is to deny, what the history of the world tells us is true, to suppose that men of ambition and talents will not continue to spring up amongst us. And, when they do, they will as naturally seek the gratification of their ruling passion, as others have *so* done before them. The question then, is, can that gratification be found in supporting and maintaining an edifice that has been erected by others? Most certainly it cannot. Many great and good men sufficiently qualified for any task they should undertake, may ever be found, whose ambition would aspire to nothing beyond a seat in Congress, a gubernatorial or a presidential chair; *but such belong not to the family of the lion, or the tribe of the eagle*. What! think you these places would satisfy an Alexander, a Caesar, or a Napoleon? Never! Towering genius disdains a beaten path. It seeks regions hitherto unexplored. It sees *no distinction* in adding story to story, upon the monuments of fame, erected to the memory of others. It *denies* that it is glory enough to serve under any chief. It *scorns* to tread in the footsteps of *any* predecessor, however illustrious. It thirsts and burns for distinction; and, if possible, it will have it, whether at the expense of emancipating slaves, or enslaving freemen. Is it unreasonable then to expect, that some man possessed of the loftiest genius, coupled with ambition sufficient to push it to its utmost stretch, will at some time, spring up among us? And when such a one does, it will require the people to be united with each other, attached to the government and laws, and generally intelligent, to successfully frustrate his designs.

Distinction will be his paramount object; and although he would as willingly, perhaps more so, acquire it by doing good as harm; yet, that opportunity being past, and nothing left to be done in the way of building up, he would set boldly to the task of pulling down.

Here then, is a probable case, highly dangerous, and such a one as could not have well existed heretofore.

Another reason which *once was*; but which, to the same extent, is *now no more*, has done much in maintaining our institutions thus far. I mean the powerful influence which the interesting scenes of the revolution had upon the *passions* of the people as distinguished from their judgment. By this influence, the jealousy, envy, and avarice, incident to our nature, and so common to a state of peace, prosperity, and conscious strength, were, for the time, in a great measure smothered and rendered inactive; while the deep rooted principles of *hate*, and the powerful motive of *revenge*, instead of being turned against each other, were directed exclusively against the British nation. And thus, from the force of circumstances, the basest principles of our nature, were either made to lie dormant, or to become the active agents in the advancement of the noblest of cause—that of establishing and maintaining civil and religious liberty.

But this state of feeling *must fade, is fading, has faded*, with the circumstances that produced it.

I do not mean to say, that the scenes of the revolution *are now* or *ever will be* entirely forgotten; but that like every thing else, they must fade upon the memory of the world, and grow more and more dim by the lapse of time. In history, we hope, they will be read of, and recounted, so long as the bible shall be read;—but even granting that they will, their influence *cannot be* what it heretofore has been. Even then, they *cannot be* so universally known, nor so vividly felt, as they were by the generation just gone to rest. At the close of that struggle, nearly every adult male had been a participator in some of its scenes. The consequence was, that of those scenes, in the form of a husband, a father, a son or a brother, a *living history was* to be found in every family—a history bearing the indubitable testimonies of its own authenticity, in the limbs mangled, in the scars of wounds received, in the midst of the very scenes related—a history, too, that could be read and understood alike by all, the wise and the ignorant, the learned and the unlearned. But *those* histories are gone. They *can* be read no more forever. They *were* a fortress of strength; but, what invading foemen could *never do*, the silent artillery of time *has done*; the levelling of its walls. They are gone. They *were* a forest of giant oaks; but the all resistless hurricane has swept over them, and left only, here and there, a lonely trunk, despoiled of its verdure, shorn of its foliage; unshading and unshaded, to murmur in a few more gentle breezes, and to combat with its mutilated limbs, a few more ruder storms, then to sink, and be no more.

They *were* the pillars of the temple of liberty; and now, that they have crumbled away, that temple must fall, unless we, their descendants, supply their places with other pillars, hewn from the solid quarry of sober reason. Passion has helped us; but can do so no more. It will in future be our enemy. Reason, cold, calculating, unimpassioned reason, must furnish all the materials for our future support and defence. Let those materials be moulded into *general intelligence, sound morality* and, in particular, *a reverence for the constitution and laws*; and, that we improved to the last; that we remained free to the last; that we revered his name to the last; that, during his long sleep, we permitted no hostile foot to pass over or desecrate his resting place; shall be that which to learn the last trump shall awaken our WASHINGTON.

Upon these let the proud fabric of freedom rest, as the rock of its basis; and as truly as has been said of the only greater institution, *"the gates of hell shall not prevail against it."*

January 27, 1838

To Mrs. Orville H. Browning

Dear Madam: Springfield, April 1. 1838.

Without appologising for being egotistical, I shall make the history of so much of my own life, as has elapsed since I saw you, the subject of this letter. And by the way I now discover, that, in order to give a full and inteligible account of the things I have done and suffered *since* I saw you, I shall necessarily have to relate some that happened *before*.

It was, then, in the autumn of 1836, that a married lady of my acquaintance, and who was a great friend of mine, being about to pay a visit to her father and other relatives residing in Kentucky, proposed to me, that on her return she would bring a sister of hers with her, upon condition that I would engage to become her brother-in-law with all convenient dispach. I, of course, accepted the proposal; for you know I could not have done otherwise, had I really been averse to it; but privately between you and me, I was most confoundedly well pleased with the project. I had seen the said sister some three years before, thought her inteligent and agreeable, and saw no good objection to plodding life through hand in hand with her. Time passed on, the lady took her journey and in due time returned, sister in company sure enough. This stomached me a little; for it appeared to me, that her coming so readily showed that she was a trifle too willing; but on reflection it occured to me, that she might have been prevailed on by her married sister to come, without any thing concerning me ever having been mentioned to her; and so I concluded that if no other objection presented itself, I would consent to wave this. All this occured upon my *hearing* of her arrival in the neighbourhood; for, be it remembered, I had not yet *seen* her, except about three years previous, as before mentioned.

In a few days we had an interview, and although I had seen her before, she did not look as my immagination had pictured her. I knew she was over-size, but she now appeared a fair match for Falstaff; I knew she was called an "old maid", and I felt no doubt of the truth of at least half of the appelation; but now, when I beheld her, I could not for my life avoid thinking of my mother; and this, not from withered features, for her skin was too full of fat, to permit its contracting in to wrinkles; but from her want of teeth, weather-beaten appearance in general, and from a kind of notion that ran in my head, that *nothing* could have commenced at the size of infancy, and reached her present bulk in less than thirtyfive or forty years; and, in short, I was not all pleased with her. But what could I do? I had told her sister that I would take her for better or for worse; and I made a point of honor and conscience in all things, to stick to my word, especially if others had been induced to act on it, which in this case, I doubted not they had, for I was now fairly convinced, that no other man on earth would have her, and hence the conclusion that they were bent on holding me to my bargain. Well, thought I, I have said it, and, be consequences what they may, it shall not be my fault if I fail to do it. At once I determined to consider her my wife; and this done, all my powers of discovery were put to the rack, in search of perfections in her, which might be fairly set-off against her defects. I tried to immagine she was handsome, which, but for her unfortunate corpulency, was actually true. Exclusive of this, no woman that I have seen, has a finer face. I also tried to convince myself, that the mind was much more to be valued than the person; and in this, she was not inferior, as I could discover, to any with whom I had been acquainted.

Shortly after this, without attempting to come to any positive understanding with her, I set out for Vandalia, where and when you first saw me. During my stay there, I had letters from her, which did not change my opinion of either her intelect or intention; but on the contrary, confirmed it in both.

All this while, although I was fixed "firm as the surge repelling rock" in my resolution, I found I was continually repenting the rashness, which had led me to make it. Through life I have been in no bondage, either real or immaginary from the thraldom of which I so much desired to be free.

After my return home, I saw nothing to change my opinion of her in any particular. She was the same and so was I. I now spent my time between planing how I might get along through life after my contemplated change of circumstances should have taken place; and how I might procrastinate the evil day for a time, which I really dreaded as much—perhaps more, than an irishman does the halter.

After all my suffering upon this deeply interesting subject, here I am, wholly unexpectedly, completely out of the "scrape"; and I now want to know, if you can guess how I got out of it. Out clear in every sense of the term; no violation of word, honor or conscience. I dont believe you can guess, and so I may as well tell you at once. As the lawyers say, it was done in the manner following, towit. After I had delayed the matter as long as I thought I could in honor do, which by the way had brought me round into the last fall, I concluded I might as well bring it to a consumation without further delay; and so I mustered my resolution, and made the proposal to her direct; but, shocking to relate, she answered, No. At first I supposed she did it through an affectation of modesty, which I thought but ill-become her, under the peculiar circumstances of her case; but on my renewal of the charge, I found she repeled it with greater firmness than before. I tried it again and again, but with the same success, or rather with the same want of success. I finally was forced to give it up, at which I verry unexpectedly found myself mortified almost beyond endurance. I was mortified, it seemed to me, in a hundred different ways. My vanity was deeply wounded by the reflection, that I had so long been too stupid to discover her intentions, and at the same time never doubting that I understood them perfectly; and also, that she whom I had taught myself to believe no body else would have, had actually rejected me with all my fancied greatness; and to cap the whole, I then, for the first time, began to suspect that I was really a little in love with her. But let it all go. I'll try and out live it. Others have been made fools of by the girls; but this can never be with truth said of me. I most emphatically, in this instance, made a fool of myself. I have now come to the conclusion never again to think of marrying; and for this reason; I can never be satisfied with any one who would be block-head enough to have me.

When you receive this, write me a long yarn about something to amuse me. Give my respects to Mr. Browning. Your sincere friend

To William Butler

Dear Butler: Vandalia, Jany. 26– 1839

Your letter of the 21st. Inst. is just received. You were in an ill-humor when you wrote that letter, and, no doubt, intended that I should be thrown into one also; which, however, I respectfully decline being done. All you have said about our having been bought up by Taylor, Wright, Turley, enemies &c I *know you would not say, seriously, in your moments of reflection*; and therefore I do not think it worth while to attempt *seriously* to prove the contrary to you. I only now say, that I am willing to pledge myself in black and white to cut my own throat from ear to ear, if, when I meet you, you shall *seriously* say, that you believe me capable of betraying my friends for any price.

The grounds of your complaint I will answer seriously. First, then, as to Athens. We *have* Allen's letter of which you speak; and although, he did not in that letter, pretend that he was specially authorized to speak for the people of Athens, he did *pretend*, that he *knew* their feelings, and that he fairly expressed them. And further; Hall & Francis of Athens are now here, and I assure you, *they* say nothing about "giving us hell". They are as good-humored as I ever saw them. About Cowardin's county. We passed the bill through the House with the lines precisely as Cowardin himself agreed they should pass. After Cowardin left, Turley insisted on having the Buffalo Heart Grove, insisting that the people of that Grove desired to go in the new county. We knew they desired no such thing; and to get rid of Turley's importunity, we promised him, that if he would get a majority of the people of the Grove to petition to go to the new county, we would let him have it. We immediately notified the people of the Grove of this promise; and we, on yesterday received a petition praying that the Grove may remain in the old county; and signed by every citizen in the grove but two; so that the grove neither is nor will be struck off to the new county. The lines, and every thing pertaining to that county are now, and will remain just as Cowardin agreed they should be. Wherein, then, has Cowardin, been betrayed, or your pledges to him violated?

Again; as to the Allenton county. You know that we could

not control the teritory proposed to be taken from Shelby & Montgomery counties. You complain that we run too far West. The justification for this is, that we *could* not get the teritory from Montgomery in any other shape, the legislature, recognizing the right of the member from that county, to divide the same as he pleased. And as to the part to be taken from Shelby, that, we could not get at all, Thornton, refusing peremptorily to let his county be divided, or curtailed in any way. Since the bill passed the House, Frink has been here (and here let me say, he is not half as mad as you would make us think) and obtained a pledge from Thornton, that if he can get a majority of Shelby county consenting to the curtailment he desires, he, Thornton, will go for it. Frink has gone to Shelby, to get petitioners, and the probability is, that we will yet be able to get from Shelby what Allenton desires. Nothing could do more credit to your heart, than the mortification you express at seeing the friends with whom you acted in getting up the remonstrance disappointed; but *surely* you ought not to blame us for being unable to accomplish impossibilities.

My respects to Mrs. Butler & Salome. Your friend in spite of your ill-nature

P.S. Judge Stone is here, and I am about to get him to help me about your Clerk-fee appropriation.

To William Butler

Friend Butler: Vandalia, Feb: 1. 1839

Your letter enclosing one to Mr. Baker, was received on yesterday evening. There is no necessity for any bad feeling between Baker & yourself. Your first letter to him was written while you were in a state of high excitement, and therefore ought not to have been construed as an emination of deliberate malice. Unfortunately however it reached Baker while he was writhing under a severe tooth-ache, and therefore he at that time was incapable of exercising that patience and reflection which the case required. The note he sent you was written while in that state of feeling, and for that reason I think you ought not to pay any serious regard to it. It is always magnanamous to recant whatever we may have said in passion; and when you and Baker shall have done this, I am sure there will no difficulty be left between you. I write this without Bakers knowledge; and I do it because nothing would be more painful to me than to see a difficulty between two of my most particular friends.

About your dissatisfaction in relation to the South East county I will now say that I all the while laboured under a mistake. When I wrote to Frink & Murphy that I would go for their county, I only meant that I would go for giving them a county as against Springfield & the old county; and it never occurred to me that I was pledging myself to one party of the new-county men against another, for I did not then know they were divided into parties. When I consented for the lines to approach Springfield nearer than the petition asked, I really thought I was confering a favour upon the new-county. And, by the way, if you will compare Frink's petition with the lines as they now stand, you will see that there is but three quarters of a township more taken from Sangamon county than the petition asked for; and as to the part from Montgomery, I have before told you we could not control that.

No news here now. Your friend as ever

To William S. Wait

Mr. William S. Wait: Vandalia, March 2. 1839

Sir: Your favour of yesterday was handed me by Mr. Dale. In relation to the Revenue law, I think there is something to be feared from the argument you suggest, though I hope the danger is not as great as you apprehend. The passage of a Revenue law at this session, is *right* within itself; and I never despair of sustaining myself before the people upon any measure that will stand a full investigation. I presume I hardly need enter into an argument to prove to *you*, that our old revenue system, raising, as it did, all the state revenue from non-resident lands, and those lands rapidly *decreasing*, by passing into the hands of resident owners, whiles the wants of the Treasury were *increasing* with the increase of population, could not longer continue to answer the purpose of it's creation. That proposition is little less than self-evident. The only question is as to sustaining the change before the people. I believe it can be sustained, because it does not increase the tax upon the *"many poor"* but upon the *"wealthy few"* by taxing the land that is worth $50 or $100 per acre, in proportion to its value, insted of, as heretofore, no more than that which was worth but $5 per acre. This valuable land, as is well known, belongs, not to the poor, but to the wealthy citizen.

On the other hand, the wealthy can not *justly* complain, because the change is equitable within itself, and also a *sine qua non* to a compliance with the Constitution. If, however, the wealthy should, regardless of the justness of the complaint, as men often are, when interest is involved in the question, complain of the change, it is still to be remembered, that *they* are not sufficiently numerous to carry the elections. Verry Respectfully

Speech on the Sub-Treasury at Springfield, Illinois

FELLOW CITIZENS:— It is peculiarly embarrassing to me to attempt a continuance of the discussion, on this evening, which has been conducted in this Hall on several preceding ones. It is so, because on each of those evenings, there was a much fuller attendance than now, without any reason for its being so, except the greater *interest* the community feel in the *Speakers* who addressed them *then*, than they do in *him* who is to do so *now*. I am, indeed, apprehensive, that the few who have attended, have done so, more to spare me of mortification, than in the hope of being interested in any thing I may be able to say. This circumstance casts a damp upon my spirits, which I am sure I shall be unable to overcome during the evening. But enough of preface.

The subject heretofore, and now to be discussed, is the Sub-Treasury scheme of the present Administration, as a means of collecting, safe-keeping, transferring and disbursing the revenues of the Nation, as contrasted with a National Bank for the same purposes. Mr. Douglass has said that we (the Whigs), have not dared to meet them (the Locos), in argument on this question. I protest against this assertion. I assert that we have again and again, during this discussion, urged facts and arguments against the Sub-Treasury, which they have neither dared to deny nor attempted to answer. But lest some may be led to believe that we really wish to avoid the question, I now propose, in my humble way, to urge those arguments again; at the same time, begging the audience to mark well the positions I shall take, and the proof I shall offer to sustain them, and that they will not again permit Mr. Douglass or his friends, to escape the force of them, by a round and groundless assertion, that we "dare not meet them in argument."

Of the Sub-Treasury then, as contrasted with a National Bank, for the before enumerated purposes, I lay down the following propositions, to wit:

1st. It will injuriously affect the community by its operation on the circulating medium.

44

2d. It will be a more expensive fiscal agent.

3d. It will be a less secure depository of the public money.

To show the truth of the first proposition, let us take a short review of our condition under the operation of a National Bank. It was the depository of the public revenues. Between the collection of those revenues and the disbursements of them by the government, the Bank was permitted to, and did actually loan them out to individuals, and hence the large amount of money annually collected for revenue purposes, which by any other plan would have been idle a great portion of time, was kept almost constantly in circulation. Any person who will reflect, that money is only valuable while in circulation, will readily perceive, that any device which will keep the government revenues, in constant circulation, instead of being locked up in idleness, is no inconsiderable advantage.

By the Sub-Treasury, the revenue is to be collected, and kept in iron boxes until the government wants it for disbursement; thus robbing the people of the use of it, while the government does not itself need it, and while the money is performing no nobler office than that of rusting in iron boxes. The natural effect of this change of policy, every one will see, is to *reduce* the quantity of money in circulation.

But again, by the Sub-Treasury scheme the revenue is to be collected in specie. I anticipate that this will be disputed. I expect to hear it said, that it is not the policy of the Administration to collect the revenue in specie. If it shall, I reply, that Mr. Van Buren, in his message recommending the Sub-Treasury, expended nearly a column of that document in an attempt to persuade Congress to provide for the collection of the revenue in specie exclusively; and he concludes with these words. "It may be safely assumed, that no motive of *convenience* to the *citizen*, requires the reception of Bank paper." In addition to this, Mr. Silas Wright, Senator from New York, and the political, personal and confidential friend of Mr. Van Buren, drafted and introduced into the Senate the first Sub-Treasury Bill, and that bill provided for ultimately collecting the revenue in specie. It is true, I know, that that clause was stricken from the bill, but it was done by the votes of the Whigs, aided by a portion only of the Van Buren Senators.

No Sub-Treasury bill has yet become a law, though two or
three have been considered by Congress, some with and some
without the specie clause; so that I admit there is room for
quibbling upon the question of whether the administration
favor the exclusive specie doctrine or not; but I take it, that
the fact that the President at first urged the specie doctrine,
and that under his recommendation the first bill introduced
embraced it, warrants us in charging it as the policy of the
party, until their head as publicly recants it, as he at first es-
poused it—I repeat then, that by the Sub-Treasury, the revenue is to be collected in *specie*. Now mark what the effect of
this must be. By all estimates ever made, there are but between 60 and 80 millions of specie in the United States. The
expenditures of the Government for the year 1838, the last for
which we have had the report, were 40 millions. Thus it is
seen, that if the whole revenue be collected in specie, it will
take more than half of all the specie in the nation to do it. By
this means more than half of all the specie belonging to the
fifteen million of souls, who compose the whole population
of the country, is thrown into the hands of the public office-
holders, and other public creditors, composing in number,
perhaps not more than one quarter of a million; leaving the
other fourteen millions and three quarters to get along as they
best can, with less than one-half of the specie of the country,
and whatever rags and shin-plasters they may be able to put,
and keep, in circulation. By this means, every office-holder,
and other public creditor, may, and most likely will, set up
shaver; and a most glorious harvest will the specie men have
of it; each specie man, upon a fair division, having to his
share, the fleecing of about 59 rag men. In all candor, let me
ask, was such a system for benefiting the few at the expense of
the many, ever before devised? And was the sacred name of
Democracy, ever before made to endorse such an enormity
against the rights of the people?

I have already said that the Sub-Treasury will reduce the
quantity of money in circulation. This position is strengthened by the recollection, that the revenue is to be collected in
specie, so that the mere amount of revenue is not all that is
withdrawn, but the amount of paper circulation that the 40
millions would serve as a basis to, is withdrawn; which would

be in a sound state at least 100 millions. When 100 millions, or more, of the circulation we now have, shall be withdrawn, who can contemplate, without terror, the distress, ruin, bankruptcy and beggary, that must follow.

The man who has purchased any article, say a horse, on credit, at 100 dollars, when there are 200 millions circulating in the country, if the quantity be reduced to 100 millions by the arrival of pay-day, will find the horse but sufficient to pay half the debt; and the other half must either be paid out of his other means, and thereby become a clear loss to him; or go unpaid, and thereby become a clear loss to his creditor. What I have here said of a single case of the purchase of a horse, will hold good in every case of a debt existing at the time a reduction in the quantity of money occurs, by whomsoever, and for whatsoever it may have been contracted. It may be said, that what the debtor loses, the creditor gains by this operation; but on examination this will be found true only to a very limited extent. It is more generally true that *all* lose by it. The *creditor*, by losing more of his debts, than he gains by the increased value of those he collects; the *debtor* by either parting with more of his property to pay his debts, than he received in contracting them; or, by entirely breaking up in his business, and thereby being thrown upon the world in idleness.

The general distress thus created, will, to be sure, be *temporary*, because whatever change may occur in the quantity of money in any community, *time* will adjust the derangement produced; but while that adjustment is progressing, all suffer more or less, and very many lose every thing that renders life desirable. Why, then, shall we suffer a severe difficulty, even though it be *but temporary*, unless we receive some equivalent for it?

What I have been saying as to the effect produced by a reduction of the quantity of money, relates to the *whole* country. I now propose to show that it would produce a *peculiar* and *permanent* hardship upon the citizens of those States and Territories in which the public lands lie. The Land Offices in those States and Territories, as all know, form the great gulf by which all, or nearly all, the money in them, is swallowed up. When the quantity of money shall be reduced, and consequently every thing under individual control brought down in proportion, the price of those lands, being fixed by law, will remain as now. Of necessity, it will follow that the *produce* or *labor* that *now* raises money sufficient to purchase 80 acres, will *then* raise but sufficient to purchase 40, or perhaps not that much. And this difficulty and hardship will last as long, in some degree, as any portion of these lands shall remain undisposed of. Knowing, as I well do, the difficulty that poor people *now* encounter in procuring homes, I hesitate not to say, that when the price of the public lands shall be doubled or trebled; or, which is the same thing, produce and labor cut down to one-half or one-third of their present prices, it will be little less than impossible for them to procure those homes at all.

In answer to what I have said as to the effect the Sub-Treasury would have upon the currency, it is often urged that the money collected for revenue purposes will *not lie idle* in the vaults of the Treasury; and, farther, that a National Bank produces greater derangement in the currency, by a system of contractions and expansions, than the Sub-Treasury would produce in any way. In reply, I need only show, that experience proves the contrary of both these propositions. It is an undisputed fact, that the late Bank of the United States, paid the Government $75,000 annually, for the *privilege* of using the public money between the times of its collection and disbursement. Can any man suppose, that the Bank would have paid this sum, annually for twenty years, and then offered to renew its obligations to do so, if in reality there was no *time* intervening between the collection and disbursement of the revenue, and consequently no privilege of *using* the money extended to it?

Again, as to the contractions and expansions of a National Bank, I need only point to the period intervening between the time that the late Bank got into successful operation and that at which the Government commenced war upon it, to show that during that period, no such contractions or expansions took place. If before, or after that period, derangement occurred in the currency, it proves nothing. The Bank could not be expected to regulate the currency, either *before* it got into successful operation, or *after* it was crippled and thrown into death convulsions, by the removal of the deposits from it, and other hostile measures of the Government against it. We do not pretend, that a National Bank can establish and maintain a sound and uniform state of currency in the country, in *spite* of the National Government; but we do say, that it has established and maintained such a currency, and can do so again, by the *aid* of that Government; and we further say, that no duty is more imperative on that Government, than the duty it owes the people, of furnishing them a sound and uniform currency.

I now leave the proposition as to the effect of the Sub-Treasury upon the currency of the country, and pass to that relative to the additional *expense* which must be incurred by it over that incurred by a National Bank, as a fiscal agent of the Government. By the late National Bank, we had the public revenue received, safely kept, transferred and disbursed, not only without expense, but we actually received of the Bank $75,000 annually for its privileges, while rendering us those services. By the Sub-Treasury, according to the estimate of the Secretary of the Treasury, who is the warm advocate of the system and which estimate is the lowest made by any one, the same services are to cost $60,000. Mr. Rives, who, to say the least, is equally talented and honest, estimates that these services, under the Sub-Treasury system, cannot cost less than $600,000. For the sake of liberality, let us suppose that the estimates of the Secretary and Mr. Rives, are the two extremes, and that their mean is about the true estimate, and we shall then find, that when to that sum is added the $75,000, which the Bank paid us, the difference between the two systems, in favor of the Bank, and against the Sub-Treasury, is $405,000 a year. This sum, though small when compared to the many millions annually expended by the General Government, is, when viewed by itself, very large; and much too large, when viewed in any light, to be thrown away once a year for nothing. It is sufficient to pay the pensions of more than 4,000 Revolutionary Soldiers, or to purchase a 40-acre tract of Government land, for each one of more than 8,000 poor families.

To the argument against the Sub-Treasury, on the score of additional expense, its friends, so far as I know, attempt no answer. They choose, so far as I can learn, to treat the throwing away $405,000 once a year, as a matter entirely too small to merit their democratic notice.

I now come to the proposition, that it would be less secure than a National Bank, as a depository of the public money. The experience of the past, I think, proves the truth of this. And here, inasmuch as I rely chiefly upon experience to establish it, let me ask, how is it that we know any thing—that any event will occur, that any combination of circumstances will produce a certain result—except by the analogies of past experience? What has once happened, will invariably happen again, when the same circumstances which combined to produce it, shall again combine in the same way. We all feel that we know that a blast of wind would extinguish the flame of the candle that stands by me. How do we know it? We have never seen this flame thus extinguished. We know it, because we have seen through all our lives, that a blast of wind extinguishes the flame of a candle whenever it is thrown fully upon it. Again, we all feel to *know* that we have to die. How? We have never died yet. We know it, because we know, or at least think we know, that of all the beings, just like ourselves, who have been coming into the world for six thousand years, not one is now living who was here two hundred years ago.

I repeat then, that we know nothing of what will happen in future, but by the analogy of experience, and that the fair analogy of past experience fully proves that the Sub-Treasury would be a less safe depository of the public money than a National Bank. Examine it. By the Sub-Treasury scheme, the public money is to be kept, between the times of its collection and disbursement, by Treasurers of the Mint, Custom-house officers, Land officers, and some new officers to be appointed in the same way that those first enumerated are. Has a year passed since the organization of the Government, that numerous defalcations have not occurred among this class of officers? Look at Swartwout with his $1,200,000, Price with his $75,000, Harris with his $109,000, Hawkins with his $100,000, Linn with his $55,000, together with some twenty-five hundred lesser lights. Place the public money again in these same hands, and will it not again go the same way? Most assuredly it will. But turn to the history of the National

Bank in this country, and we shall there see, that those Banks
performed the fiscal operations of the Government thro' a period of 40 years, received, safely kept, transferred, disbursed,
an aggregate of nearly five hundred millions of dollars; and
that, in all that time, and with all that money, not one dollar,
nor one cent, did the Government lose by them. Place the
public money again in a similar depository, and will it not
again be safe?

But, conclusive as the experience of fifty years is, that individuals are unsafe depositories of the public money, and of
forty years that National Banks are safe depositories, we are
not left to rely solely upon that experience for the truth of
those propositions. If experience were silent upon the subject,
conclusive reasons could be shown for the truth of them.

It is often urged, that to say the public money will be more
secure in a National Bank, than in the hands of individuals, as
proposed in the Sub-Treasury, is to say, that Bank directors
and Bank officers are more honest than sworn officers of the
Government. Not so. We insist on no such thing. We say that
public officers, selected with reference to their capacity and
honesty, (which by the way, we deny is the practice in these
days,) stand an equal chance, precisely, of being capable and
honest, with Bank officers selected by the same rule. We further say, that with however much care selections may be
made, there will be some unfaithful and dishonest in both
classes. The experience of the whole world, in all by-gone
times, proves this true. The Saviour of the world chose twelve
disciples, and even one of that small number, selected by
superhuman wisdom, turned out a traitor and a devil. And,
it may not be improper here to add, that Judas carried the
bag—was the Sub-Treasurer of the Saviour and his disciples.

We then, do not say, nor need we say, to maintain our
proposition, that Bank officers are more honest than Government officers, selected by the same rule. What we do say, is,
that the *interest* of the Sub-Treasurer is *against his duty*—
while the *interest* of the Bank is *on the side of its duty*. Take
instances—a Sub-Treasurer has in his hands one hundred
thousand dollars of public money; his *duty* says—"You ought
to pay this money over"—but his *interest* says, "You ought to
run away with this sum, and be a nabob the balance of your

life." And who that knows anything of human nature, doubts that, in many instances, interest will prevail over duty, and that the Sub-Treasurer will prefer opulent knavery in a foreign land, to honest poverty at home? But how different is it with a Bank. Besides the Government money deposited with it, it is doing business upon a large capital of its own. If it proves faithful to the Government, it continues its business; if unfaithful, it forfeits its charter, breaks up its business, and thereby loses more than all it can make by seizing upon the Government funds in its possession. Its *interest*, therefore, is on the side of its duty—is to be faithful to the Government, and consequently, even the dishonest amongst its managers, have no temptation to be faithless to it. Even if robberies happen in the Bank, the losses are borne by the Bank, and the Government loses nothing. It is for this reason then, that we say a Bank is the more secure. It is because of that admirable feature in the Bank system, which places the *interest* and the *duty* of the depository both on one side; whereas that feature can never enter into the Sub-Treasury system. By the latter, the *interest* of the individuals keeping the public money, will wage an eternal war with their *duty*, and in very many instances must be victorious. In answer to the argument drawn from the fact that individual depositories of public money, have always proved unsafe, it is urged that even if we had a National Bank, the money has to *pass through* the same individual hands, that it will under the Sub-Treasury. This is only partially true in fact, and wholly fallacious in argument.

It is only partially true, in fact, because by the Sub-Treasury bill, four Receivers General are to be appointed by the President and Senate. These are new officers, and consequently, it cannot be true that the money, or any portion of it, has heretofore passed thro' their hands. These four new officers are to be located at New York, Boston, Charleston and St. Louis, and consequently are to be the depositories of all the money collected at or near those points; so that more than three-fourths of the public money will fall into the keeping of these four new officers, which did not exist as officers under the National Bank system. It is only partially true, then, that the money passes through the same hands, under a National Bank, as it would do under the Sub-Treasury.

It is true, that under either system, individuals must be employed as Collectors of the Customs, Receivers at the Land Offices, &c. &c. but the difference is, that under the Bank system, the receivers of all sorts, receive the money and pay it over to the Bank once a week when the collections are large, and once a month when they are small, whereas, by the Sub-Treasury system, individuals are not only to collect the money, but they are to *keep* it also, or pay it over to other individuals equally unsafe as themselves, to be by them kept, until it is wanted for disbursement. It is during the time that it is thus lying idle in their hands, that opportunity is afforded, and temptation held out to them to embezzle and escape with it. By the Bank system, each Collector or Receiver, is to deposite in Bank all the money in his hands at the end of each month at most, and to send the Bank certificates of deposite to the Secretary of the Treasury. Whenever that certificate of deposite fails to arrive at the proper time, the Secretary *knows* that the officer thus failing, is acting the knave; and if he is himself disposed to do his duty, he has him immediately removed from office, and thereby cuts him off from the possibility of embezzling but little more than the receipts of a single month. But by the Sub-Treasury System, the money is to lie month after month in the hands of individuals; larger amounts are to accumulate in the hands of the Receivers General, and some others, by perhaps ten to one, than ever accumulated in the hands of individuals before; yet during all this time, in relation to this great stake, the Secretary of the Treasury can comparatively know nothing. Reports, to be sure, he will have, but reports are often false, and always false when made by a knave to cloak his knavery. Long experience has shown, that nothing short of an actual demand of the money will expose an adroit peculator. Ask him for reports and he will give them to your heart's content; send agents to examine and count the money in his hands, and he will borrow of a friend, merely to be counted and then returned, a sufficient sum to make the sum square. Try what you will, it will all fail till you demand the money—then, and not till then, the truth will come.

The sum of the whole matter, I take to be this: Under the Bank system, while sums of money, by the law, were permitted to lie in the hands of individuals, *for very short periods only*, many and very large defalcations occurred by those individuals. Under the Sub-Treasury system, *much larger sums* are to lie in the hands of individuals *for much longer periods*, thereby multiplying *temptation* in proportion as the sums *are larger*; and multiplying *opportunity* in proportion as the periods *are longer* to, and for, those individuals to embezzle and escape with the public treasure; and, therefore, just in the proportion, that the *temptation* and the *opportunity* are greater under the Sub-Treasury than the Bank system, will the peculations and defalcations be greater under the former than they have been under the latter. The truth of this, independent of actual experience, is but little less than self-evident. I therefore, leave it.

But it is said, and truly too, that there is to be a *Penitentiary Department* to the Sub-Treasury. This, the advocates of the system will have it, will be a *"king-cure-all."* Before I go farther, may I not ask if the Penitentiary Department, is not itself an admission that they expect the public money to be stolen? Why build the cage if they expect to catch no birds? But to the question how effectual the Penitentiary will be in preventing defalcations. How effectual have Penitentiaries heretofore been in preventing the crimes they were established to suppress? Has not confinement in them long been the legal penalty of larceny, forgery, robbery, and many other crimes, in almost all the States? And yet, are not those crimes committed weekly, daily, nay, and even hourly, in every one of those States? Again, the gallows has long been the penalty of murder, and yet we scarcely open a newspaper, that does not relate a new case of that crime. If then, the Penitentiary has ever *heretofore* failed to prevent larceny, forgery and robbery, and the gallows and halter have likewise failed to prevent murder, by what process of reasoning, I ask, is it that we are to conclude the Penitentiary will *hereafter* prevent the stealing of the public money? But our opponents seem to think they answer the charge, that the money will be stolen, fully, if they can show that they will bring the offenders to punishment. Not so. Will the punishment of the thief bring back the stolen money? No more so than the hanging of a murderer restores his victim to life. What is the object desired? Certainly not the greatest number of thieves we can catch, but that the money may not be stolen. If, then, any plan can be devised for depositing the public treasure, where it will be never stolen, never embezzled, is not that the plan to be adopted? Turn, then, to a National Bank, and you have that plan, fully and completely successful, as tested by the experience of forty years.

I have now done with the three propositions that the Sub-Treasury would injuriously affect the currency, and would be more *expensive* and *less secure* as a depository of the public money than a National Bank. How far I have succeeded in establishing their truth is for others to judge.

Omitting, for want of time, what I had intended to say as to the effect of the Sub-Treasury, to bring the public money under the more immediate control of the President, than it has ever heretofore been, I now only ask the audience, when Mr. Calhoun shall answer me, *to hold him to the questions.* Permit him not to escape them. Require him *either* to show, that the Sub-Treasury *would not* injuriously affect the *currency*, or that we should in some way, receive an equivalent for that injurious effect. Require him *either* to show that the Sub-Treasury *would not be more expensive* as a fiscal agent, than a Bank, or that we should, in some way be compensated for that additional expense. And particularly require him to show, that the public money *would be as secure* in the Sub-Treasury as in a National Bank, or that the additional *insecurity* would be over-balanced by some good result of the proposed change.

No one of them, in my humble judgment, will he be able to do; and I venture the prediction, and ask that it may be especially noted, *that he will not attempt to answer the proposition, that the Sub-Treasury would be more expensive than a National Bank as a fiscal agent of the Government.*

As a sweeping objection to a National Bank, and consequently an argument in favor of the Sub-Treasury as a substitute for it, it often has been urged, and doubtless will be again, that such a bank is unconstitutional. We have often heretofore shown, and therefore need not in detail do so again, that a majority of the Revolutionary patriarchs, whoever acted officially upon the question, commencing with Gen. Washington and embracing Gen. Jackson, the larger number of the signers of the Declaration, and of the framers of the Constitution, who were in the Congress of 1791, have decided upon their oaths that such a bank is constitutional. We have also shown that the votes of Congress have more often been in favor of than against its constitutionality. In addition to all this we have shown that the Supreme Court— that tribunal which the Constitution has itself established to decide Constitutional questions—has solemnly decided that such a bank is constitutional. Protesting that these authorities ought to settle the question—ought to be conclusive, I will not urge them further now. I now propose to take a view of the question which I have not known to be taken by anyone before. It is, that whatever objection ever has or ever can be made to the constitutionality of a bank, will apply with equal force in its whole length, breadth and proportions to the Sub-Treasury. Our opponents say, there is no *express* authority in the Constitution to establish a Bank, and therefore a Bank is unconstitutional; but we, with equal truth, may say, there is no *express* authority in the Constitution to establish a Sub-Treasury, and therefore a Sub-Treasury is unconstitutional. Who then, has the advantage of this *"express authority"* argument? Does it not cut equally both ways? Does it not wound them as deeply and as deadly as it does us?

Our position is that both are constitutional. The Constitution enumerates expressly several powers which Congress may exercise, superadded to which is a general authority "to make all laws necessary and proper," for carrying into effect all the powers vested by the Constitution of the Government of the United States. One of the express powers given Congress, is "To lay and collect taxes; duties, imposts, and excises; to pay the debts, and provide for the common defence and general welfare of the United States." Now, Congress is expressly authorized to make all laws necessary and proper for carrying this power into execution. To carry it into execution, it is indispensably necessary to collect, safely keep, transfer, and disburse a revenue. To do this, a Bank is "necessary and proper." But, say our opponents, to authorize the making of a Bank, the *necessity* must be so great, that the power just recited, would be nugatory without it; and that that *necessity* is expressly negatived by the fact, that they have got along *ten* whole years without such a *Bank*. Immediately we turn on them, and say, that that sort of *necessity* for a Sub-Treasury does not exist, because we have got along *forty* whole years without one. And this time, it may be observed, that we are not merely equal with them in the argument, but we beat them *forty* to *ten*, or which is the same thing, *four* to *one*. On examination, it will be found, that the absurd rule, which prescribes that before we can constitutionally adopt a National Bank as a fiscal agent, we must show an *indispensable necessity* for it, will exclude every sort of fiscal agent that the mind of man can conceive. A *Bank* is not *indispensable*, because we can take the *Sub-Treasury*; the *Sub-Treasury* is not indispensable because we can take the *Bank*. The rule is too absurd to need further comment. Upon the phrase *"necessary and proper,"* in the Constitution, it seems to me more reasonable to say, that *some* fiscal agent is *indispensably necessary*; but, inasmuch as no *particular sort* of agent is thus *indispensable*, because some *other* sort might be adopted, we are left to choose that sort of agent, which may be most *"proper"* on grounds of expediency.

But it is said the Constitution gives no power to Congress to pass acts of incorporation. Indeed! What is the passing an act of incorporation, but the *making of a law*? Is any one wise enough to tell? The Constitution expressly gives Congress power *"to pass all laws necessary and proper,"* &c. If, then, the passing of a Bank charter, be the *"making a law necessary and proper,"* is it not clearly within the constitutional power of Congress to do so?

I now leave the Bank and the Sub-Treasury to try to answer, in a brief way, some of the arguments which, on previous evenings here, have been urged by Messrs. Lamborn and Douglass. Mr. Lamborn admits that *"errors,"* as he charitably calls them, have occurred under the present and late administrations, but he insists that as great *"errors"* have occurred under all administrations. This we respectfully deny. We admit that errors may have occurred under all administrations; but we insist that there is *no parallel* between them and those of the two last. If they can show that their errors are no greater in number and magnitude, than those of former times, we call off the dogs.

But they can do no such thing. To be brief, I will now

attempt a contrast of the "errors" of the two latter, with those of former administrations, in relation to the public expenditures only. What I am now about to say, as to the expenditures, will be, in all cases, exclusive of payments on the National debt. By an examination of authentic public documents, consisting of the regular series of annual reports, made by all the Secretaries of the Treasury from the establishment of the Government down to the close of the year 1838, the following contrasts will be presented.

1st. The last *ten* years under Gen. Jackson and Mr. Van Buren, cost more money than the first *twenty-seven* did, (including the heavy expenses of the late British war,) under Washington, Adams, Jefferson, and Madison.

2d. The last year of J. Q. Adams' administration cost, in round numbers, *thirteen* millions, being about *one* dollar to each soul in the nation; the last (1838) of Mr. Van Buren's cost *forty* millions, being about *two dollars and fifty cents* to each soul; and being larger than the expenditure of Mr. Adams in the proportion of *five* to *two*.

3d. The highest annual expenditure during the late British war, being in 1814, and while we had in actual service rising 188,000 militia, together with the whole regular army, swelling the number to greatly over 200,000, and they to be clad, fed and transported from point to point, with great rapidity and corresponding expense, and to be furnished with arms and ammunition, and they to be transported in like manner, and at like expense, was no more in round numbers than *thirty* millions; whereas, the annual expenditure of 1838, under Mr. Van Buren, and while we were at peace with every government in the world, was *forty* millions; being over the highest year of the late and very expensive war, in the proportion of *four* to *three*.

4th. Gen. Washington administered the Government *eight* years for *sixteen* millions. Mr. Van Buren administered it *one* year (1838) for *forty* millions; so that Mr. Van Buren expended *twice and a half* as much in *one* year, as Gen. Washington did in *eight*, and being in the proportion of *twenty* to *one*—or, in other words, had Gen. Washington administered the Government *twenty* years, at the same average expense that he did for *eight*, he would have carried us through the whole *twenty*, for no more money than Mr. Van Buren has expended in getting us through the single *one* of 1838.

Other facts, equally astounding, might be presented from the same authentic document; but I deem the foregoing abundantly sufficient to establish the proposition, that there is no parallel between the *"errors"* of the present and late administrations, and those of former times, and that Mr. Van Buren is wholly out of the line of all precedents.

But, Mr. Douglass, seeing that the enormous expenditure of 1838, has no parallel in the olden times, comes in with a long list of excuses for it. This list of excuses I will rapidly examine, and show, as I think, that the few of them which are true, prove nothing; and that the majority of them are wholly untrue in fact. He first says, that the expenditures of that year were made under the appropriations of Congress— *one branch of which was a Whig body*. It is true that those expenditures were made under the appropriations of Congress; but it is *untrue* that either branch of Congress was a *Whig* body. The Senate had fallen into the hands of the administration, more than a year before, as proven by the passage of the Expunging Resolution; and at the time those appropriations were made, there were too few Whigs in that body, to make a respectable struggle, in point of numbers, upon any question. This is notorious to all. The House of Representatives that voted those appropriations, was the same that first assembled at the called session of September, 1838. Although it refused to pass the Sub-Treasury Bill, a majority of its members were elected as friends of the administration, and proved their adherence to it, by the election of a Van Buren Speaker, and two Van Buren clerks. It is clear then, that both branches of the Congress that passed those appropriations were in the hands of Mr. Van Buren's friends, so that the Whigs had no power to arrest them, as Mr. Douglass would insist. And is not the charge of extravagant expenditures, equally well sustained, if shown to have been made by a Van Buren Congress, as if shown to have been made in any other way? A Van Buren Congress passed the bill; and Mr. Van Buren himself approved them, and consequently the party are wholly responsible for them.

Mr. Douglass next says that a portion of the expenditures of that year was made for the purchase of public lands from the Indians. Now it happens that no such purchase was made during that year. It is true that some money was paid that year in pursuance of Indian treaties; but no more, or rather not as much as had been paid on the same account in each of several preceding years.

Next he says that the Florida war created many millions of this year's expenditure. This is true, and it is also true that during that and every other year that that war has existed, it has cost three or four times as much as it would have done under an honest and judicious administration of the Government. The large sums foolishly, not to say corruptly, thrown away in that war constitute one of the just causes of complaint against the administration. Take a single instance. The agents of the Government in connection with that war needed a certain Steamboat; the owner proposed to sell it for ten thousand dollars; the agents refused to give that sum, but hired the boat at one hundred dollars per day, and kept it at that hire till it amounted to ninety-two thousand dollars. This fact is not found in the public reports, but depends with me, on the verbal statement of an officer of the navy, who says he knows it to be true. That the administration ought to be credited for the *reasonable* expenses of the Florida war, we have never denied. Those *reasonable* charges, we say, could not exceed one or two millions a year. Deduct such a sum from the forty-million expenditure of 1838, and the remainder will still be without a parallel as an annual expenditure.

Again, Mr. Douglass says that the removal of the Indians to the country west of the Mississippi created much of the expenditure of 1838. I have examined the public documents in relation to this matter, and find that less was paid for the removal of Indians in that than in some former years. The whole sum expended on that account in that year did not much exceed one-quarter of a million. For this small sum, altho' we do not think the administration entitled to credit, because large sums have been expended in the same way in former years, we consent it may take one and make the most of it.

Next, Mr. Douglass says that five millions of the expenditures of 1838 consisted of the payment of the French indemnity money to its individual claimants. I have carefully

examined the public documents, and thereby find this statement to be wholly untrue. Of the forty millions of dollars
expended in 1838, I am enabled to say positively that not one
dollar consisted of payments on the French indemnities. So
much for that excuse.

Next comes the Post-office. He says that five millions were
expended during that year to sustain that department. By a
like examination of public documents, I find this also wholly
untrue. Of the so often mentioned forty millions, not one
dollar went to the Post-office. I am glad, however, that the
Post-office has been referred to, because it warrants me in di-
gressing a little to inquire how it is that that department of
the Government has become a *charge* upon the Treasury,
whereas under Mr. Adams and the Presidents before him it
not only, to use a homely phrase, cut its own fodder, but
actually threw a surplus into the Treasury. Although nothing
of the forty millions was paid on that account in 1838, it is true
that five millions are appropriated *to be so expended* in 1839;
showing clearly that the department has become a *charge*
upon the Treasury. How has this happened? I account for it
in this way. The chief expense of the Post-office Department
consists of the payments of Contractors for carrying the mail.
Contracts for carrying the mails are by law let to the lowest
bidders, after advertisement. This plan introduces competition, and insures the transportation of the mails at fair prices,
so long as it is faithfully adhered to. It has ever been adhered
to until Mr. Barry was made Postmaster-General. When he
came into office, he formed the purpose of throwing the mail
contracts into the hands of his friends, to the exclusion of his
opponents. To effect this, the plan of letting to the lowest
bidder must be evaded, and it must be done in this way: the
favorite bid less by perhaps three or four hundred per cent.
than the contract could be performed for, and consequently
shutting out all honest competition, became the contractor.
The Postmaster-General would immediately add some slight
additional duty to the contract, and under the pretense of
extra allowance for extra services run the contract to double,
triple, and often quadruple what honest and fair bidders had
proposed to take it at. In 1834 the finances of the department
had become so deranged that total concealment was no

longer possible, and consequently a committee of the Senate
were directed to make a thorough investigation of its affairs.
Their report is found in the Senate Documents of 1833–34,
Vol. 5, Doc. 422; which documents may be seen at the Secretary's office, and I presume elsewhere in the State. The report
shows numerous cases of similar import, of one of which I
give the substance. The contract for carrying the mail upon a
certain route had expired, and of course was to be let again.
The old contractor offered to take it for $300 a year, the mail
to be transported thereon three times a week, or for $600
transported daily. One James Reeside bid $40 for three times
a week, or $99 daily, and of course received the contract. On
the examination of the committee, it was discovered that
Reeside had received for the service on this route, which he
had contracted to render for less than $100, the enormous sum
of $1,999! This is but a single case. Many similar ones, covering
some ten or twenty pages of a large volume, are given in that
report. The department was found to be insolvent to the
amount of half a million, and to have been so grossly misman-
aged, or rather so corruptly managed, in almost every particular, that the best friends of the Post Master General made no
defence of his administration of it. They admitted that he was
wholly unqualified for that office; but still he was retained in
it by the President, until he resigned voluntarily about a year
afterwards. And when he resigned it what do you think became of him? Why, he sunk into obscurity and disgrace, to be
sure, you will say. No such thing. Well, then, what did become of him? Why the President immediately expressed his
high disapprobation of his almost unequalled incapacity and
corruption, by appointing him to a foreign mission, with a
salary and outfit of $18,000 a year. The party now attempt to
throw Barry off, and to avoid the responsibility of his sins.
Did not the President endorse those sins, when on the very
heel of their commission, he appointed their author to the
very highest and most honorable office in his gift, and which
is but a single step behind the very goal of American political
ambition.

I return to another of Mr. Douglass' excuses for the expenditures of 1838, at the same time announcing the pleasing
intelligence, that this is the last one. He says that ten millions

of that years expenditure, was a contingent appropriation, to prosecute an anticipated war with Great Britain, on the Maine boundary question. Few words will settle this. First: that the ten millions appropriated was not *made* till 1839, and consequently could not have been expended in 1838; and, second: although it was appropriated, it has never been expended at all. Those who heard Mr. Douglass, recollect that he indulged himself in a contemptuous expression of pity for me. "Now he's got me," thought I. But when he went on to say that five millions of the expenditure of 1838, were payments of the French indemnities, *which I knew to be untrue*; that five millions had been for the Post Office, *which I knew to be untrue*; that ten millions had been for the Maine boundary war, *which I not only knew to be untrue, but supremely ridiculous also*; and when I saw that he was stupid enough to hope, that I would permit such groundless and audacious assertions to go unexposed, I readily consented, that on the score both of veracity and sagacity, the audience should judge whether he or I were the more deserving of the world's contempt.

Mr. Lamborn insists that the difference between the Van Buren party, and the Whigs is, that although, the former sometimes err in *practice*, they are always correct in *principle*— whereas the latter are wrong in *principle*—and the better to impress this proposition, he uses a figurative expression in these words: *"The Democrats are vulnerable in the heel, but they are sound in the head and the heart."* The first branch of the figure, that is that the Democrats are vulnerable in the heel, I admit is not merely figuratively, but literally true. Who that looks but for a moment at their Swartwouts, their Prices, their Harringtons, and their hundreds of others, scampering away with the public money to Texas, to Europe, and to every spot of the earth where a villain may hope to find refuge from justice, can at all doubt that they are most distressingly affected in their *heels* with a species of *"running itch."* It seems that this malady of their heels, operates on these *sound-headed* and *honest-hearted* creatures, very much like the cork-leg, in the comic song, did on its owner: which, when he had once got started on it, the more he tried to stop it, the more it would run away. At the hazard of wearing this point thread bare, I will relate an anecdote, which seems too strikingly in point to be omitted. A witty Irish soldier, who was always boasting of his bravery, when no danger was near, but who invariably retreated without orders at the first charge of an engagement, being asked by his Captain why he did so, replied: "Captain, I have as brave a *heart* as Julius Caesar ever had; but some how or other, whenever danger approaches, my *cowardly* legs will run away with it." So with Mr. Lamborn's party. They take the public money *into* their hand for the most laudable purpose, that *wise heads* and *honest hearts* can dictate; but before they can possibly get it *out* again their rascally *"vulnerable heels"* will run away with them.

Seriously: this proposition of Mr. Lamborn is nothing more or less, than a request that his party may be tried by their *professions* instead of their *practices*. Perhaps no position that the party assumes is more liable to, or more deserving of exposure, than this very modest request; and nothing but the unwarrantable length, to which I have already extended these remarks, forbids me now attempting to expose it. For the reason given, I pass it by.

I shall advert to but one more point.

Mr. Lamborn refers to the late elections in the States, and from their results, confidently predicts, that every State in the Union will vote for Mr. Van Buren at the next Presidential election. Address *that* argument to *cowards* and to *knaves*; with the *free* and the *brave* it will effect nothing. It *may* be true, if it *must*, let it. Many free countries have lost their liberty; and *ours may* lose hers; but if she shall, be it my proudest plume, not that I was the *last* to desert, but that I *never* deserted her. I know that the great volcano at Washington, aroused and directed by the evil spirit that reigns there, is belching forth the lava of political corruption, in a current broad and deep, which is sweeping with frightful velocity over the whole length and breadth of the land, bidding fair to leave unscathed no green spot or living thing, while on its bosom are riding like demons on the waves of Hell, the imps of that evil spirit, and fiendishly taunting all those who dare resist its destroying course, with the hopelessness of their effort; and knowing this, I cannot deny that all may be swept away. Broken by it, I, too, may be; bow to it I never will. The *probability* that we may fall in the struggle *ought not* to deter us from the support of a cause we believe to be just; it *shall not* deter me. If ever I feel the soul within me elevate and expand to those dimensions not wholly unworthy of its Almighty Architect, it is when I contemplate the cause of my country, deserted by all the world beside, and I standing up boldly and alone and hurling defiance at her victorious oppressors. Here, without contemplating consequences, before High Heaven, and in the face of the world, I swear eternal fidelity to the just cause, as I deem it, of the land of my life, my liberty and my love. And who, that thinks with me, will not fearlessly adopt the oath that I take. Let none faulter, who thinks he is right, and we may succeed. But, if after all, we shall fail, be it so. We still shall have the proud consolation of saying to our consciences, and to the departed shade of our country's freedom, that the cause approved of our judgment, and adored of our hearts, in disaster, in chains, in torture, in death, we NEVER faultered in defending.

December 26, 1839

Plan of Campaign in 1840

1st. Appoint one person in each county as county captain, and take his pledge to perform promptly all the duties assigned him.

Duties of the County Captain

1st. To procure from the poll-books a separate list for each Precinct of all the names of all those persons who voted the Whig ticket in August.

2nd. To appoint one person in each Precinct as Precinct Captain, and, by a personal interview with him, procure his pledge, to perform promptly all the duties assigned him.

3rd. To deliver to each Precinct Captain the list of names as above, belonging to his Precinct; and also a written list of his duties.

Duties of the Precinct Captain.

1st. To divide the list of names delivered him by the county Captain, into Sections of ten who reside most convenient to each other.

2nd. To appoint one person of each Section as Section Captain, and by a personal interview with him, procure his pledge to perform promptly all the duties assigned him.

3rd. To deliver to each Section Captain the list of names belonging to his Section and also a written list of his duties.

Duties of the Section Captain.

1st. To see each man of his Section face to face, and procure his pledge that he will for no consideration (impossibilities excepted) stay from the polls on the first monday in November; and that he will record his vote as early on the day as possible.

2nd. To add to his Section the name of every person in his vicinity who did not vote with us in August, but who will vote with us in the fall, and take the same pledge of him, as from the others.

3rd. To *task* himself to procure at least such additional names to his Section.

c. January 1840

To John T. Stuart

Dear Stuart: Springfield, Jany. 20th. 1840.

Yours of the 5th. Inst. is recd. It is the first from you for a great while. You wish the news from here. The Legislature is in session yet, but has done nothing of importance. The following is my guess as to what *will be* done. The Internal Improvement System will be put down in a lump, without benefit of clergy. The Bank will be resusitated with some trifling modifications. Whether the canal will go ahead or stop is verry doubtful. Whether the State House will go ahead, depends upon the laws already in force.

A proposition made in the House today to throw off to the Teritory of Wisconsin about 14 of our Northern counties — decided. Ayes 11. Noes. 70.

Be sure to send me as many copies of the life of Harrison, as you can spare from other uses.

Be verry sure to procure and send me the Senate Journal of New York of September 1814. I have a newspaper article which says that that document proves that Van Buren voted against raising troops in the last war.

And, in general, send me every thing you think will be a good *"war-club."* The nomination of Harrison takes first rate. You know I am never sanguine; but I believe we will carry the state. The chance for doing so, appears to me 25 per cent better than it did for you to beat Douglass. A great many of the grocery sort of Van Buren men, as formerly, are out for Harrison. Our Irish Blacksmith Gregory, is for Harrison. I believe I may say, that all our friends think the chance of carrying the state, verry good.

You have heard that the Whigs and Locos had a political discussion shortly after the meeting of the Legislature. Well, I made a big speech, which is in progress of printing in pamphlet form. To enlighten you and the rest of the world, I shall send you a copy when it is finished.

I cant think of any thing else now. Your friend, as ever —

To Andrew McCormick

Dear Captain:

I have just learned, with utter astonishment, that you have some notion of voting for Walters. This certainly *can not* be true. It *can not* be, that one so true, firm, and unwavering as you have ever been, can for a moment think of such a thing. What! support that *pet* of all those who continually slander and abuse you, and labour, day and night, for your destruction. All our friends are ready to cut our throats about it. An angel from Heaven could not make *them* believe, that we do not connive at it. For Heaven's sake, for your friends sake, for the sake of the recollection of all the hard battles we have heretofore fought shoulder, to shoulder, do not forsake us this time. We have been told for two or three days that you were in danger; but we gave it the lie whenever we heard it. We were willing to bet our lives upon you. Stand by us this time, and nothing in our power to confer, shall ever be denied you. Surely! Surely! you do not doubt *my friendship* for you. If you do, what under Heaven can I do, to convince you. Surely you will not think those who have been your revilers, better friends than I. Read this & write me what you will do. Your friend,

c. December 1840–January 1841

To John T. Stuart

Dear Stuart: Springfield, Jany. 20th. 1841

I have had no letter from you since you left. No matter for that. What I wish now is to speak of our Post-Office. You know I desired Dr. Henry to have that place when you left; I now desire it more than ever. I have, within the last few days, been making a most discreditable exhibition of myself in the way of hypochondriaism and thereby got an impression that Dr. Henry is necessary to my existence. Unless he gets that place he leaves Springfield. You therefore see how much I am interested in the matter.

We shall shortly forward you a petition in his favour signed by all or nearly all the Whig members of the Legislature, as well as other whigs.

This, together with what you know of the Dr.'s position and merits I sincerely hope will secure him the appointment. My heart is verry much set upon it.

Pardon me for not writing more; I have not sufficient composure to write a long letter. As ever yours

To John T. Stuart

Dear Stuart: Jany. 23rd. 1841– Springfield, Ills.

Yours of the 3rd. Inst. is recd. & I proceed to answer it as well as I can, tho' from the deplorable state of my mind at this time, I fear I shall give you but little satisfaction. About the matter of the congressional election, I can only tell you, that there is a bill now before the Senate adopting the General Ticket system; but whether the party have fully determined on it's adoption is yet uncertain. There is no sign of opposition to you among our friends, and none that I can learn among our enemies; tho', of course, there will be, if the Genl. Ticket be adopted. The Chicago American, Peoria Register, & Sangamo Journal, have already hoisted your flag upon their own responsibility; & the other whig papers of the District are expected to follow immediately. On last evening there was a meeting of our friends at Butler's; and I submitted the question to them & found them unanamously in favour of having you announced as a candidate. A few of us this morning, however, concluded, that as you were already being announced in the papers, we would delay announcing you, *as by your own authority* for a week or two. We thought that to appear too keen about it might spur our opponents on about their Genl. Ticket project. Upon the whole, I think I may say with certainty, that your reelection is sure, if it be in the power of the whigs to make it so.

For not giving you a general summary of news, you *must* pardon me; it is not in my power to do so. I am now the most miserable man living. If what I feel were equally distributed to the whole human family, there would not be one cheerful face on the earth. Whether I shall ever be better I can not tell; I awfully forebode I shall not. To remain as I am is impossible; I must die or be better, it appears to me. The matter you speak of on my account, you may attend to as you say, unless you shall hear of my condition forbidding it. I say this, because I fear I shall be unable to attend to any business here, and a change of scene might help me. If I could be myself, I would rather remain at home with Judge Logan. I can write no more. Your friend, as ever—

To Joshua F. Speed

Dear Speed: Springfield, June 19th. 1841
    We have had the highest state of excitement here for a week past that our community has ever witnessed; and, although

the public feeling is now somewhat allayed, the curious affair
which aroused it, is verry far from being, even yet, cleared of
mystery. It would take a quire of paper to give you any thing
like a full account of it; and I therefore only propose a brief
outline. The chief personages in the drama, are Archibald
Fisher, supposed to be murdered; and Archibald Trailor,
Henry Trailor, and William Trailor, supposed to have murdered him. The three Trailors are brothers; the first, Arch: as
you know, lives in town; the second, Henry, in Clary's
Grove, and the third, Wm., in Warren county; and Fisher, the
supposed *murderee*, being without a family, had made his
home with William. On saturday evening, being the 29th. of
May, Fisher and William came to Henry's in a one horse
dearborn, and there staid over sunday; and on monday all
three came to Springfield, Henry on horseback, and joined
Archibald at Myers' the dutch carpenter. That evening at supper Fisher was missing, and so next morning. Some ineffectual search was made for him; and on tuesday at 1 o'clock PM.
Wm. & Henry started home without him. In a day or so
Henry and one or two of his Clary Grove neighbours came
back and searched for him again, and advertised his disappearance in the paper. The knowledge of the matter thus far,
had not been general; and here it dropped entirely till about
the 10th. Inst. when Keys received a letter from the Post Master in Warren stating that Wm. had arrived at home, and was
telling a verry mysterious and improbable story about the disappearance of Fisher, which induced the community there to
suppose that he had been disposed of unfairly. Key's made
this letter public, which immediately set the whole town and
adjoining country agog; and so it has continued until yesterday. The mass of the People commenced a systematic search
for the dead body, while Wickersham was dispatched to arrest
Henry Trailor at the Grove; and Jim Maxey, to Warren to
arrest William. On monday last Henry was brought in, and
showed an evident inclination to insinuate that he knew
Fisher to be dead, and that Arch: & Wm. had killed him. He
said he guessed the body could be found in Spring Creek
between the Beardstown road bridge and Hickoxes mill.
Away the People swept like a herd of buffaloes, and cut down
Hickoxes mill dam *nolens volens*, to draw the water out of the

pond; and then went up and down, and down and up the creek, fishing and raking, and ducking and diving for two days, and after all, no dead body found. In the mean time a sort of scuffling ground had been found in the brush in the angle or point where the road leading into the woods past the brewery, and the one leading in past the brick-yard join. From this scuffle ground, was the sign of something about the size of a man having been dragged to the edge of the thicket, where it joined the track of some small wheeled carriage which was drawn by one horse, as shown by the horse tracks. The carriage track led off towards Spring Creek. Near this drag trail, Dr. Merryman found *two hairs*, which after a long scientific examination, he pronounced to be triangular human hairs, which term, he says includes within it, the whiskers, the hairs growing under the arms and on other parts of the body; and he judged that these two were of the whiskers, because the ends were cut, showing that they had flourished in the neighbourhood of the razor's operations. On thursday last, Jim: Maxey brought in William Trailor from Warren. On the same day Arch: was arrested and put in jail. Yesterday (friday) William was put upon his examining trial before May and Lavely. Archibald and Henry were both present. Lamborn prossecuted, and Logan, Baker, and your humble servant, defended. A great many witnesses were introduced and examined; but I shall only mention those whose testimony seemed to be the most important. The first of these was Capt. Ransdell. He swore, that when William and Henry left Springfield for home on the tuesday before mentioned, they did not take the direct route, which, you know, leads by the butcher shop, but that they followed the street North untill they got opposite, or nearly opposite May's new house, after which he could not see them from where he stood; and it was afterwards proven that in about an hour after they started, they came into the street by the butcher's shop from towards the brick yard. Dr. Merryman & others swore to what is before stated about the scuffle-ground, drag-trail, whiskers, and carriage tracks. Henry was then introduced by the prossecution. He swore, that when they started for home, they went out North as Ransdell stated, and turned down West by the brick yard into the woods, and there met Archibald; that they proceeded a small distance further, where he was placed as a sentinel to watch for, and announce the approach of any one that might happen that way; that William and Arch: took the dearborn out of the road a small distance to the edge of the thicket, where they stopped, and he saw them lift the body of a man into it; that they then moved off with the carriage in the direction of Hickoxes mill, and he loitered about for something like an hour, when William returned with the carriage, but without Arch: and said that they had put *him* in a safe place; that they then went some how, he did not know exactly how, into the road close to the brewery, and proceeded on to Clary's Grove. He also stated that sometime during the day, William told him, that he and Arch: had killed Fisher the evening before; that the way they did it was by him (William) knocking him down with a club, and Arch: then choking him to death. An old man from Warren, called Dr. Gilmore, was then introduced on the part of the defence. He swore that he had known Fisher for several years; that Fisher had resided at his house a long time at each of two different spells; once while he built a barn for him, and once while he was doctored for some chronic disease; that two or three years ago, Fisher had a serious hurt in his head by the bursting of a gun, since which he has been subject to continual bad health, and occasional abberations of mind. He also stated that on last tuesday, being the same day that Maxey arrested William Trailor, he (the Dr) was from home in the early part of the day, and on his return about 11 o'clock, found Fisher at his house in bed, and apparantly verry unwell; that he asked how he had come from Springfield; that Fisher said he had come by Peoria, and also told several other places he had been at not in the direction of Peoria, which showed that he, at the time of speaking, did not know where he had been, or that he had been wandering about in a state of derangement. He further stated that in about two hours he received a note from one of William Trailor's friends, advising him of his arrest, and requesting him to go on to Springfield as a witness, to testify to the state of Fisher's health in former times; that he immediately set off, catching up two of his neighbours, as company, and riding all evening and all night, overtook Maxey & William at Lewiston in Fulton county;

that Maxey refusing to discharge Trailor upon his statement, his two neighbors returned, and he came on to Springfield. Some question being made whether the doctor's story was not a fabrication, several acquaintances of his, among whom was the same Post Master who wrote to Key's as before mentioned, were introduced as sort of compurgators, who all swore, that they knew the doctor be of good character for truth and veracity, and generally of good character in every way. Here the testimony ended, and the Trailors were discharged, Arch: and William expressing, both in word and manner their entire confidence that Fisher would be found alive at the doctor's by Galaway, Mallory, and Myers, who a day before had been dispached for that purpose; while Henry still protested that no power on earth could ever show Fisher alive. Thus stands this curious affair now. When the doctor's story was first made public, it was amusing to scan and contemplate the countenances, and hear the remarks of those who had been actively engaged in the search for the dead body. Some looked quizical, some melancholly, and some furiously angry. Porter, who had been very active, swore he always knew the man was not dead, and that *he* had not stirred an inch to hunt for him; Langford, who had taken the lead in cuting down Hickoxes mill dam, and wanted to hang Hickox for objecting, looked most awfully wo-begone; he seemed the *"wictim of hunrequited haffection"* as represented in the comic almanic we used to laugh over; and Hart, the little drayman that hauled Molly home once, said it was too *damned* bad, to have so much trouble, and no hanging after all.

I commenced this letter on yesterday, since which I received yours of the 13th. I stick to my promise to come to Louisville. Nothing new here except what I have written. I have not seen Sarah since my long trip, and I am going out there as soon as I mail this letter. Yours forever

To Mary Speed

Miss Mary Speed,   Bloomington, Illinois,
Louisville, Ky.   Sept. 27th. 1841

My Friend: Having resolved to write to some of your mother's family, and not having the express permission of any

one of them to do so, I have had some little difficulty in determining on which to inflict the task of reading what I now
feel must be a most dull and silly letter; but when I remembered that you and I were something of cronies while I was at
Farmington, and that, while there, I once was under the necessity of shutting you up in a room to prevent your committing an assault and battery upon me, I instantly decided that
you should be the devoted one.

I assume that you have not heard from Joshua & myself since we left, because I think it doubtful whether he has
written.

You remember there was some uneasiness about Joshua's
health when we left. That little indisposition of his turned out
to be nothing serious; and it was pretty nearly forgotten
when we reached Springfield. We got on board the Steam
Boat Lebanon, in the locks of the Canal about 12. o'clock. M.
of the day we left, and reached St. Louis the next monday at 8
P.M. Nothing of interest happened during the passage, except
the vexatious delays occasioned by the sand bars be thought
interesting. By the way, a fine example was presented on
board the boat for contemplating the effect of *condition* upon
human happiness. A gentleman had purchased twelve negroes
in diferent parts of Kentucky and was taking them to a farm
in the South. They were chained six and six together. A small
iron clevis was around the left wrist of each, and this fastened
to the main chain by a shorter one at a convenient distance
from, the others; so that the negroes were strung together
precisely like so many fish upon a trot-line. In this condition
they were being separated forever from the scenes of their
childhood, their friends, their fathers and mothers, and brothers and sisters, and many of them, from their wives and children, and going into perpetual slavery where the lash of the
master is proverbially more ruthless and unrelenting than any
other where; and yet amid all these distressing circumstances,
as we would think them, they were the most cheerful and
apparantly happy creatures on board. One, whose offence for
which he had been sold was an over-fondness for his wife,
played the fiddle almost continually; and the others danced,
sung, cracked jokes, and played various games with cards

from day to day. How true it is that "God tempers the wind to the shorn lamb," or in other words, that He renders the worst of human conditions tolerable, while He permits the best, to be nothing better than tolerable.

To return to the narative. When we reached Springfield, I staid but one day when I started on this tedious circuit where I now am. Do you remember my going to the city while I was in Kentucky, to have a tooth extracted, and making a failure of it? Well, that same old tooth got to paining me so much, that about a week since I had it torn out, bringing with it a bit of the jawbone; the consequence of which is that my mouth is now so sore that I can neither talk, nor eat. I am litterally "subsisting on savoury remembrances"—that is, being unable to eat, I am living upon the remembrance of the delicious dishes of peaches and cream we used to have at your house.

When we left, Miss Fanny Henning was owing you a visit, as I understood. Has she paid it yet? If she has, are you not convinced that she is one of the sweetest girls in the world? There is but one thing about her, so far as I could perceive, that I would have otherwise than as it is. That is something of a tendency to mellancholly. This, let it be observed, is a misfortune not a fault. Give her an assurance of my verry highest regard, when *you* see her.

Is little Siss Eliza Davis at your house yet? If she is kiss her "o'er and o'er again" for me.

Tell your mother that I have not got her "present" with me; but that I intend to read it regularly when I return home. I doubt not that it is really, as she says, the best cure for the "Blues" could one but take it according to the truth.

Give my respects to all your sisters (including "Aunt Emma") and brothers. Tell Mrs. Peay, of whose happy face I shall long retain a pleasant remembrance, that I have been trying to think of a name for her homestead, but as yet, can not satisfy myself with one. I shall be verry happy to receive a line from you, soon after you receive this; and, in case you choose to favour me with one, address it to Charleston, Coles Co. Ills as I shall be there about the time to receive it. Your sincere friend

To Joshua F. Speed

My Dear Speed:

Feeling, as you know I do, the deepest solicitude for the success of the enterprize you are engaged in, I adopt this as the last method I can invent to aid you, in case (which God forbid) you shall need any aid. I do not place what I am going to say on paper, because I can say it any better in that way than I could by word of mouth; but because, were I to say it orrally, before we part, most likely you would forget it at the verry time when it might do you some good. As I think it reasonable that you will feel verry badly some time between this and the final consummation of your purpose, it is intended that you shall read this just at such a time.

Why I say it is reasonable that you will feel verry badly yet, is, because of *three special causes*, added to the *general one* which I shall mention.

The general cause is, that you are *naturally of a nervous temperament*; and this I say from what I have seen of you personally, and what you have told me concerning your mother at various times, and concerning your brother William at the time his wife died.

The first special cause is, *your exposure to bad weather* on your journey, which my experience clearly proves to be verry severe on defective nerves.

The second is, *the absence of all business and conversation of friends*, which might divert your mind, and give it occasional rest from that *intensity* of thought, which will some times wear the sweetest idea thread-bare and turn it to the bitterness of death.

The third is, *the rapid and near approach of that crisis on which all your thoughts and feelings concentrate.*

If from all these causes you shall escape and go through triumphantly, without another "twinge of the soul," I shall be most happily, but most egregiously deceived.

If, on the contrary, you shall, as I expect you will at some time, be agonized and distressed, let me, who have some reason to speak with judgement on such a subject, beseech you, to ascribe it to the causes I have mentioned; and not to some false and ruinous suggestion of the Devil.

"But" you will say "do not your causes apply to every one engaged in a like undertaking?"

By no means. *The particular causes*, to a greater or less extent, perhaps do apply in all cases; but the *general one*, nervous debility, which is the key and conductor of all the particular ones, and without which *they* would be utterly harmless, though it *does* pertain to you, *does not* pertain to one in a thousand. It is out of this, that the painful difference between you and the mass of the world springs.

I know what the painful point with you is, at all times when you are unhappy. It is an apprehension that you do not love her as you should. What nonsense! — How came you to court her? Was it because you thought she desired it; and that you had given her reason to expect it? If it was for that, why did not the same reason make you court Ann Todd, and at least twenty others of whom you can think, & to whom it would apply with greater force than to *her*? Did you court her for her wealth? Why, you knew she had none. But you say you *reasoned* yourself *into* it. What do you mean by that? Was it not, that you found yourself unable to *reason* yourself *out of* it? Did you not think, and partly form the purpose, of courting her the first time you ever saw or heard of her? What had reason to do with it, at that early stage? There was nothing *at that time* for reason to work upon. Whether she was moral, aimiable, sensible, or even of good character, you did not, nor could not then know; except perhaps you might infer the last from the company you found her in. All you then did or could know of her, was her *personal appearance and deportment*; and these, if they impress at all, impress the *heart* and not the head.

Say candidly, were not those heavenly *black eyes*, the whole basis of all your early *reasoning* on the subject?

After you and I had once been at her residence, did you not go and take me all the way to Lexington and back, for no other purpose but to get to see her again, on our return, in that seeming to take a trip for that express object?

What earthly consideration would you take to find her scouting and despising you, and giving herself up to another? But of this you have no apprehension; and therefore you can not bring it home to your feelings.

I shall be so anxious about you, that I want you to write me every mail. Your friend

c. early January 1842

To Joshua F. Speed

Dear Speed: Springfield, Ills. Feby. 3– 1842–

Your letter of the 25th. Jany. came to hand to-day. You well know that I do not feel my own sorrows much more keenly than I do yours, when I know of them; and yet I assure you I was not much hurt by what you wrote me of your excessively bad feeling at the time you wrote. Not that I am less capable of sympathising with you now than ever; not that I am less your friend than ever, but because I hope and believe, that your present anxiety and distress about *her* health and *her* life, must and will forever banish those horid doubts, which I know you sometimes felt, as to the truth of your affection for her. If they can be once and forever removed, (and I almost feel a presentiment that the Almighty has sent your present affliction expressly for that object) surely, nothing can come in their stead, to fill their immeasurable measure of misery. The death scenes of those we love, are surely painful enough; but these we are prepared to, and expect to see. They happen to all, and all know they must happen. Painful as they are, they are not an unlooked-for-sorrow. Should she, as you fear, be destined to an early grave, it is indeed, a great consolation to know that she is so well prepared to meet it. Her religion, which you once disliked so much, I will venture you now prize most highly.

But I hope your melancholly bodings as to her early death, are not well founded. I even hope, that ere this reaches you, she will have returned with improved and still improving health; and that you will have met her, and forgotten the sorrows of the past, in the enjoyment of the present.

I would say more if I could; but it seems I have said enough. It really appears to me that you yourself ought to rejoice, and not sorrow, at this indubitable evidence of your undying affection for her. Why Speed, if you did not love her, although you might not wish her death, you would most calmly be resigned to it. Perhaps this point is no longer a question with you, and my pertenacious dwelling upon it, is a rude intrusion upon your feelings. If so, you must pardon me. You know the Hell I have suffered on that point, and how tender I am upon it. You know I do not mean wrong.

I have been quite clear of hypo since you left,—even better than I was along in the fall.

I have seen Sarah but once. She seemed verry cheerful, and so, I said nothing to her about what we spoke of.

Old uncle Billy Herndon is dead; and it is said this evening that uncle Ben Ferguson will not live. This I believe is all the news, and enough at that unless it were better.

Write me immediately on the receipt of this. Your friend, as ever

To Joshua F. Speed

Dear Speed: Springfield, Ills. Feby. 13. 1842—

Yours of the 1st. Inst. came to hand three or four days ago. When this shall reach you, you will have been Fanny's husband several days. You know my desire to befriend you is everlasting—that I will never cease, while I know how to do any thing.

But you will always hereafter, be on ground that I have never ocupied, and consequently, if advice were needed, I might advise wrong.

I do fondly hope, however, that you will never again need any comfort from abroad. But should I be mistaken in this— should excessive pleasure still be accompanied with a painful counterpart at times, still let me urge you, as I have ever done, to remember in the depth and even the agony of despondency, that verry shortly you are to feel well again. I am now fully convinced, that you love her as ardently as you are capable of loving. Your ever being happy in her presence, and your intense anxiety about her health, if there were nothing else, would place this beyond all dispute in my mind. I incline to think it probable, that your nerves will fail you occasionally for a while; but once you get them fairly graded now, that trouble is over forever.

I think if I were you, in case my mind were not exactly right, I would avoid being *idle*; I would immediately engage in some business, or go to making preparations for it, which would be the same thing.

If you went through the ceremony *calmly*, or even with sufficient composure not to excite alarm in any present, you are safe, beyond question, and in two or three months, to say the most, will be the happiest of men.

I hope with tolerable confidence, that this letter is a plaster for a place that is no longer sore. God grant it may be so.

I would desire you to give my particular respects to Fanny, but perhaps you will not wish her to know you have received this, lest she should desire to see it. Make her write me an answer to my last letter to her at any rate. I would set great value upon another letter from her.

Write me whenever you have leisure. Yours forever.

Address to the Washington Temperance
Society of Springfield, Illinois

Although the Temperance cause has been in progress for near twenty years, it is apparent to all, that it is, *just now*, being crowned with a degree of success, hitherto unparalleled.

The list of its friends is daily swelled by the additions of fifties, of hundreds, and of thousands. The cause itself seems suddenly transformed from a cold abstract theory, to a living, breathing, active, and powerful chieftain, going forth "conquering and to conquer." The citadels of his great adversary are daily being stormed and dismantled; his temples and his altars, where the rites of his idolatrous worship have long been performed, and where human sacrifices have long been wont to be made, are daily desecrated and deserted. The trump of the conqueror's fame is sounding from hill to hill, from sea to sea, and from land to land, and calling millions to his standard at a blast.

For this new and splendid success, we heartily rejoice. That that success is so much greater *now* than *heretofore*, is doubtless owing to rational causes; and if we would have it to continue, we shall do well to enquire what those causes are. The warfare heretofore waged against the demon of Intemperance, has, some how or other, been erroneous. Either the champions engaged, or the tactics they adopted, have not been the most proper. These champions for the most part, have been Preachers, Lawyers, and hired agents. Between these and the mass of mankind, there is a want of *approachability*, if the term be admissible, partially at least, fatal to their success. They are supposed to have no sympathy of feeling or interest, with those very persons whom it is their object to convince and persuade.

And again, it is so easy and so common to ascribe motives to men of these classes, other than those they profess to act upon. The *preacher*, it is said, advocates temperance because he is a fanatic, and desires a union of Church and State; the *lawyer*, from his pride and vanity of hearing himself speak; and the *hired agent*, for his salary. But when one, who has long been known as a victim of intemperance, bursts the fetters that have bound him, and appears before his neighbors "clothed, and in his right mind," a redeemed specimen of long lost humanity, and stands up with tears of joy trembling in eyes, to tell of the miseries *once* endured, *now* to be endured no more forever; of his once naked and starving children, now clad and fed comfortably; of a wife long weighed down with woe, weeping, and a broken heart, now restored to health, happiness, and renewed affection; and how easily it all is done, once it is resolved to be done; however simple his language, there is a logic, and an eloquence in it, that few, with human feelings, can resist. They cannot say that *he* desires a union of church and state, for he is not a church member; they can not say *he* is vain of hearing himself speak, for his whole demeanor shows, he would gladly avoid speaking at all; they cannot say *he* speaks for pay for he receives none, and asks for none. Nor can his sincerity in any way be doubted; or his sympathy for those he would persuade to imitate his example, be denied.

In my judgment, it is to the battles of this new class of champions that our late success is greatly, perhaps chiefly, owing. But, had the old school champions themselves, been of the most wise selecting, was their *system* of tactics, the most judicious? It seems to me, it was not. Too much denunciation against dram sellers and dram-drinkers was indulged in. This, I think, was both impolitic and unjust. It was *impolitic*, because, it is not much in the nature of man to be driven to any thing; still less to be driven about that which is exclusively his own business; and least of all, where such driving is to be submitted to, at the expense of pecuniary interest, or burning appetite. When the dram-seller and drinker, were incessantly told, not in the accents of entreaty and persuasion, diffidently addressed by erring man to an erring brother; but in the thundering tones of anathema and denunciation, with which the lordly Judge often groups together all the crimes of the felon's life, and thrusts them in his face just ere he passes sentence of death upon him, that *they* were the authors of all the vice and misery and crime in the land; that *they* were the manufacturers and material of all the thieves and robbers and murderers that infested the earth; that *their* houses were the workshops of the devil; and that *their persons* should be shunned by all the good and virtuous, as moral pestilences—I say, when they were told all this, and in this way, it is not wonderful that they were slow, *very slow*, to acknowledge the truth of such denunciations, and to join the ranks of their denouncers, in a hue and cry against themselves.

To have expected them to do otherwise than as they did—to have expected them not to meet denunciation with denunciation, crimination with crimination, and anathema with anathema, was to expect a reversal of human nature, which is God's decree, and never can be reversed. When the conduct of men is designed to be influenced, *persuasion*, kind, unassuming persuasion, should ever be adopted. It is an old and a true maxim, that a "drop of honey catches more flies than a gallon of gall." So with men. If you would win a man to your cause, *first* convince him that you are his sincere friend. Therein is a drop of honey that catches his heart, which, say what he will, is the great high road to his reason, and which, when once gained, you will find but little trouble in convincing his judgment of the justice of your cause, if indeed that cause really be a just one. On the contrary, assume to dictate to his judgment, or to command his action, or to mark him as one to be shunned and despised, and he will retreat within himself, close all the avenues to his head and his heart; and tho' your cause be naked truth itself, transformed to the heaviest lance, harder than steel, and sharper than steel can be made, and tho' you throw it with more than Herculean force and precision, you shall no more be able to pierce him, than to penetrate the hard shell of a tortoise with a rye straw.

Such is man, and so *must* he be understood by those who would lead him, even to his own best interest.

On this point, the Washingtonians greatly excel the temperance advocates of former times. Those whom *they* desire to convince and persuade, are their old friends and companions. They know they are not demons, nor even the worst of men. *They* know that generally, they are kind, generous and charitable, even beyond the example of their more staid and sober neighbors. *They* are practical philanthropists; and *they* glow with a generous and brotherly zeal, that mere theorizers are incapable of feeling. Benevolence and charity possess *their* hearts entirely; and out of the abundance of their hearts, their tongues give utterance. "Love through all their actions runs, and all their words are mild." In this spirit they speak and act, and in the same, they are heard and regarded. And when such is the temper of the advocate, and such of the audience, no good cause can be unsuccessful.

But I have said that denunciations against dram-sellers and dram-drinkers, are *unjust* as well as impolitic. Let us see.

I have not enquired at what period of time the use of intoxicating drinks commenced; nor is it important to know. It is sufficient that to all of us who now inhabit the world, the practice of drinking them, is just as old as the world itself,—that is, we have seen the one, just as long as we have seen the other. When all such of us, as have now reached the years of maturity, first opened our eyes upon the stage of existence, we found intoxicating liquor, recognized by every body, used by every body, and repudiated by nobody. It commonly entered into the first draught of the infant, and the last draught of the dying man. From the sideboard of the parson, down to the ragged pocket of the houseless loafer, it was constantly found. Physicians prescribed it in this, that, and the other disease. Government provided it for its soldiers and sailors; and to have a rolling or raising, a husking or hoe-down, any where without it, was *positively insufferable*.

So too, it was every where a respectable article of manufacture and of merchandize. The making of it was regarded as an honorable livelihood; and he who could make most, was the most enterprising and respectable. Large and small manufactories of it were every where erected, in which all the earthly goods of their owners were invested. Wagons drew it from town to town—boats bore it from clime to clime, and the winds wafted it from nation to nation; and merchants bought and sold it, by wholesale and by retail, with precisely the same feelings, on the part of seller, buyer, and bystander, as are felt at the selling and buying of flour, beef, bacon, or any other of the real necessaries of life. Universal public opinion not only tolerated, but recognized and adopted its use.

It is true, that even *then*, it was known and acknowledged, that many were greatly injured by it; but none seemed to think the injury arose from the *use* of a *bad thing*, but from the *abuse* of a *very good thing*. The victims to it were pitied, and compassionated, just as now are, the heirs of consumptions, and other hereditary diseases. Their failing was treated as a *misfortune*, and not as a *crime*, or even as a *disgrace*.

If, then, what I have been saying be true, is it wonderful, that *some* should think and act *now*, as *all* thought and acted *twenty years ago*? And is it *just* to assail, *contemn*, or despise them, for doing so? The universal *sense* of mankind, on any subject, is an argument, or at least an *influence* not easily overcome. The success of the argument in favor of the existence of an over-ruling Providence, mainly depends upon that sense; and men ought not, in justice, to be denounced for yielding to it, in any case, or for giving it up slowly, *especially*, where they are backed by interest, fixed habits, or burning appetites.

Another error, as it seems to me, into which the old reformers fell, was, the position that all habitual drunkards were utterly incorrigible, and therefore, must be turned adrift, and damned without remedy, in order that the grace of temperance might abound to the temperate *then*, and to all mankind some hundred years *thereafter*. There is in this something so repugnant to humanity, so uncharitable, so cold-blooded and feelingless, that it never did, nor ever can enlist the enthusiasm of a popular cause. We could not love the man who taught it—we could not hear him with patience. The heart could not throw open its portals to it. The generous man could not adopt it. It could not mix with his blood. It looked so fiendishly selfish, so like throwing fathers and brothers overboard, to lighten the boat for our security—that the noble minded shrank from the manifest meanness of the thing.

And besides this, the benefits of a reformation to be effected by such a system, were too remote in point of time, to warmly engage many in its behalf. Few can be induced to labor exclusively for posterity; and none will do it enthusiastically. Posterity has done nothing for us; and theorise on it as we may, practically we shall do very little for it, unless we are made to think, we are, at the same time, doing something for ourselves. What an ignorance of human nature does it exhibit, to ask or expect a whole community to rise up and labor for the *temporal* happiness of *others* after *themselves* shall be consigned to the dust, a majority of which community take no pains whatever to secure their own eternal welfare, at a no greater distant day? Great distance, in either time or space, has wonderful power to lull and render quiescent the human mind. Pleasures to be enjoyed, or pains to be endured, *after* we shall be dead and gone, are but little regarded, even in our *own* cases, and much less in the cases of others.

Still, in addition to this, there is something so ludicrous in *promises* of good, or *threats* of evil, a great way off, as to render the whole subject with which they are connected, easily turned into ridicule. "Better lay down that spade you're stealing, Paddy,—if you don't you'll pay for it at the day of judgment." "By the powers, if ye'll credit me so long, I'll take another, jist."

By the Washingtonians, this system of consigning the habitual drunkard to hopeless ruin, is repudiated. *They* adopt a more enlarged philanthropy. *They* go for present as well as future good. *They* labor for all *now* living, as well as all *hereafter* to live. *They* teach *hope* to all—*despair* to none. As applying to *their* cause, *they* deny the doctrine of unpardonable sin. As in Christianity it is taught, so in this *they* teach, that

> "While the lamp holds out to burn,
> The vilest sinner may return."

And, what is matter of the most profound gratulation, they, by experiment upon experiment, and example upon example, prove the maxim to be no less true in the one case than in the other. On every hand we behold those, who but yesterday, were the chief of sinners, now the chief apostles of the cause. Drunken devils are cast out by ones, by sevens, and by legions; and their unfortunate victims, like the poor possessed, who was redeemed from his long and lonely wanderings in the tombs, are publishing to the ends of the earth, how great things have been done for them.

To these *new champions*, and this *new* system of tactics, our late success is mainly owing; and to *them* we must chiefly look for the final consummation. The ball is now rolling gloriously on, and none are so able as *they* to increase its speed, and its bulk—to add to its momentum, and its magnitude. Even though unlearned in letters, for this task, none others are so well educated. To fit them for this work, they have been taught in the true school. *They* have been in *that* gulf, from which they would teach others the means of escape. *They* have passed that prison wall, which others have long declared impassable; and who that has not, shall dare to weigh opinions with *them*, as to the mode of passing.

But if it be true, as I have insisted, that those who have suffered by intemperance *personally*, and have reformed, are the most powerful and efficient instruments to push the reformation to ultimate success, it does not follow, that those who have not suffered, have no part left them to perform. Whether or not the world would be vastly benefitted by a total and final banishment from it of all intoxicating drinks, seems to me not *now* to be an open question. Three-fourths of mankind confess the affirmative with their *tongues*, and, I believe, all the rest acknowledge it in their *hearts*.

Ought *any*, then, to refuse their aid in doing what the good of the *whole* demands? Shall he, who cannot do *much*, be, for that reason, excused if he do *nothing*? "But," says one, "what good can I do by signing the pledge? I never drink even without signing." This question has already been asked and answered more than millions of times. Let it be answered once more. For the man to suddenly, or in any other way, to break off from the use of drams, who has indulged in them for a long course of years, and until his appetite for them has become ten or a hundred fold stronger, and more craving, than any natural appetite can be, requires a most powerful moral effort. In such an undertaking, he needs every moral support and influence, that can possibly be brought to his aid, and thrown around him. And not only so; but every moral prop, should be taken *from* whatever argument might rise in his mind to lure him to his backsliding. When he casts his eyes around him, he should be able to see, all that he respects, all that he admires, and all that he loves, kindly and anxiously pointing him onward; and none beckoning him back, to his former miserable "wallowing in the mire."

But it is said by some, that men will *think* and *act* for themselves; that none will disuse spirits or any thing else, merely because his neighbors do; and that *moral influence* is not that powerful engine contended for. Let us examine this. Let me ask the man who would maintain this position most stiffly, what compensation he will accept to go to church some Sunday and sit during the sermon with his wife's bonnet upon his head? Not a trifle, I'll venture. And why not? There would be nothing irreligious in it: nothing immoral, nothing uncomfortable. Then why not? Is it not because there would be something egregiously unfashionable in it? Then it is the influence of *fashion*; and what is the influence of fashion, but the influence that *other* people's actions have on our own actions, the strong inclination each of us feels to do as we see all our neighbors do? Nor is the influence of fashion confined to any particular thing or class of things. It is just as strong on one subject as another. Let us make it as unfashionable to withhold our names from the temperance pledge as for husbands to wear their wives bonnets to church, and instances will be just as rare in the one case as the other.

"But," say some, "we are no drunkards; and we shall not acknowledge ourselves such by joining a reformed drunkard's society, whatever our influence might be." Surely no Christian will adhere to this objection. If they believe, as they profess, that Omnipotence condescended to take on himself the form of sinful man, and, as such, to die an ignominious death for their sakes, surely they will not refuse submission to the infinitely lesser condescension, for the temporal, and perhaps eternal salvation, of a large, erring, and unfortunate class of their own fellow creatures. Nor is the condescension very great.

In my judgment, such of us as have never fallen victims, have been spared more from the absence of appetite, than from any mental or moral superiority over those who have. Indeed, I believe, if we take habitual drunkards as a class, their heads and their hearts will bear an advantageous comparison with those of any other class. There seems ever to have been a proneness in the brilliant, and the warm-blooded, to fall into this vice. The demon of intemperance ever seems to have delighted in sucking the blood of genius and of generosity. What one of us but can call to mind some dear relative, more promising in youth than all his fellows, who has fallen a sacrifice to his rapacity? He ever seems to have gone forth, like the Egyptian angel of death, commissioned to slay if not the first, the fairest born of every family. Shall he now be arrested in his desolating career? In that arrest, all can give aid that will; and who shall be excused that *can*, and will not? Far around as human breath has ever blown, he keeps our fathers, our brothers, our sons, and our friends, prostrate in the chains of moral death. To all the living every where, we cry, "come sound the moral resurrection trump, that these may rise and stand up, an exceeding great army"—"Come from the four winds, O breath! and breathe upon these slain, that they may live."

If the relative grandeur of revolutions shall be estimated by the great amount of human misery they alleviate, and the small amount they inflict, then, indeed, will this be the grandest the world shall ever have seen. Of our political revolution of '76, we all are justly proud. It has given us a degree of political freedom, far exceeding that of any other of the nations of the earth. In it the world has found a solution of that long mooted problem, as to the capability of man to govern himself. In it was the germ which has vegetated, and still is to grow and expand into the universal liberty of mankind.

But with all these glorious results, past, present, and to come, it had its evils too. It breathed forth famine, swam in blood and rode on fire; and long, long after, the orphan's cry, and the widow's wail, continued to break the sad silence that ensued. These were the price, the inevitable price, paid for the blessings it bought.

Turn now, to the temperance revolution. In *it*, we shall find a stronger bondage broken; a viler slavery, manumitted; a greater tyrant deposed. In *it*, more of want supplied, more disease healed, more sorrow assuaged. By *it* no orphans starving, no widows weeping. By *it*, none wounded in feeling, none injured in interest. Even the dram-maker, and dram seller, will have glided into other occupations *so* gradually, as never to have felt the shock of change; and will stand ready to join all others in the universal song of gladness.

And what a noble ally this, to the cause of political freedom. With such an aid, its march cannot fail to be on and on, till every son of earth shall drink in rich fruition, the sorrow quenching draughts of perfect liberty. Happy day, when, all appetites controled, all passions subdued, all matters subjected, *mind*, all conquering *mind*, shall live and move the monarch of the world. Glorious consummation! Hail fall of Fury! Reign of Reason, all hail!

And when the victory shall be complete—when there shall be neither a slave nor a drunkard on the earth—how proud the title of that *Land*, which may truly claim to be the birth-place and the cradle of both those revolutions, that shall have ended in that victory. How nobly distinguished that People, who shall have planted, and nurtured to maturity, both the political and moral freedom of their species.

This is the one hundred and tenth anniversary of the birth-day of Washington. We are met to celebrate this day. Washington is the mightiest name of earth—*long since* mightiest in the cause of civil liberty; *still* mightiest in moral reformation. On that name, an eulogy is expected. It cannot be. To add brightness to the sun, or glory to the name of Washington, is alike impossible. Let none attempt it. In solemn awe pronounce the name, and in its naked deathless splendor, leave it shining on.

February 22, 1842

To Joshua F. Speed

Dear Speed: Springfield, Feb: 25– 1842–

I received yours of the 12th. written the day you went down to William's place, some days since; but delayed answering it, till I should receive the promised one, of the 16th., which came last night. I opened the latter, with intense anxiety and trepidation—so much, that although it turned out better than I expected, I have hardly yet, at the distance of ten hours, become calm.

I tell you, Speed, our *forebodings*, for which you and I are rather peculiar, are all the worst sort of nonsense. I fancied, from the time I received your letter of *saturday*, that the one of *wednesday* was never to come; and yet it *did* come, and what is more, it is perfectly clear, both from it's *tone* and *handwriting*, that you were much *happier*, or, if you think the term preferable, *less miserable*, when you wrote *it*, than when you wrote the last one before. You had so obviously im-proved, at the verry time I so much feared, you would have grown worse. You say that "something indescribably horrible and alarming still haunts you." You will not say *that* three months from now, I will venture. When your nerves once get steady now, the whole trouble will be over forever. Nor should you become impatient at their being even verry slow, in becoming steady. Again; you say you much fear that that Elysium of which you have dreamed so much, is never to be realized. Well, if it shall not, I dare swear, it will not be the fault of her who is now your wife. I now have no doubt that it is the peculiar misfortune of both you and me, to dream dreams of Elysium far exceeding all that any thing earthly can realize. Far short of your dreams as you may be, no woman could do more to realize them, than that same black eyed Fanny. If you could but contemplate her through my immagination, it would appear ridiculous to you, that any one should for a moment think of being unhappy with her. My old Father used to have a saying that "If you make a bad bargain, *hug* it the tighter"; and it occurs to me, that if the bargain you have just closed can possibly be called a bad one, it is certainly the most *pleasant one* for applying that maxim to, which my fancy can, by any effort, picture.

I write another letter enclosing this, which you can show her, if she desires it. I do this, because, she would think strangely perhaps should you tell her that you receive no letters from me; or, telling her you do, should refuse to let her see them.

I close this, entertaining the confident hope, that every successive letter I shall have from you, (which I here pray may not be few, nor far between,) may show you possessing a more steady hand, and cheerful heart, than the last preceding it. As ever, your friend

To Joshua F. Speed

Dear Speed: Springfield, Feby. 25– 1842–

Yours of the 16th. Inst. announcing that Miss Fanny and you "are no more twain, but one flesh," reached me this morning. I have no way of telling how much happiness I wish you both; tho' I believe you both can conceive it. I feel somewhat jealous of both of you now; you will be so exclusively concerned for one another, that I shall be forgotten entirely. My acquaintance with Miss Fanny (I call her thus, lest you should think I am speaking of your mother) was too short for me to reasonably hope to long be remembered by her; and still, I am sure, I shall not forget her soon. Try if you can not remind her of that debt she owes me; and be sure you do not interfere to prevent her paying it.

I regret to learn that you have resolved to not return to Illinois. I shall be verry lonesome without you. How miserably things seem to be arranged in this world. If we have no friends, we have no pleasure; and if we have them, we are sure to lose them, and be doubly pained by the loss. I did hope she and you would make your home here; but I own I have no right to insist. You owe obligations to her, ten thousand times more sacred than any you can owe to others; and, in that light, let them be respected and observed. It is natural that she should desire to remain with her relatives and friends. As to friends, however, *she* could not need them any where; she would have them in abundance here.

Give my kind rememberance to Mr. Williamson and his family, particularly Miss Elizabeth—also to your Mother, brothers, and sisters. Ask little Eliza Davis if she will ride to town with me if I come there again.

And, finally, give Fanny a double reciprocation of all the love she sent me. Write me often, and believe me Yours forever

P.S. Poor Eastham is gone at last. He died a while before day this morning. They say he was verry loth to die.

No clerk is appointed yet.

To Joshua F. Speed

Dear Speed: Springfield, March 27th. 1842

Yours of the 10th. Inst. was received three or four days since. You know I am sincere, when I tell you, the pleasure it's contents gave me was and is inexpressible. As to your farm matter, I have no sympathy with you. *I* have no farm, nor ever expect to have; and, consequently, have not studied the subject enough to be much interested with it. I can only say that I am glad *you* are satisfied and pleased with it.

But on that other subject, to me of the most intense interest, whether in joy or sorrow, I never had the power to withhold my sympathy from you. It can not be told, how it now thrills me with joy, to hear you say you are *"far happier than you ever expected to be."* That much I know is enough. I know you too well to suppose your expectations were not, at least sometimes, extravagant; and if the reality exceeds them all, I say, enough, dear Lord. I am not going beyond the truth, when I tell you, that the short space it took me to read your last letter, gave me more pleasure, than the total sum of all I have enjoyed since that fatal first of Jany. '41. Since then, it seems to me, I should have been entirely happy, but for the never-absent idea, that there is *one* still unhappy whom I have contributed to make so. That still kills my soul. I can not but reproach myself, for even wishing to be happy while she is otherwise. She accompanied a large party on the Rail Road cars, to Jacksonville last monday; and on her return, spoke, so that I heard of it, of having enjoyed the trip exceedingly. God be praised for that.

You know with what sleepless vigilance I have watched you, ever since the commencement of your affair; and altho' I am now almost confident it is useless, I can not forbear once more to say that I think it is even yet possible for your spirits to flag down and leave you miserable. If they should, dont fail to remember that they can not long remain so.

One thing I can tell you which I know you will be glad to hear; and that is, that I have seen Sarah, and scrutinized her feelings as well as I could, and am fully convinced, she is far happier now, than she has been for the last fifteen months past.

You will see by the last Sangamo Journal that I made a Temperance speech on the 22. of Feb. which I claim that Fanny and you shall read as an act of charity to me; for I can not learn that any body else has read it, or is likely to. Fortunately, it is not very long and I shall deem it a sufficient compliance with my request, if one of you listens while the other reads it. As to your Lockridge matter, it is only necessary to say that there has been no court since you left, and that the next, commences to-morrow morning, during which I suppose we can not fail to get a judgement.

I wish you would learn of Everett what he will take, over and above a discharge for all trouble we have been at, to take his business out of our hands and give it to somebody else. It is impossible to collect money on that or any other claim here now; and altho' you know I am not a very petulant man, I declare I am almost out of patience with Mr. Everett's endless importunity. It seems like he not only writes all the letters he can himself; but gets every body else in Louisville and vicinity to be constantly writing to us about his claim.

I have always heard that Mr. Everett is a very clever fellow, and I am very sorry he can not be obliged; but it does seem to me he ought to know we are interested to collect his money, and therefore *would* do it if we could. I am neither joking nor in a pet when I say we would thank him to transfer his business to some other, without any compensation for what we have done, provided he will see the court cost paid, for which we are security.

The sweet violet you enclosed, came safely to hand, but it was so dry, and mashed so flat, that it crumbled to dust at the first attempt to handle it. The juice that mashed out of it, stained a place on the letter, which I mean to preserve and cherish for the sake of her who procured it to be sent. My renewed good wishes to her, in particular, and generally to all such of your relatives as know me. As ever

To Joshua F. Speed

Dear Speed: Springfield, Ills. July 4th. 1842 –
Yours of the 16th. June was received only a day or two since. It was not mailed at Louisville till the 25th. You speak of the great time that has elapsed since I wrote you. Let me explain that. Your letter reached here a day or two after I started on the circuit; I was gone five or six weeks, so that I got the letter only a few days before Butler started to your country. I thought it scarcely worth while to write you the news, which he could and would tell you more in detail. On his return, he told me you would write me soon; and so I

waited for your letter. As to my having been displeased with your advice, surely you know better than that. I know you do; and therefore I will not labour to convince you. True, that subject is painfull to me; but it is not your silence, or the silence of all the world that can make me forget it. I acknowledge the correctness of your advice too; but before I resolve to do the one thing or the other, I must regain my confidence in my own ability to keep my resolves when they are made. In that ability, you know, I once prided myself as the only, or at least the chief, gem of my character; that gem I lost—how, and when, you too well know. I have not yet regained it; and until I do, I can not trust myself in any matter of much importance. I believe now that, had you understood my case at the time, as well as I understood yours afterwards, by the aid you would have given me, I should have sailed through clear; but that does not now afford me sufficient confidence, to begin that, or the like of that, again.

You make a kind acknowledgement of your obligations to me for your present happiness. I am much pleased with that acknowledgement; but a thousand times more am I pleased to know, that you enjoy a degree of happiness, worthy of an acknowledgement. The truth is, I am not sure there was any merit, with me, in the part I took in your difficulty; I was drawn to it as by fate; if I would, I could not have done less than I did. I always was superstitious; and as part of my superstition, I believe God made me one of the instruments of bringing your Fanny and you together, which union, I have no doubt He had fore-ordained. Whatever he designs, he will do for *me* yet. "Stand *still* and see the salvation of the Lord" is my text just now. If, as you say, you have told Fanny *all*, I should have no objection to her seeing this letter, but for it's reference to our friend here. Let her seeing it, depend upon whether she has ever known any thing of my affair; and if she has not, do not let her.

I do not think I can come to Kentucky this season. I am so poor, and make so little headway in the world, that I drop back in a month of idleness, as much as I gain in a year's rowing. I should like to visit you again. I should like to see that "Sis" of yours, that was absent when I was there; tho' I suppose she would run away again, if she were to hear I was coming.

About your collecting business. We have sued Branson; and will sue the others to the next court, unless they give deeds of trust as you require. Col Allen happened in the office since I commenced this letter, and promises to give a deed of trust. He says he had made the arrangement to pay you, and would have done it, but for the going down of the Shawanee money. We did not get the note in time to sue Hall at the last Tazewell court. Lockridge's property is levied on for you. John Irwin has done nothing with that Baker & Van Bergen matter. We will not fail to bring the suits for your use, where they are in the name of James Bell & Co. I have made you a subscriber to the Journal; and also sent the number containing the temperance speech. My respect and esteem to all your friends there; and, by your permission, my love to your Fanny. Ever yours—

The "Rebecca" Letter

LETTER FROM THE LOST TOWNSHIPS.

Dear Mr. Printer: Lost Townships, Aug. 27, 1842.

I see you printed that long letter I sent you a spell ago—I'm quite encouraged by it, and can't keep from writing again. I think the printing of my letters will be a good thing all round,—it will give me the benefit of being known by the world, and give the world the advantage of knowing what's going on in the Lost Townships, and give your paper respectability besides. So here come another. Yesterday afternoon I hurried through cleaning up the dinner dishes, and stepped over to neighbor S—— to see if his wife Peggy was as well as mought be expected, and hear what they called the baby. Well, when I got there, and just turned round the corner of his log cabin, there he was setting on the door-step reading a newspaper.

'How are you Jeff,' says I,—he sorter started when he heard me, for he hadn't seen me before. 'Why,' says he, 'I'm mad as the devil, aunt Becca.'

'What about,' says I, 'aint its hair the right color? None of that nonsense, Jeff—there aint an honester woman in the Lost Township than—'

'Than who?' says he, 'what the mischief are you about?'

I began to see I was running the wrong trail, and so says I, 'O nothing, I guess I was mistaken a little, that's all. But what is it you're mad about?'

'Why,' says he, 'I've been tugging ever since harvest getting out wheat and hauling it to the river, to raise State Bank paper enough to pay my tax this year, and a little school debt I owe; and now just as I've got it, here I open this infernal Extra Register, expecting to find it full of "glorious democratic victories," and "High Comb'd Cocks," when, lo and behold, I find a set of fellows calling themselves *officers of State*, have forbidden the tax collectors and school commissioners to receive State paper at all; and so here it is, dead on my hands. I don't now believe all the plunder I've got will fetch ready cash enough to pay my taxes and that school debt.'

I was a good deal thunderstruck myself; for that was the first I had heard of the proclamation, and my old man was pretty much in the same fix with Jeff. We both stood a moment, staring at one another without knowing what to say. At last says I, 'Mr. S—— let me look at that paper.' He handed it to me, when I read the proclamation over.

'There now,' says he, 'did you ever see such a piece of impudence and imposition as that?' I saw Jeff was in a good tune for saying some ill-natured things, and so I tho't I would just argue a little on the contrary side, and make him rant a spell if I could.

'Why,' says I, looking as dignified and thoughtful as I could, 'it seems pretty tough to be sure, to have to raise silver where there's none to be raised; but then you see *"there will be danger of loss"* if it aint done.'

'Loss, damnation!' says he, 'I defy Daniel Webster, I defy King Solomon, I defy the world,—I defy—I defy—yes, I defy even you, aunt Becca, to show how the people can lose any thing by paying their taxes in State paper.' 'Well,' says I, 'you see what the *officers of State* say about it, and they are a desarnin set of men.' 'But,' says I, 'I guess you're mistaken about what the proclamation says; it don't say *the people* will lose any thing by the paper money being taken for taxes. It only says *"there will be danger of loss,"* and though it is tolerable plain that the people can't lose by paying their taxes in something they can get easier than silver, instead of having to pay silver; and though it is just as plain, that the State can't lose by taking State Bank paper, however low it may be, while she owes the Bank more than the whole revenue, and can pay that paper over on her debt, dollar for dollar; still *there is danger of loss* to the *"officers of State,"* and you know Jeff, we can't get along without *officers of State.'*

'Damn officers of State,' says he, 'that's what you whigs are always hurraing for.' 'Now don't swear so Jeff,' says I, 'you know I belong to the meetin, and swearin hurts my feelins.' 'Beg pardon, aunt Becca,' says he, 'but I do say its enough to make Dr. Goddard swear, to have tax to pay in silver, for nothing only that Ford may get his two thousand a year, and Shields his twenty four hundred a year, and Carpenter his sixteen hundred a year, and all without "danger of loss" by taking it in State paper.' 'Yes, yes, it's plain enough now what these *officers of State* mean by "danger of loss." Wash, I 'spose, actually lost fifteen hundred dollars out of the three thousand that two of these "officers of State" let him steal from the Treasury, by being compelled to take it in State paper. Wonder if we don't have a proclamation before long, commanding us to make up this loss to Wash in silver.'

And so he went on, till his breath run out, and he had to stop. I couldn't think of any thing to say just then: and so I begun to look over the paper again. 'Aye! here's another proclamation, or something like it.' 'Another!' says Jeff, 'and whose egg is it, pray?' I looked to the bottom of it, and read aloud, 'Your obedient servant, JAS SHIELDS, Auditor.'

'Aha!' says Jeff, 'one of them same three fellows again. Well read it, and let's hear what of it.' I read on till I came to where it says, *"The object of this measure is to suspend the collection of the revenue for the current year."* 'Now stop, now stop,' says he, 'that's a lie already, and I don't want to hear of it.' 'O may be not,' says I.

'I say *it—is—a—lie.—*Suspend the collection, indeed! Will the collectors that have taken their oaths to make the collection DARE to suspend it? Is there any thing in the law requiring them to perjure themselves at the bidding of Jas. Shields? Will the greedy gullet of the penitentiary be satisfied with swallowing *him* instead of all *them* if they should venture to obey him? And would he not discover some "danger of loss" and be off, about the time it came to taking their places?

'And suppose the people attempt to suspend by refusing to pay, what then? The collectors would just jerk up their horses, and cows, and the like, and sell them to the highest bidder for silver in hand, without valuation or redemption. Why, Shields didn't believe that story himself—it was never meant for the truth. If it was true, why was it not writ till five days after the proclamation? Why didn't Carlin and Carpenter sign it as well as Shields? Answer me that, aunt Becca. I say its a lie, and not a well told one at that. It grins out like a copper dollar. Shields is a fool as well as a liar. With him truth is out of the question, and as for getting a good bright passable lie out of him, you might as well try to strike fire from a cake of tallow. I stick to it, its all an infernal whig lie.'

'A *whig* lie,—Highty! Tighty!!'

'Yes, a *whig* lie; and its just like every thing the cursed British whigs do. First they'll do some devilment, and then they'll tell a lie to hide it. And they don't care how plain a lie it is; they think they can cram any sort of a one down the throats of the ignorant loco focos, as they call the democrats.'

'Why, Jeff, you're crazy—you don't mean to say Shields is a whig.'

'*Yes I do.*'

'Why, look here, the proclamation is in your own democratic paper as you call it.'

'I know it, and what of that? They only printed it to let us democrats see the deviltry the whigs are at.'

'Well, but Shields is the Auditor of this loco—I mean this democratic State.'

'So he is, and Tyler appointed him to office.'

'Tyler appointed him?'

'Yes (if you must chaw it over) Tyler appointed him, or if it wasn't him it was old granny Harrison, and that's all one. I tell you, aunt Becca, there's no mistake about his being a whig—why his very looks shows it—every thing about him shows it—if I was deaf and blind I could tell him by the smell. I seed him when I was down in Springfield last winter. They had a sort of a gatherin there one night, among the grandees, they called a fair. All the galls about town was there, and all the handsome widows, and married women, finickin about, trying to look like galls, tied as tight in the middle, and puffed out at both ends like bundles of fodder that hadn't been stacked yet, but wanted stackin pretty bad. And then they had tables all round the house kivered over with baby caps, and pin-cushions, and ten thousand such little nick-nacks, tryin to sell 'em to the fellows that were bowin and scrapin, and kungeerin about 'em. They wouldn't let no democrats in, for fear they'd disgust the ladies, or scare the little galls, or dirty the floor. I looked in at the window, and there was this same fellow Shields floatin about on the air, without heft or earthly substance, just like a lock of cat-fur where cats had been fightin.

'He was paying his money to this one and that one, and tother one, and sufferin great loss because it wasn't silver instead of State paper; and the sweet distress he seemed to be in,—his very features, in the exstatic agony of his soul, spoke audibly and distinctly—"Dear girls, *it is distressing*, but I cannot marry you all. Too well I know how much you suffer; but do, *do* remember, it is not my fault that I am *so* handsome and *so* interesting."

'As this last was expressed by a most exquisite contortion of his face, he seized hold of one of their hands and squeezed, and held on to it about a quarter of an hour. O, my good fellow, says I to myself, if that was one of our democratic galls in the Lost Township, the way you'd get a brass pin let into you, would be about up to the head. He a democrat! Fiddlesticks! I tell you, aunt Becca, he's a whig, and no mistake: nobody but a whig could make such a conceity dunce of himself.'

'Well,' says I, 'may be he is, but if he is, I'm mistaken the worst sort.

'May be so; may be so; but if I am I'll suffer by it; I'll be a democrat if it turns out that Shields is a whig; considerin you shall be a whig if he turns out a democrat.'

'A bargain, by jingoes,' says he, 'but how will we find out.'

'Why,' says I, 'we'll just write and ax the printer.' 'Agreed again,' says he, 'and by thunder if it does turn out that Shields is a democrat, I never will——'

'Jefferson,—Jefferson—'

'What do you want, Peggy.'

'Do get through your everlasting clatter some time, and bring me a gourd of water; the child's been crying for a drink this live-long hour.'

'Let it die then, it may as well die for water as to be taxed to death to fatten *officers of State.*'

Jeff run off to get the water though, just like he hadn't been sayin any thing spiteful; for he's a rall good hearted fellow, after all, once you get at the foundation of him.

I walked into the house, and 'why Peggy,' says I, 'I declare, we like to forgot you altogether.' 'O yes,' says she, 'when a body can't help themselves, every body soon forgets 'em; but thank God by day after to-morrow I shall be well enough to milk the cows and pen the calves, and wring the contrary one's tails for 'em, and no thanks to nobody.' 'Good evening, Peggy,' says I, and so I sloped, for I seed she was mad at me, for making Jeff neglect her so long.

And now Mr. Printer, will you be sure to let us know in your next paper whether this Shields is a whig or a democrat? I don't care about it for myself, for I know well enough how it is already, but I want to convince Jeff. It may do some good to let him, and others like him, know *who* and *what* these *officers of State* are. It may help to send the present hypocritical set to where they belong, and to fill the places they now disgrace with men who will do more work, for less pay, and take a fewer airs while they are doing it. It aint sensible to think that the same men who get us into trouble will change their course; and yet its pretty plain, if some change for the better is not made, its not long that neither Peggy, or I, or any of us, will have a cow left to milk, or a calf's tail to wring. Yours, truly,

Rebecca ——.

To James Shields

Jas. Shields, Esq.   Tremont, Sept. 17, 1842.

Your note of to-day was handed me by Gen. Whiteside. In that note you say you have been informed, through the medium of the editor of the Journal, that I am the author of certain articles in that paper which you deem personally abusive of you: and without stopping to enquire whether I really am the author, or to point out what is offensive in them, you demand an unqualified retraction of all that is offensive; and then proceed to hint at consequences.

Now, sir, there is in this so much assumption of facts, and so much of menace as to consequences, that I cannot submit to answer that note any farther than I have, and to add, that the consequence to which I suppose you allude, would be matter of as great regret to me as it possibly could to you. Respectfully,

Duel Instructions to Elias H. Merryman

In case Whitesides shall signify a wish to adjust this affair without further difficulty, let him know that if the present papers be withdrawn, & a note from Mr. Shields asking to know if I am the author of the articles of which he complains, and asking that I shall make him gentlemanly satisfaction, if I am the author, and this without menace, or dictation as to what that satisfaction shall be, a pledge is made, that the following answer shall be given—

"I did write the 'Lost Township' letter which appeared in the Journal of the 2nd. Inst. but had no participation, in any form, in any other article alluding to you. I wrote that, wholly for political effect. I had no intention of injuring your personal or private character or standing as a man or a gentleman; and I did not then think, and do not now think that that article, could produce or has produced that effect against you, and had I anticipated such an effect I would have forborne to write it. And I will add, that your conduct towards me, so far as I knew, had always been gentlemanly; and that I had no personal pique against you, and no cause for any."

If this should be done, I leave it with you to arrange what shall & what shall not be published.

If nothing like this is done—the preliminaries of the fight are to be—

1st. Weapons—Cavalry broad swords of the largest size, precisely equal in all respects—and such as now used by the cavalry company at Jacksonville.

2nd. Position—A plank ten feet long, & from nine to twelve inches broad to be firmly fixed on edge, on the ground, as the line between us which neither is to pass his foot over upon forfeit of his life. Next a line drawn on the ground on either side of said plank & paralel with it, each at the distance of the whole length of the sword and three feet additional from the plank; and the passing of his own such line by either party during the fight shall be deemed a surrender of the contest.

3. Time—On thursday evening at five o'clock if you can get it so; but in no case to be at a greater distance of time than friday evening at five o'clock.

4th. Place—Within three miles of Alton on the opposite side of the river, the particular spot to be agreed on by you.

Any preliminary details coming within the above rules, you are at liberty to make at your discretion; but you are in no case to swerve from these rules, or to pass beyond their limits.

September 19, 1842

To Joshua F. Speed

Dear Speed: Springfield, Oct. 5 1842—

You have heard of my duel with Shields, and I have now to inform you that the duelling business still rages in this city. Day-before-yesterday Shields challenged Butler, who accepted, and proposed fighting next morning at sun-rising in Bob. Allen's meadow, one hundred yards distance with rifles. To this, Whitesides, Shields' second, said "No" because of the law. Thus ended, duel No. 2. Yesterday, Whitesides chose to consider himself insulted by Dr. Merryman, and so, sent him a kind of *quasi* challenge inviting him to meet him at the planter's House in St. Louis on the next friday to settle their difficulty. Merryman made me his friend, and sent W. a note enquiring to know if he meant his note as a challenge, and if so, that he would, according to the law in such case made and provided, prescribe the terms of the meeting. W. Returned for answer, that if M. would meet him at the Planter's House as desired, he would challenge him. M. replied in a note, that he denied W's right to dictate time and place; but that he, M, would waive the question of *time*, and meet him at Louisiana Missouri. Upon my presenting this note to W. and stating verbally, it's contents, he declined receiving it, saying he had business at St. Louis, and it was as near as Louisiana. Merryman then directed me to notify Whitesides, that he should publish the correspondence between them with such comments as he thought fit. This I did. Thus it stood at bed time last night. This morning Whitesides, by his friend Shields, is praying for a new trial, on the ground that he was mistaken in Merrymans proposition to meet him at Louisiana Missouri thinking it was the State of Louisiana. This Merryman hoots at, and is preparing his publication—while the town is in a ferment and a street fight somewhat anticipated.

But I began this letter not for what I have been writing; but to say something on that subject which you know to be of such infinite solicitude to me. The immense suffering you endured from the first days of September till the middle of February you never tried to conceal from me, and I well understood. You have now been the husband of a lovely woman nearly eight months. That you are happier now than you were the day you married her I well know; for without, you would not be living. But I have your word for it too; and the returning elasticity of spirits which is manifested in your letters. But I want to ask a closer question—"Are you now, in *feeling* as well as *judgement*, glad you are married as you are?" From any body but me, this would be an impudent question not to be tolerated; but I know you will pardon it in me. Please answer it quickly as I feel impatient to know.

I have sent my love to your Fanny so often that I fear she is getting tired of it; however I venture to tender it again. Yours forever

To James S. Irwin

Jas. S. Irwin Esqr.   Springfield, Nov. 2 1842.

Owing to my absence, yours of the 22nd. ult. was not received till this moment.

Judge Logan & myself are willing to attend to any business

in the Supreme Court you may send us. As to fees, it is impossible to establish a rule that will apply in all, or even a great many cases. We believe we are never accused of being very unreasonable in this particular; and we would always be easily satisfied, provided we could see the money—but whatever fees we earn at a distance, if not paid *before*, we have noticed we never hear of after the work is done. We therefore, are growing a little sensitive on that point. Yours &c.

To Samuel D. Marshall

Dear Sam.   Springfield, Nov. 11th. 1842—

Yours of the 10th. Oct. enclosing five dollars was taken from the office in my absence by Judge Logan who neglected to hand it to me till about a week ago, and just an hour before I took a wife. Your other of the 3rd. Inst. is also received. The Forbes & Hill case, of which you speak has not been brought up as yet.

I have looked into the Dorman & Lane case, till I believe I understand the facts of it; and I also believe we can reverse it. In the last I may be mistaken, but I think the case, at least worth the experiment; and if Dorman will risk the cost, I will do my best for the "biggest kind of a fee" as you say, if we succeed, and nothing if we fail. I have not had a chance to consult Logan since I read your letters, but if the case comes up, I can have the use of him if I need him.

I would advise you to procure the Record and send it up immediately. Attend to the making out of the Record yourself, or most likely, the clerk will not get it all together right.

Nothing new here, except my marrying, which to me, is matter of profound wonder. Yours forever

To Richard S. Thomas

Springfield, Ills., Feb. 14, 1843.

Friend Richard: . . . Now if you should hear any one say that Lincoln don't want to go to Congress, I wish you as a personal friend of mine, would tell him you have reason to believe he is mistaken. The truth is, I would like to go very much. Still, circumstances may happen which may prevent my being a candidate.

If there are any who be my friends in such an enterprise, what I now want is that they shall not throw me away just yet. Yours as ever,

To Joshua F. Speed

Dear Speed: Springfield, March 24. 1843–

Hurst tells me that Lockridge has redeemed the land in your case, & paid him the money; and that he has written you about it. I now have the pleasure of informing you that Walters has paid me $703.25 (in gold) for you. There is something still due you from him,—I think near a hundred dollars, for which I promised him a little additional time. The gold, (except the toll) we hold subject to your order.

We had a meeting of the whigs of the county here on last monday to appoint delegates to a district convention, and Baker beat me & got the delegation instructed to go for him. The meeting, in spite of my attempt to decline it, appointed me one of the delegates; so that in getting Baker the nomination, I shall be "fixed" a good deal like a fellow who is made groomsman to the man what has cut him out, and is marrying his own dear "gal." About the prospect of your having a namesake at our house cant say, exactly yet.

To Martin S. Morris

Friend Morris: Springfield March 26th. 1843

Your letter of the 23rd. was received on yesterday morning, and for which (instead of an excuse which you thought proper to ask) I tender you my sincere thanks. It is truly gratifying to me to learn that while the people of Sangamon have cast me off my old friends of Menard who have known me longest and best of any, still retain there confidence in me. It would astonish if not amuse, the older citizens of your County who twelve years ago knew me a strange, friendless, uneducated, penniless boy, working on a flat boat—at ten dollars per month to learn that I have been put down here as the candidate of pride, wealth, and arristocratic family distinction. Yet so chiefly it was. There was too the strangest combination of church influence against me. Baker is a Campbellite, and therefore as I suppose, with few acceptions got all that church. My wife has some relatives in the Presbyterian and some in the Episcopal Churches, and therefore, whereever it would tell, I was set down as either the one or the other, whilst it was every where contended that no christian ought to go for me, because I belonged to no church, was suspected of being a deist, and had talked about fighting a duel. With all these things Baker, of course had nothing to do. Nor do I complain of them. As to his own church going for him, I think that was right enough, and as to the influences I have spoken of in the other, though they were very strong, it would be grossly untrue and unjust to charge that they acted upon them in a body or even very nearly so. I only mean that those influences levied a tax of a considerable per cent. upon my strength throughout the religious comunity.

But enough of this. You say that in choosing a candidate for Congress you have an equal right with Sangamon, and in this you are undoubtedly correct. In agreeing to withdraw if the whigs of Sangamon should go against me I did not mean that they alone were worth consulting; but that if she with her heavy delegation should be against me, it would be impossible for me to succeed—and therefore I had as well decline. And in relation to Menard having rights, permit me to fully recognize them—and to express the opinion that if she and Mason act circumspectly they will in the convention be able so far to enforce there rights as to decide absolutely which *one* of the candidates shall be successful. Let me show you the reason of this. Hardin or some other Morgan Candidate will get Morgan, Scott, & Cass—14. Baker has Sangamon already, and he or he and some one else not the Morgan man will get Putnam, Marshall, Woodford, Tazwell & Logan—which with Sangamon make 16. Then you & Mason having three, can give the victory to either man. You say you shall instruct your delegates to go for me unless I object. I certainly shall not object. That would be too plesant a compliment for me to tread in the dust. And besides if any thing

should hapen (which however is not probable) by which
Baker should be thrown out of the fight, I would be at liberty
to accept the nomination if I could get it. I do however feell
myself bound not to hinder him in any way from getting the
nomination. I should dispise myself were I to attempt it. I
think it would be proper for your meeting to appoint three
delegates, and instruct them to go for some one as first
choice, some one else as second choice, and perhaps some one
as *third*—and if in those instructions I were named as the first
choice, it would gratify me very much. If you wish to hold
the ballance of power, it is important for you to attend too,
and secure the vote of Mason also. You should be sure to have
men appointed delegates, that you know you can safely confide in. If yourself & James Short were appointed for your
County all would be safe. But whether Jims woman afair a
year ago might not be in the way of his appointment is a
question. I dont know whether you know it, but I know him
to be as honorable a man as there is in the world. You have
my permission and even request to show this letter to Short;
but to no one else unless it be a very particular friend who
you know will not speak of it. Yours as ever

P.S. Will you write me again?

To Martin S. Morris

Friend Morris: April 14th 1843.
   I have heard it insinuated that Baker has been attempting
to get you or Miles or both of you to violate the instructions
of the meeting that appointed you, and to go for him. I have
insisted, and still insist, that this can not be true. Surely Baker
would not do the like. As well might Hardin ask me to vote
for him, in the convention.
   Again, it is said there will be an attempt to get up instructions in your county, requiring you to go for Baker. This is all
wrong again. Upon the same rule, why might not I fly from
the decision against me in Sangamon and get up instructions
to their delegation to go for me. There are at least twelve
hundred whigs in the county, that took no part. And yet I

would as soon put my head in the fire as to attempt it. I should feel myself strongly dishonored by it.

Besides, if any one should get the nomination by such extraordinary means, all harmony in the district would inevitably be lost. Honest whigs (and very nearly all of them are honest) will not quietly abide such enormities. I repeat, such an attempt on Baker's part can not be true. Write, me at Springfield, how this matter is. Dont show or speak of this letter. As ever yours

To Joshua F. Speed

Dear Speed: Springfield, May 18th. 1843—
Yours of the 9th. Inst. is duly received, which I do not meet as a "bore," but as a most welcome visiter. I will answer the business part of it first. The note you enclosed on Cannan & Harlan, I have placed in Moffett's hands according to your directions. Harvey is the constable to have it. I have called three times to get the note, you mention, on B. C. Webster & Co; but did not find Hurst. I will yet get it, and do with it, as you bid. At the April court at Tazewell, I saw Hall; and he then gave me an order on Jewett to draw of him, all rent which may fall due, after the 12th. day of Jany. last, till your debt shall be paid. The rent is for the house Ransom did live in just above the Globe; and is $222 per year payable quarterly, so that one quarter fell due the 12th. April. I presented the order to Jewett, since the 12th. and he said it was right, and he would accept, it, which, however, was not done in writing for want of pen & ink at the time & place. He acknowledged that the quarter's rent was due, and said he would pay it in a short time but could not at the moment. He also said that he thought, by some former arrangement, a portion of that quarter would have to be paid to the Irwins. Thus stands the Hall matter. I think we will get the money on it, in the course of this year. You ask for the amount of interest on your Van Bergen note of $572.32, and also upon the judgement against Van assigned by Baker. The note drew 12 per cent from date, and bore date Oct. 1st. 1841. I suppose the 12 per cent ceased, at the time we bought in Walters' house

which was on the 23rd. Decr. 1842. If I count right, the interest up to that time, was $78.69 cents, which added to the principal makes $651.01. On this aggregate sum you are entitled to interest at 6 per cent only, from the said 23rd. Decr. 1842 until paid. What that will amount to, you can calculate for yourself. The judgement assigned by Baker to you for $219.80, was so assigned on the 2nd. of April 1841, and of course draws 6 per cent from that time until paid. This too you can calculate for yourself. About the 25th. of March 1843 (the precise date I dont now remember) Walters paid $703.25. This, of course must be remembered in counting interest. According to my count, there was due you of principal & interest on both claims on the 25th. of March 1843—$906.70. Walters then paid $703.25—which leaves still due you, $203.45, drawing 6 per cent from that date. Walters is promising to pay the ballance every day, but still has not done it. I think he will do it soon. Allen has gone to nothing, as Butler tells you. There are 200 acres of the tract I took the deed of trust on. The improvements I should suppose you remember as well as I. It is the stage stand on the Shelbyville road, where you always said I would'nt pay Baker's tavern bill. It seems to me it must be worth much more than the debt; but whether any body will redeem it in these hard times, I can not say.

In relation to our congress matter here, you were right in supposing I would support the nominee. Neither Baker or I, however is the man; but *Hardin*. So far as I can judge from present appearances, we shall have no split or trouble about the matter; all will be harmony. In relation to the "coming events" about which Butler wrote you, I had not *heard* one word before I got your letter; but I have so much confidence in the judgement of a Butler on such a subject, that I incline to think there may be some reality in it. What *day* does Butler appoint? By the way, how do "events" of the same sort come on in your family? Are you possessing houses and lands, and oxen and asses, and men-servants and maid-servants, and begetting sons and daughters? We are not keeping house; but boarding at the Globe tavern, which is very well kept now by a widow lady of the name of Beck. Our room (the same Dr. Wallace ocupied there) and boarding only costs four dollars a week. Ann Todd was married something more than a year since to a fellow by the name of Campbell, and who Mary says, is pretty much of a "dunce" though he has a little money & property. They live in Boonville, Mo; and have not been heard from lately enough, to enable me to say any thing about her health. I reckon it will scarcely be in our power to visit Kentucky this year. Besides poverty, and the necessity of attending to business, those "coming events" I suspect would be some what in the way. I most heartily wish you and your Fanny would not fail to come. Just let us know the time a week in advance, and we will have a room provided for you at our house, and all be merry together for awhile. Be sure to give my respects to your mother and family. Assure her, that if I ever come near her I will not fail to call and see her. Mary joins in sending love to your Fanny and you. Yours as ever

To Williamson Durley

Friend Durley: Springfield, Octr. 3. 1845

When I saw you at home, it was agreed that I should write to you and your brother Madison. Until I then saw you, I was not aware of your being what is generally called an abolitionist, or, as you call yourself, a Liberty-man; though I well knew there were many such in your county. I was glad to hear you say that you intend to attempt to bring about, at the next election in Putnam, a union of the whigs proper, and such of the liberty men, as are whigs in principle on all questions save only that of slavery. So far as I can perceive, by such union, neither party need yield any thing, on *the* point in difference between them. If the whig abolitionists of New York had voted with us last fall, Mr. Clay would now be president, whig principles in the ascendent, and Texas not annexed; whereas by the division, all that either had at stake in the contest, was lost. And, indeed, it was extremely probable, beforehand, that such would be the result. As I always understood, the Liberty-men deprecated the annexation of Texas extremely; and, this being so, why they should refuse to so cast their votes as to prevent it, even to me, seemed wonderful. What was their process of reasoning, I can only judge from what a single one of them told me. It was this: "We are not to do *evil* that *good* may come." This general, proposition is doubtless correct; but did it apply? If by your votes you could have prevented the *extention*, &c. of slavery, would it not have been *good* and not *evil* so to have used your votes, even though it involved the casting of them for a slaveholder? By the *fruit* the tree is to be known. An *evil* tree can not bring forth *good* fruit. If the fruit of electing Mr. Clay would have been to prevent the extension of slavery, could the act of electing have been *evil*?

But I will not argue farther. I perhaps ought to say that individually I never was much interested in the Texas question. I never could see much good to come of annexation; inasmuch, as they were already a free republican people on our own model; on the other hand, I never could very clearly see how the annexation would augment the evil of slavery. It always seemed to me that slaves would be taken there in about equal numbers, with or without annexation. And if more *were* taken because of annexation, still there would be just so many the fewer left, where they were taken from. It is possibly true, to some extent, that with annexation, some slaves may be sent to Texas and continued in slavery, that otherwise might have been liberated. To whatever extent this may be true, I think annexation an evil. I hold it to be a paramount duty of us in the free states, due to the Union of the states, and perhaps to liberty itself (paradox though it may seem) to let the slavery of the other states alone; while, on the other hand, I hold it to be equally clear, that we should never knowingly lend ourselves directly or indirectly, to prevent that slavery from dying a natural death—to find new places for it to live in, when it can no longer exist in the old. Of course I am not now considering what would be our duty, in cases of insurrection among the slaves.

To recur to the Texas question, I understand the Liberty men to have viewed annexation as a much greater evil than I ever did; and I, would like to convince you if I could, that they could have prevented it, without violation of principle, if they had chosen.

I intend this letter for you and Madison together; and if you and he or either shall think fit to drop me a line, I shall be pleased. Yours with respect

To Benjamin F. James

Friend James: Springfield, Nov: 17, 1845.

The paper at Pekin has nominated Hardin for Governor; and, commenting on this, the Alton paper, indirectly nominates him for Congress. It would give Hardin a great start, and perhaps use me up, if the whig papers of the District should nominate him for *Congress*. If your feelings towards me are the same as when I saw you (which I have no reason to doubt) I wish you would let nothing appear in your paper which may opperate against me. You understand.

Matters stand just as they did when I saw you. Baker is certainly off of the track, and I fear Hardin intends to be on it.

In relation to the business you wrote me of, some time since, I suppose the Marshall called on you; and we think it can be adjusted, at court, to the satisfaction of you & friend Thompson.

To Henry E. Dummer

Friend Dummer: Springfield, Nov: 18th. 1845

Before Baker left, he said to me, in accordance with what had long been an understanding between him and me, that the track for the next congressional race was clear to me, so far as he was concerned; and that he would say so publicly in any manner, and at any time I might desire. I said, in reply, that as to the manner and time, I would consider a while, and write him. I understand friend Delahay to have already informed you of the substance of the above.

I now wish to say to you that if it be consistent with your feelings, you would set a few stakes for me. I do not certainly know, but I strongly suspect, that Genl. Hardin wishes to run again. I know of no argument to give me a preference over him, unless it be "Turn about is fair play."

The Pekin paper has lately nominated or suggested Hardin's name for Governor, and the Alton paper, noticing that, indirectly nominates him for Congress. I wish you would, if you can, see that, while these things are bandied about among the papers, the Beardstown paper takes no stand that may

injure my chance, unless the conductor really prefers Genl.
Hardin, in which case, I suppose it would be fair.

Let this be confidential, and please write me in a few days.
Yours as ever

To Benjamin F. James

Friend James: Springfield, Novr. 24th. 1845

Yours of the 19th. was not received till this morning. The
error I fell into in relation to the *Pekin* paper, I discovered
myself the day after I wrote you. The way I fell into it was,
that Stuart (John T) met me in the court & told me about a
nomination having been made in the Pekin paper, and about
the comments upon it in the Alton paper; and without seeing
either paper myself, I wrote you. In writing to you, I only
meant to call your attention to the matter; and that done, I
knew all would be right with you. Of course I should not
have thought this necessary, if, at the time, I had known that
the nomination had been made in your paper. And let me
assure you, that if there is any thing in my letter indicating an
opinion that the nomination for *Governor*, which I supposed
to have been made in the Pekin paper, was opperating, or
could opperate against me, such was not my meaning. Now,
that I know that nomination was made by you, I say that it
may do me good while I do not see that it *can* do me harm.
But, while the subject is in agitation, should any of the papers
in the District nominate the same man for *Congress* that
would do me harm; and it was that which I wished to guard
against. Let me assure that I do not, for a moment, suppose,
that what you *have* done is ill-judged; or that any thing you
shall do, will be. It was not to object to the course of the
Pekin paper (as I then thought it) but to guard against any
falling into the wake of the *Alton* paper, that I wrote.

You, perhaps, have noticed the Journal's article of last week,
upon the same subject. It was written without any consultation with me, but I was told by Francis of it's purport before
it was published. I chose to let it go as it was, lest it should be
suspected that I was attempting to juggle Hardin out of
a nomination for congress by juggleing him into one for

Governor. If you, and the other papers, a little more distant from me, choose, to take the same course you have, of course I have no objection. After you shall have received this, I think we shall fully understand each other, and that our views as to the effects of these things are not dissimilar. Confidential of course   Yours as ever

To Benjamin F. James

Friend James: Springfield, Decr. 6, 1845

Yours of the 4th., informing me of Hardin's communication and letter, is received. I had ascertained that such documents had been sent you, even before I received your letter. Nor is the conclusion they lead to—the certainty that he intends to run for congress—matter of surprise to me. I was almost confident of it before. Now as to the probable result of a contest with him. To succeed, I must have 17 votes in convention. To secure these, I think I may safely claim—Sangamon 8—Menard 2—Logan 1, making 11, so that, if you and other friends can secure Dr. Boal's entire senatorial district—that is—Tazewell 4—Woodford 1 and Marshall 1, it just covers the case. Besides this, I am not without some chance in Putnam and Mason, the latter of which I verily believe I can secure by close attention. The other counties—that is to say—Morgan, Scott and Cass, he will undoubtedly get. Some of Baker's particular friends in Cass, and who are now my friends, think I could carry that county; but I do not think there is any chance for it. Upon the whole, it is my intention to give him the trial, unless clouds should rise, which are not yet discernable. This determination you need not however, as yet, announce in your paper—at least not as coming from me.

If Tazewell, Woodford & Marshall, can be made safe, all will be safe. Of the first, Tazewell, I suppose there is little or no doubt—and while I believe there is good ground of hope in Woodford & Marshall, still I am not quite so easy about them. It is desireable that a sharp look-out should be kept, and every whig met with from those counties, talked to, and initiated. If you and John H. Morrison and Niel Johnson, Dr. Shaw, and others, will see to this; together with what I have done, and will do, those counties can be saved. In doing this, let nothing be said against Hardin—nothing deserves to be said against him. Let the pith of the whole argument be *"Turn about is fair play"*

More than this, I want you to watch, and whenever you see a "moccasan track" as indian fighters say, notify me of it. You understand.

I fear I shall be of a great deal of trouble to you in this matter; but rest assured, that I *will* be grateful when I can. The Lacon paper you sent me I never got, but I learned it's contents from David Dickinson, formerly of our town, but now residing in Lacon. After I left Tremont last fall, I went up to Lacon and saw Dr. Boal, who said to me that it had always been his understanding since the Pekin convention, that the race of 1846 was to be mine. I have reason to believe, tho, I did not know, that he induced the articles in the Lacon paper. I am sure also that he or Dickinson one did, as I have never spoken to the editor on the subject. This letter is, of course, confidential; tho I should have no objection to it's being seen by a few friends, in your discretion, being *sure* first that they are friends.

Write me frequently if you can find spare time. Yours as ever

P.S. Will you not visit Springfield this winter? I should be glad of a personal interview with you.

To Robert Boal

Dear Doctor   Springfield Jany. 7 1846.

Since I saw you last fall, I have often thought of writing you as it was then understood I would, but on reflection I have always found that I had nothing new to tell you. All has happened as I then told you I expected it would—Baker's declining, Hardin's taking the track, and so on.

If Hardin and I stood precisely equal—that is, if *neither* of us had been to congress, or if we *both* had—it would only accord with what I have always done, for the sake of peace, to give way to him; and I expect I should do it. That I *can* voluntarily postpone my pretentions, when they are no more than equal to those to which they are postponed, you have yourself seen. But to yield to Hardin under present circumstances, seems to me as nothing else than yielding to one who would gladly sacrifice me altogether. This, I would rather not submit to. That Hardin is talented, energetic, usually generous and magnanimous, I have, before this, affirmed to you, and do not now deny. You know that my only argument is that "turn about is fair play". This he, practically at least, denies.

If it would not be taxing you too much, I wish you would write me, telling the aspect of things in your county, or rather your district; and also send the names of some of your whig neighbours, to whom I might, with propriety write. Unless I can get some one to do this, Hardin with his old franking list, will have the advantage of me. My reliance for a fair shake (and I want nothing more) in your county is chiefly on you, because of your position and standing, and because I am acquainted with so few others. Let this be strictly confidential, & any letter you may write me shall be the same if you desire. Let me hear from you soon. Yours truly

To Benjamin F. James

Dear James: Springfield, Jany. 16. 1846 –

A plan is on foot to change the mode of selecting the candidate for this district. The movement is intended to injure me, and if effected, most likely would injure me to some extent. I have not time to give particulars now; but I want you to let nothing prevent your getting an article in your paper, of *this week* taking strong ground for the old system, under which Hardin & Baker were nominated, without seeming to know or suspect, that any one desires to change it. I have written Dr. Henry more at length; and he will probably call & consult with you, in getting up the article; but whether he does or not dont fail, on any account, to get it in *this week*.

To John J. Hardin

Dear Genl.   Springfield, Jany. 19th. 1846

I do not wish to join in your proposal of a new plan for the selection of a whig candidate for congress, because

1st. I am entirely satisfied with the old system under which you and Baker were successively nominated and elected to congress; and because the whigs of the District are well acquainted with that system, and, so far as I know or believe, are universally satisfied with it. If the old system be thought to be vague, as to all the delegates of a county, voting the same, way; or as to instructions to them, as to whom they are to vote for; or as to filling vacancies, I am willing to join in a provision to make these matters certain.

2nd. As to your proposals that a poll shall be opened in *every* precinct, and that the whole shall take place on the *same* day, I do not personally object. They seem to me to not be unfair; and I forbear to join in proposing them, only because I rather choose to leave the decision in each county to the whigs of the county, to be made as their own judgment and convenience may dictate.

3rd. As to your proposed stipulation that all the candidates shall remain in their own counties, and restrain their friends to the same, it seems to me that on reflection you will see, the fact of your having been in congress, has, in various ways, so spread your name in the district, as to give you a decided advantage in such a stipulation. I appreciate your desire to keep down excitement; and I promise you to "keep cool" under all circumstances.

4th. I have already said I am satisfied with the old system, under which such good men have triumphed; and that I desire no departure from its principles. But if there must be a departure from it, I shall insist upon a more accurate and just apportionment of delegates, or representative votes, to the constituent body, than exists by the old; and which you propose to retain in your new plan.

If we take the entire population of the counties as shown by the late census, we shall see that by the old plan, and by your proposed new plan

Morgan county with a population of 16.541 has	8 votes
while Sangamon with 18.697—2156 greater has but	8 do
So, Scott, with 6553—has	4 do
while Tazewell with 7615—1062 greater— has but	4 do—
So, Mason with 3135 has	1. do
while Logan with 3907—772 greater has but	1. do—

And so, in a less degree, the matter runs through all the counties; being not only wrong in principle, but the advantage of it being all manifestly in your favour, with one slight exception in the comparison of two counties not here mentioned.

Again: If we take the *whig votes* of the counties as shown by the late presidential election as a basis, the thing is still worse. Take a comparison of the same six counties —

Morgan, with her 1443 whig votes has					8 votes
Sangamon with her		1837 —	394 greater only		8 do.
Mason with her		255 —	has		1 do
Logan	do	do	310 —	55 greater only.	1. do
Scott	do	do	670 —	has	4. do
Tazewell	do	do	1011.	341 greater — only	4. do —

It seems to me most obvious that the old system needs adjustment in nothing so much as in this; and still by your proposal, no notice is taken of it.

I have always been in the habit of acceding to almost any proposal that a friend would make; and I am truly sorry I can not in this.

I perhaps ought to mention that some friends at different places, are endeavouring to secure the honor of the sitting of a convention at their towns respectively; and I fear they would not feel much complimented, if we were to make a bargain that it shall sit no where. Yours as ever

My Childhood-Home I See Again

My childhood-home I see again,
  And gladden with the view;
And still as mem'ries crowd my brain,
  There's sadness in it too.

O memory! thou mid-way world
  'Twixt Earth and Paradise,
Where things decayed, and loved ones lost
  In dreamy shadows rise.

And freed from all that's gross or vile,
  Seem hallowed, pure, and bright,
Like scenes in some enchanted isle,
  All bathed in liquid light.

As distant mountains please the eye,
  When twilight chases day—
As bugle-tones, that, passing by,
  In distance die away—

As leaving some grand water-fall
  We ling'ring, list it's roar,
So memory will hallow all
  We've known, but know no more.

Now twenty years have passed away,
  Since here I bid farewell
To woods, and fields, and scenes of play
  And school-mates loved so well.

Where many were, how few remain
  Of old familiar things!
But seeing these to mind again
  The lost and absent brings.

The friends I left that parting day—
  How changed, as time has sped!
Young childhood grown, strong manhood grey,
  And half of all are dead.

I hear the lone survivors tell
  How nought from death could save,
Till every sound appears a knell,
  And every spot a grave.

I range the fields with pensive tread,
  And pace the hollow rooms;
And feel (companions of the dead)
  I'm living in the tombs.

And here's an object more of dread,
  Than ought the grave contains—
A human-form, with reason fled,
  While wretched life remains.

Poor Matthew! Once of genius bright,—
  A fortune-favored child—
Now locked for aye, in mental night,
  A haggard mad-man wild.

Poor Matthew! I have ne'er forgot
  When first with maddened will,
Yourself you maimed, your father fought,
  And mother strove to kill;

And terror spread, and neighbours ran,
  Your dang'rous strength to bind;
And soon a howling crazy man,
  Your limbs were fast confined.

How then you writhed and shrieked aloud,
  Your bones and sinnews bared;
And fiendish on the gaping crowd,
  With burning eye-balls glared.

And begged, and swore, and wept, and prayed,
  With maniac laughter joined—
How fearful are the signs displayed,
  By pangs that kill the mind!

And when at length, tho' drear and long,
  Time soothed your fiercer woes—
How plaintively your mournful song,
  Upon the still night rose.

I've heard it oft, as if I dreamed,
  Far-distant, sweet, and lone;
The funeral dirge it ever seemed
  Of reason dead and gone.

To drink it's strains, I've stole away,
  All silently and still,
Ere yet the rising god of day
  Had streaked the Eastern hill.

Air held his breath; the trees all still
  Seemed sorr'wing angels round.
Their swelling tears in dew-drops fell
  Upon the list'ning ground.

But this is past, and nought remains
  That raised you o'er the brute.
Your mad'ning shrieks and soothing strains
  Are like forever mute.

Now fare thee well: more thou the cause
  Than subject now of woe.
All mental pangs, but time's kind laws,
  Hast lost the power to know.

And now away to seek some scene
  Less painful than the last—
With less of horror mingled in
  The present and the past.

The very spot where grew the bread
  That formed my bones, I see.
How strange, old field, on thee to tread,
  And feel I'm part of thee!

c. February 1846

To John J. Hardin

Genl. J. J. Hardin: Springfield.
Dear Sir: Feb. 7. 1846—

Your second letter was duly received and, so far as it goes, it is entirely satisfactory.

I had set apart the leisure this day affords, to write you the long letter alluded to by me in my last; but on going to the Post-office, and seeing the communication in the Morgan Journal, I am almost discouraged of the hope of doing any good by it; especially when I reflect that most probably that communication was written with your knowledge, in as much as it proceeds partly on information which could only have been furnished by you.

However, as I suppose it can do no *harm*, I will proceed. Your letter, admiting my right to seek, or desire, a nomination for congress, opens with an expression of dissatisfaction with the *manner* in which you think I have endeavoured to obtain it. Now, *if I have*, sought the nomination in an *improper* manner; you have the right, to the extent, to be dissatisfied. But I deny all *impropriety* on my part, in the matter.

In the early part of your letter, you introduce the proposition made by me to you and Baker, that we should take a turn a piece; and alluding to the principle you suppose be involved in it, in an after part of your letter, you say—"As a whig I have constantly combatted such practices when practiced among the Locos; & I do not see that they are any more praise worthy, or less anti-republican, when sought to be adopted by whigs." Now, if my proposition had been that we (yourself, Baker & I) should be candidates by turns, and that we should unite our strength throughout to keep down all other candidates, I should not deny the justice of the censurable language you employ; but if you so understood it, you wholly misunderstood it. I never expressed, nor meant to express, that by such an arrangement, any one of us should be, in the least restricted in his right to support any person he might choose, in the District; but only that he should not *himself*, be a candidate out of his turn. I felt then, and it seems to me I *said* then, that even with such an arrangement, should Governor Duncan be a candidate, when you were not, it would be your *previlege* and perhaps your *duty* to go for him.

In this, the true sense of my proposition, I deny that there is any thing censurable in it—any thing but a spirit of mutual concession, for harmony's sake.

In this same connection you say, "It is, in effect, acting upon the principle that the District is a horse which each candidate may mount and ride a two mile heat without consulting any body but the grooms & Jockeys." Well, of course, you go the contrary of this principle; which is, in effect acting on the principle that the District is a horse which, the first jockey that can mount him, may whip and spur round and round, till jockey, or horse, or both, fall dead on the track. And upon your principle, there is a fact as fatal to your claims as mine, which is, that neither you nor I, but *Baker* is the jockey now in the stirrups.

"Without consulting any body but the grooms & Jockeys" is an implied charge that I wish, in some way to interfere with the right of the people to select their candidate. I do not understand it so. I, and my few friends say to the people that "Turn about is fair play." You and your friends do not meet this, and say "Turn about is *not* fair play"—but insist the argument itself, ought not to be used. Fair or unfair, why not trust the people to decide it?

In the early part of your letter you say "It is also true that you did come to my house early in September to know whether I desired to run, stating that you wanted to give Baker a race." In this you are mistaken. I did not state to you that I wanted to give Baker a race; but on the contrary I told you I believed I could get Baker off the track. I do not know that you attached any importance to what I am disavowing; but, on the contrary, I do not know but you mean it as the basis of an inference that I acted deceitfully with you, in pretending to expect a contest with Baker, when in fact I did not expect it.

It is true, that after Baker's interview with you in September, he did send a letter, by a messenger, to me at Tremont; in which letter he detailed what passed at the interview, and the result, precisely as you do, in substance; and in which letter he did urge me to relinquish my pretensions. He had before told me that he would not be a candidate, if I desired he should not; and he then repeated it; but at the same time argued that you, by having been in congress, and having taken a high stand then, would in all probability beat me; so that the sacrafice he made for me, in declining, would, in the end, do me no good. And this is as near as I ever came of hearing Baker express the determination that I should beat you, if he could not; which you say you have learned he did. When he finally determined to decline, he did express the wish that I might succeed; and he has since written his letter of declension; and when *that* is told; all I know, or believe, as to him, *is told*. If he has ever, in any way, attempted to dictate to any friend of his to go for me in preference of you, it is more than I know or believe. That he has a part assigned him to act in the drama, I know to be untrue. What I here say, is not in its nature capable of very certain proof; but it may be said, that being where he is, he can only opperate against you by letters. If he attempts this to any considerable extent, some of them will fall into the hands of your friends who will apprize you of them. Have you yet seen or heard of any?

I now quote from your letter again. "You well knew I would not be a candidate for Governor. Yet during the fall courts, whilst I learn you were obtaining pledges from all the whigs you could to support you for the next candidate, my name was run up as a candidate for Governor by one of your friends under circumstances which now leave no room for doubt that the design was to keep my name out of view for congress, so that the whigs might be more easily influenced to commit themselves to go for you."

Now this is a direct imputation that I *procured*, or *winked at*, or in some way directly or indirectly, *had a hand in*, the nominating of you for Governor; and the imputation is, to the utmost hair-breadth of it, unjust. I never *knew*, or *believed*, or had any *suspicion*, that it *was done*, or *was to be done*, until it was out, had gone to Alton, and been commented upon in the Alton paper, and came back to Springfield, and my attention was called to it by Stuart, in our circuit court room, a few days, as I remember it, after you had been here attending to the case of Thayer vs Farrell, and had left. I went immediately to the Journal office, and told them it was my wish that they should not fall in with the nomination for Governor. They showed me a little paragraph, which they had already prepared, and which was published, and seen by you, as I suppose.

The reason I had not seen the nomination in the Tazewell paper was, as I suppose, because I did not then, as I do not now, take that paper. That I was wholly *innocent* and *ignorant* of that movement, I believe, if need be, I can prove more conclusively than is often in the power of man to prove any such thing.

In the paragraph last quoted you say that the design was to keep your name out of view &c. In the general disavowal I have made, this last is, of course, included; and I now go farther, and declare, that to my recollection, I have not, in a single instance, presented my name as a candidate for congress, without, at the same time presenting yours for the same place. I have some times met a man who would express the opinion that you would yield the track to me; and some times one who believed you would be a candidate for Governor; and I invariably assured such, that you would, in my opinion, be a candidate *for congress*. And while I have thus kept your name *in view* for congress, I have not reproached you for being a candidate, or for any thing else; on the contrary I have constantly spoken of you in the most kind and commendatory terms, as to your talents, your past services, and your goodness of heart. If I falsify in this, you can convict me. The witnesses live, and can tell.

And now tell me: If you think so harshly of me because a paper under the control of one of my friends nominated *you* for Governor, *what*, or *how*, ought I to think of you because of your paper at Jacksonville doing the same thing for *me* twice? Why, you will say you had nothing to do with it; and I shall believe you; but why am I to be judged less charatably?

In another part of your letter you attempt to convict me of giving a double account as to my motive in introducing the resolution to the convention at Pekin. You say "You then told me the object was to soothe Baker's mortified feelings, and that it did not amount to a committal of any body." "Now you say the object was to give Baker the field for the next race, so as to keep the party together." I kept no copy of my letter; but I *guess* if you will turn to it, you will find that I have not, any where in it, said "the object was to give Baker the field for the next race &c" and then if you will allow that you may have committed as great a mistake, as to what I told you at Pekin, you will find yourself a good deal short of the conviction you intended. What I told you at Pekin I do not precisely recollect; but I am sure of some things I did *not* tell you or any one else. If you shall say that I told you it was *an* object with me, in introducing the resolution, to soothe Baker's feelings, I shall admit it; but if you shall say I told you that, that was *the sole* object, I deny it.

If you shall say I then told you that the passage of the resolution amounted to a committal of no one, I deny that also; but if you shall say I then told you, it amounted to a committal of no one, except the delegates, generally who voted for it, and me, particularly, who introduced it, I shall not deny it.

This much, and no more, as a committal, I always supposed it to amount to; and I guess you will be able to find nothing in my late letter to you that is inconsistent with this. And I here add, that I have not since entering this contest with you, or at any time, sought to appropriate to myself any benefit from that resolution, either as settling the succession to pass through me, or as settling a principle that shall give the succession that direction. I have said that "Turn about is fair play"; but this I have said just as I would, if that resolution had never been thought of. I should not hesitate to say publicly, that I claim nothing, in any form, through the Pekin convention, were it not that some friends have thought and spoken differently, and I dislike to rebuke them for what they have not supposed to be injustice to you, while they have meant it in kindness to me—yet, rather than be over-delicate, if you desire it, I will do it any how. I repeat, I desire *nothing* from the Pekin convention. If I am not, (in services done the party, and in capacity to serve in future) near enough your equal, when added to the fact of your having had a turn, to entitle me to the nomination, I scorn it on any and all other

grounds. The question of capacity, I opine your Morgan Journal correspondent will find little difficulty in deciding; and
probably the District may concur, with quite as little.

A good long paragraph of your letter is occupied in an argument to prove that struggles for the succession will break
down the party. It is certain that struggles between candidates, do not strengthen a party; but who are most responsible for these struggles, those who are willing to live and let
live, or those who are resolved, at all hazards, to take care of
"number one"? Take, as an example, the very case in hand.
You have (and deservedly) many devoted friends; and they
have been gratified by seeing you in congress, and taking a
stand that did high credit to you and to them. I also have a
few friends (I fear not enough) who, as well as your own,
aided in giving you that distinction. Is it natural that they
shall be greatly pleased at hearing what they helped to build
up, turned into an argument, for keeping their own favourite
down? Will they grow, and multiply on such grateful food? Is
it by such exclusiveness that you think a party will gain
strength?

In my letter to you, I reminded you that you had first at
Washington, and afterwards at Pekin, said to me that if Baker
succeeded he would most likely hang on as long as possible,
while with you it would be different. If I am not mistaken in
your having said this (and I am sure I am not) it seems you
then thought a little more favourably of "turn about" than
you seem to now. And in writing your letter you seem to
have felt this; for that is about the only part of mine, that you
have failed to notice.

After, by way of imputations upon me, you have used the
terms "management" "manoevering" and "combination"
quite freely, you, in your closing paragraph say: "For it is
mortifying to discover that those with whom I have long
acted & from whom I expected a different course, have considered it all fair to prevent my nomination to congress."
Feeling, as I do, the utter injustice of these imputations, it is
somewhat difficult to be patient under them—yet I content
myself with saying that if there is cause for mortification any
where, it is in the readiness with which you believe, and make
such charges, against one with whom you truly say you have

long acted; and in whose conduct, you have heretofore marked nothing as dishonorable.

I believe you do not mean to be unjust, or ungenerous; and I, therefore am slow to believe that you will not yet think *better* and think *differently* of this matter. Yours truly

To Benjamin F. James

Dear James: Springfield, Feb. 9. 1846

You have seen, or will see what I am inclined to think you will regard as rather an extraordinary communication in the Morgan Journal. The "excessive modesty" of it's tone is certainly admirable. As an excuse for getting before the public, the writer sets out with a pretence of answering an article which I believe appeared in the Lacon paper some time since; taking the ground that the Pekin convention had settled the rotation principle. Now whether the Pekin convention did or did not settle that principle, I care not. If I am not, in what I *have done*, and am *able to do*, for the party, near enough the equal of Genl. Hardin, to entitle me to the nomination, now that he has one, I scorn it on *any* and *all* other grounds.

So far then, as this Morgan Journal communication may relate to the Pekin convention, I rather prefer that your paper shall let it "stink and die" unnoticed.

There is, however, as you will see, another thing in the communication which is, an attempt to injure me because of my declining to reccommend the adoption of a *new plan*, for the selecting a candidate. The attempt is to make it appear that I am unwilling to have a *fair* expression of the whigs of the District upon our respective claims. Now, nothing can be more false in fact; and if Genl. Hardin, had chosen, to furnish his friend with my *written reason* for declining that part of his plan; and that friend had chosen to publish that *reason*, instead of his own construction of the act, the falsehood of his insinuation would have been most apparent. That written reason was as follows, towit:

"As to your proposals that a poll shall be opened in *every* precinct, and that the whole shall take place on the *same* day, I do not personally object. They seem to me to not be unfair;

and I forbear to join in proposing them, only because I rather choose to leave the decision in each county, to the whigs of the county, to be made as their own judgment and convenience may dictate."

I send you this as a weapon with which to demolish, what I can not but regard as a mean insinuation against me. You may use it as you please; I prefer however that you should show it to some of our friends, and not publish it, unless in your judgment it becomes rather urgently necessary.

The reason I want to keep all points of controversy out of the papers, so far as possible, is, that it will be *just all we can do*, to keep out of a quarrel—and I am resolved to do my part to keep peace. Yours truly

To Andrew Johnston

Dear Johnston: Springfield, Ills., Feb. 24, 1846.

Feeling a little poetic this evening, I have concluded to redeem my promise this evening by sending you the piece you expressed the wish to have. You find it enclosed. I wish I could think of something else to say; but I believe I can not. By the way, how would you like to see a piece of poetry of my own making? I have a piece that is almost done, but I find a deal of trouble to finish it.

Give my respects to Mr. Williams, and have him, together with yourself, to understand, that if there is any thing I can do, in connection with your business in the courts, I shall take pleasure in doing it, upon notice. Yours forever,

Remarkable Case of Arrest for Murder

In the year 1841, there resided, at different points in the State of Illinois, three brothers by the name of Trailor. Their Christian names were William, Henry and Archibald. Archibald resided at Springfield, then as now the Seat of Government of the State. He was a sober, retiring and industrious man, of about thirty years of age; a carpenter by trade, and a bachelor, boarding with his partner in business—a Mr. Myers. Henry, a year or two older, was a man of like retiring and industrious habits; had a family and resided with it on a farm at Clary's Grove, about twenty miles distant from Springfield in a North-westerly direction. William, still older, and with similar habits, resided on a farm in Warren county, distant from Springfield something more than a hundred miles in the same North-westerly direction. He was a widower, with several children. In the neighborhood of William's residence, there was, and had been for several years, a man by the name of Fisher, who was somewhat above the age of fifty; had no family, and no settled home; but who boarded and lodged a while here, and a while there, with the persons for whom he did little jobs of work. His habits were remarkably economical, so that an impression got about that he had accumulated a considerable amount of money. In the latter part of May in the year mentioned, William formed the purpose of visiting his brothers at Clary's Grove, and Springfield; and Fisher, at the time having his temporary residence at his house, resolved to accompany him. They set out together in a buggy with a single horse. On Sunday Evening they reached Henry's residence, and staid over night. On Monday Morning, being the first Monday of June, they started on to Springfield, Henry accompanying them on horse back. They reached town about noon, met Archibald, went with him to his boarding house, and there took up their lodgings for the time they should remain. After dinner, the three Trailors and Fisher left the boarding house in company, for the avowed purpose of spending the evening together in looking about the town. At supper, the Trailors had all returned, but Fisher was missing, and some inquiry was made about him. After supper, the Trailors went out professedly in search of him. One by one they returned, the last coming in after late tea time, and each stating that he had been unable to discover any thing of Fisher. The next day, both before and after breakfast, they went professedly in search again, and returned at noon, still unsuccessful. Dinner again being had, William and Henry expressed a determination to give up the search and start for their homes. This was remonstrated against by some of the boarders about the house, on the ground that Fisher was somewhere in the vicinity, and would be left without any conveyance, as he and William had come in the same buggy. The remonstrance was disregarded, and they departed for their homes respectively. Up to this time, the knowledge of Fisher's mysterious disappearance, had spread very little beyond the few boarders at Myers', and excited no considerable interest. After the lapse of three or four days, Henry returned to Springfield, for the ostensible purpose of making further search for Fisher. Procuring some of the boarders, he, together with them and Archibald, spent another day in ineffectual search, when it was again abandoned, and he returned home. No general interest was yet excited. On the Friday, week after Fisher's disappearance, the Postmaster at Springfield received a letter from the Postmaster nearest William's residence in Warren county, stating that William had returned home without Fisher, and was saying, rather boastfully, that Fisher was dead, and had willed him his money, and that he had got about fifteen hundred dollars by it. The letter further stated that William's story and conduct seemed strange; and desired the Postmaster at Springfield to ascertain and write what was the truth in the matter. The Postmaster at Springfield made the letter public, and at once, excitement became universal and intense. Springfield, at that time had a population of about 3500, with a city organization. The Attorney General of the State resided there. A purpose was forthwith formed to ferret out the mystery, in putting which into execution, the Mayor of the city, and the Attorney General took the lead. To make search for, and, if possible, find the body of the man supposed to be murdered, was resolved on as the first step. In pursuance of this, men were formed into large parties, and marched abreast, in all directions, so as to let no inch of ground in the vicinity, remain unsearched. Examinations were made of cellars, wells, and pits of all descriptions, where it was thought possible the body might be concealed. All the fresh, or tolerably fresh graves at the grave-yard were pried into, and dead horses and dead dogs were disinterred, where, in some instances, they had been buried by their partial masters.

This search, as has appeared, commenced on Friday. It continued until Saturday afternoon without success, when it was determined to dispatch officers to arrest William and Henry at their residences respectively. The officers started on Sunday Morning, meanwhile, the search for the body was continued, and rumors got afloat of the Trailors having passed, at different times and places, several gold pieces, which were readily supposed to have belonged to Fisher. On Monday, the officers sent for Henry, having arrested him, arrived with him. The Mayor and Attorney Gen'l took charge of him, and set their wits to work to elicit a discovery from him. He denied, and denied, and persisted in denying. They still plied him in every conceivable way, till Wednesday, when, protesting his own innocence, he stated that his brothers, William and Archibald had murdered Fisher; that they had killed him, without his (Henry's) knowledge at the time, and made a temporary concealment of his body; that immediately preceding his and William's departure from Springfield for home, on Tuesday, the day after Fisher's disappearance, William and Archibald communicated the fact to him, and engaged his assistance in making a permanent concealment of the body; that at the time he and William left professedly for home, they did not take the road directly, but meandering their way through the streets, entered the woods at the North West of the city, two or three hundred yards to the right of where the road where they should have travelled entered them; that penetrating the woods some few hundred yards, they halted and Archibald came a somewhat different route, on foot, and joined them; that William and Archibald then stationed him (Henry) on an old and disused road that ran near by, as a sentinel, to give warning of the approach of any intruder; that William and Archibald then removed the buggy to the edge of a dense brush thicket, about forty yards distant from his (Henry's) position, where, leaving the buggy, they entered the thicket, and in a few minutes returned with the body and placed it in the buggy; that from his station, he could and did distinctly see that the object placed in the buggy was a dead man, of the general appearance and size of Fisher; that William and Archibald then moved off with the buggy in the direction of Hickox's mill pond, and after an absence of half an hour returned, saying they had put him in a safe place; that Archibald then left for town, and he and William found their way to the road, and made for their homes. At this disclosure, all lingering credulity was broken down, and excitement rose to an almost inconceivable height. Up to this time, the well known character of Archibald had repelled and put down all suspicions as to him. Till then, those who were ready to swear that a murder had been committed, were almost as confident that Archibald had had no part in it. But now, he was seized and thrown into jail; and, indeed, his personal security rendered it by no means objectionable to him. And now came the search for the brush thicket, and the search of the mill pond. The thicket was found, and the buggy tracks at the point indicated. At a point within the thicket the signs of a struggle were discovered, and a trail from thence to the buggy track was traced. In attempting to follow the track of the buggy from the thicket, it was found to proceed in the direction of the mill pond, but could not be traced all the way. At the pond, however, it was found that a buggy had been backed down to, and partially into the water's edge. Search was now to be made in the pond; and it was made in every imaginable way. Hundreds and hundreds were engaged in raking, fishing, and draining. After much fruitless effort in this way, on Thursday Morning, the mill dam was cut down, and the water of the pond partially drawn off, and the same processes of search again gone through with. About noon of this day, the officer sent for William, returned having him in custody; and a man calling himself Dr. Gilmore, came in company with them. It seems that the officer arrested William at his own house early in the day on Tuesday, and started to Springfield with him; that after dark awhile, they reached Lewiston in Fulton county, where they stopped for the night; that late in the night this Dr. Gilmore arrived, stating that Fisher was alive at his house; and that he had followed on to give the information, so that William might be released without further trouble; that the officer, distrusting Dr. Gilmore, refused to release William, but brought him on to Springfield, and the Dr. accompanied them. On reaching Springfield, the Dr. re-asserted that

Fisher was alive, and at his house. At this the multitude for a time, were utterly confounded. Gilmore's story was communicated to Henry Trailor, who, without faltering, re-affirmed his own story about Fisher's murder. Henry's adherence to his own story was communicated to the crowd, and at once the idea started, and became nearly, if not quite universal that Gilmore was a confederate of the Trailors, and had invented the tale he was telling, to secure their release and escape. Excitement was again at its zenith. About 3 o'clock the same evening, Myers, Archibald's partner, started with a two horse carriage, for the purpose of ascertaining whether Fisher was alive, as stated by Gilmore, and if so, of bringing him back to Springfield with him. On Friday a legal examination was gone into before two Justices, on the charge of murder against William and Archibald. Henry was introduced as a witness by the prosecution, and on oath, re-affirmed his statements, as heretofore detailed; and, at the end of which, he bore a thorough and rigid cross-examination without faltering or exposure. The prosecution also proved by a respectable lady, that on the Monday evening of Fisher's disappearance, she saw Archibald whom she well knew, and another man whom she did not then know, but whom she believed at the time of testifying to be William, (then present;) and still another, answering the description of Fisher, all enter the timber at the North West of town, (the point indicated by Henry,) and after one or two hours, saw William and Archibald return without Fisher. Several other witnesses testified, that on Tuesday, at the time William and Henry professedly gave up the search for Fisher's body and started for home, they did not take the road directly, but did go into the woods as stated by Henry. By others also, it was proved, that since Fisher's disappearance, William and Archibald had passed rather an unusual number of gold pieces. The statements heretofore made about the thicket, the signs of a struggle, the buggy tracks, &c., were fully proven by numerous witnesses. At this the prosecution rested. Dr. Gilmore was then introduced by the defendants. He stated that he resided in Warren county about seven miles distant from William's residence; that on the morning of William's arrest, he was out from home and heard of the arrest, and of its being on a charge of the murder of Fisher; that on returning to his own house, he found Fisher there; that Fisher was in very feeble health, and could give no rational account as to where he had been during his absence; that he (Gilmore) then started in pursuit of the officer as before stated, and that he should have taken Fisher with him only that the state of his health did not permit. Gilmore also stated that he had known Fisher for several years, and that he had understood he was subject to temporary derangement of mind, owing to an injury about his head received in early life. There was about Dr. Gilmore so much of the air and manner of truth, that his statement prevailed in the minds of the audience and of the court, and the Trailors were discharged; although they attempted no explanation of the circumstances proven by the other witnesses. On the next Monday, Myers arrived in Springfield, bringing with him the now famed Fisher, in full life and proper person. Thus ended this strange affair; and while it is readily conceived that a writer of novels could bring a story to a more perfect climax, it may well be doubted, whether a stranger affair ever really occurred. Much of the matter remains in mystery to this day. The going into the woods with Fisher, and returning without him, by the Trailors; their going into the woods at the same place the next day, after they professed to have given up the search; the signs of a struggle in the thicket, the buggy tracks at the edge of it; and the location of the thicket and the signs about it, corresponding precisely with Henry's story, are circumstances that have never been explained.

William and Archibald have both died since—William in less than a year, and Archibald in about two years after the supposed murder. Henry is still living, but never speaks of the subject.

It is not the object of the writer of this, to enter into the many curious speculations that might be indulged upon the facts of this narrative; yet he can scarcely forbear a remark upon what would, almost certainly have been the fate of William and Archibald, had Fisher not been found alive. It seems he had wandered away in mental derangement, and, had he died in this condition, and his body been found in the vicinity, it is difficult to conceive what could have saved the Trailors from the consequence of having murdered him. Or, if he had died, and his body never found, the case against them, would have been quite as bad, for, although it is a principle of law that a conviction for murder shall not be had, unless the body of the deceased be discovered, it is to be remembered, that Henry testified he saw Fisher's dead body.

April 15, 1846

To Andrew Johnston

Tremont, April 18, 1846.

Friend Johnston: Your letter, written some six weeks since, was received in due course, and also the paper with the parody. It is true, as suggested it might be, that I have never seen Poe's "Raven"; and I very well know that a parody is almost entirely dependent for its interest upon the reader's acquaintance with the original. Still there is enough in the polecat, self-considered, to afford one several hearty laughs. I think four or five of the last stanzas are decidedly funny, particularly where Jeremiah "scrubbed and washed, and prayed and fasted."

I have not your letter now before me; but, from memory, I think you ask me who is the author of the piece I sent you, and that you do so ask as to indicate a slight suspicion that I myself am the author. Beyond all question, I am not the author. I would give all I am worth, and go in debt, to be able to write so fine a piece as I think that is. Neither do I know who is the author. I met it in a straggling form in a newspaper last summer, and I remember to have seen it once before, about fifteen years ago, and this is all I know about it. The piece of poetry of my own which I alluded to, I was led to write under the following circumstances. In the fall of 1844, thinking I might aid some to carry the State of Indiana for Mr. Clay, I went into the neighborhood in that State in which I was raised, where my mother and only sister were buried, and from which I had been absent about fifteen years. That part of the country is, within itself, as unpoetical as any spot of the earth; but still, seeing it and its objects and inhabitants aroused feelings in me which were certainly poetry; though whether my expression of those feelings is poetry is quite another question. When I got to writing, the change of subjects divided the thing into four little divisions or cantos, the first only of which I send you now and may send the others hereafter. Yours truly,

My childhood's home I see again,
  And sadden with the view;
And still, as memory crowds my brain,
  There's pleasure in it too.

O Memory! thou midway world
  'Twixt earth and paradise,
Where things decayed and loved ones lost
  In dreamy shadows rise,

And, freed from all that's earthly vile,
  Seem hallowed, pure, and bright,
Like scenes in some enchanted isle
  All bathed in liquid light.

As dusky mountains please the eye
  When twilight chases day;
As bugle-notes that, passing by,
  In distance die away;

As leaving some grand waterfall,
  We, lingering, list its roar—
So memory will hallow all
  We've known, but know no more.

Near twenty years have passed away
  Since here I bid farewell
To woods and fields, and scenes of play,
  And playmates loved so well.

Where many were, but few remain
  Of old familiar things;
But seeing them, to mind again
  The lost and absent brings.

The friends I left that parting day,
   How changed, as time has sped!
Young childhood grown, strong manhood gray,
   And half of all are dead.

I hear the loved survivors tell
   How nought from death could save,
Till every sound appears a knell,
   And every spot a grave.

I range the fields with pensive tread,
   And pace the hollow rooms,
And feel (companion of the dead)
   I'm living in the tombs.

Handbill Replying to Charges of Infidelity

To the Voters of the Seventh Congressional District.

FELLOW CITIZENS:

A charge having got into circulation in some of the neighborhoods of this District, in substance that I am an open scoffer at Christianity, I have by the advice of some friends concluded to notice the subject in this form. That I am not a member of any Christian Church, is true; but I have never denied the truth of the Scriptures; and I have never spoken with intentional disrespect of religion in general, or of any denomination of Christians in particular. It is true that in early life I was inclined to believe in what I understand is called the "Doctrine of Necessity"—that is, that the human mind is impelled to action, or held in rest by some power, over which the mind itself has no control; and I have sometimes (with one, two or three, but never publicly) tried to maintain this opinion in argument. The habit of arguing thus however, I have, entirely left off for more than five years. And I add here, I have always understood this same opinion to be held by several of the Christian denominations. The foregoing, is the whole truth, briefly stated, in relation to myself, upon this subject.

I do not think I could myself, be brought to support a man for office, whom I knew to be an open enemy of, and scoffer at, religion. Leaving the higher matter of eternal consequences, between him and his Maker, I still do not think any man has the right thus to insult the feelings, and injure the morals, of the community in which he may live. If, then, I was guilty of such conduct, I should blame no man who should condemn me for it; but I do blame those, whoever they may be, who falsely put such a charge in circulation against me.

July 31, 1846.

To Allen N. Ford

Springfield, August 11th, 1846.

Mr. Ford:—I see in your paper of the 8th inst. a communication in relation to myself, of which it is perhaps expected of me to take some notice.

Shortly before starting on my tour through yours, and the other Northern counties of the District, I was informed by letter from Jacksonville that Mr. Cartwright was whispering the charge of infidelity against me in that quarter. I at once wrote a contradiction of it, and sent it to my friends there, with the request that they should publish it or not, as in their discretion they might think proper, having in view the extent of the circulation of the charge, as also the extent of credence it might be receiving. They did not publish it. After my return from your part of the District, I was informed that he had been putting the same charge in circulation against me in some of the neighborhoods in our own, and one or two of the adjoining counties. I believe nine persons out of ten had not heard the charge at all; and, in a word, its extent of circulation was just such as to make a public notice of it appear uncalled for; while it was not entirely safe to leave it unnoticed. After some reflection, I published the little hand-bill, herewith enclosed, and sent it to the neighborhoods above referred to.

I have little doubt now, that to make the same charge—to slyly sow the seed in select spots—was the chief object of his mission through your part of the District, at a time when he knew I could not contradict him, either in person or by letter before the election. And, from the election returns in your county, being so different from what they are in parts where Mr. Cartwright and I are both well known, I incline to the belief that he has succeeded in deceiving some honest men there.   .

As to Mr. Woodward, "our worthy commissioner from Henry," spoken of by your correspondent, I must say it is a little singular that he should know so much about me, while, if I ever saw *him*, or heard of him, save in the communication in your paper, I have forgotten it. If Mr. Woodward has given such assurance of my character as your correspondent asserts, I can still suppose him to be a worthy man; he may have believed what he said; but there is, even in that charitable view of his case, one lesson in morals which he might, not without profit, learn of even me—and that is, never to add the weight of his character to a charge against his fellow man, without *knowing* it to be true. I believe it is an established maxim in morals that he who makes an assertion without knowing whether it is true or false, is guilty of falsehood; and the accidental truth of the assertion, does not justify or excuse him. This maxim ought to be particularly held in view, when we contemplate an attack upon the reputation of our neighbor. I suspect it will turn out that Mr. Woodward got his information in relation to me, from Mr. Cartwright; and I here aver, that he, Cartwright, never heard me utter a word in any way indicating my opinions on religious matters, in his life.

It is my wish that you give this letter, together with the accompanying hand-bill, a place in your paper. Yours truly,

To Andrew Johnston

Friend Johnson: Springfield, Sept. 6th. 1846

You remember when I wrote you from Tremont last spring, sending you a little canto of what I called poetry, I promised to bore you with another some time. I now fulfil the promise. The subject of the present one is an insane man. His name is

Matthew Gentry. He is three years older than I, and when we were boys we went to school together. He was rather a bright lad, and the son of *the* rich man of our very poor neighbourhood. At the age of nineteen he unaccountably became furiously mad, from which condition he gradually settled down into harmless insanity. When, as I told you in my other letter I visited my old home in the fall of 1844, I found him still lingering in this wretched condition. In my poetizing mood I could not forget the impressions his case made upon me. Here is the result—

But here's an object more of dread
    Than ought the grave contains—
A human form with reason fled,
    While wretched life remains.

Poor Matthew! Once of genius bright,
    A fortune-favored child—
Now locked for aye, in mental night,
    A haggard mad-man wild.

Poor Matthew! I have ne'er forgot,
    When first, with maddened will,
Yourself you maimed, your father fought,
    And mother strove to kill;

When terror spread, and neighbours ran,
    Your dange'rous strength to bind;
And soon, a howling crazy man
    Your limbs were fast confined.

How then you strove and shrieked aloud,
    Your bones and sinews bared;
And fiendish on the gazing crowd,
    With burning eye-balls glared—

And begged, and swore, and wept and prayed
    With maniac laugh joined—
How fearful were those signs displayed
    By pangs that killed thy mind!

And when at length, tho' drear and long,
    Time soothed thy fiercer woes,

How plaintively thy mournful song
   Upon the still night rose.

I've heard it oft, as if I dreamed,
   Far distant, sweet, and lone—
The funeral dirge, it ever seemed
   Of reason dead and gone.

To drink it's strains, I've stole away,
   All stealthily and still,
Ere yet the rising God of day
   Had streaked the Eastern hill.

Air held his breath; trees, with the spell,
   Seemed sorrowing angels round,
Whose swelling tears in dew-drops fell
   Upon the listening ground.

But this is past; and nought remains,
   That raised thee o'er the brute.
Thy piercing shrieks, and soothing strains,
   Are like, forever mute.

Now fare thee well—more thou the *cause*,
   Than *subject* now of woe.
All mental pangs, by time's kind laws,
   Hast lost the power to know.

O death! Thou awe-inspiring prince,
   That keepst the world in fear;
Why dost thou tear more blest ones hence,
   And leave him ling'ring here?

If I should ever send another, the subject will be a "Bear hunt." Yours as ever

To Joshua F. Speed

Dear Speed: Springfield, Octr. 22nd. 1846

   Owing to my absence, yours of the 10th. Inst. was not received until yesterday. Since then I have been devoting myself to arive at a correct conclusion upon your matter of business. It may be that you do not precisely understand the nature and result of the suit against you and Bell's estate. It is a chancery suit, and has been brought to a final decree, in which, you are treated as a nominal party only. The decree is, that Bell's administrator pay the Nelson Fry debt, out of the proceeds of Bell's half of the store. So far, you are not injured; because you are released from the debt, without having paid any thing, and Hurst is in no way left liable to you, because the debt he & Bell undertook to pay, is, or will be, paid without your paying it, or any part of it. The question, then, is, "How are you injured?" By diverting so much of the assets of Bell's estate, to the payment of the Fry debt, the general assets are lessened, and so, will pay a smaller dividend to general creditors; one of which creditors I suppose you are, in effect, as assignor of the note to W. P. Speed. It incidentally enlarges your liability to W. P. Speed; and to that extent, you are injured. How much will this be? I think, $100– or $120– being the dividend of 25 or 30 per cent, that Hurst's half of the Fry debt, would pay on the W. P. S. debt. Hurst's undertaking was, in effect, that he would pay the *whole* of the Fry debt, if Bell did not pay any part of it; but it was not his undertaking, that if Bell should pay the whole of it, he would refund the whole, so that Bell should be the better able to pay his other debts. You are not losing on the Fry debt, because that is, or will be paid; but your loss will be on the W. P. S. debt,—a debt that Hurst is under no obligation to indemnify you against. Hurst is bound to account to Bell's estate, for one half of the Fry debt; because he owed half, and Bell's estate pays all; and if, upon such accounting any thing is due the estate from Hurst, it will swell the estate, and so far enlarge the dividend to the W. P. S. debt. But when Bell's estate shall call Hurst to account, he will I am informed show that the estate, after paying the whole of the Fry debt is still indebted to him. If so, not much, if any thing can come from that quarter—nothing, unless it can be so turned, as to compel him pay *all* he owes the estate, and take a *dividend* only, upon what the estate owes him. If you had paid the Fry debt yourself, you could then turn on Hurst and make him refund you; but this would only bring you where you started from, excepting it would leave Bell's estate able to pay a larger dividend; and Hurst would then turn upon the estate to contribute one half, which would enlarge the indebtedness of the estate in the same proportion, and so reduce the dividend again. I believe the only thing that can be done for your advantage in the matter, is for Bell's administrator to call Hurst to account for one half the Fry debt, and then fight off, the best he can, Hurst's claim of indebtedness against the estate.

I should be much pleased to see you here again; but I must, in candour, say I do not perceive how your personal presence would do any good in the business matter.

You, no doubt, assign the suspension of our correspondence to the true philosophical cause, though it must be confessed, by both of us, that this is rather a cold reason for allowing a friendship, such as ours, to die by degrees. I propose now, that, on the receipt of this, you shall be considered in my debt, and under obligation to pay soon, and that neither shall remain long in arrears hereafter. Are you agreed?

Being elected to Congress, though I am very grateful to our friends, for having done it, has not pleased me as much as I expected.

We have another boy, born the 10th. of March last. He is very much such a child as Bob was at his age—rather of a longer order. Bob is "short and low," and, I expect, always will be. He talks very plainly—almost as plainly as any body. He is quite smart enough. I some times fear he is one of the little rare-ripe sort, that are smarter at about five than ever after. He has a great deal of that sort of mischief, that is the offspring of much animal spirits. Since I began this letter a messenger came to tell me, Bob was lost; but by the time I reached the house, his mother had found him, and had him whiped—and, by now, very likely he is run away again.

Mary has read your letter, and wishes to be remembered to Mrs. S. and you, in which I most sincerely join her. As ever Yours—

To Andrew Johnston

Springfield, February 25, 1847.

Dear Johnston: Yours of the 2d of December was duly delivered to me by Mr. Williams. To say the least, I am not at all

displeased with your proposal to publish the poetry, or dog-
gerel, or whatever else it may be called, which I sent you. I
consent that it may be done, together with the third canto,
which I now send you. Whether the prefatory remarks in my
letter shall be published with the verses, I leave entirely to
your discretion; but let names be suppressed by all means. I
have not sufficient hope of the verses attracting any favorable
notice to tempt me to risk being ridiculed for having written
them.

Why not drop into the paper, at the same time, the "half
dozen stanzas of your own"? Or if, for any reason, it suit your
feelings better, send them to me, and I will take pleasure in
putting them in the paper here. Family well, and nothing
new. Yours sincerely,

The Bear Hunt

A wild-bear chace, didst never see?
  Then hast thou lived in vain.
Thy richest bump of glorious glee,
  Lies desert in thy brain.

When first my father settled here,
  'Twas then the frontier line:
The panther's scream, filled night with fear
  And bears preyed on the swine.

But wo for Bruin's short lived fun,
  When rose the squealing cry;
Now man and horse, with dog and gun,
  For vengeance, at him fly.

A sound of danger strikes his ear;
  He gives the breeze a snuff:
Away he bounds, with little fear,
  And seeks the tangled *rough*.

On press his foes, and reach the ground,
  Where's left his half munched meal;
The dogs, in circles, scent around,
  And find his fresh made trail.

With instant cry, away they dash,
  And men as fast pursue;
O'er logs they leap, through water splash,
  And shout the brisk halloo.

Now to elude the eager pack,
  Bear shuns the open ground;
Through matted vines, he shapes his track
  And runs it, round and round.

The tall fleet cur, with deep-mouthed voice,
  Now speeds him, as the wind;
While half-grown pup, and short-legged fice,
  Are yelping far behind.

And fresh recruits are dropping in
  To join the merry *corps*:

147

With yelp and yell,—a mingled din—
 The woods are in a roar.

And round, and round the chace now goes,
 The world's alive with fun;
Nick Carter's horse, his rider throws,
 And more, Hill drops his gun.

Now sorely pressed, bear glances back,
 And lolls his tired tongue;
When as, to force him from his track,
 An ambush on him sprung.

Across the glade he sweeps for flight,
 And fully is in view.
The dogs, new-fired, by the sight,
 Their cry, and speed, renew.

The foremost ones, now reach his rear,
 He turns, they dash away;
And circling now, the wrathful bear,
 They have him full at bay.

At top of speed, the horse-men come,
 All screaming in a row.
"Whoop! Take him Tiger. Seize him Drum."
 Bang,—bang—the rifles go.

And furious now, the dogs he tears,
 And crushes in his ire.
Wheels right and left, and upward rears,
 With eyes of burning fire.

But leaden death is at his heart,
 Vain all the strength he plies.
And, spouting blood from every part,
 He reels, and sinks, and dies.

And now a dinsome clamor rose,
 'Bout who should have his skin;
Who first draws blood, each hunter knows,
 This prize must always win.

But who did this, and how to trace
 What's true from what's a lie,

Like lawyers, in a murder case
    They stoutly *argufy*.

Aforesaid fice, of blustering mood,
    Behind, and quite forgot,
Just now emerging from the wood,
    Arrives upon the spot.

With grinning teeth, and up-turned hair—
    Brim full of spunk and wrath,
He growls, and seizes on dead bear,
    And shakes for life and death.

And swells as if his skin would tear,
    And growls and shakes again;
And swears, as plain as dog can swear,
    That he has won the skin.

Conceited whelp! we laugh at thee—
    Nor mind, that not a few
Of pompous, two-legged dogs there be,
    Conceited quite as you.

before February 25, 1847

Fragments on the Tariff

Whether the protective policy shall be finally abandoned, is now the question.

Discussion and experience already had; and question now in greater dispute than ever.

Has there not been some great error in the mode of discussion?

Propose a single issue of fact, namely—"From 1816 to the present, have protected articles cost us more, of labour, during the *higher*, than during the *lower* duties upon them?"

Introduce the evidence.

Analyze this issue, and try to show that it embraces the *true* and the whole question of the protective policy.

Intended as a test of *experience*.

The *period* selected, is fair; because it is a period of peace—a period sufficiently long to furnish a fair average under all other causes operating on prices—a period in which various modifications of higher and lower duties have occurred.

Protected articles, only are embraced. Show that *these only* belong to the question.

The *labour* price only is embraced. Show this to be correct.

———

I suppose the true effect of duties upon prices to be as follows: If a certain duty be levied upon an article which, by nature can not be produced in this country, as three cents a pound upon coffee, the effect will be, that the consumer will pay one cent more per pound than before, the producer will take one cent less, and the merchant one cent less in profits— in other words, the burthen of the duty will be distributed over consumption, production, and commerce, and not confined to either. But if a duty amounting to full protection be levied upon an article which can be produced here with as little labour, as elsewhere, as iron, that article will ultimately, and at no distant day, in consequence of such duty, be sold to our people cheaper than before, at least by the amount of the cost of *carrying* it from abroad.

. . . as to useless labour. Before proceeding however, it may be as well to give a specimen of what I conceive to be useless labour. I say, then, that all *carrying*, & incidents of carrying, of articles from the place of their production, to a *distant* place for consumption, which articles could be produced of as good quality, in sufficient quantity, and with as little labour, at the place of consumption, as at the place carried from, is useless labour. Applying this principle to our own country by an example, let us suppose that A and B, are a Pennsylvania farmer, and a Pennsylvania iron-maker, whose lands are adjoining. Under the protective policy A is furnishing B with bread and meat, and vegetables, and fruits, and food for horses and oxen, and fresh supplies of horses and oxen themselves occasionally, and receiving, in exchange, all the iron, iron utensils, tools, and implements he needs. In this process of exchange, each receives the *whole* of that which the other parts with—and the reward of labour between them is perfect; each receiving the product of just so much labour, as he has himself bestowed on what he parts with for it. But the change comes. The protective policy is abandoned, and A determines to buy his iron and iron manufactures of C. in Europe. This he can only do by a direct or an indirect exchange of the produce of his farm for them. We will suppose the direct exchange is adopted. In this A desires to exchange ten barrels of flour the precise product of one hundred days labour, for the largest quantity of iron &c that he can get; C, also wishes to exchange the precise product, in iron, of one hundred days labour, for the greatest quantity of flour he can get. In intrinsic value the things to be so exchanged are precisely equal. But before this exchange can take place, the flour must be carried from Pennsylvania to England, and the iron from England to Pennsylvania. The flour starts; the waggoner who hauls it to Philadelphia, takes a part of it to pay him for his labour; then a merchant there takes a little more for storage and forwarding commission, and another takes a little more for insurance; and then the ship-owner carries it across the water, and takes a little more of it for his trouble; still before it reaches C. it is tolled two or three times more for storage, drayage, commission and so on, so that when C. gets it, there are but seven & a half barrels of it left. The iron too, in its transit from England to Penna., goes through the same process of tolling, so that when it reaches A there is but three quarters of it left. The result of this case is, that A. and C. have each parted with one hundred days labour, and each received but seventyfive in return. That the carrying in this case, was introduced by A ceasing to buy of B, and turning to C; that it was utterly useless; and that it is ruinous in its effects, upon A, are all little less than self evident. "But," asks one, "if A is now only getting three quarters as much iron from C for ten barrels of flour as he used to get of B, why does he not turn back to B?" The answer is "B has quit making iron, and so, has none to sell." "But why did B quit making?" "Because A quit buying of him, and he had no other customer to sell to." "But surely A. did not cease buying of B. with the *expectation* of buying of C. on harder terms?" "Certainly not. Let me tell you how that was. When B was making iron as well as C, B had but *one* customer, this farmer A. C had *four* customers in Europe."

It seems to be an opinion very generally entertained, that

the condition of a nation, is *best*, whenever it can *buy cheapest*; but this is not necessarily true, because if, at the same time, and by the same cause, it is compelled to *sell* correspondingly cheap, nothing is gained. Then, it is said, the best condition is, when we can *buy cheapest*, and *sell dearest*; but this again, is not necessarily true; because, with both these, we might have scarcely any thing to sell—or, which is the same thing, to buy with. To illustrate this, suppose a man in the present state of things is labouring the year round, at ten dollars per month, which amounts in the year to $120—a change in affairs enables him to buy supplies at half the former price, to get fifty dollars per month for his labour; but at the same time deprives him of employment during all the months of the year but one. In this case, though goods have fallen one half, and labour risen five to one, it is still plain, that at the end of the year, the labourer is twenty dollars poorer, than under the old state of things.

These reflections show, that to reason and act correctly on this subject, we must look not merely to *buying* cheap, nor yet to buying cheap *and* selling dear; but also to having constant employment, so that we may have the largest possible amount of something to sell. This matter of employment can only be secured by an ample, steady, and certain market, to sell the products of labour in.

But let us yield the point, and admit that, by abandoning the protective policy, our farmers can purchase their supplies of manufactured articles *cheaper* than by continuing it; and then let us see whether, even at that, they will, upon the whole, be gainers by the change. To simplify this question, let us suppose the whole agricultural interest of the country to be in the hands of one man, who has one hundred labourers in his employ; the whole manufacturing interest, to be in the hands of one other man, who has twenty labourers in his employ. The farmer owns all the plough and pasture land, and the manufacturer, all the iron-mines, and coal-banks, and sites of water power. Each is pushing on in his own way, and obtaining supplies from the other so far as he needs—that is, the manufacturer, is buying of the farmer all the cotten he can use in his cotten factory, all the wool he can use in his woollen establishment, all the bread and meat, as well as all the fruits and vegetables which are necessary for himself and all his hands in all his departments; all the corn, and oats, and hay, which are necessary for all his horses and oxen, as well as fresh supplies of horses and oxen themselves, to do all his heavy hauling about his iron works and generally of every sort. The farmer, in turn, is buying of the manufacturer all the iron, iron tools, wooden tools, cotten goods, woolen goods &c &c. that he needs in his business and for his hands. But after awhile farmer discovers that, were it not for the protective policy, he could buy all these supplies cheaper from a European manufacturer, owing to the fact that the price of labour is only one quarter as high there as here. He and his hands are a majority of the whole; and therefore have the legal and moral right to have their interest first consulted. They throw off the protective policy, and farmer ceases buying of home manufacturer. Verry soon, however, he discovers, that to *buy*, even at the cheaper rate, requires something to buy with, and some how or other, he is falling short in this particular.

————

In the early days of the world, the Almighty said to the first of our race "In the sweat of thy face shalt thou eat bread"; and since then, if we except the *light* and the *air* of heaven, no good thing has been, or can be enjoyed by us, without having first cost labour. And, inasmuch as most good things are produced by labour, it follows that all such things of right belong to those whose labour has produced them. But it has so happened in all ages of the world, that *some* have laboured, and *others* have, without labour, enjoyed a large proportion of the fruits. This is wrong, and should not continue. To secure to each labourer the whole product of his labour, or as nearly as possible, is a most worthy object of any good government. But then the question arises, how can a government best, effect this? In our own country, in it's present condition, will the protective principle *advance* or *retard* this object? Upon this subject, the habits of our whole species fall into three great classes—*useful* labour, *useless* labour and *idleness*. Of these the first only is meritorious; and to it all the products of labour rightfully belong; but the two latter, while they exist, are heavy pensioners upon the first, robbing it of a large portion of it's just rights. The only remedy for this is to, as far as possible, drive *useless* labour and *idleness* out of existence. And, first, as to useless labour. Before making war upon this, we must learn to distinguish it from the *useful*. It appears to me, then, that all labour done *directly* and *incidentally* in *carrying* articles to their place of consumption, which could have been produced in sufficient abundance, *with as little labour, at the place of consumption*, as at the place they were carried from, is useless labour. Let us take a few examples of the application of this principle to our own country. Iron & every thing made of iron, can be produced, in sufficient abundance, and with as little labour, in the United States, as any where else in the world; therefore, all labour done in bringing iron & it's fabrics from a foreign country to the United States, is useless labour. The same precisely may be said of cotten, wool, and of their fabrics respectively, as well as many other articles. While the uselessness of the carrying labour is equally true of all the articles mentioned, and of many others not mentioned, it is, perhaps, more glaringly obvious in relation to the cotten goods we purchase from abroad. The raw cotten, from which they are made, itself grows in our own country; is carried by land and by water to England, is there spun, wove, dyed, stamped &c; and then carried back again and worn in the very country where it grew, and partly by the very persons who grew it. Why should it not be spun, wove &c. in the very neighbourhood where it both grows and is consumed, and the carrying about thereby dispensed with? Has nature interposed any obstacle? Are not all the agents— animal power, water power, and steam power—as good and as abundant here as elsewhere? Will not as small an amount of human labour answer here as elsewhere? We may easily see that the cost of this useless labour is very heavy. It includes, not only the cost of the actual carriage, but also the insurances of every kind, and the profits the merchants through whose hands it passes. All these create a heavy burthen necessarily falling upon the useful labour connected with such articles, either *depressing* the price to the *producer*, or enhancing it to the *consumer*, or, what is more probable, doing both in part. A supposed case, will serve to illustrate several points now to the purpose. A, in the interior of South Carolina, has one hundred pounds of cotten, which we suppose to be the precise product of one mans labour for twenty days; B, in Manchester, England, has one hundred yards of cotten cloth, the precise product of the same amount of labour. This lot of cotten, and lot of cloth are precisely equal to each other in their intrinsic value. But A. wishes to part with his cotten for the largest quantity of cloth he can get; B, also wishes to part with his cloth for the greatest quantity of cotten he can get. An exchange is therefore necessary; but before this can be effected, the cotten must be carried to Manchester, and the cloth to South Carolina. The cotten starts to Manchester; the man that hauls it to Charleston in his waggon, takes a little of it out to pay him for his trouble; the merchant, who stores it a while before the ship is ready to sail, takes a little out, for his trouble; the ship-owner, who carries it across the water, takes a little out for his trouble, still before it gets to Manchester, it is tolled two or three times more for drayage, storage, commission, and so on; so that when it reaches B's hands there are but seventyfive pounds of it left. The cloth, too, in it's transit from Manchester to South Carolina goes through the same process of tolling, so that when it reaches A there are but seventyfive yards of it. Now, in this case, A. and B. have each parted with twenty days labour; and each received but fifteen in return. But now let us suppose that B. has removed to the side of A's farm, in South Carolina, and has there made his lot of cloth. Is it not clear that he and A. can then exchange their cloth & cotten, each getting the *whole* of what the other parts with?

This supposed case shows the utter uselessness of the carrying labour in all similar cases, and also the direct burthen it imposes upon useful labour. And whoever will take up the train of reflection suggested by this case, and run it out to the full extent of it's just application, will be astonished, at the amount of useless labour he will thus discover to be done in this very way. I am mistaken, if it is not in fact many times over equal to all the real want in the world. This useless labour I would have discontinued, and those engaged in it, added to the class of useful labourers. If I be asked whether I would destroy all commerce, I answer "Certainly not"—I would continue it where it is *necessary*, and *discontinue* it, where it is not. An instance: I would continue commerce so far as it is employed in bringing us coffee, and I would discontinue it so far as it is employed in bringing us cotten goods.

But let us yield the point, and admit that, by abandoning to protective policy, our farmers can purchase their supplies of manufactured articles *cheaper* than before; and then let us see whether, even at that, the farmers will, upon the whole, be gainers by the change. To simplify this question, let us suppose our whole population to consist of but twenty men. Under the prevalence of the protective policy, fifteen of these are farmers, one is a miller, one manufactures iron, one, implements from iron, one cotten goods, and one woolen goods. The farmers discover, that, owing to labour only costing one quarter as much in Europe as here, they can buy iron, iron implements, cotten goods, & woolen goods cheaper, when brought from Europe, than when made by their neighbours. They are the majority, and therefore have both the legal and moral right to have their interest first consulted. They throw off the protective policy, and cease buying these articles of their neighbours. But they soon discover that to buy, and at the cheaper rate, requires something to buy with. Falling short in this particular, one of these farmers, takes a load of wheat to the miller, and gets it made into flour, and starts, as had been his custom, to the iron furnace; he approaches the well known spot, but, strange to say, all is cold and still as death—no smoke rises, no furnace roars, no anvil rings. After some search he finds the owner of the desolate place, and calls out to him, "Come, Vulcan, dont you want to buy a load of flour?" "Why" says Vulcan "I am hungry enough, to be sure—have'nt tasted bread for a week—but then you see my works are stopped, and I have nothing to give for your flour." "But, Vulcan, why dont you go to work and get something?" "I am ready to do so; will you hire me, farmer?" "Oh, no; I could only set you to raising wheat, and you see I have more of that already than I can get any thing for." "But give me employment, and send your flour to Europe for a market." "Why, Vulcan, how silly you talk. Dont you know they raise wheat in Europe as well as here, and that *labour* is so cheap there as to fix the price of flour there so low as scarcely to pay the long carriage of it from here, leaving nothing whatever to me." "But, farmer, could'nt you pay to raise and prepare garden stuffs, and fruits, such as radishes, cabages, irish and sweet potatoes, cucumbers, water-melons and musk-melons, plumbs, pears, peaches, apples, and the like; all these are good things and used to sell well." "So they did use to sell well, but it was to *you* we sold them, and now you tell us you have nothing to buy with. Of course I can not sell such things to the other farmers, because each of them raises enough for himself, and, in fact, rather wishes to sell than to buy. Neither can I send them to Europe for a market; because, to say nothing of European markets being stocked with such articles at lower prices than I can afford, they are of such a nature as to rot before they could reach there. The truth is, Vulcan, I am compelled to quit raising these things altogether, except a few for my own use, and this leaves part of my own time idle on my hands, instead of my finding employment for you."

If at any time all *labour* should cease, and all existing provisions be equally divided among the people, at the end of a single year there could scarcely be one human being left alive—all would have perished by want of subsistence.

So again, if upon such division, all that *sort* of labour, which produces provisions, should cease, and each individual should take up so much of his share as he could, and carry it continually around his habitation, although in this carrying, the amount of labour going on might be as great as ever, so long as it could last, at the end of the year the result would be precisely the same—that is, none would be left living.

The first of these propositions shows, that universal *idleness* would speedily result in universal *ruin*; and the second shows, that *useless labour* is, in this respect, the same as idleness.

I submit, then, whether it does not follow, that *partial* idleness, and partial *useless labour*, would, in the proportion of their extent, in like manner result, in partial ruin—whether, if *all* should subsist upon the labour that *one half* should perform, it would not result in very scanty allowance to the whole.

Believing that these propositions, and the conclusions I

draw from them can not be successfully controverted, I, for the present, assume their correctness, and proceed to try to show, that the abandonment of the protective policy by the American Government, must result in the increase of both useless labour, and idleness; and so, in proportion, must produce want and ruin among our people.

(The foregoing scraps about protection were written by Lincoln, between his election to Congress in 1846, and taking his seat in Dec. 1847)

"Spot" Resolutions in the U.S. House of Representatives

Whereas the President of the United States, in his message of May 11th. 1846, has declared that "The Mexican Government not only refused to receive him" (the envoy of the U.S.) "or listen to his propositions, but, after a long continued series of menaces, have at last invaded *our teritory*, and shed the blood of our fellow *citizens* on *our own soil*"

And again, in his message of December 8, 1846 that "We had ample cause of war against Mexico, long before the breaking out of hostilities. But even then we forbore to take redress into our own hands, until Mexico herself became the aggressor by invading *our soil* in hostile array, and shedding the blood of our *citizens*"

And yet again, in his message of December 7– 1847 that "The Mexican Government refused even to hear the terms of adjustment which he" (our minister of peace) "was authorized to propose; and finally, under wholly unjustifiable pretexts, involved the two countries in war, by invading the teritory of the State of Texas, striking the first blow, and shedding the blood of our *citizens* on *our own soil*"

And whereas this House desires to obtain a full knowledge of all the facts which go to establish whether the particular spot of soil on which the blood of our *citizens* was so shed, was, or was not, *our own soil*, at that time; therefore

Resolved by the House of Representatives, that the President of the United States be respectfully requested to inform this House —

First: Whether the spot of soil on which the blood of our *citizens* was shed, as in his messages declared, was, or was not, within the teritories of Spain, at least from the treaty of 1819 until the Mexican revolution

Second: Whether that spot is, or is not, within the teritory which was wrested from Spain, by the Mexican revolution.

Third: Whether that spot is, or is not, within a settlement of people, which settlement had existed ever since long before the Texas revolution, until it's inhabitants fled from the approach of the U.S. Army.

Fourth: Whether that settlement is, or is not, isolated from any and all other settlements, by the Gulf of Mexico, and the Rio Grande, on the South and West, and by wide uninhabited regions on the North and East.

Fifth: Whether the *People* of that settlement, or a *majority* of them, or *any* of them, had ever, previous to the bloodshed, mentioned in his messages, submitted themselves to the government or laws of Texas, or of the United States, by *consent*, or by *compulsion*, either by accepting office, or voting at elections, or paying taxes, or serving on juries, or having process served upon them, or in *any other way*.

Sixth: Whether the People of that settlement, did, or did not, flee from the approach of the United States Army, leaving unprotected their homes and their growing crops, *before* the blood was shed, as in his messages stated; and whether the first blood so shed, was, or was not shed, within the *inclosure* of the People, or some of them, who had thus fled from it.

Seventh: Whether our *citizens*, whose blood was shed, as in his messages declared, were, or were not, at that time, *armed* officers, and *soldiers*, sent into that settlement, by the military order of the President through the Secretary of War—and

Eighth: Whether the military force of the United States, including those *citizens*, was, or was not, so sent into that settlement, after Genl. Taylor had, more than once, intimated to the War Department that, in his opinion, no such movement was necessary to the defence or protection of Texas.

December 22, 1847

To William H. Herndon

Washington, January 8, 1848.

Dear William: Your letter of December 27 was received a day or two ago. I am much obliged to you for the trouble you have taken, and promise to take in my little business there. As to speech-making, by way of getting the hang of the House I made a little speech two or three days ago on a post-office question of no general interest. I find speaking here and elsewhere about the same thing. I was about as badly scared, and no worse, as I am when I speak in court. I expect to make one within a week or two, in which I hope to succeed well enough to wish you to see it.

It is very pleasant to learn from you that there are some who desire that I should be reëlected. I most heartily thank them for their kind partiality; and I can say, as Mr. Clay said of the annexation of Texas, that "personally I would not object" to a reëlection, although I thought at the time, and still think, it would be quite as well for me to return to the law at the end of a single term. I made the declaration that I would not be a candidate again, more from a wish to deal fairly with others, to keep peace among our friends, and to keep the district from going to the enemy, than for any cause personal to myself; so that, if it should so happen that nobody else wishes to be elected, I could not refuse the people the right of sending me again. But to enter myself as a competitor of others, or to authorize any one so to enter me, is what my word and honor forbid.

I got some letters intimating a probability of so much difficulty amongst our friends as to lose us the district; but I remember such letters were written to Baker when my own case was under consideration, and I trust there is no more ground for such apprehension now than there was then. Remember I am always glad to receive a letter from you. Most truly your friend,

Speech in the U.S. House of Representatives on the War with Mexico

Mr. Chairman:

Some, if not all the gentlemen on, the other side of the House, who have addressed the committee within the last two days, have spoken rather complainingly, if I have rightly understood them, of the vote given a week or ten days ago, declaring that the war with Mexico was unnecessarily and unconstitutionally commenced by the President. I admit that such a vote should not be given, in mere party wantonness, and that the one given, is justly censurable, if it have no other, or better foundation. I am one of those who joined in that vote; and I did so under my best impression of the *truth* of the case. How I got this impression, and how it may possibly be removed, I will now try to show. When the war began, it was my opinion that all those who, because of knowing too *little*, or because of knowing too *much*, could not conscientiously approve the conduct of the President, in the beginning of it, should, nevertheless, as good citizens and patriots, remain silent on that point, at least till the war should be ended. Some leading democrats, including Ex President Van Buren, have taken this same view, as I understand them; and I adhered to it, and acted upon it, until since I took my seat here; and I think I should still adhere to it, were it not that the President and his friends will not allow it to be so. Besides the continual effort of the President to argue every silent vote given for supplies, into an endorsement of the justice and wisdom of his conduct—besides that singularly candid paragraph, in his late message in which he tells us that Congress, with great unanimity, only two in the Senate and fourteen in the House dissenting, had declared that, "by the act of the Republic of Mexico, a state of war exists between that Government and the United States," when the same journals that informed him of this, also informed him, that when that declaration stood disconnected from the question of supplies, sixtyseven in the House, and not fourteen merely, voted against it—besides this open attempt to prove, by telling the *truth*, what he could not prove by telling the

whole truth—demanding of all who will not submit to be misrepresented, in justice to themselves, to speak out—besides
all this, one of my colleagues (Mr. Richardson) at a very early
day in the session brought in a set of resolutions, expressly
endorsing the original justice of the war on the part of the
President. Upon these resolutions, when they shall be put on
their passage I shall be *compelled* to vote; so that I can not be
silent, if I would. Seeing this, I went about preparing myself
to give the vote understandingly when it should come. I carefully examined the President's messages, to ascertain what he
himself had said and proved upon the point. The result of this
examination was to make the impression, that taking for true,
all the President states as facts, he falls far short of proving his
justification; and that the President would have gone farther
with his proof, if it had not been for the small matter, that the
truth would not permit him. Under the impression thus
made, I gave the vote before mentioned. I propose now to
give, concisely, the process of the examination I made, and
how I reached the conclusion I did. The President, in his first
war message of May 1846, declares that the soil was *ours* on
which hostilities were commenced by Mexico; and he repeats
that declaration, almost in the same language, in each successive annual message, thus showing that he esteems that point,
a highly essential one. In the importance of that point, I entirely agree with the President. To my judgment, it is the *very
point*, upon which he should be justified, or condemned. In
his message of Decr. 1846, it seems to have occurred to him,
as is certainly true, that title—ownership—to soil, or any
thing else, is not a simple fact; but is a conclusion following
one or more simple facts; and that it was incumbent upon
him, to present the facts, from which he concluded, the soil
was ours, on which the first blood of the war was shed.

Accordingly a little below the middle of page twelve in the
message last referred to, he enters upon that task; forming an
issue, and introducing testimony, extending the whole, to a
little below the middle of page fourteen. Now I propose to
try to show, that the whole of this,—issue and evidence—is,
from beginning to end, the sheerest deception. The issue, as
he presents it, is in these words "But there are those who,
conceding all this to be true, assume the ground that the true

western boundary of Texas is the Nueces, instead of the Rio Grande; and that, therefore, in marching our army to the east bank of the latter river, we passed the Texan line, and invaded the teritory of Mexico." Now this issue, is made up of two affirmatives and no negative. The main deception of it is, that it assumes as true, that *one* river or the *other* is necessarily the boundary; and cheats the superficial thinker entirely out of the idea, that *possibly* the boundary is somewhere *between* the two, and not actually at either. A further deception is, that it will let in *evidence*, which a true issue would exclude. A true issue, made by the President, would be about as follows "I say, the soil *was ours*, on which the first blood was shed; there are those who say it was not."

I now proceed to examine the Presidents evidence, as applicable to such an issue. When that evidence is analized, it is all included in the following propositions:

1. That the Rio Grande was the Western boundary of Louisiana as we purchased it of France in 1803.

2 That the Republic of Texas always *claimed* the Rio Grande, as her Western boundary.

3 That by various acts, she had claimed it *on paper*.

4. That Santa Anna, in his treaty with Texas, recognised the Rio Grande, as her boundary.

5. That Texas *before*, and the U. S. *after*, annexation had *exercised* jurisdiction *beyond* the Nueces—*between* the two rivers.

6 That our Congress, *understood* the boundary of Texas to extend beyond the Nueces.

Now for each of these in it's turn.

His first item is, that the Rio Grande was the Western boundary of Louisiana, as we purchased it of France in 1803; and seeming to expect this to be disputed, he argues over the amount of nearly a page, to prove it true; at the end of which he lets us know, that by the treaty of 1819, we sold to Spain the whole country from the Rio Grande eastward, to the Sabine. Now, admitting for the present, that the Rio Grande, was the boundary of Louisiana, what, under heaven, had that to do with the *present* boundary between us and Mexico? How, Mr. Chairman, the line, that once divided your land from mine, can *still* be the boundary between us, *after* I have sold my land to you, is, to me, beyond all comprehension. And how any man, with an honest purpose only, of proving the truth, could ever have *thought* of introducing such a fact to prove such an issue, is equally incomprehensible. His next piece of evidence is that "The Republic of Texas always *claimed* this river (Rio Grande) as her western boundary." That is not true, in fact. Texas *has* claimed it, but she has not *always* claimed it. There is, at least, one distinguished exception. Her state constitution,—the republic's most solemn, and well considered act—that which may, without impropriety, be called her last will and testament revoking all others—makes no such claim. But suppose she had always claimed it. Has not Mexico always claimed the contrary? so that there is but *claim* against *claim*, leaving nothing proved, until we get back of the claims, and find which has the better *foundation*. Though not in the order in which the President presents his evidence, I now consider that class of his statements, which are, in substance, nothing more than that Texas has, by various acts of her convention and congress, claimed the Rio Grande, as her boundary, *on paper*. I mean here what he says about the fixing of the Rio Grande as her boundary in her old constitution (not her state constitution) about forming congressional districts, counties &c &c. Now all of this is but naked *claim*; and what I have already said about claims is strictly applicable to this. If I should claim your land, by word of mouth, that certainly would not make it mine; and if I were to claim it by a deed which I had made myself, and with which, you had had nothing to do, the claim would be quite the same, in substance—or rather, in utter nothingness. I next consider the President's statement that Santa Anna in his *treaty* with Texas, recognised the Rio Grande, as the western boundary of Texas. Besides the position, so often taken that Santa Anna, while a prisoner of war—a captive—*could* not bind Mexico by a treaty, which I deem conclusive—besides this, I wish to say something in relation to this treaty, so called by the President, with Santa Anna. If any man would like to be amused by a sight of that *little* thing, which the President calls by that *big* name, he can have it, by turning to Niles' Register volume 50, page 336. And if any one should suppose that Niles' Register is a curious repository of so mighty a document, as a solemn treaty between nations, I can only say that I learned, to a tolerable degree of certainty, by enquiry at the State Department, that the President himself, never saw it any where else. By the way, I believe I should not err, if I were to declare, that during the first ten years of the existence of that document, it was never, by any body, *called* a treaty—that it was never so called, till the President, in his extremity, attempted, by so calling it, to wring something from it in justification of himself in connection with the Mexican war. It has none of the distinguishing features of a treaty. It does not call itself a treaty. Santa Anna does not therein, assume to bind Mexico; he assumes only to act as the President-Commander-in-chief of the Mexican Army and Navy; stipulates that the then present hostilities should cease, and that he would not *himself* take up arms, nor *influence* the Mexican people to take up arms, against Texas during the existence of the war of independence. He did not recognise the independence of Texas; he did not assume to put an end to the war; but clearly indicated his expectation of it's continuance; he did not say one word about boundary, and, most probably, never thought of it. It *is* stipulated therein that the Mexican forces should evacuate the teritory of Texas, *passing to the other side of the Rio Grande*; and in another article, it is stipulated that, to prevent collisions between the armies, the Texan army should not approach nearer than within five leagues—of *what* is not said—but clearly, from the object stated it is—of the Rio Grande. Now, if this is a treaty, recognising the Rio Grande, as the boundary of Texas, it contains the singular feature, of stipulating, that Texas shall not go within five leagues of *her own* boundary.

Next comes the evidence of Texas before annexation, and the United States, afterwards, *exercising* jurisdiction *beyond* the Nueces, and *between* the two rivers. This actual *exercise* of jurisdiction, is the very class or quality of evidence we want. It is excellent so far as it goes; but does it go far enough? He tells us it went *beyond* the Nueces; but he does not tell us it went *to* the Rio Grande. He tells us, jurisdiction was exercised *between* the two rivers, but he does not tell us it was exercised over *all* the teritory between them. Some simple minded people, think it is *possible*, to cross one river and go *beyond* it

without going *all the way* to the next—that jurisdiction may
be exercised *between* two rivers without covering *all* the country between them. I know a man, not very unlike myself, who
exercises jurisdiction over a piece of land between the Wabash
and the Mississippi; and yet so far is this from being *all* there
is between those rivers, that it is just one hundred and fiftytwo feet long by fifty wide, and no part of it much within a
hundred miles of either. He has a neighbour between him
and the Mississippi,—that is, just across the street, in that
direction—whom, I am sure, he could neither *persuade* nor
force to give up his habitation; but which nevertheless, he
could certainly annex, if it were to be done, by merely standing on his own side of the street and *claiming* it, or even,
sitting down, and writing a *deed* for it.

But next the President tells us, the Congress of the United
States *understood* the state of Texas they admitted into the
union, to extend *beyond* the Nueces. Well, I suppose they did.
I certainly so understood it. But how *far* beyond? That Congress did *not* understand it to extend clear to the Rio Grande,
is quite certain by the fact of their joint resolutions, for admission, expressly leaving all questions of boundary to future
adjustment. And it may be added, that Texas herself, is proved
to have had the same understanding of it, that our Congress
had, by the fact of the exact conformity of her new constitution, to those resolutions.

I am now through the whole of the President's evidence;
and it is a singular fact, that if any one should declare the
President sent the army into the midst of a settlement of Mexican people, who had never submited, by consent or by
force, to the authority of Texas or of the United States, and
that *there*, and *thereby*, the first blood of the war was shed,
there is not one word in all the President has said, which
would either admit or deny the declaration. This strange
omission, it does seem to me, could not have occurred but by
design. My way of living leads me to be about the courts of
justice; and there, I have sometimes seen a good lawyer,
struggling for his client's neck, in a desparate case, employing
every artifice to work round, befog, and cover up, with many
words, some point arising in the case, which he *dared* not
admit, and yet *could* not deny. Party bias may help to make it

appear so; but with all the allowance I can make for such bias, it still does appear, to me, that just such, and from just such necessity, is the President's struggle in this case.

Some time after my colleague (Mr. Richardson) introduced the resolutions I have mentioned, I introduced a preamble, resolution, and interrogatories, intended to draw the President out, if possible, on this hitherto untrodden ground. To show their relevancy, I propose to state my understanding of the true rule for ascertaining the boundary between Texas and Mexico. It is, that *wherever* Texas was *exercising* jurisdiction, was hers; and *wherever Mexico* was exercising jurisdiction, was hers; and that *whatever* separated the actual exercise of jurisdiction of the one, from that of the other, was the true boundary between them. If, as is probably true, Texas was exercising jurisdiction along the western bank of the Nueces, and Mexico was exercising it along the eastern bank of the Rio Grande, then *neither* river was the boundary; but the uninhabited country between the two, was. The extent of our territory in that region depended, not on any *treaty-fixed* boundary (for no treaty had attempted it) but on revolution. Any people anywhere, being inclined and having the power, have the *right* to rise up, and shake off the existing government, and form a new one that suits them better. This is a most valuable,—a most sacred right—a right, which we hope and believe, is to liberate the world. Nor is this right confined to cases in which the whole people of an existing government, may choose to exercise it. Any portion of such people that *can*, *may* revolutionize, and make their *own*, of so much of the territory as they inhabit. More than this, a *majority* of any portion of such people may revolutionize, putting down a *minority*, intermingled with, or near about them, who may oppose their movement. Such minority, was precisely the case, of the tories of our own revolution. It is a quality of revolutions not to go by *old* lines, or *old* laws; but to break up both, and make new ones. As to the country now in question, we bought it of France in 1803, and sold it to Spain in 1819, according to the President's statements. After this, all Mexico, including Texas, revolutionized against Spain; and still later, Texas revolutionized against Mexico. In my view, just so far as she carried her revolution, by obtaining the *actual*, willing or unwilling, submission of the people, *so far*, the country was hers, and no farther. Now sir, for the purpose of obtaining the very best evidence, as to whether Texas had actually carried her revolution, to the place where the hostilities of the present war commenced, let the President answer the interrogatories, I proposed, as before mentioned, or some other similar ones. Let him answer, fully, fairly, and candidly. Let him answer with *facts*, and not with arguments. Let him remember he sits where Washington sat, and so remembering, let him answer, as Washington would answer. As a nation *should* not, and the Almighty *will* not, be evaded, so let him attempt no evasion—no equivocation. And if, so answering, he can show that the soil was ours, where the first blood of the war was shed—that it was not within an inhabited country, or, if within such, that the inhabitants had submitted themselves to the civil authority of Texas, or of the United States, and that the same is true of the site of Fort Brown, then I am with him for his justification. In that case I, shall be most happy to reverse the vote I gave the other day. I have a selfish motive for desiring that the President may do this. I expect to give some votes, in connection with the war, which, without his so doing, will be of doubtful propriety in my own judgment, but which will be free from the doubt if he does so. But if he *can* not, or *will* not do this—if on any pretence, or no pretence, he shall refuse or omit it, then I shall be fully convinced, of what I more than suspect already, that he is deeply conscious of being in the wrong—that he feels the blood of this war, like the blood of Abel, is crying to Heaven against him. That originally having some strong motive— what, I will not stop now to give my opinion concerning—to involve the two countries in a war, and trusting to escape scrutiny, by fixing the public gaze upon the exceeding brightness of military glory—that attractive rainbow, that rises in showers of blood—that serpent's eye, that charms to destroy—he plunged into it, and has swept, *on* and *on*, till, disappointed in his calculation of the ease with which Mexico might be subdued, he now finds himself, he knows not where. How like the half insane mumbling of a fever-dream, is the whole war part of his late message! At one time telling us that Mexico has nothing whatever, that we can get, but teritory; at another, showing us how we can support the war, by levying contributions on Mexico. At one time, urging the national honor, the security of the future, the prevention of foreign interference, and even, the good of Mexico herself, as among the objects of the war; at another, telling us, that "to reject indemnity, by refusing to accept a cession of teritory, would be to abandon all our just demands, and to wage the war, bearing all it's expenses, *without a purpose or definite object*." So then, the national honor, security of the future, and every thing but teritorial indemnity, may be considered the *no-purposes*, and *indefinite*, objects of the war! But, having it now settled that teritorial indemnity is the only object, we are urged to seize, by legislation here, all that he was content to take, a few months ago, and the whole province of lower California to boot, and to still carry on the war—to take *all* we are fighting for, and *still* fight on. Again, the President is resolved, under all circumstances, to have full teritorial indemnity for the expenses of the war; but he forgets to tell us how we are to get the *excess*, after those expenses shall have surpassed the value of the *whole* of the Mexican teritory. So again, he insists that the separate national existence of Mexico, shall be maintained; but he does not tell us *how* this can be done, after we shall have taken *all* her teritory. Lest the questions, I here suggest, be considered speculative merely, let me be indulged a moment in trying to show they are not. The war has gone on some twenty months; for the expenses of which, together with an inconsiderable old score, the President now claims about one half of the Mexican teritory; and that, by far the better half, so far as concerns our ability to make any thing out of it. *It* is comparatively uninhabited; so that we could establish land offices in it, and raise some money in that way. But the other half is already inhabited, as I understand it, tolerably densely for the nature of the country; and all it's lands, or all that are valuable, already appropriated as private property. How then are we to make any thing out of these lands with this incumbrance on them? or how, remove the incumbrance? I suppose no one will say we should kill the people, or drive them out, or make slaves of them, or even confiscate their property. How then can we make much out of this part of the teritory? If the prossecution of the war has, in expenses, already equalled the *better* half of the country, how long it's future prosecution, will be in equalling, the less valuable half, is not a *speculative*, but a *practical* question, pressing closely upon us. And yet it is a question which the President seems to never have thought of. As to the mode of terminating the war, and securing peace, the President is equally wandering and indefinite. First, it is to be done by a more vigorous prossecution of the war in the vital parts of the enemies country; and, after apparently, talking himself tired, on this point, the President drops down into a half despairing tone, and tells us that "with a people distracted and divided by contending factions, and a government subject to constant changes, by successive revolutions, *the continued success of our arms may fail to secure a satisfactory peace.*" Then he suggests the propriety of wheedling the Mexican people to desert the counsels of their own leaders, and trusting in our protection, to set up a government from which we can secure a satisfactory peace; telling us, that *"this may become the only mode of obtaining such a peace."* But soon he falls into doubt of this too; and then drops back on to the already half abandoned ground of "more vigorous prossecution." All this shows that the President is, in no wise, satisfied with his own positions. First he takes up one, and in attempting to argue us *into* it, he argues himself *out* of it; then seizes another, and goes through the same process; and then, confused at being able to think of nothing new, he snatches up the old one again, which he has some time before cast off. His mind, tasked beyond it's power, is running hither and thither, like some tortured creature, on a burning surface, finding no position, on which it can settle down, and be at ease.

Again, it is a singular omission in this message, that it, no where intimates *when* the President expects the war to terminate. At it's beginning, Genl. Scott was, by this same President, driven into disfavor, if not disgrace, for intimating that peace could not be conquered in less than three or four months. But now, at the end of about twenty months, during which time our arms have given us the most splendid successes—every department, and every part, land and water, officers and privates, regulars and volunteers, doing all that men *could* do, and hundreds of things which it had ever before been thought men could *not* do,—after all this, this same President gives us a long message, without showing us, that, *as to the end*, he himself, has, even an immaginary conception. As I have before said, he knows not where he is. He is a bewildered, confounded, and miserably perplexed man. God grant he may be able to show, there is not something about his conscience, more painful than all his mental perplexity!

January 12, 1848

To Jonathan R. Diller

Friend Diller: Washington Jany. 19 1848

Your letter of the 27th. Decr. was received only the day before yesterday. The very best I can do with your case, I will. Send to me just as soon as you can, the affidavit of one of your clerks, showing the number of mails you receive per week; the number you send away per week; the number of pounds weight of mails you handle daily, besides that stopping at your own office; the number of hands, including yourself, you have to constantly employ; and what you pay them; how many hours out of the twentyfour you are obliged to be up and at work; and how much you have to pay annually, besides clerk-hire, for matters connected with the office, which the Govt. does not allow you for. Whether Govt. allows for room-rent, candles, and fuel, I dont know, but if it does not, these will fall in the item last mentioned. If, in this way you can show that your compensation is too small, I think I can get it increased; but the bare fact that you get less than you used to do, will not enable me to get along. We have had one such case, which was sneered out of court. I am really interested for you, & wish you to lose no time in doing as I tell you. Show this letter to Logan, and get him to frame the affidavit—adding any thing that may occur to you or him which I may have forgotten.

Tell Hickox I received his claim, and will do the best with it I can; but that I fear I can not get along with it.

I am kept very busy here; and one thing that perplexes me more than most any thing else, are the cases of whigs calling on me to get them appointments to places in the army, from the President. There are two great obstacles in the way which they do not seem to understand—first, the President has no such appointments to give—and secondly, if he had, he could hardly be expected to give them to whigs, at the solicitation of a whig Member of Congress. Yours truly

To William H. Herndon

Dear William: Washington, Feb. 1— 1848

Your letter of the 19th. ult. was received last night, and for which I am much obliged. The only thing in it that I wish to talk to you about at once, is that, because of my vote for Mr. Ashmun's amendment, you fear that you and I disagree about the war. I regret this, not because of any fear we shall remain disagreed, after you shall have read this letter, but because, if *you* misunderstand, I fear other good friends will also. That vote affirms that the war was unnecessarily and unconstitutionally commenced by the President; and I will stake my life, that if you had been in my place, you would have voted just as I did. Would you have voted what you felt you knew to be a lie? I know you would not. Would you have gone out of the House—skulked the vote? I expect not. If you had skulked one vote, you would have had to skulk many more, before the end of the session. Richardson's resolutions, introduced before I made any move, or gave any vote upon the subject, make the direct question of the justice of the war; so that no man can be silent if he would. You are compelled to speak; and your only alternative is to tell the *truth* or tell a *lie*. I can not doubt which you would do.

This vote, has nothing to do, in determining my votes on the questions of supplies. I have always intended, and still intend, to vote supplies; perhaps not in the precise form recommended by the President, but in a better form for all purposes, except locofoco party purposes. It is in this particular you seem to be mistaken. The locos are untiring in their effort to make the impression that all who vote supplies, or take part in the war, do, of necessity, approve the Presidents conduct in the beginning of it; but the whigs have, from the beginning, made and kept the distinction between the two. In the very first act, nearly all the whigs voted *against* the preamble declaring that war existed by the act of Mexico, and yet nearly all of them voted *for* the supplies. As to the whig men who have participated in the war, so far as they have spoken to my hearing, they do not hesitate to denounce, as unjust, the Presidents conduct in the beginning of the war. They do not suppose that such denunciation, is dictated by undying hatred to them, as the Register would have it believed. There are two such whigs on this floor, Col. Haskell, and Major Gaines. The former, fought as a Col. by the side of Col. Baker at Cerro Gordo, and stands side by side with me, in the vote, that you seem to be dissatisfied with. The latter, the history of whose capture with Cassius Clay, you well know, had not arrived here when that vote was given; but as I understand, he stands ready to give just such a vote, whenever an occasion shall present. Baker too, who is now here, says the truth is undoubtedly that way, and whenever he shall speak out, he will say so. Col. Donaphin too, the favourite whig of Missouri, and who over ran all Northern Mexico, on his return home in a public speech at St. Louis, condemned the administration in relation to the war as I remember. G. T. M Davis, who has been through almost the whole war, declares in favour of Mr. Clay, from which I infer that he adopts the sentiments of Mr. Clay, generally at least. On the other hand, I have heard of but one whig, who has been to the war, attempting to justify the President's conduct. That one is Capt. Bishop, editor of the Charleston Courier, and a very clever fellow.

I do not mean this letter for the public, but for you. Before it reaches you, you will have seen and read my pamphlet speech, and perhaps, scared anew, by it. After you get over your scare, read it over again, sentence by sentence, and tell me honestly what you think of it. I condensed all I could for fear of being cut off by the hour rule, and when I got through, I had spoke but 45 minutes. Yours forever

To William H. Herndon

Dear William: Washington, Feb: 2. 1848

I just take up my pen to say, that Mr. Stephens of Georgia, a little slim, pale-faced, consumptive man, with a voice like Logan's has just concluded the very best speech, of an hour's length, I ever heard.

My old, withered, dry eyes, are full of tears yet.

If he writes it out any thing like he delivered it, our people shall see a good many copies of it. Yours truly

To Josephus Hewett

Dear Hewett: Washington, Feb. 13. 1848.

Your whig representative from Mississippi, P. W. Tompkins, has just shown me a letter of yours to him. I am jealous because you did not write to me. Perhaps you have forgotten me. Dont you remember a long black fellow who rode on horseback with you from Tremont to Springfield nearly ten years ago, swiming your horses over the Mackinaw on the trip? Well, I am that same one fellow yet. I was once of your opinion, expressed in your letter, that presidential electors should be dispensed with; but a more thorough knowledge of the causes that first introduced them, has made me doubt. Those causes were briefly these. The convention that framed the constitution had this difficulty: the small states wished to so frame the new government as that they might be equal to the large ones regardless of the inequality of population; the large ones insisted on equality in proportion to population. They compromised it, by basing the House of Representatives on *population*, and the Senate on *states* regardless of population; and the executive on both principles, by electors in each state, equal in numbers to her senators *and* representatives. Now, throw away the machinery of electors, and the compromise is broken up, and the whole yielded to the principle of the large states. There is one thing more. In the slave states, you have representatives, and consequently, electors, partly upon the basis of your black population, which would be swept away by the change you seem to think desireable. Have you ever reflected on these things?

But to come to the main point, I wish you to know that I have made a speech in congress, and that I want you to be *enlightened* by reading it; to further which object, I send a copy of the speech by this mail.

For old acquaintance sake, if for nothing else, be sure to write me on receiving this. I was very near forgetting to tell you that on my being introduced to Genl. Quitman, and telling him I was from Springfield, Illinois, he at once remarked "Then you are acquainted with my valued friend Hewett of Natchez," and on being assured I was, he said just such things about you as I like to hear said about my own valued friends. Yours as ever

To William H. Herndon

Dear William: Washington, Feb. 15. 1848

Your letter of the 29th. Jany. was received last night. Being exclusively a constitutional argument, I wish to submit some reflections upon it in the same spirit of kindness that I know actuates you. Let me first state what I understand to be your position. It is, that if it shall become *necessary, to repel invasion*, the President may, without violation of the Constitution, cross the line, and *invade* the teritory of another country; and that whether such *necessity* exists in any given case, the President is to be the *sole* judge.

Before going further, consider well whether this is, or is not your position. If it is, it is a position that neither the President himself, nor any friend of his, so far as I know, has ever taken. Their only positions are first, that the soil was *ours* where hostilities commenced, and second, that whether it was rightfully *ours* or not, *Congress had annexed it*, and the President, for that reason was bound to defend it, both of which are as clearly proved to be false in fact, as you can prove that your house is not mine. That soil was not ours; and Congress did not annex or attempt to annex it. But to return to your position: Allow the President to invade a neighboring nation, whenever *he* shall deem it necessary to repel an invasion, and you allow him to do so, *whenever he may choose to say* he deems it necessary for such purpose—and you allow him to make war at pleasure. Study to see if you can fix *any limit* to his power in this respect, after you have given him so much as you propose. If, to-day, he should choose to say he thinks it necessary to invade Canada, to prevent the British from invading us, how could you stop him? You may say to him, "I see no probability of the British invading us" but he will say to you "be silent; I see it, if you dont."

The provision of the Constitution giving the war-making power to Congress, was dictated, as I understand it, by the following reasons. Kings had always been involving and impoverishing their people in wars, pretending generally, if not always, that the good of the people was the object. This, our Convention understood to be the most oppressive of all Kingly oppressions; and they resolved to so frame the Constitution that *no one man* should hold the power of bringing this oppression upon us. But your view destroys the whole matter, and places our President where kings have always stood. Write soon again. Yours truly,

To Thomas S. Flournoy

Hon: T. S. Florney,   H. R. Feb: 17. 1848—
Dear Sir:

In answer to your enquiries, I have to say I am in favor of Gen: Taylor as the whig candidate for the Presidency because I am satisfied we can elect him, that he would give us a whig administration, and that we can not elect any other whig.

In Illinois, his being our candidate, would *certainly* give us one additional member of Congress, if not more; and *probably* would give us the electoral vote of the state. That with him, we can, in that state, make great inroads among the rank and file of the democrats, to my mind is certain; but the majority against us there, is so great, that I can no more than express my *belief* that we can carry the state. Very respectfully

To Usher F. Linder

Dear Linder: Washington, Feb. 20. 1848—

In law it is good policy to never *plead* what you *need* not, lest you oblige yourself to *prove* what you *can* not. Reflect on this well before you proceed. The application I mean to make of this rule is, that you should simply go for Genl. Taylor; because by this, you can take some democrats, and lose no whigs; but if you go also for Mr. Polk on the origin and mode of prossecuting the war, you will still take some democrats, but you will lose more whigs, so that in the sum of the opperation you will be loser. This is at least my opinion; and if you will look round, I doubt, if you do not discover such to be the fact amongst your own neighbors. Further than this: By justifying Mr. Polk's mode of prossecuting the war, you put yourself in opposition to Genl. Taylor himself, for we all know he has declared for, and, in fact originated, the defensive line policy.

You know I mean this in kindness, and wish it to be confidential. Yours as ever

To Solomon Lincoln

Mr. Solomon Lincoln,   Washington,
Dear Sir: March 6— 1848

Your letter to Mr. Hale, in which you do me the honor of making some kind enquiries concerning me, has been handed me by Mr. Hale, with the request that I should give you the desired information. I was born Feb: 12th. 1809 in Hardin county, Kentucky. My father's name is *Thomas*; my grandfather's was *Abraham*,—the same of my own. My grandfather went from Rockingham county in Virginia, to Kentucky, about the year 1782; and, two years afterwards, was killed by the indians. We have a vague tradition, that my great-grand father went from Pennsylvania to Virginia; and that he was a quaker. Further back than this, I have never heard any thing. It may do no harm to say that "Abraham" and "Mordecai" are common names in our family; while the name "Levi" so common among the Lincolns of New England, I have not known in any instance among us.

Owing to my father being left an orphan at the age of six years, in poverty, and in a new country, he became a wholly uneducated man; which I suppose is the reason why I know so little of our family history. I believe I can say nothing more that would at all interest you. If you shall be able to trace any connection between yourself and me, or, in fact, whether you shall or not, I should be pleased to have a line from you at any time. Very respectfully

To Usher F. Linder

Friend Linder: Washington, March 22– 1848–

Yours of the 15th. is just received, as was a day or two ago, one from Dunbar on the same subject. Although I address this to you alone, I intend it for you, Dunbar, and Bishop, and wish you to show it to them. In Dunbar's letter, and in Bishop's paper, it is assumed that Mr. Crittenden's position on the war is correct. Well, so I think. Please wherein is my position different from his? Has *he* ever approved the President's conduct in the beginning of the war, or his mode or objects in prossecuting it? Never. He condemns both. True, he votes supplies, and so do I. What, then, is the difference, except that he is a great man and I am a small one?

Towards the close of your letter you ask three questions, the first of which is "Would it not have been just as easy to have elected Genl. Taylor without opposing the war as by opposing it?" I answer, I suppose it would, if we could do *neither*—could be *silent* on the question; but the Locofocos here will not let the whigs be *silent*. Their very first act in congress was to present a preamble declaring that war existed by the act of Mexico, and the whigs were obliged to vote on it—and this policy is followed up by them; so that they are compelled to *speak* and their only option is whether they will, when they do speak, tell the *truth*, or tell a foul, villainous, and bloody falsehood. But, while on this point, I protest against your calling the condemnation of Polk "opposing the war." In thus assuming that all must be opposed to the war, even though they vote supplies, who do not endorse Polk, with due deference I say I think you fall into one of the artfully set traps of Locofocoism.

Your next question is "And suppose we could succeed in proving it a wicked and unconstitutional war, do we not thereby strip Taylor and Scott of more than half their laurels?" Whether it would so strip them is not matter of demonstration, but of *opinion* only; and my opinion is that it would not; but as your opinion seems to be different, let us call in some others as umpire. There are in this H.R. some more than forty members who support Genl. Taylor for the Presidency, every one of whom has voted that the war was "unnecessarily and unconstitutionally commenced by the President" every one of whom has spoken to the same effect, who has spoken at all, and not one of whom supposes he thereby strips Genl. of any laurels. More than this; two of these, Col. Haskell and Major Gaines, themselves fought in Mexico; and yet they vote and speak just as the rest of us do, without ever dreaming that they "strip" themselves of any laurels. There may be others, but Capt. Bishop is the only intelligent whig who has been to Mexico, that I have heard of taking different ground.

Your third question is "And have we as a party, ever gained any thing, by falling in company with abolitionists?" Yes. We gained our only national victory by falling in company with them in the election of Genl. Harrison. Not that we fell into abolition doctrines; but that we took up a man whose position induced them to join us in his election. But this question is not so significant as a *question*, as it is as a charge of abolitionism against those who have chosen to speak their minds against the President. As you and I perhaps would again differ as to the justice of this charge, let us once more call in our umpire. There are in this H.R. whigs from the slave states as follows: one from Louisiana, one from Mississippi, one from Florida, two from Alabama, four from Georgia, five from Tennessee, six from Kentucky, six from North Carolina, six from Virginia, four from Maryland and one from Delaware, making thirtyseven in all, and all slave-holders, every one of whom votes the commencement of the war "unnecessary and unconstitutional" and so falls subject to your charge of abolitionism!

"En passant" these are all *Taylor* men, except one in Tenn. two in Ky, one in N.C. and one in Va. Besides which we have one in Ills—two in Ia, three in Ohio, five in Penn. four in N.J. and one in Conn. While this is less than half the whigs of the H.R. it is three times as great as the strength of any other one candidate.

You are mistaken in your impression that any one has communicated expressions of yours and Bishop's to me. In my letter to Dunbar, I only spoke from the impression made by seeing in the paper that you and he were, "in the degree, though not in the extreme" on the same tack with Latshaw. Yours as ever

To David Lincoln

Dear Sir,   Washington, April 2nd. 1848

Last evening I was much gratified by receiving and reading your letter of the 30th. of March. There is no longer any doubt that your uncle Abraham, and my grandfather was the same man. His family did reside in Washington county, Kentucky, just as you say you found them in 1801 or 2. The oldest son, uncle Mordecai, near twenty years ago, removed from Kentucky to Hancock county, Illinois, where within a year or two afterwards, he died, and where his surviving children now live. His two sons there now are Abraham & Mordecai; and their Post-office is "La Harp."

Uncle Josiah, farther back than my recollection, went from Kentucky to Blue River in Indiana. I have not heard from him in a great many years, and whether he is still living I can not say. My recollection of what I have heard is, that he has several daughters & only one son, Thomas. Their Post-office is "Corydon, Harrisson county, Indiana."

My father, Thomas, is still living, in Coles county Illinois, being in the 71st. year of his age. His Post-office is Charleston, Coles co. Ill. I am his only child. I am now in my 40th. year; and I live in Springfield, Sangamon county, Illinois. This is the outline of my grandfather's family in the West.

I think my father has told me that grandfather had four

brothers, Isaac, Jacob, John and Thomas. Is that correct? and which of them was your father? Are any of them alive? I am quite sure that Isaac resided on Wataga, near a point where Virginia and Tennessee join; and that he has been dead more than twenty, perhaps thirty, years. Also, that Thomas removed to Kentucky, near Lexington, where he died a good while ago.

What was your grandfather's christian name? Was he or not, a Quaker? About what *time* did he emigrate from Berks county, Pa. to Virginia? Do you know any thing of your family (or rather I may now say, *our* family) farther back than your grandfather?

If it be not too much trouble to you, I shall be much pleased to hear from you again. Be assured I will call on you, should any thing ever bring me near you. I shall give your respects to Gov. McDowell, as you desire. Very truly yours—

To Mary Todd Lincoln

Dear Mary: Washington, April 16— 1848—

In this troublesome world, we are never quite satisfied. When you were here, I thought you hindered me some in attending to business; but now, having nothing but business—no variety—it has grown exceedingly tasteless to me. I hate to sit down and direct documents, and I hate to stay in this old room by myself. You know I told you in last sunday's letter, I was going to make a little speech during the week; but the week has passed away without my getting a chance to do so; and now my interest in the subject has passed away too. Your second and third letters have been received since I wrote before. Dear Eddy thinks father is *"gone tapila."* Has any further discovery been made as to the breaking into your grand-mother's house? If I were she, I would not remain there alone. You mention that your uncle John Parker is likely to be at Lexington. Dont forget to present him my very kindest regards.

I went yesterday to hunt the little plaid stockings, as you

wished; but found that McKnight has quit business, and Allen had not a single pair of the description you give, and only one plaid pair of any sort that I thought would fit "Eddy's dear little feet." I have a notion to make another trial to-morrow morning. If I could get them, I have an excellent chance of sending them. Mr. Warrick Tunstall, of St. Louis is here. He is to leave early this week, and to go by Lexington. He says he knows you, and will call to see you; and he voluntarily asked, if I had not some package to send to you.

I wish you to enjoy yourself in every possible way; but is there no danger of wounding the feelings of your good father, by being so openly intimate with the Wickliffe family?

Mrs. Broome has not removed yet; but she thinks of doing so to-morrow. All the house—or rather, all with whom you were on decided good terms—send their love to you. The others say nothing.

Very soon after you went away, I got what I think a very pretty set of shirt-bosom studs—modest little ones, jet, set in gold, only costing 50 cents a piece, or 1.50 for the whole.

Suppose you do not prefix the "Hon" to the address on your letters to me any more. I like the letters very much, but I would rather they should not have that upon them. It is not necessary, as I suppose you have thought, to have them to come free.

And you are entirely free from head-ache? That is good—good—considering it is the first spring you have been free from it since we were acquainted. I am afraid you will get so well, and fat, and young, as to be wanting to marry again. Tell Louisa I want her to watch you a little for me. Get weighed, and write me how much you weigh.

I did not get rid of the impression of that foolish dream about dear Bobby till I got your letter written the same day. What did he and Eddy think of the little letters father sent them? Dont let the blessed fellows forget father.

A day or two ago Mr. Strong, here in Congress, said to me that Matilda would visit here within two or three weeks. Suppose you write her a letter, and enclose it in one of mine; and if she comes I will deliver it to her, and if she does not, I will send it to her. Most affectionately

To Archibald Williams

Dear Williams: Washington, April 30. 1848.

I have not seen in the papers any evidence of a movement to send a delegate from your circuit to the June convention. I wish to say that I think it all important that a delegate should be sent. Mr. Clay's chance for an election, is just no chance at all. He might get New-York; and that would have elected in 1844, but it will not now; because he must now, at the least, lose Tennessee, which he had then, and, in addition, the fifteen *new* votes of Florida, Texas, Iowa, and Wisconsin. I know our good friend Browning, is a great admirer of Mr. Clay, and I therefore fear, he is favoring his nomination. If he is, ask him to discard feeling, and try if he can possibly, as a matter of judgment, count the votes necessary to elect him.

In my judgment, we can elect nobody but Gen; Taylor; and we can not elect him without a nomination. Therefore, dont fail to send a delegate. Your friend as ever

To John M. Peck

Rev: J. M. Peck.   Washington,
Dear Sir: May 21 – 1848 –

On last evening I received a copy of the Belleville Advocate, with the appearance of having been sent by a private hand; and, inasmuch as it contains your oration on the occasion of the celebrating of the battle of Buena Vista, and is postmarked at Rock-Spring, I can not doubt that it is to you, I am indebted for this, courtesy. I own that finding in the oration a laboured justification of the administration on the origin of the Mexican war, disappoints me—disappoints me, because it is the first effort of the kind I have known, made by one appearing to me to be, intelligent, right-minded, and *impartial*. It is this disappointment that prompts me to address you, briefly, on the subject. I do not propose any extended review. I do not quarrel with your *brief* exhibition of facts; I presume it is correct so far as it goes; but it is so brief, as to exclude some facts quite as material in my judgment, to a just conclusion, as any it includes. For instance, you say "Paredes came into power the last of December 1845, and from that moment, all hopes of avoiding war by negociation vanished." A little further on, refering to this and other preceding statements, you say "All this transpired three months before Gen: Taylor marched across the desert of the Nueces." These two statements are substantially correct; and you evidently intend to have it infered that Gen: Taylor was sent across the desert, in *consequence* of the destruction of all hope of peace, in the overthrow of Herara by Paredes. Is not that the inference you intend? If so, the material fact you have excluded is, that Gen: Taylor was *ordered* to cross the desert on the 13th. of January 1846, and *before* the news of Herara's fall reached Washington—*before* the administration, which gave the order, had any knowledge that Herara had fallen. Does not this fact cut up your inference by the roots? Must you not find some other excuse for that order, or give up the case? All that part of the three months you speak of, which transpired *after* the 13th. of January, was expended in the order's going *from* Washington *to* Gen: Taylor, in his preparations *for* the march, and in the *actual* march across the desert; and not in the president's waiting to hear the knell of peace, in the fall of Herara, or for any other object. All this is to be found in the very documents you seem to have used.

One other thing: Although you say, at one point, "I shall briefly exhibit *facts* and *leave* each person to perceive the just application to the principles already laid down, to the case in hand" you very soon get to making applications yourself—in one instance, as follows: "In view of *all* the facts, the conviction to my mind is irresistable, that the Government of the United States committed no aggression on Mexico." Not in view of *all* the facts. There are facts which you have kept out of view. It is a fact, that the United States Army, in marching to the Rio Grande, marched into a peaceful Mexican settlement, and frightened the inhabitants away from their homes and their growing crops.

It is a fact, that Fort Brown, opposite Matamoras, was built by that army, within a Mexican cotten-field, on which, at the time the army reached it, a young cotten crop was growing and which crop was wholly destroyed, and the field itself greatly, and permanently injured, by ditches, embankments, and the like.

It is a fact, that when the Mexicans captured Capt. Thornton and his command, they found and captured them within another Mexican field.

Now I wish to bring these facts to your notice, and to ascertain what is the result of your reflections upon them. If you *deny* that they *are* facts, I think I can furnish proof which shall convince you that you are mistaken.

If you *admit* that they are facts, then I shall be obliged for a reference to any law of language, law of states, law of nations, law of morals, law of religion,—any law human or divine, in which an authority can be found for saying those facts constitute *"no aggression."*

Possibly you consider those acts too small for notice. Would you venture to so consider them, had they been committed by any nation on earth, against the humblest of our people? I know you would not. Then I ask, is the precept "Whatsoever ye would that men should do to you, do ye even so to them" obsolete?—of no force?—of no application?

I shall be pleased if you can find leisure to write me. Yours truly

To William H. Herndon

Dear William   Washington, June 12. 1848—

On my return from Philadelphia, where I had been attending the nomination of "Old Rough"—I found your letter in a mass of others, which had accumulated in my absence. By many, and often, it had been said they would not abide the nomination of Taylor; but since the deed has been done, they are fast falling in, and in my opinion we shall have a most overwhelming, glorious, triumph. One unmistakable sign is, that all the odds and ends are with us—Barnburners, Native Americans, Tyler men, disappointed office seeking locofocos, and the Lord knows what. This is important, if in nothing else, in showing which way the wind blows. Some of the sanguine men here, set down all the states as certain for Taylor, but Illinois, and it as doubtful. Can not something be done, even in Illinois? Taylor's nomination takes the locos on the blind side. It turns the war thunder against them. The war is now to them, the gallows of Haman, which they built for us, and on which they are doomed to be hanged themselves.

Excuse this short letter. I have so many to write, that I can not devote much time to any one. Yours as ever

To Mary Todd Lincoln

My dear wife: Washington, June 12. 1848—

On my return from Philadelphia, yesterday, where, in my anxiety I had been led to attend the whig convention I found your last letter. I was so tired and sleepy, having ridden all night, that I could not answer it till to-day; and now I have to do so in the H.R. The leading matter in your letter, is your wish to return to this side of the Mountains. Will you be a *good girl* in all things, if I consent? Then come along, and that as *soon* as possible. Having got the idea in my head, I shall be impatient till I see you. You will not have money enough to bring you; but I presume your uncle will supply you, and I will refund him here. By the way you do not mention whether you have received the fifty dollars I sent you. I do not much fear but that you got it; because the want of it would have induced you say something in relation to it. If your uncle is already at Lexington, you might induce him to start on earlier than the first of July; he could stay in Kentucky longer on his return, and so make up for lost time. Since I began this letter, the H.R. has passed a resolution for adjourning on the 17th. July, which probably will pass the Senate. I hope this letter will not be disagreeable to you; which, together with the circumstances under which I write, I hope will excuse me for not writing a longer one. Come on just as soon as you can. I want to see you, and our dear—*dear* boys very much. Every body here wants to see our dear Bobby. Affectionately

Speech in the U.S. House of Representatives on Internal Improvements

In committee of the whole on the state of the union, on the civil and diplomatic appropriation bill—

Mr. Chairman

I wish at all times in no way to practice any fraud upon the House or the committee, and I also desire to do nothing which may be very disagreeable to any of the members. I therefore state in advance that my object in taking the floor is to make a speech on the general subject of internal improvements; and if I am out of order in doing so, I give the chair the oppertunity of so deciding, and I will take my seat.

The Chair: I will not undertake to anticipate what the gentleman may say on the subject of internal improvements. He will, therefore, proceed in his remarks, and if any question of order shall be made, the chair will then decide it.

Mr. Lincoln: At an early day of this session the president sent us what may properly be called an internal improvement veto message. The late democratic convention which sat at Baltimore, and which nominated Gen: Cass for the presidency, adopted a set of resolutions, now called the democratic platform, among which is one in these words:

"That the constitution does not confer upon the general government the power to commence, and carry on a general system of internal improvements"

Gen: Cass, in his letter accepting the nomination, holds this language:

"I have carefully read the resolutions of the Democratic National convention, laying down the platform of our political faith, and I adhere to them as firmly, as I approve them cordially."

These things, taken together, show that the question of internal improvements is now more distinctly made—has become more intense—than at any former period. It can no longer be avoided. The veto message, and the Baltimore resolution, I understand to be, in substance, the same thing; the latter being the mere general statement, of which the former is the amplification—the bill of particulars. While I know there are many democrats, on this floor and elsewhere, who disapprove that message, I understand that all who shall vote for Gen: Cass, will thereafter be counted as having approved it—as having endorsed all it's doctrines. I suppose all, or nearly all the democrats will vote for him. Many of them will do so, not because they like his position on this question, but because they prefer him, being wrong in this, to another whom they consider farther wrong on other questions. In this way, the internal improvement democrats are to be, by a sort of forced consent, carried over, and arrayed against themselves on this measure of policy. Gen: Cass, once elected, will not trouble himself to make a constitutional argument, or, perhaps, any argument at all, when he shall veto a river or harbor bill; he will consider it a sufficient answer to all democratic murmers, to point to Mr. Polk's message, and to the "democratic platform." This being the case, the question of improvements is verging to a final crisis; and the friends of the policy must now battle, and battle manfully, or surrender all. In this view, humble as I am, I wish to review, and contest as well as I may, the general positions of this veto message. When I say *general* positions, I mean to exclude from consideration so much as relates to the present embarrassed state of the Treasury in consequence of the Mexican war.

Those general positions are: That internal improvements ought not to be made by the general government—

1. Because they would overwhelm the Treasury.

2. Because, while their *burthens* would be general, their *benefits* would be *local* and *partial*; involving an obnoxious inequality—and

3. Because they would be unconstitutional.

4. Because the states may do enough by the levy and collection of tonnage duties—or if not

5. That the constitution may be amended.

"Do nothing at all, lest you do something wrong" is the sum of these positions—is the sum of this message. And this, with the exception of what is said about constitutionality, applying as forcibly to making improvements by state authority, as by the national authority. So that we must abandon the improvements of the country altogether, by any, and every authority, or we must resist, and repudiate the doctrines of this message. Let us attempt the latter.

The first position is, that a system of internal improvements would overwhelm the treasury.

That, in such a system there is a *tendency* to undue expansion, is not to be denied. Such tendency is founded in the nature of the subject. A member of congress will prefer voting for a bill which contains an appropriation for his district, to voting for one which does not; and when a bill shall be expanded till every district shall be provided for, that it will be too greatly expanded, is obvious. But is this any more true in congress, than in a state legislature? If a member of congress must have an appropriation for his district, so, a member of a legislature must have one for his county. And if one will overwhelm the national treasury, so the other will overwhelm the state treasury. Go where we will, the difficulty is the same. Allow it to drive us from the halls of congress, and it will, just as easily, drive us from the state legislatures.

Let us, then, grapple with it, and test it's strength. Let us, judging of the future by the past, ascertain whether there may not be, in the discretion of congress, a sufficient power to limit, and restrain this expansive tendency, within reasonable, and proper bounds. The president himself values the evidence of the past. He tells us that at a certain point of our history, more than two hundred millions of dollars had been, *applied for*, to make improvements; and this he does to prove that the treasury would be overwhelmed by such a system. Why did he not tell us how much was *granted*? Would not that have been better evidence? Let us turn to it, and see what it proves. In the message, the president tells us that "During the four succeeding years, embraced by the administration of president Adams, the power not only to appropriate money, but to apply it, under the direction and authority of the General Government, as well to the construction of roads, as to the improvement of harbors and rivers, was fully asserted and exercised"

This, then, was the period of greatest enormity. These, if any, must have been the days of the two hundred millions. And how much do you suppose was really expended for improvements, during that four years? Two hundred millions?

One hundred? Fifty? Ten? Five? No sir, less than two millions. As shown by authentic documents, the expenditures on
improvements, during 1825 1826—1827 and 1828, amounted
to $1-879-627-01. These four years were the period of Mr.
Adams' administration, nearly, and substantially. This fact
shows, that when the power to make improvements "was
fully asserted and exercised" the congress *did* keep within reasonable limits; and what has been done, it seems to me, can
be done again.

Now for the second position of the message, namely, that
the burthens of improvements would be *general*, while their
benefits would be *local* and *partial*, involving an obnoxious inequality. That there is some degree of truth in this position, I
shall not deny. No commercial object of government patronage can be so exclusively *general*, as to not be of some peculiar
local advantage; but, on the other hand, nothing is so *local*, as
to not be of some general advantage. The Navy, as I understand it, was established, and is maintained at a great annual
expense, partly to be ready for war when war shall come, but
partly also, and perhaps chiefly, for the protection of our
commerce on the high seas. This latter object is, for all I can
see, in principle, the same as internal improvements. The driving a pirate from the track of commerce on the broad ocean,
and the removing a snag from it's more narrow path in the
Mississippi river, can not, I think, be distinguished in principle. Each is done to save life and property, and for nothing
else.

The Navy, then, is the most general in it's benefits of all
this class of objects; and yet even the Navy is of some peculiar
advantage to Charleston, Baltimore, Philadelphia, New-York
and Boston, beyond what it is to the interior towns of Illinois. The next most general object I can think of would be
improvements on the Mississippi river and it's tributaries.
They touch thirteen of our states, Pennsylvania, Virginia,
Kentucky, Tennessee, Mississippi, Louisiana, Arkansas, Missouri, Illinois, Indiana, Ohio, Wisconsin and Iowa. Now I
suppose it will not be denied, that these thirteen states are a
little more interested in improvements on that great river,
than are the remaining seventeen. These instances of the
Navy, and the Mississippi river, show clearly that there is

something of local advantage in the most general objects. But the converse is also true. Nothing is so *local* as to not be of some *general* benefit. Take, for instance, the Illinois and Michigan canal. Considered apart from it's effects, it is perfectly local. Every inch of it is within the state of Illinois. That canal was first opened for business last April. In a very few days we were all gratified to learn, among other things, that sugar had been carried from New-Orleans through this canal to Buffalo in New-York. This sugar took this route, doubtless because it was cheaper than the old route. Supposing the benefit of the reduction in the cost of carriage to be shared between seller and buyer, the result is, that the New Orleans merchant sold his sugar a little *dearer*; and the people of Buffalo sweetened their coffee a little *cheaper*, than before—a benefit resulting *from* the canal, not to Illinois where the canal *is*, but to Louisiana and New-York where it is *not*. In other transactions Illinois will, of course, have her share, and perhaps the larger share too, in the benefits of the canal; but the instance of the sugar clearly shows that the *benefits* of an improvement, are by no means confined to the particular locality of the improvement itself.

The just conclusion from all this is, that if the nation refuse to make improvements, of the more general kind, because their benefits may be somewhat local, a state may, for the same reason, refuse to make an improvement of a local kind, because it's benefits may be somewhat general. A state may well say to the nation "If you will do nothing for me, I will do nothing for you." Thus it is seen, that if this argument of "inequality" is sufficient any where,—it is sufficient every where; and puts an end to improvements altogether. I hope and believe, that if both the nation and the states would, in good faith, in their respective spheres, do what they could in the way of improvements, what of inequality might be produced in one place, might be compensated in another, and that the sum of the whole might not be very unequal.

But suppose, after all, there should be some degree of inequality. Inequality is certainly never to be embraced for it's own sake; but is every good thing to be discarded, which may be inseparably connected with some degree of it? If so, we must discard all government. This capitol is built at the

public expense, for the public benefit; but does any one
doubt that it is of some peculiar local advantage to the property holders, and business people of Washington? Shall we
remove it for this reason? and if so, where shall we set it
down, and be free from the difficulty? To make sure of our
object, shall we locate it nowhere? and have congress hereafter to hold it's sessions, as the loafer lodged "in spots
about"? I make no special allusion to the present president
when I say there are few stronger cases in this world, of
"burthen to the many, and benefit to the few"—of "inequality"—than the presidency itself is by some thought to be.
An honest laborer digs coal at about seventy cents a day,
while the president digs abstractions at about seventy dollars
a day. The *coal* is clearly worth more than the *abstractions*,
and yet what a monstrous inequality in the prices! Does the
president, for this reason, propose to abolish the presidency?
He *does* not, and he *ought* not. The true rule, in determining
to embrace, or reject any thing, is not whether it have *any*
evil in it; but whether it have more of evil, than of good.
There are few things *wholly* evil, or *wholly* good. Almost
every thing, especially of governmental policy, is an inseparable
compound of the two; so that our best judgment of the pre-
ponderance between them is continually demanded. On this
principle the president, his friends, and the world generally,
act on most subjects. Why not apply it, then, upon this
question? Why, as to improvements, magnify the *evil*, and
stoutly refuse to see any *good* in them?

Mr. Chairman, on the third position of the message, the
constitutional question, I have not much to say. Being the
man I am, and speaking when I do, I feel, that in any attempt
at an original constitutional argument, I should not be, and
ought not to be, listened to patiently. The ablest, and the best
of men, have gone over the whole ground long ago. I shall
attempt but little more than a brief notice of what some of
them have said. In relation to Mr. Jeffersons views, I read
from Mr. Polk's veto message—

President Jefferson, in his message to Congress in 1806, recommended
an amendment of the constitution, with a view to apply an anticipated
surplus in the Treasury "to the great purposes of the public education,
roads, rivers, canals, and such other objects of public improvements as it

may be thought proper to add to the constitutional enumeration of the federal powers;" and he adds: "I suppose an amendment to the constitution, by consent of the States, necessary, because the objects now recommended are not among those enumerated in the constitution, and to which it permits the public moneys to be applied." In 1825, he repeated, in his published letters, the opinion that no such power has been conferred upon Congress.

I introduce this, not to controvert, just now, the constitutional opinion, but to show that on the question of *expediency*, Mr. Jeffersons opinion was against the present president— that this opinion of Mr. Jefferson, in one branch at least, is, in the hands of Mr. Polk, like McFingal's gun: — "Bears wide, and kicks the owner over."

But to the constitutional question—In 1826, Chancellor Kent first published his Commentaries on American Law. He devoted a portion of one of the lectures to the question of the authority of congress to appropriate public moneys for internal improvements. He mentions that the question had never been brought under judicial consideration, and proceeds to give a brief summary of the discussions it had undergone between the legislative, and executive branches of the government. He shows that the legislative branch had usually been *for*, and the executive against the power, till the period of Mr. J. Q. Adams' administration, at which point he considers the executive influence as withdrawn from opposition, and added to the support of the power. In 1844 the chancellor published a new edition of his commentaries, in which he adds some notes of what had transpired on the question since 1826. I have not time to read the original text, or the notes; but the whole may be found on page 267, and the two or three following pages of the first volume of the edition of 1844. As what Chancellor Kent seems to consider the sum of the whole, I read from one of the notes:

"Mr. Justice Story, in his commentaries on the constitution of the United States, vol. ii p 429–440, and again p 519–538 has stated at large the arguments for and against the proposition, that congress have a constitutional authority to lay taxes, and to apply the power to regulate commerce as a means directly to encourage and protect domestic manufactures; and without giving any opinion of his own on the contested

doctrine, he has left the reader to draw his own conclusions. I
should think, however, from the arguments as stated, that every mind which has taken no part in the discussions, and felt
no prejudice or teritorial bias on either side of the question,
would deem the arguments in favor of the congressional
power vastly superior." It will be seen, that in this extract the
power to make improvements is not directly mentioned; but
by examining the context, both of Kent and Story, it will be
seen that the power mentioned in the extract, and the power
to make improvements are regarded as identical. It is not to
be denied that many great and good men have been *against*
the power; but it is insisted that quite as many, as great and as
good, have been *for* it; and it is shown that, on a full survey of
the whole, Chancellor Kent was of opinion that the arguments of the latter were *vastly* superior. This is but the opinion of a man, but who was that man? He was one of the
ablest and most learned lawyers of his age, or of any age. It is
no disparagement to Mr. Polk, nor, indeed to any one who
devotes much time to politics, to be placed far behind Chancellor Kent as a lawyer. His attitude was most favorable to
correct conclusions. He wrote coolly, and in retirement. He
was struggling to rear a durable monument of fame; and he
well knew that *truth* and thoroughly sound reasoning were
the only sure foundations. Can the party opinion of a party
president, on a law question, as this purely is, be at all compared, or set in in opposition to that of such a man, in such
an attitude, as Chancellor Kent?

This constitutional question will probably never be better
settled than it is, until it shall pass under judicial consideration; but I do think no man, who is clear on the questions
of expediency, needs feel his conscience much pricked upon
this.

Mr. Chairman, the president seems to think that enough
may be done, in the way of improvements, by means of tonnage duties, under state authority, with the consent of the
General Government. Now I suppose this matter of tonnage
duties is well enough in it's own sphere. I suppose it may be
efficient, and perhaps, *sufficient*, to make slight improvements
and repairs, in harbors already in use, and not much out of
repair. But if I have any correct general idea of it, it must be

wholly inefficient for any generally benificent purposes of improvement. I know very little, or rather nothing at all, of the practical matter of levying and collecting tonnage duties; but I suppose one of it's principles must be, to lay a duty for the improvement of any particular harbor, *upon the tonnage coming into that harbor*. To do otherwise—to collect money in *one* harbor, to be expended on improvements in *another*, would be an extremely aggravated form of that inequality which the president so much deprecates. If I be right in this, how could we make any entirely new improvement by means of tonnage duties? How make a road, a canal, or clear a greatly obstructed river? The idea that we could, involves the same absurdity of the irish bull about the new boots—"I shall niver git em on" says Patrick "till I wear em a day or two, and strech em a little." We shall never make a canal by tonnage duties, until it shall already have been made awhile, so the tonnage can get into it.

After all, the president, concludes that possibly there may be some great objects of improvements which can not be effected by tonnage duties, and which, therefore, may be expedient for the General Government to take in hand. Accordingly he suggests, in case any such be discovered, the propriety of amending the constitution. Amend it for what? If, like Mr. Jefferson, the president thought improvements *expedient*, but not constitutional, it would be natural enough for him to recommend such an amendment; but hear what he says in this very message:

"In view of these portentous consequences, I can not but think that this course of legislation should be arrested, even were there nothing to forbid it in the fundamental laws of our union."

For what, then, would *he* have the constitution amended? With *him* it is a proposition to remove *one* impediment, merely to be met by *others*, which, in his opinion, can not be removed—to enable congress to do what, in his opinion they ought not to do, if they could!—(Here Mr. Meade, of Virginia, enquired if Mr. L. understood the president to be opposed, on grounds of expediency to any and every improvement; to which Mr. L. answered) In the very part of his message of which I am speaking, I understand him as

giving some vague expression in favor of some possible objects of improvements; but in doing so, I understand him to
be directly in the teeth of his own arguments, in other parts
of it. Neither the president, nor any one, can possibly specify
an improvement, which shall not be clearly liable to one or
another of the objections he has urged on the score of expediency. I have shown, and might show again, that no work—
no object—can be so general, as to dispense it's benefits with
precise equality; and this inequality, is chief among the "portentous consequences" for which he declares that improvements should be arrested. No sir, when the president
intimates that something, in the way of improvements, may
properly be done by the General Government, he is shrinking
from the conclusions to which his own arguments would
force him. He feels that the improvements of this broad and
goodly land, are a mighty interest; and he is unwilling to confess to the people, or perhaps to himself, that he has built an
argument which, when pressed to it's conclusions, entirely
annihilates this interest.

I have already said that no one, who is satisfied of the expediency of making improvements, needs be much uneasy in his
conscience about it's constitutionality. I wish now to submit
a few remarks on the general proposition of amending the
constitution. As a general rule, I think, we would much better
let it alone. No slight occasion should tempt us to touch it.
Better not take the first step, which may lead to a habit of
altering it. Better, rather, habituate ourselves to think of it, as
unalterable. It can scarcely be made better than it is. New
provisions, would introduce new difficulties, and thus create,
and increase appetite for still further change. No sir, let it
stand as it is. New hands have never touched it. The men who
made it, have done their work, and have passed away. Who
shall improve, on what *they* did?

Mr. Chairman, for the purpose of reviewing this message in
the least possible time, as well as for the sake of distinctness, I
had analized it's arguments, as well as I could, and reduced
them to the propositions I have stated. I have now examined
them in detail. I wish to detain the committee only a little
while longer with some general remarks upon the subject of
improvements. That the subject is a difficult one, can not be

denied. Still it is no more difficult in congress, than in the
state legislatures, in the counties, or in the smallest municipal
districts, which any where exist. All can recur to instances of
this difficulty in the case of county-roads, bridges, and the
like. One man is offended because a road passes over his land,
and another is offended because it does *not* pass over his; one
is dissatisfied because the bridge, for which he is taxed,
crosses the river on a different road from that which leads
from his house to town; another can not bear that the county
should be got in debt for these same roads and bridges; while
not a few struggle hard to have roads located over their lands,
and then stoutly refuse to let them be opened until they are
first paid the damages. Even between the different wards, and
streets, of towns and cities, we find this same wrangling, and
difficulty. Now these are no other than the very difficulties,
against which and out of which, the president constructs his
objections of "inequality" "speculation" and "crushing the
treasury." There is but a single alternative about them; they
are *sufficient*, or they are *not*. If sufficient, they are sufficient
out of congress as well as *in* it, and there is the end. We must
reject them, as insufficient, or lie down and do nothing, by
any authority. Then, difficulty though there be, let us meet,
and encounter it.

> Attempt the end, and never stand to doubt;
> Nothing so hard, but search will find it out.

Determine that the thing can and shall be done, and then we
shall find the way. The tendency to undue expansion is unquestionably the chief difficulty. How to do *something*, and
still not do *too much*, is the desideratum. Let each contribute
his mite in the way of suggestion. The late Silas Wright, in a
letter to the Chicago convention, contributed his, which was
worth something; and I now contribute mine, which may be
worth nothing. At all events, it will mislead nobody, and,
therefore will do no harm. I would not borrow money. I am
against an overwhelming, crushing system. Suppose, that at
each session, congress shall first determine *how much* money
can, for that year, be spared for improvements; then appor-
tion that sum to the most *important* objects. So far all is easy;
but how shall we determine which *are* the most important?

On this question comes the collision of interests. *I* shall be slow to acknowledge, that *your* harbor, or *your* river is more important than *mine*—and *vice versa*. To clear this difficulty, let us have that same statistical information, which the gentleman from Ohio (Mr. Vinton) suggested at the beginning of this session. In that information, we shall have a stern, unbending basis of *facts*—a basis, in nowise subject to whim, caprice, or local interest. The pre-limited amount of means, will save us from doing *too much*, and the statistics, will save us from doing, what we do, in *wrong places*. Adopt, and adhere to this course, and it seems to me, the difficulty is cleared.

One of the gentlemen from South Carolina (Mr. Rhett) very much deprecates these statistics. He particularly objects, as I understand him, to counting all the pigs and chickens in the land. I do not perceive much force in the objection. It is true that if every thing be enumerated, a portion of such statistics may not be very useful to this object. Such products of the country as are to be *consumed* where they are *produced*, need no roads or rivers—no means of transportation, and have no very proper connection with this subject. The *surplus*—that which is produced in *one* place, to be consumed in *another*; the capacity of each locality for producing a *greater* surplus; the natural means of transportation, and their susceptability of improvement; the hindrances, delays, and losses of life and property during transportation, and the causes of each, would be among the most valuable statistics in this connection. From these, it would readily appear where a given amount of expenditure would do the most good. These statistics might be equally accessable, as they would be equally useful, to both the nation and the states. In this way, and by these means, let the nation take hold of the larger works, and the states the smaller ones; and thus, working in a meeting direction, discreetly, but steadily and firmly, what is made unequal in one place may be equalized in another, extravagance avoided, and the whole country put on that career of prosperity, which shall correspond with it's extent of teritory, it's natural resources, and the intelligence and enterprize of it's people.

June 20, 1848

To William H. Herndon

Dear William: Washington, June 22. 1848—

Last night I was attending a sort of caucus of the whig members held in relation to the coming presidential election. The whole field of the Nation was scanned, and all is high hope and confidence. Illinois is expected to better her condition in this race. Under these circumstances, judge how heart-sickening it was to come to my room and find and read your discouraging letter of the 15th. We have made no gains, but have lost "A. R. Robinson, *Turner*, Campbell, and four or five more." Tell Arney to re-consider, if he would be saved. Baker and I used to do something, but I think you attach more importance to our absence than is just. There is another cause. In 1840, for instance, we had two senators and five representatives in Sangamon; now we have part of one senator, and two representatives. With quite one third more people than we had then, we have only half the sort of offices which are sought by men of the speaking sort of talent. This, I think, is the chief cause. Now as to the young men. You must not wait to be brought forward by the older men. For instance do you suppose that I should ever have got into notice if I had waited to be hunted up and pushed forward by older men. You young men get together and form a Rough & Ready club, and have regular meetings and speeches. Take in every body that you can get, Harrison Grimsley, Z. A. Enos, Lee Kimball, and C. W. Matheny will do well to begin the thing, but as you go along, gather up all the shrewd wild boys about town, whether just of age, or little under age—Chris: Logan, Reddick Ridgely, Lewis Zwizler, and hundreds such. Let every one play the part he can play best—some speak, some sing, and all hollow. Your meetings will be of evenings; the older men, and the women will go to hear you; so that it will not only contribute to the election of "Old Zach" but will be an interesting pastime, and improving to the intellectual faculties of all engaged. Dont fail to do this.

You ask me to send you all the speeches made about "Old Zac" the war &c. &c. Now this makes me a little impatient. I have regularly sent you the Congressional Globe and Appendix, and you can not have examined them, or you would have discovered that they contain every speech made by every man, in both Houses of Congress, on every subject, during this session. Can I send any more? Can I send speeches that nobody has made? Thinking it would be most natural that the newspapers would feel interested to give at least some of the speeches to their readers, I, at the beginning of the session made arrangement to have one copy of the Globe and Appendix regularly sent to each whig paper of our district. And yet, with the exception of my own little speech, which was published in two only of the then five, now four whig papers, I do not remember having seen a single speech, or even an extract from one, in any single one of those papers. With equal and full means on both sides, I will venture that the State Register has thrown before it's readers more of Locofoco speeches in a month, than all the whig papers of the district, have done of whig speeches during the session.

If you wish a full understanding of the beginning of the war, I repeat what I believe I said to you in a letter once before, that the whole, or nearly so is to be found in the speech of Dixon of Connecticut. This I sent you in Pamphlet, as well as in the Globe. Examine and study every sentence of that speech thoroughly, and you will understand the whole subject.

You ask how Congress came to declare that war existed by the act of Mexico. Is it possible you dont understand that yet? You have at least twenty speeches in your possession that fully explain it. I will, however, try it once more. The news reached Washington of the commencement of hostilities on the Rio Grande, and of the great peril of Gen: Taylor's army. Every body, whig and democrat, was for sending them aid, in men and money. It was necessary to pass a bill for this. The Locos had a majority in both Houses, and they brought in a bill with a preamble, saying—*Whereas* war exists by the act of Mexico, therefore we send Gen: Taylor men and money. The whigs moved to strike out the preamble, so that they could vote to send the men and money, without saying any thing about how the war commenced; but, being in the minority they were voted down, and the preamble was retained. Then, on the passage of the bill, the question came upon them, "shall we vote *for* preamble and bill both together, or against both together." They could not vote *against* sending help to Gen: Taylor, and therefore they voted *for* both together. Is there any difficulty in understanding this? Even my little speech, shows how this was; and if you will go to the Library you may get the Journals of 1845–6, in which you can find the whole for yourself.

We have nothing published yet with special reference to the Taylor race; but we soon will have, and then I will send them to every body. I made an Internal Improvement speech day-before-yesterday, which I shall send home as soon as I can get it written out and printed, and which I suppose nobody will read. Your friend as ever

To Horace Greeley

Washington, June 27, 1848.

Friend Greeley: In the "Tribune" of yesterday I discovered a little editorial paragraph in relation to Colonel Wentworth of Illinois, in which, in relation to the boundary of Texas, you say: "All Whigs and many Democrats having ever contended it stopped at the Nueces." Now this is a mistake which I dislike to see go uncorrected in a leading Whig paper. Since I have been here, I know a large majority of such Whigs of the House of Representatives as have spoken on the question have not taken that position. Their position, and in my opinion the true position, is that the boundary of Texas extended just so far as American settlements taking part in her revolution extended; and that as a matter of fact those settlements did extend, at one or two points, beyond the Nueces, but not anywhere near the Rio Grande at any point. The "stupendous desert" between the valleys of those two rivers, and not either river, has been insisted on by the Whigs as the true boundary.

Will you look at this? By putting us in the position of insisting on the line of the Nueces, you put us in a position which, in my opinion, we cannot maintain, and which therefore gives the Democrats an advantage of us. If the degree of arrogance is not too great, may I ask you to examine what I said on this very point in the printed speech I send you. Yours truly,

To Mary Todd Lincoln

My dear wife: Washington, July 2. 1848.

Your letter of last sunday came last night. On that day (sunday) I wrote the principal part of a letter to you, but did not finish it, or send it till tuesday, when I had provided a draft for $100 which I sent in it. It is now probable that on that day (tuesday) you started to Shelbyville; so that when the money reaches Lexington, you will not be there. Before leaving, did you make any provision about letters that might come to Lexington for you? Write me whether you got the draft, if you shall not have already done so, when this reaches you. Give my kindest regards to your uncle John, and all the family. Thinking of them reminds me that I saw your acquaintance, Newton, of Arkansas, at the Philadelphia Convention. We had but a single interview, and that was so brief, and in so great a multitude of strange faces, that I am quite sure I should not recognize him, if I were to meet him again. He was a sort of Trinity, three in one, having the right, in his own person, to cast the three votes of Arkansas. Two or three days ago I sent your uncle John, and a few of our other friends each a copy of the speech I mentioned in my last letter; but I did not send any to you, thinking you would be on the road here, before it would reach you. I send you one now. Last wednesday, P. H. Hood & Co, dunned me for a little bill of $5.38 cents, and Walter Harper & Co, another for $8.50 cents, for goods which they say you bought. I hesitated to pay them, because my recollection is that you told me when you went away, there was nothing left unpaid. Mention in your next letter whether they are right.

Mrs. Richardson is still here; and what is more, has a baby—so Richardson says, and he ought to know. I believe Mary Hewett has left here and gone to Boston. I met her on the street about fifteen or twenty days ago, and she told me she was going soon. I have seen nothing of her since.

The music in the Capitol grounds on saturdays, or, rather, the interest in it, is dwindling down to nothing. Yesterday evening the attendance was rather thin. Our two girls, whom you remember seeing first at Carusis, at the exhibition of the Ethiopian Serenaders, and whose peculiarities were the wearing of black fur bonnets, and never being seen in close company with other ladies, were at the music yesterday. One of them was attended by their brother, and the other had a member of Congress in tow. He went home with her; and if I were to guess, I would say, he went away a somewhat altered man—most likely in his pockets, and in some other particular. The fellow looked conscious of guilt, although I believe he was unconscious that every body around knew who it was that had caught him.

I have had no letter from home, since I wrote you before, except short business letters, which have no interest for you.

By the way, you do not intend to do without a girl, because the one you had has left you? Get another as soon as you can to take charge of the dear codgers. Father expected to see you all sooner; but let it pass; stay as long as you please, and come when you please. Kiss and love the dear rascals. Affectionately

To William H. Herndon

Dear William: Washington, July 10, 1848

Your letter covering the newspaper slips, was received last night. The subject of that letter is exceedingly painful to me; and I can not but think there is some mistake in your impression of the motives of the old men. I suppose I am now one of the old men—and I declare on my veracity, which I think is good with you, that nothing could afford me more satisfaction than to learn that you and others of my young friends at home, were doing battle in the contest, and endearing themselves to the people, and taking a stand far above any I have ever been able to reach, in their admiration. I can not conceive that other old men feel differently. Of course I can not demonstrate what I say; but I was young once, and I am sure I was never ungenerously thrust back. I hardly know what to say. The way for a young man to rise, is to improve himself every way he can, never suspecting that any body wishes to hinder him. Allow me to assure you, that suspicion and jealousy never did help any man in any situation. There may sometimes be ungenerous attempts to keep a young man down; and they will succeed too, if he allows his mind to be diverted from its true channel to brood over the attempted injury. Cast about, and see if this feeling has not injured every person you have ever known to fall into it.

Now, in what I have said, I am sure you will suspect nothing but sincere friendship. I would save you from a fatal error. You have been a laborious, studious young man. You are far better informed on almost all subjects than I have ever been. You can not fail in any laudable object, unless you allow your mind to be improperly directed. I have some the advantage of you in the world's experience, merely by being older; and it is this that induces me to advise.

You still seem to be a little mistaken about the Congressional Globe and Appendix. They contain *all* of the speeches that are published in any way. My speech, and Dayton's speech, which you say you got in pamphlet form, are both, word for word, in the Appendix. I repeat again all are there. Your friend, as ever

To William H. Herndon

Dear William: Washington, July 11− 1848
    Yours of the 3rd. is this moment received; and I hardly need say, it gives unalloyed pleasure. I now almost regret writing the serious, long faced letter, I wrote yesterday; but let the past as nothing be. Go it while you're young!
    I write this in the confusion of the H.R, and with several other things to attend to. I will send you about eight different speeches this evening; and as to kissing a pretty girl, I know one very pretty one, but I guess she wont let me kiss her. Yours forever

Speech in the U.S. House of Representatives on the Presidential Question

GEN: TAYLOR AND THE VETO

Mr. Speaker

Our democratic friends seem to be in great distress because they think our candidate for the Presidency dont suit *us*. Most of them can not find out that Gen: Taylor has any principles at all; some, however, have discovered that he has *one*, but that that one is entirely wrong. This one principle, is his position on the veto power. The gentleman from Tennessee (Mr. Stanton) who has just taken his seat, indeed, has said there is very little if any difference on this question between Gen: Taylor and all the Presidents; and he seems to think it sufficient detraction from Gen: Taylor's position on it, that it has nothing new in it. But all others, whom I have heard speak, assail it furiously. A new member from Kentucky (Mr. Clark) of very considerable ability, was in particular concern about it. He thought it altogether novel, and unprecedented, for a President, or a Presidential candidate to think of approving bills whose constitutionality may not be entirely clear to his own mind. He thinks the ark of our safety is gone, unless Presidents shall always veto such bills, as in their judgment, may be of *doubtful* constitutionality. However clear congress may be of their authority to pass any particular act, the gentleman from Kentucky thinks the President must veto it if *he* has *doubts* about it. Now I have neither time nor inclination to argue with the gentleman on the veto power as an original question; but I wish to show that Gen: Taylor, and not he, agrees with the earlier statesmen on this question. When the bill chartering the first bank of the United States passed Congress, it's constitutionality was questioned. Mr. Madison, then in the House of Representatives, as well as others, had opposed it on that ground. Gen: Washington, as President, was called on to approve or reject it. He sought and obtained on the constitutional question the separate written opinions of Jefferson, Hamilton, and Edmund Randolph; they then being respectively Secretary of State, Secretary of the Treasury, and Attorney General. Hamilton's opinion was for the

power; while Randolph's and Jefferson's were both against it.
Mr. Jefferson, after giving his opinion decidedly against the
constitutionality of that bill, closes his letter with the paragraph which I now read:

"It must be admitted, however, that, unless the President's
mind, on a view of every thing, which is urged for and
against this bill, is tollerably clear that it is unauthorized by
the constitution; if the *pro* and the *con* hang so even as to
ballance his judgment, a just respect for the wisdom of the
legislature, would naturally decide the ballance in favor of
their opinion: it is chiefly for cases, where they are clearly
misled by error, ambition, or interest, that the constitution
has placed a check in the negative of the President.

February 15– 1791–   Thomas Jefferson–"

Gen: Taylor's opinion, as expressed in his Allison letter, is
as I now read:

"The power given by the veto, is a high conservative
power; but in my opinion, should never be exercised except
in cases of clear violation of the constitution, or manifest
haste, and want of consideration by congress."

It is here seen that, in Mr. Jefferson's opinion, if on the
constitutionality of any given bill, the President *doubts*, he is
not to veto it, as the gentleman from Kentucky would have
him to do, but is to defer to congress, and approve it. And if
we compare the opinions of Jefferson and Taylor, as expressed
in these paragraphs, we shall find them more exactly alike,
than we can often find any two expressions, having any litteral
difference. None but interested fault-finders, I think, can discover any substantial variation.

TAYLOR ON MEASURES OF POLICY

But gentlemen on the other side are unanamously agreed
that Gen: Taylor has no other principles. They are in utter
darkness as to his opinions on any of the questions of policy
which occupy the public attention. But is there any doubt as
to what he will *do* on the prominent questions, if elected? Not
the least. It is not possible to know what he will, or would
do, in every immaginable case; because many questions have

passed away, and others doubtless will arise which none of us have yet thought of; but on the prominent questions of Currency, Tariff, internal improvements, and Wilmot Proviso, Gen: Taylor's course is at least as well defined as is Gen: Cass'. Why, in their eagerness to get at Gen: Taylor, several democratic members here, have desired to know whether, in case of his election, a bankrupt law is to be established. Can they tell us Gen: Cass' opinion on this question? (Some member answered "He is against it") Aye, how do you know he is? There is nothing about it in the Platform, nor elsewhere that I have seen. If the gentleman knows of any thing, which I do not, he can show it. But to return: Gen: Taylor, in his Allison letter, says

"Upon the subject of the tariff, the currency, the improvements of our great high-ways, rivers, lakes, and harbors, the will of the people, as expressed through their representatives in congress, ought to be respected and carried out by the executive."

Now this is the whole matter. In substance, it is this: The people say to Gen: Taylor "If you are elected, shall we have a national bank?" He answers "*Your* will, gentlemen, not *mine*" "What about the Tariff?" "Say yourselves." "Shall our rivers and harbours be improved?" "Just as you please" "If you desire a bank, an alteration of the tariff, internal improvements, any, or all, I will not hinder you; if you do not desire them, I will not attempt to force them on you" "Send up your members of congress from the various districts, with opinions according to your own; and if they are for these measures, or any of them, I shall have nothing to oppose; if they are not for them, I shall not, by any appliances whatever, attempt to dragoon them into their adoption." Now, can there be any difficulty in understanding this? To you democrats, it may not seem like principle; but surely you can not fail to perceive the position plainly enough. The distinction between it, and the position of your candidate is broad and obvious; and I admit, you have a clear right to show it is wrong if you can; but you have no right to pretend you can not see it at all. We see it; and to us it appears like principle, and the best sort of principle at that—the principle of allowing the people to do as they

please with their own business. My friend from Indiana
(C. B. Smith) has aptly asked "Are you willing to trust the
people?" Some of you answered, substantially "We are willing
to trust the people; but the President is as much the representative of the people as Congress." In a certain sense, and to a
certain extent, he is the representative of the people. He is
elected by them, as well as congress is. But can he, in the
nature of things, know the wants of the people, as well as
three hundred other men, coming from all the various localities of the nation? If so, where is the propriety of having a
congress? That the constitution gives the President a negative
on legislation, all know; but that this negative should be so
combined with platforms, and other appliances, as to enable
him, and, in fact, almost compel him, to take the whole of
legislation into his own hands, is what we object to, is what
Gen: Taylor objects to, and is what constitutes the broad distinction between you and us. To thus transfer legislation, is
clearly to take it from those who understand, with minute-
ness, the interests of the people, and give it to one who does
not, and can not so well understand it. I understand your
idea, that if a Presidential candidate avow his opinion upon a
given question, or rather, upon all questions, and the people,
with full knowledge of this, elect him, they thereby distinctly
approve all those opinions. This, though plausable, is a most
pernicious deception. By means of it, measures are adopted or
rejected, contrary to the wishes of the whole of one party, and
often nearly half of the other. The process is this. Three, four,
or half a dozen questions are prominent at a given time; the
party selects it's candidate, and he takes his position on each
of these questions. On all but one, his positions have already
been endorsed at former elections, and his party fully committed to them; but that one is new, and a large portion of them
are against it. But what are they to do? The whole are strung
together; and they must take all, or reject all. They can not
take what they like, and leave the rest. What they are already
committed to, being the majority, they shut their eyes, and
gulp the whole. Next election, still another is introduced in
the same way. If we run our eyes along the line of the past,
we shall see that almost, if not quite all the articles of the
present democratic creed, have been at first forced upon the

party in this very way. And just now, and just so, opposition to internal improvements is to be established, if Gen: Cass shall be elected. Almost half the democrats here, are for improvements; but they will vote for Cass, and if he succeeds, their votes will have aided in closing the doors against improvements. Now this is a process which we think is wrong. We prefer a candidate, who, like Gen: Taylor, will allow the people to have their own way, regardless of his private opinions; and I should think the internal improvement democrats, at least, ought to prefer such a candidate. He would force nothing on them which they dont want, and he would allow them to have improvements, which their own candidate, if elected, will not.

Mr. Speaker, I have said Gen: Taylors position is as well defined, as is that of Gen: Cass. In saying this I admit I do not certainly know what he would do on the Wilmot Proviso. I am a Northern man, or rather, a Western free state man, with a constituency I believe to be, and with personal feelings I know to be, against the extension of slavery. As such, and with what information I have, I hope and *believe*, Gen: Taylor, if elected, would not veto the Proviso. *But* I do not *know* it. Yet, if I knew he would, I still would vote for him. I should do so, because, in my judgment, his election alone, can defeat Gen: Cass; and because, *should* slavery thereby go to the teritory we now have, just so much will certainly happen by the election of Cass; and, in addition, a course of policy, leading to new wars, new acquisitions of teritory and still further extensions of slavery. One of the two is to be President; which is preferable?

But there is as much doubt of Cass on improvements, as there is of Taylor on the Proviso. I have no doubt myself of Gen: Cass on this question; but I know the democrats differ among themselves as to his position. My internal improvement colleague (Mr. Wentworth) stated on this floor the other day that he was satisfied Cass was for improvements, because he had voted for all the bills that he (Mr. W.) had. So far so good; but Mr. Polk vetoed some of these very bills, the Baltimore convention passed a set of resolutions, among other things, approving these vetoes, and Gen: Cass declares, in his letter accepting the nomination, that he has carefully read these resolutions, and that he adheres to them as firmly as he approves them cordially. In other words, Gen: Cass voted for the bills, and thinks the President did right to veto them; and his friends here are amiable enough to consider him as being on one side or the other, just as one or the other may correspond with their own respective inclinations. My colleague admits that the platform declares against the constitutionality of a general system of improvements, and that Gen: Cass endorses the platform; but he still thinks Gen: Cass is in favor of some sort of improvements. Well, what are they? As he is against *general* objects, those he is for, must be *particular* and *local*. Now this is taking the subject precisely by the wrong end. *Particularity*—expending the money of the *whole* people, for an object, which will benefit only a *portion* of them—is the greatest real objection to improvements, and has been so held by Gen: Jackson, Mr. Polk, and all others, I believe, till now. But now, behold, the objects most general,—nearest free from this objection, are to be rejected, while those most liable to it, are to be embraced. To return; I can not help believing that Gen: Cass, when he wrote his letter of acceptance, well understood he was to be claimed by the advocates of both sides of this question, and that he then closed the door against all further expressions of opinion, purposely to retain the benefits of that double position. His subsequent equivocation at Cleveland, to my mind, proves such to have been the case.

One word more, and I shall have done with this branch of the subject. You democrats, and your candidate, in the main are in favor of laying down, in advance, a platform—a set of party positions, as a unit; and then of enforcing the people, by every sort of appliance, to ratify them, however unpalatable some of them may be. We, and our candidate, are in favor of making Presidential elections, and the legislation of the country, distinct matters; so that the people can elect whom they please, and afterwards, legislate just as they please, without any hindrance, save only so much as may guard against infractions of the constitution, undue haste, and want of consideration. The difference between us, is clear as noonday. That we are right, we can not doubt. We hold the true republican position. In leaving the people's business in their hands, we can not be wrong. We are willing, and even anxious, to go to the people, on this issue.

OLD HORSES AND MILITARY COAT TAILS

But I suppose I can not reasonably hope to convince you that we have any principles. The most I can expect, is to assure you that we think we have, and are quite contented with them. The other day, one of the gentlemen from Georgia (Mr. Iverson) an eloquent man, and a man of learning, so far as I could judge, not being learned, myself, came down upon us astonishingly. He spoke in what the Baltimore American calls the "scathing and withering style." At the end of his second severe flash, I was struck blind, and found myself feeling with my fingers for an assurance of my continued physical existence. A little of the bone was left, and I gradually revived. He eulogised Mr. Clay in high and beautiful terms, and then declared that we had deserted all our principles, and had turned Henry Clay out, like an old horse to root. This is terribly severe. It can not be answered by argument; at least, I can not so answer it. I merely wish to ask the gentleman if the whigs are the only party he can think of, who some times turn old horses out to root. Is not a certain Martin Van Buren, an old horse which your own party have turned out to root? and is he not rooting a little to your discomfort about now? But in not nominating Mr. Clay, we deserted our principles, you say. Ah! in what? Tell us, ye men of principles, what principle we violated. We say you did violate principle in discarding Van Buren, and we can tell you how. You violated the primary, the cardinal, the one great living principle of all Democratic representative government—the principle, that the representative is bound to carry out the known will of his constituents. A large majority of the Baltimore Convention of 1844, were, by their constituents, instructed to procure Van Buren's nomination if they could. In violation, in utter, glaring contempt of this, you rejected him—rejected him, as the gentleman from New-York (Mr. Birdsall) the other day, expressly admitted, for *availability*—that same "General availability" which you charge upon us, and daily chew over here, as something exceedingly odious and unprincipled. But the gentleman from Georgia (Mr. Iverson) gave us a second speech yesterday, all well considered, and put down in writing, in which Van Buren was scathed and withered a "few" for his present position and movements. I can not remember the gentlemans precise language; but I do remember he put Van Buren down, down, till he got him where he was finally to "stink" and "rot."

Mr. Speaker, it is no business, or inclination of mine, to defend Martin Van Buren. In the war of extermination now waging between him and his old admirers, I say, devil take the hindmost—and the foremost. But there is no mistaking the origin of the breach; and if the curse of "stinking" and "rotting" is to fall on the first and greatest violators of principle in the matter, I disinterestedly suggest, that the gentleman from Georgia, and his present co-workers, are bound to take it upon themselves.

But the gentleman from Georgia further says we have deserted all our principles, and taken shelter under Gen: Taylor's military coat-tail; and he seems to think this is exceedingly degrading. Well, as his faith is, so be it unto him. But can he remember no other military coat tail under which a certain other party have been sheltering for near a quarter of a century? Has he no acquaintance with the ample military coat tail of Gen: Jackson? Does he not know that his own party have run the five last Presidential races under that coat-tail? and that they are now running the sixth, under the same cover? Yes sir, that coat tail was used, not only for Gen: Jackson himself; but has been clung to, with the gripe of death, by every democratic candidate since. You have never ventured, and dare not now venture, from under it. Your campaign papers have constantly been "Old Hickories" with rude likenesses of the old general upon them; hickory poles, and hickory brooms, your never-ending emblems; Mr. Polk himself was "Young Hickory" "Little Hickory" or something so; and even now, your campaign paper here, is proclaiming that Cass and Butler are of the true "Hickory stripe." No sir, you dare not give it up.

Like a horde of hungry ticks you have stuck to the tail of the Hermitage lion to the end of his life; and you are still sticking to it, and drawing a loathsome sustenance from it, after he is dead. A fellow once advertised that he had made a discovery by which he could make a new man out of an old one, and have enough of the stuff left to make a little yellow dog. Just such a discovery has Gen: Jackson's popularity been to you. You not only twice made President of him out of it, but you have had enough of the stuff left, to make Presidents of several comparatively small men since; and it is your chief reliance now to make still another.

Mr. Speaker, old horses, and military coat-tails, or tails of any sort, are not figures of speech, such as I would be the first to introduce into discussions here; but as the gentleman from Georgia has thought fit to introduce them, he, and you, are welcome to all you have made, or can make, by them. If you have any more old horses, trot them out; any more tails, just cock them, and come at us.

I repeat, I would not introduce this mode of discussion here; but I wish gentlemen on the other side to understand, that the use of degrading figures is a game at which they may not find themselves able to take all the winnings. (We give it up). Aye, you give it up, and well you may; but for a very different reason from that which you would have us understand. The point—the power to hurt—of all figures, consists in the *truthfulness* of their application; and, understanding this, you may well give it up. They are weapons which hit you, but miss us.

MILITARY TAIL OF THE GREAT MICHIGANDER

But in my hurry I was very near closing on the subject of military tails before I was done with it. There is one entire article of the sort I have not discussed yet; I mean the military tail you democrats are now engaged in dovetailing onto the great Michigander. Yes sir, all his biographers (and they are legion) have him in hand, tying him to a military tail, like so many mischievous boys tying a dog to a bladder of beans. True, the material they have is very limited; but they drive at it, might and main. He *in*vaded Canada without resistance, and he *out*vaded it without pursuit. As he did both under orders, I suppose there was, to him, neither credit or discredit in them; but they constitute a large part of the tail. He was not at Hull's surrender, but he was close by; he was volunteer aid to Gen: Harrison on the day of the battle of the Thames;

and, as you said in 1840, Harrison was picking huckleberries two miles off while the battle was fought, I suppose it is a just conclusion with you, to say Cass was aiding Harrison to pick huckleberries. This is about all, except the mooted question of the broken sword. Some authors say he broke it, some say he threw it away, and some others, who ought to know, say nothing about it. Perhaps it would be a fair historical compromise to say, if he did not break it, he did n't do any thing else with it.

By the way, Mr. Speaker, did you know I am a military hero? Yes sir; in the days of the Black Hawk war, I fought, bled, and came away. Speaking of Gen: Cass' career, reminds me of my own. I was not at Stillman's defeat, but I was about as near it, as Cass was to Hulls surrender; and, like him, I saw the place very soon afterwards. It is quite certain I did not break my sword, for I had none to break; but I bent a musket pretty badly on one occasion. If Cass broke his sword, the idea is, he broke it in desperation; I bent the musket by accident. If Gen: Cass went in advance of me in picking huckleberries, I guess I surpassed him in charges upon the wild onions. If he saw any live, fighting indians, it was more than I did; but I had a good many bloody struggles with the musquetoes; and, although I never fainted from loss of blood, I can truly say I was often very hungry. Mr. Speaker, if I should ever conclude to doff whatever our democratic friends may suppose there is of black cockade federalism about me, and thereupon, they shall take me up as their candidate for the Presidency, I protest they shall not make fun of me, as they have of Gen: Cass, by attempting to write me into a military hero.

CASS ON THE WILMOT PROVISO

While I have Gen: Cass in hand, I wish to say a word about his political principles. As a specimen, I take the record of his progress on the Wilmot Proviso. In the Washington Union, of March 2nd. 1847, there is a report of a speech of Gen: Cass, made the day before, in the Senate, on the Wilmot Proviso, during the delivery of which, Mr. Miller, of New Jersey, is reported to have interupted him as follows, towit:

"Mr. Miller expressed his great surprise at the change in the

sentiments of the senator from Michigan, who had been regarded as the great champion of freedom in the North West,
of which he was a distinguished ornament. Last year the senator from Michigan was understood to be decidedly in favor
of the Wilmot Proviso; and, as no reason had been stated for
the change, he (Mr. M.) could not refrain from the expression
of his extreme surprise."

To this, Gen: Cass is reported to have replied as follows,
towit:

"Mr. Cass said that the course of the senator from New-
Jersey was most extraordinary. Last year he (Mr. C) should
have voted for the proposition had it come up. But circumstances had altogether changed. The honorable senator then
read several passages from the remarks, as given above, which
he had committed to writing, in order to refute such a charge
as that of the senator from New-Jersey."

In the "remarks above committed to writing" is one numbered 4 as follows, towit

"4th. Legislation now would be wholly inoperative, because no teritory hereafter to be acquired can be governed,
without an act of congress providing for its government. And
such an act, on it's passage, would open the whole subject,
and leave the congress, called on to pass it, free to exercise it's
own discretion, entirely uncontrolled by any declaration
found on the statute book."

In Niles' Register, Vol. 73, page 293, there is a letter of
Gen: Cass to A.O.P. Nicholson, of Nashville, Tenn. dated
Decr. 24th. 1847, from which, the following are correct ex-
tracts —

"The Wilmot Proviso has been before the country some
time. It has been repeatedly discussed in congress, and by the
public press. I am strongly impressed with the opinion that a
great change has been going on in the public mind upon this
subject — in my own as well as others; and that doubts are
resolving themselves into convictions, that the principle it involves should be kept out of the national legislature, and left
to the people of the confederacy in their respective local
governments."   *   *   *

"Briefly, then, I am opposed to the exercise of any jurisdiction by congress over this matter; and I am in favor of leaving

the people of any teritory which may be hereafter acquired, the right to regulate it themselves, under the general principles of the constitution; Because

1. I do not see in the constitution any grant of the requisite power to congress; and I am not disposed to extend a doubtful precedent beyond it's necessity—the establishment of teritorial governments when needed—leaving to the inhabitants all the rights compatable with the relations they bear to the confederation."

These extracts show that, in 1846, Gen: Cass was for the Proviso *at once*; that in March 1847, he was still for it, *but not just then*; and that, in Decr. 1847 he was *against* it altogether. This is a true index to the whole man. When the question was raised in 1846, he was in a blustering hurry to take ground for it. He sought to be in advance, and to avoid the uninteresting position of a mere follower; but soon he began to see glimpses of the great democratic ox-gad waving in his face, and to hear, indistinctly, a voice saying "Back" "Back sir" "Back a little." He shakes his head, and bats his eyes, and blunders back to his position of March 1847; but still the gad waves, and the voice grows more distinct, and sharper still "Back sir" "Back I say" "Further back"; and back he goes, to the position of Decr. 1847, at which the gad is still, and the voice soothingly says "So" "Stand at that."

Have no fears, gentlemen, of your candidate. He exactly suits you, and we congratulate you upon it. However much you may be distressed about *our* candidate, you have all cause to be contented and happy with your own. If elected, he may not maintain all, or even any of his positions previously taken; but he will be sure to do whatever the party exigency, for the time being, may require; and that is precisely what you want. He and Van Buren are the same "manner of men"; and, like Van Buren, he will never desert *you*, till you first desert *him*.

CASS ON WORKING AND EATING

Mr. Speaker, I adopt the suggestion of a friend, that Gen: Cass is a General of splendidly successful *charges*—charges, to be sure, not upon the public enemy, but upon the public Treasury.

He, was governor of Michigan Teritory, and ex-officio, superintendent of indian affairs, from the 9th. of October 1813 till the 31st. of July 1831, a period of seventeen years, nine months, and twentytwo days. During this period, he received from the U.S. Treasury, for personal services, and personal expenses, the aggregate sum of $96.028, being an average of $14.79 cents per day, for every day of the time. This large sum was reached, by assuming that he was doing service, and incurring expenses, at several different *places*, and in several different *capacities* in the *same* place, all at the same *time*. By a correct analysis of his accounts, during that period, the following propositions may be deduced—

First: He was paid in *three* different capacities during the *whole* of the time—that is to say—

1. As governor's salary, at the rate per year of $2000.

2. As estimated for office-rent, clerk-hire, fuel &c in superintendence of indian affairs *in* Michigan, at the rate per year of $1500

3. As compensation and expenses, for various miscellaneous, items of indian service *out* of Michigan, an average per year of—$625

Second: During *part* of the time, that is, from the 9th. of October 1813, to the 29th. of May 1822, he was paid in *four* different capacities—that is to say—

The three as above, and, in addition thereto, the commutation of ten rations per day, amounting, per year, to $730.

Third: During *another* part of the time, that is, from the beginning of 1822 to the 31st. of July 1831, he was also paid in *four* different capacities, that is to say—The *first* three, as above (the rations being dropped after the 29th. of May 1822) and, in addition thereto, for superintending indian agencies at Piqua, Ohio, Fort Wayne, Indiana, and Chicago, Illinois, at the rate per year of $1500. It should be observed here, that the last item, commencing at the beginning of 1822; and the item of rations, ending on the 29th. of May 1822, lap on each other, during so much of the time as lies between those two dates.

Fourth: Still another part of the time, that is, from the 31st. of October 1821 to the 29th. of May 1822, he was paid in *six* different capacities—that is to say—

The three first, as above, the item of rations, as above; and, in addition thereto, another item of ten rations per day, while at Washington, settling his accounts, being at the rate per year of $730.

And also, an allowance for expenses traveling to and from Washington, and while there, of $1022, being at the rate per year of $1793.

Fifth: And yet during the little portion of the time which lies between the 1st. of Jany. 1822, and the 29th. of May 1822, he was paid in *seven* different capacities, that is to say—

The six, last mentioned, and also, at the rate of $1500 per year, for the Piqua, Fort Wayne, and Chicago service, as mentioned above.

These accounts have already been discussed some here; but when we are amongst them, as when we are in the Patent Office, we must peep about a good while before we can see all the curiosities. I shall not be tedious with them. As to the large item of $1500 per year amounting in the aggregate, to $26.715 for office-rent, clerk-hire, fuel &c. I barely wish to remark that, so far as I can discover in the public documents, there is no evidence, by word or inference, either from any disinterested witness or of Gen: Cass himself, that he ever rented, or kept a separate office; ever hired or kept a clerk; or ever used any extra amount of fuel &c. in consequence of his indian services. Indeed, Gen. Cass' entire silence in regard to these items, in his two long letters urging his claims upon the government, is, to my mind, almost conclusive that no such items had any real existence.

But I have introduced Gen: Cass' accounts here chiefly to show the wonderful physical capacities of the man. They show that he not only did the labor of several men at the same *time*; but that he often did it at several *places*, many hundreds of miles apart, at the same time. And, at eating too, his capacities are shown to be quite as wonderful. From October 1821 to May 1822, he ate ten rations a day in Michigan, ten rations a day here in Washington, and near five dollars worth a day on the road between the two places! And then there is an important discovery in his example—the art of being paid for what one eats, instead of having to pay for it. Hereafter if any nice young man shall owe a bill which he can not pay in any other way, he can just board it out. Mr. Speaker, we have all heard of the animal standing in doubt between two stacks of hay, and starving to death. The like of that would never happen to Gen: Cass; place the stacks a thousand miles apart, he would stand stock still midway between them, and eat them both at once; and the green grass along the line would be apt to suffer some too at the same time. By all means, make him President, gentlemen. He will feed you bounteously, — if — if there is any left after he shall have helped himself.

THE WHIGS AND THE WAR

But, as Gen: Taylor is, par excellence, the hero of the Mexican war; and, as you democrats say we whigs have always opposed the war, you think it must be very awkward and embarrassing for us to go for Gen: Taylor. The declaration that we have always opposed the war, is true or false, accordingly as one may understand the term "opposing the war." If to say "the war was unnecessarily and unconstitutionally commenced by the President" be opposing the war, then the whigs have very generally opposed it. Whenever they have spoken at all, they have said this; and they have said it on what has appeared good reason to them. The marching an army into the midst of a peaceful Mexican settlement, frightening the inhabitants away, leaving their growing crops, and other property to destruction, to *you* may appear a perfectly amiable, peaceful, unprovoking procedure; but it does not appear so to *us*. So to call such an act, to us appears no other than a naked, impudent absurdity, and we speak of it accordingly. But if, when the war had begun, and had become the cause of the country, the giving of our money and our blood, in common with yours, was support of the war, then it is not true that we have always opposed the war. With few individual exceptions, you have constantly had our votes here for all the necessary supplies. And, more than this, you have had the services, the blood, and the lives of our political bretheren in every trial, and on every field. The beardless boy, and the mature man — the humble and the distinguished, you have had them. Through suffering and death, by disease, and in battle, they have endured, and fought, and fell with you. Clay and Webster each gave a son, never to be returned. From the state of my own residence, besides other worthy but less known whig names, we sent Marshall, Morrison, Baker, and Hardin; they all fought, and one fell; and in the fall of that one, we lost our best whig man. Nor were the whigs few in number, or laggard in the day of danger. In that fearful, bloody, breathless struggle at Buena Vista, where each man's hard task was to beat back five foes or die himself, of the five high officers who perished, four were whigs.

In speaking of this, I mean no odious comparison between the lion-hearted whigs and democrats who fought there. On other occasions, and among the lower officers and privates on *that* occasion, I doubt not the proportion was different. I wish to do justice to all. I think of all those brave men as Americans, in whose proud fame, as an American, I too have a share. Many of them, whigs and democrats, are my constituents and personal friends; and I thank them—more than thank them—one and all, for the high, imperishable honor they have confered on our common state.

But the distinction between the cause of the *President* in beginning the war, and the cause of the *country* after it was begun, is a distinction which you can not perceive. To you the President, and the country, seems to be all one. You are interested to see no distinction between them; and I venture to suggest that possibly your interest blinds you a little. We see the distinction, as we think, clearly enough; and our friends who have fought in the war have no difficulty in seeing it also. What those who have fallen would say were they alive and here, of course we can never know; but with those who have returned there is no difficulty. Col: Haskell, and Major Gaines, members here, both fought in the war; and one of them underwent extraordinary perils and hardships; still they, like all other whigs here, vote, on the record, that the war was unnecessarily and unconstitutionally commenced by the President. And even Gen: Taylor himself, the noblest Roman of them all, has declared that as a citizen, and particularly as a soldier, it is sufficient for him to know that his country is at war with a foreign nation, to do all in his power to bring it to a speedy and honorable termination, by the most vigorous and energetic opperations, without enquiring about it's justice, or any thing else connected with it.

Mr. Speaker, let our democratic friends be comforted with the assurance, that we are content with our position, content with our company, and content with our candidate; and that although they, in their generous sympathy, think we ought to be miserable, we really are not, and that they may dismiss the great anxiety they have on *our* account.

DIVIDED GANGS OF HOGS

Mr. Speaker, I see I have but three minutes left, and this forces me to throw out one whole branch of my subject. A single word on still another. The democrats are kind enough to frequently remind us that we have some dissensions in our ranks. Our good friend from Baltimore, immediately before me (Mr. McLane) expressed some doubt the other day as to which branch of our party, Gen: Taylor would ultimately fall into the hands of. That was a new idea to me. I knew we had dissenters, but I did not know they were trying to get our candidate away from us. I would like to say a word to our dissenters, but I have not the time. Some such *we* certainly have; have *you* none, gentlemen democrats? Is it all union and harmony in *your* ranks?—no bickerings?—no divisions? If there be doubt as to which of our divisions will get our candidate, is there no doubt as to which of your candidates will get your party? I have heard some things from New-York; and if they are true, one might well say of your party there, as a drunken fellow once said when he heard the reading of an indictment for hog-stealing. The clerk read on till he got to, and through the words "did steal, take, and carry away, ten boars, ten sows, ten shoats, and ten pigs" at which he exclaimed "Well, by golly, that is the most equally divided gang of hogs, I ever did hear of." If there is any *other* gang of hogs more equally divided than the democrats of New-York are about this time, I have not heard of it.

July 27, 1848

To William Schouler

Washington, August 28, 1848.
Friend Schouler,—Your letter of the 21st was received two or three days ago, and for which please accept my thanks,

both for your courtesy and the encouraging news in it. The news we are receiving here now from all parts is on the look-up. We have had several letters from Ohio to-day, all encouraging. Two of them inform us that Hon. C. B. Smith, on his way here, addressed a larger and more enthusiastic audience, at Cincinnati, than has been seen in that city since 1840. Smith himself wrote one of the letters; and he says the signs are decidedly good. Letters from the Reserve are of the same character. The tone of the letters—free from despondency—full of hope—is what particularly encourages me. If a man is scared when he writes, I think I can detect it, when I see what he writes.

I would rather not be put upon explaining how Logan was defeated in my district. In the first place I have no particulars from there, my friends, supposing I am on the road home, not having written me. Whether there was a full turn out of the voters I have as yet not learned. The most I can now say is that a good many Whigs, without good cause, as I think, were unwilling to go for Logan, and some of them so wrote me before the election. On the other hand Harris was a Major of the war, and fought at Cerro Gordo, where several Whigs of the district fought with him. These two facts and their effects, I presume tell the whole story. That there is any political change against us in the district I cannot believe; because I wrote some time ago to every county of the district for an account of changes; and, in answer I got the names of four against us, eighty-three for us. I dislike to predict, but it seems to me the district must and will be found right side up again in November. Yours truly,

Fragment on Niagara Falls

Niagara-Falls! By what mysterious power is it that millions and millions, are drawn from all parts of the world, to gaze upon Niagara Falls? There is no mystery about the thing itself. Every effect is just such as any inteligent man knowing the causes, would anticipate, without it. If the water moving onward in a great river, reaches a point where there is a perpendicular jog, of a hundred feet in descent, in the bottom of the river,—it is plain the water will have a violent and continuous plunge at that point. It is also plain the water, thus plunging, will foam, and roar, and send up a mist, continuously, in which last, during sunshine, there will be perpetual rain-bows. The mere physical of Niagara Falls is only this. Yet this is really a very small part of that world's wonder. It's power to excite reflection, and emotion, is it's great charm. The geologist will demonstrate that the plunge, or fall, was once at Lake Ontario, and has worn it's way back to it's present position; he will ascertain how *fast* it is wearing now, and so get a basis for determining how *long* it has been wearing back from Lake Ontario, and finally demonstrate by it that this world is at least fourteen thousand years old. A philosopher of a slightly different turn will say Niagara Falls is only the lip of the basin out of which pours all the surplus water which rains down on two or three hundred thousand square miles of the earth's surface. He will estimate with approximate accuracy, that five hundred thousand tons of water, falls with it's full weight, a distance of a hundred feet each minute—thus exerting a force equal to the lifting of the same weight, through the same space, in the same time. And then the further reflection comes that this vast amount of water, constantly pouring *down*, is supplied by an equal amount constantly *lifted up*, by the sun; and still he says, "If this much is lifted up, for *this one* space of two or three hundred thousand square miles, an equal amount must be lifted for every other equal space"; and he is overwhelmed in the contemplation of the vast power the sun is constantly exerting in quiet, noiseless operation of lifting water *up* to be rained *down* again.

But still there is more. It calls up the indefinite past. When Columbus first sought this continent—when Christ suffered on the cross—when Moses led Israel through the Red-Sea— nay, even, when Adam first came from the hand of his Maker—then as now, Niagara was roaring here. The eyes of that species of extinct giants, whose bones fill the mounds of America, have gazed on Niagara, as ours do now. Cotemporary with the whole race of men, and older than the first man, Niagara is strong, and fresh to-day as ten thousand years ago. The Mammoth and Mastadon—now so long dead, that fragments of their monstrous bones, alone testify, that they ever lived, have gazed on Niagara. In that long—long time, never still for a single moment. Never dried, never froze, never slept, never rested,

late September 1848?

To Thomas Lincoln and John D. Johnston

My dear father: Washington, Decr. 24th. 1848–

Your letter of the 7th. was received night before last. I very cheerfully send you the twenty dollars, which sum you say is necessary to save your land from sale. It is singular that you should have forgotten a judgment against you; and it is more singular that the plaintiff should have let you forget it so long, particularly as I suppose you have always had property enough to satisfy a judgment of that amount. Before you pay it, it would be well to be sure you have not paid it; or, at least, that you can not prove you have paid it. Give my love to Mother, and all the connections. Affectionately your Son

Dear Johnston:

Your request for eighty dollars, I do not think it best, to comply with now. At the various times when I have helped you a little, you have said to me "We can get along very well now" but in a very short time I find you in the same difficulty again. Now this can only happen by some defect in your *conduct*. What that defect is, I think I know. You are not *lazy*, and still you *are* an *idler*. I doubt whether since I saw you, you have done a good whole day's work, in any one day. You do not very much dislike to work; and still you do not work much, merely because it does not seem to you that you could get much for it. This habit of uselessly wasting time, is the whole difficulty; and it is vastly important to you, and still more so to your children that you should break this habit. It is more important to them, because they have longer to live, and can keep out of an idle habit before they are in it; easier than they can get out after they are in.

You are now in need of some ready money; and what I propose is, that you shall go to work, "tooth and nails" for some body who will give you money for it. Let father and your boys take charge of things at home — prepare for a crop, and make the crop; and you go to work for the best money wages, or in discharge of any debt you owe, that you can get. And to secure you a fair reward for your labor, I now promise you, that for every dollar you will, between this and the first of next May, get for your own labor, either in money, or in your own indebtedness, I will then give you one other dollar. By this, if you hire yourself at ten dollars a month, from me you will get ten more, making twenty dollars a month for your work. In this, I do not mean you shall go off to St. Louis, or the lead mines, or the gold mines, in California, but I mean for you to go at it for the best wages you can get close to home in Coles county. Now if you will do this, you will soon be out of debt, and what is better, you will have a habit that will keep you from getting in debt again. But if I should now clear you out, next year you will be just as deep in as ever. You say you would almost give your place in Heaven for $70 or $80. Then you value your place in Heaven very cheaply for I am sure you can with the offer I make you get the seventy or eighty dollars for four or five months work. You say if I furnish you the money you will deed me the land, and, if you dont pay the money back, you will deliver possession. Nonsense! If you cant now live *with* the land, how will you then live without it? You have always been kind to me, and I do not now mean to be unkind to you. On the contrary, if you will but follow my advice, you will find it worth more than eight times eighty dollars to you. Affectionately Your brother

To Walter Davis

Friend Walter: Washington, Jan: 5. 1849

Your letter is received. When I last saw you I said, that if the distribution of the offices should fall into my hands, you should have *something*; and I now say as much, but can say no more. I know no more now than I knew when you saw me, as to whether the present officers will be removed, or, if they shall, whether *I* shall be allowed to name the persons to fill them. It will perhaps be better for both you and me, for you to say nothing about this.

I shall do what I can about the Land claim on your brother Thomas' account. Yours as ever

To William H. Herndon

Dear William   Washington, Jan. 5. 1849

Your two letters were received last night. I have a great many letters to write, and so can not write very long ones. There must be some mistake about Walter Davis saying I promised him the Post-Office; I did not so promise him. I did tell him, that if the distribution of the offices should fall into my hands, he should have *something*; and if I shall be convinced he has said any more than this, I shall be disappointed. I said this much to him, because, as I understand, he is of *good character*, is one of the *young* men, is of the *mechanics*, an always *faithful*, and never *troublesome* whig, and is *poor*, with the support of a widow mother thrown almost exclusively on him by the death of his brother. If these are wrong reasons, then I have been wrong; but I have certainly not been selfish in it; because in my greatest need of friends he was against me and for Baker. Yours as ever

P. S. Let the above be confidential

To C. U. Schlater

Mr. C. U. Schlater: Washington,
Dear Sir: Jan: 5. 1849

Your note, requesting my "signature with a sentiment" was received, and should have been answered long since, but that it was mislaid. I am not a very sentimental man; and the best sentiment I can think of is, that if you collect the signatures of all persons who are no less distinguished than I, you will have a very undistinguishing mass of names. Very respectfully

Proposal in the U.S. House of Representatives for Abolition of Slavery in the District of Columbia

Mr. LINCOLN appealed to his colleague [Mr. WENT-WORTH] to withdraw his motion, to enable him to read a proposition which he intended to submit, if the vote should be reconsidered.

Mr. WENTWORTH again withdrew his motion for that purpose.

Mr. LINCOLN said, that by the courtesy of his colleague, he would say, that if the vote on the resolution was reconsidered, he should make an effort to introduce an amendment, which he should now read.

And Mr. L. read as follows:

Strike out all before and after the word "Resolved" and insert the following, towit: That the Committee on the District of Columbia be instructed to report a bill in substance as follows, towit:

Section 1 Be it enacted by the Senate and House of Representatives of the United States of America, in Congress assembled: That no person not now within the District of Columbia, nor now owned by any person or persons now resident within it, nor hereafter born within it, shall ever be held in slavery within said District.

Section 2. That no person now within said District, or now owned by any person, or persons now resident within the same, or hereafter born within it, shall ever be held in slavery without the limits of said District: *Provided*, that officers of the government of the United States, being citizens of the slave-holding states, coming into said District on public business, and remaining only so long as may be reasonably necessary for that object, may be attended into, and out of, said District, and while there, by the necessary servants of themselves and their families, without their right to hold such servants in service, being thereby impaired.

Section 3. That all children born of slave mothers within said District on, or after the first day of January in the year of our Lord one thousand, eight hundred and fifty shall be free;

but shall be reasonably supported and educated, by the respective owners of their mothers or by their heirs or representatives, and shall owe reasonable service, as apprentices, to such owners, heirs and representatives until they respectively arrive at the age of —— years when they shall be entirely free; and the municipal authorities of Washington and Georgetown, within their respective jurisdictional limits, are hereby empowered and required to make all suitable and necessary provisions for enforcing obedience to this section, on the part of both masters and apprentices.

Section 4. That all persons now within said District lawfully held as slaves, or now owned by any person or persons now resident within said District, shall remain such, at the will of their respective owners, their heirs and legal representatives: *Provided* that any such owner, or his legal representative, may at any time receive from the treasury of the United States the full value of his or her slave, of the class in this section mentioned, upon which such slave shall be forthwith and forever free: and *provided further* that the President of the United States, the Secretary of State, and the Secretary of the Treasury shall be a board for determining the value of such slaves as their owners may desire to emancipate under this section; and whose duty it shall be to hold a session for the purpose, on the first monday of each calendar month; to receive all applications; and, on satisfactory evidence in each case, that the person presented for valuation, is a slave, and of the class in this section mentioned, and is owned by the applicant, shall value such slave at his or her full cash value, and give to the applicant an order on the treasury for the amount; and also to such slave a certificate of freedom.

Section 5 That the municipal authorities of Washington and Georgetown, within their respective jurisdictional limits, are hereby empowered and required to provide active and efficient means to arrest, and deliver up to their owners, all fugitive slaves escaping into said District.

Section 6 That the election officers within said District of Columbia, are hereby empowered and required to open polls at all the usual places of holding elections, on the first monday of April next, and receive the vote of every free white male citizen above the age of twentyone years, having resided within said District for the period of one year or more next preceding the time of such voting, for, or against this act; to proceed, in taking said votes, in all respects not herein specified, as at elections under the municipal laws; and, with as little delay as possible, to transmit correct statements of the votes so cast to the President of the United States. And it shall be the duty of the President to canvass said votes immediately, and, if a majority of them be found to be for this act, to forthwith issue his proclamation giving notice of the fact; and this act shall only be in full force and effect on, and after the day of such proclamation.

Section 7.   That involuntary servitude for the punishment of crime, whereof the party shall have been duly convicted shall in no wise be prohibited by this act.

Section 8.   That for all the purposes of this act the jurisdictional limits of Washington are extended to all parts of the District of Columbia not now included within the present limits of Georgetown.

Mr. LINCOLN then said, that he was authorized to say, that of about fifteen of the leading citizens of the District of Columbia to whom this proposition had been submitted, there was not one but who approved of the adoption of such a proposition. He did not wish to be misunderstood. He did not know whether or not they would vote for this bill on the first Monday of April; but he repeated, that out of fifteen persons to whom it had been submitted, he had authority to say that every one of them desired that some proposition like this should pass.

January 10, 1849

To David Davis

Dear Davis: Washington, Feb. 12. 1849

Your letter of the 24th. Jany. is received; and I have more cause to thank you for it, than you would suppose. Out of more than three hundred letters received this session, yours is the second one manifesting the least interest for me personally. I do not much doubt that I could take the Land-office if I would. It also would make me more money than I can otherwise make. Still, when I remember that taking the office would be a final surrender of the law, and that every man in the state, who wants it himself, would be snarling at me about it, I shrink from it.

Baker has just looked over my shoulder, and seen that I am writing to you. He says to me to tell you he has received your letter, and will obey it's requirements as far as he can.

I scarcely know where to send this letter; but I supose it may be best to send it to Bloomington. Your friend as ever

To Joshua F. Speed

Dear Speed: Washington, Feb: 20. 1849.

Your letter of the 13th. was received yesterday. I showed it to Baker. I did this because he knew I had written you, and was expecting an answer; and he still enquired what I had received; so that I could not well keep it a secret. Besides this, I knew the contents of the letter would not affect him as you seemed to think it would. He knows he did not make a favorable impression while in Congress, and he and I had talked it over frequently. He tells me to write you that he has too much self-esteem to be put out of humor with himself by the opinion of any man who does not know him better than Mr. Crittenden does; and that he thinks you ought to have known it. The letter will not affect him the least in regard to either Mr. Crittenden or you. He understands you to have acted the part of a discreet friend; and he intends to make Mr. Crittenden think better of him, hereafter. I am flattered to learn that Mr. Crittenden has any recollection of me which is not unfavorable; and for the manifestation of your kindness towards me, I sincerely thank you. Still there is nothing about me which would authorize me to think of a first class office; and a second class one would not compensate me for being snarled at by others who want it for themselves. I believe that, so far as the whigs in congress, are concerned, I could have the Genl. Land office almost by common consent; but then Sweet, and Don: Morrison, and Browning, and Cyrus Edwards all want it. And what is worse, while I think I could easily take it myself, I fear I shall have trouble to get it for any other man in Illinois. The reason is, that McGaughey, an Indiana ex-member of congress is here after it; and being personally known, he will be hard to beat by any one who is not.

Baker showed me your letter, in which you make a passing allusion to the Louisville Post Office. I have told Garnett Duncan I am for you. I like to open a letter of yours, and I therefore hope you will write me again on the receipt of this.

Give my love, to Mrs. Speed. Yours as ever

P.S. I have not read the Frankfort papers this winter; and consequently do not know whether you have made a speech. If you have, and it has been printed send me a copy.

To Charles R. Welles

C. R. Welles, Esq.   Washington,
Dear Sir: Feb: 20. 1849

This is tuesday evening, and your letter enclosing the one of Young & Brothers to you, saying the money you sent by me to them had not been received, came to hand last saturday night. The facts, which are perfectly fresh in my recollection, are these: you gave me the money in a letter (open I believe) directed to Young & Brothers. To make it more secure than it would be in my hat, where I carry most all my packages, I put it in my trunk. I had a great many jobs to do in St. Louis; and by the very extra care I had taken of yours, overlooked it. On the Steam Boat near the mouth of the Ohio, I opened the trunk, and discovered the letter. I then began to cast about for some safe hand to send it back by. Mr. Yeatman, Judge Pope's son-in-law, and step-son of Mr. Bell of Tennessee, was on board, and was to return immediately to St. Louis from the Mouth of Cumberland. At my request, he took the letter and promised to deliver it—and I heard no more about it till I received your letter on saturday. It so happens that Mr. Yeatman is now in this city; I called on him last night about it; he said he remembered my giving him the letter, and he could remember nothing more of it. He told me he would try to refresh his memory, and see me again concerning it to-day—which however he has not done. I will try to see him to-morrow and write you again. He is a young man, as I understand, of unquestioned, and unquestionable character;

and this makes me fear some pick-pocket on the boat may have seen me give him the letter, and slipped it from him. In this way, never seeing the letter again, he would, naturally enough, never think of it again. Yours truly

To William B. Warren and Others

Gentlemen: Springfield, Ills. April 7. 1849

In answer to your note concerning the General Land-Office I have to say that, if the office can be secured to Illinois by my consent to accept it, and not otherwise, I give that consent. Some months since I gave my word to secure the appointment to that office of Mr. Cyrus Edwards, if in my power, in case of a vacancy; and more recently I stipulated with Col. Baker that if Mr. Edwards and Col. J.L.D. Morrison could arrange with each other for one of them to withdraw, we would jointly recommend the other. In relation to these pledges, I must not only be chaste but above suspicion. If the office shall be tendered to me, I must be permitted to say "Give it to Mr. Edwards, or, if so agreed by them, to Col. Morrison, and I decline it; if not, I accept." With this understanding, you are at liberty to procure me the offer of the appointment if you can; and I shall feel complimented by your effort, and still more by it's success. It should not be overlooked that Col. Baker's position entitles him to a large share of control in this matter; however, one of your number, Col. Warren, knows that Baker has at all times been ready to recommend me, if I would consent. It must also be understood that if at any time, previous to an appointment being made, I shall learn that Mr. Edwards & Col. Morrison have agreed, I shall at once carry out my stipulation with Col. Baker, as above stated. Yours truly

To William B. Preston

Hon: W. B. Preston: Springfield, Ills.
Dear Sir: April 20. 1849.

No member of the cabinet knows so well as yourself, the

great anxiety I felt for Gen: Taylor's election, and consequently none could so well appreciate my anxiety for the
success of his administration. Therefore I address you. It is
seen here that the government advertising, or a great part of
it, is given to the Democratic papers. This gives offence to
the Whig papers; and, if persisted in, will leave the administration without any newspaper support whatever. It causes,
or will cause, the Whig editors to fall off, while the Democratic ones will not be brought in by it. I suppose Gen: Taylor, because both of his declarations, and his inclination, will
not go the doctrine of removals very strongly; and hence the
greater reason, when an office or a job is not already in democratic hands, that it should be given to a Whig. Even at
this, full half the government patronage will still be in the
hands of our opponents at the end of four years; and if still
less than this is done for our friends, I think they will have
just cause to complain, and I verily believe the administration can not be sustained. The enclosed paragraph is from
the leading Whig paper in this state. I think it is injudicious,
and should not have appeared; still there is no keeping men
silent when they feel they are wronged by their friends. As
the subject of this paragraph pertains to the War Department, I would have written Mr. Crawford, but that it might
have appeared obtrusive, I having no personal acquaintance
with him. I am sure *you* will not be offended. Your Obt.
Servt.

To Josiah M. Lucas

J. M. Lucas, Esq   Springfield Ills. April 25, 1849.
    Dear Sir: Your letter of the 15th is just received. Like you,
I fear the Land Office is not going as it should; but I know
nothing I can do. In my letter written three days ago, I told
you the Department understands my wishes. As to Butterfield, he is my personal friend, and is qualified to do the
duties of the office; but of the quite one hundred Illinoisians,
equally well qualified, I do not know one with less claims to
it. In the first place, what you say about Lisle Smith, is the
first intimation I have had of any one man in Illinois de-

siring Butterfield to have any office. Now, I think if any
thing be given the state, it should be so given as to gratify
our friends, and to stimulate them to future exertions. As to
Mr. Clay having recommended him, that is *"quid pro quo."*
He fought for Mr. Clay against Gen Taylor to the bitter end
as I understand; and I do not believe I misunderstand. Lisle
Smith too, was a Clay delegate at Philadelphia; and against
my most earnest entreaties, took the lead in filling two vacancies, from my own district with Clay men. It will now
mortify me deeply if Gen. Taylors administration shall trample all my wishes in the dust merely to gratify these men.
Yours as ever

To William B. Preston

Hon: W. B. Preston: Springfield, Ills.
Dear Sir: May 16. 1849
    It is a delicate matter to oppose the wishes of a friend;
and consequently I address you on the subject I now do,
with no little hesitation. Last night I received letters from
different persons at Washington assuring me it was not improbable that Justin Butterfield, of Chicago, Ills, would be
appointed Commissioner of the Genl. Land-Office. It was to
avert this very thing, that I called on you at your rooms one
sunday evening shortly after you were installed, and be-
sought you that, so far as in your power, no man from Illinois should be appointed to any high office, without my
being at least heard on the question. You were kind enough
to say you thought my request a reasonable one. Mr. Butterfield is my friend, is well qualified, and, I suppose, would be
faithful in the office. So far, good. But now for the objections. In 1840 we fought a fierce and laborious battle in
Illinois, many of us spending almost the entire year in the
contest. The general victory came, and with it, the appointment of a set of drones, including this same Butterfield, who
had never spent a dollar or lifted a finger in the fight. The
place he got was that of District Attorney. The defection of
Tyler came, and then B. played off and on, and kept the

office till after Polk's election. Again, winter and spring before the last, when you and I were almost sweating blood to
have Genl. Taylor nominated, this same man was ridiculing
the idea, and going for Mr. Clay; and when Gen: T. was
nominated, if he went out of the city of Chicago to aid in
his election, it is more than I ever heard, or believe. Yet,
when the election is secured, by other men's labor, and even
against his effort, why, he is the first man on hand for the
best office that our state lays any claim to. Shall this thing
be? Our whigs will throw down their arms, and fight no
more, if the fruit of their labor is thus disposed of. If there
is one man in this state who desires B's appointment to any
thing, I declare I have not heard of him. What influence op-
perates for him, I can not conceive. Your position makes it a
matter of peculiar interest to you, that the administration
shall be successful; and be assured, nothing can more endanger it, than making appointments through old-hawker foreign influences, which offend, rather than gratify, the people
immediately interested in the offices.

   Can you not find time to write me, even half as long a
letter as this? I shall be much gratified if you will. Your Obt.
Servt.

To Duff Green

Dear General: Springfield, Ills. May 18. 1849
   I learn from Washington that a man by the name of Butterfield will probably be appointed Commissioner of the General
Land-Office. This ought not to be. That is about the only
crumb of patronage which Illinois expects; and I am sure the
mass of Gen: Taylor's friends here, would quite as lief see it
go East of the Alleghanies, or West of the Rocky mountains,
as into that man's hands. They are already sore on the subject
of his getting office. In the great contest of /40 he was not
seen or heard of; but when the victory came, three or four old
drones, including him, got all the valuable offices, through
what influence no one has yet been able to tell. I believe the
only time he has been very active, was last spring a year, in
opposition to Gen: Taylor's nomination.

Now can not you get the ear of Gen: Taylor? Ewing is for B; and therefore he must be avoided. Preston I think will favor you. Mr. Edwards has written me offering to decline, but I advised him not to do so. Some kind friends think I ought to be an applicant; but I am for Mr. Edwards. Try to defeat B; and in doing so, use Mr. Edwards, J.L.D. Morrison, or myself, whichever you can to best advantage. Write me, and let this be confidential. Yours truly

To Joseph Gillespie

Dear Gillespie: Springfield, Ills. May 19. 1849

Butterfield will be Commissioner of the Genl. Land Office, unless prevented by strong and speedy efforts. Ewing is for him; and he is only not appointed yet because Old Zach hangs fire. I have reliable information of this. Now, if you agree with me, that his appointment would *dissatisfy*, rather than gratify the whigs of this state; that it would slacken their energies in future contests, that his appointment in /41 is an old sore with them which they will not patiently have re-opened—in a word, that his appointment now would be a fatal blunder to the administration, and our political ruin here in Ills—write Mr. Crittenden to that effect. He can control the matter. Were you to write Ewing, I fear the President would never hear of your letter. This may be mere suspicion. You might write directly to Old Zach; you will be the judge of the propriety of that. Not a moment's time is to be lost. Let this be confidential, except with Mr. Edwards & a few others, whom you know I would trust just as I do you. Yours as ever

To Elisha Embree

CONFIDENTIAL

Hon E. Embree   Springfield, Ills.
Dear Sir: May 25– 1849

I am about to ask a favor of you—one which, I hope will not cost you much. I understand the General Land Office is about to be given to Illinois; and that Mr. Ewing desires Justin Butterfield, of Chicago, to be the man. I give you my word, the appointment of Mr. B. will be an egregious political blunder. It will give offence to the whole whig party here, and be worse than a dead loss to the administration, of so much of it's patronage. Now, if you can conscientiously do so, I wish you to write General Taylor at once, saying that either *I, or the man I recommend,* should, in your opinion, be appointed to that office, if any one from Illinois shall be. I restrict my request to Ills. because you may have a man of your own, in your own state; and I do not ask to interfere with that. Your friend as ever

To Josiah B. Herrick

Dr. J. B. Herrick   Springfield,
Dear Sir: June 3. 1849
   It is now certain that either Mr. Butterfield or I will be Commissioner of the General Land-Office. If you are willing to give me the preference, please write me to that effect, at Washington, whither I am going. There is not a moment of time to be lost. Yours truly

To Thomas Ewing

Hon. Secretary of the Interior   Washington, June 22. 1849
Dear Sir,
   This morning, on my mentioning to you, I had an intimation my old friend, Cyrus Edwards, had placed on file something ill-natured against me, you had the kindness, as I remember, to volunteer the remark, in my defense, that but for my devotion to Mr. Edwards, manifested by withholding my own name for his benefit, I would now, in your opinion, be the Commissioner. If, in this, my memory serves me correctly, you will greatly oblige me, by saying as much on paper, with anything additional to the same point, which may occur to you. It will enable me, I think, to remove from the mind of

one of my most highly valued friends, a bad impression, which is now the only thing much painful to me personally, in this whole matter.   Your Obt Servt

To Joseph Gillespie

Dear Gillespie: Springfield, Ills, July 13th. 1849
Your letter of the 9th. of June in which you manifest some apprehension that your writing directly to Gen: Taylor had been regarded as improper, was received by me at Washington. I feel I owe you an apology for not answering it sooner. You committed no error in writing directly to the President; half the letters, or nearly so, on the subject of appointments, are so addressed. The President assorts them, and sends them to the Departments to which they belong respectively. Whether he reads them first, or only so far as to ascertain what subject they are on, I have not learned.

Mr. Edwards is angry with me; and, in which, he is wronging me very much. He wrote a letter against me & in favor of Butterfield, which was filed in the Department. Ever since I discovered this, I have had a conflict of feeling, whether to write him or not; and, so far, I have remained silent. If he knew of your letters to me of the 9th. of May, and to the President of the 23rd. I suspect he would be angry with you too. Both those letters would help defend me with him; but I will not hazzard your interest by letting him know of them. To avoid that, I write you a separate letter which I wish you would show him when it may be convenient.

You will please accept my sincere thanks for the very flattering terms in which you speak of me in your letter to the President. I withdrew the papers on file in my behalf, by which means your letter is now in my possession. Yours as ever

To Joseph Gillespie

Dear Gillespie: Springfield, July 13. 1849.
Mr. Edwards is unquestionably offended with me, in connection with the matter of the General Land-Office. He wrote a letter against me, which was filed at the Department. The

better part of one's life consists of his friendships; and, of these, mine with Mr. Edwards was one of the most cherished. I have not been false to it. At a word, I could have had the office any time before the Department was committed to Mr. Butterfield—at least Mr. Ewing & the President say as much. That word I forebore to speak, partly for other reasons, but chiefly for Mr. Edwards' sake. Losing the office that he might gain it, I was always for; but to lose his *friendship* by the effort for him, would oppress me very much, were I not sustained by the utmost consciousness of rectitude. I first determined to be an applicant, unconditionally, on the 2nd. of June; and I did so then upon being informed by a Telegraphic despach, that the question was narrowed down to Mr. B. and myself, and that the Cabinet had postponed the appointment three weeks for my benefit. Not doubting, that Mr. Edwards was wholly out of the question, I nevertheless would not then have become an applicant, had I supposed he would thereby be brought to suspect me of treachery to him. Two or three days afterwards a conversation with Levi Davis convinced me Mr. E. was dissatisfied; but I was then too far in to get out. His own letter, written on the 25th. of April, after I had fully informed him of all that had passed up to within a few days of that time, gave assurance I had that entire confidence from him, which I felt my uniform and strong friendship for him entitled me to. Among other things it says "whatever course your judgment may dictate as proper to be pursued, shall never be excepted to by me." I also had had a letter from Washington, saying Chambers of the Republican had brought a rumor then that, Mr. E. had declined in my favor, which rumor I judged came from Mr. E himself, as I had not then breathed of his letter, to any living creature.

In saying I had never before the 2nd. of June determined to be an applicant, *unconditionally*, I mean to admit that before then, I had said substantially I would take the office rather than it should be lost to the state, or given to one in the state whom the whigs did not want; but I aver that in every instance in which I spoke of myself, I intended to keep, and now believe I did keep, Mr. E. ahead of myself. Mr. Edwards' first suspicion was that I had allowed Baker to overreach me, as his friend, in behalf of Don: Morrison. I knew

this was a mistake; and the result has proved it. I understand
his view now is, that if I had gone to open war with Baker I
could have ridden him down, and had the thing all my own
way. I believe no such thing. With Baker & some strong men
from the Military tract, & elsewhere for Morrison; and we
and some strong men from the Wabash & elsewhere for Mr.
E, it was not possible for either to succeed. I *believed* this in
March, and I *know* it now. The only thing which gave either
any chance was the very thing Baker & I proposed—an adjustment with themselves.

You may wish to know how Butterfield finally beat me. I
can not tell you particulars now, but will, when I see you. In
the mean time let it be understood I am not greatly dissatisfied. I wish the office had been so bestowed as to encourage
our friends in future contests, and I regret exceedingly Mr.
Edwards' feelings towards me. These two things away, I
should have no regrets—at least I think I would not.

Write me soon. Your friend, as ever

To John M. Clayton

Hon. J. M. Clayton.   Springfield, Ill., July 28, 1849.

Dear Sir: It is with some hesitation I presume to address
this letter—and yet I wish not only you, but the whole cabinet, and the President too, would consider the subject matter
of it. My being among the People while you and they are not,
will excuse the apparent presumption. It is understood that
the President at first adopted, as a general rule, to throw the
responsibility of the appointments upon the respective Departments; and that such rule is adhered to and practised
upon. This course I at first thought proper; and, of course, I
am not now complaining of it. Still I am disappointed with
the effect of it on the public mind. It is fixing for the President the unjust and ruinous character of being a mere man of
straw. This must be arrested, or it will damn us all inevitably.
It is said Gen. Taylor and his officers held a council of war, at
Palo Alto (I believe); and that he then fought the battle
against unanimous opinion of those officers. This fact (no
matter whether rightfully or wrongfully) gives him more

popularity than ten thousand submissions, however really wise and magnanimous those submissions may be.

The appointments need be no better than they have been, but the public must be brought to understand, that they are the *President's* appointments. He must occasionally say, or seem to say, "by the Eternal," "I take the responsibility." Those phrases were the "Samson's locks" of Gen. Jackson, and we dare not disregard the lessons of experience. Your Ob't Sev't

To John M. Clayton

Hon: J. M. Clayton,   Springfield, Illinois,
Secretary of State.   Augt. 21st. 1849

Dear Sir: Your letter of the 10th. Inst., notifying me of my appointment as Secretary of the Teritory of Oregon, and accompanied by a Commission, has been duly received. I respectfully decline the office.

I shall be greatly obliged if the place be offered to Simeon Francis, of this place. He will accept it, is capable, and would be faithful in the discharge of it's duties. He is the principal editor of the oldest, and what I think may be fairly called, the leading Whig paper of the state,—the Illinois Journal. His good business habits are proved by the facts, that the paper has existed eighteen years, all the time weekly, and part of it, tri-weekly, and daily, and has not failed to issue regularly in a single instance.

Some time in May last, I think, Mr. Francis addressed a letter to Mr. Ewing, which, I was informed while at Washington in June, had been seen by the cabinet, and very highly approved. You possibly may remember it. He has, for a long time desired to go to Oregon; and I think his appointment would give general satisfaction   Your Obt. Servt.

To John M. Clayton

Hon J. M. Clayton.   Springfield, Illinois,
Secretary of State   Sept. 16– 1849

Dear Sir: I send you a paper recommending Simeon Francis for the appointment of Secretary for the Oregon Teritory.

I know I have no right to claim the disposal of the office; but I do think, under all the circumstances, that he ought to receive the appointment. If a long course of uniform and efficient action as a whig editor; if an honesty unimpeached, and qualifications undisputed; if the fact that he has advanced to the meridian of life without ever before asking for an office, be considerations of importance with the Administration, I can not but feel that the appointment, while it will do him justice, will also do honor to the Administration. Your Obt. Servt.

To John Addison

Springfield, Illinois,
John Addison, Esq.   September 27, 1849.
My dear Sir: Your letter is received. I can not but be grateful to you and all other friends who have interested themselves in having the governorship of Oregon offered to me; but on as much reflection as I have had time to give the subject, I cannot consent to accept it. I have an ever abiding wish to serve you; but as to the secretaryship, I have already recommended our friend Simeon Francis, of the "Journal." Please present my respects to G.T.M. Davis generally, and my thanks especially for his kindness in the Oregon matter. Yours as ever,

To Thomas Ewing

Hon Thomas Ewing   Springfield Sept. 27th. 1849.
I respectfully decline Governorship of Oregon; I am still anxious that, Simeon Frances shall be secretary of that Territory

To Thomas Ewing

Hon. T. Ewing Secretary etc.   Springfield, Ills
Dear Sir: Oct. 13, 1849
I have just received a letter from a friend at Washington, from which the following is an extract. "Again —— told me

that there was a clique in Springfield determined to prevent Butterfield's confirmation; and, that Lincoln would give a thousand dollars to have it done, but, says ——, one of the company who meets with them, keeps Butterfield *weekly* posted etc."

This annoys me a little. I am unwilling for the Administration to believe or suspect such a thing. I write this therefore, to assure you that I am neither privy to, nor cognizant of, any such clique; and that I most potently disbelieve in the existence of any such. I opposed the appointment of Mr. B. because I believed it would be a matter of discouragement to our active, working friends here, and I opposed it for no other reason. I never did, in any true sense, want the office myself. Since Mr. B's appointment, having no personal ill-will to him, and believing it to be for the interest of the Administration and of our cause generally, I have constantly desired his confirmation. I have seen in the Newspapers but one matter of complaint against him, and in that (the matter of the Land Warrants) I believe he is right. What I am here saying depends on my word alone; but I think Mr. B. himself, if appealed to, will not say he disbelieves me. Your Obt. Servt.

To George W. Rives

G. W. Rives, Esq   Springfield,
Dear Sir: Decr. 15– 1849

On my return from Kentucky, I found your letter of the 7th. of November, and have delayed answering it till now, for the reason I now briefly state. From the beginning of our acquaintance I had felt the greatest kindness for you, and had supposed it was reciprocated on your part. Last summer, under circumstances which I mentioned to you, I was painfully constrained to withhold a recommendation which you desired; and shortly afterwards I learned, in such way as to believe it, that you were indulging open abuse of me. Of course my feelings were wounded. On receiving your last letter, the question occurred whether you were attempting to *use* me, at

the same time you would *injure* me, or whether you might
not have been misrepresented to me. If the former, I ought
not to answer you; if the latter I ought, and so I have remained in suspense. I now enclose you a letter which you may
use if you think fit. Yours &c.

To John D. Johnston

Dear Brother   Springfield, Feb. 23 1850
    Your letter about a mail contract was received yesterday. I
have made out a bid for you at $120, guaranteed it myself, got
our PM here to certify it, and sent it on. Your former letter,
concerning some man's claim for a pension was also received.
I had the claim examined by those who are practised in such
matters, & they decide he can not get a pension.
    As you make no mention of it, I suppose you had not
learned that we lost our little boy. He was sick fiftytwo days
& died the morning of the first day of this month. It was not
our *first*, but our second child. We miss him very much. Your
Brother in haste

To the Editors of the Illinois Journal

Editors of the Illinois Journal: Springfield,
Gentlemen—   June 5, 1850.
    An article in the Tazewell Mirror in which my name is
prominently used, makes me fear that my position, with reference to the next Congressional election in this District, is
misunderstood, and that such misunderstanding may work injury to the cause of our friends. I therefore take occasion to
say that I neither seek, expect, or desire a nomination for a
seat in the next Congress; that I prefer my name should not
be brought forward in that connection; and that I would now
peremptorily forbid the use of it, could I feel entirely at liberty to do so. I will add, that in my opinion, the whigs of the
district have several other men, any one of whom they *can*
elect, and that too quite as *easily* as they could elect me. I

therefore shall be obliged, if any such as may entertain a preference for me, will, at once turn their attention to making a choice from others. Let a Convention be held at a suitable time, and in good feeling, make a nomination; and I venture the prediction we will show the District once more *right side up*. Your obd't servant,

Notes on the Practice of Law

I am not an accomplished lawyer. I find quite as much material for a lecture, in those points wherein I have failed, as in those wherein I have been moderately successful.

The leading rule for the lawyer, as for the man, of every calling, is *diligence*. Leave nothing for to-morrow, which can be done to-day. Never let your correspondence fall behind. Whatever piece of business you have in hand, before stopping, do all the labor pertaining to it which can *then* be done. When you bring a common-law suit, if you have the facts for doing so, write the declaration at once. If a law point be involved, examine the books, and note the authority you rely on, upon the declaration itself, where you are sure to find it when wanted. The same of defences and pleas. In business not likely to be litigated—ordinary collection cases, foreclosures, partitions, and the like,—make all examinations of titles, and note them, and even draft orders and decrees in advance. This course has a tripple advantage; it avoids omissions and neglect, *saves* your labor, when once done; performs the labor out of court when you *have* leisure, rather than in court, when you have not. Extemporaneous speaking should be practiced and cultivated. It is the lawyer's avenue to the public. However able and faithful he may be in other respects, people are slow to bring him business, if he cannot make a speech. And yet there is not a more fatal error to young lawyers, than relying too much on speech-making. If any one, upon his rare powers of speaking, shall claim exemption from the drudgery of the law, his case is a failure in advance.

Discourage litigation. Persuade your neighbors to compromise whenever you can. Point out to them how the *nominal*

winner is often a *real* loser—in fees, and expenses, and waste
of time. As a peace-maker the lawyer has a superior opertunity of being a good man. There will still be business enough.

Never stir up litigation. A worse man can scarcely be found
than one who does this. Who can be more nearly a fiend than
he who habitually overhauls the Register of deeds, in search
of defects in titles, whereon to stir up strife, and put money in
his pocket? A moral tone ought to be infused into the profession, which should drive such men out of it.

The matter of fees is important far beyond the mere question of bread and butter involved. Properly attended to fuller
justice is done to both lawyer and client. An exorbitant fee
should never be claimed. As a general rule, never take your
whole fee in advance, nor any more than a small retainer.
When fully paid before hand, you are more than a common
mortal if you can feel the same interest in the case, as if something was still in prospect for you, as well as for your client.
And when you lack interest in the case, the job will very likely
lack skill and diligence in the performance. Settle the *amount*
of fee, and take a note in advance. Then you will feel that you
are working for something, and you are sure to do your work
faithfully and well. Never sell a fee-note—at least, not before
the consideration service is performed. It leads to negligence
and dishonesty—negligence, by losing interest in the case,
and dishonesty in refusing to refund, when you have allowed
the consideration to fail.

There is a vague popular belief that lawyers are necessarily
dishonest. I say *vague*, because when we consider to what extent *confidence*, and *honors* are reposed in, and conferred upon
lawyers by the people, it appears improbable that their *impression* of dishonesty is very distinct and vivid. Yet the impression, is common—almost universal. Let no young man,
choosing the law for a calling, for a moment yield to this
popular belief. Resolve to be honest at all events; and if, in
your own judgment, you can not be an honest lawyer, resolve
to be honest without being a lawyer. Choose some other occupation, rather than one in the choosing of which you do, in
advance, consent to be a knave.

Eulogy on Zachary Taylor at Chicago, Illinois

GENERAL ZACHARY TAYLOR, the eleventh elected President of the United States, is dead. He was born Nov. 2nd, 1784, in Orange county, Virginia; and died July the 9th 1850, in the sixty-sixth year of his age, at the White House in Washington City. He was the second son of Richard Taylor, a Colonel in the army of the revolution. His youth was passed among the pioneers of Kentucky, whither his parents emigrated soon after his birth; and where his taste for military life, probably inherited, was greatly stimulated. Near the commencement of our last war with Great Britain, he was appointed by President Jefferson, a lieutenant in the 7th regiment of Infantry. During the war, he served under Gen. Harrison in his North Western campaign against the Indians; and, having been promoted to a captaincy, was intrusted with the defence of Fort Harrison, with fifty men, half of them unfit for duty. A strong party of Indians, under the Prophet, brother of Tecumseh, made a midnight attack on the Fort; but Taylor, though weak in his force, and without preparation, was resolute, and on the alert; and, after a battle, which lasted till after daylight, completely repulsed them. Soon after, he took a prominent part in the expedition under Major Gen. Hopkins against the Prophet's town; and, on his return, found a letter from President Madison, who had succeeded Mr. Jefferson, conferring on him a major's brevet for his gallant defence of Fort Harrison.

After the close of the British war, he remained in the frontier service of the West, till 1818. He was then transferred to the Southern frontier, where he remained, most of the time in active service till 1826. In 1819, and during his service in the South, he was promoted to the rank of lieutenant colonel. In 1826 he was again sent to the North West, where he continued until 1836. In 1832, he was promoted to the rank of a colonel. In 1836 he was ordered to the South to engage in what is well known as the Florida War. In the autumn of 1837, he fought and conquered in the memorable battle of Okeechobee, one of the most desperate struggles known to the annals of Indian warfare. For this, he was honored with the rank of Brigadier

General; and, in 1838 was appointed to succeed Gen. Jessup in command of the forces in Florida. In 1841 he was ordered to Fort Gibson to take command of the Second Military department of the United States; and in September, 1844, was directed to hold the troops between the Red River and the Sabine in readiness to march as might be indicated by the Charge of the United States, near Texas. In 1845 his forces were concentrated at Corpus Christi.

In obedience to orders, in March 1846, he planted his troops on the Rio Grande opposite Mattamoras. Soon after this, and near this place, a small detachment of Gen. Taylor's forces, under Captain Thornton, was cut to pieces by a party of Mexicans. Open hostilities being thus commenced, and Gen. Taylor being constantly menaced by Mexican forces vastly superior to his own, in numbers, his position became exceedingly critical. Having erected a fort, he might defend himself against great odds while he could remain within it; but his provisions had failed, and there was no supply nearer than Point Isabel, between which and the new fort, the country was open to, and full of, armed Mexicans. His resolution was at once taken. He garrisoned Fort Brown, (the new fort) with a force of about four hundred; and, putting himself at the head of the main body of his troops, marched forthwith for Point Isabel. He met no resistance on his march. Having obtained his supplies, he began his return march, to the relief of Fort Brown, which he at first knew, would be, and then knew had been besieged by the enemy, immediately upon his leaving it. On the first or second day of this return march, the Mexican General, Arista, met General Taylor in front, and offered battle. The Mexicans numbered six or eight thousand, opposed to whom were about two thousand Americans. The moment was a trying one. Comparatively, Taylor's forces were but a handful; and few, of either officers or men, had ever been under fire. A brief council was held; and the result was, the battle commenced. The issue of that contest all remember—remember with mingled sensations of pride and sorrow, that then, American valor and powers triumphed, and then the gallant and accomplished, and noble Ringgold fell.

The Americans passed the night on the field. The General

knew the enemy was still in his fort; and the question rose upon him, whether to advance or retreat. A council was again held; and, it is said, the General overruled the majority, and resolved to advance. Accordingly in the morning, he moved rapidly forward. At about four or five miles from Fort Brown he again met the enemy in force, who had selected his position, and made some hasty fortification. Again the battle commenced, and raged till toward nightfall, when the Mexicans were entirely routed, and the General with his fatigued and bleeding, and reduced battalions marched into Fort Brown. There was a joyous meeting. A brief hour before, whether all *within* the fort had perished, all *without* feared, but none could tell—while the incessant roar of artillery, wrought those *within* to the highest pitch of apprehension, that their brethren *without* were being massacred to the last man. And now the din of battle nears the fort and sweeps obliquely by; a gleam of hope flies through the half imprisoned few; they fly to the wall; every eye is strained—it is—it is—the stars and stripes are still aloft! Anon the anxious brethren meet; and while hand strikes hand, the heavens are rent with a loud, long, glorious, gushing cry of victory! victory!! victory!!!

Soon after these two battles, Gen. Taylor was breveted a Major General in the U.S. Army.

In the mean time, war having been declared to exist between the United States and Mexico, provisions were made to reinforce Gen. Taylor; and he was ordered to march into the interior of Mexico. He next marched upon Monterey, arriving there on the 19th of September. He commenced an assault upon the city, on the 21st, and on the 23d was about carrying it at the point of the bayonet, when Gen. Ampudia capitulated. Taylor's forces consisted of 425 officers, and 9,220 men. His artillery consisted of one 10 inch mortar, two 24 pound Howitzers, and four light field batteries of four guns—the mortar being the only piece serviceable for the siege. The Mexican works were armed with forty-two pieces of cannon, and manned with a force of at least 7000 troops of the line, and from 2000 to 3000 irregulars.

Next we find him advancing farther into the interior of Mexico, at the head of 5,400 men, not more than 600 being regular troops.

At Agua Nueva he received intelligence that Santa Anna, the greatest military chieftain of Mexico, was advancing after him; and he fell back to Buena Vista, a strong position a few miles in advance of Saltillo. On the 22nd of Feb., 1847, the battle, now called the battle of Buena Vista, was commenced by Santa Anna at the head of 20,000 well appointed soldiers. This was Gen. Taylor's great battle. The particulars of it are familiar to all. It continued through the 23d; and although Gen. Taylor's defeat seemed to be inevitable, yet he succeeded by skill, and by the courage and devotion of his officers and men, in repulsing the overwhelming forces of the enemy, and throwing them back into the desert. This was the battle of the chiefest interest fought during the Mexican war. At the time it was fought, and for some weeks after, Gen. Taylor's communication with the United States was cut off; and the road was in possession of parties of the enemy. For many days after full intelligence of it, should have been in all parts of this country, nothing certain, concerning it, was known, while vague and painful rumors were afloat, that a great battle had been fought, and that Gen. Taylor, and his whole force had been annihilated.

At length the truth came, with its thrilling details of victory and blood—of glory and grief. A bright and glowing page was added to our Nation's history; but then too, in eternal silence, lay Clay, and Mc'Kee, and Yell, and Lincoln, and our own beloved Hardin.

This also was Gen. Taylor's *last* battle. He remained in active service in Mexico, till the autumn of the same year, when he returned to the United States.

Passing in review, Gen. Taylor's military history, some striking peculiarities will appear. No one of the six battles which he fought, excepting perhaps, that of Monterey, presented a field, which would have been selected by an ambitious captain upon which to gather laurels. So far as fame was concerned, the prospect—the promise in advance, was, "you may lose, but you can not win." Yet Taylor, in his blunt business-like view of things, seems never to have thought of this.

It did not happen to Gen. Taylor once in his life, to fight a battle on equal terms, or on terms advantageous to himself—

and yet he was never beaten, and never retreated. In *all*, the odds was greatly against him; in each, defeat seemed inevitable; and yet *in all*, he triumphed. Wherever he has led, while the battle still raged, the issue was painfully doubtful; yet in *each* and *all*, when the din had ceased, and the smoke had blown away, our country's flag was still seen, fluttering in the breeze.

Gen. Taylor's battles were not distinguished for brilliant military manoeuvers; but in all, he seems rather to have conquered by the exercise of a sober and steady judgment, coupled with a dogged incapacity to understand that defeat was possible. His rarest military trait, was a combination of negatives—absence of *excitement* and absence of *fear*. He could not be *flurried*, and he could not be *scared*.

In connection with Gen. Taylor's military character, may be mentioned his relations with his brother officers, and his soldiers. Terrible as he was to his country's enemies, no man was so little disposed to have difficulty with his friends. During the period of his life, *duelling* was a practice not quite uncommon among gentlemen in the peaceful avocations of life, and still more common, among the officers of the Army and Navy. Yet, so far as I can learn, a *duel* with Gen. Taylor, has never been talked of.

He was alike averse to *sudden*, and to *startling* quarrels; and he pursued no man with *revenge*. A notable, and a noble instance of this, is found in his conduct to the gallant and now lamented Gen. Worth. A short while before the battles of the 8th and 9th of May, some questions of precedence arose between Worth, (then a colonel) and some other officer, which question it seems Gen. Taylor's duty to decide. He decided against Worth. Worth was greatly offended, left the Army, came to the United States, and tendered his resignation to the authorities at Washington. It is said, that in his passionate feeling, he hesitated not to speak harshly and disparagingly of Gen. Taylor. He was an officer of the highest character; and his word, on military subjects, and about military men, could not, with the country, pass for nothing. In this absence from the army of Col. Worth, the unexpected turn of things brought on the battles of the 8th and 9th. He was deeply mortified—in almost absolute desperation—at having lost the opportunity of being present, and taking part in those battles. The laurels won by his previous service, in his own eyes, seemed withering away. The Government, both *wisely* and *generously*, I think, declined accepting his resignation; and he returned to Gen. Taylor. Then came Gen. Taylor's *opportunity* for revenge. The battle of Monterey was approaching, and even at hand. Taylor *could* if he *would*, so place Worth in that battle, that his name would scarcely be noticed in the report. But no. He felt it was due to the service, to assign the real post of honor to some one of the best officers; he knew Worth was one of the best, and he felt that it was *generous* to allow him, then and there, to retrieve his secret loss. Accordingly he assigned to Col. Worth in that assault, what was *par excellence*, the post of honor; and, the duties of which, he executed so well, and so brilliantly, as to eclipse, in that battle, even Gen. Taylor himself.

As to Gen. Taylor's relations with his soldiers, details would be endless. It is perhaps enough to say—and it is far from the *least* of his honors that we can *truly* say—that of the many who served with him through the long course of forty years, all testify to the uniform kindness, and his constant care for, and hearty sympathy with, their every want and every suffering; while none can be found to declare, that he was ever a tyrant anywhere, in anything.

Going back a little in point of time, it is proper to say that so soon as the news of the battles of the 8th and 9th of May 1846, had fairly reached the United States, Gen. Taylor began to be named for the next Presidency, by letter writers, newspapers, public meetings and conventions in various parts of the country.

These nominations were generally put forth as being of a no-party character. Up to this time I think it highly probable—nay, almost certain, that Gen. Taylor had never thought of the Presidency in connection with himself. And there is reason for believing that the first intelligence of these nominations rather *amused* than *seriously* interested him. Yet I should be insincere, were I not to confess, that in my opinion, the repeated, and steady manifestations in his favor, *did* beget in his mind a laudable ambition to reach the high distinction of the Presidential chair.

As the time for the Presidential canvass approached, it was seen that general nominations, combining anything near the number of votes necessary to an election, could not be made without some pretty strong and decided reference to party politics. Accordingly, in the month of May, 1848, the great Democratic party nominated as their candidate, an able and distinguished member of their own party, on strictly party grounds. Almost immediately following this, the Whig party, in general convention, nominated Gen. Taylor as their candidate. The election came off in the November following; and though there was also a third candidate, the two former only, received any vote in the electoral college. Gen. Taylor, having the majority of them was duly elected; and he entered on the duties of that high and responsible office, March 5th, 1849. The incidents of his administration up to the time of his death, are too familiar and too fresh to require any direct repetition.

The Presidency, even to the most experienced politicians, is no bed of roses; and Gen. Taylor like others, found thorns within it. No human being can fill that station and escape censure. Still I hope and believe when Gen. Taylor's official conduct shall come to be viewed in the calm light of history, he will be found to have *deserved* as little as any who have succeeded him.

Upon the death of Gen. Taylor, as it would in the case of the death of any President, we are naturally led to consider what will be its effect, politically, upon the country. I will not pretend to believe that all the wisdom, or all the patriotism of the country, died with Gen. Taylor. But we know that *wisdom* and *patriotism*, in a public office, under institutions like ours, are wholly inefficient and worthless, unless they are sustained by the confidence and devotion of the people. And I confess my apprehensions, that in the death of the late President, we have lost a degree of that confidence and devotion, which will not soon again pertain to any successor. Between public measures regarded as antagonistic, there is often less real difference in its bearing on the public weal, than there is between the dispute being *kept up*, or being *settled* either way. I fear the one *great* question of the day, is not now so likely to be partially acquiesced in by the different sections of the Union, as it would have been, could Gen. Taylor have been spared to us. Yet, under all circumstances, trusting to our Maker, and through his wisdom and beneficence, to the great body of our people, we will not despair, nor despond.

In Gen. Taylor's general public relation to his country, what will strongly impress a close observer, was his unostentatious, self-sacrificing, long enduring devotion to his *duty*. He indulged in no recreations, he visited no public places, seeking applause; but quietly, as the earth in its orbit, he was always at his post. Along our whole Indian frontier, thro' summer and winter, in sunshine and storm, like a sleepless sentinel, *he* has *watched*, while *we* have *slept* for forty long years. How well might the dying hero say at last, "I have done my duty, I am ready to go."

Nor can I help thinking that the American people, in electing Gen. Taylor to the presidency, thereby showing their high appreciation, of his sterling, but unobtrusive qualities, did their *country* a service, and *themselves* an imperishable honor. It is *much* for the young to know, that treading the hard path of duty, as he trod it, *will* be noticed, and *will* lead to high places.

But he is gone. The conqueror at last is conquered. The fruits of his labor, his name, his memory and example, are all that is left us—his example, verifying the great truth, that "he that humbleth himself, shall be exalted" teaching, that to serve one's country with a singleness of purpose, gives assurance of that country's gratitude, secures its best honors, and makes "a dying bed, soft as downy pillows are."

The death of the late President may not be without its use, in reminding us, that *we*, too, must die. Death, abstractly considered, is the same with the high as with the low; but practically, we are not so much aroused to the contemplation of our own mortal natures, by the fall of *many* undistinguished, as that of *one* great, and well known, name. By the latter, we are forced to muse, and ponder, sadly.

"Oh, why should the spirit of mortal be proud"

So the multitude goes, like the flower or the weed,
That withers away to let others succeed;
So the multitude comes, even those we behold,
To repeat every tale that has often been told.

For we are the same, our fathers have been,
We see the same sights our fathers have seen;
We drink the same streams and see the same sun
And run the same course our fathers have run.

They loved; but the story *we* cannot unfold;
They scorned, but the heart of the haughty is cold;
They grieved, but no wail from their slumbers will come,
They joyed, but the tongue of their gladness is dumb.

They died! Aye, they died; we things that are now;
That work on the turf that lies on their brow,
And make in their dwellings a transient abode,
Meet the things that they met on their pilgrimage road.

Yea! hope and despondency, pleasure and pain,
Are mingled together in sun-shine and rain;
And the smile and the tear, and the song and the dirge,
Still follow each other, like surge upon surge.

'Tis the wink of an eye, 'tis the draught of a breath,
From the blossoms of health, to the paleness of death.
From the gilded saloon, to the bier and the shroud.
Oh, why should the spirit of mortal be proud!

July 25, 1850

To John D. Johnston

Dear Brother: Springfield, Jany. 12. 1851—
    On the day before yesterday I received a letter from Har-
riett, written at Greenup. She says she has just returned from
your house; and that Father is very low, and will hardly recover. She also says you have written me two letters; and that
although you do not expect me to come now, you wonder
that I do not write. I received both your letters, and although
I have not answered them, it is not because I have forgotten
them, or been uninterested about them—but because it appeared to me I could write nothing which could do any good.
You already know I desire that neither Father or Mother shall

be in want of any comfort either in health or sickness while they live; and I feel sure you have not failed to use my name, if necessary, to procure a doctor, or any thing else for Father in his present sickness. My business is such that I could hardly leave home now, if it were not, as it is, that my own wife is sick abed. (It is a case of baby-sickness, and I suppose is not dangerous.) I sincerely hope Father may yet recover his health; but at all events tell him to remember to call upon, and confide in, our great, and good, and merciful Maker; who will not turn away from him in any extremity. He notes the fall of a sparrow, and numbers the hairs of our heads; and He will not forget the dying man, who puts his trust in Him. Say to him that if we could meet now, it is doubtful whether it would not be more painful than pleasant; but that if it be his lot to go now, he will soon have a joyous meeting with many loved ones gone before; and where the rest of us, through the help of God, hope ere-long to join them.

Write me again when you receive this. Affectionately

To Andrew McCallen

Andrew McCallen.   Springfield, Ills.
Dear Sir: July. 4. 1851.
    I have news from Ottawa, that we *win* our Galatin & Saline county case. As the dutch Justice said, when he married folks "Now, vere ish my hundred tollars" Yours truly

To John D. Johnston

Dear Brother: Shelbyville, Novr. 4. 1851
    When I came into Charleston day-before yesterday I learned that you are anxious to sell the land where you live, and move to Missouri. I have been thinking of this ever since; and can not but think such a notion is utterly foolish. What can you do in Missouri, better than here? Is the land any richer? Can you there, any more than here, raise corn, & wheat & oats, without work? Will any body there, any more

than here, do your work for you? If you intend to go to work, there is no better place than right where you are; if you do not intend to go to work, you can not get along any where. Squirming & crawling about from place to place can do no good. You have raised no crop this year, and what you really want is to sell the land, get the money and spend it— part with the land you have, and my life upon it, you will never after, own a spot big enough to bury you in. Half you will get for the land, you spend in moving to Missouri, and the other half you will eat and drink, and wear out, & no foot of land will be bought. Now I feel it is my duty to have no hand in such a piece of foolery. I feel that it is so even on your own account; and particularly on *Mother's* account. The Eastern forty acres I intend to keep for Mother while she lives—if you *will not cultivate it*; it will rent for enough to support her—at least it will rent for something. Her Dower in the other two forties, she can let you have, and no thanks to me.

Now do not misunderstand this letter. I do not write it in any unkindness. I write it in order, if possible, to get you to *face* the truth—which truth is, you are destitute because you have *idled* away all your time. Your thousand pretences for not getting along better, are all non-sense—they deceive no body but yourself. *Go to work* is the only cure for your case.

A word for Mother:

Chapman tells me he wants you to go and live with him. If I were you I would try it awhile. If you get tired of it (as I think you will not) you can return to your own home. Chapman feels very kindly to you; and I have no doubt he will make your situation very pleasant. Sincerely your Son

To John D. Johnston

Dear Brother: Shelbyville, Novr. 9. 1851
    When I wrote you before I had not received your letter. I still think as I did; but if the land can be sold so that I get three hundred dollars to put to interest for mother, I will not object if she does not. But before I will make a deed, the

money must be had, or secured, beyond all doubt, at ten per cent.

As to Abram, I do not want him *on my own account*; but I understand he wants to live with me so that he can go to school, and get a fair start in the world, which I very much wish him to have. When I reach home, if I can make it convenient to take him, I will take him, provided there is no mistake between us as to the object and terms of my taking him. In haste As ever

To John D. Johnston

Dear Brother   Springfield, Novr. 25. 1851.

Your letter of the 22nd. is just received. Your proposal about selling the East forty acres of land is all that I want or could claim for *myself*; but I am not satisfied with it on *Mother's* account. I want her to have her living, and I feel that it is my duty, to some extent, to see that she is not wronged. She had a right of Dower (that is, the use of one third for life) in the other two forties; but, it seems, she has already let you take that, hook and line. She now has the use of the whole of the East forty, as long as she lives; and if it be sold, of course, she is intitled to the interest on *all* the money it brings, as long as she lives; but you propose to sell it for three hundred dollars, take one hundred away with you, and leave her two hundred, at 8 per cent, making her the *enormous* sum of 16 dollars a year. Now, if you are satisfied with treating her in that way, I am not. It is true, that you are to have that forty for two hundred dollars, *at* Mother's death; but you are not to have it *before*. I am confident that land can be made to produce for Mother, at least $30 a year, and I can not, to oblige any living person, consent that she shall be put on an allowance of sixteen dollars a year. Yours &c

Eulogy on Henry Clay at Springfield, Illinois

On the fourth day of July, 1776, the people of a few feeble and oppressed colonies of Great Britain, inhabiting a portion of the Atlantic coast of North America, publicly declared their national independence, and made their appeal to the justice of their cause, and to the God of battles, for the maintainance of that declaration. That people were few in numbers, and without resources, save only their own wise heads and stout hearts. Within the first year of that declared independence, and while its maintainance was yet problematical—while the bloody struggle between those resolute rebels, and their haughty would-be masters, was still waging, of undistinguished parents, and in an obscure district of one of those colonies, Henry Clay was born. The infant nation, and the infant child began the race of life together. For three quarters of a century they have travelled hand in hand. They have been companions ever. The nation has passed its perils, and is free, prosperous, and powerful. The child has reached his manhood, his middle age, his old age, and is dead. In all that has concerned the nation the man ever sympathised; and now the nation mourns for the man.

The day after his death, one of the public Journals, opposed to him politically, held the following pathetic and beautiful language, which I adopt, partly because such high and exclusive eulogy, originating with a political friend, might offend good taste, but chiefly, because I could not, in any language of my own, so well express my thoughts—

"Alas! who can realize that Henry Clay is dead! Who can realize that never again that majestic form shall rise in the council-chambers of his country to beat back the storms of anarchy which may threaten, or pour the oil of peace upon the troubled billows as they rage and menace around? Who can realize, that the workings of that mighty mind have ceased—that the throbbings of that gallant heart are stilled— that the mighty sweep of that graceful arm will be felt no more, and the magic of that eloquent tongue, which spake as spake no other tongue besides, is hushed—hushed forever! Who can realize that freedom's champion—the champion of a civilized world, and of all tongues and kindreds and people, has indeed fallen! Alas, in those dark hours, which, as they come in the history of all nations, must come in ours—those hours of peril and dread which our land has experienced, and which she may be called to experience again—to whom now may her people look up for that council and advice, which only wisdom and experience and patriotism can give, and which only the undoubting confidence of a nation will receive? Perchance, in the whole circle of the great and gifted of our land, there remains but one on whose shoulders the mighty mantle of the departed statesman may fall—one, while we now write, is doubtless pouring his tears over the bier of his brother and his friend—brother, friend ever, yet in political sentiment, as far apart as party could make them. Ah, it is at times like these, that the petty distinctions of mere party disappear. We see only the great, the grand, the noble features of the departed statesman; and we do not even beg permission to bow at his feet and mingle our tears with those who have ever been his political adherents—we do not beg this permission—we claim it as a right, though we feel it as a privilege. Henry Clay belonged to his country—to the world, mere party cannot claim men like him. His career has been national—his fame has filled the earth—his memory will endure to 'the last syllable of recorded time.'

"Henry Clay is dead!—He breathed his last on yesterday at twenty minutes after eleven, in his chamber at Washington. To those who followed his lead in public affairs, it more appropriately belongs to pronounce his eulogy, and pay specific honors to the memory of the illustrious dead—but all Americans may show the grief which his death inspires, for, his character and fame are national property. As on a question of liberty, he knew no North, no South, no East, no West, but only the Union, which held them all in its sacred circle, so now his countrymen will know no grief, that is not as widespread as the bounds of the confederacy. The career of Henry Clay was a public career. From his youth he has been devoted to the public service, at a period too, in the world's history justly regarded as a remarkable era in human affairs. He witnessed in the beginning the throes of the French Revolution. He saw the rise and fall of Napoleon. He was called upon to legislate for America, and direct her policy when all Europe was the battle-field of contending dynasties, and when the struggle for supremacy imperilled the rights of all neutral nations. His voice, spoke war and peace in the contest with Great Britain.

"When Greece rose against the Turks and struck for liberty, his name was mingled with the battle-cry of freedom. When South America threw off the thraldom of Spain, his speeches were read at the head of her armies by Bolivar. His name has been, and will continue to be, hallowed in two hemispheres, for it is —

> 'One of the few the immortal names
> That were not born to die,'

"To the ardent patriot and profound statesman, he added a quality possessed by few of the gifted on earth. His eloquence has not been surpassed. In the effective power to move the heart of man, Clay was without an equal, and the heaven born endowment, in the spirit of its origin, has been most conspicuously exhibited against intestine feud. On at least three important occasions, he has quelled our civil commotions, by a power and influence, which belonged to no other statesman of his age and times. And in our last internal discord, when this Union trembled to its center — in old age, he left the shades of private life and gave the death blow to fraternal strife, with the vigor of his earlier years in a series of Senatorial efforts, which in themselves would bring immortality, by challenging comparison with the efforts of any statesman in any age. He exorcised the demon which possessed the body politic, and gave peace to a distracted land. Alas! the achievement cost him his life! He sank day by day to the tomb — his pale, but noble brow, bound with a triple wreath, put there by a grateful country. May his ashes rest in peace, while his spirit goes to take its station among the great and good men who preceded him!"

While it is customary, and proper, upon occasions like the present, to give a brief sketch of the life of the deceased; in the case of Mr. Clay, it is less necessary than most others; for his biography has been written and re-written, and read, and re-read, for the last twenty-five years; so that, with the exception of a few of the latest incidents of his life, all is as well known, as it can be. The short sketch which I give is, therefore merely to maintain the connection of this discourse.

Henry Clay was born on the 12th of April 1777, in Hanover county, Virginia. Of his father, who died in the fourth or fifth year of Henry's age, little seems to be known, except that he was a respectable man, and a preacher of the baptist persuasion. Mr. Clay's education, to the end of his life, was comparatively limited. I say *"to the end of his life,"* because I have understood that, from time to time, he added something to his education during the greater part of his whole life. Mr. Clay's lack of a more perfect early education, however it may be regretted generally, teaches at least one profitable lesson; it teaches that in this country, one can scarcely be so poor, but that, if he *will*, he *can* acquire sufficient education to get through the world respectably. In his twenty-third year Mr. Clay was licenced to practice law, and emigrated to Lexington, Kentucky. Here he commenced and continued the practice till the year 1803, when he was first elected to the Kentucky Legislature. By successive elections he was continued in the Legislature till the latter part of 1806, when he was elected to fill a vacancy, of a single session, in the United States Senate. In 1807 he was again elected to the Kentucky House of Representatives, and by that body, chosen its speaker. In 1808 he was re-elected to the same body. In 1809 he was again chosen to fill a vacancy of two years in the United States Senate. In 1811 he was elected to the United States House of Representatives, and on the first day of taking his seat in that body, he was chosen its speaker. In 1813 he was again elected Speaker. Early in 1814, being the period of our last British war, Mr. Clay was sent as commissioner, with others, to negotiate a treaty of peace, which treaty was concluded in the latter part of the same year. On his return from Europe he was again elected to the lower branch of Congress, and on taking his seat in December 1815 was called to his old post—the speaker's chair, a position in which he was retained, by successive elections, with one brief intermission, till the inauguration of John Q. Adams in March 1825. He was then appointed Secretary of State, and occupied that important station till the

inauguration of Gen. Jackson in March 1829. After this he returned to Kentucky, resumed the practice of the law, and
continued it till the Autumn of 1831, when he was by the
Legislature of Kentucky, again placed in the United States
Senate. By a re-election he was continued in the Senate till
he resigned his seat, and retired, in March 1842. In December 1849 he again took his seat in the Senate, which he again
resigned only a few months before his death.

By the foregoing it is perceived that the period from the
beginning of Mr. Clay's official life, in 1803, to the end of it in
1852, is but one year short of half a century; and that the sum
of all the intervals in it, will not amount to ten years. But
mere duration of time in office, constitutes the smallest part
of Mr. Clay's history. Throughout that long period, he has
constantly been the most loved, and most implicitly followed
by friends, and the most dreaded by opponents, of all living
American politicians. In all the great questions which have
agitated the country, and particularly in those great and fearful crises, the Missouri question—the Nullification question,
and the late slavery question, as connected with the newly
acquired territory, involving and endangering the stability of
the Union, his has been the leading and most conspicuous
part. In 1824 he was first a candidate for the Presidency, and
was defeated; and, although he was successively defeated for
the same office in 1832, and in 1844, there has never been a
moment since 1824 till after 1848 when a very large portion of
the American people did not cling to him with an enthusiastic
hope and purpose of still elevating him to the Presidency.
With other men, to be defeated, was to be forgotten; but to
him, defeat was but a trifling incident, neither changing him,
or the world's estimate of him. Even those of both political
parties, who have been preferred to him for the highest office,
have run far briefer courses than he, and left him, still shining,
high in the heavens of the political world. Jackson, Van
Buren, Harrison, Polk, and Taylor, all rose *after*, and set long
before him. The spell—the long enduring spell—with which
the souls of men were bound to him, is a miracle. Who can
compass it? It is probably true he owed his pre-eminence to
no one quality, but to a fortunate combination of several.
He was surpassingly eloquent; but many eloquent men fail

utterly; and they are not, as a class, generally successful. His judgment was excellent; but many men of good judgment, live and die unnoticed. His will was indomitable; but this quality often secures to its owner nothing better than a character for useless obstinacy. These then were Mr. Clay's leading qualities. No one of them is very uncommon; but all taken together are rarely combined in a single individual; and this is probably the reason why such men as Henry Clay are so rare in the world.

Mr. Clay's eloquence did not consist, as many fine specimens of eloquence does, of types and figures—of antithesis, and elegant arrangement of words and sentences; but rather of that deeply earnest and impassioned tone, and manner, which can proceed only from great sincerity and a thorough conviction, in the speaker of the justice and importance of his cause. This it is, that truly touches the chords of human sympathy; and those who heard Mr. Clay, never failed to be moved by it, or ever afterwards, forgot the impression. All his efforts were made for practical effect. He never spoke merely to be heard. He never delivered a Fourth of July Oration, or an eulogy on an occasion like this. As a politician or statesman, no one was so habitually careful to avoid all sectional ground. Whatever he did, he did for the whole country. In the construction of his measures he ever carefully surveyed every part of the field, and duly weighed every conflicting interest. Feeling, as he did, and as the truth surely is, that the world's best hope depended on the continued Union of these States, he was ever jealous of, and watchful for, whatever might have the slightest tendency to separate them.

Mr. Clay's predominant sentiment, from first to last, was a deep devotion to the cause of human liberty—a strong sympathy with the oppressed every where, and an ardent wish for their elevation. With him, this was a primary and all controlling passion. Subsidiary to this was the conduct of his whole life. He loved his country partly because it was his own country, but mostly because it was a free country; and he burned with a zeal for its advancement, prosperity and glory, because he saw in such, the advancement, prosperity and glory, of human liberty, human right and human nature. He desired the prosperity of his countrymen partly because they were his countrymen, but chiefly to show to the world that freemen could be prosperous.

That his views and measures were always the wisest, needs not to be affirmed; nor should it be, on this occasion, where so many, thinking differently, join in doing honor to his memory. A free people, in times of peace and quiet—when pressed by no common danger—naturally divide into parties. At such times, the man who is of neither party, is not—cannot be, of any consequence. Mr. Clay, therefore, was of a party. Taking a prominent part, as he did, in all the great political questions of his country for the last half century, the wisdom of his course on many, is doubted and denied by a large portion of his countrymen; and of such it is not now proper to speak particularly. But there are many others, about his course upon which, there is little or no disagreement amongst intelligent and patriotic Americans. Of these last are the War of 1812, the Missouri question, Nullification, and the now recent compromise measures. In 1812 Mr. Clay, though not unknown, was still a young man. Whether we should go to war with Great Britain, being the question of the day, a minority opposed the declaration of war by Congress, while the majority, though apparently inclining to war, had, for years, wavered, and hesitated to act decisively. Meanwhile British aggressions multiplied, and grew more daring and aggravated. By Mr. Clay, more than any other man, the struggle was brought to a decision in Congress. The question, being now fully before congress, came up, in a variety of ways, in rapid succession, on most of which occasions Mr. Clay spoke. Adding to all the logic, of which the subject was susceptible, that noble inspiration, which came to him as it came to no other, he aroused, and nerved, and inspired his friends, and confounded and bore-down all opposition. Several of his speeches, on these occasions, were reported, and are still extant; but the best of these all never was. During its delivery the reporters forgot their vocations, dropped their pens, and sat enchanted from near the beginning to quite the close. The speech now lives only in the memory of a few old men; and the enthusiasm with which they cherish their recollection of it is absolutely astonishing. The precise language of this speech we shall never know; but we do know—we cannot help

knowing, that, with deep pathos, it pleaded the cause of the
injured sailor—that it invoked the genius of the revolution—
that it apostrophised the names of Otis, of Henry and of
Washington—that it appealed to the interest, the pride, the
honor and the glory of the nation—that it shamed and
taunted the timidity of friends—that it scorned, and scouted,
and withered the temerity of domestic foes—that it bearded
and defied the British Lion—and rising, and swelling, and
maddening in its course, it sounded the onset, till the charge,
the shock, the steady struggle, and the glorious victory, all
passed in vivid review before the entranced hearers.

Important and exciting as was the War question, of 1812, it
never so alarmed the sagacious statesmen of the country for
the safety of the republic, as afterwards did the Missouri question. This sprang from that unfortunate source of discord—
negro slavery. When our Federal Constitution was adopted,
we owned no territory beyond the limits or ownership of the
states, except the territory North-West of the River Ohio, and
East of the Mississippi. What has since been formed into the
States of Maine, Kentucky, and Tennessee, was, I believe,
within the limits of or owned by Massachusetts, Virginia, and
North Carolina. As to the North Western Territory, provision
had been made, even before the adoption of the Constitution,
that slavery should never go there. On the admission of the
States into the Union carved from the territory we owned
before the constitution, no question—or at most, no considerable question—arose about slavery—those which were
within the limits of or owned by the old states, following,
respectively, the condition of the parent state, and those
within the North West territory, following the previously
made provision. But in 1803 we purchased Louisiana of the
French; and it included with much more, what has since been
formed into the State of Missouri. With regard to it, nothing
had been done to forestall the question of slavery. When,
therefore, in 1819, Missouri, having formed a State constitution, without excluding slavery, and with slavery already actually existing within its limits, knocked at the door of the
Union for admission, almost the entire representation of the
non-slaveholding states, objected. A fearful and angry struggle instantly followed. This alarmed thinking men, more than

any previous question, because, unlike all the former, it divided the country by geographical lines. Other questions had
their opposing partizans in all localities of the country and in
almost every family; so that no division of the Union could
follow such, without a separation of friends, to quite as great
an extent, as that of opponents. Not so with the Missouri
question. On this a geographical line could be traced which,
in the main, would separate opponents only. This was the
danger. Mr. Jefferson, then in retirement wrote:

"I had for a long time ceased to read newspapers, or to pay
any attention to public affairs, confident they were in good
hands, and content to be a passenger in our bark to the shore
from which I am not distant. But this momentous question,
like a fire bell in the night, awakened, and filled me with terror. I considered it at once as the knell of the Union. It is
hushed, indeed, for the moment. But this is a reprieve only,
not a final sentence. A geographical line, co-inciding with a
marked principle, moral and political, once conceived, and
held up to the angry passions of men, will never be obliter-
ated; and every irritation will mark it deeper and deeper. I can
say, with conscious truth, that there is not a man on earth
who would sacrifice more than I would to relieve us from this
heavy reproach, in any *practicable* way. The cession of that
kind of property, for so it is misnamed, is a bagatelle which
would not cost me a second thought, if, in that way, a general
emancipation, and *expatriation* could be effected; and, gradually, and with due sacrifices I think it might be. But as it is,
we have the wolf by the ears and we can neither hold him,
nor safely let him go. Justice is in one scale, and self-
preservation in the other."

Mr. Clay was in congress, and, perceiving the danger, at
once engaged his whole energies to avert it. It began, as I
have said, in 1819; and it did not terminate till 1821. Missouri
would not yield the point; and congress—that is, a majority
in congress—by repeated votes, showed a determination to
not admit the state unless it should yield. After several fail-
ures, and great labor on the part of Mr. Clay to so present the
question that a majority could consent to the admission, it
was, by a vote, rejected, and as all seemed to think, finally. A
sullen gloom hung over the nation. All felt that the rejection

of Missouri, was equivalent to a dissolution of the Union: because those states which already had, what Missouri was rejected for refusing to relinquish, would go with Missouri. All deprecated and deplored this, but none saw how to avert it. For the judgment of Members to be convinced of the necessity of yielding, was not the whole difficulty; each had a constituency to meet, and to answer to. Mr. Clay, though worn down, and exhausted, was appealed to by members, to renew his efforts at compromise. He did so, and by some judicious modifications of his plan, coupled with laborious efforts with individual members, and his own over-mastering eloquence upon the floor, he finally secured the admission of the State. Brightly, and captivating as it had previously shown, it was now perceived that his great eloquence, was a mere embellishment, or, at most, but a helping hand to his inventive genius, and his devotion to his country in the day of her extreme peril.

After the settlement of the Missouri question, although a portion of the American people have differed with Mr. Clay, and a majority even, appear generally to have been opposed to him on questions of ordinary administration, he seems constantly to have been regarded by all, as *the* man for a crisis. Accordingly, in the days of Nullification, and more recently in the re-appearance of the slavery question, connected with our territory newly acquired of Mexico, the task of devising a mode of adjustment, seems to have been cast upon Mr. Clay, by common consent—and his performance of the task, in each case, was little else than a literal fulfilment of the public expectation.

Mr. Clay's efforts in behalf of the South Americans, and afterwards, in behalf of the Greeks, in the times of their respective struggles for civil liberty are among the finest on record, upon the noblest of all themes; and bear ample corroboration of what I have said was his ruling passion—a love of liberty and right, unselfishly, and for their own sakes.

Having been led to allude to domestic slavery so frequently already, I am unwilling to close without referring more particularly to Mr. Clay's views and conduct in regard to it. He ever was, on principle and in feeling, opposed to slavery. The very earliest, and one of the latest public efforts of his life, separated by a period of more than fifty years, were both made in favor of gradual emancipation of the slaves in Kentucky. He did not perceive, that on a question of human right, the negroes were to be excepted from the human race. And yet Mr. Clay was the owner of slaves. Cast into life where slavery was already widely spread and deeply seated, he did not perceive, as I think no wise man has perceived, how it could be at *once* eradicated, without producing a greater evil, even to the cause of human liberty itself. His feeling and his judgment, therefore, ever led him to oppose both extremes of opinion on the subject. Those who would shiver into fragments the Union of these States; tear to tatters its now venerated constitution; and even burn the last copy of the Bible, rather than slavery should continue a single hour, together with all their more halting sympathisers, have received, and are receiving their just execration; and the name, and opinions, and influence of Mr. Clay, are fully, and, as I trust, effectually and enduringly, arrayed against them. But I would also, if I could, array his name, opinions, and influence against the opposite extreme—against a few, but an increasing number of men, who, for the sake of perpetuating slavery, are beginning to assail and to ridicule the white-man's charter of freedom—the declaration that "all men are created free and equal." So far as I have learned, the first American, of any note, to do or attempt this, was the late John C. Calhoun; and if I mistake not, it soon after found its way into some of the messages of the Governors of South Carolina. We, however, look for, and are not much shocked by, political eccentricities and heresies in South Carolina. But, only last year, I saw with astonishment, what purported to be a letter of a very distinguished and influential clergyman of Virginia, copied, with apparent approbation, into a St. Louis newspaper, containing the following, to me, very extraordinary language—

"I am fully aware that there is a text in some Bibles that is not in mine. Professional abolitionists have made more use of it, than of any passage in the Bible. It came, however, as I trace it, from Saint Voltaire, and was baptized by Thomas Jefferson, and since almost universally regarded as canonical authority *'All men are born free and equal.'*

"This is a genuine coin in the political currency of our

generation. I am sorry to say that I have never seen two men of whom it is true. But I must admit I never saw the Siamese twins, and therefore will not dogmatically say that no man ever saw a proof of this sage aphorism."

This sounds strangely in republican America. The like was not heard in the fresher days of the Republic. Let us contrast with it the language of that truly national man, whose life and death we now commemorate and lament. I quote from a speech of Mr. Clay delivered before the American Colonization Society in 1827.

"We are reproached with doing mischief by the agitation of this question. The society goes into no household to disturb its domestic tranquility; it addresses itself to no slaves to weaken their obligations of obedience. It seeks to affect no man's property. It neither has the power nor the will to affect the property of any one contrary to his consent. The execution of its scheme would augment instead of diminishing the value of the property left behind. The society, composed of free men, concerns itself only with the free. Collateral consequences we are not responsible for. It is not this society which has produced the great moral revolution which the age exhibits. What would they, who thus reproach us, have done? If they would repress all tendencies towards liberty, and ultimate emancipation, they must do more than put down the benevolent efforts of this society. They must go back to the era of our liberty and independence, and muzzle the cannon which thunders its annual joyous return. They must renew the slave trade with all its train of atrocities. They must suppress the workings of British philanthropy, seeking to meliorate the condition of the unfortunate West Indian slave. They must arrest the career of South American deliverance from thraldom. They must blow out the moral lights around us, and extinguish that greatest torch of all which America presents to a benighted world—pointing the way to their rights, their liberties, and their happiness. And when they have achieved all those purposes their work will be yet incomplete. They must penetrate the human soul, and eradicate the light of reason, and the love of liberty. Then, and not till then, when universal darkness and despair prevail, can you perpetuate slavery, and repress all sympathy, and all humane, and benevolent efforts among free men, in behalf of the unhappy portion of our race doomed to bondage."

The American Colonization Society was organized in 1816. Mr. Clay, though not its projector, was one of its earliest members; and he died, as for the many preceding years he had been, its President. It was one of the most cherished objects of his direct care and consideration; and the association of his name with it has probably been its very greatest collateral support. He considered it no demerit in the society, that it tended to relieve slave-holders from the troublesome presence of the free negroes; but this was far from being its whole merit in his estimation. In the same speech from which I have quoted he says: "There is a moral fitness in the idea of returning to Africa her children, whose ancestors have been torn from her by the ruthless hand of fraud and violence. Transplanted in a foreign land, they will carry back to their native soil the rich fruits of religion, civilization, law and liberty. May it not be one of the great designs of the Ruler of the universe, (whose ways are often inscrutable by short-sighted mortals,) thus to transform an original crime, into a signal blessing to that most unfortunate portion of the globe?" This suggestion of the possible ultimate redemption of the African race and African continent, was made twenty-five years ago. Every succeeding year has added strength to the hope of its realization. May it indeed be realized! Pharaoh's country was cursed with plagues, and his hosts were drowned in the Red Sea for striving to retain a captive people who had already served them more than four hundred years. May like disasters never befall us! If as the friends of colonization hope, the present and coming generations of our countrymen shall by any means, succeed in freeing our land from the dangerous presence of slavery; and, at the same time, in restoring a captive people to their long-lost father-land, with bright prospects for the future; and this too, so gradually, that neither races nor individuals shall have suffered by the change, it will indeed be a glorious consummation. And if, to such a consummation, the efforts of Mr. Clay shall have contributed, it will be what he most ardently wished, and none of his labors will have been more valuable to his country and his kind.

But Henry Clay is dead. His long and eventful life is closed.

Our country is prosperous and powerful; but could it have been quite all it has been, and is, and is to be, without Henry Clay? Such a man the times have demanded, and such, in the providence of God was given us. But he is gone. Let us strive to deserve, as far as mortals may, the continued care of Divine Providence, trusting that, in future national emergencies, He will not fail to provide us the instruments of safety and security.

July 6, 1852

Speech to the Scott Club of Springfield, Illinois

GENTLEMEN:—Unlike our young friend who has just taken his seat, I do not appear before you on a flattering invitation, or on any invitation at all; but, on the contrary I am about to address you, by your permission, given me at my own special request. Soon after the Democratic nomination for President and vice-President in June last at Baltimore, it was announced somewhat ostentatiously, as it seemed to me, that Judge Douglas would, previous to the election, make speeches in favor of those nominations, in twenty-eight of the thirty-one States. Since then, and as I suppose, in part performance of this undertaking, he has actually made one speech at Richmond, Virginia. This speech has been published, with high commendations, in at least one of the democratic papers in this state, and I suppose it has been, and will be, in most of the others. When I first saw it, and read it, I was reminded of old times—of the times when Judge Douglas was not so much greater man than all the rest of us, as he now is—of the Harrison campaign, twelve years ago, when I used to hear, and *try* to answer many of his speeches; and believing that the Richmond speech though marked with the same species of "shirks and quirks" as the old ones, was not marked with any greater ability, I was seized with a strong inclination to attempt an answer to it; and this inclination it was that prompted me to seek the privilege of addressing you on this occasion. In the speech, so far as I propose noticing it now, the Judge rebukes the whigs for calling Gen. Pierce "a fainting General;" eulogizes Gen. Scott's military character; denounces the whig platform, except as to the slavery question, which he says is a plank stolen from the democratic platform; charges that Gen. Scott's nomination was forced on the South by the North on a sectional issue; charges Gen. Scott with duplicity, and intent to deceive in his letter of acceptance; attempts to ridicule Gen. Scott's views on naturalization; charges that Gen. Scott, in his letter of acceptance, has pledged himself to proscription; denounces as dangerous the election of military men to the Presidency; says the hand of Providence saved us from our first and only military administration; speaks of Mr. Fillmore and his administration. In addition to these specific points, a constant repetition of something more than insinuations and yet something less than direct charges, that Gen. Scott is wholly under the control of Seward of New York; and that abolitionism is controlling the whole whig party, forms a sort of key-note to the whole speech. As a further characteristic of the speech, it may be noted that a very small portion of it is devoted to Pierce, and almost the whole of it to attacks upon Scott.

As I desire to say something on each of these matters, and as the evening is already partially spent, I propose going only about halfway through, reserving the remainder for a subsequent meeting. As to the Judge's rebuke of the whigs for calling Pierce "a fainting General," in which he insists that they mean to impute cowardice to Gen. Pierce, and that it is cowardly and false in them to cast such an imputation, I have only to say that, Gen. Pierce's history being as it is, the attempt to set him up as a great General, is simply ludicrous and laughable; and that the free merry people of the country have laughed at it, and will continue to laugh at it, in spite of the querulous scolding of Judge Douglas or of anybody else; and further, that if the Judge has any real honest indignation against unjust imputations of cowardice, he will find a much ampler field for the indulgence of it against his own friends, who are everywhere seeking by reference to an old affair with Gen. Jackson, to throw such an imputation upon Gen. Scott.

As to the Judge's eulogy on Gen. Scott's military character, in which he says "I will not depreciate his merits as a soldier, because truth and honor forbid it," I have but to remark that whoever will read the speech through and carefully note the imputations implying ignorance and stupidity, and duplicity and knavery, against Gen. Scott in almost every paragraph, will I think, conclude that the eulogy on his military character, was dictated quite as much by the Judge's view of the party impolicy of assailing that character, as by a love of truth and honor.

In denouncing the whig platform generally, the Judge gives no reason other than that it is "a whig concern" and that all democrats are presumed to be opposed to it. This needs no answer other than that for the same reason all whigs are presumed to be in favor of it. But as to the slavery question, the Judge says it was a plank stolen from the democratic platform. On what authority does he make this declaration? Upon what fact, or what reasoning from facts does he base it? I had understood and now understand, as the indelibly written history of the country, that the compromise measures were not party measures—that for praise or blame, they belonged to neither party to the exclusion of the other; but that the chief leaders in their origin and adoption were whigs and not democrats. I had thought that the pen of history had written, acknowledged, and recorded it as facts, that Henry Clay, more than any other man, or perhaps more than any other ten men, was the originator of that system of measures; and that he together with Webster and Pearce of Maryland, (not Gen. Pierce,) were its most efficient supporters in its progress. I knew, or supposed I knew, that democrats, numerous and distinguished, gave it able and efficient support; and I have not sought, or known of any whig seeking to deprive them of the credit of it. Among these last Judge Douglas himself was not the least. After the close of the session of Congress at which these measures were passed, Judge Douglas visited Chicago, in this State, and the measures, if not the Judge himself, were there clamorously assailed. He succeeded in getting a hearing at a public meeting, and made a speech which silenced his adversaries, and gave him a triumph most complete. It was afterwards written out and published. I saw a copy, and read it once hastily, and glanced over it a second time. I do not now remember seeing anything in it to condemn, and I do remember that I considered it a very able production—by far superior to any thing I had ever seen from Judge Douglas, and comparing favorably with any thing from any source, which I had seen, on that general subject. The reading of it afforded me a good deal of pleasure; and I never said, or inclined to say any thing in disparagement of it. But as the Judge, in his Richmond speech, has thought fit to speak so confidently, and, in my judgment so unjustly, of stealing, I will venture to suggest that if he had stolen none of the ideas of Henry Clay and Daniel Webster, and other whigs, which he had been listening to for the last preceding six or eight months, he might not have been able to get up quite so creditable a speech at Chicago as he did.

But the Judge asserts in substance, that the nomination of Scott was forced on the south by the north, on a sectional issue; and he argues that such a nomination is exceedingly perilous to the safety of the Union. As evidence that the nomination was forced on the south by the north, the Judge says, "every southern delegation voted against him more than fifty times, day after day, and night after night." This is not quite correct, for one, two, or more of the Virginia delegation voted for Scott every ballot after the first; but call it substantially correct to say that the Southern delegations did not vote for Scott, does it follow, in the sense the Judge would have us to understand, that they voted *against* Scott? If so, then, by the same rule, in the democratic Convention, every delegation north and south, voted against Gen. Pierce thirty-four times.

Now, according to the Judge's logic, the nomination of Pierce was *forced* on the whole country by some mysterious and invisible agency, "a defiance of the thirty-four times repeated protest and remonstrance of the delegates from ALL the States of the Union represented in the Convention." Still the Judge thinks the nomination of Scott, made in compliance with the original preference of nearly half the whig convention, is extremely perilous to the safety of the Union; but that the nomination of Pierce, made contrary to the original preference of every man in the democratic Convention (and every man out of it, I presume) is to be the very salvation of the Union!!! It may be said that although every member of the democratic convention preferred some other man, finally they all honorably surrendered their preferences and united on Pierce. Very well, if the whole democratic convention could honorably, and without being forced, go over to Pierce, why could not HALF the whig convention, as honorably and as free from force, go over to Scott?

But, according to the Judge's view, Scott's nomination was not only forced upon the south, but was forced upon it, *on a sectional issue*. Now, in point of fact, at the time the nomination was made, there was no issue, except as to who should be the *men* to lead the campaign upon a set of principles previously put in writing and acquiesced in by the whole convention; and those principles, too, being precisely such as the south demanded. When the platform, which I understand to be just such as the south desired, was voted upon by the convention—the whole south, and more than half the north voted for, and adopted it, by a vote of 226 to 66; those who voted against it made no further opposition to it. On the adoption of the platform arose the only sectional issue which came before the convention, and by the vote it passed from an issue into a decision, and left no issue before the convention, except as to men. It is proper to notice too, that on the first ballot for a candidate for the presidency, Scott's vote only lacked one of doubling the numbers of all the votes cast against the platform; so that of Scott's original friends in the convention, more than half *may* have been, and within one of half *must* have been original platform men. If Scott should throw himself into the hands exclusively of those who originally preferred him, to be controlled by the majority of them, in utter disregard of all those who originally preferred others, it is still probable that the majority would lead him to adopt the platform or union view of the slavery question.

But the gist of all the Judge's views is, that Scott's nomination, made as it was, is more perilous to the safety of the Union, than all the scenes through which we have recently passed in connection with the slavery question. Well, we ought all to be startled at the view of "peril to the Union," but it may be a little difficult for some shortsighted mortals to perceive such peril in the *nomination of* Scott. Mark you, it is the *nomination* and not the *election*, which produces the peril. The Judge does not say the election, and he cannot mean the election, because he constantly assures us there is no prospect of Scott's election. He could not be so alarmed at what he is so sure will never happen. In plain truth I suppose he did mean the election, so far as he meant anything; but feeling that his whole proposition was mere nonsense, he did not think of it distinctly enough to enable him to speak with any precision.

As one point in support of his charge of duplicity against Gen. Scott, Judge Douglas attempts to show that Gen. Scott in his letter of acceptance, framed language studiously for the

purpose of enabling men north and south to read it one way
or the other, as the public pulse should beat in their particular
localities, and he insists that the language so designed will be
so used. He quotes Scott's language as follows, "I accept the
nomination, with the resolutions annexed," and then he criti-
cises it as follows: "Now gentlemen I desire to know what is
the meaning of the words 'with the resolutions annexed.'
Does he mean that he approves the resolutions? If so, why
did he not say so, as the candidate for the Vice Presidency,
Mr. Graham, did in his letter of acceptance? Or why did he
not do as that gallant and honest man, Frank Pierce did, and
say, 'I accept the nomination upon the platform adopted by
the convention, not because this is expected of me as a candidate, but because the principles *it* embraces command the
approbation of my judgement.'

"There you have (continues the Judge) an honest man
speaking from an honest heart, without any equivocation, dis-
simulation, or mental reservation. Here you find that Gen.
Scott accepts the nomination with the resolution annexed—
that is to say, using language susceptible of two constructions—one at the North, and another at the South. In the
North it will be said he accepts the nomination notwithstanding the platform; that he accepts it although he defies the
platform; that he accepts it although he spits upon the platform. At the South it will be said he accepts it with the approval of the platform. I submit the question to you whether
that language was not framed studiously for the purpose of
enabling men, North and South to read it one way or the
other as the public pulse should beat in their particular localities. Again, I submit to you, was it the General-in-chief of
the armies who fought the battles in Mexico, that conceived
this part of the letter, or was it his commander-in-chief, Gen.
Seward, who dictated it?" [Great applause.]

What wonderful acumen the Judge displays on the construction of language!!! According to this criticism of his, the
word "with" is equivalent to the word "notwithstanding,"
and also to the phrases, "although I defy," and "although I
spit upon." Verily these are wonderful substitutes for the
word "with." When the builders of the tower of Babel got
into difficulty about language, if they had just called on Judge

Douglas, he would, at once, have construed away the difficulty, and enabled them to finish the structure, upon the truly democratic platform on which they were building. Suppose, gentlemen, you were to amuse yourselves some leisure hour, by selecting sentences, from well known compositions, each containing the word "with" and by striking it out, and inserting alternately, the Judge's substitutes, and then testing whether the sense is changed.

As an example, take a sentence from an old and well known book, not much suspected for duplicity, or equivocal language; which sentence is as follows:

"And Enoch walked *with* God; and he was not, for God took him."

Try, for yourselves, how Judge Douglas' substitutes for the word "with" will affect this sentence. Let Judge Douglas be brought to understand that he can advance the interest of a locofoco candidate for the presidency by criticising this sentence; and forthwith he will hie away to the African church in Richmond, Virginia, and make a great speech, in which he will find great difficulty in understanding the meaning of the words "walked with God." He will contrast it, greatly to its disadvantage, with the language of that *gallant* and *honest* man, Frank Pierce! He will show that it is, and was designed to be, susceptible of two constructions, one at the North, and another at the South; that at the North the word "with" will be read "NOTWITHSTANDING," "ALTHOUGH HE DEFIES," "ALTHOUGH HE SPITS UPON;" and finally he will thrill, and electrify, and throw into spasms of ecstasy his African church auditors by suggesting that such monstrous duplicity could not have been conceived by Enoch or Moses, but must have been dictated by Gen. Seward!!!

As another example, take from Judge Douglas' ratification speech a sentence in relation to the democratic platform and the democratic ticket, Pierce and King, which is as follows:

"With such a platform, and with such a ticket, a glorious victory awaits us."

Now according to the Judge's rule of criticising Gen. Scott's language, the above sentence of his will, without perversion of meaning admit of being read in each of the following ways:

"NOTWITHSTANDING such a platform, and notwithstanding such a ticket, a glorious victory awaits us."

"ALTHOUGH WE DEFY such a platform, and although we defy such a ticket, a glorious victory awaits us."

"ALTHOUGH WE SPIT UPON such a platform, and although we spit upon such a ticket, a glorious victory awaits us."

Similar examples might be found without end; but the foregoing are enough, if indeed anything was wanting to show the utter absurdity of the Judge's criticism. Can any two fair minded men differ about the meaning of this part of Gen. Scott's letter? Do his friends, north and south, read it differently, as Judge Douglas asserts they will? Nothing is too absurd for the malice of his fault finding enemies; but where among his millions of friends can a single one be found who is supporting him because he understands him to defy, and spit upon the Whig platform?

Judge Douglas also perceives the same duplicity in Gen. Scott's language about the Public Lands, and about Naturalization; but his criticisms upon it, are so similar to that which I have already reviewed, that I am willing to trust my review of the one, to stand as answer to the whole.

But, in addition to the charge of duplicity, the Judge also seizes upon what Gen. Scott says about naturalization, on which to base a charge of ignorance and stupidity against Gen. Scott. Scott, in his letter of acceptance, suggests the propriety of so altering the naturalization laws as to admit to the rights of citizenship, such foreigners as may serve one year in time of war, in the land or naval service of the United States. The Judge insists that it is uncertain whether the General means this to be an *addition* to the present laws on the subject, or a *substitute* for them; but by a few brief dashes, he argues himself into the belief that the General means his proposition to be a substitute—to embrace the *only* law on naturalization; and then the Judge bewails the supposed condition of things, when the numbers of the army and navy must either be swelled to a million, or the bulk of the foreigners must remain unnaturalized, and without rights of citizenship among us. He admits the General does not say that he intends his proposition to embrace the only law; but inasmuch as he does not say the contrary, he must so mean it, because, the Judge argues, to maintain the present laws, and such as Scott proposes, *together*, would be unconstitutional. He quotes from the constitution, and shows that there can be but *one* uniform rule of naturalization; and swelling with indignation, he grows severe on Gen. Scott, and asks, "Is it possible that this candidate for the presidency never read the constitution?" He insists that to add Scott's proposition to the present laws, would establish *two* rules because it would admit one person on one set of reasons and another person on another; and hence the unconstitutionality. Now it so happens that the first Congress which ever sat under the constitution, composed in a great part of the same men who made the constitution, passed a naturalization law, in which it was provided that adult aliens should come in on one set of reasons; that their minor children should come in on another set; and that such particular foreigners as had been proscribed by any State, should come in, if at all, on still another set. Will Judge Douglas sneeringly ask if the framers of *this law* never read the Constitution? Since the passage of the first law, there have been some half a dozen acts modifying, adding to, and substituting, the preceding acts; and there has never been a moment from that day to this, when, by the existing system, different persons might not have become naturalized on different sets of reasons.

Would it be discourteous to Judge Douglas to retort his question upon him, and ask, "Is it possible that this candidate for a nomination to the Presidency never read the naturalization laws?" Cases under these laws, have frequently arisen in the courts, and some of them have gone to and passed through, the Supreme Court of the United States. Certainly in some, probably in every one of these cases, one of the parties could have gained his suit by establishing that the laws were unconstitutional; and yet I believe Judge Douglas is the first man who has been found wise enough or enough otherwise, as the case may be, to even suggest their unconstitutionality.

Even those adopted citizens, whose votes have given Judge Douglas all his consequence, came in under these very laws. Would not the Judge have considered the holding those laws unconstitutional, and those particular votes illegal, as more deplorable, than even an army and navy, a million strong?

If the Judge finds no cause to regret this part of his assault, upon the General, I certainly think that the General needs not.

> The man recovered of the bite,
> The dog it was that died.

[The Club adjourned to Wednesday evening August 26, on which evening the Speech was concluded as follows:]

When I spoke on a previous evening, I was not aware of what I have since learned, that Mr. Edwards, in his address to you, had, to some extent, reviewed Judge Douglas' Richmond speech. Had I known this, I probably should have abstained from selecting it as the subject of my remarks; because I dislike the appearance of unfairness of two attacking one. After all, however, as the Judge is a giant, and Edwards and I are but common mortals, it may not be very unfair. And then it is to be considered too, that in attempting to answer the Judge, we do not assail him personally; but we are only trying to meet his mode of conducting the assault which the whole party are making upon Gen. Scott.

Taking up the Richmond speech at the point where I left it, the next charge is that Gen. Scott has pledged himself to a course of proscription. This charge the Judge makes in the following language—

"Gen. Scott, in his letter of acceptance,— in cunning and adroit language—solemnly pledges himself that no democrat shall ever hold office under his administration; but that abolition whigs may do so without the slightest hindrance."

Upon this the Judge indulges himself in a long comment, in the course of which he falls into a strain of wailing pathos which Jeremiah in his last days might envy, for the old soldier democrats to be turned out of office by Gen. Scott. And finally he winds up with the use of Clayton's name in such connection, as to insinuate that he, as Secretary of State under Gen. Taylor, had been exceedingly proscriptive.

In the first place, I think it will be in vain, any fair minded man will search for any such solemn pledge in the letter of acceptance, as Judge Douglas attributes to it. Indeed, the

Judge himself seems to have thought it would not be quite safe to his reputation to leave his allegation without furnishing it the means of escape from a charge which might be brought against it; for he immediately adds, "This is my translation of that part of his letter." He then quotes from the letter, as follows —

"In regard to the general policy of the administration, if elected I should, of course, look among those who may approve that policy for the agents to carry it into execution; and I should seek to cultivate harmony and fraternal sentiments throughout the whig party, without attempting to reduce its members by proscription to exact conformity to my own views."

Now it appears to me the Judge's translation of this may be called a very *free* translation—a translation enjoying a perfect freedom from all the restraint of justice and fair dealing. So far from having solemnly pledged himself that no democrat should ever hold office, the evident sense of the sentence shows that he was not speaking or thinking of the democrats at all—that he was merely giving an assurance that difference of opinion among whigs should not be regarded, except in the higher offices through which the general policy of the administration is to be conducted.

But suppose the translation is correct, I still should like to hear from the Judge where are the democratic office holders who are to be made to "walk the plank" by Gen. Scott, after having told us in this very speech that the Taylor and Fillmore administrations have proscribed nearly every democrat in office. The Judge's pathos on this subject reminds me of a little rumor I heard at Washington about the time of Gen. Taylor's inauguration. The Senate was democratic and could reject all the nominations. The rumor was that the democratic clerks from Illinois, appealed to our democratic delegation to save them their places if possible; but that the delegation told them no; "we prefer your heads should fall; the sight of your blood will aid us to regain our lost power." Judge Douglas was then at the head of our delegation, and will know better than I whether the rumor was true.

A word now about Clayton, and his proscriptive disposition and practices, as insinuated by Judge Douglas. It is

matter of public history, that on Saturday night before Taylor
was inaugurated Monday, Mr. Polk nominated Edward Hannegan, a democrat, as minister to Prussia, and that the Senate
confirmed the nomination; and that Clayton, a few days after
becoming Secretary of State, to which department such appointments belong, allowed him to go, and receive the outfit
and salary of $18,000. This is public history, about which
there is no disputing. But the more private history, as I have
heard and believe it, and as I believe Judge Douglas, knows it,
is still more favorable to Clayton's character for generosity. It
is that Mr. Clayton induced Mr. Polk to make the appointment, by an assurance that the new administration would not
revoke it. Hannegan had been a Senator from Indiana six
years, and, in that time, had done his state some credit, and
gained some reputation for himself; but in the end, was un-
dermined and superseded by a man who will never do either.
He was the son of an Irishman, with a bit of the brogue still
lingering on his tongue; and with a very large share of that
sprightliness and generous feeling, which generally character-
ize Irishmen who have had anything of a fair chance in the
world. He was personally a great favorite with Senators, and
particularly so with Mr. Clayton, although of opposite politics. He was now broken down politically and pecuniarily;
and Mr. Clayton, disregarding the ties of party came to his
relief. With a knowledge of the exact truth on this subject,
how could Judge Douglas find it in his heart to so try to
prejudice the nation against John M. Clayton? Poor Hannegan! Since his return, in a heated, and unguarded moment, he
spilled the life of a favorite brother-in-law, and for which he is
now enduring the tortures of deepest mental agony; yet I
greatly mistake his nature, if, ever to be released from his extreme misery, he could be induced to assail John M. Clayton,
as one wanting in liberality and generosity.

Next Judge Douglas runs a tilt at Gen. Scott as a military
politician, commencing with the interrogatory "Why has the
whig party forgotten with an oblivion so complete all that
it once said about military politicians?" I retort the question, and ask, why has the *democratic* party forgotten with
an oblivion so complete all that *it* once said about military
politicians?

But the Judge proceeds to contrast Scott with General Pierce and with all our General presidents, except Taylor; and he succeeds in showing that Scott differs from them, in having held a military commission longer than any of them; in holding such a commission when nominated for the presidency, in not having been a physician or farmer and in not having held civil office. He does not stop to point *how* any of these differences is material to the question of his qualification for the presidency; but he seems to assume that disqualification must necessarily follow from these facts. Let us not adopt this conclusion too hastily. Let us examine the premises. He has held a military commission a long time—over forty years. If you assert that this has bred in him a thirst for war, and a distaste for peace, "the known incidents of a long public life" abundantly prove the contrary. Among them are his successful efforts for peace and against war in the South Carolina Nullification question, on the burning of the Caroline, and on the Maine boundary question. The mere fact that he held a military commission when he was nominated, I presume no one will seriously contend proves anything to the point. Nor is it perceived how the being a physician or farmer, should qualify a man for office. Whatever of sound views of government is acquired by the physician and farmer, is acquired not in their regular occupations, but by reading and reflection in the hours of relaxation from their regular occupations. It is probable that the leisure time for such reading and reflection would, in time of peace, be quite as abundant with an officer of the army, as with a physician or farmer.

But Gen. Scott has not held civil office, and General Pierce has; and this is the great point. Well, let us examine this too. Gen. Pierce has been in the State Legislature and in congress; and I misread his history if it does not show him to have had just sufficient capacity, and no more, of setting his foot down in the track, as his partizan leader lifted his out of it—and so trudging along in the party team without a single original tho't or independent action. Scott, on the contrary, has on many occasions, been placed in the lead, when originality of thought and independence of action, both of the highest order, have been indispensable to success; and yet he failed in none. What he has performed in these stations bears much stronger resemblance to the duties he would have to perform as president, than any thing Gen. Pierce has ever done. Indeed they were literally, in every instance, executive duties— functions delegated to Gen. Scott by the president, because the president could not perform them in person. Is it not great folly to suppose that the manner of performing them is any less a test of his capacity for civil administration than it would be if he had held a civil office at the time? They say we rely solely on Gen. Scott's military reputation. Throw it aside then. In comparing the candidates let no consideration be given to military reputations. Let it be alike forgotten that Gen. Pierce ever fainted, or that Gen. Scott ever made a "fuss" or wore a "feather." Let them be placed in the scales solely on what they have done, giving evidence of capacity for civil administration; and let him kick the beam who is found lightest.

But, we cannot help observing the fact, that the democrats, with all their present horror of military candidates, have themselves put a general on the track. Why is this? It must have been by *accident* or by *design*; and it could not have been by accident, because I understand the party has become very philosophical, and it would be very unphilosophical to do such a thing by *accident*. It was by design, then. Let us try to trace it. They made their nomination before we made ours; but they knew we *ought*, and therefore concluded we *would*, not nominate Gen. Scott, and they shaped their course accordingly. They said "confound these old generals, is there no way of beating them? In 1840 we thought it would be mere sport to beat Harrison. We charged that his friends kept him in a cage; that he was an abolitionist, so far as he had sense enough to be anything; and we called him a petticoat general, and an old granny; but the election showed we had not hit upon the true philosophy. Again when Taylor was put up, we did not venture to call him an old granny, but we insisted he was not a whig; and, to help along, we put up a general against him, relying on our accustomed confidence in the capacity of the people to *not see* the difference between one who *is* a general, and one who is *called* a general, but we failed again. History is philosophy teaching by example, and if we regard the examples it has given us, we must try something new, before we can succeed in beating a general for the presidency."

Accordingly they nominated Pierce. It soon came to light that the first thing ever urged in his favor as a candidate was his having given a strange boy a cent to buy candy with. An examination of the official reports of his doings as a general in Mexico, showed him to have been the victim of a most extraordinary scene of mishap, which though it might by possibility have so happened with a brave and skillful general, left no considerable evidence that he was such. Forthwith also appears a biographical sketch of him, in which he is represented, at the age of seventeen, to have spelled "but" for his father, who was unable to spell it for himself. By the way I *do* wish Frank had not been present on that trying occasion. I have a great curiosity to know how "old dad" would have spelled that difficult word, if he had been left entirely to himself. But the biography also represents him as cutting at the enemy's flying cannon balls with his sword in the battles of Mexico, and calling out, "Boys there's a game of ball for you;" and finally that he added enough to a balance due him to raise the whole to three hundred dollars, and treated his men.

When I first saw these things I suspected they had been put forward by mischievous whigs; but very soon I saw the biography published at length in a veritable democratic paper, conducted by a man whose party fidelity and intelligent cooperation with his party, I know to be beyond suspicion. Then I was puzzled. But now we have a letter from Gen. Shields, in which, speaking of Pierce and himself, he says, "As we approached the enemy's position, directly under his fire, we encountered a deep ditch, or rather a deep narrow, slimy canal, which had been previously used for the purpose of irrigation. It was no time to hesitate, so we both plunged in. The horse I happened to ride that day was a light active Mexican horse. This circumstance operated in my favor, and enabled me to extricate myself and horse after considerable difficulty. Pierce, on the contrary, was mounted on a large, heavy American horse, and man and horse both sank down and rolled over in the ditch. There I was compelled to leave him . . .

After struggling there, I cannot say how long, he extricated himself from his horse, and hurried on foot to join his command, &c."

Now, what right had a brigadier general, when approaching the enemy's position, and directly under his fire, to sink down and roll over in a deep slimy canal and struggle there before he got out, how long, another brigadier general cannot tell, when the whole of both their brigades got across that same "slimy canal," without any difficulty worth mentioning? I say, Judge Douglas, "Is *this* manoeuvre sanctioned by Scott's Infantry Tactics as adopted in the army?" This ludicrous scene in Gen. Pierce's career had not been told of before; and the telling of it by Gen. Shields, looks very much like a pertinacious purpose to "pile up" the ridiculous. This explains the new plan or system of tactics adopted by the democracy. It is to ridicule and burlesque the whole military character out of credit; and this to kill Gen. Scott with vexation. Being philosophical and literary men, they have read, and remembered, how the institution of chivalry was ridiculed out of existence by its fictitious votary Don Quixote. They also remember how our own "militia trainings" have been "laughed to death" by fantastic parades and caricatures upon them. We remember one of these parades ourselves here, at the head of which, on horse-back, figured our old friend Gordon Abrams, with a pine wood sword, about nine feet long, and a paste-board cocked hat, from front to rear about the length of an ox yoke, and very much the shape of one turned bottom upwards; and with spurs having rowels as large as the bottom of a teacup, and shanks a foot and a half long. That was the last militia muster here. Among the rules and regulations, no man is to wear more than five pounds of cod-fish for epaulets, or more than thirty yards of bologna sausages for a sash; and no two men are to dress alike, and if any two should dress alike the one that dresses most alike is to be fined, (I forget how much). Flags they had too, with devices and mottoes, one of which latter is, "We'll fight till we run, and we'll run till we die."

Now, in the language of Judge Douglas, "I submit to you gentlemen," whether there is not great cause to fear that on some occasion when Gen. Scott suspects no danger, suddenly Gen. Pierce will be discovered charging upon him, holding a huge roll of candy in one hand for a spy-glass; with B U T labelled on some appropriate part of his person; with Abrams' long pine sword cutting in the air at imaginary cannon balls, and calling out "boys there's a game of ball for you," and over all streaming the flag, with the motto, "We'll fight till we faint, and I'll treat when it's over."

It is calculated that such opposition will take "Old Fuss and Feathers" by surprise. He has thought of, and prepared himself for, all the ordinary modes of assault—for over-reachings, and underminings; for fires in front and fires in the rear; but I guess this would be a fire on the "blind side"—totally unlooked for by him. Unless the opposition should, once more sink down, and roll over, in that deep slimy canal, I cannot conceive what is to save Gen. Scott.

But Judge Douglas alluding to the death of General Taylor says it was the hand of Providence which saved us from our first and only military administration. This reminds me of Judge Douglas' so much wanted confidence in the people. The people had elected Gen. Taylor; and, as is appointed to all men once to do, he died. Douglas chooses to consider this a special interference of Providence, against the people, and in favor of Locofocoism. After all, his confidence in the people seems to go no farther than this, that they may be safely trusted with their own affairs, provided Providence retains, and exercises a sort of veto upon their acts, whenever they fall into the "marvelous hallucination," as the Judge calls it, of electing some one to office contrary to the dictation of a democratic convention. The people have fallen into this hallucination in two of the presidential elections of the four since the retirement of Gen. Jackson. The present struggle is for the best three in five. Let us stand by our candidate as faithfully as he has always stood by our country, and I much doubt if we do not perceive a slight abatement in Judge Douglas' confidence in Providence, as well as in the people. I suspect that confidence is not more firmly fixed with the Judge than it was with the old woman, whose horse ran away with her in a buggy. She said she trusted in Providence till the britchen broke; and then she didn't know what on airth *to* do. The chance is the Judge will see the breechen break, and then he can at his leisure, bewail the fate of loco-focoism, as the victim of misplaced confidence.

Speaking of Mr. Fillmore, the Judge calls him, "a man who, previous to that time (his accession to the presidency) had never furnished such proofs of superiority of statesmanship as to cause him to be looked to as a candidate for the first office." O ho! Judge; it is you, is it, that thinks a man should furnish *proof of superiority of statesmanship*, before he is looked to as a candidate for the first office? Do please show us those proofs in the case of your "gallant and honest man, Frank Pierce." Do please name a single one that you consider such. What good thing, or even *part* of good thing has the country ever enjoyed, which originated with him? What evil thing has ever been averted by him? Compare his proofs of statesmanship with those of Mr. Fillmore, up to the times respectively when their names were first connected with presidential elections. Mr. Fillmore, if I remember rightly, had not been in Congress so long as Mr. or Gen. Pierce; yet he did acquire the distinction of being placed at the head of one of the most important Committees; and as its Chairman, was the principal member of the H.R. in maturing the tariff of 1842. On the other hand, Gen. Pierce was in Congress six whole years, without being the chairman of any committee at all; and it was at the beginning of his seventh year when he was first placed at the head of one; and then it was a comparatively unimportant one. To show by comparison, to the people of Illinois, the estimate in which Mr. Pierce was held, let me mention, that Douglas and McClernand were each, placed at the head of an important committee, at the commencement of their second term; while it was not till the commencement of Pierce's fourth term, or rather of the fourth congress of which he had been a member, that he was admitted to the head of a less important one. I have no doubt that Col. Mc-Clernand is as much the superior of Pierce as this difference in the estimation in which they were held in Congress, would indicate. I have glanced over the Journals a little to ascertain if I could, what it is, or was, that Gen. Pierce had originated; and the most noted of any thing I could see, was a proposition to plead the Statute of Limitations against certain Revolutionary claims; and even this I believe he did not succeed in having adopted. There is one good democrat in our town who I apprehend would turn against Pierce if he only knew of this; for I have several times heard him insist that there is nothing but unmitigated rascality in Statutes of Limitation.

Judge Douglas says Mr. Fillmore, as president, "did no harm to the country," and he says this in such connection as to show that he regards it a disparagement to an administration to be able to say no more for it, than that it "did no harm to the country." And please Judge, is not an administration that "does no harm," the very *beau ideal* of a democratic administration? Is not the very idea of *beneficence*, unjust, inexpedient, and unconstitutional, in your view? Take the present democratic platform, and it does not propose to do a single thing. It is full of declarations as to what ought *not* to be done, but names no one to be done. If there is in it, even an inference in favor of any positive action by the democracy, should they again get into power, it only extends to the collecting a sufficient revenue to pay their own salaries, including perhaps, constructive mileage to Senators. Propose a course of policy that shall ultimately supplant the monstrous folly of bringing untold millions of iron, thousands of miles across water and land, which our own hills and mountains are groaning with the best quality in the world, and in quantity sufficient for ten such worlds, and the cry instantly is "no." Propose to remove a snag, a rock, or a sand-bar from a lake or river, and the cry still is "no."

I have seen in a dirty little democratic issue, called "papers for the people," what is there called a "democratic Battle Hymn." The first stanza of the delectable production runs as follows:

> "Sturdy and strong, we march along,
> Millions on millions of freemen bold;
> Raising the dead, with our iron tread—
> The noble dead, of the days of old!"

Now I do not wish to disturb the poet's delicious reverie, but I will thank him to inform me, at his earliest convenience, whether among the "noble dead" he saw "stirred up" there were any from the hulls of flats and keels, and brigs, and steam boats, which had gone to the bottom on questions of constitutionality?

After speaking rather kindly of Mr. Fillmore, the Judge proceeds to find fault with "certain features" of his administration, for which, he says, the Whig party is responsible, even more than Mr. Fillmore. This is palpably absurd. The Whigs hold no department of the government but the executive, and that is in the hands of Mr. Fillmore. What can they be responsible for which he is not? What led the Judge to make this absurd declaration is equally plain. He knew the Whigs of Virginia were partial to Mr. Fillmore, and he supposed to hold him up as a good man sacrificed, might excite his friends against Scott; but suddenly it occurs to him it will not do to leave the thing in such shape, as that the Whig party may claim it as an indorsement, to any extent, of a Whig administration. It was with some regret, that the Judge could do no more for lack of time than merely glance at these "certain features." He had before, in his ratification speech at Washington, glanced at the same features, not having sufficient *time* to consider them at length. It is to be hoped that in some one of the twenty-seven speeches yet to come, he will find *time* to be a little more specific.

One of these "certain features" is that the proper satisfaction was not insisted upon, for the shooting of the Americans in Cuba last year. He says that, whether they were right or wrong, they were, by a treaty stipulation, entitled to a trial, which was not given them. Now whether there is a treaty stipulation that American citizens shall not be punished in the Spanish dominions, without a fair trial, I know not; but it strikes me as most remarkable that there should be. Without any express treaty stipulation, it would seem to me to be a plain principle of public law. The question is, did the principle apply to these fifty men? Were they "American citizens" in the sense of that principle? The position they had assumed was, that they were oppressed Spanish subjects, and as such, had a right to revolutionize the Spanish government in Cuba. They had renounced our authority and our protection; and we had no more legal right to demand satisfaction for their treatment, than if they had been native born Cubans. Their butchery was, as it seemed to me, most unnecessary, and inhuman. They were fighting against one of the worst governments in the world; but their fault was, that the real people of Cuba had not asked for their assistance; were neither desirous of, nor fit for civil liberty.

But suppose I am mistaken, and that satisfaction should have been demanded of Spain for the shooting of the fifty in Cuba. What should have been the nature of the satisfaction? Not pecuniary certainly? A disavowal of the act by the government, with the punishment of perpetrators? The very nature of the case made this impossible. The satisfaction, if sought at all, must have been sought in war. If Judge Douglas thought it cause for war, upon him rests the responsibility of not bringing a proposition before the Senate to declare war. I suppose he knows that under the constitution, Congress, and not the president, declares war. Does not his omission to move in the matter, in Congress, coupled with his greediness to agitate it before ratification meetings, and African church audiences, prove that he feels much greater concern for a presidential election, than he does to vindicate the honor of the nation, or to avenge the blood of its citizens?

The extravagant expenditures of the present administration is another of the Judge's "certain features." On this subject his language is very general, for want of *time* no doubt. At the "ratification" he says, "You find the expenditures nearly doubled, running up to about sixty millions of dollars a year, in times of profound peace." At Richmond he says, "I should like to know why a whig administration costs more in a profound peace than a democratic administration does during a great war." I have not had the opportunity to investigate this subject as I would like to do before undertaking to speak upon it; but I have learned enough to feel confident that the expenditures (of 1850–51 for instance) have not, by any plausible mode of estimating them, amounted to sixty millions, or to more than the expenditures of a "democratic administration in a great war," by at least ten millions of dollars.

I take the following from a paper which, is not often misled, and never intentionally misleads others—the National Intelligencer: —

"In the discussions which have taken place, in the newspaper and elsewhere, on the financial question, an attempt has been made to hold the present administration responsible for an alleged large *increase* of the expenditures of the Government. With the growth of the Government, and the additional cost of governing newly acquired and distant territories, it could not well be otherwise than that the expenses of the Government must be somewhat increased, but not to anything like the amount at which it has been stated; as, for example in the "Union" of a few days ago, in which the expenditures of Government were charged to have reached fifty two millions of dollars, instead of the thirty seven millions which they had reached at one period of the Van Buren administration.

"Let us briefly analyze this sweeping charge. It is not true, in the first place, that the expenditures of the Government last year amounted so high as fifty millions. In so large an expenditure, however, a few millions more or less would by some persons be thought to make little difference. But the *actual* payments during the year amounted to only forty eight millions of dollars, instead of fifty two millions (or fifty millions, as estimated by others,) as will be seen by the following statement, made up from authentic materials:

"The *payment* (net expenses) of the Government for fiscal year 1850 and 1851 were $48 005,878
From which *deduct*—

One Mexican instalment	$3 242 400	
Mexican indemnity claims	2 516 691	5 759,091
		42 246,787
Duties *refunded* on sugar and molasses wrong fully collected (see decisions of Supreme Court).	$ 513 850	
Debentures	867 268	
Excess of duties	896 024	
Expenses of collecting the revenues and sales of lands	2 051 708	4 328,845
		38 917,936
Census expenses	672 500	
Three and five per cent. funds to states, and repayment of lands erroneously sold	74 345	
Smithsonian Institution	30 910	777,755
		37 140 177
And mail service—Navy Department.		1 303,365
		35,837 812
Payments to volunteers.		635 380
		$35,201,432

"Of the expenditures of the last year nearly six millions of dollars, it will be seen, went to pay in part for our little property in California.

"The duties refunded, and the expenses of collecting the revenues, &c., amounting to more than four millions of dollars, would, under *former Administrations*, according to the then existing laws, have been paid by and deducted from the revenue by collectors. Now every thing is paid into the Treasury and repaid to the employees, &c.

"The items under the third division of the above statement are surely not 'ordinary expenses' of Government.

"The revenue from the Ocean Mail Steamers not appearing in the *receipts* of the Treasury, the fourth item of the above should not be added to the expenses.

"The volunteers (comprising the fifth item) ought to have been paid years ago. Why, then, does that hold a place in the account of 'ordinary expenses' of the Government?

"A just computation of the 'ordinary' expenditures of the Government for the year 1851 is, therefore, by this analysis, reduced to little more than thirty five millions of dollars, being a less annual amount, as before stated, than the Government expenditure had risen to before the Whigs had ever had any effective share in the administration of the General Government."

By this it appears that in this twice made assault upon the administration, Judge Douglas is only mistaken about twenty five millions of dollars—a mere trifle for a giant!

I come now to the key-notes of the Richmond speech— Seward—Abolition—free soil, &c. &c. It is amusing to observe what a "Raw Head and Bloody Bones" Seward is to universal Locofocoism. That they do really hate him there is no mistake; but that they do not choose to tell the true reason of their hatred, is manifest from the vagueness of their attacks upon him. His supposed proclamation of a "higher law" is the only specific charge I have seen for a long time. I never read the speech in which that proclamation is said to have been made; so that I cannot by its connection, judge of its import and purpose; and I therefore have only to say of it now, that in so far as it may attempt to foment a disobedience to the constitution, or to the constitutional laws of the country, it has my unqualified condemnation. But this is not the true ground of democratic hatred to Seward; else they would not so fondly cherish so many "higher law" men in their own ranks. The real secret is this: whoever does not get the State of New York will not be elected president. In 1848, in New York, Taylor had 218 538 votes—Cass 114 319, and free soilism, under Van Buren 120 497, Taylor only lacking 16 234 of beating them both. Now in 1852, the free soil organization is broken up, Van Buren has gone back to Locofocoism, and his 120 thousand votes are the stakes for which the game in New York is being played. If Scott can get nine thousand of them he carries the State, and is elected; while Pierce is beaten unless he can get about one hundred and eleven thousand of them. Pierce has all the leaders, and can carry a majority; but that won't do—he cannot live unless he gets nearly all. Standing in the way of this Seward is thought to be the greatest obstacle. In this division of free soil effects, they greatly fear he may be able to get as many as nine out of each hundred, which is more than they can bear; and hence their insane malice against him. The indispensable necessity with the democrats of getting these New York free soil votes, to my mind, explains why they nominated a man who "loathes the Fugitive Slave Law." In December or January last Gen. Pierce made a speech, in which, according to two different news paper reports, published at the time in his vicinity and never questioned by him or any one else till after the nomination, he publicly declared his loathing of the Slave law. Now we shall allow ourselves to be very green, if we conclude the democratic convention did not know of this when they nominated him. On the contrary, its supposed efficacy to win free soil votes, was the very thing that secured his nomination. His Southern allies will continue to bluster and pretend to disbelieve the report, but they would not, for any consideration, have him to contradict it. And he will not contradict it—mark me, *he will not contradict it*. I see by the despatches he has already written a letter on the subject; but I have not seen the letter, or any quotation from it. When we shall see it, we shall also see it does not contradict the report—that is, it will not specifically deny the charge that he declared his loathing for the Fugitive Slave

Law. I know it will not, because I know the *necessity* of the party will not permit it to be done. The letter will deal in generalities, and will be framed with a view of having it to pass at the South for a denial; but the specific point will not be made and met.

And this being the necessity of the party, and its action and attitude in relation to it, is it not particularly bright—in Judge Douglas to stand up before a slave-holding audience, and make flings at the Whigs about free soil and abolition! Why Pierce's only chance for presidency, is to be born into it, as a cross between New York old hunkerism, and free soilism, the latter predominating in the offspring. Marryat, in some one of his books, describes the sailors, weighing anchor, and singing:

> "Sally is a bright Mullatter,
>   Oh Sally Brown—
> Pretty gal, but can't get at her,
>   Oh, Sally Brown."

Now, should Pierce ever be President, he will, politically speaking, not only be a mulatto; but he will be a good deal darker one than Sally Brown.

August 14 and 26, 1852

To Charles R. Welles

C. R. Welles, Esq.   Bloomington,
Dear Sir   Sept. 27. 1852.
    I am in a little trouble here. I am trying to get a decree for our "Billy the Barber" for the conveyance of certain town lots sold to him by Allen, Gridly and Prickett. I made you a party, as administrator of Prickett, but the Clerk omitted to put your name in the writ, and so you are not served. Billy will blame me, if I do not get the thing fixed up this time. If, therefore, you will be so kind as to sign the authority below, and send it to me by *return mail*, I shall be greatly obliged, and will be careful that you shall not be involved, or your rights invaded by it. Yours as ever

To Lewis M. Hays

L. M. Hays Esq.   Springfield,
Dear Sir: Oct. 27. 1852

Yours of Sept. 30th. just received. At our court, just past; I could have got a judgment against Turley, if I had pressed to the utmost; but I am really sorry for him—*poor* and a *cripple* as he is. He begged time to try to find evidence to prove that the deceased on his death bed, ordered the note to be given up to him or destroyed. I do not suppose he will get any such evidence, but I allowed him till next court to try. Yours &c

To Thompson R. Webber

T. R. Webber, Esq–   Bloomington,
My dear Sir: Sept. 12. 1853.

On my arrival here to court, I find that McLean county has assessed the land and other property of the Central Railroad, for the purpose of county taxation. An effort is about to be made to get the question of the right to so tax the Co. before the court, & ultimately before the Supreme Court, and the Co. are offering to engage me for them. As this will be the same question I have had under consideration for you, I am somewhat trammelled by what has passed between you and me; feeling that you have the prior right to my services; if you choose to secure me a fee something near such as I can get from the other side. The question, in its magnitude, to the Co. on the one hand, and the counties in which the Co. has land, on the other, is the largest law question that can now be got up in the State; and therefore, in justice to myself, I can not afford, if I can help it, to miss a fee altogether. If you choose to release me; say so by return mail, and there an end. If you wish to retain me, you better get authority from your court, come directly over in the Stage, and make common cause with this county. Very truly your friend

To Mason Brayman

M. Brayman, Esq   Pekin, Ills.
Dear Sir: Oct. 3, 1853.

Neither the county of McLean nor any one on it's behalf, has yet made any engagement with me in relation to it's suit with the Illinois Central Railroad, on the subject of taxation. I am now free to make an engagement for the Road; and if you think fit you may "count me in" Please write me, on receipt of this. I shall be here at least ten days. Yours truly

To James F. Joy

J. F. Joy, Esq   Springfield,
Dear Sir—   Jany. 25– 1854.

Yours of the 20th. is just received, and I suppose, ere this, you have received my answer to your despatch on the same subject. It is my impression the case will not be brought up for trial before the meeting of the Legislature, but I can not get the *promise* of the court to that effect. I can only venture to say the *first of February*; but as this day draws nearer, I can see farther ahead, and will try to notify you again.

Allow me to suggest that it is not safe to regard the case too lightly. A great stake is involved, and it will be fiercely contended for. I think we shall carry it; but I have a suspicion that the *feeling* of some of the Judges is against us.

I suppose you are aware that the point to be made against us, that the Constitution *secures* to the counties the right to tax all property, *beyond* the *power* of the Legislature to take it away. Yours truly

To Jesse Lincoln

Springfield, Illinois, April 1, 1854.

My Dear Sir: On yesterday I had the pleasure of receiving your letter of the 16th of March. From what you say there can be no doubt that you and I are of the same family. The history of your family, as you give it, is precisely what I have always heard, and partly know, of my own. As you have supposed, I am the grandson of your uncle Abraham; and the story of his death by the Indians, and of Uncle Mordecai, then fourteen years old, killing one of the Indians, is the legend more strongly than all others imprinted upon my mind and memory. I am the son of grandfather's youngest son, Thomas. I have often heard my father speak of his uncle Isaac residing at Watauga (I think), near where the then States of Virginia, North Carolina, and Tennessee join,—you seem now to be some hundred miles or so west of that. I often saw Uncle Mordecai, and Uncle Josiah but once in my life; but I never resided near either of them. Uncle Mordecai died in 1831 or 2, in Hancock County, Illinois, where he had then recently removed from Kentucky, and where his children had also removed, and still reside, as I understand. Whether Uncle Josiah is dead or living, I cannot tell, not having heard from him for more than twenty years. When I last heard of him he was living on Big Blue River, in Indiana (Harrison Co., I think), and where he had resided ever since before the beginning of my recollection. My father (Thomas) died the 17th of January, 1851, in Coles County, Illinois, where he had resided twenty years. I am his only child. I have resided here, and hereabouts, twenty-three years. I am forty-five years of age, and have a wife and three children, the oldest eleven years. My wife was born and raised at Lexington, Kentucky; and my connection with her has sometimes taken me there, where I have heard the older people of her relations speak of your uncle Thomas and his family. He is dead long ago, and his descendants have gone to some part of Missouri, as I recollect what I was told. When I was at Washington in 1848, I got up a correspondence with David Lincoln, residing at Sparta, Rockingham County, Virginia, who, like yourself, was a first cousin of my father; but I forget, if he informed me, which of my grandfather's brothers was his father. With Col. Crozier, of whom you speak, I formed quite an intimate acquaintance, for a short one, while at Washington; and when you meet him again I will thank you to present him my respects. Your present governor, Andrew Johnson, was also at Washington while I was; and he told me of there being people of the name of Lincoln in Carter County, I think. I can no longer claim to be a young man myself; but I infer that, as you are of the same generation as my father, you are some older. I shall be very glad to hear from you again. Very truly your relative,

Fragments on Government

The legitimate object of government, is to do for a community of people, whatever they need to have done, but can not do, *at all*, or can not, *so well do*, for themselves—in their separate, and individual capacities.

In all that the people can individually do as well for themselves, government ought not to interfere.

The desirable things which the individuals of a people can not do, or can not well do, for themselves, fall into two classes: those which have relation to *wrongs*, and those which have not. Each of these branch off into an infinite variety of subdivisions.

The first—that in relation to wrongs—embraces all crimes, misdemeanors, and non-performance of contracts. The other embraces all which, in its nature, and without wrong, requires combined action, as public roads and highways, public schools, charities, pauperism, orphanage, estates of the deceased, and the machinery of government itself.

From this it appears that if all men were just, there still would be *some*, though not *so much*, need of government.

———

Government is a combination of the people of a country to effect certain objects by joint effort. The best framed and best administered governments are necessarily expensive; while by errors in frame and maladministration most of them are more onerous than they need be, and some of them very oppressive. Why, then, should we have government? Why not each individual take to himself the whole fruit of his labor, without having any of it taxed away, in services, corn, or money? Why not take just so much land as he can cultivate with his own hands, without buying it of any one?

The legitimate object of government is "to do for the people what needs to be done, but which they can not, by individual effort, do at all, or do so well, for themselves." There are many such things—some of them exist independently of the injustice in the world. Making and maintaining roads, bridges, and the like; providing for the helpless young and afflicted; common schools; and disposing of deceased men's property, are instances.

But a far larger class of objects springs from the injustice of men. If one people will make war upon another, it is a necessity with that other to unite and coöperate for defense. Hence the military department. If some men will kill, or beat, or constrain others, or despoil them of property, by force, fraud, or noncompliance with contracts, it is a common object with peaceful and just men to prevent it. Hence the criminal and civil departments.

———

dent truth. Made so plain by our good Father in Heaven, that all *feel* and *understand* it, even down to brutes and creeping insects. The ant, who has toiled and dragged a crumb to his nest, will furiously defend the fruit of his labor, against whatever robber assails him. So plain, that the most dumb and stupid slave that ever toiled for a master, does constantly *know* that he is wronged. So plain that no one, high or low, ever does mistake it, except in a plainly *selfish* way; for although volume upon volume is written to prove slavery a very good thing, we never hear of the man who wishes to take the good of it, *by being a slave himself.*

Most governments have been based, practically, on the denial of equal rights of men, as I have, in part, stated them; *ours* began, by *affirming* those rights. *They* said, some men are too *ignorant*, and *vicious*, to share in government. Possibly so, said we; and, by your system, you would always keep them ignorant, and vicious. We proposed to give *all* a chance; and we expected the weak to grow stronger, the ignorant, wiser; and all better, and happier together.

We made the experiment; and the fruit is before us. Look at it—think of it. Look at it, in it's aggregate grandeur, of extent of country, and numbers of population—of ship, and steamboat, and rail-

1854?

Fragment on Slavery

If A. can prove, however conclusively, that he may, of right, enslave B.—why may not B. snatch the same argument, and prove equally, that he may enslave A?—

You say A. is white, and B. is black. It is *color*, then; the lighter, having the right to enslave the darker? Take care. By this rule, you are to be slave to the first man you meet, with a fairer skin than your own.

You do not mean *color* exactly?—You mean the whites are *intellectually* the superiors of the blacks, and, therefore have the right to enslave them? Take care again. By this rule, you are to be slave to the first man you meet, with an intellect superior to your own.

But, say you, it is a question of *interest*; and, if you can make it your *interest*, you have the right to enslave another. Very well. And if he can make it his interest, he has the right to enslave you.

1854?

To John M. Palmer

(CONFIDENTIAL)

Hon. J. M. Palmer.   Springfield,
Dear Sir.   Sept. 7. 1854

You know how anxious I am that this Nebraska measure shall be rebuked and condemned every where. Of course I hope something from your position; yet I do not expect you to do any thing which may be wrong in your own judgment; nor would I have you do anything personally injurious to yourself. You are, and always have been, *honestly*, and *sincerely* a democrat; and I know how painful it must be to an honest sincere man, to be urged by his party to the support of a measure, which on his conscience he believes to be wrong. You have had a severe struggle with yourself, and you have determined *not* to swallow the *wrong*. Is it not just to yourself that you should, in a few public speeches, state your reasons, and thus justify yourself? I wish you would; and yet I say "dont do it, if you think it will injure you." You may have given your word to vote for Major Harris, and if so, of course you will stick to it. But allow me to suggest that you should avoid speaking of this; for it probably would induce some of your friends, in like manner, to cast their votes. You understand. And now let me beg your pardon for obtruding this letter upon you, to whom I have ever been opposed in politics. Had your party omitted to make Nebraska a test of party fidelity; you probably would have been the Democratic candidate for congress in the district. You deserved it, and I believe it would have been given you. In that case I should have been quit, happy that Nebraska was to be rebuked at all events. I still should have voted for the whig candidate; but I should have made no speeches, written no letters; and you would have been elected by at least a thousand majority. Yours truly

To Richard J. Oglesby

R. J. Oglesby, Esq.   Confidential
Dear Sir: Springfield, Sept. 8, 1854.
    You perhaps know how anxious I am for Yates' re-election in this District. I understand his enemies are getting up a charge against him, that while he passes for a temperate man, he is in the habit of drinking secretly—and that they calculate on proving an instance of the charge by you. If, indeed, you have told them any thing, I can not help thinking they have misunderstood what you did tell them. Other things being equal, I would much prefer a temperate man, to an intemperate one; still I do not make my vote depend absolutely upon the question of whether a candidate does or does not *taste* liquor.

Thousands and thousands of us, in point of fact, have known Yates for more than twenty years; and as I have never seen him drink liquor, nor act, or speak, as if he had been drinking, nor smelled it on his breath, nor heard any man say *he* ever had and as he has been twice elected to congress without any such thing being discovered I can not but think such a charge as the above must be incorrect. Will you please write me, and tell me what the truth of this matter is? I will reciprocate at any time. Yours truly

Editorial in the Illinois Journal

THE 14TH SECTION.

The following is the 14th section of the Kansas-Nebraska law. It repeals the Missouri Compromise; and then puts in a declaration that it is not intended by this repeal to legislate slavery in or exclude it therefrom, the territory.

SEC. 14. That the constitution, and all the laws of the United States which are not locally inapplicable, shall have the same force and effect within said territory of Nebraska as elsewhere in the United States, except the 8th section of the act preparatory to the admission of Missouri into the Union, approved March sixth, eighteen hundred and twenty, which being inconsistent with the principles of non-intervention by congress with slavery in the States and Territories as recognized by the legislation of eighteen hundred and fifty, commonly called the compromise measures, is hereby declared inoperative and void; it being the true intent and meaning of this act not to legislate slavery into any territory or State, nor to exclude it therefrom, but to leave the people thereof perfectly free to form and regulate their domestic institutions in their own way, subject only to the constitution of the United States: Provided, that nothing herein contained shall be construed to revive or put in force any law or regulation which may have existed prior to the act of sixth of March, eighteen hundred and twenty, either protecting, establishing, prohibiting, or abolishing slavery.

The state of the case in a few words, is this: The Missouri Compromise excluded slavery from the Kansas-Nebraska territory. The repeal opened the territories to slavery. If there is any meaning to the declaration in the 14th section, that it does not mean to legislate slavery into the territories, it is this: that it does not require slaves to be sent there. The Kansas and Nebraska territories are now as open to slavery as Mississippi or Arkansas were when they were territories.

To illustrate the case—Abraham Lincoln has a fine meadow, containing beautiful springs of water, and well fenced, which John Calhoun had agreed with Abraham (originally owning the land in common) should be his, and the agreement had been consummated in the most solemn manner, regarded by both as sacred. John Calhoun, however, in the course of time, had become owner of an extensive herd of cattle—the prairie grass had become dried up and there was no convenient water to be had. John Calhoun then looks with a longing eye on Lincoln's meadow, and goes to it and throws down the fences, and exposes it to the ravages of his starving and famishing cattle. "You rascal," says Lincoln, "what have you done? what do you do this for?" "Oh," replies Calhoun, "everything is right. I have taken down your fence; but nothing more. It is my true intent and meaning not to drive my cattle into your meadow, nor to exclude them therefrom, but to leave them perfectly free to form their own notions of the feed, and to direct their movements in their own way!"

Now would not the man who committed this outrage be deemed both a knave and a fool,—a knave in removing the restrictive fence, which he had solemnly pledged himself to sustain;—and a fool in supposing that there could be one man found in the country to believe that he had not pulled down the fence for the purpose of opening the meadow for his cattle?

September 11, 1854

Speech on the Kansas-Nebraska Act at Peoria, Illinois

MR. LINCOLN'S SPEECH.

On Monday, October 16, Senator DOUGLAS, by appointment, addressed a large audience at Peoria. When he closed he was greeted with six hearty cheers; and the band in attendance played a stirring air. The crowd then began to call for LINCOLN, who, as Judge Douglas had announced was, by agreement, to answer him. Mr. Lincoln then took the stand, and said—

"I do not arise to speak now, if I can stipulate with the audience to meet me here at half past 6 or at 7 o'clock. It is now several minutes past five, and Judge Douglas has spoken over three hours. If you hear me at all, I wish you to hear me thro'. It will take me as long as it has taken him. That will carry us beyond eight o'clock at night. Now every one of you who can remain that long, can just as well get his supper, meet me at seven, and remain one hour or two later. The Judge has already informed you that he is to have an hour to reply to me. I doubt not but you have been a little surprised to learn that I have consented to give one of his high reputation and known ability, this advantage of me. Indeed, my consenting to it, though reluctant, was not wholly unselfish; for I suspected if it were understood, that the Judge was entirely done, you democrats would leave, and not hear me; but by giving him the close, I felt confident you would stay for the fun of hearing him skin me."

The audience signified their assent to the arrangement, and adjourned to 7 o'clock P.M., at which time they re-assembled, and Mr. LINCOLN spoke substantially as follows:

The repeal of the Missouri Compromise, and the propriety of its restoration, constitute the subject of what I am about to say.

As I desire to present my own connected view of this subject, my remarks will not be, specifically, an answer to Judge Douglas; yet, as I proceed, the main points he has presented will arise, and will receive such respectful attention as I may be able to give them.

I wish further to say, that I do not propose to question the patriotism, or to assail the motives of any man, or class of men; but rather to strictly confine myself to the naked merits of the question.

I also wish to be no less than National in all the positions I may take; and whenever I take ground which others have thought, or may think, narrow, sectional and dangerous to the Union, I hope to give a reason, which will appear sufficient, at least to some, why I think differently.

And, as this subject is no other, than part and parcel of the larger general question of domestic-slavery, I wish to MAKE and to KEEP the distinction between the EXISTING institution, and the EXTENSION of it, so broad, and so clear, that no honest man can misunderstand me, and no dishonest one, successfully misrepresent me.

In order to a clear understanding of what the Missouri Compromise is, a short history of the preceding kindred subjects will perhaps be proper. When we established our independence, we did not own, or claim, the country to which this compromise applies. Indeed, strictly speaking, the confederacy then owned no country at all; the States respectively owned the country within their limits; and some of them owned territory beyond their strict State limits. Virginia thus owned the North-Western territory—the country out of which the principal part of Ohio, all Indiana, all Illinois, all Michigan and all Wisconsin, have since been formed. She also owned (perhaps within her then limits) what has since been formed into the State of Kentucky. North Carolina thus owned what is now the State of Tennessee; and South Carolina and Georgia, in separate parts, owned what are now Mississippi and Alabama. Connecticut, I think, owned the little remaining part of Ohio—being the same where they now send Giddings to Congress, and beat all creation at making cheese. These territories, together with the States themselves, constituted all the country over which the confederacy then claimed any sort of jurisdiction. We were then living under the Articles of Confederation, which were superceded by the Constitution several years afterwards. The question of ceding these territories to the general government was set on foot. Mr. Jefferson, the author of the Declaration of Independence, and otherwise a chief actor in the revolution; then a delegate in Congress; afterwards twice President; who was, is, and perhaps will continue to be, the most distinguished politician of our history; a Virginian by birth and continued residence, and withal, a slave-holder; conceived the idea of taking that occasion, to prevent slavery ever going into the north-western territory. He prevailed on the Virginia Legislature to adopt his views, and to cede the territory, making the prohibition of slavery therein, a condition of the deed. Congress accepted the cession, with the condition; and in the first Ordinance (which the acts of Congress were then called) for the government of the territory, provided that slavery should never be permitted therein. This is the famed ordinance of '87 so often spoken of. Thenceforward, for sixty-one years, and until in 1848, the last scrap of this territory came into the Union as the State of Wisconsin, all parties acted in quiet obedience to this ordinance. It is now what Jefferson foresaw and intended—the happy home of teeming millions of free, white, prosperous people, and no slave amongst them.

Thus, with the author of the declaration of Independence, the policy of prohibiting slavery in new territory originated. Thus, away back of the constitution, in the pure fresh, free breath of the revolution, the State of Virginia, and the National congress put that policy in practice. Thus through sixty odd of the best years of the republic did that policy steadily work to its great and beneficent end. And thus, in those five states, and five millions of free, enterprising people, we have before us the rich fruits of this policy. But *now* new light breaks upon us. Now congress declares this ought never to have been; and the like of it, must never be again. The sacred right of self government is grossly violated by it! We even find some men, who drew their first breath, and every other breath of their lives, under this very restriction, now live in dread of absolute suffocation, if they should be restricted in the "sacred right" of taking slaves to Nebraska. That *perfect* liberty they sigh for—the liberty of making slaves of other people—Jefferson never thought of; their own father never thought of; they never thought of themselves, a year ago. How fortunate for them, they did not sooner become sensible of their great misery! Oh, how difficult it is to treat with respect, such assaults upon all we have ever really held sacred.

But to return to history. In 1803 we purchased what was then called Louisiana, of France. It included the now states of Louisiana, Arkansas, Missouri, and Iowa; also the territory of Minnesota, and the present bone of contention, Kansas and Nebraska. Slavery already existed among the French at New Orleans; and, to some extent, at St. Louis. In 1812 Louisiana came into the Union as a slave state, without controversy. In 1818 or '19, Missouri showed signs of a wish to come in with slavery. This was resisted by northern members of Congress; and thus began the first great slavery agitation in the nation. This controversy lasted several months, and became very angry and exciting; the House of Representatives voting steadily for the prohibition of slavery in Missouri, and the Senate voting as steadily against it. Threats of breaking up the Union were freely made; and the ablest public men of the day became seriously alarmed. At length a compromise was made, in which, like all compromises, both sides yielded something. It was a law passed on the 6th day of March, 1820, providing that Missouri might come into the Union *with* slavery, but that in all the remaining part of the territory purchased of France, which lies north of 36 degrees and 30 minutes north latitude, slavery should never be permitted. This provision of law, *is the Missouri Compromise.* In excluding slavery North of the line, the same language is employed as in the Ordinance of '87. It directly applied to Iowa, Minnesota, and to the present bone of contention, Kansas and Nebraska. Whether there should or should not, be slavery south of that line, nothing was said in the law; but Arkansas constituted the principal remaining part, south of the line; and it has since been admitted as a slave state without serious controversy. More recently, Iowa, north of the line, came in as a free state without controversy. Still later, Minnesota, north of the line, had a territorial organization without controversy. Texas principally south of the line, and West of Arkansas; though originally within the purchase from France, had, in 1819, been traded off to Spain, in our treaty for the acquisition of Florida. It had thus become a part of Mexico. Mexico revolutionized and became independent of Spain. American citizens began settling rapidly, with their slaves in the southern part of Texas. Soon they revolutionized against Mexico, and established an independent government of their own, adopting a constitution, with slavery, strongly resembling the constitutions of our slave states. By still another rapid move, Texas, claiming a boundary much further West, than when we parted with her in 1819, was brought back to the United States, and admitted into the Union as a slave state. There then was little or no settlement in the northern part of Texas, a considerable portion of which lay north of the Missouri line; and in the resolutions admitting her into the Union, the Missouri restriction was expressly extended westward across her territory. This was in 1845, only nine years ago.

Thus originated the Missouri Compromise; and thus has it been respected down to 1845. And even four years later, in 1849, our distinguished Senator, in a public address, held the following language in relation to it:

"The Missouri Compromise had been in practical operation for about a quarter of a century, and had received the sanction and approbation of men of all parties in every section of the Union. It had allayed all sectional jealousies and irritations growing out of this vexed question, and harmonized and tranquilized the whole country. It had given to Henry Clay, as its prominent champion, the proud sobriquet of the *"Great Pacificator"* and by that title and for that service, his political friends had repeatedly appealed to the people to rally under his standard, as a presidential candidate, as the man who had exhibited the patriotism and the power to suppress, an unholy and treasonable agitation, and preserve the Union. He was not aware that any man or any party from any section of the Union, had ever urged as an objection to Mr. Clay, that he was the great champion of the Missouri Compromise. On the contrary, the effort was made by the opponents of Mr. Clay, to prove that he was not entitled to the exclusive merit of that great patriotic measure, and that the honor was equally due to others as well as to him, for securing its adoption—that it had its origin in the hearts of all patriotic men, who desired to preserve and perpetuate the blessings of our glorious Union—an origin akin that of the constitution of the United States, conceived in the same spirit of fraternal affection, and calculated to remove forever, the only danger, which seemed to threaten, at some distant day, to sever the social bond of union. All the evidences of public opinion at that day, seemed to indicate that this Compromise had been canonized in the hearts of the American people, as a sacred thing which no ruthless hand would ever be reckless enough to disturb."

I do not read this extract to involve Judge Douglas in an inconsistency. If he afterwards thought he had been wrong, it was right for him to change. I bring this forward merely to show the high estimate placed on the Missouri Compromise by all parties up to so late as the year 1849.

But, going back a little, in point of time, our war with Mexico broke out in 1846. When Congress was about adjourning that session, President Polk asked them to place two millions of dollars under his control, to be used by him in the recess, if found practicable and expedient, in negociating a treaty of peace with Mexico, and acquiring some part of her territory. A bill was duly got up, for the purpose, and was progressing swimmingly, in the House of Representatives, when a member by the name of David Wilmot, a democrat from Pennsylvania, moved as an amendment "Provided that in any territory thus acquired, there shall never be slavery."

This is the origin of the far-famed "Wilmot Proviso." It created a great flutter; but it stuck like wax, was voted into the bill, and the bill passed with it through the House. The Senate, however, adjourned without final action on it and so both appropriation and proviso were lost, for the time. The war continued, and at the next session, the president renewed his request for the appropriation, enlarging the amount, I think, to three million. Again came the proviso; and defeated the measure. Congress adjourned again, and the war went on. In Dec., 1847, the new congress assembled. I was in the lower House that term. The "Wilmot Proviso" or the principle of it, was constantly coming up in some shape or other, and I think I may venture to say I voted for it at least forty times; during the short term I was there. The Senate, however, held it in check, and it never became law. In the spring of 1848 a treaty of peace was made with Mexico; by which we obtained that portion of her country which now constitutes the territories of New Mexico and Utah, and the now state of California. By this treaty the Wilmot Proviso was defeated, as so far as it was intended to be, a condition of the acquisition of territory. Its friends however, were still determined to find some way to restrain slavery from getting into the new country. This new acquisition lay directly West of our old purchase from France, and extended west to the Pacific ocean—and was so situated that if the Missouri line should be extended straight West, the new country would be divided by such extended line, leaving some North and some South of it. On Judge Douglas' motion a bill, or provision of a bill, passed the Senate to so extend the Missouri line. The Proviso men in the House, including myself, voted it down, because by implication, it gave up the Southern part to slavery, while we were bent on having it *all* free.

In the fall of 1848 the gold mines were discovered in California. This attracted people to it with unprecedented rapidity, so that on, or soon after, the meeting of the new congress in Dec., 1849, she already had a population of nearly a hundred thousand, had called a convention, formed a state constitution, excluding slavery, and was knocking for admission into the Union. The Proviso men, of course were for letting her in, but the Senate, always true to the other side would not consent to her admission. And there California stood, kept *out* of the Union, because she would not let slavery *into* her borders. Under all the circumstances perhaps this was not wrong. There were other points of dispute, connected with the general question of slavery, which equally needed adjustment. The South clamored for a more efficient fugitive slave law. The North clamored for the abolition of a peculiar species of slave trade in the District of Columbia, in connection with which, in view from the windows of the capitol, a sort of negro-livery stable, where droves of negroes were collected, temporarily kept, and finally taken to Southern markets, precisely like droves of horses, had been openly maintained for fifty years. Utah and New Mexico needed territorial governments; and whether slavery should or should not be prohibited within them, was another question. The indefinite Western boundary of Texas was to be settled. She was received a slave state; and consequently the farther West the slavery men could push her boundary, the more slave country they secured. And the farther East the slavery opponents could thrust the boundary back, the less slave ground was secured. Thus this was just as clearly a slavery question as any of the others.

These points all needed adjustment; and they were all held up, perhaps wisely to make them help to adjust one another. The Union, now, as in 1820, was thought to be in danger; and devotion to the Union rightfully inclined men to yield somewhat, in points where nothing else could have so inclined them. A compromise was finally effected. The south got their new fugitive-slave law; and the North got California, (the far best part of our acquisition from Mexico,) as a free State. The south got a provision that New Mexico and Utah, *when admitted as States*, may come in *with* or *without* slavery as they may then choose; and the north got the slave-trade abolished in the District of Columbia. The north got the western boundary of Texas, thence further back eastward than the south desired; but, in turn, they gave Texas ten millions of dollars, with which to pay her old debts. This is the Compromise of 1850.

Preceding the Presidential election of 1852, each of the great political parties, democrats and whigs, met in convention, and adopted resolutions endorsing the compromise of '50; as a "finality," a final settlement, so far as these parties could make it so, of all slavery agitation. Previous to this, in 1851, the Illinois Legislature had indorsed it.

During this long period of time Nebraska had remained, substantially an uninhabited country, but now emigration to, and settlement within it began to take place. It is about one third as large as the present United States, and its importance so long overlooked, begins to come into view. The restriction of slavery by the Missouri Compromise directly applies to it; in fact, was first made, and has since been maintained, expressly for it. In 1853, a bill to give it a territorial government passed the House of Representatives, and, in the hands of Judge Douglas, failed of passing the Senate only for want of time. This bill contained no repeal of the Missouri Compromise. Indeed, when it was assailed because it did not contain such repeal, Judge Douglas defended it in its existing form.

On January 4th, 1854, Judge Douglas introduces a new bill to give Nebraska territorial government. He accompanies this bill with a report, in which last, he expressly recommends that the Missouri Compromise shall neither be affirmed nor repealed.

Before long the bill is so modified as to make two territories instead of one; calling the Southern one Kansas.

Also, about a month after the introduction of the bill, on the judge's own motion, it is so amended as to declare the Missouri Compromise inoperative and void; and, substantially, that the People who go and settle there may establish slavery, or exclude it, as they may see fit. In this shape the bill passed both branches of congress, and became a law.

This is the *repeal* of the Missouri Compromise. The foregoing history may not be precisely accurate in every particular; but I am sure it is sufficiently so, for all the uses I shall attempt to make of it, and in it, we have before us, the chief material enabling us to correctly judge whether the repeal of the Missouri Compromise is right or wrong.

I think, and shall try to show, that it is wrong; wrong in its direct effect, letting slavery into Kansas and Nebraska—and wrong in its prospective principle, allowing it to spread to every other part of the wide world, where men can be found inclined to take it.

This *declared* indifference, but as I must think, covert *real* zeal for the spread of slavery, I can not but hate. I hate it because of the monstrous injustice of slavery itself. I hate it because it deprives our republican example of its just influence in the world—enables the enemies of free institutions, with plausibility, to taunt us as hypocrites—causes the real friends of freedom to doubt our sincerity, and especially because it forces so many really good men amongst ourselves into an open war with the very fundamental principles of civil liberty—criticising the Declaration of Independence, and insisting that there is no right principle of action but *self-interest*.

Before proceeding, let me say I think I have no prejudice against the Southern people. They are just what we would be in their situation. If slavery did not now exist amongst them, they would not introduce it. If it did now exist amongst us, we should not instantly give it up. This I believe of the masses north and south. Doubtless there are individuals, on both sides, who would not hold slaves under any circumstances; and others who would gladly introduce slavery anew, if it were out of existence. We know that some southern men do free their slaves, go north, and become tip-top abolitionists; while some northern ones go south, and become most cruel slave-masters.

When southern people tell us they are no more responsible for the origin of slavery, than we; I acknowledge the fact. When it is said that the institution exists; and that it is very difficult to get rid of it, in any satisfactory way, I can understand and appreciate the saying. I surely will not blame them for not doing what I should not know how to do myself. If all earthly power were given me, I should not know what to do, as to the existing institution. My first impulse would be to free all the slaves, and send them to Liberia,—to their own native land. But a moment's reflection would convince me, that whatever of high hope, (as I think there is) there may be in this, in the long run, its sudden execution is impossible. If they were all landed there in a day, they would all perish in the next ten days; and there are not surplus shipping and surplus money enough in the world to carry them there in many times ten days. What then? Free them all, and keep them among us as underlings? Is it quite certain that this betters their condition? I think I would not hold one in slavery, at any rate; yet the point is not clear enough for me to denounce people upon. What next? Free them, and make them politically and socially, our equals? My own feelings will not admit of this; and if mine would, we well know that those of the great mass of white people will not. Whether this feeling accords with justice and sound judgment, is not the sole question, if indeed, it is any part of it. A universal feeling, whether well or ill-founded, can not be safely disregarded. We can not, then, make them equals. It does seem to me that systems of gradual emancipation might be adopted; but for their tardiness in this, I will not undertake to judge our brethren of the south.

When they remind us of their constitutional rights, I acknowledge them, not grudgingly, but fully, and fairly; and I would give them any legislation for the reclaiming of their fugitives, which should not, in its stringency, be more likely to carry a free man into slavery, than our ordinary criminal laws are to hang an innocent one.

But all this, to my judgment, furnishes no more excuse for permitting slavery to go into our own free territory, than it would for reviving the African slave trade by law. The law which forbids the bringing of slaves *from* Africa; and that which has so long forbid the taking them *to* Nebraska, can hardly be distinguished on any moral principle; and the repeal of the former could find quite as plausible excuses as that of the latter.

The arguments by which the repeal of the Missouri Compromise is sought to be justified, are these:

First, that the Nebraska country needed a territorial government.

Second, that in various ways, the public had repudiated it, and demanded the repeal; and therefore should not now complain of it.

And lastly, that the repeal establishes a principle, which is intrinsically right.

I will attempt an answer to each of them in its turn.

First, then, if that country was in need of a territorial organization, could it not have had it as well without as with the repeal? Iowa and Minnesota, to both of which the Missouri restriction applied, had, without its repeal, each in succession, territorial organizations. And even, the year before, a bill for Nebraska itself, was within an ace of passing, without the repealing clause; and this in the hands of the same men who are now the champions of repeal. Why no necessity then for the repeal? But still later, when this very bill was first brought in, it contained no repeal. But, say they, because the public had demanded, or rather commanded the repeal, the repeal was to accompany the organization, whenever that should occur.

Now I deny that the public ever demanded any such thing—ever repudiated the Missouri Compromise—ever commanded its repeal. I deny it, and call for the proof. It is not contended, I believe, that any such command has ever been given in express terms. It is only said that it was done *in principle*. The support of the Wilmot Proviso, is the first fact mentioned, to prove that the Missouri restriction was re-

pudiated in *principle*, and the second is, the refusal to extend
the Missouri line over the country acquired from Mexico.
These are near enough alike to be treated together. The one
was to exclude the chances of slavery from the *whole* new acquisition by the lump; and the other was to reject a division
of it, by which one *half* was to be given up to those chances.
Now whether this was a repudiation of the Missouri line, in
principle, depends upon whether the Missouri law contained
any *principle* requiring the line to be extended over the country acquired from Mexico. I contend it did not. I insist that it
contained no general principle, but that it was, in every sense,
specific. That its terms limit it to the country purchased from
France, is undenied and undeniable. It could have no principle beyond the intention of those who made it. They did not
intend to extend the line to country which they did not own.
If they intended to extend it, in the event of acquiring additional territory, why did they not say so? It was just as easy to
say, that "in all the country west of the Mississippi, which we
now own, *or may hereafter acquire* there shall never be
slavery," as to say, what they did say; and they would have
said it if they had meant it. An intention to extend the law is
not only not mentioned in the law, but is not mentioned in
any contemporaneous history. Both the law itself, and the history of the times are a blank as to any *principle* of extension;
and by neither the known rules for construing statutes and
contracts, nor by common sense, can any such *principle* be
inferred.

Another fact showing the *specific* character of the Missouri
law—showing that it intended no more than it expressed—
showing that the line was not intended as a universal dividing
line between free and slave territory, present and prospective—north of which slavery could never go—is the fact that
by that very law, Missouri came in as a slave state, *north* of the
line. If that law contained any prospective *principle*, the whole
law must be looked to in order to ascertain what the *principle*
was. And by this rule, the south could fairly contend that
inasmuch as they got one slave state north of the line at the
inception of the law, they have the right to have another
given them *north* of it occasionally—now and then in the indefinite westward extension of the line. This demonstrates the

absurdity of attempting to deduce a prospective *principle* from the Missouri Compromise line.

When we voted for the Wilmot Proviso, we were voting to keep slavery *out* of the whole Mexican acquisition; and little did we think we were thereby voting, to let it *into* Nebraska, laying several hundred miles distant. When we voted against extending the Missouri line, little did we think we were voting to destroy the old line, then of near thirty years standing. To argue that we thus repudiated the Missouri Compromise is no less absurd than it would be to argue that because we have, so far, forborne to acquire Cuba, we have thereby, *in principle*, repudiated our former acquisitions, and determined to throw them out of the Union! No less absurd than it would be to say that because I may have refused to build an addition to my house, I thereby have decided to destroy the existing house! And if I catch you setting fire to my house, you will turn upon me and say I INSTRUCTED you to do it! The most conclusive argument, however, that, while voting for the Wilmot Proviso, and while voting against the EXTENSION of the Missouri line, we never thought of disturbing the original Missouri Compromise, is found in the facts, that there was then, and still is, an unorganized tract of fine country, nearly as large as the state of Missouri, lying immediately west of Arkansas, and south of the Missouri Compromise line; and that we never attempted to prohibit slavery as to it. I wish particular attention to this. It adjoins the original Missouri Compromise line, by its northern boundary; and consequently is part of the country, into which, by implication, slavery was permitted to go, by that compromise. There it has lain open ever since, and there it still lies. And yet no effort has been made at any time to wrest it from the south. In all our struggles to prohibit slavery within our Mexican acquisitions, we never so much as lifted a finger to prohibit it, as to this tract. Is not this entirely conclusive that at all times, we have held the Missouri Compromise as a sacred thing; even when against ourselves, as well as when for us?

Senator Douglas sometimes says the Missouri line itself was, *in principle*, only an extension of the line of the ordinance of '87—that is to say, an extension of the Ohio river. I think this is weak enough on its face. I will remark, however that, as a glance at the map will show, the Missouri line is a long way farther South than the Ohio; and that if our Senator, in proposing his extension, had stuck to the *principle* of jogging southward, perhaps it might not have been voted down so readily.

But next it is said that the compromises of '50 and the ratification of them by both political parties, in '52, established a *new principle*, which required the repeal of the Missouri Compromise. This again I deny. I deny it, and demand the proof. I have already stated fully what the compromises of '50 are. The particular part of those measures, for which the virtual repeal of the Missouri compromise is sought to be inferred (for it is admitted they contain nothing about it, in express terms) is the provision in the Utah and New Mexico laws, which permits them when they seek admission into the Union as States, to come in with or without slavery as they shall then see fit. Now I insist this provision was made for Utah and New Mexico, and for no other place whatever. It had no more direct reference to Nebraska than it had to the territories of the moon. But, say they, it had reference to Nebraska, *in principle*. Let us see. The North consented to this provision, not because they considered it right in itself; but because they were compensated—paid for it. They, at the same time, got California into the Union as a free State. This was far the best part of all they had struggled for by the Wilmot Proviso. They also got the area of slavery somewhat narrowed in the settlement of the boundary of Texas. Also, they got the slave trade abolished in the District of Columbia. For all these desirable objects the North could afford to yield something; and they did yield to the South the Utah and New Mexico provision. I do not mean that the whole North, or even a majority, yielded, when the law passed; but enough yielded, when added to the vote of the South, to carry the measure. Now can it be pretended that the *principle* of this arrangement requires us to permit the same provision to be applied to Nebraska, *without any equivalent at all*? Give us another free State; press the boundary of Texas still further back, give us another step toward the destruction of slavery in the District, and you present us a similar case. But ask us not to repeat, for nothing, what you paid for in the first instance. If you wish the thing again, pay again. That is the *principle* of the compromises of '50, if indeed they had any principles beyond their specific terms—it was the system of equivalents.

Again, if Congress, at that time, intended that all future territories should, when admitted as States, come in with or without slavery, at their own option, why did it not say so? With such an universal provision, all know the bills could not have passed. Did they, then—could they—establish a *principle* contrary to their own intention? Still further, if they intended to establish the principle that wherever Congress had control, it should be left to the people to do as they thought fit with slavery why did they not authorize the people of the District of Columbia at their adoption to abolish slavery within these limits? I personally know that this has not been left undone, because it was unthought of. It was frequently spoken of by members of Congress and by citizens of Washington six years ago; and I heard no one express a doubt that a system of gradual emancipation, with compensation to owners, would meet the approbation of a large majority of the white people of the District. But without the action of Congress they could say nothing; and Congress said "no." In the measures of 1850 Congress had the subject of slavery in the District expressly in hand. If they were then establishing the *principle* of allowing the people to do as they please with slavery, why did they not apply the *principle* to that people?

Again, it is claimed that by the Resolutions of the Illinois Legislature, passed in 1851, the repeal of the Missouri compromise was demanded. This I deny also. Whatever may be worked out by a criticism of the language of those resolutions, the people have never understood them as being any more than an endorsement of the compromises of 1850; and a release of our Senators from voting for the Wilmot Proviso. The whole people are living witnesses, that this only, was their view. Finally, it is asked "If we did not mean to apply the Utah and New Mexico provision, to all future territories, what did we mean, when we, in 1852, endorsed the compromises of '50?"

For myself, I can answer this question most easily. I meant not to ask a repeal, or modification of the fugitive slave law. I meant not to ask for the abolition of slavery in the District of

Columbia. I meant not to resist the admission of Utah and New Mexico, even should they ask to come in as slave States. I meant nothing about additional territories, because, as I understood, we then had no territory whose character as to slavery was not already settled. As to Nebraska, I regarded its character as being fixed, by the Missouri compromise, for thirty years—as unalterably fixed as that of my own home in Illinois. As to new acquisitions I said "sufficient unto the day is the evil thereof." When we make new acquisitions, we will, as heretofore, try to manage them some how. That is my answer. That is what I meant and said; and I appeal to the people to say, each for himself, whether that was not also the universal meaning of the free States.

And now, in turn, let me ask a few questions. If by any, or all these matters, the repeal of the Missouri Compromise was commanded, why was not the command sooner obeyed? Why was the repeal omitted in the Nebraska bill of 1853? Why was it omitted in the original bill of 1854? Why, in the accompanying report, was such a repeal characterized as a *departure* from the course pursued in 1850? and its continued omission recommended?

I am aware Judge Douglas now argues that the subsequent express repeal is no substantial alteration of the bill. This argument seems wonderful to me. It is as if one should argue that white and black are not different. He admits, however, that there is a literal change in the bill; and that he made the change in deference to other Senators, who would not support the bill without. This proves that those other Senators thought the change a substantial one; and that the Judge thought their opinions worth deferring to. His own opinions, therefore, seem not to rest on a very firm basis even in his own mind—and I suppose the world believes, and will continue to believe, that precisely on the substance of that change this whole agitation has arisen.

I conclude then, that the public never demanded the repeal of the Missouri compromise.

I now come to consider whether the repeal, with its avowed principle, is intrinsically right. I insist that it is not. Take the particular case. A controversy had arisen between the advocates and opponents of slavery, in relation to its establishment within the country we had purchased of France. The southern, and then best part of the purchase, was already in as a slave State. The controversy was settled by also letting Missouri in as a slave State; but with the agreement that within all the remaining part of the purchase, North of a certain line, there should never be slavery. As to what was to be done with the remaining part south of the line, nothing was said; but perhaps the fair implication was, that it should come in with slavery if it should so choose. The southern part, except a portion heretofore mentioned, afterwards did come in with slavery, as the State of Arkansas. All these many years since 1820, the Northern part had remained a wilderness. At length settlements began in it also. In due course, Iowa, came in as a free State, and Minnesota was given a territorial government, without removing the slavery restriction. Finally the sole remaining part, North of the line, Kansas and Nebraska, was to be organized; and it is proposed, and carried, to blot out the old dividing line of thirty-four years standing, and to open the whole of that country to the introduction of slavery. Now, this, to my mind, is manifestly unjust. After an angry and dangerous controversy, the parties made friends by dividing the bone of contention. The one party first appropriates her own share, beyond all power to be disturbed in the possession of it; and then seizes the share of the other party. It is as if two starving men had divided their only loaf; the one had hastily swallowed his half, and then grabbed the other half just as he was putting it to his mouth!

Let me here drop the main argument, to notice what I consider rather an inferior matter. It is argued that slavery will not go to Kansas and Nebraska, *in any event*. This is a *palliation*—a *lullaby*. I have some hope that it will not; but let us not be too confident. As to climate, a glance at the map shows that there are five slave States—Delaware, Maryland, Virginia, Kentucky, and Missouri—and also the District of Columbia, all north of the Missouri compromise line. The census returns of 1850 show that, within these, there are 867,276 slaves—being more than one-fourth of all the slaves in the nation.

It is not climate, then, that will keep slavery out of these territories. Is there any thing in the peculiar nature of the country? Missouri adjoins these territories, by her entire western boundary, and slavery is already within every one of her western counties. I have even heard it said that there are more slaves, in proportion to whites, in the north western county of Missouri, than within any county of the State. Slavery pressed entirely up to the old western boundary of the State, and when, rather recently, a part of that boundary, at the north-west was moved out a little farther west, slavery followed on quite up to the new line. Now, when the restriction is removed, what is to prevent it from going still further? Climate will not. No peculiarity of the country will—nothing in *nature* will. Will the disposition of the people prevent it? Those nearest the scene, are all in favor of the extension. The yankees, who are opposed to it may be more numerous; but in military phrase, the battle-field is too far from *their* base of operations.

But it is said, there now is *no* law in Nebraska on the subject of slavery; and that, in such case, taking a slave there, operates his freedom. That *is* good book-law; but is not the rule of actual practice. Wherever slavery is, it has been first introduced without law. The oldest laws we find concerning it, are not laws introducing it; but *regulating* it, as an already existing thing. A white man takes his slave to Nebraska now; who will inform the negro that he is free? Who will take him before court to test the question of his freedom? In ignorance of his legal emancipation, he is kept chopping, splitting and plowing. Others are brought, and move on in the same track. At last, if ever the time for voting comes, on the question of slavery, the institution already in fact exists in the country, and cannot well be removed. The facts of its presence, and the difficulty of its removal will carry the vote in its favor. Keep it out until a vote is taken, and a vote in favor of it, can not be got in any population of forty thousand, on earth, who have been drawn together by the ordinary motives of emigration and settlement. To get slaves into the country simultaneously with the whites, in the incipient stages of settlement, is the precise stake played for, and won in this Nebraska measure.

The question is asked us, "If slaves will go in, notwithstanding the general principle of law liberates them, why would they not equally go in against positive statute law?—

go in, even if the Missouri restriction were maintained?" I answer, because it takes a much bolder man to venture in, with his property, in the latter case, than in the former—because the positive congressional enactment is known to, and respected by all, or nearly all; whereas the negative principle that *no* law is free law, is not much known except among lawyers. We have some experience of this practical difference. In spite of the Ordinance of '87, a few negroes were brought into Illinois, and held in a state of quasi slavery; not enough, however to carry a vote of the people in favor of the institution when they came to form a constitution. But in the adjoining Missouri country, where there was no ordinance of '87—was no restriction—they were carried ten times, nay a hundred times, as fast, and actually made a slave State. This is fact—naked fact.

Another LULLABY argument is, that taking slaves to new countries does not increase their number—does not make any one slave who otherwise would be free. There is some truth in this, and I am glad of it, but it is not WHOLLY true. The African slave trade is not yet effectually suppressed; and if we make a reasonable deduction for the white people amongst us, who are foreigners, and the descendants of foreigners, arriving here since 1808, we shall find the increase of the black population out-running that of the white, to an extent unaccountable, except by supposing that some of them too, have been coming from Africa. If this be so, the opening of new countries to the institution, increases the demand for, and augments the price of slaves, and so does, in fact, make slaves of freemen by causing them to be brought from Africa, and sold into bondage.

But, however this may be, we know the opening of new countries to slavery, tends to the perpetuation of the institution, and so does KEEP men in slavery who otherwise would be free. This result we do not FEEL like favoring, and we are under no legal obligation to suppress our feelings in this respect.

Equal justice to the south, it is said, requires us to consent to the extending of slavery to new countries. That is to say, inasmuch as you do not object to my taking my hog to Nebraska, therefore I must not object to you taking your slave.

Now, I admit this is perfectly logical, if there is no difference between hogs and negroes. But while you thus require me to deny the humanity of the negro, I wish to ask whether you of the south yourselves, have ever been willing to do as much? It is kindly provided that of all those who come into the world, only a small percentage are natural tyrants. That percentage is no larger in the slave States than in the free. The great majority, south as well as north, have human sympathies, of which they can no more divest themselves than they can of their sensibility to physical pain. These sympathies in the bosoms of the southern people, manifest in many ways, their sense of the wrong of slavery, and their consciousness that, after all, there is humanity in the negro. If they deny this, let me address them a few plain questions. In 1820 you joined the north, almost unanimously, in declaring the African slave trade piracy, and in annexing to it the punishment of death. Why did you do this? If you did not feel that it was wrong, why did you join in providing that men should be hung for it? The practice was no more than bringing wild negroes from Africa, to sell to such as would buy them. But you never thought of hanging men for catching and selling wild horses, wild buffaloes or wild bears.

Again, you have amongst you, a sneaking individual, of the class of native tyrants, known as the "SLAVE-DEALER." He watches your necessities, and crawls up to buy your slave, at a speculating price. If you cannot help it, you sell to him; but if you can help it, you drive him from your door. You despise him utterly. You do not recognize him as a friend, or even as an honest man. Your children must not play with his; they may rollick freely with the little negroes, but not with the "slave-dealers" children. If you are obliged to deal with him, you try to get through the job without so much as touching him. It is common with you to join hands with the men you meet; but with the slave dealer you avoid the ceremony— instinctively shrinking from the snaky contact. If he grows rich and retires from business, you still remember him, and still keep up the ban of non-intercourse upon him and his family. Now why is this? You do not so treat the man who deals in corn, cattle or tobacco.

And yet again; there are in the United States and territories, including the District of Columbia, 433,643 free blacks. At $500 per head they are worth over two hundred millions of dollars. How comes this vast amount of property to be running about without owners? We do not see free horses or free cattle running at large. How is this? All these free blacks are the descendants of slaves, or have been slaves themselves, and they would be slaves now, but for SOMETHING which has operated on their white owners, inducing them, at vast pecuniary sacrifices, to liberate them. What is that SOMETHING? Is there any mistaking it? In all these cases it is your sense of justice, and human sympathy, continually telling you, that the poor negro has some natural right to himself—that those who deny it, and make mere merchandise of him, deserve kickings, contempt and death.

And now, why will you ask us to deny the humanity of the slave? and estimate him only as the equal of the hog? Why ask us to do what you will not do yourselves? Why ask us to do for *nothing*, what two hundred million of dollars could not induce you to do?

But one great argument in the support of the repeal of the Missouri Compromise, is still to come. That argument is "the sacred right of self government." It seems our distinguished Senator has found great difficulty in getting his antagonists, even in the Senate to meet him fairly on this argument—some poet has said

"Fools rush in where angels fear to tread."

At the hazzard of being thought one of the fools of this quotation, I meet that argument—I rush in, I take that bull by the horns.

I trust I understand, and truly estimate the right of self-government. My faith in the proposition that each man should do precisely as he pleases with all which is exclusively his own, lies at the foundation of the sense of justice there is in me. I extend the principles to communities of men, as well as to individuals. I so extend it, because it is politically wise, as well as naturally just: politically wise, in saving us from broils about matters which do not concern us. Here, or at Washington, I would not trouble myself with the oyster laws of Virginia, or the cranberry laws of Indiana.

The doctrine of self government is right—absolutely and eternally right—but it has no just application, as here attempted. Or perhaps I should rather say that whether it has such just application depends upon whether a negro is *not* or *is* a man. If he is *not* a man, why in that case, he who *is* a man may, as a matter of self-government, do just as he pleases with him. But if the negro *is* a man, is it not to that extent, a total destruction of self-government, to say that he too shall not govern *himself*? When the white man governs himself that is self-government; but when he governs himself, and also governs *another* man, that is *more* than self-government—that is despotism. If the negro is a *man*, why then my ancient faith teaches me that "all men are created equal;" and that there can be no moral right in connection with one man's making a slave of another.

Judge Douglas frequently, with bitter irony and sarcasm, paraphrases our argument by saying "The white people of Nebraska are good enough to govern themselves, *but they are not good enough to govern a few miserable negroes!!*"

Well I doubt not that the people of Nebraska are, and will continue to be as good as the average of people elsewhere. I do not say the contrary. What I do say is, that no man is good enough to govern another man, *without that other's consent.* I say this is the leading principle—the sheet anchor of American republicanism. Our Declaration of Independence says:

"We hold these truths to be self evident: that all men are created equal; that they are endowed by their Creator with certain inalienable rights; that among these are life, liberty and the pursuit of happiness. That to secure these rights, governments are instituted among men, DERIVING THEIR JUST POWERS FROM THE CONSENT OF THE GOVERNED."

I have quoted so much at this time merely to show that according to our ancient faith, the just powers of governments are derived from the consent of the governed. Now the relation of masters and slaves is, PRO TANTO, a total violation of this principle. The master not only governs the slave without his consent; but he governs him by a set of rules altogether different from those which he prescribes for himself. Allow ALL the governed an equal voice in the government, and that, and that only is self government.

Let it not be said I am contending for the establishment of political and social equality between the whites and blacks. I have already said the contrary. I am not now combating the argument of NECESSITY, arising from the fact that the blacks are already amongst us; but I am combating what is set up as MORAL argument for allowing them to be taken where they have never yet been—arguing against the EXTENSION of a bad thing, which where it already exists, we must of necessity, manage as we best can.

In support of his application of the doctrine of self-government, Senator Douglas has sought to bring to his aid the opinions and examples of our revolutionary fathers. I am glad he has done this. I love the sentiments of those old-time men; and shall be most happy to abide by their opinions. He shows us that when it was in contemplation for the colonies to break off from Great Britain, and set up a new government for themselves, several of the states instructed their delegates to go for the measure PROVIDED EACH STATE SHOULD BE ALLOWED TO REGULATE ITS DOMESTIC CONCERNS IN ITS OWN WAY. I do not quote; but this in substance. This was right. I see nothing objectionable in it. I also think it probable that it had some reference to the existence of slavery amongst them. I will not deny that it had. But had it, in any reference to the carrying of slavery into NEW COUNTRIES? That is the question; and we will let the fathers themselves answer it.

This same generation of men, and mostly the same individuals of the generation, who declared this principle—who declared independence—who fought the war of the revolution through—who afterwards made the constitution under which we still live—these same men passed the ordinance of '87, declaring that slavery should never go to the north-west territory. I have no doubt Judge Douglas thinks they were very inconsistent in this. It is a question of discrimination between them and him. But there is not an inch of ground left for his claiming that their opinions—their example—their authority—are on his side in this controversy.

Again, is not Nebraska, while a territory, a part of us? Do we not own the country? And if we surrender the control of it, do we not surrender the right of self-government? It is part of ourselves. If you say we shall not control it because it is ONLY part, the same is true of every other part; and when all the parts are gone, what has become of the whole? What is then left of us? What use for the general government, when there is nothing left for it to govern?

But you say this question should be left to the people of Nebraska, because they are more particularly interested. If this be the rule, you must leave it to each individual to say for himself whether he will have slaves. What better moral right have thirty-one citizens of Nebraska to say, that the thirty-second shall not hold slaves, than the people of the thirty-one States have to say that slavery shall not go into the thirty-second State at all?

But if it is a sacred right for the people of Nebraska to take and hold slaves there, it is equally their sacred right to buy them where they can buy them cheapest; and that undoubtedly will be on the coast of Africa; provided you will consent to not hang them for going there to buy them. You must remove this restriction too, from the sacred right of self-government. I am aware you say that taking slaves from the States to Nebraska, does not make slaves of freemen; but the African slave-trader can say just as much. He does not catch free negroes and bring them here. He finds them already slaves in the hands of their black captors, and he honestly buys them at the rate of about a red cotton handkerchief a head. This is very cheap, and it is a great abridgement of the sacred right of self-government to hang men for engaging in this profitable trade!

Another important objection to this application of the right of self-government, is that it enables the first FEW, to deprive the succeeding MANY, of a free exercise of the right of self-government. The first few may get slavery IN, and the subsequent many cannot easily get it OUT. How common is the remark now in the slave States—"If we were only clear of our slaves, how much better it would be for us." They are actually deprived of the privilege of governing themselves as they would, by the action of a very few, in the beginning. The same thing was true of the whole nation at the time our constitution was formed.

Whether slavery shall go into Nebraska, or other new territories, is not a matter of exclusive concern to the people who may go there. The whole nation is interested that the best use shall be made of these territories. We want them for the homes of free white people. This they cannot be, to any considerable extent, if slavery shall be planted within them. Slave States are places for poor white people to remove FROM; not to remove TO. New free States are the places for poor people to go to and better their condition. For this use, the nation needs these territories.

Still further; there are constitutional relations between the slave and free States, which are degrading to the latter. We are under legal obligations to catch and return their runaway slaves to them—a sort of dirty, disagreeable job, which I believe, as a general rule the slave-holders will not perform for one another. Then again, in the control of the government— the management of the partnership affairs—they have greatly the advantage of us. By the constitution, each State has two Senators—each has a number of Representatives; in proportion to the number of its people—and each has a number of presidential electors, equal to the whole number of its Senators and Representatives together. But in ascertaining the number of the people, for this purpose, five slaves are counted as being equal to three whites. The slaves do not vote; they are only counted and so used, as to swell the influence of the white people's votes. The practical effect of this is more aptly shown by a comparison of the States of South Carolina and Maine. South Carolina has six representatives, and so has Maine; South Carolina has eight presidential electors, and so has Maine. This is precise equality so far; and, of course they are equal in Senators, each having two. Thus in the control of the government, the two States are equals precisely. But how are they in the number of their white people? Maine has 581,813—while South Carolina has 274,567. Maine has twice as many as South Carolina, and 32,679 over. Thus each white man in South Carolina is more than the double of any man in Maine. This is all because South Carolina, besides her free people, has 384,984 slaves. The South Carolinian has precisely the same advantage over the white man in every other free State, as well as in Maine. He is more than the double of any one of us in this crowd. The same advantage, but not to the same extent, is held by all the citizens of the slave States, over those of the free; and it is an absolute truth, without an exception, that there is no voter in any slave State, but who has more legal power in the government, than any voter in any free State. There is no instance of exact equality; and the disadvantage is against us the whole chapter through. This principle, in the aggregate, gives the slave States, in the present Congress, twenty additional representatives—being seven more than the whole majority by which they passed the Nebraska bill.

Now all this is manifestly unfair; yet I do not mention it to complain of it, in so far as it is already settled. It is in the constitution; and I do not, for that cause, or any other cause, propose to destroy, or alter, or disregard the constitution. I stand to it, fairly, fully, and firmly.

But when I am told I must leave it altogether to OTHER PEOPLE to say whether new partners are to be bred up and brought into the firm, on the same degrading terms against me, I respectfully demur. I insist, that whether I shall be a whole man, or only, the half of one, in comparison with others, is a question in which I am somewhat concerned; and one which no other man can have a sacred right of deciding for me. If I am wrong in this—if it really be a sacred right of self-government, in the man who shall go to Nebraska, to decide whether he will be the EQUAL of me or the DOUBLE of me, then after he shall have exercised that right, and thereby shall have reduced me to a still smaller fraction of a man than I already am, I should like for some gentleman deeply skilled in the mysteries of sacred rights, to provide himself with a microscope, and peep about, and find out, if he can, what has become of my sacred rights! They will surely be too small for detection with the naked eye.

Finally, I insist, that if there is ANY THING which it is the duty of the WHOLE PEOPLE to never entrust to any hands but their own, that thing is the preservation and perpetuity, of their own liberties, and institutions. And if they shall think, as I do, that the extension of slavery endangers them, more than any, or all other causes, how recreant to themselves, if they submit the question, and with it, the fate of their country, to a mere hand-full of men, bent only on temporary self-interest. If this question of slavery extension were an insignificant one—one having no power to do harm—it might be shuffled aside in this way. But being, as it is, the great Behemoth of danger, shall the strong gripe of the nation be loosened upon him, to entrust him to the hands of such feeble keepers?

I have done with this mighty argument, of self-government. Go, sacred thing! Go in peace.

But Nebraska is urged as a great Union-saving measure. Well I too, go for saving the Union. Much as I hate slavery, I would consent to the extension of it rather than see the Union dissolved, just as I would consent to any GREAT evil, to avoid a GREATER one. But when I go to Union saving, I must believe, at least, that the means I employ has some adaptation to the end. To my mind, Nebraska has no such adaptation.

"It hath no relish of salvation in it."

It is an aggravation, rather, of the only one thing which ever endangers the Union. When it came upon us, all was peace and quiet. The nation was looking to the forming of new bonds of Union; and a long course of peace and prosperity seemed to lie before us. In the whole range of possibility, there scarcely appears to me to have been any thing, out of which the slavery agitation could have been revived, except the very project of repealing the Missouri compromise. Every inch of territory we owned, already had a definite settlement of the slavery question, and by which, all parties were pledged to abide. Indeed, there was no uninhabited country on the continent, which we could acquire; if we except some extreme northern regions, which are wholly out of the question. In this state of case, the genius of Discord himself, could scarcely have invented a way of again getting us by the ears, but by turning back and destroying the peace measures of the past. The councils of that genius seem to have prevailed, the Missouri compromise was repealed; and here we are, in the midst of a new slavery agitation, such, I think, as we have never seen before. Who is responsible for this? Is it those who resist the measure; or those who, causelessly, brought it forward, and pressed it through, having reason to know, and, in fact, knowing it must and would be so resisted? It could not but be expected by its author, that it would be looked upon as a measure for the extension of slavery, aggravated by a gross breach of faith. Argue as you will, and long as you will, this is the naked FRONT and ASPECT, of the measure. And in this aspect, it could not but produce agitation. Slavery is founded in the selfishness of man's nature—opposition to it, is his love of justice. These principles are an eternal antagonism; and when brought into collision so fiercely, as slavery extension brings them, shocks, and throes, and convulsions must ceaselessly follow. Repeal the Missouri compromise—repeal all compromises—repeal the declaration of independence— repeal all past history, you still can not repeal human nature. It still will be the abundance of man's heart, that slavery extension is wrong; and out of the abundance of his heart, his mouth will continue to speak.

The structure, too, of the Nebraska bill is very peculiar. The people are to decide the question of slavery for themselves; but WHEN they are to decide; or HOW they are to decide; or whether, when the question is once decided, it is to remain so, or is it to be subject to an indefinite succession of new trials, the law does not say, Is it to be decided by the first dozen settlers who arrive there? or is it to await the arrival of a hundred? Is it to be decided by a vote of the people? or a vote of the legislature? or, indeed by a vote of any sort? To these questions, the law gives no answer. There is a mystery about this; for when a member proposed to give the legislature express authority to exclude slavery, it was hooted down by the friends of the bill. This fact is worth remembering. Some yankees, in the east, are sending emigrants to Nebraska, to exclude slavery from it; and, so far as I can judge, they expect the question to be decided by voting, in some way or other. But the Missourians are awake too. They are within a stone's throw of the contested ground. They hold meetings, and pass resolutions, in which not the slightest allusion to voting is made. They resolve that slavery already exists in the territory; that more shall go there; that they, remaining in Missouri will protect it; and that abolitionists shall be hung, or driven away. Through all this, bowie-knives and six-shooters are seen plainly enough; but never a glimpse of the ballot-box. And, really, what is to be the result of this? Each party WITHIN, having numerous and determined backers WITHOUT, is it not probable that the contest will come to blows, and bloodshed? Could there be a more apt invention to bring about collision and violence, on the slavery question, than this Nebraska project is? I do not charge, or believe, that such was intended by Congress; but if they had literally formed a ring, and placed champions within it to fight out the controversy, the fight could be no more likely to come off, than it is. And if this fight should begin, is it likely to take a very peaceful, Union-saving turn? Will not the first drop of blood so shed, be the real knell of the Union?

The Missouri Compromise ought to be restored. For the sake of the Union, it ought to be restored. We ought to elect a House of Representatives which will vote its restoration. If by any means, we omit to do this, what follows? Slavery may or may not be established in Nebraska. But whether it be or not, we shall have repudiated—discarded from the councils of the Nation—the SPIRIT of COMPROMISE; for who after this will ever trust in a national compromise? The spirit of mutual concession—that spirit which first gave us the constitution, and which has thrice saved the Union—we shall have strangled and cast from us forever. And what shall we have in lieu of it? The South flushed with triumph and tempted to excesses; the North, betrayed, as they believe, brooding on wrong and burning for revenge. One side will provoke; the other resent. The one will taunt, the other defy; one aggresses, the other retaliates. Already a few in the North, defy all constitutional restraints, resist the execution of the fugitive slave law, and even menace the institution of slavery in the states where it exists.

Already a few in the South, claim the constitutional right to take to and hold slaves in the free states—demand the revival of the slave trade; and demand a treaty with Great Britain by which fugitive slaves may be reclaimed from Canada. As yet they are but few on either side. It is a grave question for the lovers of the Union, whether the final destruction of the Missouri Compromise, and with it the spirit of all compromise will or will not embolden and embitter each of these, and fatally increase the numbers of both.

But restore the compromise, and what then? We thereby

restore the national faith, the national confidence, the national feeling of brotherhood. We thereby reinstate the spirit of concession and compromise—that spirit which has never failed us in past perils, and which may be safely trusted for all the future. The south ought to join in doing this. The peace of the nation is as dear to them as to us. In memories of the past and hopes of the future, they share as largely as we. It would be on their part, a great act—great in its spirit, and great in its effect. It would be worth to the nation a hundred years' purchase of peace and prosperity. And what of sacrifice would they make? They only surrender to us, what they gave us for a consideration long, long ago; what they have not now, asked for, struggled or cared for; what has been thrust upon them, not less to their own astonishment than to ours.

But it is said we cannot restore it; that though we elect every member of the lower house, the Senate is still against us. It is quite true, that of the Senators who passed the Nebraska bill, a majority of the whole Senate will retain their seats in spite of the elections of this and the next year. But if at these elections, their several constituencies shall clearly express their will against Nebraska, will these senators disregard their will? Will they neither obey, nor make room for those who will?

But even if we fail to technically restore the compromise, it is still a great point to carry a popular vote in favor of the restoration. The moral weight of such a vote can not be estimated too highly. The authors of Nebraska are not at all satisfied with the destruction of the compromise—an endorsement of this PRINCIPLE, they proclaim to be the great object. With them, Nebraska alone is a small matter—to establish a principle, for FUTURE USE, is what they particularly desire.

That future use is to be the planting of slavery wherever in the wide world, local and unorganized opposition can not prevent it. Now if you wish to give them this endorsement— if you wish to establish this principle—do so. I shall regret it; but it is your right. On the contrary if you are opposed to the principle—intend to give it no such endorsement—let no wheedling, no sophistry, divert you from throwing a direct vote against it.

Some men, mostly whigs, who condemn the repeal of the Missouri Compromise, nevertheless hesitate to go for its restoration, lest they be thrown in company with the abolitionist. Will they allow me as an old whig to tell them good humoredly, that I think this is very silly? Stand with anybody that stands RIGHT. Stand with him while he is right and PART with him when he goes wrong. Stand WITH the abolitionist in restoring the Missouri Compromise; and stand AGAINST him when he attempts to repeal the fugitive slave law. In the latter case you stand with the southern disunionist. What of that? you are still right. In both cases you are right. In both cases you oppose the dangerous extremes. In both you stand on middle ground and hold the ship level and steady. In both you are national and nothing less than national. This is good old whig ground. To desert such ground, because of any company, is to be less than a whig—less than a man—less than an American.

I particularly object to the NEW position which the avowed principle of this Nebraska law gives to slavery in the body politic. I object to it because it assumes that there CAN be MORAL RIGHT in the enslaving of one man by another. I object to it as a dangerous dalliance for a free people—a sad evidence that, feeling prosperity we forget right—that liberty, as a principle, we have ceased to revere. I object to it because the fathers of the republic eschewed, and rejected it. The argument of "Necessity" was the only argument they ever admitted in favor of slavery; and so far, and so far only as it carried them, did they ever go. They found the institution existing among us, which they could not help; and they cast blame upon the British King for having permitted its introduction. BEFORE the constitution, they prohibited its introduction into the north-western Territory—the only country we owned, then free from it. AT the framing and adoption of the constitution, they forbore to so much as mention the word "slave" or "slavery" in the whole instrument. In the provision for the recovery of fugitives, the slave is spoken of as a "PERSON HELD TO SERVICE OR LABOR." In that prohibiting the abolition of the African slave trade for twenty years, that trade is spoken of as "The migration or importation of such persons as any of the States NOW EXISTING, shall think proper to admit," &c. These are the only provisions alluding to slavery. Thus, the thing is hid away, in the constitution, just as an afflicted man hides away a wen or a cancer, which he dares not cut out at once, lest he bleed to death; with the promise, nevertheless, that the cutting may begin at the end of a given time. Less than this our fathers COULD not do; and MORE they WOULD not do. Necessity drove them so far, and farther, they would not go. But this is not all. The earliest Congress, under the constitution, took the same view of slavery. They hedged and hemmed it in to the narrowest limits of necessity.

In 1794, they prohibited an out-going slave-trade—that is, the taking of slaves FROM the United States to sell.

In 1798, they prohibited the bringing of slaves from Africa, INTO the Mississippi Territory—this territory then comprising what are now the States of Mississippi and Alabama. This was TEN YEARS before they had the authority to do the same thing as to the States existing at the adoption of the constitution.

In 1800 they prohibited AMERICAN CITIZENS from trading in slaves between foreign countries—as, for instance, from Africa to Brazil.

In 1803 they passed a law in aid of one or two State laws, in restraint of the internal slave trade.

In 1807, in apparent hot haste, they passed the law, nearly a year in advance, to take effect the first day of 1808—the very first day the constitution would permit—prohibiting the African slave trade by heavy pecuniary and corporal penalties.

In 1820, finding these provisions ineffectual, they declared the trade piracy, and annexed to it, the extreme penalty of death. While all this was passing in the general government, five or six of the original slave States had adopted systems of gradual emancipation; and by which the institution was rapidly becoming extinct within these limits.

Thus we see, the plain unmistakable spirit of that age, towards slavery, was hostility to the PRINCIPLE, and toleration, ONLY BY NECESSITY.

But NOW it is to be transformed into a "sacred right." Nebraska brings it forth, places it on the high road to extension and perpetuity; and, with a pat on its back, says to it, "Go, and God speed you." Henceforth it is to be the chief jewel of the nation—the very figure-head of the ship of State. Little by little, but steadily as man's march to the grave, we have been giving up the OLD for the NEW faith. Near eighty years ago we began by declaring that all men are created equal; but now from that beginning we have run down to the other declaration, that for SOME men to enslave OTHERS is a "sacred right of self-government." These principles can not stand together. They are as opposite as God and mammon; and whoever holds to the one, must despise the other. When Pettit, in connection with his support of the Nebraska bill, called the Declaration of Independence "a self-evident lie" he only did what consistency and candor require all other Nebraska men to do. Of the forty odd Nebraska Senators who sat present and heard him, no one rebuked him. Nor am I apprized that any Nebraska newspaper, or any Nebraska orator, in the whole nation, has ever yet rebuked him. If this had been said among Marion's men, Southerners though they were, what would have become of the man who said it? If this had been said to the men who captured André, the man who said it, would probably have been hung sooner than André was. If it had been said in old Independence Hall, seventy-eight years ago, the very door-keeper would have throttled the man, and thrust him into the street.

Let no one be deceived. The spirit of seventy-six and the spirit of Nebraska, are utter antagonisms; and the former is being rapidly displaced by the latter.

Fellow countrymen—Americans south, as well as north, shall we make no effort to arrest this? Already the liberal party throughout the world, express the apprehension "that the one retrograde institution in America, is undermining the principles of progress, and fatally violating the noblest political system the world ever saw." This is not the taunt of enemies, but the warning of friends. Is it quite safe to disregard it—to despise it? Is there no danger to liberty itself, in discarding the earliest practice, and first precept of our ancient faith? In our greedy chase to make profit of the negro, let us beware, lest we "cancel and tear to pieces" even the white man's charter of freedom.

Our republican robe is soiled, and trailed in the dust. Let

us repurify it. Let us turn and wash it white, in the spirit, if not the blood, of the Revolution. Let us turn slavery from its claims of "moral right," back upon its existing legal rights, and its arguments of "necessity." Let us return it to the position our fathers gave it; and there let it rest in peace. Let us re-adopt the Declaration of Independence, and with it, the practices, and policy, which harmonize with it. Let north and south—let all Americans—let all lovers of liberty everywhere—join in the great and good work. If we do this, we shall not only have saved the Union; but we shall have so saved it, as to make, and to keep it, forever worthy of the saving. We shall have so saved it, that the succeeding millions of free happy people, the world over, shall rise up, and call us blessed, to the latest generations.

At Springfield, twelve days ago, where I had spoken substantially as I have here, Judge Douglas replied to me—and as he is to reply to me here, I shall attempt to anticipate him, by noticing some of the points he made there.

He commenced by stating I had assumed all the way through, that the principle of the Nebraska bill, would have the effect of extending slavery. He denied that this was INTENDED, or that this EFFECT would follow.

I will not re-open the argument upon this point. That such was the intention, the world believed at the start, and will continue to believe. This was the COUNTENANCE of the thing; and, both friends and enemies, instantly recognized it as such. That countenance can not now be changed by argument. You can as easily argue the color out of the negroes' skin. Like the "bloody hand" you may wash it, and wash it, the red witness of guilt still sticks, and stares horribly at you.

Next he says, congressional intervention never prevented slavery, any where—that it did not prevent it in the north west territory, nor in Illinois—that in fact, Illinois came into the Union as a slave State—that the principle of the Nebraska bill expelled it from Illinois, from several old States, from every where.

Now this is mere quibbling all the way through. If the ordinance of '87 did not keep slavery out of the north west territory, how happens it that the north west shore of the Ohio river is entirely free from it; while the south east shore, less than a mile distant, along nearly the whole length of the river, is entirely covered with it?

If that ordinance did not keep it out of Illinois, what was it that made the difference between Illinois and Missouri? They lie side by side, the Mississippi river only dividing them; while their early settlements were within the same latitude. Between 1810 and 1820 the number of slaves in Missouri INCREASED 7,211; while in Illinois, in the same ten years, they DECREASED 51. This appears by the census returns. During nearly all of that ten years, both were territories—not States. During this time, the ordinance forbid slavery to go into Illinois; and NOTHING forbid it to go into Missouri. It DID go into Missouri, and did NOT go into Illinois. That is the fact. Can any one doubt as to the reason of it?

But, he says, Illinois came into the Union as a slave State. Silence, perhaps, would be the best answer to this flat contradiction of the known history of the country. What are the facts upon which this bold assertion is based? When we first acquired the country, as far back as 1787, there were some slaves within it, held by the French inhabitants at Kaskaskia. The territorial legislation, admitted a few negroes, from the slave States, as indentured servants. One year after the adoption of the first State constitution the whole number of them was—what do you think? just 117—while the aggregate free population was 55,094—about 470 to one. Upon this state of facts, the people framed their constitution prohibiting the further introduction of slavery, with a sort of guaranty to the owners of the few indentured servants, giving freedom to their children to be born thereafter, and making no mention whatever, of any supposed slave for life. Out of this small matter, the Judge manufactures his argument that Illinois came into the Union as a slave State. Let the facts be the answer to the argument.

The principles of the Nebraska bill, he says, expelled slavery from Illinois? The principle of that bill first planted it here—that is, it first came, because there was no law to prevent it—first came before we owned the country; and finding it here, and having the ordinance of '87 to prevent its increasing, our people struggled along, and finally got rid of it as best they could.

But the principle of the Nebraska bill abolished slavery in several of the old States. Well, it is true that several of the old States, in the last quarter of the last century, did adopt systems of gradual emancipation, by which the institution has finally become extinct within their limits; but it MAY or MAY NOT be true that the principle of the Nebraska bill was the cause that led to the adoption of these measures. It is now more than fifty years, since the last of these States adopted its system of emancipation. If Nebraska bill is the real author of these benevolent works, it is rather deplorable, that he has, for so long a time, ceased working all together. Is there not some reason to suspect that it was the principle of the REVOLUTION, and not the principle of Nebraska bill, that led to emancipation in these old States? Leave it to the people of those old emancipating States, and I am quite sure they will decide, that neither that, nor any other good thing, ever did, or ever will come of Nebraska bill.

In the course of my main argument, Judge Douglas interrupted me to say, that the principle of the Nebraska bill was very old; that it originated when God made man and placed good and evil before him, allowing him to choose for himself, being responsible for the choice he should make. At the time I thought this was merely playful; and I answered it accordingly. But in his reply to me he renewed it, as a serious argument. In seriousness then, the facts of this proposition are not true as stated. God did not place good and evil before man, telling him to make his choice. On the contrary, he did tell him there was one tree, of the fruit of which, he should not eat, upon pain of certain death. I should scarcely wish so strong a prohibition against slavery in Nebraska.

But this argument strikes me as not a little remarkable in another particular—in its strong resemblance to the old argument for the "Divine right of Kings." By the latter, the King is to do just as he pleases with his white subjects, being responsible to God alone. By the former the white man is to do just as he pleases with his black slaves, being responsible to God alone. The two things are precisely alike; and it is but natural that they should find similar arguments to sustain them.

I had argued, that the application of the principle of self-government, as contended for, would require the revival of the African slave trade—that no argument could be made in favor of a man's right to take slaves to Nebraska, which could not be equally well made in favor of his right to bring them from the coast of Africa. The Judge replied, that the constitution requires the suppression of the foreign slave trade; but does not require the prohibition of slavery in the territories. That is a mistake, in point of fact. The constitution does NOT require the action of Congress in either case; and it does AUTHORIZE it in both. And so, there is still no difference between the cases.

In regard to what I had said, the advantage the slave States have over the free, in the matter of representation, the Judge replied that we, in the free States, count five free negroes as five white people, while in the slave States, they count five slaves as three whites only; and that the advantage, at last, was on the side of the free States.

Now, in the slave States, they count free negroes just as we do; and it so happens that besides their slaves, they have as many free negroes as we have, and thirty-three thousand over. Thus their free negroes more than balance ours; and their advantage over us, in consequence of their slaves, still remains as I stated it.

In reply to my argument, that the compromise measures of 1850, were a system of equivalents; and that the provisions of no one of them could fairly be carried to other subjects, without its corresponding equivalent being carried with it, the Judge denied out-right, that these measures had any connection with, or dependence upon, each other. This is mere desperation. If they have no connection, why are they always spoken of in connection? Why has he so spoken of them, a thousand times? Why has he constantly called them a SERIES of measures? Why does everybody call them a compromise? Why was California kept out of the Union, six or seven months, if it was not because of its connection with the other measures? Webster's leading definition of the verb "to compromise" is "to adjust and settle a difference, by mutual agreement with concessions of claims by the parties." This conveys precisely the popular understanding of the word compromise. We knew, before the Judge told us, that these measures passed separately, and in distinct bills; and that no two of them were passed by the votes of precisely the same members. But we also know, and so does he know, that no one of them could have passed both branches of Congress but for the understanding that the others were to pass also. Upon this understanding each got votes, which it could have got in no other way. It is this fact, that gives to the measures their true character; and it is the universal knowledge of this fact, that has given them the name of compromise so expressive of that true character.

I had asked "If in carrying the provisions of the Utah and New Mexico laws to Nebraska, you could clear away other objection, how can you leave Nebraska 'perfectly free' to introduce slavery BEFORE she forms a constitution—during her territorial government?—while the Utah and New Mexico laws only authorize it WHEN they form constitutions, and are admitted into the Union?" To this Judge Douglas answered that the Utah and New Mexico laws, also authorized it BEFORE; and to prove this, he read from one of their laws, as follows: "That the legislative power of said territory shall extend to all rightful subjects of legislation consistent with the constitution of the United States and the provisions of this act."

Now it is perceived from the reading of this, that there is nothing express upon the subject; but that the authority is sought to be implied merely, for the general provision of "all rightful subjects of legislation." In reply to this, I insist, as a legal rule of construction, as well as the plain popular view of the matter, that the EXPRESS provision for Utah and New Mexico coming in with slavery if they choose, when they shall form constitutions, is an EXCLUSION of all implied authority on the same subject—that Congress, having the subject distinctly in their minds, when they made the express provision, they therein expressed their WHOLE meaning on that subject.

The Judge rather insinuated that I had found it convenient to forget the Washington territorial law passed in 1853. This was a division of Oregon, organizing the northern part, as the territory of Washington. He asserted that, by this act, the ordinance of '87 theretofore existing in Oregon, was repealed; that nearly all the members of Congress voted for it, beginning in the H.R., with Charles Allen of Massachusetts, and ending with Richard Yates, of Illinois; and that he could not understand how those who now oppose the Nebraska bill, so voted then, unless it was because it was then too soon after both the great political parties had ratified the compromises of 1850, and the ratification therefore too fresh, to be then repudiated.

Now I had seen the Washington act before; and I have carefully examined it since; and I aver that there is no repeal of the ordinance of '87, or of any prohibition of slavery, in it. In express terms, there is absolutely nothing in the whole law upon the subject—in fact, nothing to lead a reader to THINK of the subject. To my judgment, it is equally free from every thing from which such repeal can be legally implied; but however this may be, are men now to be entrapped by a legal implication, extracted from covert language, introduced perhaps, for the very purpose of entrapping them? I sincerely wish every man could read this law quite through, carefully watching every sentence, and every line, for a repeal of the ordinance of '87 or any thing equivalent to it.

Another point on the Washington act. If it was intended to be modelled after the Utah and New Mexico acts, as Judge Douglas, insists, why was it not inserted in it, as in them, that Washington was to come in with or without slavery as she may choose at the adoption of her constitution? It has no such provision in it; and I defy the ingenuity of man to give a reason for the omission, other than that it was not intended to follow the Utah and New Mexico laws in regard to the question of slavery.

The Washington act not only differs vitally from the Utah and New Mexico acts; but the Nebraska act differs vitally from both. By the latter act the people are left "perfectly free" to regulate their own domestic concerns, &c.; but in all the former, all their laws are to be submitted to Congress, and if disapproved are to be null. The Washington act goes even further; it absolutely prohibits the territorial legislation, by very strong and guarded language, from establishing banks, or borrowing money on the faith of the territory. Is this the sacred right of self-government we hear vaunted so much? No sir, the Nebraska bill finds no model in the acts of '50 or the Washington act. It finds no model in any law from Adam till today. As Phillips says of Napoleon, the Nebraska act is grand, gloomy, and peculiar; wrapped in the solitude of its own originality; without a model, and without a shadow upon the earth.

In the course of his reply, Senator Douglas remarked, in substance, that he had always considered this government was made for the white people and not for the negroes. Why, in point of mere fact, I think so too. But in this remark of the Judge, there is a significance, which I think is the key to the great mistake (if there is any such mistake) which he has made in this Nebraska measure. It shows that the Judge has no very vivid impression that the negro is a human; and consequently has no idea that there can be any moral question in legislating about him. In his view, the question of whether a new country shall be slave or free, is a matter of as utter indifference, as it is whether his neighbor shall plant his farm with tobacco, or stock it with horned cattle. Now, whether this view is right or wrong, it is very certain that the great mass of mankind take a totally different view. They consider slavery a great moral wrong; and their feelings against it, is not evanescent, but eternal. It lies at the very foundation of their sense of justice; and it cannot be trifled with. It is a great and durable element of popular action, and, I think, no statesman can safely disregard it.

Our Senator also objects that those who oppose him in this measure do not entirely agree with one another. He reminds me that in my firm adherence to the constitutional rights of the slave States, I differ widely from others who are co-operating with me in opposing the Nebraska bill; and he says it is not quite fair to oppose him in this variety of ways. He should remember that he took us by surprise—astounded us—by this measure. We were thunderstruck and stunned; and we reeled and fell in utter confusion. But we rose each fighting, grasping whatever he could first reach—a scythe—a pitchfork—a chopping axe, or a butcher's cleaver. We struck in the direction of the sound; and we are rapidly closing in upon him. He must not think to divert us from our purpose, by showing us that our drill, our dress, and our weapons, are not entirely perfect and uniform. When the storm shall be past, he shall find us still Americans; no less devoted to the continued Union and prosperity of the country than heretofore.

Finally, the Judge invokes against me, the memory of Clay and of Webster. They were great men; and men of great deeds. But where have I assailed them? For what is it, that their life-long enemy, shall now make profit, by assuming to defend them against me, their life-long friend? I go against the repeal of the Missouri compromise; did they ever go for it? They went for the compromise of 1850; did I ever go against them? They were greatly devoted to the Union; to the small measure of my ability, was I ever less so? Clay and Webster were dead before this question arose; by what authority shall our Senator say they would espouse his side of it, if alive? Mr. Clay was the leading spirit in making the Missouri compromise; is it very credible that if now alive, he would take the lead in the breaking of it? The truth is that some support from whigs is now a necessity with the Judge, and for thus it is, that the names of Clay and Webster are now invoked. His old friends have deserted him in such numbers as to leave too few to live by. He came to his own, and his own received him not, and Lo! he turns unto the Gentiles.

A word now as to the Judge's desperate assumption that the compromises of '50 had no connection with one another; that Illinois came into the Union as a slave state, and some other similar ones. This is no other than a bold denial of the history of the country. If we do not know that the Compromises of '50 were dependent on each other; if we do not know that Illinois came into the Union as a free state—we do not know any thing. If we do not know these things, we do not know that we ever had a revolutionary war, or such a chief as Washington. To deny these things is to deny our national axioms, or dogmas, at least; and it puts an end to all argument. If a man will stand up and assert, and repeat, and re-assert, that two and two do not make four, I know nothing in the power of argument that can stop him. I think I can answer the Judge so long as he sticks to the premises; but when he flies from them, I can not work an argument into the consistency of a maternal gag, and actually close his mouth with it. In such a case I can only commend him to the seventy thousand answers just in from Pennsylvania, Ohio and Indiana.

To Charles Hoyt

Mr. Charles Hoyt   Clinton, DeWitt Co.
Dear Sir: Nov. 10. 1854
    You used to express a good deal of partiality for me; and if you are still so, now is the time. Some friends here are really for me, for the U.S. Senate; and I should be very grateful if you could make a mark for me among your members. Please write me at all events, giving me the names, post-offices, and *"political position"* of members round about you. Direct to Springfield.
    Let this be confidential. Yours truly

To Jonathan Y. Scammon

J. Y. Scammon, Esq   Clinton, DeWitt Co. Nov. 10 1854
My dear Sir:
    Some partial friends here are for me for the U.S. Senate; and it would be very foolish, and very false, for me to deny that I would be pleased with an election to that Honorable body. If you know nothing, and feel nothing to the contrary, please make a mark for me with the members. Write me, at all events. Direct to Springfield.
    Let this be confidential.
Yours as ever

To Jacob Harding

Harding, Esq   Clinton, DeWitt Co.
My dear Sir   Nov. 11. 1854

    I have a suspicion that a whig has been elected to the Legislature from Edgar. If this is not so, why then *"nix cum arous"* but if it is so, then could you not make a mark with him for me, for U.S. Senator?—I really have some chance. Please write me at Springfield, giving me the names, post-offices, and political positions, of your representative and senator, whoever they may be.

    Let this be confidential. Yours truly

To Noah W. Matheny

N. W. Matheny: Springfield,
Clerk of the county court   Novr. 25— 1854
    of Sangamon County, Illinois

    Sir: I hereby decline to accept the office of Representative in the General Assembly, for the said county of Sangamon, to which office I am reported to have been elected on the 7th. of Novr. Inst. I therefore desire that you notify the Governor of this vacancy, in order that legal steps be taken to fill the same. Your Obt. Servt.

To Ichabod Codding

(COPY)

I. Codding, Esq   Springfield,
Dear Sir   Novr. 27. 1854

    Your note of the 13th. requesting my attendance of the Republican State Central Committee, on the 17th. Inst. at Chicago, was, owing to my absence from home, received on the evening of that day (17th) only. While I have pen in hand allow me to say I have been perplexed some to understand why my name was placed on that committee. I was not consulted on the subject; nor was I apprized of the appointment, until I discovered it by accident two or three weeks afterwards. I suppose my opposition to the principle of slavery is as strong as that of any member of the Republican party; but I had also supposed that the *extent* to which I feel authorized to carry that opposition, practically; was not at all satisfactory to that party. The leading men who organized that party, were present, on the 4th. of Oct. at the discussion between Douglas and myself at Springfield, and had full oppertunity to not misunderstand my position. Do I misunderstand theirs? Please write, and inform me. Yours truly

To Hugh Lemaster

Hugh LeMaster, Esq.   Springfield,
My dear Sir: Nov. 29, 1854.

I have got it into my head to try to be U.S. Senator, and I wish somehow to get at your Whig member, Mr. Babcock. I am not acquainted with him—could you not make or cause to be made, a mark with him for me? Would not Judge Kellogg lend a helping hand? J. P. Boris, I venture to hope, would be willing to give a lift. Please write me at all events; and let this be confidential, so far as practicable. Yours as ever,

To Joseph Gillespie

J. Gillespie, Esq   Springfield,
My dear Sir   Dec: 1– 1854

I have really got it into my head to try to be United States Senator; and if I could have your support my chances would be reasonably good. But I know, and acknowledge, that you have as just claims to the place as I have; and therefore I do not ask you to yield to me, if you are thinking of becoming a candidate yourself. If, however, you are not, then I should like to be remembered affectionately by you; and also, to have you make a mark for me with the Anti-Nebraska members, down your way. If you know, and have no objection to tell, let me know whether Trumbull intends to make a push. If he does, I suppose the two men in St. Clair, and one or both in Madison will be for him.

We have the Legislature clearly enough on joint ballot; but the Senate is very close; and Calhoun told me to-day that the Nebraska men will stave off the election if they can. Even if we get into joint vote, we shall have difficulty to unite our forces.

Please write me, and let this be confidential   Your friend as ever

To Elihu B. Washburne

Hon: E. B. Washburne.   Springfield, Ills.
My dear Sir: Dec: 11, 1854

Your note of the 5th. is just received. It is too true that by the official returns Allen beats Col Archer one vote. There is a report to-day that there is a mistake in the returns from Clay county, giving Allen sixty votes more than he really has; but this, I fear is itself a mistake. I have just examined the returns from that county at the Secretarie's office, and find that the agregate vote for Sheriff only falls short, by three votes, of the agregate as reported, of Allen & Archer's vote. Our friends, however, are hot on the track; and will probe the matter to the bottom.

As to my own matter, things continue to look reasonably well. I wrote your friend, George Gage; and, three days ago, had an answer from him, in which he talks out plainly, as your letter taught me to expect. To-day I had a letter from Turner. He says he is not committed, & will not be until he sees how most effectually to oppose slavery extension.

I have not ventured to write all the members in your district, lest some of them should be offended by the indelicacy of the thing—that is, coming from a total stranger. Could you not drop some of them a line? Very truly your friend,

To Elihu B. Washburne

Hon: E. B. Washburne   Springfield,
My dear Sir: Dec: 14, 1854
 So far as I am concerned, there must be something wrong
about U.S. Senator, at Chicago. My most intimate friends
there do not answer my letters; and I can not get a word from
them. Wentworth has a knack of knowing things better than
most men. I wish you would pump him, and write me what
you get from him. Please do this as soon as you can, as the
time is growing short. Don't let *any one* know I have written
you this; for there may be those opposed to me, nearer about
you than you think. Very truly Yours &c

To Elihu B. Washburne

(CONFIDENTIAL)

Hon: E. B. Washburne.   Springfield,
My dear Sir: Dec: 6– 1855
 I telegraphed you as to the organization of the two houses.
T. J. Turner, elected Speaker 40 to 24. House not full. Dr.
Richmond of Schuyler was his opponent. Anti-Nebraska also
elected all the other officers of the H.R. In the Senate, Anti-
Nebraska elected George T. Brown, of the Alton Courier,
Secretary; and Dr. Ray of the Galena Jeffersonian, one of the
clerks. In fact they elected all the officers; but some of them
were Nebraska men elected over the regular Nebraska nominees. It is said that by this, they get one or two Nebraska
Senators to go for bringing on the Senatorial election. I can
not vouch for this. As to the Senatorial election I think very
little more is known than was before the meeting of the Legislature. Besides the ten or a dozen, on our side, who are
willing to be known as candidates, I think there are fifty secretly watching for a chance. I do not know that it is much
advantage to have the largest number of votes at the start. If I
did know this to be an advantage I should feel better; for I
can not doubt but I have more committals than any other one
man. Your District comes up tolerably well for me; but not
unanamously by any means—George Gage is for me, as you

know. J. H. Adams is not committed to me but I think will be for me. Mr. Talcott will not be for me as a first choice. Dr. Little and Mr. Sargent are openly for me. Prof– Pinckney is for me, but wishes to be quiet. Dr. Whitney writes me that Rev: Mr. Lawrence will be for me; and his manner to me so indicates; but he has not spoken it out. Mr. Swan, I have some slight hopes of. Turner says he is not committed; and I shall get him whenever I can make it appear to be his interest to go for me. Dr. Lyman and old Mr. Diggins will never go for me as a first choice. M. P. Sweet is here as a candidate; and I understand he claims that he has 22 members committed to him. I think some part of his estimate must be based on insufficient evidence; as I can not well see where they are to be found; and as I can learn the name of one only—Day of La Salle. Still, it may be so. There are more than 22 Anti-Nebraska members who are not committed to me. Tell Norton that Mr. Strunk and Mr. Wheeler come out plump for me; and for which I thank him. Judge Parks I have decided hopes for; but he says he is not committed. I understand myself as having 26 committals; and I do not think any other one man has ten—may be mistaken though. The whole Legislature stands,

Senate	—	A.N.	13	N.	12—
H.R.		"	<u>44</u>	"	<u>31</u>—
			57		43
			<u>43</u>		

14 maj. All here, but Kinney, of St. Clair.

Our special election here is plain enough when understood. Our adversaries pretended to be running no candidate, secretly notified all their men to be on hand; and, favored by a very rainy day got a complete snap judgment on us. In Novr. Sangamon gave Yates 2166 votes. On the rainy day she gave our man only 984—leaving him 82 votes behind. After all, the result is not of the least consequence. The Locos kept up a great chattering over it till the organization of the HR. since which they all seem to have forgotten it.

G's letter to L. I think has not been received. Ask him if he sent it. Yours as ever

January 6, 1855

To Richard Yates

Dear Yates   Springfield, Jany. 14, 1855

Your letter of the 8th. is just received. The Bissell movement of which you speak, I have had my eye upon, ever since
before the commencement of the session; and it is now perhaps as dangerous a card as we have to play against. There is
no danger, as I think, of the A. N. men uniting on him, but
the danger is that the Nebraska men, failing to do better, will
turn onto him *en masse*, and then a few A. N. men, wanting a
pretext only, will join on him, pretending to believe him an
A. N. man. He can not get a single *sincere* Anti Nebraska
vote. At least, so I think. At the meeting of the Legislature we
had 57 to their 43, nominally. But Kinny did not attend which
left us only 56. Then Trapp of St. Clair went over, leaving us
only 55, and raising them to 44. Next Osgood of the Senate
went over, reducing us to 54 and raising them to 45. It is now
said Kinny will be here soon, putting us up to 55 again; and so
we stand now nominally. What mines, and pitfalls they have
under us we do not know; but we understand they claim to
have 48 votes. If they have that number, it is only that they
have already got some men whom we have all along suspected
they would get; and we hope they have reached the bottom
of the rotten material. In this too, we may be mistaken. This
makes a squally case of it.

As to myself personally I may start with 20 or 25 votes, but
I think I can, in a few ballots, get up to 48 if an election is not
sooner made by the other side. But how I am to get the three
additional votes I do not yet see. It seems to me the men that
their votes are to come from will not go to the other side
unless they should be led off on the Bissell trick. If the election should be protracted, a general scramble may ensue, and
your chance will be as good as that of *any other* I suppose. It is
said Govr. Matteson is trying his hand; and as his success
would make a Governor of Koerner, he may be expected to
favor this movement. I suppose the election will commence
on the 31st. and when it will end I am sure I have no idea.
Very truly Yours

To Elihu B. Washburne

Hon: E. B. Washburne—   Springfield,
My dear Sir: Feby. 9— 1855

The agony is over at last; and the result you doubtless know. I write this only to give you some particulars to explain what might appear difficult of understanding. I began with 44 votes, Shields 41, and Trumbull 5—yet Trumbull was elected. In fact 47 different members voted for me—getting three new ones on the second ballot, and losing four old ones. How came my 47 to yield to T's 5? It was Govr. Matteson's work. He has been secretly a candidate ever since (before even) the fall election. All the members round about the canal were Anti-Nebraska; but were, nevertheless nearly all democrats, and old personal friends of his. His plan was to privately impress them with the belief that he was as good Anti-Nebraska as any one else—at least could be secured to be so by instructions, which could be easily passed. In this way he got from four to six of that sort of men to really prefer his election to that of any other man—all "sub rosa" of course. One notable instance of this sort was with Mr. Strunk of Kankakee. At the beginning of the session he came a volunteer to tell me he was for me & would walk a hundred miles to elect me; but lo, it was not long before he leaked it out that he was going for me the first few ballots & then for Govr. Matteson.

The Nebraska men, of course, were not for Matteson; but when they found they could elect no avowed Nebraska man they tardily determined, to let him get whomever of our men he could by whatever means he could and ask him no questions. In the mean time Osgood, Don. Morrison & Trapp of St. Clair had openly gone over from us. With the united Nebraska force, and their recruits, open & covert, it gave Matteson more than enough to elect him. We saw into it plainly ten days ago; but with every possible effort, could not head it off. All that remained of the Anti Nebraska force, excepting Judd, Cook, Palmer, Baker & Allen of Madison, & two or three of the secret Matteson men, would go into caucus, & I could get the nomination of that caucus. But the three Senators & one of the two representatives above named "could never vote for a whig" and this incensed some twenty whigs to "think" they would never vote for the man of the five. So we stood, and so we went into the fight yesterday; the Nebraska men very confident of the election of Matteson, though denying that he was a candidate; and we very much believing also, that they would elect him. But they wanted first to make a show of good faith to Shields by voting for him a few times, and our secret Matteson men also wanted to make a show of good faith by voting with us a few times. So we led off. On the seventh ballot, I think, the signal was given to the Neb. men, to turn on to Matteson, which they acted on to a man, with one exception; my old friend Strunk going with them giving him 44 votes. Next ballot the remaining Neb. man, & one pretended Anti- went on to him, giving him 46. The next still another giving him 47, wanting only three of an election. In the mean time, our friends with a view of detaining our expected bolters had been turning from me to Trumbull till he had risen to 35 & I had been reduced to 15. These would never desert me except by my direction; but I became satisfied that if we could prevent Matteson's election one or two ballots more, we could not possibly do so a single ballot after my friends should begin to return to me from Trumbull. So I determined to strike at once; and accordingly advised my remaining friends to go for him, which they did & elected him on that the 10th. ballot.

Such is the way the thing was done. I think you would have done the same under the circumstances; though Judge Davis, who came down this morning, declares he never would have consented to the 47 men being controlled by the 5. I regret my defeat moderately, but I am not nervous about it. I could have headed off every combination and been elected, had it not been for Matteson's double game—and his defeat now gives me more pleasure than my own gives me pain. On the whole, it is perhaps as well for our general cause that Trumbull is elected. The Neb. men confess that they hate it worse than any thing that could have happened. It is a great consolation to see them worse whipped than I am. I tell them it is their own fault—that they had abundant opertunity to choose between him & me, which they declined, and instead forced it on me to decide between him & Matteson.

With my grateful acknowledgments for the kind, active, and continued interest you have taken for me in this matter, allow me to subscribe myself   Yours forever

To William H. Henderson

Hon: W. H. Henderson: Springfield, Ills.
My dear Sir: Feby. 21– 1855

Your letter of the 4th. covering a lot of old deeds was received only two days ago. Wilton says he has the order but can not lay his hand upon it easily, and can not take time to make a thorough search, until he shall have gone to & returned from Chicago. So I lay the papers by, and wait.

The election is over, the Session is ended, and I am *not* Senator. I have to content myself with the honor of having been the first choice of a large majority of the fiftyone members who finally made the election. My larger number of friends had to surrender to Trumbull's smaller number, in order to prevent the election of Matteson, which would have been a Douglas victory. I started with 44 votes & T. with 5. It was rather hard for the 44 to have to surrender to the 5—and a less good humored man than I, perhaps would not have consented to it—and it would not have been done without my consent. I could not, however, let the whole political result go to ruin, on a point merely personal to myself.

Your son, kindly and firmly stood by me from first to last; and for which he has my everlasting gratitude. Your friend as ever

To Owen Lovejoy

Hon: Owen Lovejoy: Springfield,
My dear Sir: August 11– 1855

Yours of the 7th. was received the day before yesterday. Not even *you* are more anxious to prevent the extension of slavery than I; and yet the political atmosphere is such, just now, that I fear to do any thing, lest I do wrong. Know-nothingism has not yet entirely tumbled to pieces—nay, it is even a little encouraged by the late elections in Tennessee, Kentucky & Alabama. Until we can get the elements of this organization, there is not sufficient materials to successfully combat the Nebraska democracy with. We can not get them so long as they cling to a hope of success under their own organization; and I fear an open push by us now, may offend them, and tend to prevent our ever getting them. About us here, they are mostly my old political and personal friends; and I have hoped their organization would die out without the painful necessity of my taking an open stand against them. Of their principles I think little better than I do of those of the slavery extensionists. Indeed I do not perceive how any one professing to be sensitive to the wrongs of the negroes, can join in a league to degrade a class of white men.

I have no objection to "fuse" with any body provided I can fuse on ground which I think is right; and I believe the opponents of slavery extension could now do this, if it were not for this K.N.ism. In many speeches last summer I advised those who did me the honor of a hearing to "stand with any body who stands right"—and I am still quite willing to follow my own advice. I lately saw, in the Quincy Whig, the report of a preamble and resolutions, made by Mr. Williams, as chairman of a committee, to a public meeting and adopted by the meeting. I saw them but once, and have them not now at command; but so far as I can remember them, they occupy about the ground I should be willing to "fuse" upon.

As to my personal movements this summer, and fall, I am quite busy trying to pick up my lost crumbs of last year. I shall be here till September; then to the circuit till the 20th. then to Cincinnati, awhile, after a Patent right case; and back to the circuit to the end of November. I can be seen here any time this month; and at Bloomington at any time from the 10th. to the 17th. of September. As to an extra session of the Legislature, I should know no better how to bring that about, than to lift myself over a fence by the straps of my boots. Yours truly

To George Robertson

Hon: Geo. Robertson   Springfield, Ills.
Lexington, Ky.   Aug. 15. 1855

My dear Sir: The volume you left for me has been received. I am really grateful for the honor of your kind remembrance, as well as for the book. The partial reading I have already given it, has afforded me much of both pleasure and instruction. It was new to me that the exact question which led to the Missouri compromise, had arisen before it arose in regard to Missouri; and that you had taken so prominent a part in it. Your short, but able and patriotic speech upon that occasion, has not been improved upon since, by those holding the same views; and, with all the lights you then had, the views you took appear to me as very reasonable.

You are not a friend of slavery in the abstract. In that speech you spoke of *"the peaceful extinction of slavery"* and used other expressions indicating your belief that the thing was, at some time, to have an end. Since then we have had thirty six years of experience; and this experience has demonstrated, I think, that there is no peaceful extinction of slavery in prospect for us. The signal failure of Henry Clay, and other good and great men, in 1849, to effect any thing in favor of gradual emancipation in Kentucky, together with a thousand other signs, extinguishes that hope utterly. On the question of liberty, as a principle, we are not what we have been. When we were the political slaves of King George, and wanted to be free, we called the maxim that "all men are created equal" a self evident truth; but now when we have grown fat, and have lost all dread of being slaves ourselves, we have become so greedy to be *masters* that we call the same maxim "a self-evident lie" The fourth of July has not quite dwindled away; it is still a great day —*for burning fire-crackers!!!*

That spirit which desired the peaceful extinction of slavery, has itself become extinct, with the *occasion*, and the *men* of the Revolution. Under the impulse of that occasion, nearly half the states adopted systems of emancipation at once; and it is a significant fact, that not a single state has done the like since. So far as peaceful, voluntary emancipation is concerned, the condition of the negro slave in America, scarcely less terrible to the contemplation of a free mind, is now as fixed, and hopeless of change for the better, as that of the lost souls of the finally impenitent. The Autocrat of all the Russias will resign his crown, and proclaim his subjects free republicans sooner than will our American masters voluntarily give up their slaves.

Our political problem now is "Can we, as a nation, continue together *permanently—forever*—half slave, and half free?" The problem is too mighty for me. May God, in his mercy, superintend the solution. Your much obliged friend, and humble servant

To Joshua F. Speed

Dear Speed: Springfield, Aug: 24, 1855

You know what a poor correspondent I am. Ever since I received your very agreeable letter of the 22nd. of May I have been intending to write you in answer to it. You suggest that in political action now, you and I would differ. I suppose we would; not quite as much, however, as you may think. You know I dislike slavery; and you fully admit the abstract wrong of it. So far there is no cause of difference. But you say that sooner than yield your legal right to the slave—especially at the bidding of those who are not themselves interested, you would see the Union dissolved. I am not aware that *any one* is bidding you to yield that right; very certainly *I* am not. I leave that matter entirely to yourself. I also acknowledge *your* rights and *my* obligations, under the constitution, in regard to your slaves. I confess I hate to see the poor creatures hunted down, and caught, and carried back to their stripes, and unrewarded toils; but I bite my lip and keep quiet. In 1841 you and I had together a tedious low-water trip, on a Steam Boat from Louisville to St. Louis. You may remember, as I well do, that from Louisville to the mouth of the Ohio there were, on board, ten or a dozen slaves, shackled together with irons. That sight was a continual torment to me; and I see something like it every time I touch the Ohio, or any other slave-border. It is hardly fair for you to assume, that I have no interest in a thing which has, and continually exercises, the power of making me miserable. You ought rather to appreciate how much the great body of the Northern people do crucify their feelings, in order to maintain their loyalty to the constitution and the Union.

I do oppose the extension of slavery, because my judgment and feelings so prompt me; and I am under no obligation to the contrary. If for this you and I must differ, differ we must. You say if you were President, you would send an army and hang the leaders of the Missouri outrages upon the Kansas elections; still, if Kansas fairly votes herself a slave state, she must be admitted, or the Union must be dissolved. But how if she votes herself a slave state *unfairly*—that is, by the very means for which you say you would hang men? Must she still be admitted, or the Union be dissolved? That will be the phase of the question when it first becomes a practical one. In your assumption that there may be a *fair* decision of the slavery question in Kansas, I plainly see you and I would differ about the Nebraska-law. I look upon that enactment not as a *law*, but as *violence* from the beginning. It was conceived in violence, passed in violence, is maintained in violence, and is being executed in violence. I say it was *conceived* in violence, because the destruction of the Missouri Compromise, under the circumstances, was nothing less than violence. It was *passed* in violence, because it could not have passed at all but for the votes of many members, in violent disregard of the known will of their constituents. It is *maintained* in violence because the elections since, clearly demand it's repeal, and this demand is openly disregarded. *You* say men ought to be hung for the way they are executing that law; and *I* say the way it is being executed is quite as good as any of its antecedents. It is being executed in the precise way which was intended from the first; else why does no Nebraska man express astonishment or condemnation? Poor Reeder is the only public man who has been silly enough to believe that any thing like fairness was ever intended; and he has been bravely undeceived.

That Kansas will form a Slave constitution, and, with it, will ask to be admitted into the Union, I take to be an already settled question; and so settled by the very means you so pointedly condemn. By every principle of law, ever held by any court, North or South, every negro taken to Kansas is free; yet in utter disregard of this—in the spirit of violence merely—that beautiful Legislature gravely passes a law to hang men who shall venture to inform a negro of his legal rights. This is the substance, and real object of the law. If, like Haman, they should hang upon the gallows of their own building, I shall not be among the mourners for their fate.

In my humble sphere, I shall advocate the restoration of the Missouri Compromise, so long as Kansas remains a territory; and when, by all these foul means, it seeks to come into the Union as a Slave-state, I shall oppose it. I am very loth, in any case, to withhold my assent to the enjoyment of property *acquired*, or *located*, in good faith; but I do not admit that *good faith*, in taking a negro to Kansas, to be held in slavery, is a *possibility* with any man. Any man who has sense enough to be the controller of his own property, has too much sense to misunderstand the outrageous character of this whole Nebraska business. But I digress. In my opposition to the admission of Kansas I shall have some company; but we may be beaten. If we are, I shall not, on that account, attempt to dissolve the Union. On the contrary, if we succeed, there will be enough of us to take care of the Union. I think it probable, however, we shall be beaten. Standing as a unit among yourselves, you can, directly, and indirectly, bribe enough of our men to carry the day—as you could on an open proposition to establish monarchy. Get hold of some man in the North, whose position and ability is such, that he can make the support of your measure—whatever it may be—a *democratic party necessity*, and the thing is done. *Appropos* of this, let me tell you an anecdote. Douglas introduced the Nebraska bill in January. In February afterwards, there was a call session of the Illinois Legislature. Of the one hundred members composing the two branches of that body, about seventy were democrats. These latter held a caucus, in which the Nebraska bill was talked of, if not formally discussed. It was thereby discovered that just three, and no more, were in favor of the measure. In a day or two Douglas' orders came on to have resolutions passed approving the bill; and they were passed by large majorities!!! The truth of this is vouched for by a bolting democratic member. The masses too, democratic as well as whig, were even, nearer unanamous against it; but as soon as the party necessity of supporting it, became apparent, the way the democracy began to see the *wisdom* and *justice* of it, was perfectly astonishing.

You say if Kansas fairly votes herself a free state, as a christian you will rather rejoice at it. All decent slave-holders *talk* that way; and I do not doubt their candor. But they never *vote* that way. Although in a private letter, or conversation, you will express your preference that Kansas shall be free, you would vote for no man for Congress who would say the same thing publicly. No such man could be elected from any district in any slave-state. You think Stringfellow & Co ought to be hung; and yet, at the next presidential election you will vote for the exact type and representative of Stringfellow. The slave-breeders and slave-traders, are a small, odious and detested class, among you; and yet in politics, they dictate the course of all of you, and are as completely your masters, as you are the masters of your own negroes.

You enquire where I now stand. That is a disputed point. I think I am a whig; but others say there are no whigs, and that I am an abolitionist. When I was at Washington I voted for the Wilmot Proviso as good as forty times, and I never heard of any one attempting to unwhig me for that. I now do no more than oppose the *extension* of slavery.

I am not a Know-Nothing. That is certain. How could I be? How can any one who abhors the oppression of negroes, be in favor of degrading classes of white people? Our progress in degeneracy appears to me to be pretty rapid. As a nation, we began by declaring that *"all men are created equal."* We now practically read it "all men are created equal, *except negroes.*" When the Know-Nothings get control, it will read "all men are created equal, except negroes, *and foreigners, and catholics.*" When it comes to this I should prefer emigrating to some country where they make no pretence of loving liberty—to Russia, for instance, where despotism can be taken pure, and without the base alloy of hypocracy.

Mary will probably pass a day or two in Louisville in October. My kindest regards to Mrs. Speed. On the leading subject of this letter, I have more of her sympathy than I have of yours.

And yet let say I am   Your friend forever

To Isham Reavis

Isham Reavis, Esq.   Springfield,
My dear Sir: Novr. 5— 1855
    I have just reached home, and found your letter of the 23rd. ult. I am from home too much of my time, for a young man to read law with me advantageously. If you are resolutely determined to make a lawyer of yourself, the thing is more than half done already. It is but a small matter whether you read *with* any body or not. I did not read with any one. Get the books, and read and study them till, you understand them in their principal features; and that is the main thing. It is of no consequence to be in a large town while you are reading. I read at New-Salem, which never had three hundred people living in it. The *books*, and your *capacity* for understanding them, are just the same in all places. Mr. Dummer is a very clever man and an excellent lawyer (much better than I, in law-learning); and I have no doubt he will cheerfully tell you what books to read, and also loan you the books.
    Always bear in mind that your own resolution to succeed, is more important than any other one thing. Very truly Your friend

To Richard P. Morgan

R. P. Morgan, Esq   Springfield, Feby. 13, 1856
    Dear Sir: Says Tom to John "Heres your old rotten wheelbarrow" "Ive broke it, usin on it" "I wish *you* would mend it, case I shall want to borrow it this arter-noon."
    Acting on this as a precedent, I say "Heres your old "chalked hat" "I wish you would take it, and send me a new one, case I shall want to use it the first of March" Yours truly

To George P. Floyd

Mr. George P. Floyd,   Springfield, Illinois,
Quincy, Illinois.   February 21, 1856.

Dear Sir: I have just received yours of 16th, with check on Flagg & Savage for twenty-five dollars. You must think I am a high-priced man. You are too liberal with your money.

Fifteen dollars is enough for the job. I send you a receipt for fifteen dollars, and return to you a ten-dollar bill. Yours truly,

Speech at Bloomington, Illinois

Abraham Lincoln, of Sangamon, came upon the platform amid deafening applause. He enumerated the pressing reasons of the present movement. He was here ready to fuse with anyone who would unite with him to oppose slave power; spoke of the bugbear disunion which was so vaguely threatened. It was to be remembered that the *Union must be preserved in the purity of its principles as well as in the integrity of its territorial parts*. It must be "Liberty and Union, now and forever, one and inseparable." The sentiment in favor of white slavery now prevailed in all the slave state papers, except those of Kentucky, Tennessee and Missouri and Maryland. Such was the progress of the National Democracy. Douglas once claimed against him that Democracy favored more than his principles, the individual rights of man. Was it not strange that he must stand there now to defend those rights against their former eulogist? The Black Democracy were endeavoring to cite Henry Clay to reconcile old Whigs to their doctrine, and repaid them with the very cheap compliment of National Whigs.

May 29, 1856

To Lyman Trumbull

Hon: Lyman Trumbull   Springfield, June 7, 1856

My dear Sir: The news of Buchanan's nomination came yesterday; and a good many whigs, of conservative feelings, and slight pro-slavery proclivities, withal, are inclining to go for him, and will do it, unless the Anti-Nebraska nomination shall be such as to divert them. The man to effect that object is Judge McLean; and his nomination would save every whig, except such as have already gone over hook and line, as Singleton, Morrison, Constable, & others. J. T. Stuart, Anthony Thornton, James M. Davis (the old settler) and others like them, will heartily go for McLean, but will every one go for Buchanan, as against Chase, Banks, Seward, Blair or Fremont. I think they would stand Blair or Fremont for Vice-President—but not more.

Now there is a grave question to be considered. Nine tenths of the Anti-Nebraska votes have to come from old whigs. In setting stakes, is it safe to totally disregard them? Can we possibly win, if we do so? So far they have been disregarded. I need not point out the instances.

I think I may trust you to believe I do not say this on my own personal account. I am *in*, and shall go for any one nominated unless he be *"platformed"* expressly, or impliedly, on some ground which I may think wrong.

Since the nomination of Bissell we are in good trim in Illinois, save at the point I have indicated. If we can save pretty nearly all the whigs, we shall elect him, I think, by a very large majority.

I address this to you, because your influence in the Anti-Nebraska nomination will be greater than that of any other Illinoian.

Let this be confidential. Yours very truly

To Lyman Trumbull

Hon. L. Trumbull   Springfield, June 27, 1856
Dear Sir:

Yours of the 15th was received a few days ago. It would have been easier for us here, I think, had we got McLean; but as it is, I am not without high hopes for the state. I think we shall elect Bissell, at all events—and, if we can get rid of the Fillmore ticket, we shall carry the state for Fremont also.

Yesterday the Buchanan State ratification came off here. I do not think it proves much; but it really was a failure. There were not fifty—I think not thirty—persons, from other counties; and of the citizens of Sangamon, there were not more in town than there usually are on Saturdays. At night they spoke at the State-House; and they had no greater crowd than could be gathered any night on an hour's notice. Great effort had b[   ] from a distance, an[   ] from our ranks. Of th[   ] got Charley Constable, John Hogan from St. Louis, and no body else. Linder, and Singleton, and Webb, and Don Morrison, all missing. The old democratic speakers were old uncle Jimmy Barret, Moulton of Shelby, Vandeveer of Christian, and McClernand, all told.

Give my respects to Mrs. T. and believe [   ]

To David Davis

Dear Judge: Springfield, July 7. 1856

When I heard that Swett was beaten, and Lovejoy nominated, it turned me blind. I was, by invitation, on my way to Princeton; and I really thought of turning back. However, on reaching that region, and seeing the people there—their great enthusiasm for Lovejoy—considering the activity they will carry into the contest with him—and their great disappointment, if he should now be torn from them, I really think it best to let the matter stand. It is not my business to advise in the case; and if it were, I am not sure I am capable of giving the best advice; but I know, saying what I do, will not be offensive to you. Show this to Gridley and other friends, *or not*, just as you may judge whether it do good or harm.
Yours as ever

To James Berdan

James Berdan, Esq.   Springfield,
My dear Sir: July 10. 1856

I have just received your letter of yesterday; and I shall take the plan you suggest into serious consideration. I expect to go to Chicago about the 15th., and I will then confer with other friends upon the subject. A union of our strength, to be effected in some way, is indispensable to our carrying the State against Buchanan. The inherent obstacle to any plan of union, lies in the fact that of those germans which we now have with us, large numbers will fall away, so soon as it is seen that their votes, cast with us, may *possibly* be used to elevate Mr. Fillmore.

If this inherent difficulty were out of the way, one small improvement on your plan occurs to me. It is this. Let Fremont and Fillmore men unite on one entire ticket, with the understanding that that ticket, if elected, shall cast the vote of the State, for whichever of the two shall be known to have received the larger number of electoral votes, in the other states.

This plan has two advantages. It carries the electoral vote of the State where it will do most good; and it also saves the waste vote, which, according to your plan would be lost, and would be equal to two in the general result. But there may be disadvantages also, which I have not thought of. Your friend, as ever

To James W. Grimes

Hon. J. W. Grimes   Springfield, Ills.
My dear Sir: July 12, 1856

Yours of the 29th. of June was duly received. I did not answer it, because it plagued me. This morning I received another, from Judd and Peck, written by consultation with you.

Now let me tell you why I am plagued.

First I can hardly spare the time.

Secondly, I am superstitious. I have scarcely known a party, preceding an election, to call in help from the neighboring states, but they lost the state. Last fall our friends had Wade of Ohio, & others in Maine; and they lost the state. Last Spring, our adversaries had New-Hampshire full of South Carolinians, and *they* lost the State. And so generally. It seems to stir up more enemies than friends.

Have the enemy called in any foreign help. If they have a foreign champion there, I should have no objection to drive a nail in his track. I shall reach Chicago on the night of the 15th. to attend a little business in court. Consider the things I have suggested, and write me at Chicago. Especially write me whether Browning consents to visit you. Your Obt. Servt.

On Sectionalism

It is constantly objected to Fremont & Dayton, that they are supported by a *sectional* party, who, by their *sectionalism*, endanger the National Union. This objection, more than all others, causes men, really opposed to slavery extension, to hesitate. Practically, it is the most difficult objection we have to meet.

For this reason, I now propose to examine it, a little more carefully than I have heretofore done, or seen it done by others.

First, then, what is the question between the parties, respectively represented by Buchanan and Fremont?

Simply this: *"Shall slavery be allowed to extend into U.S. teritories, now legally free?"* Buchanan says it *shall*; and Fremont says it shall *not*.

That is the *naked* issue, and the *whole* of it. Lay the respective platforms side by side; and the difference between them, will be found to amount to precisely that.

True, each party charges upon the other, *designs* much beyond what is involved in the issue, as stated; but as these charges can not be fully proved either way, it is probably better to reject them on both sides, and stick to the naked issue, as it is clearly made up on the record.

And now, to restate the question *"Shall slavery be allowed to extend into U.S. teritories, now legally free?"* I beg to know *how one* side of that question is more sectional than the other? Of course I expect to effect nothing with the man who makes this charge of sectionalism, without caring whether it is just or not. But of the *candid, fair*, man who has been puzzled with this charge, I do ask how is *one* side of this question, more *sectional*, than the other? I beg of him to consider well, and answer calmly.

If one side be as sectional as the other, nothing is gained, as to sectionalism, by changing sides; so that each must choose sides of the question on some other ground—as I should think, according, as the one side or the other, shall appear nearest right.

If he shall really think slavery *ought* to be extended, let him go to Buchanan; if he think it ought *not* let him go to Fremont.

But, Fremont and Dayton, are both residents of the free-states; and this fact has been vaunted, in high places, as excessive *sectionalism*.

While interested individuals become *indignant* and *excited*, against this manifestation of *sectionalism*, I am very happy to know, that the Constitution remains calm—keeps cool—upon the subject. It does say that President and Vice President shall be resident of different states; but it does not say one must live in a *slave*, and the other in a *free* state.

It has been a *custom* to take one from a slave, and the other from a free state; but the custom has not, at all been uniform. In 1828 Gen. Jackson and Mr. Calhoun, both from slave-states, were placed on the same ticket; and Mr. Adams and Dr. Rush both from the free-states, were pitted against them. Gen: Jackson and Mr. Calhoun were elected; and qualified and served under the election; yet the whole thing never suggested the idea of sectionalism.

In 1841, the president, Gen. Harrison, died, by which Mr. Tyler, the Vice-President & a slave state man, became president. Mr. Mangum, another slave-state man, was placed in the Vice Presidential chair, served out the term, and no fuss about it—no sectionalism thought of.

In 1853 the present president came into office. He is a free-state man. Mr. King, the new Vice President elect, was a slave state man; but he died without entering on the duties of his office. At first, his vacancy was filled by Atchison, another slave-state man; but he soon resigned, and the place was supplied by Bright, a free-state man. So that right now, and for the year and a half last past, our president and vice-president are both actually free-state men.

But, it is said, the friends of Fremont, avow the purpose of electing him exclusively by free-state votes, and that this is unendurable *sectionalism*.

This statement of fact, is not exactly true. With the friends of Fremont, it is an *expected necessity*, but it is not an *"avowed purpose,"* to elect him, if at all, principally, by free state votes;

but it is, with equal intensity, true that Buchanan's friends expect to elect him, if at all, chiefly by slave-state votes.

Here, again, the sectionalism, is just as much on one side as the other.

The thing which gives most color to the charge of Sectionalism, made against those who oppose the spread of slavery into free teritory, is the fact that *they* can get no votes in the slave-states, while their opponents get all, or nearly so, in the slave-states, and also, a large number in the free States. To state it in another way, the Extensionists, can get votes all over the Nation, while the Restrictionists can get them only in the free states.

This being the fact, *why* is it so? It is not because one *side* of the question dividing them, is more sectional than the *other*; nor because of any difference in the mental or moral structure of the people North and South. It is because, in that question, the people of the South have an immediate palpable and immensely great pecuniary interest; while, with the people of the North, it is merely an abstract question of moral right, with only *slight*, and *remote* pecuniary interest added.

The slaves of the South, at a moderate estimate, are worth a thousand millions of dollars. Let it be permanently settled that this property may extend to new teritory, without restraint, and it greatly *enhances*, perhaps quite *doubles*, its value at once. This immense, palpable pecuniary interest, on the question of extending slavery, unites the Southern people, as one man. But it can not be demonstrated that the *North* will gain a dollar by restricting it.

Moral principle is all, or nearly all, that unites us of the North. Pity 'tis, it is so, but this is a looser bond, than pecuniary interest. Right here is the plain cause of *their perfect* union and *our want* of it. And see how it works. If a Southern man aspires to be president, they choke him down instantly, in order that the glittering prize of the presidency, may be held up, on Southern terms, to the greedy eyes of Northern ambition. With this they tempt us, and break in upon us.

The democratic party, in 1844, elected a Southern president. Since then, they have neither had a Southern candidate for *election*, or *nomination*. Their Conventions of 1848–1852 and 1856, have been struggles exclusively among *Northern* men, each vieing to out-bid the other for the Southern vote—the South standing calmly by to finally cry going, going, gone, to the highest bidder; and, at the same time, to make its power more distinctly seen, and thereby to secure a still higher bid at the next succeeding struggle.

"Actions speak louder than words" is the maxim; and, if true, the South now distinctly says to the North "Give us the *measures*, and you take the *men*"

The total withdrawal of Southern aspirants, for the presidency, multiplies the number of Northern ones. These last, in competing with each other, commit themselves to the utmost verge that, through their own greediness, they have the least hope their Northern supporters will bear. Having got committed, in a race of competetion, necessity drives them into union to sustain themselves. Each, at first secures all he can, on personal attachments to him, and through *hopes* resting on him personally. Next, they unite with one another, and with the perfectly banded South, to make the offensive position they have got into, "a party measure." This done, large additional numbers are secured.

When the repeal of the Missouri compromise was first proposed, at the North there was litterally *"nobody"* in favor of it. In February 1854 our Legislature met in call, or extra, session. From them Douglas sought an indorsement of his then pending measure of Repeal. In our Legislature were about 70 democrats to 30 whigs. The former held a caucus, in which it was resolved to give Douglas the desired indorsement. Some of the members of that caucus bolted—would not stand it—and they now divulge the secrets. They say that the caucus fairly confessed that the Repeal was wrong; and they placed their determination to indorse it, solely on the ground that it was *necessary* to sustain Douglas. Here we have the direct evidence of how the Nebraska-bill obtained it's strength in Illinois. It was given, not in a sense of right, but in the teeth of a sense of wrong, to *sustain Douglas*. So Illinois was divided. So New England, for Pierce; Michigan for Cass, Pensylvania for Buchanan, and all for the Democratic party.

And when, by such means, they have got a large portion

of the Northern people into a position contrary to their own honest impulses, and sense of right; they have the impudence to turn upon those who do stand firm, and call them *sectional*.

Were it not too serious a matter, this cool impudence would be laughable, to say the least.

Recurring to the question *"Shall slavery be allowed to extend into U.S. teritory now legally free?"*

This *is* a sectional question—that is to say, it is a question, in its nature calculated to divide the American people geographically. Who is to *blame* for that? *who* can help it? Either side *can* help it; but how? Simply by *yielding* to the other side. There is no other way. In the whole range of *possibility*, there is no other way. Then, which side shall yield? To this again, there can be but one answer—the side which is in the *wrong*. True, we differ, as to which side *is* wrong; and we boldly say, let all who really think slavery ought to spread into free teritory, openly go over against us. There is where they rightfully belong.

But why should any go, who really think slavery ought not to spread? Do they really think the *right* ought to yield to the *wrong*? Are they afraid to stand by the *right*? Do they fear that the constitution is too weak to sustain them in the right? Do they really think that by right surrendering to wrong, the hopes of our constitution, our Union, and our liberties, can possibly be bettered?

c. July 1856

To Lyman Trumbull

Hon: L. Trumbull: Springfield,
My dear Sir   Aug: 11. 1856

I have just returned from speaking at Paris and Grandview in Edgar county—& Charleston and Shelbyville, in Coles and Shelby counties. Our whole trouble along there has been & is Fillmoreism. It loosened considerably during the week, not under my preaching, but under the election returns from Mo. Ky. Ark. & N.C. I think we shall ultimately get all the Fillmore men, who are realy anti-slavery extension—the rest will probably go to Buchanan where they rightfully belong; if they do not, so much the better for us. The great difficulty with anti-slavery extension Fillmore men, is that they suppose Fillmore as good as Fremont on that question; and it is a delicate point to argue them out of it, they are so ready to think you are *abusing* Mr. Fillmore.

Mr. Conkling showed me a letter of yours, from which I infer you will not be in Ills. till 11th. Sept. But for that I was going to write you to make appointments at Paris, Charleston, Shelbyville, Hillsboro, &c. immediately after the adjournment. They were tolerably well satisfied with my work along there; but they believe with me, that you can touch some points that I can not; and they are very anxious to have you do it. Yours as ever

Speech at Kalamazoo, Michigan

Fellow countrymen:—Under the Constitution of the U.S. another Presidential contest approaches us. All over this land—that portion at least, of which I know much—the people are assembling to consider the proper course to be adopted by them. One of the first considerations is to learn what the people differ about. If we ascertain what we differ about, we shall be better able to decide. The question of slavery, at the present day, should be not only the greatest question, but very nearly the sole question. Our opponents, however, prefer that this should not be the case. To get at this question, I will occupy your attention but a single moment. The question is simply this:—Shall slavery be spread into the new Territories, or not? This is the naked question. If we should support Fremont successfully in this, it may be charged that we will not be content with restricting slavery in the new territories. If we should charge that James Buchanan, by his platform, is bound to extend slavery into the territories, and that he is in favor of its being thus spread, we should be puzzled to prove it. We believe it, nevertheless. By taking the issue as I present it, whether it shall be permitted as an issue, is made up between the parties. Each takes his own stand. This is the question: Shall the Government of the United States prohibit slavery in the United States.

We have been in the habit of deploring the fact that slavery exists amongst us. We have ever deplored it. Our forefathers did, and they declared, as we have done in later years, the blame rested on the mother Government of Great Britain. We constantly condemn Great Britain for not preventing slavery from coming amongst us. She would not interfere to prevent it, and so individuals were enabled to introduce the institution without opposition. I have alluded to this, to ask you if this is not exactly the policy of Buchanan and his friends, to place this government in the attitude then occupied by the government of Great Britain—placing the nation in the position to authorize the territories to reproach it, for refusing to allow them to hold slaves. I would like to ask your attention, any gentleman to tell me when the people of Kansas are going to decide. When are they to do it? How are they to do it? I asked that question two years ago—when, and how are they to do it? Not many weeks ago, our new Senator from Illinois, (Mr. Trumbull) asked Douglas how it could be done. Douglas is a great man—at keeping from answering questions he don't want to answer. He would not answer. He said it was a question for the Supreme Court to decide. In the North, his friends argue that the people can decide it at any time. The Southerners say there is no power in the people, whatever. We know that from the time that white people have been allowed in the territory, they have brought slaves with them. Suppose the people come up to vote as freely, and with as perfect protection as we could do it here. Will they be at liberty to vote their sentiments? If they can, then all that has ever been said about our provincial ancestors is untrue, and they could have done so, also. We know our Southern friends say that the General Government cannot interfere. The people, say they, have no right to interfere. They could as truly say,—"It is amongst us—we cannot get rid of it."

But I am afraid I waste too much time on this point. I take it as an illustration of the principle, that slaves are admitted into the territories. And, while I am speaking of Kansas, how will that operate? Can men vote truly? We will suppose that there are ten men who go into Kansas to settle. Nine of these are opposed to slavery. One has ten slaves. The slaveholder is a good man in other respects; he is a good neighbor, and being a wealthy man, he is enabled to do the others many neighborly kindnesses. They like the man, though they don't like the system by which he holds his fellow-men in bondage. And here let me say, that in intellectual and physical structure, our Southern brethren do not differ from us. They are, like us, subject to passions, and it is only their odious institution of slavery, that makes the breach between us. These ten men of whom I was speaking, live together three or four years; they intermarry; their family ties are strengthened. And who wonders that in time, the people learn to look upon slavery with complacency? This is the way in which slavery is planted, and gains so firm a foothold. I think this is a strong card that the Nebraska party have played, and won upon, in this game.

I suppose that this crowd are opposed to the admission of slavery into Kansas, yet it is true that in all crowds there are some who differ from the majority. I want to ask the Buchanan men, who are against the spread of slavery, if there be any present, why not vote for the man who is against it? I understand that Mr. Fillmore's position is precisely like Buchanan's. I understand that, by the Nebraska bill, a door has been opened for the spread of slavery in the Territories. Examine, if you please, and see if they have ever done any such thing as try to shut the door. It is true that Fillmore tickles a few of his friends with the notion that he is not the cause of the door being opened. Well; it brings him into this position: he tries to get both sides, one by denouncing those who opened the door, and the other by hinting that he doesn't care a fig for its being open. If he were President, he would have one side or the other—he would either restrict slavery or not. Of course it would be so. There could be no middle way. You who hate slavery and love freedom, why not, as Fillmore and Buchanan are on the same ground, vote for Fremont? Why not vote for the man who takes your side of the question? "Well," says Buchanier, "it is none of our business." But is it not *our* business? There are several reasons why I think it is our business. But let us see how it is. Others have urged these reasons before, but they are still of use. By our Constitution we are represented in Congress in proportion to numbers, and in counting the numbers that give us our representatives, three slaves are counted as two people. The State of Maine has six representatives in the lower house of Congress. In strength South Carolina is equal to her. But stop! Maine has *twice as many* white people, and 32,000 to boot! And is that fair? I don't complain of it. This regulation was put in force when the exigencies of the times demanded it, and could not have been avoided. Now, one man in South Carolina is the same as two men here. Maine should have twice as many men in Congress as South Carolina. It is a fact that any man in South Carolina has more influence and power in Congress today than any two now before me. The same thing is true of all slave States, though it may not be in the same proportion. It is a truth that cannot be denied, that in all the free States no white man is the equal of the white man of the slave States.

But this is in the Constitution, and we must stand up to it. The question, then is, "Have we no interest as to whether the white man of the North shall be the equal of the white man of the South?" Once when I used this argument in the presence of Douglas, he answered that in the North the black man was counted as a full man, and had an equal vote with the white, while at the South they were counted at but three-fifths. And Douglas, when he had made this reply, doubtless thought he had forever silenced the objection.

Have we no interest in the free Territories of the United States—that they should be kept open for the homes of free white people? As our Northern States are growing more and more in wealth and population, we are continually in want of an outlet, through which it may pass out to enrich our country. In this we have an interest—a deep and abiding interest. There is another thing, and that is the mature knowledge we have—the greatest interest of all. It is the doctrine, that the people are to be driven from the maxims of our free Government, that despises the spirit which for eighty years has celebrated the anniversary of our national independence.

We are a great empire. We are eighty years old. We stand at once the wonder and admiration of the whole world, and we must enquire what it is that has given us so much prosperity, and we shall understand that to give up that one thing, would be to give up all future prosperity. This cause is that every man can make himself. It has been said that such a race of prosperity has been run nowhere else. We find a people on the North-east, who have a different government from ours, being ruled by a Queen. Turning to the South, we see a people who, while they boast of being free, keep their fellow beings in bondage. Compare our Free States with either, shall we say here that we have no interest in keeping that principle alive? Shall we say—"Let it be." No—we have an interest in the maintenance of the principles of the Government, and without this interest, it is worth nothing. I have noticed in Southern newspapers, particularly the Richmond *Enquirer*, the Southern view of the Free States. They insist that slavery has a right to spread. They defend it upon principle. They insist that their slaves are far better off than Northern freemen. What a mistaken view do these men have of Northern laborers! They think that men are always to remain laborers here—but there is no such class. The man who labored for another last year, this year labors for himself, and next year he will hire others to labor for him. These men don't understand when they think in this manner of Northern free labor. When these reasons can be introduced, tell me not that we have no interest in keeping the Territories free for the settlement of free laborers.

I pass, then, from this question. I think we have an ever growing interest in maintaining the free institutions of our country.

It is said that our party is a sectional party. It has been said in high quarters that if Fremont and Dayton were elected the Union would be dissolved. The South do not think so. I believe it! I believe it! It is a shameful thing that the subject is talked of so much. Did we not have a Southern President and Vice-President at one time? And yet the Union has not yet been dissolved. Why, at this very moment, there is a Northern President and Vice-President. Pierce and King were elected, and King died without ever taking his seat. The Senate elected a Northern man from their own numbers, to perform the duties of the Vice-President. He resigned his seat, however, as soon as he got the job of making a slave State out of Kansas. Was not that a great mistake?

(A voice.—"He didn't mean that!")

Then why didn't he speak what he did mean? Why did not he speak what he ought to have spoken? That was the very thing. He should have spoken manly, and we should then have known where to have found him. It is said we expect to elect Fremont by Northern votes. Certainly we do not think the South will elect him. But let us ask the question differently. Does not Buchanan expect to be elected by Southern votes? Fillmore, however, will go out of this contest the most national man we have. He has no prospect of having a single vote on either side of Mason and Dixon's line, to trouble his poor soul about. (Laughter and cheers.)

We believe that it is right that slavery should not be tolerated in the new territories, yet we cannot get support for this doctrine, except in one part of the country. Slavery is looked upon by men in the light of dollars and cents. The estimated worth of the slaves at the South is $1,000,000,000, and in a very few years, if the institution shall be admitted into the territories, they will have increased fifty per cent in value.

Our adversaries charge Fremont with being an abolitionist. When pressed to show proof, they frankly confess that they can show no such thing. They then run off upon the assertion that his supporters are abolitionists. But this they have never attempted to prove. I know of no word in the language that has been used so much as that one "abolitionist," having no definition. It has no meaning unless taken as designating a person who is abolishing something. If that be its signification, the supporters of Fremont are not abolitionists. In Kansas all who come there are perfectly free to regulate their own social relations. There has never been a man there who was an abolitionist—for what was there to be abolished? People there had perfect freedom to express what they wished on the subject, when the Nebraska bill was first passed. Our friends in the South, who support Buchanan, have five disunion men to one at the North. This disunion is a sectional question. Who is to blame for it? Are we? I don't care how you express it. This government is sought to be put on a new track. Slavery is to be made a ruling element in our government. The question can be avoided in but two ways. By the one, we must submit, and allow slavery to triumph, or, by the other, we must triumph over the black demon. We have chosen the latter manner. If you of the North wish to get rid of this question, you must decide between these two ways—submit and vote for Buchanan, submit and vote that slavery is a just and good thing and immediately get rid of the question; or unite with us, and help us to triumph. We would all like to have the question done away with, but we cannot submit.

They tell us that we are in company with men who have long been known as abolitionists. What care we how many may feel disposed to labor for our cause? Why do not you, Buchanan men, come in and use your influence to make our party respectable? (Laughter.) How is the dissolution of the Union to be consummated? They tell us that the Union is in danger. Who will divide it? Is it those who make the charge? Are they themselves the persons who wish to see this result? A majority will never dissolve the Union. Can a minority do it? When this Nebraska bill was first introduced into Congress, the sense of the Democratic party was outraged. That party has ever prided itself, that it was the friend of individual, universal freedom. It was that principle upon which they carried their measures. When the Kansas scheme was conceived, it was natural that this respect and sense should have been outraged. Now I make this appeal to the Democratic citizens here. Don't you find yourself making arguments in support of these measures, which you never would have made before? Did you ever do it before this Nebraska bill compelled you to do it? If you answer this in the affirmative, see how a whole party have been turned away from their love of liberty! And now, my Democratic friends, come forward. Throw off these things, and come to the rescue of this great principle of equality. Don't interfere with anything in the Constitution. That must be maintained, for it is the only safeguard of our liberties. And not to Democrats alone do I make this appeal, but to all who love these great and true principles. Come, and keep coming! Strike, and strike again! So sure as God lives, the victory shall be yours. (Great cheering.)

August 27, 1856

Letter to Fillmore Men

Dear Sir,   Springfield, Sept. 8, 1856

I understand you are a Fillmore man. Let me prove to you that every vote withheld from Fremont, and given to Fillmore, *in this state*, actually lessens Fillmore's chance of being President.

Suppose Buchanan gets *all* the slave states, and Pennsylvania, and *any other* one state besides; *then he is elected*, no matter who gets all the rest.

But suppose Fillmore gets the two slave states of Maryland and Kentucky; *then* Buchanan *is not* elected; Fillmore goes into the House of Representatives, and may be made President by a compromise.

But suppose again Fillmore's friends throw away a few thousand votes on him, in *Indiana* and *Illinois*, it will inevitably give these states to Buchanan, which will more than compensate him for the loss of Maryland and Kentucky; will elect him, and leave Fillmore no chance in the H.R. or out of it.

This is as plain as the adding up of the weights of three small hogs. As Mr. Fillmore has no possible chance to carry Illinois *for himself*, it is plainly his interest to let Fremont take it, and thus keep it out of the hands of Buchanan. Be not deceived. *Buchanan* is the hard horse to beat in this race. Let him have Illinois, and nothing can beat him; *and he will get Illinois*, if men persist in throwing away votes upon Mr. Fillmore.

Does some one persuade, you that Mr. Fillmore can carry Illinois? Nonsense! There are over seventy newspapers in Illinois opposing Buchanan, only three or four of which support Mr. Fillmore, *all* the rest going for Fremont. Are not these newspapers a fair index of the proportion of the voters. If not, tell me why.

Again, of these three or four Fillmore newspapers, *two* at least, are supported, in part, by the Buchanan men, as I understand. Do not they know where the shoe pinches? They know the Fillmore movement helps *them*, and therefore they help *it*.

Do think these things over, and then act according to your judgment. Yours very truly,

(Confidential)

To Henry O'Conner

Henry O'Conner,   Springfield,
Muscatine Iowa.   Sept. 14, 1856

Dear Sir   Yours, inviting me to attend a mass meeting on the 23rd. Inst. is received. It would be very pleasant to strike hands with the Fremonters of Iowa, who have led the van so splendidly, in this grand charge which we hope and believe will end in a most glorious victory. All thanks, all honor to Iowa!!

But Iowa is out of all danger, and it is no time for us, when the battle still rages, to pay holy-day visits to Iowa. I am sure you will excuse me for remaining in Illinois, where much hard work is still to be done. Yours very truly

To Julian M. Sturtevant

Rev. J. M. Sturtevant   Springfield,
Jacksonville, Ills   Sept. 27. 1856

My dear Sir: Owing to absence yours of the 16th. was not received till the day-before yesterday. I thank you for your good opinion of me personally, and still more for the deep interest you take in the cause of our common country. It pains me a little that you have deemed it necessary to point out to me how I may be compensated for throwing myself in the breach now. This assumes that I am merely calculating the chances of personal advancement. Let me assure you that I decline to be a candidate for congress, on my clear conviction, that my running would *hurt*, & not *help* the cause. I am willing to make any personal sacrafice, but I am not willing to do, what in my own judgment, is, a sacrafice of the cause itself. Very truly Yours

On Stephen Douglas

Twenty-two years ago Judge Douglas and I first became acquainted. We were both young then; he a trifle younger than I. Even then, we were both ambitious; I, perhaps, quite as much so as he. With *me*, the race of ambition has been a failure—a flat failure; with *him* it has been one of splendid success. His name fills the nation; and is not unknown, even, in foreign lands. I affect no contempt for the high eminence he has reached. So reached, that the oppressed of my species, might have shared with me in the elevation, I would rather stand on that eminence, than wear the richest crown that ever pressed a monarch's brow.

c. December 1856

Portion of Speech at Republican Banquet in Chicago, Illinois

We have another annual Presidential Message. Like a rejected lover, making merry at the wedding of his rival, the President felicitates hugely over the late Presidential election. He considers the result a signal triumph of good principles and good men, and a very pointed rebuke of bad ones. He says the people did it. He forgets that the "people," as he complacently calls only those who voted for Buchanan, are in a minority of the whole people, by about four hundred thousand voters—one full tenth of all the voters. Remembering this, he might perceive that the "Rebuke" may not be quite as durable as he seems to think—that the majority may not choose to remain permanently rebuked by that minority.

The President thinks the great body of us Fremonters, being ardently attached to liberty, in the abstract, were duped by a few wicked and designing men. There is a slight difference of opinion on this. We think *he*, being ardently attached to the hope of a second term, *in the concrete*, was duped by men who had liberty every way. He is in the cat's paw. By much dragging of chestnuts from the fire for others to eat, his claws are burnt off to the gristle, and he is thrown aside as unfit for further use. As the fool said to King Lear, when his daughters had turned him out of doors, "He's a shelled pea's cod."

So far as the President charges us "with a desire to change the domestic institutions of existing States;" and of "doing every thing in our power to deprive the Constitution and the laws of moral authority," for the whole party, on *belief*, and for myself, on *knowledge* I pronounce the charge an unmixed, and unmitigated falsehood.

Our government rests in public opinion. Whoever can change public opinion, can change the government, practically just so much. Public opinion, on any subject, always has a *"central idea,"* from which all its minor thoughts radiate. That "central idea" in our political public opinion, at the beginning was, and until recently has continued to be, "the equality of men." And although it was always submitted patiently to whatever of inequality there seemed to be as matter of actual necessity, its constant working has been a steady progress towards the practical equality of all men. The late Presidential election was a struggle, by one party, to discard that central idea, and to substitute for it the opposite idea that slavery is right, in the abstract, the workings of which, as a central idea, may be the perpetuity of human slavery, and its extension to all countries and colors. Less than a year ago, the Richmond *Enquirer*, an avowed advocate of slavery, regardless of color, in order to favor his views, invented the phrase, "State equality," and now the President, in his Message, adopts the *Enquirer's* catch-phrase, telling us the people "have asserted the constitutional equality of each and all of the States of the Union as States." The President flatters himself that the new central idea is completely inaugurated; and so, indeed, it is, so far as the mere fact of a Presidential election can inaugurate it. To us it is left to know that the majority of the people have not yet declared for it, and to hope that they never will.

All of us who did not vote for Mr. Buchanan, taken together, are a majority of four hundred thousand. But, in the late contest we were divided between Fremont and Fillmore. Can we not come together, for the future. Let every one who really believes, and is resolved, that free society is not, *and shall not be*, a failure, and who can conscientiously declare that in the past contest he has done only what he thought best— let every such one have charity to believe that every other one can say as much. Thus let bygones be bygones. Let past differences, as nothing be; and with steady eye on the real issue, let us reinaugurate the good old "central ideas" of the Republic. We *can* do it. The human heart *is* with us—God is with us. We shall again be able not to declare, that "all States as States, are equal," nor yet that "all citizens as citizens are equal," but to renew the broader, better declaration, including both these and much more, that "all *men* are created equal."

December 10, 1856

Notes for Speech at Chicago, Illinois

With the future of this party, the approaching city election will have something to do—not, indeed, to the extent of making or breaking it, but still to help or to hurt it.

Last year the city election here was lost by our friends; and none can safely say, but that fact lost us the electoral ticket at the State election.

Although Chicago recovered herself in the fall, there was no general confidence that she could do so; and the Spring election encouraged our enemies, and haunted and depressed our friends to the last.

Let it not be so again.

Let minor differences, and personal preferences, if there be such; go to the winds.

Let it be seen by the result, that the cause of free-men and free-labor is stronger in Chicago that day, than ever before.

Let the news go forth to our thirteen hundred thousand bretheren, to gladden, and to multiply them; and to insure and accelerate that consumation, upon which the happy destiny of all men, everywhere, depends.

We were without party history, party pride, or party idols.

We were a collection of individuals, but recently in political hostility, one to another; and thus subject to all that distrust, and suspicion, and jealousy could do.

Every where in the ranks of the common enemy, were old party and personal friends, jibing, and jeering, and framing deceitful arguments against us.

We were scarcely met at all on the real issue.

Thousands avowed our principles, but turned from us, professing to believe we *meant* more than we *said*.

No argument, which was true in fact, made any head-way against us. This we know.

We were constantly charged with seeking an amalgamation of the white and black races; and thousands turned from us, not believing the charge (no one believed it) but *fearing* to face it themselves.

February 28, 1857

To Newton Deming and George P. Strong

Messrs. N.D. & G.P. Strong   Springfield, May 25, 1857.
Gentlemen

Yours of the 22nd is just received. The admiralty case now stands on appeal to the circuit court and consequently, can only be tried by Judge McLean; and I understand he will remain here only one week, commencing the first Monday of June. Of course, the other side will press for a hearing during that week.

I have just been to see Stuart & Edwards and they suggest that you see the plaintiff's lawyer in St. Louis (I forget his name) and make an arrangement with him as to a day of taking up the case, and notify us.

I do not think any defence has been presented based on the fact of Messrs Page & Bacon having purchased under the Deed of Trust. *Quere.* Does not the Libellant's right, attach to the specific *thing*—this case—regardless of who may own them?

There is no longer any difficult question of *jurisdiction* in the Federal courts; they have jurisdiction in all possible cases, except such as might redound to the benefit of a "nigger" in some way.

Seriously, I wish you to prepare, on the question jurisdiction as well as you can; for I fear the later decisions are against us. I understand they have some new Admiralty Books here, but I have not examined them. Yours truly

On the Dred Scott Case

What would be the effect of this, if it should ever be the creed of a dominant party in the nation? Let us analyse, and consider it.

It affirms that, whatever the Supreme Court may decide as to the constitutional restriction on the power of a teritorial Legislature, in regard to slavery in the teritory, must be obeyed, and enforced by all the departments of the federal government.

Now, if this is sound, as to this particular constitutional question, it is equally sound of *all* constitutional questions; so that the proposition substantially, is "Whatever decision the Supreme court makes on *any* constitutional question, must be obeyed, and enforced by all the departments of the federal government."

Again, it is not the full scope of this creed, that if the Supreme court, having the particular question before them, shall decide that Dred Scott is a slave, the executive department must enforce the decision against Dred Scott. If this were it's full scope, it is presumed, no one would controvert it's correctness. But in this narrow scope, there is no room for the Legislative department to enforce the decision; while the creed affirms that *all* the departments must enforce it. The creed, then, has a broader scope; and what is it? It is this; that so soon as the Supreme court decides that Dred Scott is a slave, the whole community must decide that not only Dred Scott, but that *all* persons in like condition, are rightfully slaves

June? 1857

Speech on the Dred Scott Decision at Springfield, Illinois

FELLOW CITIZENS:—I am here to-night, partly by the invitation of some of you, and partly by my own inclination. Two weeks ago Judge Douglas spoke here on the several subjects of Kansas, the Dred Scott decision, and Utah. I listened to the speech at the time, and have read the report of it since. It was intended to controvert opinions which I think just, and to assail (politically, not personally,) those men who, in common with me, entertain those opinions. For this reason I wished then, and still wish, to make some answer to it, which I now take the opportunity of doing.

I begin with Utah. If it prove to be true, as is probable, that the people of Utah are in open rebellion to the United States, then Judge Douglas is in favor of repealing their territorial organization, and attaching them to the adjoining States for judicial purposes. I say, too, if they are in rebellion, they ought to be somehow coerced to obedience; and I am not now prepared to admit or deny that the Judge's mode of coercing them is not as good as any. The Republicans can fall in with it without taking back anything they have ever said. To be sure, it would be a considerable backing down by Judge Douglas from his much vaunted doctrine of self-government for the territories; but this is only additional proof of what was very plain from the beginning, that that doctrine was a mere deceitful pretense for the benefit of slavery. Those who could not see that much in the Nebraska act itself, which forced Governors, and Secretaries, and Judges on the people of the territories, without their choice or consent, could not be made to see, though one should rise from the dead to testify.

But in all this, it is very plain the Judge evades the only question the Republicans have ever pressed upon the Democracy in regard to Utah. That question the Judge well knows to be this: "If the people of Utah shall peacefully form a State Constitution tolerating polygamy, will the Democracy admit them into the Union?" There is nothing in the United States Constitution or law against polygamy; and why is it not a part of the Judge's "sacred right of self-government" for that people to have it, or rather to *keep* it, if they choose? These questions, so far as I know, the Judge never answers. It might involve the Democracy to answer them either way, and they go unanswered.

As to Kansas. The substance of the Judge's speech on Kansas is an effort to put the free State men in the wrong for not voting at the election of delegates to the Constitutional Convention. He says: *"There is every reason to hope and believe that the law will be fairly interpreted and impartially executed, so as to insure to every bona fide inhabitant the free and quiet exercise of the elective franchise."*

It appears extraordinary that Judge Douglas should make such a statement. He knows that, by the law, no one can vote who has not been registered; and he knows that the free State men place their refusal to vote on the ground that but few of them have been registered. It is *possible* this is not true, but Judge Douglas knows it is asserted to be true in letters, newspapers and public speeches, and borne by every mail, and blown by every breeze to the eyes and ears of the world. He knows it is boldly declared that the people of many whole counties, and many whole neighborhoods in others, are left unregistered; yet, he does not venture to contradict the declaration, nor to point out how they *can* vote without being registered; but he just slips along, not seeming to know there is any such question of fact, and complacently declares: "There is every reason to hope and believe that the law will be fairly and impartially executed, so as to insure to every *bona fide* inhabitant the free and quiet exercise of the elective franchise."

I readily agree that if all had a chance to vote, they ought to have voted. If, on the contrary, as they allege, and Judge Douglas ventures not to particularly contradict, few only of the free State men had a chance to vote, they were perfectly right in staying from the polls in a body.

By the way since the Judge spoke, the Kansas election has come off. The Judge expressed his confidence that all the Democrats in Kansas would do their duty—including "free state Democrats" of course. The returns received here as yet are very incomplete; but so far as they go, they indicate that only about one sixth of the registered voters, have really voted; and this too, when not more, perhaps, than one half of the rightful voters have been registered, thus showing the thing to have been altogether the most exquisite farce ever enacted. I am watching with considerable interest, to ascertain what figure "the free state Democrats" cut in the concern. Of course they voted—all democrats do their duty—and of course they did not vote for slave-state candidates. We soon shall know how many delegates *they* elected, how many candidates they had, pledged for a free state; and how many votes were cast for them.

Allow me to barely whisper my suspicion that there were no such things in Kansas "as free state Democrats"—that they were altogether mythical, good only to figure in newspapers and speeches in the free states. If there should prove to be one real living free state Democrat in Kansas, I suggest that it might be well to catch him, and stuff and preserve his skin, as an interesting specimen of that soon to be extinct variety of the genus, Democrat.

And now as to the Dred Scott decision. That decision declares two propositions—first, that a negro cannot sue in the U.S. Courts; and secondly, that Congress cannot prohibit slavery in the Territories. It was made by a divided court—dividing differently on the different points. Judge Douglas does not discuss the merits of the decision; and, in that respect, I shall follow his example, believing I could no more improve on McLean and Curtis, than he could on Taney.

He denounces all who question the correctness of that decision, as offering violent resistance to it. But who resists it? Who has, in spite of the decision, declared Dred Scott free, and resisted the authority of his master over him?

Judicial decisions have two uses—first, to absolutely determine the case decided, and secondly, to indicate to the public how other similar cases will be decided when they arise. For the latter use, they are called "precedents" and "authorities."

We believe, as much as Judge Douglas, (perhaps more) in obedience to, and respect for the judicial department of government. We think its decisions on Constitutional questions, when fully settled, should control, not only the particular cases decided, but the general policy of the country, subject to be disturbed only by amendments of the Constitution as provided in that instrument itself. More than this would be revolution. But we think the Dred Scott decision is erroneous. We know the court that made it, has often over-ruled its own decisions, and we shall do what we can to have it to over-rule this. We offer no *resistance* to it.

Judicial decisions are of greater or less authority as precedents, according to circumstances. That this should be so, accords both with common sense, and the customary understanding of the legal profession.

If this important decision had been made by the unanimous concurrence of the judges, and without any apparent partisan bias, and in accordance with legal public expectation, and with the steady practice of the departments throughout our history, and had been in no part, based on assumed historical facts which are not really true; or, if wanting in some of these, it had been before the court more than once, and had there been affirmed and re-affirmed through a course of years, it then might be, perhaps would be, factious, nay, even revolutionary, to not acquiesce in it as a precedent.

But when, as it is true we find it wanting in all these claims to the public confidence, it is not resistance, it is not factious, it is not even disrespectful, to treat it as not having yet quite established a settled doctrine for the country—But Judge Douglas considers this view awful. Hear him:

"The courts are the tribunals prescribed by the Constitution and created by the authority of the people to determine, expound and enforce the law. Hence, whoever resists the final decision of the highest judicial tribunal, aims a deadly blow to our whole Republican system of government—a blow, which if successful would place all our rights and liberties at the mercy of passion, anarchy and violence. I repeat, therefore, that if resistance to the decisions of the Supreme Court of the United States, in a matter like the points decided in the Dred Scott case, clearly within their jurisdiction as defined by the Constitution, shall be forced upon the country as a political issue, it will become a distinct and naked issue between the friends and the enemies of the Constitution—the friends and the enemies of the supremacy of the laws."

Why this same Supreme court once decided a national bank

to be constitutional; but Gen. Jackson, as President of the United States, disregarded the decision, and vetoed a bill for a re-charter, partly on constitutional ground, declaring that each public functionary must support the Constitution, *"as he understands it."* But hear the General's own words. Here they are, taken from his veto message:

"It is maintained by the advocates of the bank, that its constitutionality, in all its features, ought to be considered as settled by precedent, and by the decision of the Supreme Court. To this conclusion I cannot assent. Mere precedent is a dangerous source of authority, and should not be regarded as deciding questions of constitutional power, except where the acquiescence of the people and the States can be considered as well settled. So far from this being the case on this subject, an argument against the bank might be based on precedent. One Congress in 1791, decided in favor of a bank; another in 1811, decided against it. One Congress in 1815 decided against a bank; another in 1816 decided in its favor. Prior to the present Congress, therefore the precedents drawn from that source were equal. If we resort to the States, the expressions of legislative, judicial and executive opinions against the bank have been probably to those in its favor as four to one. There is nothing in precedent, therefore, which if its authority were admitted, ought to weigh in favor of the act before me."

I drop the quotations merely to remark that all there ever was, in the way of precedent up to the Dred Scott decision, on the points therein decided, had been against that decision. But hear Gen. Jackson further—

"If the opinion of the Supreme court covered the whole ground of this act, it ought not to control the co-ordinate authorities of this Government. The Congress, the executive and the court, must each for itself be guided by its own opinion of the Constitution. Each public officer, who takes an oath to support the Constitution, swears that he will support it as he understands it, and not as it is understood by others."

Again and again have I heard Judge Douglas denounce that bank decision, and applaud Gen. Jackson for disregarding it. It would be interesting for him to look over his recent speech, and see how exactly his fierce philippics against us for resisting Supreme Court decisions, fall upon his own head. It will call to his mind a long and fierce political war in this country, upon an issue which, in his own language, and, of course, in his own changeless estimation, was "a distinct and naked issue between the friends and the enemies of the Constitution," and in which war he fought in the ranks of the enemies of the Constitution.

I have said, in substance, that the Dred Scott decision was, in part, based on assumed historical facts which were not really true; and I ought not to leave the subject without giving some reasons for saying this; I therefore give an instance or two, which I think fully sustain me. Chief Justice Taney, in delivering the opinion of the majority of the Court, insists at great length that negroes were no part of the people who made, or for whom was made, the Declaration of Independence, or the Constitution of the United States.

On the contrary, Judge Curtis, in his dissenting opinion, shows that in five of the then thirteen states, to wit, New Hampshire, Massachusetts, New York, New Jersey and North Carolina, free negroes were voters, and, in proportion to their numbers, had the same part in making the Constitution that the white people had. He shows this with so much particularity as to leave no doubt of its truth; and, as a sort of conclusion on that point, holds the following language:

"The Constitution was ordained and established by the people of the United States, through the action, in each State, of those persons who were qualified by its laws to act thereon in behalf of themselves and all other citizens of the State. In some of the States, as we have seen, colored persons were among those qualified by law to act on the subject. These colored persons were not only included in the body of 'the people of the United States,' by whom the Constitution was ordained and established; but in at least five of the States they had the power to act, and, doubtless, did act, by their suffrages, upon the question of its adoption."

Again, Chief Justice Taney says: "It is difficult, at this day to realize the state of public opinion in relation to that unfortunate race, which prevailed in the civilized and enlightened portions of the world at the time of the Declaration of Independence, and when the Constitution of the United States was framed and adopted." And again, after quoting from the

Declaration, he says: "The general words above quoted would seem to include the whole human family, and if they were used in a similar instrument at this day, would be so understood."

In these the Chief Justice does not directly assert, but plainly assumes, as a fact, that the public estimate of the black man is more favorable *now* than it was in the days of the Revolution. This assumption is a mistake. In some trifling particulars, the condition of that race has been ameliorated; but, as a whole, in this country, the change between then and now is decidedly the other way; and their ultimate destiny has never appeared so hopeless as in the last three or four years. In two of the five States—New Jersey and North Carolina—that then gave the free negro the right of voting, the right has since been taken away; and in a third—New York—it has been greatly abridged; while it has not been extended, so far as I know, to a single additional State, though the number of the States has more than doubled. In those days, as I understand, masters could, at their own pleasure, emancipate their slaves; but since then, such legal restraints have been made upon emancipation, as to amount almost to prohibition. In those days, Legislatures held the unquestioned power to abolish slavery in their respective States; but now it is becoming quite fashionable for State Constitutions to withhold that power from the Legislatures. In those days, by common consent, the spread of the black man's bondage to new countries was prohibited; but now, Congress decides that it *will* not continue the prohibition, and the Supreme Court decides that it *could* not if it would. In those days, our Declaration of Independence was held sacred by all, and thought to include all; but now, to aid in making the bondage of the negro universal and eternal, it is assailed, and sneered at, and construed, and hawked at, and torn, till, if its framers could rise from their graves, they could not at all recognize it. All the powers of earth seem rapidly combining against him. Mammon is after him; ambition follows, and philosophy follows, and the Theology of the day is fast joining the cry. They have him in his prison house; they have searched his person, and left no prying instrument with him. One after another they have closed the heavy iron doors upon him, and now they have him, as it were, bolted in with a lock of a hundred keys, which can never be unlocked without the concurrence of every key; the keys in the hands of a hundred different men, and they scattered to a hundred different and distant places; and they stand musing as to what invention, in all the dominions of mind and matter, can be produced to make the impossibility of his escape more complete than it is.

It is grossly incorrect to say or assume, that the public estimate of the negro is more favorable now than it was at the origin of the government.

Three years and a half ago, Judge Douglas brought forward his famous Nebraska bill. The country was at once in a blaze. He scorned all opposition, and carried it through Congress. Since then he has seen himself superseded in a Presidential nomination, by one indorsing the general doctrine of his measure, but at the same time standing clear of the odium of its untimely agitation, and its gross breach of national faith; and he has seen that successful rival Constitutionally elected, not by the strength of friends, but by the division of adversaries, being in a popular minority of nearly four hundred thousand votes. He has seen his chief aids in his own State, Shields and Richardson, politically speaking, successively tried, convicted, and executed, for an offense not their own, but his. And now he sees his own case, standing next on the docket for trial.

There is a natural disgust in the minds of nearly all white people, to the idea of an indiscriminate amalgamation of the white and black races; and Judge Douglas evidently is basing his chief hope, upon the chances of being able to appropriate the benefit of this disgust to himself. If he can, by much drumming and repeating, fasten the odium of that idea upon his adversaries, he thinks he can struggle through the storm. He therefore clings to this hope, as a drowning man to the last plank. He makes an occasion for lugging it in from the opposition to the Dred Scott decision. He finds the Republicans insisting that the Declaration of Independence includes ALL men, black as well as white; and forthwith he boldly denies that it includes negroes at all, and proceeds to argue gravely that all who contend it does, do so only because they want to vote, and eat, and sleep, and marry with negroes! He will have it that they cannot be consistent else. Now I protest against that counterfeit logic which concludes that, because I do not want a black woman for a *slave* I must necessarily want her for a *wife*. I need not have her for either, I can just leave her alone. In some respects she certainly is not my equal; but in her natural right to eat the bread she earns with her own hands without asking leave of any one else, she is my equal, and the equal of all others.

Chief Justice Taney, in his opinion in the Dred Scott case, admits that the language of the Declaration is broad enough to include the whole human family, but he and Judge Douglas argue that the authors of that instrument did not intend to include negroes, by the fact that they did not at once, actually place them on an equality with the whites. Now this grave argument comes to just nothing at all, by the other fact, that they did not at once, *or ever afterwards*, actually place all white people on an equality with one or another. And this is the staple argument of both the Chief Justice and the Senator, for doing this obvious violence to the plain unmistakable language of the Declaration. I think the authors of that notable instrument intended to include *all* men, but they did not intend to declare all men equal *in all respects*. They did not mean to say all were equal in color, size, intellect, moral developments, or social capacity. They defined with tolerable distinctness, in what respects they did consider all men created equal—equal in "certain inalienable rights, among which are life, liberty, and the pursuit of happiness." This they said, and this meant. They did not mean to assert the obvious untruth, that all were then actually enjoying that equality, nor yet, that they were about to confer it immediately upon them. In fact they had no power to confer such a boon. They meant simply to declare the *right*, so that the *enforcement* of it might follow as fast as circumstances should permit. They meant to set up a standard maxim for free society, which should be familiar to all, and revered by all; constantly looked to, constantly labored for, and even though never perfectly attained, constantly approximated, and thereby constantly spreading and deepening its influence, and augmenting the happiness and value of life to all people of all colors everywhere. The assertion that "all men are created equal" was of no practical use in effecting our separation from Great Britain; and it was placed in the Declaration, not for that, but for future use. Its authors meant it to be, thank God, it is now proving itself, a stumbling block to those who in after times might seek to turn a free people back into the hateful paths of despotism. They knew the proneness of prosperity to breed tyrants, and they meant when such should re-appear in this fair land and commence their vocation they should find left for them at least one hard nut to crack.

I have now briefly expressed my view of the *meaning* and *objects* of that part of the Declaration of Independence which declares that "all men are created equal."

Now let us hear Judge Douglas' view of the same subject, as I find it in the printed report of his late speech. Here it is:

"No man can vindicate the character, motives and conduct of the signers of the Declaration of Independence, except upon the hypothesis that they referred to the white race alone, and not to the African, when they declared all men to have been created equal—that they were speaking of British subjects on this continent being equal to British subjects born and residing in Great Britain—that they were entitled to the same inalienable rights, and among them were enumerated life, liberty and the pursuit of happiness. The Declaration was adopted for the purpose of justifying the colonists in the eyes of the civilized world in withdrawing their allegiance from the British crown, and dissolving their connection with the mother country."

My good friends, read that carefully over some leisure hour, and ponder well upon it—see what a mere wreck—mangled ruin—it makes of our once glorious Declaration.

"They were speaking of British subjects on this continent being equal to British subjects born and residing in Great Britain!" Why, according to this, not only negroes but white people outside of Great Britain and America are not spoken of in that instrument. The English, Irish and Scotch, along with white Americans, were included to be sure, but the French, Germans and other white people of the world are all gone to pot along with the Judge's inferior races.

I had thought the Declaration promised something better than the condition of British subjects; but no, it only meant that we should be *equal* to them in their own oppressed and *unequal* condition. According to that, it gave no promise that having kicked off the King and Lords of Great Britain, we should not at once be saddled with a King and Lords of our own.

I had thought the Declaration contemplated the progressive improvement in the condition of all men everywhere; but no, it merely "was adopted for the purpose of justifying the colonists in the eyes of the civilized world in withdrawing their allegiance from the British crown, and dissolving their connection with the mother country." Why, that object having been effected some eighty years ago, the Declaration is of no practical use now—mere rubbish—old wadding left to rot on the battle-field after the victory is won.

I understand you are preparing to celebrate the "Fourth," to-morrow week. What for? The doings of that day had no reference to the present; and quite half of you are not even descendants of those who were referred to at that day. But I suppose you will celebrate; and will even go so far as to read the Declaration. Suppose after you read it once in the old fashioned way, you read it once more with Judge Douglas' version. It will then run thus: "We hold these truths to be self-evident that all British subjects who were on this continent eighty-one years ago, were created equal to all British subjects born and *then* residing in Great Britain."

And now I appeal to all—to Democrats as well as others, —are you really willing that the Declaration shall be thus frittered away?—thus left no more at most, than an interesting memorial of the dead past? thus shorn of its vitality, and practical value; and left without the *germ* or even the *suggestion* of the individual rights of man in it?

But Judge Douglas is especially horrified at the thought of the mixing blood by the white and black races: agreed for once—a thousand times agreed. There are white men enough to marry all the white women, and black men enough to marry all the black women; and so let them be married. On this point we fully agree with the Judge; and when he shall show that his policy is better adapted to prevent amalgamation than ours we shall drop ours, and adopt his. Let us see. In 1850 there were in the United States, 405,751, mulattoes. Very few of these are the offspring of whites and *free* blacks;

nearly all have sprung from black *slaves* and white masters. A separation of the races is the only perfect preventive of amalgamation but as an immediate separation is impossible the next best thing is to *keep* them apart *where* they are not already together. If white and black people never get together in Kansas, they will never mix blood in Kansas. That is at least one self-evident truth. A few free colored persons may get into the free States, in any event; but their number is too insignificant to amount to much in the way of mixing blood. In 1850 there were in the free states, 56,649 mulattoes; but for the most part they were not born there—they came from the slave States, ready made up. In the same year the slave States had 348,874 mulattoes all of home production. The proportion of free mulattoes to free blacks—the only colored classes in the free states—is much greater in the slave than in the free states. It is worthy of note too, that among the free states those which make the colored man the nearest to equal the white, have, proportionably the fewest mulattoes the least of amalgamation. In New Hampshire, the State which goes farthest towards equality between the races, there are just 184 Mulattoes while there are in Virginia—how many do you think? 79,775, being 23,126 more than in all the free States together.

These statistics show that slavery is the greatest source of amalgamation; and next to it, not the elevation, but the degeneration of the free blacks. Yet Judge Douglas dreads the slightest restraints on the spread of slavery, and the slightest human recognition of the negro, as tending horribly to amalgamation.

This very Dred Scott case affords a strong test as to which party most favors amalgamation, the Republicans or the dear Union-saving Democracy. Dred Scott, his wife and two daughters were all involved in the suit. We desired the court to have held that they were citizens so far at least as to entitle them to a hearing as to whether they were free or not; and then, also, that they were in fact and in law really free. Could we have had our way, the chances of these black girls, ever mixing their blood with that of white people, would have been diminished at least to the extent that it could not have been without their consent. But Judge Douglas is delighted to have them decided to be slaves, and not human enough to have a hearing, even if they were free, and thus left subject to the forced concubinage of their masters, and liable to become the mothers of mulattoes in spite of themselves—the very state of case that produces nine tenths of all the mulattoes— all the mixing of blood in the nation.

Of course, I state this case as an illustration only, not meaning to say or intimate that the master of Dred Scott and his family, or any more than a per centage of masters generally, are inclined to exercise this particular power which they hold over their female slaves.

I have said that the separation of the races is the only perfect preventive of amalgamation. I have no right to say all the members of the Republican party are in favor of this, nor to say that as a party they are in favor of it. There is nothing in their platform directly on the subject. But I can say a very large proportion of its members are for it, and that the chief plank in their platform—opposition to the spread of slavery—is most favorable to that separation.

Such separation, if ever effected at all, must be effected by colonization; and no political party, as such, is now doing anything directly for colonization. Party operations at present only favor or retard colonization incidentally. The enterprise is a difficult one; but "when there is a will there is a way;" and what colonization needs most is a hearty will. Will springs from the two elements of moral sense and self-interest. Let us be brought to believe it is morally right, and, at the same time, favorable to, or, at least, not against, our interest, to transfer the African to his native clime, and we shall find a way to do it, however great the task may be. The children of Israel, to such numbers as to include four hundred thousand fighting men, went out of Egyptian bondage in a body.

How differently the respective courses of the Democratic and Republican parties incidentally bear on the question of forming a will—a public sentiment—for colonization, is easy to see. The Republicans inculcate, with whatever of ability they can, that the negro is a man; that his bondage is cruelly wrong, and that the field of his oppression ought not to be enlarged. The Democrats deny his manhood; deny, or dwarf to insignificance, the wrong of his bondage; so far as possible, crush all sympathy for him, and cultivate and excite hatred and disgust against him; compliment themselves as Union-savers for doing so; and call the indefinite outspreading of his bondage "a sacred right of self-government."

The plainest print cannot be read through a gold eagle; and it will be ever hard to find many men who will send a slave to Liberia, and pay his passage while they can send him to a new country, Kansas for instance, and sell him for fifteen hundred dollars, and the rise.

June 26, 1857

To James W. Grimes

His Excellency,   Springfield, Ills.
James W. Grimes   Aug: 1857.

Dear Sir   Yours of the 14th. is received and I am much obliged for the legal information you give.

You can scarcely be more anxious than I, that the next election in Iowa shall result in favor of the Republicans. I lost nearly all the working part of last year, giving my time to the canvass; and I am altogether too poor to lose two years together. I am engaged in a suit in the U.S. Court at Chicago, in which the Rock-Island Bridge Co. is a party. The trial is to commence the 8th. of September, and probably will last two or three weeks. During the trial it is not improbable that all hands may come over and take a look at the Bridge, & if it were possible to make it hit right, I could then speak at Davenport. My courts go right on without cessation till late in November. Write me again, pointing out the most striking points of difference between your old, and new constitutions; and also whether Democratic and Republican party lines were drawn in the adoption of it; & which were for, and which against it. If by possibility I could get over amongst you, it might be of some advantage to know these things in advance. Yours very truly

after August 14, 1857

Speech to the Jury in the Rock Island Bridge Case, Chicago, Illinois

THIRTEENTH DAY

Tuesday, September 22d, 1857.

Mr. A. Lincoln addressed the jury: He said he did not purpose to assail anybody, that he expected to grow earnest as he proceeded, but not ill-natured. There is some conflict of testimony in the case, but one quarter of such a number of witnesses, seldom agree, and even if all had been on one side some discrepancy might have been expected. We are to try and reconcile them, and to believe that they are not intentionally erroneous, as long as we can. He had no prejudice against steamboats or steamboatmen, nor any against St. Louis, for he supposed they went about as other people would do in their situation. St. Louis as a commercial place, may desire that this bridge should not stand, as it is adverse to her commerce, diverting a portion of it from the river; and it might be that she supposed that the additional cost of railroad transportation upon the productions of Iowa, would force them to go to St. Louis if this bridge were removed. The meetings in St. Louis were connected with this case, only as some witnesses were in it and thus had some prejudice add color to their testimony.

The last thing that would be pleasing to him would be, to have one of these great channels, extending almost from where it never freezes to where it never thaws, blocked up. But there is a travel from East to West, whose demands are not less important than that of the river. It is growing larger and larger, building up new countries with a rapidity never before seen in the history of the world. He alluded to the astonishing growth of Illinois, having grown within his memory to a population of a million and a half, to Iowa and the other young and rising communities of the Northwest.

This current of travel has its rights, as well as that north and south. If the river had not the advantage in priority and legislation, we could enter into free competition with it and we would surpass it. This particular line has a great importance, and the statement of its business during little less than a year shows this importance. It is in evidence that from September 8, 1856, to August 8, 1857, 12,586 freight cars and 74,179 passengers passed over this bridge. Navigation was closed four days short of four months last year, and during this time, while the river was of no use, this road and bridge were equally valuable. There is, too, a considerable portion of time, when floating or thin ice makes the river useless, while the bridge is as useful as ever. This shows that this bridge must be treated with respect in this court and is not to be kicked about with contempt.

The other day Judge Wead alluded to the strife of the contending interests, and even a dissolution of the Union. Mr. Lincoln thought the proper mood for all parties in this affair, is to "live and let live," and then we will find a cessation of this trouble about the bridge. What mood were the steamboat men in when this bridge was burned? Why there was a shouting, a ringing of bells and whistling on all the boats as it fell. It was a jubilee, a greater celebration than follows an excited election.

The first thing I will proceed to is the record of Mr. Gurney and the complaint of Judge Wead, that it did not extend back over all the time from the completion of the bridge. The principal part of the navigation after the bridge was burned passed through the span. When the bridge was repaired and the boats were a second time confined to the draw, it was provided that this record should be kept. That is the simple history of that book.

From April 19, 1856, to May 6—17 days—there were 20 accidents, and all the time since then, there has been but 20 hits, including 7 accidents; so that the dangers of this place are tapering off, and, as the boatmen get cool, the accidents get less. We may soon expect, if this ratio is kept up, that there will be no accidents at all.

Judge Wead said, while admitting that the floats went straight through, there was a difference between a float and a boat, but I do not remember that he indulged us with an argument in support of this statement. Is it because there is a difference in size? Will not a small body and a large one, float the same way, under the same influence? True, a flat boat would float faster than an egg-shell, and the egg-shell might be blown away by the wind, but if under the *same influence* they would go the same way. Logs, floats, boards, various things, the witnesses say all show the same current. Then is not this test reliable? At all depths too, the direction of the current is the same. A series of these floats would make a line as long as a boat, and would show any influence upon any part, and all parts of the boat.

I will now speak of the angular position of the piers. What is the amount of the angle? The course of the river is a curve and the pier is straight. If a line is produced from the upper end of the long pier straight with the pier to a distance of 350 feet, and a line is drawn from a point in the channel opposite this point to the head of the pier, Col. Mason says they will form an angle of 20 degrees; but the angle if measured at the pier, is 7 degrees—that is, we would have to move the pier 7 degrees, and then it would be exactly straight with the current. Would that make the navigation better or worse? The witnesses of the plaintiffs seemed to think it was only necessary to say that the pier was angling to the current, and that settled the matter. Our more careful and accurate witnesses say, that though they had been accustomed to seeing the piers placed straight with the current, yet, they could see that here the current has been made straight by us, in having made this slight angle—that the water now runs just right now—that it is straight and cannot be improved. They think that if the pier was changed the eddy would be divided, and the navigation improved; and that as it is, the bridge is placed in the best manner possible.

I am not now going to discuss the question what is a material obstruction? We do not very greatly differ about the law. The cases produced here, are, I suppose, proper to be taken into consideration by the Court in instructing the jury. Some of them I think are not exactly in point, but still I am willing to trust his honor, Judge McLean, and take his instructions as law.

What is *reasonable* skill and care? This is a thing of which the jury are to judge. I differ from them in saying that they are bound to exercise no more care than they took before the building of the bridge. If we are allowed by the Legislature to build a bridge, which will require them to do more than before, when a pilot comes along, it is unreasonable for him to dash on, heedless of this structure, which has been *legally put there*. The Afton came there on the 5th, and lay at Rock Island until next morning. When the boat lies up, the pilot has a holiday, and would not any of these jurors have then gone around there, and got acquainted with the place? Parker has shown here that he does not understand the draw. I heard him say that the fall from the head to the foot of that pier was four feet! He needs information. He could have gone there that day and have seen there was no such fall. He should have discarded passion, and the chances are that he would have had no disaster at all. He was bound to make himself acquainted with it.

McCammon says that "the current and the swell coming from the long pier, drove her against the long pier." Drove her towards the very pier from which the current came! It is an absurdity, an impossibility. The only reconciliation I can find for this contradiction, is in a current which White says strikes out from the long pier, and then, like a ram's horn, turns back, and this might have acted somehow in this manner.

It is agreed by all that the plaintiffs' boat was destroyed; that it was destroyed upon the head of the short pier; that she moved from the channel, where she was, with her bow above the head of the long pier, till she struck the short one, swung around under the bridge, and there was crowded under the bridge and destroyed.

I shall try to prove that the average velocity of the current through the draw with the boat in it, should be five and a half miles an hour; that it is slowest at the head of the pier,— swiftest at the foot of the pier. Their lowest estimate, in evidence, is six miles an hour, their highest twelve miles. This was the testimony of men who had made no experiment— only conjecture. We have adopted the most exact means. The water runs swiftest in high water, and we have taken the point of nine feet above low water. The water, when the Afton was lost, was seven feet above low water, or at least a foot lower than our time. Brayton and his assistants timed the instruments—the best known instruments for measuring currents. They timed them under various circumstances, and they found the current five miles an hour, and no more. They found that the water, at the upper end, ran slower than five miles; that below it was swifter than five miles, but that the average was five miles. Shall men, who have taken no care, who conjecture, some of whom speak of twenty miles an hour be believed, against those who have had such a favorable and well-improved opportunity? They should not even *qualify* the result. Several men have given their opinions as to the distance of the Carson, and I suppose if *one* should go and *measure* that distance, you would believe him in preference to all of them.

These measurements were made when the boat was not in the draw. It has been ascertained what is the area of the cross-section of the stream, and the area of the face of the piers, and the engineers say, that the piers being put there will increase the current proportionably as the space is decreased. So with the boat in the draw. The depth of the channel was 22 feet, the width 116 feet—multiply these and you have the square feet across the water of the draw, viz.: 2,552 feet. The Afton was 35 feet wide and drew five feet, making a fourteenth of the sum. Now one-fourteenth of five miles is five-fourteenths of one mile—about one-third of a mile—the increase of the current. We will call the current 5½ miles per hour.

The next thing I will try to prove that is that the plaintiffs' boat had power to run six miles an hour in that current. It has been testified that she was a strong, swift boat, able to run eight miles an hour up stream in a current of four miles an hour, and fifteen miles down stream. Strike the average and you will find what is her average—about 11½ miles. Take the 5½, miles which is the speed of the current in the draw, and it leaves the power of the boat in that draw at six miles an hour, 528 feet per minute, and 8⅘ feet to the second.

Next I propose to show that there are no cross currents. I know their witnesses say that there are cross currents—that, as one witness says, there are three cross currents and two eddies. So far as mere statement without experiment, and mingled with mistakes can go, they have proved. But can these men's testimony be compared with the nice, exact, thorough experiments of our witnesses. Can you believe that these floats go across the currents? It is inconceiveable that they could not have discovered every possible current. How do boats find currents that floats cannot discover? We assume the position then that those cross currents are not there. My next proposition is that the Afton passed between the S. B. Carson and Iowa shore. That is undisputed.

Next I shall show that she struck first the short pier, then the long pier, then the short one again and there she stopped. Mr. Lincoln cited the testimony of eighteen witnesses on this point. How did the boat strike Baker when she went in! Here is an endless variety of opinion. But ten of them say what pier she struck; three of them testify that she struck first the short, then the long, then the short pier for the last time. None of the rest substantially contradict this. I assume that these men have got the truth, because I believe it an established fact.

My next proposition is that after she struck the short and long pier and before she got back to the short pier the boat got right with her bow out. So says the Pilot Parker—that he "got her through until her starboard wheel passed the short pier." This would make her head about even with the head of the long pier. He says her head was as high or higher than the head of the long pier. Other witnesses confirm this one. The final stroke was in the splash door, aft the wheel. Witnesses differ but the majority say that she struck thus.

Court adjourned.

FOURTEENTH DAY

Wednesday, September 23, 1857.

Mr. A. Lincoln resumed. He said he should conclude as soon as possible. He said the colored map of the plaintiffs, which was brought in during the advanced stages of the trial, showed itself that the cross currents alleged did not exist; that the current as represented would drive an ascending boat to the long pier, but not to the short pier as they urged. He explained from a model of a boat where the splash door is, just behind the wheel. The boat struck on the lower shoulder of the short pier, as she swung round, in the splash door, then as she went on round she struck the point or end of the pier, where she rested. Her engineers say the starboard wheel then was rushing round rapidly. Then the boat must have struck the upper point of the pier so far back as not to disturb the wheel. It is forty feet from the stern of the Afton to the splash door, and thus it appears that she had but forty feet to go to clear the pier.

How was it that the Afton, with all her power, flanked over from the channel to the short pier without moving one inch ahead? Suppose she was in the middle of the draw, her wheel would have been 31 feet from the short pier. The reason she went over thus is, her starboard wheel was not working. I shall try to establish the fact that that wheel was not running, and, that after she struck, she went ahead strong on this same wheel. Upon the last point the witnesses agree—that the starboard wheel was running after she struck—and no witnesses say that it was running while she was out in the draw flanking over. Mr. Lincoln read from the testimony of various witnesses to prove that the starboard wheel was not working while she was out in the stream. Other witnesses show that the captain said something of the machinery of the wheel, and the inference is that he knew the wheel was not working. The fact is undisputed, that she did not move one inch ahead, while she was moving this 31 feet sideways. There is evidence proving that the current there is only five miles an hour, and the only explanation is that her power was not all used—that only one wheel was working. The pilot says he ordered the engineers to back her out. The engineers differ from him and say that they kept one going ahead. The bow was so swung that the current pressed it over; the pilot pressed the stern over with the rudder, though not so fast but that the bow gained on it, and, only one wheel being in motion, the boat merely stood still so far as motion up and down is concerned, and thus she was thrown upon this pier.

The Afton came into the draw after she had just passed the Carson, and, as the Carson no doubt kept the true course, the Afton going around her, got out of the proper way, got across the current, into the eddy which is west of a straight line drawn down from the long pier, was compelled to resort to these changes of wheels, which she did not do with sufficient adroitness to save her. Was it not her own fault that she entered wrong? so far, wrong that she never got right. Is the defence to blame for that?

For several days we were entertained with depositions about boats "smelling a bar." Why did the Afton then, after she had come up smelling so close to the long pier sheer off so strangely? When she got to the centre of the very nose she was smelling, she seems suddenly to have lost her sense of smell and flanks over to the short pier.

Mr. Lincoln said there was no practicability in the project of building a tunnel under the river, for there is not a tunnel that is a successful project, in the world. A suspension bridge cannot be built so high, but that the chimneys of the boats will grow up till they cannot pass. The steamboatmen will take pains to make them grow. The cars of a railroad, cannot, without immense expense, rise high enough to get even with a suspension bridge, or go low enough to get down through a tunnel. Such expense is unreasonable.

The plaintiffs have to establish that the bridge is a material obstruction, and that they managed their boat with reasonable care and skill. As to the last point, high winds have nothing to do with it, for it was not a windy day. They must show "due skill and care." Difficulties going down stream, will not do, for they were going up stream. Difficulties with barges in tow, have nothing to do with it, for they had no barge. He said he had much more to say, many things he could suggest to the jury, but he would close to save time.

On the Republican Party

Upon those men who are, in sentiment, opposed to the spread, and nationalization of slavery, rests the task of preventing it. The Republican organization is the embodyment of that sentiment; though, as yet, it by no means embraces all the individuals holding that sentiment. The party is newly formed; and in forming, old party ties had to be broken, and the attractions of party pride, and influential leaders were wholly wanting. In spite of old differences, prejudices, and animosities, it's members were drawn together by a paramount common danger. They formed and manouvered in the face of the deciplined enemy, and in the teeth of all his per-

sistent misrepresentations. Of course, they fell far short of
gathering in all of their own. And yet, a year ago, they stood
up, an army over thirteen hundred thousand strong. That
army is, to-day, the best hope of the nation, and of the world.
Their work is before them; and from which they may not
guiltlessly turn away.

c. November 1857

To Lyman Trumbull

Hon: Lyman Trumbull.   Chicago, Nov. 30. 1857.
    Dear Sir: Herewith you find duplicates of a notice which I
wish to be served upon the Miss French, or now Mrs. Gray,
who married the late Franklin C. Gray. You understand what
person I mean.
    Please hand her one copy, and note on the other that you
have done so, the date of service, and your signature & return
it to me at Springfield.
    What think you of the probable *"rumpus"* among the de-
mocracy over the Kansas constitution? I think the Republicans should stand clear of it. In their view both the President
and Douglas are wrong; and they should not espouse the
cause of either, because they may consider the other a little
the farther wrong of the two.
    From what I am told here, Douglas tried, before leaving, to
draw off some Republicans on this dodge, and even succeeded in making some impression on one or two. Yours very
truly

Draft of a Speech

    From time to time, ever since the Chicago "Times" and
"Illinois State Register" declared their opposition to the Lecompton constitution, and it began to be understood that
Judge Douglas was also opposed to it, I have been accosted
by friends of his with the question, "What do you think
now?" Since the delivery of his speech in the Senate, the

question has been varied a little. "Have you read Douglas's speech?" "Yes." "Well, what do you think of it?" In every instance the question is accompanied with an anxious inquiring stare, which asks, quite as plainly as words could, "Can't you go for Douglas now?" Like boys who have set a bird-trap, they are watching to see if the birds are picking at the bait and likely to go under.

I think, then, Judge Douglas knows that the Republicans wish Kansas to be a free State. He knows that they know, if the question be fairly submitted to a vote of the people of Kansas, it will be a free State; and he would not object at all if, by drawing their attention to this particular fact, and himself becoming vociferous for such fair vote, they should be induced to drop their own organization, fall into rank behind him, and form a great free-State Democratic party.

But before Republicans do this, I think they ought to require a few questions to be answered on the other side. If they so fall in with Judge Douglas, and Kansas shall be secured as a free State, there then remaining no cause of difference between him and the regular Democracy, will not the Republicans stand ready, haltered and harnessed, to be handed over by him to the regular Democracy, to filibuster indefinitely for additional slave territory,—to carry slavery into all the States, as well as Territories, under the Dred Scott decision, construed and enlarged from time to time, according to the demands of the regular slave Democracy,—and to assist in reviving the African slave-trade in order that all may buy negroes where they can be bought cheapest, as a clear incident of that "sacred right of property," now held in some quarters to be above all constitutions?

By so falling in, will we not be committed to or at least compromitted with, the Nebraska policy?

If so, we should remember that Kansas is saved, not by that policy or its authors, but in spite of both—by an effort that cannot be kept up in future cases.

Did Judge Douglas help any to get a free-State majority into Kansas? Not a bit of it—the exact contrary. Does he now express any wish that Kansas, or any other place, shall be free? Nothing like it. He tells us, in this very speech, expected to be so palatable to Republicans, that he cares not whether slavery is voted down or voted up. His whole effort is devoted to clearing the ring, and giving slavery and freedom a fair fight. With one who considers slavery just as good as freedom, this is perfectly natural and consistent.

But have Republicans any sympathy with such a view? They think slavery is wrong; and that, like every other wrong which some men will commit if left alone, it ought to be prohibited by law. They consider it not only morally wrong, but a "deadly poison" in a government like ours, professedly based on the equality of men. Upon this radical difference of opinion with Judge Douglas, the Republican party was organized. There is all the difference between him and them now that there ever was. He will not say that he has changed; have you?

Again, we ought to be informed as to Judge Douglas's present opinion as to the inclination of Republicans to marry with negroes. By his Springfield speech we know what it was last June; and by his resolution dropped at Jacksonville in September we know what it was then. Perhaps we have something even later in a Chicago speech, in which the danger of being "stunk out of church" was descanted upon. But what is his opinion on the point now? There is, or will be, a sure sign to judge by. If this charge shall be silently dropped by the judge and his friends, if no more resolutions on the subject shall be passed in Douglas Democratic meetings and conventions, it will be safe to swear that he is courting. Our "witching smile" has "caught his youthful fancy"; and henceforth Cuffy and he are rival beaux for our gushing affections.

We also ought to insist on knowing what the judge now thinks on "Sectionalism." Last year he thought it was a "clincher" against us on the question of Sectionalism, that we could get no support in the slave States, and could not be allowed to speak, or even breathe, south of the Ohio River.

In vain did we appeal to the justice of our principles. He would have it that the treatment we received was conclusive evidence that we deserved it. He and his friends would bring speakers from the slave States to their meetings and conventions in the free States, and parade about, arm in arm with them, breathing in every gesture and tone, "How we national apples do swim!" Let him cast about for this particular evidence of his own nationality now. Why, just now, he and Frémont would make the closest race imaginable in the Southern States.

In the present aspect of affairs what ought the Republicans to do? I think they ought not to oppose any measure merely because Judge Douglas proposes it. Whether the Lecompton constitution should be accepted or rejected is a question upon which, in the minds of men not committed to any of its antecedents, and controlled only by the Federal Constitution, by republican principles, and by a sound morality, it seems to me there could not be two opinions. It should be throttled and killed as hastily and as heartily as a rabid dog. What those should do who are committed to all its antecedents is their business, not ours. If, therefore, Judge Douglas's bill secures a fair vote to the people of Kansas, without contrivance to commit any one farther, I think Republican members of Congress ought to support it. They can do so without any inconsistency. They believe Congress ought to prohibit slavery wherever it can be done without violation of the Constitution or of good faith. And having seen the noses counted, and actually knowing that a majority of the people of Kansas are against slavery, passing an act to secure them a fair vote is little else than prohibiting slavery in Kansas by act of Congress.

Congress cannot dictate a constitution to a new State. All it can do at that point is to secure the people a fair chance to form one for themselves, and then to accept or reject it when they ask admission into the Union. As I understand, Republicans claim no more than this. But they do claim that Congress can and ought to keep slavery out of a Territory, up to the time of its people forming a State constitution; and they should now be careful to not stultify themselves to any extent on that point.

I am glad Judge Douglas has, at last, distinctly told us that he cares not whether slavery be voted down or voted up. Not so much that this is any news to me; nor yet that it may be slightly new to some of that class of his friends who delight to say that they "are as much opposed to slavery as anybody."

I am glad because it affords such a true and excellent definition of the Nebraska policy itself. That policy, honestly administered, is exactly that. It seeks to bring the people of the
nation to not care anything about slavery. This is Nebraskaism in its abstract purity—in its very best dress.

Now, I take it, nearly everybody does care something about
slavery—is either for it or against it; and that the statesmanship of a measure which conforms to the sentiments of nobody might well be doubted in advance.

But Nebraskaism did not originate as a piece of statesmanship. General Cass, in 1848, invented it, as a political manoeu-
ver, to secure himself the Democratic nomination for the
presidency. It served its purpose then, and sunk out of sight.
Six years later Judge Douglas fished it up, and glozed it over
with what he called, and still persists in calling, "sacred rights
of self-government."

Well, I, too, believe in self-government as I understand it;
but I do not understand that the privilege one man takes of
making a slave of another, or holding him as such, is any part
of "self-government." To call it so is, to my mind, simply absurd and ridiculous. I am for the people of the whole nation
doing just as they please in all matters which concern the
whole nation; for those of each part doing just as they choose
in all matters which concern no other part; and for each individual doing just as he chooses in all matters which concern
nobody else. This is the principle. Of course I am content
with any exception which the Constitution, or the actually
existing state of things, makes a necessity. But neither the
principle nor the exception will admit the indefinite spread
and perpetuity of human slavery.

I think the true magnitude of the slavery element in this
nation is scarcely appreciated by any one. Four years ago the
Nebraska policy was adopted, professedly, to drive the agitation of the subject into the Territories, and out of every other
place, and especially out of Congress.

When Mr. Buchanan accepted the presidential nomination,
he felicitated himself with the belief that the whole thing
would be quieted and forgotten in about six weeks. In his
inaugural, and in his Silliman letter, at their respective dates,
he was just not quite in reach of the same happy consum-

mation. And now, in his first annual message, he urges the acceptance of the Lecompton constitution (not quite satisfactory to him) on the sole ground of getting this little unimportant matter out of the way.

Meanwhile, in those four years, there has really been more angry agitation of this subject, both in and out of Congress, than ever before. And just now it is perplexing the mighty ones as no subject ever did before. Nor is it confined to politics alone. Presbyterian assemblies, Methodist conferences, Unitarian gatherings, and single churches to an indefinite extent, are wrangling, and cracking, and going to pieces on the same question. Why, Kansas is neither the whole nor a tithe of the real question.

A house divided against itself cannot stand.

I believe the government cannot endure permanently half slave and half free. I expressed this belief a year ago; and subsequent developments have but confirmed me. I do not expect the Union to be dissolved. I do not expect the house to fall; but I do expect it will cease to be divided. It will become all one thing or all the other. Either the opponents of slavery will arrest the further spread of it, and put it in course of ultimate extinction; or its advocates will push it forward till it shall become alike lawful in all the States, old as well as new. Do you doubt it? Study the Dred Scott decision, and then see how little even now remains to be done. That decision may be reduced to three points.

The first is that a negro cannot be a citizen. That point is made in order to deprive the negro, in every possible event, of the benefit of that provision of the United States Constitution which declares that "the citizens of each State shall be entitled to all privileges and immunities of citizens in the several States."

The second point is that the United States Constitution protects slavery, as property, in all the United States territories, and that neither Congress, nor the people of the Territories, nor any other power, can prohibit it at any time prior to the formation of State constitutions.

This point is made in order that the Territories may safely be filled up with slaves, before the formation of State constitutions, thereby to embarrass the free-State sentiment, and enhance the chances of slave constitutions being adopted.

The third point decided is that the voluntary bringing of Dred Scott into Illinois by his master, and holding him here a long time as a slave, did not operate his emancipation—did not make him free.

This point is made, not to be pressed immediately; but if acquiesced in for a while, then to sustain the logical conclusion that what Dred Scott's master might lawfully do with Dred in the free State of Illinois, every other master may lawfully do with any other one or one hundred slaves in Illinois, or in any other free State. Auxiliary to all this, and working hand in hand with it, the Nebraska doctrine is to educate and mold public opinion to "not care whether slavery is voted up or voted down." At least Northern public opinion must cease to care anything about it. Southern public opinion may, without offense, continue to care as much as it pleases.

Welcome, or unwelcome, agreeable, or disagreeable, whether this shall be an entire slave nation, *is* the issue before us. Every incident—every little shifting of scenes or of actors—only clears away the intervening trash, compacts and consolidates the opposing hosts, and brings them more and more distinctly face to face. The conflict will be a severe one; and it will be fought through by those who *do* care for the result, and not by those who do not care—by those who are *for*, and those who are against a legalized national slavery. The combined charge of Nebraskaism, and Dred Scottism must be repulsed, and rolled back. The deceitful cloak of "self-government" wherewith "the sum of all villanies" seeks to protect and adorn itself, must be torn from it's hateful carcass. That burlesque upon judicial decisions, and slander and profanation upon the honored names, and sacred history of republican America, must be overruled, and expunged from the books of authority.

To give the victory to the right, not *bloody bullets*, but *peaceful ballots* only, are necessary. Thanks to our good old constitution, and organization under it, these alone are necessary. It only needs that every right thinking man, shall go to the polls, and without fear or prejudice, *vote* as he *thinks*.

c. late December 1857

To Lyman Trumbull

Hon. Lyman Trumbull.   Bloomington, Dec. 28. 1857 –

Dear Sir: What does the New-York Tribune mean by it's constant eulogising, and admiring, and magnifying Douglas? Does it, in this, speak the sentiments of the republicans at Washington? Have they concluded that the republican cause, generally, can be best promoted by sacraficing us here in Illinois? If so we would like to know it soon; it will save us a great deal of labor to surrender at once.

As yet I have heared of no republican here going over to Douglas; but if the Tribune continues to din his praises into the ears of it's five or ten thousand republican readers in Illinois, it is more than can be hoped that all will stand firm.

I am not complaining. I only wish a fair understanding. Please write me at Springfield. Your Obt. Servt.

To Owen Lovejoy

Hon: O. Lovejoy.   Springfield,
Dear Sir   March 8. 1858.

I have just returned from court in one of the counties of your District, where I had an inside view that few will have who correspond with you; and I feel it rather a duty to say a word to you about it.

Your danger *has been* that democracy would wheedle some republican to run against you without a nomination, relying mainly on democratic votes. I have seen the strong men who could make the most trouble in that way, and find that they view the thing in the proper light, and will not consent to be so used. But they have been urgently tempted by the enemy; and I think it is still the point for you to guard most vigilantly. I think it is not expected that you can be beaten for a nomination; but do not let what I say, as to that, lull you.

Now, let this be strictly confidential; not that there is anything wrong in it; but that I have some highly valued friends who would not like me any the better for writing it. Yours very truly

P.S. Be glad to hear from you.

To Ozias M. Hatch

Hon: O. M. Hatch   Lincoln, March 24. 1858
My dear Sir:

It is next to impossible for me to leave here now. I received your letter and inclosures. My judgment is that we must never sell old friends to buy old enemies. Let us have a State convention, in which we can have a full consultation; and till which, let us all stand firm, making no committals as to strange and new combinations. This is the sum of all the counsel I could give if with you; and you are at liberty to show to discreet friends.

Yours very truly

To Elihu B. Washburne

Hon. E. B. Washburne,   Urbana, Ills.
My dear Sir: April 26. 1858.

I am rather a poor correspondent, but I think perhaps I ought to write you a letter just now. I am here at this time; but I was at home during the sitting of the two democratic conventions. The day before the conventions I received a letter from Chicago having, among other things, on other subjects, the following in it:

"A reliable republican, but an old line whig lawyer, in this city told me to-day that *he himself had seen* a letter from one of our republican congressmen, advising us all to go for the re-election of Judge Douglass. He said he was injoined to keep the author a secret & he was going to do so. From him I learnt that he was not an old line democrat, or abolitionist. This narrows the contest down to the congressmen from the Galena and Fulton Dists."

The above is a litteral copy of all the letter contained on that subject. The morning of the conventions Mr. Herndon showed me your letter of the 15th. to him, which convinced me that the story in the letter from Chicago was based upon some mistake, misconstruction of language, or the like. Several of our friends were down from Chicago, and they had something of the same story amongst them, some half suspecting that you were inclined to favor Douglas, and others thinking there was an effort to wrong you.

I thought neither was exactly the case; that the whole had originated in some misconstruction, coupled with a high degree of sensitiveness on the point, and that the whole matter was not worth another moment's consideration.

Such is my opinion now, and I hope you will have no concern about it. I have written this because Charley Wilson told me he was writing you, and because I expect Dr. Ray, (who was a little excited about the matter) has also written you; and because I think, I perhaps, have taken a calmer view of the thing than they may have done. I am satisfied you have done no wrong, and nobody has intended any wrong to you.

A word about the conventions. The democracy parted in not a very encouraged state of mind.

On the contrary, our friends, a good many of whom were present, parted in high spirits. They think if we do not triumph the fault will be our own, and so I really think. Your friend as ever

To Jediah F. Alexander

J. F. Alexander, Esq   Springfield,
Greenville, Ills.   May 15. 1858

My dear Sir   I reached home a week ago and found yours of the 1st. inviting me to name a time to meet and address a political meeting in Bond county. It is too early, considering that when I once begin making political speeches I shall have no respite till November. The *labor* of that I might endure, but I really can not spare the time from my business.

Nearer the time I will try to meet the people of Bond, if they desire.

I will only say now that, as I understand, there remains all the difference there ever was between Judge Douglas & the Republicans—*they* insisting that Congress *shall*, and *he* insisting that congress *shall not*, keep slavery out of the Teritories *before & up to the time* they form State constitutions. No republican has ever contended that, *when* a constitution is to be formed, any but the *people* of the teritory shall form it. Re-publican's have never contended that congress should *dictate* a constitution to any state or teritory; but they have contended that the people should be *perfectly* free to form their constitu-tion in their own way—as *perfectly* free from the *presence* of *slavery* amongst them, as from every other improper influence.

In voting together in opposition to a constitution being forced upon the people of Kansas, neither Judge Douglas nor the Republicans, has conceded anything which was ever in dispute between them. Yours very truly

To Elihu B. Washburne

Hon. E. B. Washburne   Springfield,
My dear Sir   May 27– 1858–

Yours requesting me to return you the now some what noted "Charley Wilson letter" is received; and I herewith re-turn that letter.

Political matters just now bear a very *mixed* and *incongruous* aspect. For several days the signs have been that Douglas and the President had probably burned the hatchet, Doug's friends at Washington going over to the President's side, and his friends here & South of here, talking as if there never had been any serious difficulty, while the President himself does nothing for his own peculiar friends here. But this morning my partner, Mr. Herndon, receives a letter from Mr. Medill of the Chicago Tribune, showing the writer to be in great alarm at the prospect North of Republicans going over to Douglas, on the idea that Douglas is going to assume steep free-soil ground, and furiously assail the administration on the stump when he comes home. There certainly is a double game being played some how. Possibly—even *probably*—Douglas is temporarily deceiving the President in order to crush out the 8th. of June convention here. Unless he plays his double game more successfully than we have often seen done, he can not carry many republicans North, without at the same time losing a larger number of his old friends South.

Let this be confidential. Yours as ever

To Stephen A. Hurlbut

S. A. Hurlbut, Esq   Springfield,
My dear Sir   June 1. 1858.

Yours of the 29th. of May is just received. I suppose it is hardly necessary that any expression of preference for U.S. Senator, should be given at the county, or other local conventions and meetings. When the Republicans of the whole State get together at the State convention, the thing will then be thought of, and something will or will not be done, according as the united judgment may dictate.

I do not find republicans from the old *democratic* ranks more inclined to Douglas than those from the old whig ranks—indeed I find very little of such inclination in either class; but of that little, the larger portion, falling under my observation, has been among old whigs. The republicans from the old democratic ranks, constantly say to me "Take care of your old whigs, and have no fears for us." I am much obliged to you for your letter; and shall be pleased to see you at the convention. Yours very truly,

To Charles L. Wilson

Charles L. Wilson, Esq.   Springfield,
My Dear Sir   June 1. 1858.

Yours of yesterday, with the inclosed newspaper slip, is received. I have never said, or thought more, as to the inclination of some of our Eastern republican friends to favor Douglas, than I expressed in your hearing on the evening of the 21st. April, at the State Library in this place. I have believed—do believe now—that Greely, for instance, would be rather pleased to see Douglas re-elected over me or any other republican; and yet I do not believe it is so, because of any secret arrangement with Douglas. It is because he thinks Douglas' superior position, reputation, experience, and *ability*, if you please, would more than compensate for his lack of a pure republican position, and therefore, his re-election do the general cause of republicanism, more good, than would

the election of any one of our better undistinguished pure
republicans. I do not know how *you* estimate Greely, but *I*
consider him incapable of corruption, or falsehood. He denies
that he directly is taking part in favor of Douglas, and I believe him. Still his *feeling* constantly manifests itself in his
paper, which, being so extensively read in Illinois, is, and will
continue to be, a drag upon us. I have also thought that
Govr. Seward too, feels about as Greely does; but not being a
newspaper editor, his feeling, in this respect, is not much
manifested. I have no idea that he is, by conversations or by
letters, urging Illinois republicans to vote for Douglas.

As to myself, let me pledge you my word that neither I, nor
any friend of mine so far as I know, has been setting stake
against Gov. Seward. No combination has been made *with*
me, or *proposed* to me, in relation to the next Presidential candidate. The same thing is true in regard to the next Governor
of our State. I am not directly or indirectly committed to any
one; nor has any one made any advance to me upon the subject. I have had many free conversations with John Wentworth; but he never dropped a remark that led me to suspect
that he wishes to be Governor. Indeed, it is due to truth to
say that while he has uniformly expressed himself for me, he
has never hinted at any condition.

The signs are that we shall have a good convention on the
16th. and I think our prospects generally, are improving some
every day. I believe we need nothing so much as to get rid of
unjust suspicions of one another. Yours very truly

To Samuel Wilkinson

Samuel Wilkinson Esq   Springfield,
My dear Sir   June 10. 1858
    Yours of the 26th. May came to hand *only* last night. *I know*
of no effort to unite the Reps. & Buc. men, and *believe* there
is none. Of course the Republicans do not try to keep the
common enemy from dividing; but, so far as I *know*, or *believe*, they will not unite with either branch of the division.
Indeed it is difficult for me to see, on what ground they could

unite; but it is useless to spend words, there is simply nothing of it. It is a trick of our enemies to try to excite all sorts of suspicions and jealosies amongst us. We hope that our Convention on the 16th. bringing us together, and letting us hear each other talk will put an end to most of this. Yours truly

"House Divided" Speech at Springfield, Illinois

The Speech, immediately succeeding, was delivered, June 16, 1858 at Springfield Illinois, at the close of the Republican State convention held at that time and place; and by which convention Mr. Lincoln had been named as their candidate for U. S. Senator.

Senator Douglas was not present.

Mr. PRESIDENT and Gentlemen of the Convention.

If we could first know *where* we are, and *whither* we are tending, we could then better judge *what* to do, and *how* to do it.

We are now far into the *fifth* year, since a policy was initiated, with the *avowed* object, and *confident* promise, of putting an end to slavery agitation.

Under the operation of that policy, that agitation has not only, *not ceased*, but has *constantly augmented*.

In *my* opinion, it *will* not cease, until a *crisis* shall have been reached, and passed.

"A house divided against itself cannot stand."

I believe this government cannot endure, permanently half *slave* and half *free*.

I do not expect the Union to be *dissolved*—I do not expect the house to *fall*—but I *do* expect it will cease to be divided.

It will become *all* one thing, or *all* the other.

Either the *opponents* of slavery, will arrest the further spread of it, and place it where the public mind shall rest in the belief that it is in course of ultimate extinction; or its *advocates* will push it forward, till it shall become alike lawful in *all* the States, *old* as well as *new*—*North* as well as *South*.

Have we no *tendency* to the latter condition?

Let any one who doubts, carefully contemplate that now almost complete legal combination—piece of *machinery* so to speak—compounded of the Nebraska doctrine, and the Dred Scott decision. Let him consider not only *what work* the machinery is adapted to do, and *how well* adapted; but also, let him study the *history* of its construction, and trace, if he can, or rather *fail*, if he can, to trace the evidences of design, and concert of action, among its chief bosses, from the beginning.

The new year of 1854 found slavery excluded from more than half the States by State Constitutions, and from most of the national territory by Congressional prohibition.

Four days later, commenced the struggle, which ended in repealing that Congressional prohibition.

This opened all the national territory to slavery; and was the first point gained.

But, so far, *Congress* only, had acted; and an *indorsement* by the people, *real* or apparent, was indispensable, to *save* the point already gained, and give chance for more.

This necessity had not been overlooked; but had been provided for, as well as might be, in the notable argument of *"squatter sovereignty,"* otherwise called *"sacred right of self government,"* which latter phrase, though expressive of the only rightful basis of any government, was so perverted in this attempted use of it as to amount to just this: That if any *one* man, choose to enslave *another*, no *third* man shall be allowed to object.

That argument was incorporated into the Nebraska bill itself, in the language which follows: *"It being the true intent and meaning of this act not to legislate slavery into any Territory or state, nor to exclude it therefrom; but to leave the people thereof perfectly free to form and regulate their domestic institutions in their own way, subject only to the Constitution of the United States."*

Then opened the roar of loose declamation in favor of "Squatter Sovereignty," and "Sacred right of self government."

"But," said opposition members, "let us be more *specific*— let us *amend* the bill so as to expressly declare that the people of the territory *may* exclude slavery." "Not we," said the friends of the measure; and down they voted the amendment.

While the Nebraska bill was passing through congress, a *law case*, involving the question of a negroe's freedom, by reason of his owner having voluntarily taken him first into a free state and then a territory covered by the congressional prohibition, and held him as a slave, for a long time in each, was passing through the U.S. Circuit Court for the District of Missouri; and both Nebraska bill and law suit were brought to a decision in the same month of May, 1854. The negroe's name was "Dred Scott," which name now designates the decision finally made in the case.

Before the *then* next Presidential election, the law case came *to*, and was argued *in* the Supreme Court of the United States; but the *decision* of it was deferred until *after* the election. Still, *before* the election, Senator Trumbull, on the floor of the Senate, requests the leading advocate of the Nebraska bill to state *his opinion* whether the people of a territory can constitutionally exclude slavery from their limits; and the latter answers, "That is a question for the Supreme Court."

The election came. Mr. Buchanan was elected, and the *indorsement*, such as it was, secured. That was the *second* point gained. The indorsement, however, fell short of a clear popular majority by nearly four hundred thousand votes, and so, perhaps, was not overwhelmingly reliable and satisfactory.

The *outgoing* President, in his last annual message, as impressively as possible *echoed back* upon the people the *weight* and *authority* of the indorsement.

The Supreme Court met again; *did not* announce their decision, but ordered a re-argument.

The Presidential inauguration came, and still no decision of the court; but the *incoming* President, in his inaugural address, fervently exhorted the people to abide by the forthcoming decision, *whatever it might be*.

Then, in a few days, came the decision.

The reputed author of the Nebraska bill finds an early occasion to make a speech at this capitol indorsing the Dred Scott Decision, and vehemently denouncing all opposition to it.

The new President, too, seizes the early occasion of the Silliman letter to *indorse* and strongly *construe* that decision, and to express his *astonishment* that any different view had ever been entertained.

At length a squabble springs up between the President and the author of the Nebraska bill, on the *mere* question of *fact*, whether the Lecompton constitution was or was not, in any just sense, made by the people of Kansas; and in that squabble the latter declares that all he wants is a fair vote for the people, and that he *cares* not whether slavery be voted *down* or voted *up*. I do not understand his declaration that he cares not whether slavery be voted down or voted up, to be intended by him other than as an *apt definition* of the *policy* he would impress upon the public mind—the *principle* for which he declares he has suffered much, and is ready to suffer to the end.

And well may he cling to that principle. If he has any parental feeling, well may he cling to it. That principle, is the only *shred* left of his original Nebraska doctrine. Under the Dred Scott decision, "squatter sovereignty" squatted out of existence, tumbled down like temporary scaffolding—like the mould at the foundry served through one blast and fell back into loose sand—helped to carry an election, and then was kicked to the winds. His late *joint* struggle with the Republicans, against the Lecompton Constitution, involves nothing of the original Nebraska doctrine. That struggle was made on a point, the right of a people to make their own constitution, upon which he and the Republicans have never differed.

The several points of the Dred Scott decision, in connection with Senator Douglas' "care not" policy, constitute the piece of machinery, in its *present* state of advancement. This was the third point gained.

The *working* points of that machinery are:

First, that no negro slave, imported as such from Africa, and no descendant of such slave can ever be a *citizen* of any State, in the sense of that term as used in the Constitution of the United States.

This point is made in order to deprive the negro, in every possible event, of the benefit of this provision of the United States Constitution, which declares that—

"The citizens of each State shall be entitled to all privileges and immunities of citizens in the several States."

Secondly, that "subject to the Constitution of the United States," neither *Congress* nor a *Territorial Legislature* can exclude slavery from any United States territory.

This point is made in order that individual men may *fill up* the territories with slaves, without danger of losing them as property, and thus to enhance the chances of *permanency* to the institution through all the future.

Thirdly, that whether the holding a negro in actual slavery in a free State, makes him free, as against the holder, the

United States courts will not decide, but will leave to be decided by the courts of any slave State the negro may be forced into by the master.

This point is made, not to be pressed *immediately*; but, if acquiesced in for a while, and apparently *indorsed* by the people at an election, *then* to sustain the logical conclusion that what Dred Scott's master might lawfully do with Dred Scott, in the free State of Illinois, every other master may lawfully do with any other *one*, or one *thousand* slaves, in Illinois, or in any other free State.

Auxiliary to all this, and working hand in hand with it, the Nebraska doctrine, or what is left of it, is to *educate* and *mould* public opinion, at least *Northern* public opinion, to not *care* whether slavery is voted *down* or voted *up*.

This shows exactly where we now *are*; and *partially* also, whither we are tending.

It will throw additional light on the latter, to go back, and run the mind over the string of historical facts already stated. Several things will *now* appear less *dark* and *mysterious* than they did *when* they were transpiring. The people were to be left "perfectly free" "subject only to the Constitution." What the *Constitution* had to do with it, outsiders could not *then* see. Plainly enough *now*, it was an exactly fitted *niche*, for the Dred Scott decision to afterwards come in, and declare the *perfect freedom* of the people, to be just no freedom at all.

Why was the amendment, expressly declaring the right of the people to exclude slavery, voted down? Plainly enough *now*, the adoption of it, would have spoiled the niche for the Dred Scott decision.

Why was the court decision held up? Why, even a Senator's individual opinion withheld, till *after* the Presidential election? Plainly enough *now*, the speaking out *then* would have damaged the *"perfectly free"* argument upon which the election was to be carried.

Why the *outgoing* President's felicitation on the indorsement? Why the delay of a reargument? Why the incoming President's *advance* exhortation in favor of the decision?

These things *look* like the cautious *patting* and *petting* a spirited horse, preparatory to mounting him, when it is dreaded that he may give the rider a fall.

And why the hasty after indorsements of the decision by the President and others?

We can not absolutely *know* that all these exact adaptations are the result of preconcert. But when we see a lot of framed timbers, different portions of which we know have been gotten out at different times and places and by different workmen—Stephen, Franklin, Roger and James, for instance—and when we see these timbers joined together, and see they exactly make the frame of a house or a mill, all the tenons and mortices exactly fitting, and all the lengths and proportions of the different pieces exactly adapted to their respective places, and not a piece too many or too few—not omitting even scaffolding—or, if a single piece be lacking, we can see the place in the frame exactly fitted and prepared to yet bring such piece in—in *such* a case, we find it impossible to not *believe* that Stephen and Franklin and Roger and James all understood one another from the beginning, and all worked upon a common *plan* or *draft* drawn up before the first lick was struck.

It should not be overlooked that, by the Nebraska bill, the people of a *State* as well as *Territory*, were to be left *"perfectly free" "subject only to the Constitution."*

Why mention a *State*? They were legislating for *territories*, and not *for* or *about* States. Certainly the people of a State *are* and *ought to be* subject to the Constitution of the United States; but why is mention of this *lugged* into this merely *territorial* law? Why are the people of a *territory* and the people of a *state* therein *lumped* together, and their relation to the Constitution therein treated as being *precisely* the same?

While the opinion of *the Court*, by Chief Justice Taney, in the Dred Scott case, and the separate opinions of all the concurring Judges, expressly declare that the Constitution of the United States neither permits Congress nor a Territorial legislature to exclude slavery from any United States territory, they all *omit* to declare whether or not the same Constitution permits a *state*, or the people of a State, to exclude it.

Possibly, this was a mere *omission*; but who can be *quite* sure, if McLean or Curtis had sought to get into the opinion a declaration of unlimited power in the people of a *state* to exclude slavery from their limits, just as Chase and Macy sought to get such declaration, in behalf of the people of a territory, into the Nebraska bill—I ask, who can be quite *sure* that it would not have been voted down, in the one case, as it had been in the other.

The nearest approach to the point of declaring the power of a State over slavery, is made by Judge Nelson. He approaches it more than once, using the precise idea, and *almost* the language too, of the Nebraska act. On one occasion his exact language is, "except in cases where the power is restrained by the Constitution of the United States, the law of the State is supreme over the subject of slavery within its jurisdiction."

In what *cases* the power of the *states is* so restrained by the U.S. Constitution, is left an *open* question, precisely as the same question, as to the restraint on the power of the *territories* was left open in the Nebraska act. Put *that* and *that* together, and we have another nice little niche, which we may, ere long, see filled with another Supreme Court decision, declaring that the Constitution of the United States does not permit a *state* to exclude slavery from its limits.

And this may especially be expected if the doctrine of "care not whether slavery be voted *down* or voted *up*," shall gain upon the public mind sufficiently to give promise that such a decision can be maintained when made.

Such a decision is all that slavery now lacks of being alike lawful in all the States.

Welcome or unwelcome, such decision *is* probably coming, and will soon be upon us, unless the power of the present political dynasty shall be met and overthrown.

We shall *lie down* pleasantly dreaming that the people of *Missouri* are on the verge of making their State *free*; and we shall *awake* to the *reality*, instead, that the *Supreme* Court has made *Illinois* a *slave* State.

To meet and overthrow the power of that dynasty, is the work now before all those who would prevent that consummation.

That is *what* we have to do.

But *how* can we best do it?

There are those who denounce us *openly* to their *own* friends, and yet whisper *us softly*, that *Senator Douglas* is the *aptest* instrument there is, with which to effect that object. *They* do *not* tell us, nor has *he* told us, that he *wishes* any such object to be effected. They wish us to *infer* all, from the facts, that he now has a little quarrel with the present head of the dynasty; and that he has regularly voted with us, on a single point, upon which, he and we, have never differed.

They remind us that *he* is a very *great man*, and that the largest of *us* are very small ones. Let this be granted. But "a *living dog* is better than a *dead lion*." Judge Douglas, if not a *dead* lion *for this work*, is at least a *caged* and *toothless* one. How can he oppose the advances of slavery? He don't *care* anything about it. His avowed *mission is impressing* the "public heart" to *care* nothing about it.

A leading Douglas Democratic newspaper thinks Douglas' superior talent will be needed to resist the revival of the African slave trade.

Does Douglas believe an effort to revive that trade is approaching? He has not said so. Does he *really* think so? But if it is, how can he resist it? For years he has labored to prove it a *sacred right* of white men to take negro slaves into the new territories. Can he possibly show that it is *less* a sacred right to *buy* them where they can be bought cheapest? And, unquestionably they can be bought *cheaper in Africa* than in *Virginia*.

He has done all in his power to reduce the whole question of slavery to one of a mere *right of property*; and as such, how can *he* oppose the foreign slave trade—how can he refuse that trade in that "property" shall be "perfectly free"—unless he does it as a *protection* to the home production? And as the home *producers* will probably not *ask* the protection, he will be wholly without a ground of opposition.

Senator Douglas holds, we know, that a man may rightfully be *wiser to-day* than he was *yesterday*—that he may rightfully *change* when he finds himself wrong.

But, can we for that reason, run ahead, and *infer* that he *will* make any particular change, of which he, himself, has given no intimation? Can we *safely* base *our* action upon any such *vague* inference?

Now, as ever, I wish to not *misrepresent* Judge Douglas' *position*, question his *motives*, or do ought that can be personally offensive to him.

Whenever, *if ever*, he and we can come together on *principle* so that *our great cause* may have assistance from *his great ability*, I hope to have interposed no adventitious obstacle.

But clearly, he is not *now* with us—he does not *pretend* to be—he does not *promise* to *ever* be.

Our cause, then, must be intrusted to, and conducted by its own undoubted friends—those whose hands are free, whose hearts are in the work—who *do care* for the result.

Two years ago the Republicans of the nation mustered over thirteen hundred thousand strong.

We did this under the single impulse of resistance to a common danger, with every external circumstance against us.

Of *strange*, *discordant*, and even, *hostile* elements, we gathered from the four winds, and *formed* and fought the battle through, under the constant hot fire of a disciplined, proud, and pampered enemy.

Did we brave all *then*, to *falter* now?—*now*—when that same enemy is *wavering*, dissevered and belligerent?

The result is not doubtful. We shall not fail—if we stand firm, we shall not fail.

Wise councils may *accelerate* or *mistakes delay* it, but, sooner or later the victory is *sure* to come.

To John L. Scripps

Jno. L. Scripps, Esq   Springfield,
My dear Sir   June 23, 1858

Your kind note of yesterday is duly received. I am much flattered by the estimate you place on my late speech; and yet I am much mortified that any part of it should be construed so differently from any thing intended by me. The language, "place it where the public mind shall rest in the belief that it is in course of ultimate extinction," I used deliberately, not dreaming then, nor believing now, that it asserts, or intimates, any power or purpose, to interfere with slavery in the States where it exists. But, to not cavil about language, I declare that whether the clause used by me, will bear such construction or not, I never so intended it. I have declared a thousand times, and now repeat that, in my opinion, neither the General Government, nor any other power outside of the slave states, can constitutionally or rightfully interfere with slaves or slavery where it already exists. I believe that whenever the effort to spread slavery into the new teritories, by whatever means, and into the free states themselves, by Supreme court decisions, shall be fairly headed off, the institution will then be in course of ultimate extinction; and by the language used I meant only this.

I do not intend this for publication; but still you may show it to any one you think fit. I think I shall, as you suggest, take some early occasion to publicly repeat the declaration I have already so often made as before stated. Yours very truly

To Lyman Trumbull

Hon. Lyman Trumbull   Springfield,
My dear Sir: June 23, 1858

Your letter of the 16th. reached me only yesterday. We had already seen, by Telegraph, a report of Douglas' general onslaught upon every body but himself. I have this morning seen the Washington Union, in which I think the Judge is rather worsted in regard to that onslaught.

In relation to the charge of an alliance between the Republicans and Buchanan men in this state, if being rather pleased to see a division in the ranks of the democracy, and not doing anything to prevent it, be such alliance, then there is such alliance—at least that is true of me. But if it be intended to charge that there is any alliance by which there is to be any concession of principle on either side, or furnishing of the sinews, or partition of offices, or swopping of votes, to any extent; or the doing of anything, great or small, on the one side, for a consideration, express or implied, on the other, no such thing is true so far as I know or believe.

Before this reaches you, you will have seen the proceedings of our Republican State Convention. It was really a grand affair, and was, in all respects, all that our friends could desire.

The resolution in effect nominating me for Senator I

suppose was passed more for the object of closing down upon this everlasting croaking about Wentworth, than anything else.

The signs look reasonably well. Our State ticket, I think, will be elected without much difficulty. But, with the advantages they have of us, we shall be very hard run to carry the Legislature.

We shall greet your return home with great pleasure. Yours very truly

To Joseph Medill

J Medill, Esq   Springfield,
My dear Sir   June 25 1858

Your note of the 23rd. did not reach me till last evening. The Times article I saw yesterday morning. I will give you a brief history of facts, upon which you may rely with entire confidence, and from which you can frame such articles or paragraphs as you see fit.

I was in Congress but a single term. I was a candidate when the Mexican war broke out—and I then took the ground, which I never varied from, that the Administration had done wrong in getting us into the war, but that the Officers and soldiers who went to the field must be supplied and sustained at all events. I was elected the first Monday of August 1846, but, in regular course, only took my seat December 6, 1847. In the interval all the battles had been fought, and the war was substantially ended, though our army was still in Mexico, and the treaty of peace was not finally concluded till May 30. 1848. Col. E. D. Baker had been elected to congress from the same district, for the regular term next preceding mine; but having gone to Mexico himself, and having resigned his seat in Congress, a man by the name of John Henry, was elected to fill Baker's vacancy, and so came into Congress before I did. On the 23rd. day of February 1847 (the very day I believe, Col. John Hardin was killed at Buena Vista, and certainly more than nine months before I took a seat in congress) a bill corresponding with great accuracy to that mentioned by the Times, passed the House of Representatives, and *John Henry* voted against it, as may be seen in the Journal of that session at pages 406–7. The bill became a law; and is found in the U.S. Statutes at Large—Vol. 9. page 149.

This I suppose is the real origin of the Times' attack upon me. In its' blind rage to assail me, it has seized on a vague recollection of Henry's vote, and appropriated it to me. I scarcely think any one is quite vile enough to make such a charge in such terms, without some slight belief in the truth of it.

Henry was my personal and political friend; and, as I thought, a very good man; and when I first learned of that vote, I well remember how astounded and mortified I was. This very bill, voted against by Henry, passed into a law, and made the appropriations for the year ending June 30. 1848—extending a full month beyond the actual and formal ending of the war. When I came into congress, money was needed to meet the appropriations made, and to be made; and accordingly on the 17th. day of Feb. 1848, a bill to borrow 18.500 000. passed the House of Representatives, for which I voted, as will appear by the Journal of that session page 426, 427. The act itself, reduced to 16.000 000 (I suppose in the Senate) is found in U.S. Statutes at Large Vol. 9– 217.

Again, on the 8th. of March 1848, a bill passed the House of Representatives, for which I voted, as may be seen by the Journal 520–521. It passed into a law, and is found in U.S. Statutes at Large Page 215 and forward. The last section of the act, on page 217—contains an appropriation of 800 000. for clothing the volunteers.

It is impossible to refer to all the votes I gave but the above I think are sufficient as specimens; and you may safely deny that I ever gave any vote for withholding any supplies whatever, from officers or soldiers of the Mexican war. I have examined the Journals a good deal; and besides I can not be mistaken; for I had my eye always upon it. I must close to get this into the mail. Yours very truly

Fragment on the Struggle Against Slavery

I have never professed an indifference to the honors of official station; and were I to do so now, I should only make

myself ridiculous. Yet I have never failed—do not now fail—
to remember that in the republican cause there is a higher aim
than that of mere office. I have not allowed myself to forget
that the abolition of the Slave-trade by Great Brittain, was
agitated a hundred years before it was a final success; that the
measure had it's open fire-eating opponents; it's stealthy
"dont care" opponents; it's dollar and cent opponents; it's
inferior race opponents; its negro equality opponents; and its
religion and good order opponents; that all these opponents
got offices, and their adversaries got none. But I have also
remembered that though they blazed, like tallow-candles for a
century, at last they flickered in the socket, died out, stank in
the dark for a brief season, and were remembered no more,
even by the smell. School-boys know that Wilbeforce, and
Granville Sharpe, helped that cause forward; but who can
now name a single man who labored to retard it? Remembering these things I can not but regard it as possible that the
higher object of this contest may not be completely attained
within the term of my natural life.

c. July 1858

Speech at Chicago, Illinois

The succeeding speech was delivered by Mr. Lincoln, on Satur-
day Evening, July 10, 1858, at Chicago, Illinois.
Senator Douglas was not present.

My Fellow Citizens:—On yesterday evening, upon the occasion of the reception given to Senator Douglas, I was furnished with a seat very convenient for hearing him, and was
otherwise very courteously treated by him and his friends, and
for which I thank him and them. During the course of his
remarks my name was mentioned in such a way, as I suppose
renders it at least not improper that I should make some sort
of reply to him. I shall not attempt to follow him in the precise order in which he addressed the assembled multitude
upon that occasion, though I shall perhaps do so in the main.

A QUESTION OF VERACITY — THE ALLIANCE.

There was one question to which he asked the attention of
the crowd, which I deem of somewhat less importance—at
least of propriety for me to dwell upon—than the others,
which he brought in near the close of his speech, and which I
think it would not be entirely proper for me to omit attending to, and yet if I were not to give some attention to it now,
I should probably forget it altogether. [Applause]. While I am
upon this subject, allow me to say that I do not intend to
indulge in that inconvenient mode sometimes adopted in
public speaking, of reading from documents; but I shall depart from that rule so far as to read a little scrap from his
speech, which notices this first topic of which I shall speak—
that is, provided I can find it in the paper. (Examines the
Press and Tribune of this morning). A voice—"Get out your
specs."

I have made up my mind to appeal to the people against the combination that has been made against me!—the Republican leaders have
formed an alliance, an unholy and unnatural alliance, with a portion of
unscrupulous federal office-holders. I intend to fight that allied army
wherever I meet them. I know they deny the alliance, but yet these men
who are trying to divide the Democratic party for the purpose of electing a Republican Senator in my place, are just as much the agents and
tools of the supporters of Mr. Lincoln. Hence I shall deal with this allied

army just as the Russians dealt with the allies at Sebastopol—that is, the Russians did not stop to inquire, when they fired a broadside, whether it hit an Englishman, a Frenchman, or a Turk. Nor will I stop to inquire, nor shall I hesitate, whether my blows shall hit these Republican leaders or their allies who are holding the federal offices and yet acting in concert with them.

Well now, gentlemen, is not that very alarming? [Laughter.] Just to think of it! right at the outset of his canvass, I, a poor, kind, amiable, intelligent, [laughter] gentleman, [laughter and renewed cheers] I am to be slain in this way. Why, my friend, the Judge, is not only, as it turns out, not a dead lion, nor even a living one—he is the rugged Russian Bear! [Roars of laughter and loud applause.]

But if they will have it—for he says that we deny it—that there is any such alliance, as he says there is—and I don't propose hanging very much upon this question of veracity— but if he will have it that there is such an alliance—that the Administration men and we are allied, and we stand in the attitude of English, French and Turk, he occupying the position of the Russian, in that case, I beg that he will indulge us while we barely suggest to him, that these allies took Sebastopol. [Long and tremendous applause.]

Gentlemen, only a few more words as to this alliance. For my part, I have to say, that whether there be such an alliance, depends, so far as I know, upon what may be a right definition of the term *alliance*. If for the Republican party to see the other great party to which they are opposed divided among themselves, and not try to stop the division and rather be glad of it—if that is an alliance I confess I am in; but if it is meant to be said that the Republicans had formed an alliance going beyond that, by which there is contribution of money or sacrifice of principle on the one side or the other, so far as the Republican party is concerned, if there be any such thing, I protest that I neither know anything of it, nor do I believe it. I will however say—as I think this branch of the argument is lugged in—I would before I leave it, state, for the benefit of those concerned, that one of those same Buchanan men did once tell me of an argument that he made for his opposition to Judge Douglas. He said that a friend of our Senator Douglas had been talking to him, and had among other things said to him: "Why, you don't want to beat Douglas?" "Yes," said he "I do want to beat him, and I will tell you why. I believe his original Nebraska bill was right in the abstract, but it was wrong in the time that it was brought forward. It was wrong in the application to a territory in regard to which the question had been settled; it was brought forward at a time when nobody asked him; it was tendered to the South when the South had not asked for it, but when they could not well refuse it; and for this same reason he forced that question upon our party: it has sunk the best men all over the nation, everywhere; and now when our President, struggling with the difficulties of this man's getting up, has reached the very hardest point to turn in the case, he deserts him, and I am for putting him where he will trouble us no more." [Applause.]

Now, gentlemen, that is not my argument—that is not my argument at all. I have only been stating to you the argument of a Buchanan man. You will judge if there is any force in it. [Applause.]

WHAT IS POPULAR SOVEREIGNTY?

Popular sovereignty! everlasting popular sovereignty! [Laughter and continued cheers.] Let us for a moment inquire into this vast matter of popular sovereignty. What is popular sovereignty? We recollect that at an early period in the history of this struggle, there was another name for this same thing—*Squatter Sovereignty*. It was not exactly Popular Sovereignty but Squatter Sovereignty. What do those terms mean? What do those terms mean when used now? And vast credit is taken by our friend, the Judge, in regard to his support of it, when he declares the last years of his life have been, and all the future years of his life shall be, devoted to this matter of popular sovereignty. What is it? Why, it is the sovereignty of the people! What was Squatter Sovereignty? I suppose if it had any significance at all it was the right of the people to govern themselves, to be sovereign of their own affairs while they were squatted down in a country not their own, while they had squatted on a territory that did not belong to them, in the sense that a State belongs to the people who inhabit it—when it belonged to the nation—such right to govern themselves was called "Squatter Sovereignty."

Now I wish you to mark. What has become of that Squatter Sovereignty? What has become of it? Can you get anybody to tell you now that the people of a territory have any authority to govern themselves, in regard to this mooted question of Slavery, before they form a State Constitution? No such thing at all, although there is a general running fire, and although there has been a hurrah made in every speech on that side, assuming that policy had given the people of a territory the right to govern themselves upon this question; yet the point is dodged. To-day it has been decided—no more than a year ago it was decided by the Supreme Court of the United States, and is insisted upon to-day, that the people of a territory have no right to exclude Slavery from a territory, that if any one man chooses to take slaves into a territory, all the rest of the people have no right to keep them out. This being so, and this decision being made one of the points that the Judge approved, and one in the approval of which he says he means to keep me down—put me down I should not say, for I have never been up. He says he is in favor of it, and sticks to it, and expects to win his battle on that decision, which says that there is no such thing as Squatter Sovereignty; but that any one man may take slaves into a territory, and all the other men in the territory may be opposed to it, and yet by reason of the constitution they cannot prohibit it. When that is so, how much is left of this vast matter of Squatter Sovereignty I should like to know?—(a voice)—"it has all gone."

When we get back, we get to the point of the right of the people to make a constitution. Kansas was settled, for example, in 1854. It was a territory yet, without having formed a Constitution, in a very regular way, for three years. All this time negro slavery could be taken in by any few individuals, and by that decision of the Supreme Court, which the Judge approves, all the rest of the people cannot keep it out; but when they come to make a Constitution they may say they will not have Slavery. But it is there; they are obliged to tolerate it in some way, and all experience shows that it will be so—for they will not take the negro slaves and absolutely deprive the owners of them. All experience shows this to be so. All that space of time that runs from the beginning of the settlement of the Territory until there is sufficiency of people to make a State Constitution—all that portion of time popular sovereignty is given up. The seal is absolutely put down upon it by the Court decision, and Judge Douglas puts his own upon the top of that, yet he is appealing to the people to give him vast credit for his devotion to popular sovereignty. (Applause.)

Again, when we get to the question of the right of the people to form a State Constitution as they please, to form it with Slavery or without Slavery—if that is anything new, I confess I don't know it. Has there ever been a time when anybody said that any other than the people of a Territory itself should form a Constitution? What is now in it, that Judge Douglas should have fought several years of his life, and pledged himself to fight all the remaining years of his life for? Can Judge Douglas find anybody on earth that said that anybody else should form a constitution for a people? (A voice, "Yes.") Well, I should like you to name him; I should like to know who he was. (Same voice—"John Calhoun.")

Mr. Lincoln—No, sir, I never heard of even John Calhoun saying such a thing. He insisted on the same principle as Judge Douglas; but his mode of applying it in fact, was wrong. It is enough for my purpose to ask this crowd, when ever a Republican said anything against it? They never said anything against it, but they have constantly spoken for it; and whosoever will undertake to examine the platform, and the speeches of responsible men of the party, and of irresponsible men, too, if you please, will be unable to find one word from anybody in the Republican ranks, opposed to that Popular Sovereignty which Judge Douglas thinks that he has invented. [Applause.] I suppose that Judge Douglas will claim in a little while, that he is the inventor of the idea that the people should govern themselves: [cheers and laughter]; that nobody ever thought of such a thing until he brought it forward. We do remember, that in that old Declaration of Independence, it is said that "We hold these truths to be self-evident that all men are created equal; that they are endowed by their Creator with certain inalienable rights; that among these are life, liberty, and the pursuit of happiness; that to secure these rights, governments are instituted among men, deriving their just powers from the consent of the governed." There is the origin of Popular Sovereignty. [Loud applause]. Who, then, shall come in at this day and claim that he invented it. [Laughter and applause.]

LECOMPTON CONSTITUTION.

The Lecompton Constitution connects itself with this question, for it is in this matter of the Lecompton Constitution that our friend Judge Douglas claims such vast credit. I agree that in opposing the Lecompton Constitution so far as I can perceive, he was right. ["Good," "good."] I do not deny that at all; and gentlemen, you will readily see why I could not deny it, even if I wanted to. But I do not wish to; for all the Republicans in the nation opposed it, and they would have opposed it just as much without Judge Douglas' aid, as with it. They had all taken ground against it long before he did. Why, the reason that he urges against that Constitution, I urged against him a year before. I have the printed speech in my hand. The argument that he makes, why that Constitution should not be adopted, that the people were not fairly represented nor allowed to vote, I pointed out in a speech a year ago, which I hold in my hand now, that no fair chance was to be given to the people. ["Read it," "read it."] I shall not waste your time by trying to read it. ["Read it," "read it."] Gentlemen, reading from speeches is a very tedious business, particularly for an old man that has to put on spectacles, and the more so if the man be so tall that he has to bend over to the light. [Laughter.]

A little more, now, as to this matter of popular sovereignty and the Lecompton Constitution. The Lecompton Constitution, as the Judge tells us, was defeated. The defeat of it was a good thing or it was not. He thinks the defeat of it was a good thing, and so do I, and we agree in that. Who defeated it?

A voice—Judge Douglas.

Mr. Lincoln—Yes, he furnished himself, and if you suppose he controlled the other Democrats that went with him, he furnished *three* votes, while the Republicans furnished *twenty*. [Applause.]

That is what he did to defeat it. In the House of Representatives he and his friends furnished some twenty votes, and the Republicans furnished *ninety odd*. [Loud applause.] Now who was it that did the work?

A voice—Douglas.

Mr. Lincoln—Why, yes, Douglas did it! To be sure he did. Let us, however, put that proposition another way. The Republicans could not have done it without Judge Douglas. Could he have done it without them. [Applause.] Which could have come the nearest to doing it without the other? [Renewed applause. "That's it," "that's it;" "good," "good."]

A voice—Who killed the bill?

Another voice—Douglas.

Mr. Lincoln—Ground was taken against it by the Republicans long before Douglas did it. The proportion of opposition to that measure is about five to one.

A Voice—"Why don't they come out on it?"

Mr. Lincoln—You don't know what you are talking about, my friend. I am quite willing to answer any gentleman in the crowd who asks an *intelligent* question. [Great applause.]

Now, who in all this country has ever found any of our friends of Judge Douglas' way of thinking, and who have acted upon this main question, that has ever thought of uttering a word in behalf of Judge Trumbull? A voice—"we have." I defy you to show a printed resolution passed in a Democratic meeting—I take it upon myself to defy any man to show a printed resolution of a Democratic meeting, large or small, in favor of Judge Trumbull, or any of the five to one Republicans who beat that bill. Every thing must be for the Democrats! They did every thing, and the five to one that really did the thing, they snub over, and they do not seem to remember that they have an existence upon the face of the earth. [Applause.]

LINCOLN AND DOUGLAS.

Gentlemen: I fear that I shall become tedious, (Go on, go on.) I leave this branch of the subject to take hold of another. I take up that part of Judge Douglas' speech in which he respectfully attended to me. [Laughter.]

Judge Douglas made two points upon my recent speech at Springfield. He says they are to be the issues of this campaign. The first one of these points he bases upon the language in a speech which I delivered at Springfield, which I believe I can quote correctly from memory. I said there that "we are now far into the fifth year since a policy was instituted for the avowed object and with the confident promise of putting an end to slavery agitation; under the operation of that policy, that agitation had only not ceased, but has constantly augmented."—(A voice)—"That's the very language." "I believe it will not cease until a crisis shall have been reached and passed. A house divided against itself cannot stand. I believe this government cannot endure permanently half slave and half free." [Applause.] "I do not expect the Union to be dissolved,"—I am quoting from my speech—"I do not expect the house to fall, but I do expect it will cease to be divided. It will become all one thing or the other. Either the opponents of slavery will arrest the spread of it, and place it where the public mind shall rest in the belief that it is in the course of ultimate extinction, or its advocates will push it forward until it shall become alike lawful in all the States, North as well as South." [Good, good.]

What is the paragraph. In this paragraph which I have quoted in your hearing, and to which I ask the attention of all, Judge Douglas thinks he discovers great political heresy. I want your attention particularly to what he has inferred from it. He says I am in favor of making all the States of this Union uniform in all their internal regulations; that in all their domestic concerns I am in favor of making them entirely uniform. He draws this inference from the language I have quoted to you. He says that I am in favor of making war by the North upon the South for the extinction of slavery; that I am also in favor of inviting (as he expresses it) the South to a war upon the North, for the purpose of nationalizing slavery. Now, it is singular enough, if you will carefully read that passage over, that I did not say that I was in favor of anything in it. I only said what I expected would take place. I made a prediction only—it may have been a foolish one perhaps. I did not even say that I desired that slavery should be put in course of ultimate extinction. I do say so now, however, [great applause] so there need be no longer any difficulty about that. It may be written down in the great speech. [Applause and laughter.]

Gentlemen, Judge Douglas informed you that this speech of mine was probably carefully prepared. I admit that it was. I am not master of language; I have not a fine education; I am not capable of entering into a disquisition upon dialectics, as I believe you call it; but I do not believe the language I employed bears any such construction as Judge Douglas put upon it. But I don't care about a quibble in regard to words. I know what I meant, and I will not leave this crowd in doubt, if I can explain it to them, what I really meant in the use of that paragraph.

I am not, in the first place, unaware that this Government has endured eighty-two years, half slave and half free. I know that. I am tolerably well acquainted with the history of the country, and I know that it has endured eighty-two years, half slave and half free. I *believe* — and that is what I meant to allude to there — I *believe* it has endured because, during all that time, until the introduction of the Nebraska Bill, the public mind did rest, all the time, in the belief that slavery was in course of ultimate extinction. ["Good!" "Good!" and applause.] That was what gave us the rest that we had through that period of eighty-two years; at least, so I believe. I have always hated slavery, I think as much as any Abolitionist. [Applause.] I have been an Old Line Whig. I have always hated it, but I have always been quiet about it until this new era of the introduction of the Nebraska Bill began. I always believed that everybody was against it, and that it was in course of ultimate extinction. (Pointing to Mr. Browning, who stood near by.) Browning thought so; the great mass of the nation have rested in the belief that slavery was in course of ultimate extinction. They had reason so to believe.

The adoption of the Constitution and its attendant history led the people to believe so; and that such was the belief of the framers of the Constitution itself. Why did those old men, about the time of the adoption of the Constitution, decree that Slavery should not go into the new Territory, where it had not already gone? Why declare that within twenty years the African Slave Trade, by which slaves are supplied, might

be cut off by Congress? Why were all these acts? I might enu-
merate more of these acts—but enough. What were they but
a clear indication that the framers of the Constitution intended and expected the ultimate extinction of that institution. [Cheers.] And now, when I say, as I said in my speech
that Judge Douglas has quoted from, when I say that I think
the opponents of slavery will resist the farther spread of it,
and place it where the public mind shall rest with the belief
that it is in course of ultimate extinction, I only mean to say,
that they will place it where the founders of this Government
originally placed it.

I have said a hundred times, and I have now no inclination
to take it back, that I believe there is no right, and ought to
be no inclination in the people of the free States to enter into
the slave States, and interfere with the question of slavery at
all. I have said that always. Judge Douglas has heard me say
it—if not quite a hundred times, at least as good as a hundred times; and when it is said that I am in favor of interfering with slavery where it exists, I know it is unwarranted by
anything I have ever *intended*, and, as I believe, by anything I
have ever *said*. If, by any means, I have ever used language
which could fairly be so construed, (as, however, I believe I
never have,) I now correct it.

[Here the shouts of the Seventh Ward Delegation announced that they were coming in procession. They were received with enthusiastic cheers.]

So much, then, for the inference that Judge Douglas draws,
that I am in favor of setting the sections at war with one
another. I know that I never meant any such thing, and I
believe that no fair mind can infer any such thing from anything I have ever said. ["Good," "good."]

Now in relation to his inference that I am in favor of a
general consolidation of all the local institutions of the various States. I will attend to that for a little while, and try to
inquire, if I can, how on earth it could be that any man could
draw such an inference from anything I said. I have said, very
many times, in Judge Douglas' hearing, that no man believed
more than I in the principle of self-government; that it lies at
the bottom of all my ideas of just government, from beginning to end. I have denied that his use of that term applies

properly. But for the thing itself, I deny that any man has ever gone ahead of me in his devotion to the principle, whatever he may have done in efficiency in advocating it. I think that I have said it in your hearing—that I believe each individual is naturally entitled to do as he pleases with himself and the fruit of his labor, so far as it in no wise interferes with any other man's rights—[applause]—that each community, as a State, has a right to do exactly as it pleases with all the concerns within that State that interfere with the rights of no other State, and that the general government, upon principle, has no right to interfere with anything other than that general class of things that does concern the whole. I have said that at all times. I have said, as illustrations, that I do not believe in the right of Illinois to interfere with the cranberry laws of Indiana, the oyster laws of Virginia, or the Liquor Laws of Maine. I have said these things over and over again, and I repeat them here as my sentiments.

How is it, then, that Judge Douglas infers, because I hope to see slavery put where the public mind shall rest in the belief that it is in the course of ultimate extinction, that I am in favor of Illinois going over and interfering with the cranberry laws of Indiana? What can authorize him to draw any such inference? I suppose there might be one thing that at least enabled *him* to draw such an inference that would not be true with me or with many others, that is, because he looks upon all this matter of slavery as an exceedingly little thing—this matter of keeping one-sixth of the population of the whole nation in a state of oppression and tyranny unequalled in the world. He looks upon it as being an exceedingly little thing—only equal to the question of the cranberry laws of Indiana—as something having no moral question in it—as something on a par with the question of whether a man shall pasture his land with cattle, or plant it with tobacco—so little and so small a thing, that he concludes, if I could desire that anything should be done to bring about the ultimate extinction of that little thing, I must be in favor of bringing about an amalgamation of all the other little things in the Union. Now, it so happens—and there, I presume, is the foundation of this mistake—that the Judge thinks thus; and it so happens that there is a vast portion of the American people that do *not*

look upon that matter as being this very little thing. They
look upon it as a vast moral evil; they can prove it is such by
the writings of those who gave us the blessings of liberty
which we enjoy, and that they so looked upon it, and not as
an evil merely confining itself to the States where it is situated; and while we agree that, by the Constitution we as-
sented to, in the States where it exists we have no right to
interfere with it because it is in the Constitution and we are
by both duty and inclination to stick by that Constitution in
all its letter and spirit from beginning to end. [Great
applause.]

So much then as to my disposition—my wish—to have
all the State legislatures blotted out, and to have one general
consolidated government, and a uniformity of domestic regulations in all the States, by which I suppose it is meant if
we raise corn here, we must make sugar cane grow here too,
and we must make those which grow North, grow in the
South. All this I suppose he understands I am in favor of
doing. Now, so much for all this nonsense—for I must call
it so. The Judge can have no issue with me on a question of
establishing uniformity in the domestic regulations of the
States.

DRED SCOTT DECISION.

A little now on the other point—the Dred Scott Decision.
Another one of the issues he says that is to be made with me,
is upon his devotion to the Dred Scott Decision, and my opposition to it.

I have expressed heretofore, and I now repeat, my opposition to the Dred Scott Decision, but I should be allowed to
state the nature of that opposition, and I ask your indulgence
while I do so. What is fairly implied by the term Judge Douglas has used "resistance to the Decision?" I do not resist it. If
I wanted to take Dred Scott from his master, I would be
interfering with property, and that terrible difficulty that
Judge Douglas speaks of, of interfering with property, would
arise. But I am doing no such thing as that, but all that I am
doing is refusing to obey it as a political rule. If I were in
Congress, and a vote should come up on a question whether
slavery should be prohibited in a new territory, in spite of

that Dred Scott decision, I would vote that it should. [Applause; "good for you;" "we hope to see it;" "that's right."]

Mr. Lincoln—That is what I would do. ["You will have a chance soon."] Judge Douglas said last night, that before the decision he might advance his opinion, and it might be contrary to the decision when it was made; but after it was made he would abide by it until it was reversed. Just so! We let this property abide by the decision, but we will try to reverse that decision. [Loud applause—cries of "good."] We will try to put it where Judge Douglas would not object, for he says he will obey it until it is reversed. Somebody has to reverse that decision, since it is made, and we mean to reverse it, and we mean to do it peaceably.

What are the uses of decisions of courts? They have two uses. As rules of property they have two uses. First—they decide upon the question before the court. They decide in this case that Dred Scott is a slave. Nobody resists that. Not only that, but they say to everybody else, that persons standing just as Dred Scott stands is as he is. That is, they say that when a question comes up upon another person it will be so decided again, unless the court decides in another way, [cheers—cries of "good,"] unless the court overrules its decision. [Renewed applause]. Well, we mean to do what we can to have the court decide the other way. That is one thing we mean to try to do.

The sacredness that Judge Douglas throws around this decision, is a degree of sacredness that has never been before thrown around any other decision. I have never heard of such a thing. Why, decisions apparently contrary to that decision, or that good lawyers thought were contrary to that decision, have been made by that very court before. It is the first of its kind; it is an astonisher in legal history. [Laughter.] It is a new wonder of the world. [Laughter and applause.] It is based upon falsehood in the main as to the facts—allegations of facts upon which it stands are not facts at all in many instances, and no decision made on any question—the first instance of a decision made under so many unfavorable circumstances—thus placed has ever been held by the profession as law, and it has always needed confirmation before the lawyers regarded it as settled law. But Judge Douglas will have it that all hands must take this extraordinary decision, made under these extraordinary circumstances, and give their vote in Congress in accordance with it, yield to it and obey it in every possible sense. Circumstances alter cases. Do not gentlemen here remember the case of that same Supreme Court, some twenty-five or thirty years ago, deciding that a National Bank was constitutional? I ask, if somebody does not remember that a National Bank was declared to be constitutional? ["Yes," "yes"] Such is the truth, whether it be remembered or not. The Bank charter ran out, and a re-charter was granted by Congress. That re-charter was laid before General Jackson. It was urged upon him, when he denied the constitutionality of the bank, that the Supreme Court had decided that it was constitutional; and that General Jackson then said that the Supreme Court had no right to lay down a rule to govern a co-ordinate branch of the government, the members of which had sworn to support the Constitution—that each member had sworn to support that Constitution as he understood it. I will venture here to say, that I have heard Judge Douglas say that he approved of General Jackson for that act. What has now become of all his tirade about "resistance to the Supreme Court?" ["Gone up," "Gone to the Theatre."]

My fellow citizens, getting back a little, for I pass from these points, when Judge Douglas makes his threat of annihilation upon the "alliance." He is cautious to say that that warfare of his is to fall upon the leaders of the Republican party. Almost every word he utters and every distinction he makes, has its significance. He means for the Republicans that do not count themselves as leaders, to be his friends; he makes no fuss over them; it is the leaders that he is making war upon. He wants it understood that the mass of the Republican party are really his friends. It is only the leaders that are doing something, that are intolerant, and that requires extermination at his hands. As this is clearly and unquestionably the light in which he presents that matter, I want to ask your attention, addressing myself to the Republicans here, that I may ask you some questions, as to where you, as the Republican party, would be placed if you sustained Judge Douglas in his present position by a re-election? I do not claim, gentlemen, to be unselfish, I do not pretend that I would not like to go to the United States Senate, (laughter), I make no such hypocritical pretense, but I do say to you that in this mighty issue, it is nothing to you—nothing to the mass of the people of the nation, whether or not Judge Douglas or myself shall ever be heard of after this night, it may be a trifle to either of us, but in connection with this mighty question, upon which hang the destinies of the nation, perhaps, it is absolutely nothing; but where will you be placed if you re-endorse Judge Douglas? Don't you know how apt he is—how exceedingly anxious he is at all times to seize upon anything and everything to persuade you that something *he* has done *you* did yourselves? Why, he tried to persuade you last night that our Illinois Legislature instructed him to introduce the Nebraska bill. There was nobody in that legislature ever thought of such a thing; and when he first introduced the bill, he never thought of it; but still he fights furiously for the proposition, and that he did it because there was a standing instruction to our Senators to be always introducing Nebraska bills. [Laughter and applause] He tells you he is for the Cincinnati platform, he tells you he is for the Dred Scott decision. He tells you, not in his speech last night, but substantially in a former speech, that he cares not if slavery is voted up or down—he tells you the struggle on Lecompton is past—it may come up again or not, and if it does he stands where he stood when in spite of him and his opposition you built up the Republican party. If you endorse him you tell him you do not care whether slavery be voted up or down, and he will close, or try to close your mouths with his declaration repeated by the day, the week, the month and the year. Is that what you mean? (cries of "no," one voice "yes.") Yes, I have no doubt you who have always been for him if you mean that. No doubt of that (a voice "hit him again") soberly I have said, and I repeat it I think in the position in which Judge Douglas stood in opposing the Lecompton Constitution he was right, he does not know that it will return, but if it does we may know where to find him, and if it does not we may know where to look for him and that is on the Cincinnati platform. Now I could ask the Republican party after all the hard names that Judge Douglas has called them by—all his repeated charges of their inclination to marry with and hug negroes—all his declarations of Black Republicanism—by the way we are improving, the black has got rubbed off—but with all that, if he be endorsed by Republican votes where do you stand? Plainly you stand ready saddled, bridled and harnessed and waiting to be driven over to the slavery extension camp of the nation [a voice "we will hang ourselves first"]—just ready to be driven over tied together in a lot—to be driven over, every man with a rope around his neck, that halter being held by Judge Douglas. That is the question. If Republican men have been in earnest in what they have done, I think they had better not do it, but I think that the Republican party is made up of those who, as far as they can peaceably, will oppose the extension of slavery, and who will hope for its ultimate extinction. If they believe it is wrong in grasping up the new lands of the continent, and keeping them from the settlement of free white laborers, who want the land to bring up their families upon; if they are in earnest, although they may make a mistake, they will grow restless, and the time will come when they will come back again and re-organize, if not by the same name, at least upon the same principles as their party now has. It is better, then, to save the work while it is begun. You have done the labor; maintain it—keep it. If men choose to serve you, go with them; but as you have made up your organization upon principle, stand by it; for, as surely as God reigns over you, and has inspired your mind, and given you a sense of propriety, and continues to give you hope, so surely you will still cling to these ideas, and you will at last come back again after your wanderings, merely to do your work over again. [Loud applause.]

We were often—more than once at least—in the course of Judge Douglas' speech last night, reminded that this government was made for white men—that he believed it was made for white men. Well, that is putting it into a shape in which no one wants to deny it, but the Judge then goes into his passion for drawing inferences that are not warranted. I protest, now and forever, against that counterfeit logic which presumes that because I do not want a negro woman for a slave, I do necessarily want her for a wife. [Laughter and cheers.] My understanding is that I need not have her for either, but as God made us separate, we can leave one another alone and do one another much good thereby. There are white men enough to marry all the white women, and enough black men to marry all the black women, and in God's name let them be so married. The Judge regales us with the terrible enormities that take place by the mixture of races; that the inferior race bears the superior down. Why, Judge, if we do not let them get together in the Territories they won't mix there. [Immense applause.]

A voice—"Three cheers for Lincoln." [The cheers were given with a hearty good will.]

Mr. Lincoln—I should say at least that that is a self evident truth.

Now, it happens that we meet together once every year, sometime about the 4th of July, for some reason or other. These 4th of July gatherings I suppose have their uses. If you will indulge me, I will state what I suppose to be some of them.

We are now a mighty nation, we are thirty—or about thirty millions of people, and we own and inhabit about one-fifteenth part of the dry land of the whole earth. We run our memory back over the pages of history for about eighty-two years and we discover that we were then a very small people in point of numbers, vastly inferior to what we are now, with a vastly less extent of country,—with vastly less of everything we deem desirable among men,—we look upon the change as exceedingly advantageous to us and to our posterity, and we fix upon something that happened away back, as in some way or other being connected with this rise of prosperity. We find a race of men living in that day whom we claim as our fathers and grandfathers; they were iron men, they fought for the principle that they were contending for; and we understood that by what they then did it has followed that the degree of prosperity that we now enjoy has come to us. We hold this annual celebration to remind ourselves of all the good done in this process of time of how it was done and who did it, and how we are historically connected with it; and we go from these meetings in better humor with ourselves—we feel more attached the one to the other, and more firmly bound to the country we inhabit. In every way we are better men in the age, and race, and country in which we live for these celebrations. But after we have done all this we have not yet reached the whole. There is something else connected with it. We have besides these men—descended by blood from our ancestors—among us perhaps half our people who are not descendants at all of these men, they are men who have come from Europe—German, Irish, French and Scandinavian—men that have come from Europe themselves, or whose ancestors have come hither and settled here, finding themselves our equals in all things. If they look back through this history to trace their connection with those days by blood, they find they have none, they cannot carry themselves back into that glorious epoch and make themselves feel that they are part of us, but when they look through that old Declaration of Independence they find that those old men say that "We hold these truths to be self-evident, that all men are created equal," and then they feel that that moral sentiment taught in that day evidences their relation to those men, that it is the father of all moral principle in them, and that they have a right to claim it as though they were blood of the blood, and flesh of the flesh of the men who wrote that Declaration, (loud and long continued applause) and so they are. That is the electric cord in that Declaration that links the hearts of patriotic and liberty-loving men together, that will link those patriotic hearts as long as the love of freedom exists in the minds of men throughout the world. [Applause.]

Now, sirs, for the purpose of squaring things with this idea of "don't care if slavery is voted up or voted down," for sustaining the Dred Scott decision [A voice—"Hit him again"], for holding that the Declaration of Independence did not mean anything at all, we have Judge Douglas giving his exposition of what the Declaration of Independence means, and we have him saying that the people of America are equal to the people of England. According to his construction, you Germans are not connected with it. Now I ask you in all soberness, if all these things, if indulged in, if ratified, if confirmed and endorsed, if taught to our children, and repeated to them, do not tend to rub out the sentiment of liberty in the country, and to transform this Government into a government of some other form. Those arguments that are made, that the inferior race are to be treated with as much allowance as they are capable of enjoying; that as much is to be done for them as their condition will allow. What are these arguments? They are the arguments that kings have made for enslaving the people in all ages of the world. You will find that all the arguments in favor of king-craft were of this class; they always bestrode the necks of the people, not that they wanted to do it, but because the people were better off for being ridden. That is their argument, and this argument of the Judge is the same old serpent that says you work and I eat, you toil and I will enjoy the fruits of it. Turn in whatever way you will—whether it come from the mouth of a King, an excuse for enslaving the people of his country, or from the mouth of men of one race as a reason for enslaving the men of another race, it is all the same old serpent, and I hold if that course of argumentation that is made for the purpose of convincing the public mind that we should not care about this, should be granted, it does not stop with the negro. I should like to know if taking this old Declaration of Independence, which declares that all men are equal upon principle and making exceptions to it where will it stop. If one man says it does not mean a negro, why not another say it does not mean some other man? If that declaration is not the truth, let us get the Statute book, in which we find it and tear it out! Who is so bold as to do it! [Voices—"me" "no one," &c.] If it is not true let us tear it out! [cries of "no, no,"] let us stick to it then, [cheers] let us stand firmly by it then. [Applause.]

It may be argued that there are certain conditions that make necessities and impose them upon us, and to the extent that a necessity is imposed upon a man he must submit to it. I think that was the condition in which we found ourselves when we established this government. We had slavery among us, we could not get our constitution unless we permitted them to remain in slavery, we could not secure the good we did secure if we grasped for more, and having by necessity submitted to that much, it does not destroy the principle that is the charter of our liberties. Let that charter stand as our standard.

My friend has said to me that I am a poor hand to quote Scripture. I will try it again, however. It is said in one of the admonitions of the Lord, "As your Father in Heaven is perfect, be ye also perfect." The Savior, I suppose, did not expect that any human creature could be perfect as the Father in Heaven; but He said, "As your Father in Heaven is perfect, be ye also perfect." He set that up as a standard, and he who did most towards reaching that standard, attained the highest degree of moral perfection. So I say in relation to the principle that all men are created equal, let it be as nearly reached as we can. If we cannot give freedom to every creature, let us do nothing that will impose slavery upon any other creature. [Applause.] Let us then turn this government back into the channel in which the framers of the Constitution originally placed it. Let us stand firmly by each other. If we do not do so we are turning in the contrary direction, that our friend Judge Douglas proposes—not intentionally—as working in the traces tend to make this one universal slave nation. [A voice—"that is so."] He is one that runs in that direction, and as such I resist him.

My friends, I have detained you about as long as I desired to do, and I have only to say, let us discard all this quibbling about this man and the other man—this race and that race and the other race being inferior, and therefore they must be placed in an inferior position—discarding our standard that we have left us. Let us discard all these things, and unite as one people throughout this land, until we shall once more stand up declaring that all men are created equal.

My friends, I could not, without launching off upon some new topic, which would detain you too long, continue to-night. [Cries of "go on."] I thank you for this most extensive audience that you have furnished me to-night. I leave you, hoping that the lamp of liberty will burn in your bosoms until there shall no longer be a doubt that all men are created free and equal.

Mr. Lincoln retired amid a perfect torrent of applause and cheers.

To Gustave P. Koerner

Hon. G. Koerner: Springfield,
My dear Sir July 15. 1858

I have just been called on by one of our german republicans here, to ascertain if Mr. Hecker could not be prevailed on to visit this region, and address the germans, at this place, and a few others at least. Please ascertain & write me. He would, of course, have to be paid something. Find out from him about how much.

I have just returned from Chicago. Douglas took nothing by his motion there. In fact, by his rampant indorsement of the Dred Scott decision he drove back a few republicans who were favorably inclined towards him. His tactics just now, in part is, to make it appear that he is having a triumphal entry into; and march through the country; but it is all as bombastic and hollow as Napoleon's bulletins sent back from his campaign in Russia. I was present at his reception in Chicago, and it certainly was very large and imposing; but judging from the opinions of others better acquainted with faces there, and by the strong call for me to speak, when he closed, I really believe we could have voted him down in that very crowd. Our meeting, twentyfour hours after, called only twelve hours before it came together and got up without trumpery, was nearly as large, and five times as enthusiastic.

I write this, for your private eye, to assure you that there is no solid shot, in these bombastic parades of his. Yours very truly

Speech at Springfield, Illinois

Delivered, as indicated by the heading.
Senator Douglas not present.

FELLOW CITIZENS:—Another election, which is deemed an important one, is approaching, and, as I suppose, the Republican party will, without much difficulty elect their State ticket. But in regard to the Legislature, we, the Republicans, labor under some disadvantages. In the first place, we have a Legislature to elect upon an apportionment of the representation made several years ago, when the proportion of the population was far greater in the South (as compared with the North) than it now is; and inasmuch as our opponents hold almost entire sway in the South, and we a correspondingly large majority in the North, the fact that we are now to be represented as we were years ago, when the population was different, is to us a very great disadvantage. We had, in the year 1855, according to law, a census or enumeration of the inhabitants, taken for the purpose of a new apportionment of representation. We know what a fair apportionment of representation upon that census would give us. We know that it could not if fairly made, fail to give the Republican party from six to ten more members of the Legislature than they can probably get as the law now stands. It so happened at the last session of the Legislature, that our opponents, holding the control of both branches of the Legislature, steadily refused to give us such an apportionment as we were rightfully entitled to have upon the census already taken. The Legislature steadily refused to give us such an apportionment as we were rightfully entitled to have upon the census taken of the population of the State. The Legislature would pass no bill upon that subject, except such as was at least as unfair to us as the old one, and in which, in some instances, two men in the Democratic regions were allowed to go as far towards sending a member to the Legislature as three were in the Republican regions. Comparison was made at the time as to representative and senatorial districts, which completely demonstrated that such was the fact. Such a bill was passed, and tendered to the Republican Governor for his signature; but principally for the reasons I have stated, he withheld his approval, and the bill fell without becoming a law.

Another disadvantage under which we labor is, that there are one or two Democratic Senators who will be members of the next Legislature, and will vote for the election of Senator, who are holding over in districts in which we could, on all reasonable calculation, elect men of our own, if we only had the chance of an election. When we consider that there are but twenty five Senators in the Senate, taking two from the side where they rightfully belong and adding them to the other, is to us a disadvantage not to be lightly regarded. Still, so it is; we have this to contend with. Perhaps there is no ground of complaint on our part. In attending to the many things involved in the last general election for President, Governor, Auditor, Treasurer, Superintendent of Public Instruction, Members of Congress, of the Legislature, County officers, and so on, we allowed these things to happen by want of sufficient attention, and we have no cause to complain of our adversaries, so far as this matter is concerned. But we have some cause to complain of the refusal to give us a fair apportionment.

There is still another disadvantage under which we labor, and to which I will ask your attention. It arises out of the relative positions of the two persons who stand before the State as candidates for the Senate. Senator Douglas is of world wide renown. All the anxious politicians of his party, or who have been of his party for years past, have been looking upon him as certainly, at no distant day, to be the President of the United States. They have seen in his round, jolly, fruitful face, postoffices, landoffices, marshalships, and cabinet appointments, chargeships and foreign missions, bursting and sprouting out in wonderful exuberance ready to be laid hold of by their greedy hands. [Great laughter.] And as they have been gazing upon this attractive picture so long, they cannot, in the little distraction that has taken place in the party, bring themselves to give up the charming hope; but with greedier anxiety they rush about him, sustain him, and give him marches, triumphal entries, and receptions beyond what even in the days of his highest prosperity they could have brought about in his favor. On the contrary nobody has ever expected me to be President. In my poor, lean, lank, face, nobody has ever seen that any cabbages were sprouting out. [Tremendous cheering and laughter.] These are disadvantages all, taken together, that the Republicans labor under. *We* have to fight this battle upon principle, and upon principle alone. I am, in a certain sense, made the standard-bearer in behalf of the Republicans. I was made so merely because there had to be some one so placed—I being in no wise, preferable to any other one of the twenty-five— perhaps a hundred we have in the Republican ranks. Then I say I wish it to be distinctly understood and borne in mind, that we have to fight this battle without many—perhaps without any—of the external aids which are brought to bear against us. So I hope those with whom I am surrounded have principle enough to nerve themselves for the task and leave nothing undone, that can be fairly done, to bring about the right result.

After Senator Douglas left Washington, as his movements were made known by the public prints, he tarried a considerable time in the city of New York; and it was heralded that, like another Napoleon, he was lying by, and framing the plan of his campaign. It was telegraphed to Washington City, and published in the *Union*, that he was framing his plan for the purpose of going to Illinois to pounce upon and annihilate the treasonable and disunion speech which Lincoln had made here on the 16th of June. Now, I do suppose that the Judge really spent some time in New York maturing the plan of the campaign, as his friends heralded for him. I have been able, by noting his movements since his arrival in Illinois, to discover evidences confirmatory of that allegation. I think I have been able to see what are the material points of that plan. I will, for a little while, ask your attention to some of them. What I shall point out, though not showing the whole plan, are, nevertheless, the main points, as I suppose.

They are not very numerous. The first is Popular Sovereignty. The second and third are attacks upon my speech made on the 16th of June. Out of these three points—drawing within the range of Popular Sovereignty the question of the Lecompton Constitution—he makes his principal assault. Upon these his successive speeches are substantially one and the same. On this matter of Popular Sovereignty I wish to be a little careful. Auxiliary to these main points, to be sure, are their thunderings of cannon, their marching and music, their fizzlegigs and fireworks; but I will not waste time with them. They are but the little trappings of the campaign.

Coming to the substance—the first point—"Popular Sovereignty." It is to be labelled upon the cars in which he travels; put upon the hacks he rides in; to be flaunted upon the arches he passes under, and the banners which wave over him. It is to be dished up in as many varieties as a French cook can produce soups from potatoes. Now, as this is so great a staple of the plan of the campaign, it is worth while to examine it carefully; and if we examine only a very little, and do not allow ourselves to be misled, we shall be able to see that the whole thing is the most arrant Quixotism that was ever enacted before a community. What is the matter of Popular Sovereignty? The first thing, in order to understand it, is to get a good definition of what it is, and after that to see how it is applied.

I suppose almost every one knows, that in this controversy, whatever has been said, has had reference to the question of negro slavery. We have not been in a controversy about the right of the people to govern themselves in the *ordinary* matters of domestic concern in the States and Territories. Mr. Buchanan in one of his late messages, (I think when he sent up the Lecompton Constitution,) urged that the main points to which the public attention had been directed, was not in regard to the great variety of small domestic matters, but was directed to the question of negro slavery; and he asserts, that if the people had had a fair chance to vote on that question, there was no reasonable ground of objection in regard to minor questions. Now, while I think that the people had *not* had given, or offered them, a fair chance upon that slavery question; still, if there had been a fair submission to a vote upon that main question, the President's proposition would have been true to the uttermost. Hence, when hereafter, I speak of popular sovereignty, I wish to be understood as applying what I say to the question of slavery only, not to other minor domestic matters of a Territory or a State.

Does Judge Douglas, when he says that several of the past

years of his life have been devoted to the question of "popular sovereignty," and that all the remainder of his life shall be devoted to it, does he mean to say that he has been devoting his life to securing to the people of the territories the right to exclude slavery from the territories? If he means so to say, he means to deceive; because he and every one knows that the decision of the Supreme Court, which he approves and makes especial ground of attack upon me for disapproving, forbids the people of a territory to exclude slavery. This covers the whole ground, from the settlement of a territory till it reaches the degree of maturity entitling it to form a State Constitution. So far as all that ground is concerned, the Judge is not sustaining popular sovereignty, but absolutely opposing it. He sustains the decision which declares that the popular will of the territories has no constitutional power to exclude slavery during their territorial existence. [Cheers] This being so, the period of time from the first settlement of a territory till it reaches the point of forming a State Constitution, is not the thing that the Judge has fought for or is fighting for, but on the contrary, he has fought for, and is fighting for, the thing that annihilates and crushes out that same popular sovereignty.

Well, so much being disposed of, what is left? Why, he is contending for the right of the people, when they come to make a State Constitution, to make it for themselves, and precisely as best suits themselves. I say again, that is Quixotic. I defy contradiction when I declare that the Judge can find no one to oppose him on that proposition. I repeat, there is nobody opposing that proposition on *principle*. Let me not be misunderstood. I know that, with reference to the Lecompton Constitution, I may be misunderstood; but when you understand me correctly, my proposition will be true and accurate. Nobody is opposing, or has opposed, the right of the people, when they form a Constitution, to form it for themselves. Mr. Buchanan and his friends have not done it; they, too, as well as the Republicans and the Anti-Lecompton Democrats, have not done it; but, on the contrary, they together have insisted on the right of the people to form a Constitution for themselves. The difference between the Buchanan men on the one hand, and the Douglas men and the Republicans on the other, has not been on a question of principle, but on a question of *fact*.

The dispute was upon the question of fact, whether the Lecompton Constitution had been fairly formed by the people or not. Mr. Buchanan and his friends have not contended for the contrary principle any more than the Douglas men or the Republicans. They have insisted that whatever of small irregularities existed in getting up the Lecompton Constitution, were such as happen in the settlement of all new Territories. The question was, was it a fair emanation of the people? It was a question of fact, and not of principle. As to the principle, all were agreed. Judge Douglas voted with the Republicans upon that matter of fact.

He and they, by their voices and votes, denied that it was a fair emanation of the people. The Administration affirmed that it was. With respect to the evidence bearing upon that question of fact, I readily agree that Judge Douglas and the Republicans had the right on their side, and that the Administration was wrong. But I state again that as a matter of principle there is no dispute upon the right of a people in a Territory, merging into a State to form a Constitution for themselves without outside interference from any quarter. This being so, what is Judge Douglas going to spend his life for? Is he going to spend his life in maintaining a principle that nobody on earth opposes? [Cheers.] Does he expect to stand up in majestic dignity, and go through his *apotheosis* and become a god, in the maintaining of a principle which neither a man nor a mouse in all God's creation is opposing? [Tremendous cheering.] Now something in regard to the Lecompton Constitution more specially; for I pass from this other question of popular sovereignty as the most errant humbug that has ever been attempted on an intelligent community.

As to the Lecompton Constitution, I have already said that on the question of fact as to whether it was a fair emanation of the people or not, Judge Douglas with the Republicans and some Americans had greatly the argument against the Administration; and while I repeat this, I wish to know what there is in the opposition of Judge Douglas to the Lecompton Constitution that entitles him to be considered the only opponent to

it—as being *par excellence* the very *quintessence* of that opposition. I agree to the rightfulness of his opposition. He in the
Senate and his class of men there formed the number *three*
and no more. In the House of Representatives his class of
men—the anti Lecompton Democrats—formed a number of
about twenty. It took one hundred and twenty to defeat the
measure against one hundred and twelve. Of the votes of that
one hundred and twenty, Judge Douglas' friends furnished
twenty, to add to which, there were six Americans and ninety-
four Republicans. I do not say that I am precisely accurate
in their numbers, but I am sufficiently so for any use I am
making of it.

Why is it that twenty shall be entitled to all the credit of
doing that work, and the hundred none of it? Why, if, as
Judge Douglas says, the honor is to be divided and due credit
is to be given to other parties, why is just so much given as is
consonant with the wishes, the interests and advancement of
the twenty? My understanding is, when a common job is
done, or a common enterprise prosecuted, if I put in five dollars to your one, I have a right to take out five dollars to your
one. But he does not so understand it. He declares the dividend of credit for defeating Lecompton upon a basis which
seems unprecedented and incomprehensible.

Let us see. Lecompton in the raw was defeated. It afterwards took a sort of cooked up shape, and was passed in the
English bill. It is said by the Judge that the defeat was a
good and proper thing. If it was a good thing, why is he
entitled to more credit than others, for the performance of
that good act, unless there was something in the antecedents
of the Republicans that might induce every one to expect
them to join in that good work, and at the same time, something leading them to doubt that he would? Does he place
his superior claim to credit, on the ground that he performed a good act which was never expected of him? He
says I have a proneness for quoting scripture. If I should do
so now, it occurs that perhaps he places himself somewhat
upon the ground of the parable of the lost sheep which went
astray upon the mountains, and when the owner of the hundred sheep found the one that was lost, and threw it upon
his shoulders, and came home rejoicing, it was said that

there was more rejoicing over the one sheep that was lost and had been found, than over the ninety and nine in the fold. [Great cheering, renewed cheering.] The application is made by the Saviour in this parable, thus, "Verily, I say unto you, there is more rejoicing in heaven over one sinner that repenteth, than over ninety and nine just persons that need no repentance." [Cheering.]

And now, if the Judge claims the benefit of this parable, *let him repent.* [Vociferous applause.] Let him not come up here and say: I am the only just person; and you are the ninety-nine sinners! *Repentance,* before *forgiveness* is a provision of the Christian system, and on that condition alone will the Republicans grant his forgiveness. [Laughter and cheers.]

How will he prove that we have ever occupied a different position in regard to the Lecompton Constitution or any principle in it? He says he did not make his opposition on the ground as to whether it was a free or slave constitution, and he would have you understand that the Republicans made their opposition because it ultimately became a slave constitution. To make proof in favor of himself on this point, he reminds us that he opposed Lecompton before the vote was taken declaring whether the State was to be free or slave. But he forgets to say that our Republican Senator Trumbull, made a speech against Lecompton, even before he did.

Why did he oppose it? Partly, as he declares, because the members of the Convention who framed it were not fairly elected by the people; that the people were not allowed to vote unless they had been registered; and that the people of whole counties, in some instances, were not registered. For these reasons he declares the constitution was not an emanation, in any true sense, from the people. He also has an additional objection as to the mode of submitting the constitution back to the people. But bearing on the question of whether the delegates were fairly elected, a speech of his, made something more than twelve months ago, from this stand, becomes important. It was made a little while before the election of the delegates who made Lecompton. In that speech he declared there was every reason to hope and believe the election would be fair; and if any one failed to vote, it would be his own culpable fault.

I, a few days after, made a sort of answer to that speech. In that answer, I made, substantially, the very argument with which he combatted his Lecompton adversaries in the Senate last winter. I pointed to the facts that the people could not vote without being registered, and that the time for registering had gone by. I commented on it as wonderful that Judge Douglas could be ignorant of these facts, which every one else in the nation so well knew.

I now pass from popular sovereignty and Lecompton. I may have occasion to refer to one or both.

When he was preparing his plan of campaign, Napoleon like, in New York, as appears by two speeches I have heard him deliver since his arrival in Illinois, he gave special attention to a speech of mine, delivered here on the 16th of June last. He says that he carefully read that speech. He told us that at Chicago a week ago last night, and he repeated it at Bloomington last night. Doubtless, he repeated it again to-day, though I did not hear him. In the two first places— Chicago and Bloomington—I heard him; to-day I did not. [A voice—Yes; he said the same thing.] He said he had carefully examined that speech; *when*, he did not say; but there is no reasonable doubt it was when he was in New York preparing his plan of campaign. I am glad he did read it carefully. He says it was evidently prepared with great care. I freely admit it was prepared with care. I claim not to be more free from errors than others—perhaps scarcely so much; but I was very careful not to put anything in that speech as a matter of fact, or make any inferences which did not appear to me to be true, and fully warrantable. If I had made any mistake I was willing to be corrected; if I had drawn any inference in regard to Judge Douglas, or any one else, which was not warranted, I was fully prepared to modify it as soon as discovered. I planted myself upon the truth, and the truth only, so far as I knew it, or could be brought to know it.

Having made that speech with the most kindly feeling towards Judge Douglas, as manifested therein, I was gratified when I found that he had carefully examined it, and had detected no error of fact, nor any inference against him, nor any misrepresentations, of which he thought fit to complain. In neither of the two speeches I have mentioned, did he make any such complaint. I will thank any one who will inform me that he, in his speech to day, pointed out anything I had stated, respecting him, as being erroneous. I presume there is no such thing. I have reason to be gratified that the care and caution used in that speech, left it so that he, most of all others interested in discovering error, has not been able to point out one thing against him which he could say was wrong. He seizes upon the doctrines he supposes to be included in that speech, and declares that upon them will turn the issues of this campaign. He then quotes, or attempts to quote, from my speech. I will not say that he willfully misquotes, but he does fail to quote accurately. His attempt at quoting is from a passage which I believe I can quote accurately from memory. I shall make the quotation now, with some comments upon it, as I have already said, in order that the Judge shall be left entirely without excuse for misrepresenting me. I do so now, as I hope, for the last time. I do this in great caution, in order that if he repeats his misrepresentation, it shall be plain to all that he does so willfully. If, after all, he still persists, I shall be compelled to reconstruct the course I have marked out for myself, and draw upon such humble resources as I have, for a new course, better suited to the real exigencies of the case. I set out in this campaign, with the intention of conducting it strictly as a gentleman, in substance at least, if not in the outside polish. The latter I shall never be, but that which constitutes the inside of a gentleman I hope I understand, and am not less inclined to practice than others. [Cheers.] It was my purpose and expectations that this canvass would be conducted upon principle, and with fairness on both sides; and it shall not be my fault, if this purpose and expectation shall be given up.

He charges, in substance, that I invite a war of sections; that I propose all the local institutions of the different States shall become consolidated and uniform. What is there in the language of that speech which expresses such purpose, or bears such construction? I have again and again said that I would not enter into any of the States to disturb the institution of slavery. Judge Douglas said, at Bloomington, that I used language most able and ingenious for concealing what I really meant; and that while I had protested against entering into the slave States, I nevertheless did mean to go on the banks of Ohio and throw missiles into Kentucky to disturb them in their domestic institutions.

I said, in that speech, and I meant no more, that the institution of slavery ought to be placed in the very attitude where the framers of this Government placed it, and left it. I do not understand that the framers of our Constitution left the people of the free States in the attitude of firing bombs or shells into the slave States. I was not using that passage for the purpose for which he infers I did use it. I said: "We are now far advanced into the fifth year since a policy was created for the avowed object and with the confident promise of putting an end to slavery agitation. Under the operation of that policy that agitation has not only not ceased, but has constantly augmented. In my opinion it will not cease till a crisis shall have been reached and passed. 'A house divided against itself can not stand.' I believe that this Government cannot endure permanently half slave and half free. It will become all one thing or all the other. Either the opponents of slavery will arrest the further spread of it, and place it where the public mind shall rest in the belief that it is in the course of ultimate extinction, or its advocates will push it forward till it shall become alike lawful in all the States, old as well as new, North as well as South."

Now you all see, from that quotation, I did not express my *wish* on anything. In that passage I indicated no wish or purpose of my own; I simply expressed my *expectation*. Cannot the Judge perceive the distinction between a *purpose* and an *expectation*. I have often expressed an expectation to die, but I have never expressed a *wish* to die. I said at Chicago, and now repeat, that I am quite aware this government has endured, half slave and half free, for eighty-two years. I understand that little bit of history. I expressed the opinion I did, because I perceived—or thought I perceived—a new set of causes introduced. I did say, at Chicago, in my speech there, that I do wish to see the spread of slavery arrested and to see it placed where the public mind shall rest in the belief that it is in course of ultimate extinction. I said that because I supposed, when the public mind shall rest in that belief, we shall have peace on the slavery question. I have believed—and now believe—the public mind did rest on that belief up to the introduction of the Nebraska bill.

Although I have ever been opposed to slavery, so far I rested in the hope and belief that it was in course of ultimate extinction. For that reason, it had been a minor question with me. I might have been mistaken; but I had believed, and now believe, that the whole public mind, that is the mind of the great majority, had rested in that belief up to the repeal of the Missouri Compromise. But upon that event, I became convinced that either I had been resting in a delusion, or the institution was being placed on a new basis—a basis for making it perpetual, national and universal. Subsequent events have greatly confirmed me in that belief. I believe that bill to be the beginning of a conspiracy for that purpose. So believing, I have since then considered that question a paramount one. So believing, I have thought the public mind will never rest till the power of Congress to restrict the spread of it, shall again be acknowledged and exercised on the one hand, or on the other, all resistance be entirely crushed out. I have expressed that opinion, and I entertain it to-night. It is denied that there is any tendency to the nationalization of slavery in these States.

Mr. Brooks, of South Carolina, in one of his speeches, when they were presenting him with canes, silver plate, gold pitchers and the like, for assaulting Senator Sumner, distinctly affirmed his opinion that when this Constitution was formed, it was the belief of no man that slavery would last to the present day.

He said, what I think, that the framers of our Constitution placed the institution of slavery where the public mind rested in the hope that it was in course of ultimate extinction. But he went on to say that the men of the present age, by their experience, have become wiser than the framers of the Constitution; and the invention of the cotton gin had made the perpetuity of slavery a necessity in this country.

As another piece of evidence tending to the same point:— Quite recently in Virginia, a man—the owner of slaves— made a will providing that after his death certain of his slaves should have their freedom if they should so choose, and go to Liberia, rather than remain in slavery. They chose to be liberated. But the persons to whom they would descend as property, claimed them as slaves. A suit was instituted, which finally came to the Supreme Court of Virginia, and was therein decided against the slaves, upon the ground that a negro cannot make a choice—that they had no legal power to choose—could not perform the condition upon which their freedom depended.

I do not mention this with any purpose of criticising, but to connect it with the arguments as affording additional evidence of the change of sentiment upon this question of slavery in the direction of making it perpetual and national. I argue now as I did before, that there is such a tendency, and I am backed not merely by the facts, but by the open confession in the Slave States.

And now as to the Judge's inference, that because I wish to see slavery placed in the course of ultimate extinction—placed where our fathers originally placed it—I wish to annihilate the State Legislatures—to force cotton to grow upon the tops of the Green Mountains—to freeze ice in Florida—to cut lumber on the broad Illinois prairies—that I am in favor of all these ridiculous and impossible things.

It seems to me it is a complete answer to all this, to ask, if, when Congress did have the fashion of restricting slavery from free territory; when courts did have the fashion of deciding that taking a slave into a free country made him free—I say it is a sufficient answer, to ask, if any of this ridiculous nonsense about consolidation, and uniformity, did actually follow. Who heard of any such thing, because of the Ordinance of '87? because of the Missouri Restriction? because of the numerous court decisions of that character?

Now, as to the Dred Scott decision; for upon that he makes his last point at me. He boldly takes ground in favor of that decision.

This is one-half the onslaught, and one-third of the entire plan of the campaign. I am opposed to that decision in a certain sense, but not in the sense which he puts on it. I say that in so far as it decided in favor of Dred Scott's master and against Dred Scott and his family, I do not propose to disturb or resist the decision.

I never have proposed to do any such thing. I think, that in respect for judicial authority, my humble history would not suffer in a comparison with that of Judge Douglas. He would have the citizen conform his vote to that decision; the Member of Congress, his; the President, his use of the veto power. He would make it a rule of political action for the people and all the departments of the government. I would not. By resisting it as a political rule, I disturb no right of property, create no disorder, excite no mobs.

When he spoke at Chicago, on Friday evening of last week, he made this same point upon me. On Saturday evening I replied and reminded him of a Supreme Court decision which he opposed for at least several years. Last night, at Bloomington, he took some notice of that reply; but entirely forgot to remember that part of it.

He renews his onslaught upon me, forgetting to remember that I have turned the tables against himself on that very point. I renew the effort to draw his attention to it. I wish to stand erect before the country as well as Judge Douglas, on this question of judicial authority; and therefore I add something to the authority in favor of my own position. I wish to show that I am sustained by authority, in addition to that heretofore presented. I do not expect to convince the Judge. It is part of the plan of his campaign, and he will cling to it with a desperate gripe. Even, turn it upon him—turn the sharp point against him, and gaff him through—he will still cling to it till he can invent some new dodge to take the place of it.

In public speaking it is tedious reading from documents; but I must beg to indulge the practice to a limited extent. I shall read from a letter written by Mr. Jefferson in 1820, and now to be found in the seventh volume of his correspondence, at page 177. It seems he had been presented by a gentleman of the name of Jarvis with a book, or essay, or periodical, called the "Republican," and he was writing in acknowledgement of the present, and noting some of its contents. After expressing the hope that the work will produce a favorable effect upon the minds of the young, he proceeds to say:

That it will have this tendency may be expected, and for that reason I feel an urgency to note what I deem an error in it, the more requiring notice as your opinion is strengthened by that of many others. You seem in pages 84 and 148, to consider the judges as the ultimate arbiters of all constitutional questions—a very dangerous doctrine indeed and one which would place us under the despotism of an oligarchy. Our judges are as honest as other men, and not more so. They have, with others, the same passions for party, for power, and the privilege of their corps. Their maxim is, "boni judicis est ampliare jurisdictionem"; and their power is the more dangerous as they are in office for life, and not responsible, as the other functionaries are, to the elective control. The Constitution has erected no such single tribunal, knowing that to whatever hands confided, with the corruptions of time and party, its members would become despots. It has more wisely made all the departments co-equal and co-sovereign within themselves.

Thus we see the power claimed for the Supreme Court by Judge Douglas, Mr. Jefferson holds, would reduce us to the despotism of an oligarchy.

Now, I have said no more than this—in fact, never quite so much as this—at least I am sustained by Mr. Jefferson.

Let us go a little further. You remember we once had a national bank. Some one owed the bank a debt; he was sued and sought to avoid payment, on the ground that the bank was unconstitutional. The case went to the Supreme Court, and therein it was decided that the bank was constitutional. The whole Democratic party revolted against that decision. General Jackson himself asserted that he, as President, would not be bound to hold a national bank to be constitutional, even though the Court had decided it to be so. He fell in precisely with the view of Mr. Jefferson, and acted upon it under his official oath, in vetoing a charter for a national bank. The declaration that Congress does not possess this constitutional power to charter a bank, has gone into the Democratic platform, at their national conventions, and was brought forward and reaffirmed in their last convention at Cincinnati. They have contended for that declaration, in the very teeth of the Supreme Court, for more than a quarter of a century. In fact, they have reduced the decision to an absolute nullity. That decision, I repeat, is repudiated in the Cincinnati platform; and still, as if to show that effrontery can go no farther, Judge Douglas vaunts in the very speeches in which he denounces me for opposing the Dred Scott decision, that he stands on the Cincinnati platform.

Now, I wish to know what the Judge can charge upon me, with respect to decisions of the Supreme Court which does not lie in all its length, breadth, and proportions at his own door. The plain truth is simply this: Judge Douglas is *for* Supreme Court decisions when he likes and against them when he does not like them. He is for the Dred Scott decision because it tends to nationalize slavery—because it is part of the original combination for that object. It so happens, singularly enough, that I never stood opposed to a decision of the Supreme Court till this. On the contrary, I have no recollection that he was ever particularly in favor of one till this. He never was in favor of any, nor opposed to any, till the present one, which helps to nationalize slavery.

Free men of Sangamon—free men of Illinois—free men everywhere—judge ye between him and me, upon this issue.

He says this Dred Scott case is a very small matter at most—that it has no practical effect; that at best, or rather, I suppose, at worst, it is but an abstraction. I submit that the proposition that the thing which determines whether a man is free or a slave, is rather *concrete* than *abstract*. I think you would conclude that it was, if your liberty depended upon it, and so would Judge Douglas if his liberty depended upon it. But suppose it was on the question of spreading slavery over the new territories that he considers it as being merely an abstract matter, and one of no practical importance. How has the planting of slavery in new countries always been effected? It has now been decided that slavery cannot be kept out of our new territories by any legal means. In what does our new territories now differ in this respect, from the old colonies when slavery was first planted within them? It was planted as Mr. Clay once declared, and as history proves true, by individual men in spite of the wishes of the people; the mother government refusing to prohibit it, and withholding from the people of the colonies the authority to prohibit it for themselves. Mr. Clay says this was one of the great and just causes of complaint against Great Britain by the colonies, and the best apology we can now make for having the institution amongst us. In that precise condition our Nebraska politicians have at last suc-

ceeded in placing our own new territories; the government
will not prohibit slavery within them, nor allow the people
to prohibit it.

I defy any man to find any difference between the policy
which originally planted slavery in these colonies and that
policy which now prevails in our own new Territories. If it
does not go into them, it is only because no individual wishes
it to go. The Judge indulged himself, doubtless, to-day, with
the question as to what I am going to do with or about the
Dred Scott decision. Well, Judge, will you please tell me what
you did about the Bank decision? Will you not graciously allow us to do with the Dred Scott decision precisely as you did
with the Bank decision? You succeeded in breaking down the
moral effect of that decision; did you find it necessary to
amend the Constitution? or to set up a court of negroes in
order to do it?

There is one other point. Judge Douglas has a very affec-
tionate leaning towards the Americans and old Whigs. Last
evening, in a sort of weeping tone, he described to us a death
bed scene. He had been called to the side of Mr. Clay, in his
last moments, in order that the genius of "popular sovereignty" might duly descend from the dying man and settle
upon him, the living and most worthy successor. He could do
no less than promise that he would devote the remainder of
his life to "popular sovereignty;" and then the great statesman
departs in peace. By this part of the "plan of the campaign,"
the Judge has evidently promised himself that tears shall be
drawn down the cheeks of all old Whigs, as large as half
grown apples.

Mr. Webster, too, was mentioned; but it did not quite
come to a death-bed scene, as to him. It would be amusing, if
it were not disgusting, to see how quick these compromise-
breakers administer on the political effects of their dead adversaries, trumping up claims never before heard of, and
dividing the assets among themselves. If I should be found
dead tomorrow morning, nothing but my insignificance could
prevent a speech being made on my authority, before the end
of next week. It so happens that in that "popular sovereignty"
with which Mr. Clay was identified, the Missouri Compromise was expressly reserved; and it was a little singular if

Mr. Clay cast his mantle upon Judge Douglas on purpose to have that compromise repealed.

Again, the Judge did not keep faith with Mr. Clay when he first brought in his Nebraska bill. He left the Missouri Compromise unrepealed, and in his report accompanying the bill, he told the world he did it on purpose. The manes of Mr. Clay must have been in great agony, till thirty days later, when "popular sovereignty" stood forth in all its glory.

One more thing. Last night Judge Douglas tormented himself with horrors about my disposition to make negroes perfectly equal with white men in social and political relations. He did not stop to show that I have said any such thing, or that it legitimately follows from any thing I have said, but he rushes on with his assertions. I adhere to the Declaration of Independence. If Judge Douglas and his friends are not willing to stand by it, let them come up and amend it. Let them make it read that all men are created equal except negroes. Let us have it decided, whether the Declaration of Independence, in this blessed year of 1858, shall be thus amended. In his construction of the Declaration last year he said it only meant that Americans in America were equal to Englishmen in England. Then, when I pointed out to him that by that rule he excludes the Germans, the Irish, the Portuguese, and all the other people who have come amongst us since the Revolution, he reconstructs his construction. In his last speech he tells us it meant Europeans.

I press him a little further, and ask if it meant to include the Russians in Asia? or does he mean to exclude that vast population from the principles of our Declaration of Independence? I expect ere long he will introduce another amendment to his definition. He is not at all particular. He is satisfied with any thing which does not endanger the nationalizing of negro slavery. It may draw white men down, but it must not lift negroes up. Who shall say, "I am the superior, and you are the inferior?"

My declarations upon this subject of negro slavery may be misrepresented, but can not be misunderstood. I have said that I do not understand the Declaration to mean that all men were created equal in all respects. They are not our equal in color; but I suppose that it does mean to declare that all men are equal in some respects; they are equal in their right to "life, liberty, and the pursuit of happiness." Certainly the negro is not our equal in color—perhaps not in many other respects; still, in the right to put into his mouth the bread that his own hands have earned, he is the equal of every other man, white or black. In pointing out that more has been given you, you can not be justified in taking away the little which has been given him. All I ask for the negro is that if you do not like him, let him alone. If God gave him but little, that little let him enjoy.

When our Government was established, we had the institution of slavery among us. We were in a certain sense compelled to tolerate its existence. It was a sort of necessity. We had gone through our struggle and secured our own independence. The framers of the Constitution found the institution of slavery amongst their other institutions at the time. They found that by an effort to eradicate it, they might lose much of what they had already gained. They were obliged to bow to the necessity. They gave power to Congress to abolish the slave trade at the end of twenty years. They also prohibited it in the Territories where it did not exist. They did what they could and yielded to the necessity for the rest. I also yield to all which follows from that necessity. What I would most desire would be the separation of the white and black races.

One more point on this Springfield speech which Judge Douglas says he has read so carefully. I expressed my belief in the existence of a conspiracy to perpetuate and nationalize slavery. I did not profess to know it, nor do I now. I showed the part Judge Douglas had played in the string of facts, constituting to my mind, the proof of that conspiracy. I showed the parts played by others.

I charged that the people had been deceived into carrying the last Presidential election, by the impression that the people of the Territories might exclude slavery if they chose, when it was known in advance by the conspirators, that the Court was to decide that neither Congress nor the people could so exclude slavery. These charges are more distinctly made than any thing else in the speech.

Judge Douglas has carefully read and re-read that speech. He has not, so far as I know, contradicted those charges. In the two speeches which I heard he certainly did not. On his own tacit admission I renew that charge. I charge him with having been a party to that conspiracy and to that deception for the sole purpose of nationalizing slavery.

Mr. Lincoln sat down amidst loud and continued cheering.

July 17, 1858

To John Mathers

Jno. Mathers, Esq.   Springfield,
My dear Sir: July 20 1858
Your kind and interesting letter of the 19th. was duly received. Your suggestions as to placing one's self on the offensive, rather than the *defensive*, are certainly correct. That is a point which I shall not disregard. I spoke here on Saturday-night. The speech, not very well reported, appears in the State Journal of this morning. You, doubtless, will see it; and I hope you will perceive in it, that I am already improving. I would mail you a copy now, but I have not one at hand.

I thank you for your letter; and shall be pleased to hear from you again. Yours very truly

To Stephen A. Douglas

Hon. S. A. Douglas   Chicago, Ills.
My Dear Sir   July 24, 1858.
Will it be agreeable to you to make an arrangement for you and myself to divide time, and address the same audiences during the present canvass? Mr. Judd, who will hand you this, is authorized to receive your answer; and, if agreeable to you, to enter into the terms of such arrangement. Your Obt. Servt

To Joseph Gillespie

Hon. J. Gillespie.   Springfield,
My dear Sir   July 25. 1858.

Your doleful letter of the 18th. was received on my return
from Chicago last night. I do hope you are worse scared than
hurt, though you ought to know best. We must not lose that
district. We must make a job of it, and save it. Lay hold of the
proper agencies and secure all the Americans you can, at once.
I do hope, on closer inspection, you will find they are not half
gone. Make a little test. Run down one of the poll-books of
the Edwardsville precinct, and take the first hundred known
American names. Then quietly ascertain how many of them
are actually going for Douglas. I think you will find less than
fifty. But even if you find fifty, make sure of the other fifty—
that is, make sure of all you can at all events. We will set other
agencies to work, which shall compensate for the loss of a
good many Americans. Dont fail to check the stampede at
once. Trumbull, I think will be with you before long. There is
much he can not do, and *some* he can. I have reason to hope
there will be other help of an appropriate kind. Write me
again. Yours as ever

To Gustave P. Koerner

Hon. G. Koerner   Springfield,
My dear Sir,   July 25. 1858.

Yours of late date was duly received. Many germans here
are anxious to have Mr. Hecker come; but I suppose your
judgement is best. I write this mostly because I learn we are
in great danger in Madison. It is said half the Americans are
going for Douglas; and that slam will ruin us if not counter-
acted. It appears to me this fact of itself, would make it, at
least no harder for us to get accessions from the Germans. We
must make a special job of Madison. Every edge must be
made to cut. Can not you, Canisius, and some other influential Germans set a plan on foot that shall gain us accession
from the Germans, and see that, at the election, none are
cheated in their ballots? Gillespie thinks that thing is some-

times practiced on the German in Madison. Others of us must find the way to save as many Americans as possible. Still others must do other things. Nothing must be left undone. Elsewhere things look reasonably well. Please write me. Yours as ever

To Stephen A. Douglas

Hon. S. A. Douglas   Springfield,
Dear Sir   July 29. 1858

Yours of the 24th. in relation to an arrangement to divide time and address the same audiences, is received; and, in apology for not sooner replying, allow me to say that when I sat by you at dinner yesterday I was not aware that you had answered my note, nor certainly, that my own note had been presented to you. An hour after I saw a copy of your answer in the Chicago Times; and, reaching home, I found the original awaiting me. Protesting that your insinuations of attempted unfairness on my part are unjust; and with the hope that you did not very considerately make them, I proceed to reply. To your statement that "It has been suggested recently that an arrangement had been made to bring out a third candidate for the U. S. Senate who, with yourself, should canvass the state in opposition to me &c." I can only say that such suggestion must have been made by yourself; for certainly none such has been made by, or to me; or otherwise, to my knowledge. Surely you did not *deliberately* conclude, as you insinuate, that I was expecting to draw you into an arrangement, of terms to be agreed on by yourself, by which a third candidate, and my self, "in concert, might be able to take the opening and closing speech in every case."

As to your surprise that I did not sooner make the proposal to divide time with you, I can only say I made it as soon as I resolved to make it. I did not know but that such proposal would come from you; I waited respectfully to see. It may have been well known to you that you went to Springfield for the purpose of agreeing on the plan of campaign; but it was not so known to me. When your appointments were announced in the papers, extending only to the 21st. of August, I, for the first time, considered it certain that you would make no proposal to me; and then resolved, that if my friends concurred, I would make one to you. As soon thereafter as I could see and consult with friends satisfactorily, I did make the proposal. It did not occur to me that the proposed arrangement could derange your plan, after the latest of your appointments already made. After that, there was, before the election, largely over two months of clear time.

For you to say that we have already spoken at Chicago and Springfield, and that on both occasions I had the concluding speech, is hardly a fair statement. The truth rather is this. At Chicago, July 9th, you made a carefully prepared conclusion on my speech of June 16th.; twentyfour hours after I made a hasty conclusion on yours of the 9th.; you had six days to prepare, and concluded on me again at Bloomington on the 16th.; twentyfour hours after I concluded on you again at Springfield. In the mean time you had made another conclusion on me at Springfield, which I did not hear, and of the contents of which I knew nothing when I spoke; so that your speech made in day-light, and mine at night of the 17th. at Springfield were both made in perfect independence of each other. The dates of making all these speeches, will show, I think, that in the matter of time for preparation, the advantage has all been on your side; and that none of the external circumstances have stood to my advantage.

I agree to an arrangement for us to speak at the seven places you have named, and at your own times, provided you name the times at once, so that I, as well as you, can have to myself the time not covered by the arrangement. As to other details, I wish perfect reciprocity, and no more. I wish as much time as you, and that conclusions shall alternate. That is all. Your obedient Servant

P.S. As matters now stand, I shall be at no more of your exclusive meetings; and for about a week from to-day a letter from you will reach me at Springfield.

To Henry Asbury

Henry Asbury, Esq   Springfield,
My dear Sir   July 31. 1858.

Yours of the 28th. is received. The points you propose to press upon Douglas, he will be very hard to get up to. But I think you labor under a mistake when you say no one cares how he answers. This implies that it is equal with him whether he is injured here or at the South. That is a mistake. He cares nothing for the South—he knows he is already dead there. He only leans Southward now to keep the Buchanan party from growing in Illinois. You shall have hard work to get him directly to the point whether a teritorial Legislature has or has not the power to exclude slavery. But if you succeed in bringing him to it, though he will be compelled to say it possesses no such power; he will instantly take ground that slavery can not actually exist in the teritories, unless the people desire it, and so give it protective teritorial legislation. If this offends the South he will let it offend them; as at all events he means to hold on to his chances in Illinois. You will soon learn by the papers that both the Judge and myself, are to be in Quincy on the 13th. of October, when & where I expect the pleasure of seeing you. Yours very truly

To Stephen A. Douglas

Hon. S. A. Douglas: Springfield,
Dear Sir   July 31. 1858.

Yours of yesterday, naming places, times, and terms, for joint discussions between us, was received this morning. Although, by the terms, as you propose, you take *four* openings and closes to my *three*, I accede, and thus close the arrangement. I direct this to you at Hillsboro; and shall try to have both your letter and this, appear in the Journal and Register of Monday morning. Your Obt. Servt.

On Slavery and Democracy

As I would not be a *slave*, so I would not be a *master*. This expresses my idea of democracy. Whatever differs from this, to the extent of the difference, is no democracy.

1858?

To Jediah F. Alexander

J. F. Alexander, Esq   Springfield,
My dear Sir   Aug. 2. 1858.

I should be with Judge Douglas at your town on the 4th. had he not intimated in his published letter, that my presence would be considered an intrusion. I shall soon publish a string of appointments following his present track, which will bring me to Greenville about the 11th. of Sept. I hope to have Judge Trumbull with me. Yours truly

To Burton C. Cook

Hon: B. C. Cook   Springfield,
My dear Sir   Aug. 2. 1858 –

I have a letter from a very true friend, and intelligent man, insisting that there is a plan on foot in La Salle and Bureau, to run Douglas republicans for Congress, and for the Legislature in those counties, if they can only get the encouragement of our folks nominating pretty extreme abolitionists. It is thought they will do nothing if our folks nominate men, who are not very obnoxious to the charge of abolitionism. Please have your eye upon this.

Signs are looking pretty fair. Yours very truly

To William H. Grigsby

Wm. H. Grigsby, Esq.   Springfield,
My dear Sir: Aug: 3. 1858

Yours of the 14th. of July, desiring a situation in my law office, was received several days ago. My partner, Mr. Herndon, controls our office in this respect, and I have known of his declining at least a dozen applications like yours within the last three months.

If you wish to be a lawyer, attach no consequence to the *place* you are in, or the *person* you are with; but get books, sit down anywhere, and go to reading for yourself. That will make a lawyer of you quicker than any other way. Yours Respectfully,

To Henry E. Dummer

Friend Dummer   Springfield, Aug: 5. 1858

Yours, not dated, just received. No accident preventing, I shall be at Beardstown on the 12th. I thank you for the contents of your letter generally. I have not time now to notice the various points you suggest; but I will say I do not understand the Republican party to be committed to the proposition "No more slave States." I think they are not so committed. Most certainly they prefer there should be no more; but I know there are many of them who think we are under obligation to admit slave states from Texas, if such shall be presented for admission; but I think the party as such is not committed either way. Your friend as ever

Portion of Speech at Havana, Illinois

A QUESTION OF MUSCLE

I am informed, that my distinguished friend yesterday became a little excited, nervous, perhaps, [laughter] and he said something about *fighting*, as though referring to a pugilistic encounter between him and myself. Did anybody in this audience hear him use such language? [Cries of yes.] I am informed, further, that somebody in *his* audience, rather more excited, or nervous, than himself, took off his coat, and offered to take the job off Judge Douglas' hands, and fight Lincoln himself. Did anybody here witness that warlike proceeding? [Laughter, and cries of yes.] Well, I merely desire to say that I shall fight neither Judge Douglas nor his second. [Great laughter.] I shall not do this for two reasons, which I will now explain. In the first place, a fight would *prove* nothing which is in issue in this contest. It might establish that Judge Douglas is a more muscular man than myself, or it might demonstrate that I am a more muscular man than Judge Douglas. But this question is not referred to in the Cincinnati platform, nor in either of the Springfield platforms. [Great laughter.] Neither result would prove him right or me wrong. And so of the gentleman who volunteered to do his fighting for him. If my fighting Judge Douglas would not prove anything, it would certainly prove nothing for me to fight his bottle-holder. [Continued laughter.]

My second reason for not having a personal encounter with the Judge is, that I don't believe he wants it himself. [Laughter.] He and I are about the best friends in the world, and when we get together he would no more think of fighting me than of fighting his wife. Therefore, ladies and gentlemen, when the Judge talked about fighting, he was not giving vent to any ill-feeling of his own, but merely trying to excite—well, *enthusiasm* against me on the part of his audience. And as I find he was tolerably successful, we will call it quits. [Cheers and laughter.]

TWO UPON ONE

One other matter of trifling consequence, and I will proceed. I understand that Judge Douglas yesterday referred to the fact that both Judge Trumbull and myself are making speeches throughout the State to beat him for the Senate, and that he tried to create a sympathy by the suggestion that this was playing *two upon one* against him. It is true that Judge Trumbull has made a speech in Chicago, and I believe he intends to co-operate with the Republican Central Committee in their arrangements for the campaign to the extent of making other speeches in different parts of the State. Judge Trumbull is a Republican, like myself, and he naturally feels a lively interest in the success of his party. Is there anything wrong about that? But I will show you how little Judge Douglas's appeal to your sympathies amounts to. At the next general election, two years from now, a Legislature will be elected which will have to choose a successor to Judge Trumbull. Of course there will be an effort to fill his place with a Democrat. This person, whoever he may be, is probably out making stump-speeches against me, just as Judge Douglas is. It may be one of the present Democratic members of the lower house of Congress—but who ever he is, I can tell you he has got to make some stump speeches now, or his party will not nominate him for the seat occupied by Judge Trumbull. Well, are not Judge Douglas and this man playing *two upon one* against me, just as much as Judge Trumbull and I are playing *two upon one* against Judge Douglas? [Laughter.] And if it happens that there are two Democratic aspirants for Judge Trumbull's place, are they not playing *three upon one* against me, just as we are playing *two upon one* against Judge Douglas? [Renewed laughter.]

August 14, 1858

Draft of a Speech

When Douglas ascribes such to me, he does so, not by argument, but by mere burlesque on the art and name of argument—by such fantastic arrangements of words as prove "horse-chestnuts to be chestnut horses." In the main I shall trust an intelligent community to learn my objects and aims from what I say and do myself, rather than from what Judge Douglas may say of me. But I must not leave the judge just yet. When he has burlesqued me into a position which I never thought of assuming myself, he will, in the most benevolent and patronizing manner imaginable, compliment me by saying "he has no doubt I am perfectly conscientious in it." I thank him for that word "conscientious." It turns my attention to the wonderful evidences of conscience he manifests. When he assumes to be the first discoverer and sole advocate of the right of a people to govern themselves, he is conscientious. When he affects to understand that a man, putting a hundred slaves through under the lash, is simply governing himself, he is more conscientious. When he affects not to

know that the Dred Scott decision forbids a territorial legislature to exclude slavery, he is most conscientious. When, as in
his last Springfield speech, he declares that I say, unless I shall
play my batteries successfully, so as to abolish slavery in every
one of the States, the Union shall be dissolved, he is absolutely bursting with conscience. It is nothing that I have never
said any such thing. With some men it might make a difference; but consciences differ in different individuals. Judge
Douglas has a greater conscience than most men. It corresponds with his other points of greatness. Judge Douglas
amuses himself by saying I wish to go into the Senate on my
qualifications as a prophet. He says he has known some other
prophets, and does not think very well of them. Well, others
of us have also known some prophets. We know one who
nearly five years ago prophesied that the "Nebraska bill"
would put an end to slavery agitation in next to no time—
one who has renewed that prophecy at least as often as
quarter-yearly ever since; and still the prophecy has not been
fulfilled. That one might very well go out of the Senate on his
qualifications as a false prophet.

Allow me now, in my own way, to state with what aims
and objects I did enter upon this campaign. I claim no extraordinary exemption from personal ambition. That I like
preferment as well as the average of men may be admitted.
But I protest I have not entered upon this hard contest solely,
or even chiefly, for a mere personal object. I clearly see, as I
think, a powerful plot to make slavery universal and perpetual
in this nation. The effort to carry that plot through will be
persistent and long continued, extending far beyond the senatorial term for which Judge Douglas and I are just now
struggling. I enter upon the contest to contribute my humble
and temporary mite in opposition to that effort.

At the Republican State convention at Springfield I made a
speech. That speech has been considered the opening of the
canvass on my part. In it I arrange a string of incontestable
facts which, I think, prove the existence of a conspiracy to
nationalize slavery. The evidence was circumstantial only; but
nevertheless it seemed inconsistent with every hypothesis,
save that of the existence of such conspiracy. I believe the
facts can be explained to-day on no other hypothesis. Judge

Douglas can so explain them if any one can. From warp to woof his handiwork is everywhere woven in.

At New York he finds this speech of mine, and devises his plan of assault upon it. At Chicago he develops that plan. Passing over, unnoticed, the obvious purport of the whole speech, he cooks up two or three issues upon points not discussed by me at all, and then authoritatively announces that these are to be the issues of the campaign. Next evening I answer, assuring him that he misunderstands me—that he takes issues which I have not tendered. In good faith I try to set him right. If he really has misunderstood my meaning, I give him language that can no longer be misunderstood. He will have none of it. At Bloomington, six days later, he speaks again, and perverts me even worse than before. He seems to have grown confident and jubilant, in the belief that he has entirely diverted me from my purpose of fixing a conspiracy upon him and his co-workers. Next day he speaks again at Springfield, pursuing the same course, with increased confidence and recklessness of assertion. At night of that day I speak again. I tell him that as he has carefully read my speech making the charge of conspiracy, and has twice spoken of the speech without noticing the charge, upon his own tacit admission I renew the charge against him. I call him, and take a default upon him. At Clifton, ten days after, he comes in with a plea. The substance of that plea is that he never passed a word with Chief Justice Taney as to what his decision was to be in the Dred Scott case; that I ought to know that he who affirms what he does not know to be true falsifies as much as he who affirms what he does know to be false; and that he would pronounce the whole charge of conspiracy a falsehood, were it not for his own self-respect!

Now I demur to this plea. Waiving objection that it was not filed till after default, I demur to it on the merits. I say it does not meet the case. What if he did not pass a word with Chief Justice Taney? Could he not have as distinct an understanding, and play his part just as well, without directly passing a word with Taney, as with it? But suppose we construe this part of the plea more broadly than he puts it himself— suppose we construe it, as in an answer in chancery, to be a denial of all knowledge, information, or belief of such conspiracy. Still I have the right to prove the conspiracy, even against his answer; and there is much more than the evidence of two witnesses to prove it by. Grant that he has no knowledge, information, or belief of such conspiracy, and what of it? That does not disturb the facts in evidence. It only makes him the dupe, instead of a principal, of conspirators.

What if a man may not affirm a proposition without knowing it to be true? I have not affirmed that a conspiracy does exist. I have only stated the evidence, and affirmed my belief in its existence. If Judge Douglas shall assert that I do not believe what I say, then he affirms what he cannot know to be true, and falls within the condemnation of his own rule.

Would it not be much better for him to meet the evidence, and show, if he can, that I have no good reason to believe the charge? Would not this be far more satisfactory than merely vociferating an intimation that he may be provoked to call somebody a liar?

So far as I know, he denies no fact which I have alleged. Without now repeating all those facts, I recall attention to only a few of them. A provision of the Nebraska bill, penned by Judge Douglas, is in these words:

> It being the true intent and meaning of this act not to legislate slavery into any Territory or State, nor exclude it therefrom, but to leave the people thereof perfectly free to form and regulate their domestic institutions in their own way, subject only to the Constitution of the United States.

In support of this the argument, evidently prepared in advance, went forth: "Why not let the people of a Territory have or exclude slavery, just as they choose? Have they any less sense or less patriotism when they settle in the Territories than when they lived in the States?"

Now the question occurs: Did Judge Douglas, even then, intend that the people of a Territory should have the power to exclude slavery? If he did, why did he vote against an amendment expressly declaring they might exclude it? With men who then knew and intended that a Supreme Court decision should soon follow, declaring that the people of a Territory could not exclude slavery, voting down such an amendment was perfectly rational. But with men not expecting or desiring such a decision, and really wishing the people to have such power, voting down such an amendment, to my mind, is wholly inexplicable.

That such an amendment was voted down by the friends of the bill, including Judge Douglas, is a recorded fact of the case. There was some real reason for so voting it down. What that reason was, Judge Douglas can tell. I believe that reason was to keep the way clear for a court decision, then expected to come, and which has since come, in the case of Dred Scott. If there was any other reason for voting down that amendment, Judge Douglas knows of it and can tell it. Again, in the before-quoted part of the Nebraska bill, what means the provision that the people of the "State" shall be left perfectly free, subject only to the Constitution? Congress was not therein legislating for, or about, States or the people of States. In that bill the provision about the people of "States" is the odd half of something, the other half of which was not yet quite ready for exhibition. What is that other half to be? Another Supreme Court decision, declaring that the people of a State cannot exclude slavery, is exactly fitted to be that other half. As the power of the people of the Territories and of the States is cozily set down in the Nebraska bill as being the same: so the constitutional limitations on that power will then be judicially held to be precisely the same in both Territories and States—that is, that the Constitution permits neither a Territory nor a State to exclude slavery.

With persons looking forward to such additional decision, the inserting a provision about States in the Nebraska bill was perfectly rational; but to persons not looking for such decision it was a puzzle. There was a real reason for inserting such provision. Judge Douglas inserted it, and therefore knows, and can tell, what that real reason was.

Judge Douglas's present course by no means lessens my belief in the existence of a purpose to make slavery alike lawful in all the States. This can be done by a Supreme Court decision holding that the United States Constitution forbids a State to exclude slavery; and probably it can be done in no other way. The idea of forcing slavery into a free State, or out of a slave State, at the point of the bayonet, is alike nonsensical. Slavery can only become extinct by being restricted to its present limits, and dwindling out. It can only become national by a Supreme Court decision. To such a decision, when it comes, Judge Douglas is fully committed. Such a decision acquiesced in by the people effects the whole object. Bearing this in mind, look at what Judge Douglas is doing every day. For the first sixty-five years under the United States Constitution, the practice of government had been to exclude slavery from the new free Territories. About the end of that period Congress, by the Nebraska bill, resolved to abandon this practice; and this was rapidly succeeded by a Supreme Court decision holding the practice to have always been unconstitutional. Some of us refuse to obey this decision as a political rule. Forthwith Judge Douglas espouses the decision, and denounces all opposition to it in no measured terms. He adheres to it with extraordinary tenacity; and under rather extraordinary circumstances. He espouses it not on any opinion of his that it is right within itself. On this he forbears to commit himself. He espouses it exclusively on the ground of its binding authority on all citizens—a ground which commits him as fully to the next decision as to this. I point out to him that Mr. Jefferson and General Jackson were both against him on the binding political authority of Supreme Court decisions. No response. I might as well preach Christianity to a grizzly bear as to preach Jefferson and Jackson to him.

I tell him I have often heard him denounce the Supreme Court decision in favor of a national bank. He denies the accuracy of my recollection—which seems strange to me, but I let it pass.

I remind him that he, even now, indorses the Cincinnati platform, which declares that Congress has no constitutional power to charter a bank; and that in the teeth of a Supreme Court decision that Congress has such power. This he cannot deny; and so he remembers to forget it.

I remind him of a piece of Illinois history about Supreme Court decisions—of a time when the Supreme Court of Illinois, consisting of four judges, because of one decision made, and one expected to be made, were overwhelmed by the adding of five new judges to their number; that he, Judge Douglas, took a leading part in that onslaught, ending in his sitting down on the bench as one of the five added judges. I suggest to him that as to his questions how far judges have to be catechized in advance, when appointed under such circumstances, and how far a court, so constituted, is prostituted beneath the contempt of all men, no man is better posted to answer than he, having once been entirely through the mill himself.

Still no response, except "Hurrah for the Dred Scott decision!" These things warrant me in saying that Judge Douglas adheres to the Dred Scott decision under rather extraordinary circumstances—circumstances suggesting the question, "Why does he adhere to it so pertinaciously? Why does he thus belie his whole past life? Why, with a long record more marked for hostility to judicial decisions than almost any living man, does he cling to this with a devotion that nothing can baffle?" In this age, and this country, public sentiment is every thing. *With* it, nothing can fail; *against* it, nothing can succeed. Whoever moulds public sentiment, goes deeper than he who enacts statutes, or pronounces judicial decisions. He makes possible the inforcement of these, else impossible.

Judge Douglas is a man of large influence. His bare opinion goes far to fix the opinion of others. Besides this, thousands hang their hopes upon forcing their opinions to agree with his. It is a party necessity with them to *say* they agree with him; and there is danger they will repeat the saying till they really come to believe it. Others dread, and shrink from his denunciations, his sarcasms, and his ingenious misrepresentations. The susceptable young hear lessons from him, such as their fathers never heared when they were young.

If, by all these means, he shall succeed in moulding public sentiment to a perfect accordance with his own—in bringing all men to indorse all court decisions, without caring to know whether they are right or wrong—in bringing all tongues to as perfect a silence as his own, as to there being any wrong in slavery—in bringing all to declare, with him, that they care not whether slavery be voted down or voted up—that if any people want slaves they have a right to have them—that negroes are not men—have no part in the declaration of Independence—that there is no moral question about slavery—that liberty and slavery are perfectly consistent—indeed, necessary accompaniments—that for a strong man to declare himself the *superior* of a weak one, and thereupon enslave the weak one, is the very *essence* of liberty—the most sacred right of self-government—when, I say, public sentiment shall be brought to all this, in the name of heaven, what barrier will be left against slavery being made lawful every where? Can you find *one* word of his, opposed to it? Can you *not* find many strongly favoring it? If for his life—for his eternal salvation—he was solely striving for that end, could he find any means so well adapted to reach the end?

If our Presidential election, by a mere plurality, and of doubtful significance, brought one Supreme Court decision, that no power can exclude slavery from a Teritory; how much more shall a public sentiment, in exact accordance with the sentiments of Judge Douglas bring another that no power can exclude it from a State?

And then, the negro being doomed, and damned, and forgotten, to everlasting bondage, is the white man quite certain that the tyrant demon will not turn upon him too?

c. August 1858

First Lincoln-Douglas Debate, Ottawa, Illinois

First joint debate: —August 21– 1858, at Ottawa, Illinois.
Senator Douglas' two speeches taken from the Chicago Times;
Mr. Lincoln's, from the Press & Tribune.

MR. DOUGLAS' SPEECH.

Ladies and gentlemen: I appear before you to-day for the purpose of discussing the leading political topics which now agitate the public mind. By an arrangement between Mr. Lincoln and myself, we are present here to-day for the purpose of having a joint discussion as the representatives of the two great political parties of the State and Union, upon the principles in issue between these parties and this vast concourse of people shows the deep feeling which pervades the public mind in regard to the questions dividing us.

Prior to 1854 this country was divided into two great political parties, known as the Whig and Democratic parties. Both were national and patriotic, advocating principles that were universal in their application. An old line Whig could proclaim his principles in Louisiana and Massachusetts alike. Whig principles had no boundary sectional line, they were not limited by the Ohio river, nor by the Potomac, nor by the line of the free and slave States, but applied and were proclaimed wherever the Constitution ruled or the American flag waved over the American soil. (Hear him, and three cheers.) So it was, and so it is with the great Democratic party, which, from the days of Jefferson until this period, has proven itself to be the historic party of this nation. While the Whig and Democratic parties differed in regard to a bank, the tariff, distribution, the specie circular and the sub-treasury, they agreed on the great slavery question which now agitates the Union. I say that the Whig party and the Democratic party agreed on this slavery question while they differed on those matters of expediency to which I have referred. The Whig party and the Democratic party jointly adopted the Compromise measures of 1850 as the basis of a proper and just solution of this slavery question in all its forms. Clay was the great leader, with Webster on his right and Cass on his left, and sustained by the patriots in the Whig and Democratic ranks, who had devised and enacted the Compromise measures of 1850.

In 1851, the Whig party and the Democratic party united in Illinois in adopting resolutions endorsing and approving the principles of the compromise measures of 1850, as the proper adjustment of that question. In 1852, when the Whig party assembled in Convention at Baltimore for the purpose of nominating a candidate for the Presidency, the first thing it did was to declare the compromise measures of 1850, in substance and in principle, a suitable adjustment of that question. (Here the speaker was interrupted by loud and long continued applause.) My friends, silence will be more acceptable to me in the discussion of these questions than applause. I desire to address myself to your judgment, your understanding, and your consciences, and not to your passions or your enthusiasm. When the Democratic convention assembled in Baltimore in the same year, for the purpose of nominating a Democratic candidate for the Presidency, it also adopted the compromise measures of 1850 as the basis of Democratic action. Thus you see that up to 1853–'54, the Whig party and the Democratic party both stood on the same platform with regard to the slavery question. That platform was the right of the people of each State and each Territory to decide their local and domestic institutions for themselves, subject only to the federal constitution.

During the session of Congress of 1853–'54, I introduced into the Senate of the United States a bill to organize the Territories of Kansas and Nebraska on that principle which had been adopted in the compromise measures of 1850, approved by the Whig party and the Democratic party in Illinois in 1851, and endorsed by the Whig party and the Democratic party in national convention in 1852. In order that there might be no misunderstanding in relation to the principle involved in the Kansas and Nebraska bill, I put forth the true intent and meaning of the act in these words: "It is the true intent and meaning of this act not to legislate slavery into any State or Territory, or to exclude it therefrom, but to leave the people thereof perfectly free to form and regulate their domestic institutions in their own way, subject only to the federal constitution." Thus, you see, that up to 1854, when the Kansas and Nebraska bill was brought into Congress for the purpose of carrying out the principles which both parties had up to that time endorsed and approved, there had been no division in this country in regard to that principle except the opposition of the abolitionists. In the House of Representatives of the Illinois Legislature, upon a resolution asserting that principle, every Whig and every Democrat in the House voted in the affirmative, and only four men voted against it, and those four were old line Abolitionists. (Cheers.)

In 1854, Mr. Abraham Lincoln and Mr. Trumbull entered into an arrangement, one with the other, and each with his respective friends, to dissolve the old Whig party on the one hand, and to dissolve the old Democratic party on the other, and to connect the members of both into an Abolition party under the name and disguise of a Republican party. (Laughter and cheers, hurrah for Douglas.) The terms of that arrangement between Mr. Lincoln and Mr. Trumbull have been published to the world by Mr. Lincoln's special friend, James H. Matheny, Esq., and they were that Lincoln should have Shields' place in the U.S. Senate, which was then about to become vacant, and that Trumbull should have my seat when my term expired. (Great laughter.) Lincoln went to work to abolitionize the Old Whig party all over the State, pretending that he was then as good a Whig as ever; (laughter) and Trumbull went to work in his part of the State preaching Abolitionism in its milder and lighter form, and trying to abolitionize the Democratic party, and bring old Democrats handcuffed and bound hand and foot into the Abolition camp. ("Good," "hurrah for Douglas," and cheers.) In pursuance of the arrangement, the parties met at Springfield in October, 1854, and proclaimed their new platform. Lincoln was to bring into the Abolition camp the old line Whigs, and transfer them over to Giddings, Chase, Ford, Douglass and Parson Lovejoy, who were ready to receive them and christen them in their new faith. (Laughter and cheers.) They laid down on that occasion a platform for their new Republican party, which was to be thus constructed. I have the resolutions of their State convention then held, which was the first mass State Convention ever held in Illinois by the Black Republican party, and I now hold them in my hands and will read a part of them, and cause the others to be printed. Here is the most important and material resolution of this Abolition platform.

1. *Resolved,* That we believe this truth to be self-evident, that when parties become subversive of the ends for which they are established, or incapable of restoring the government to the true principles of the constitution, it is the right and duty of the people to dissolve the political bands by which they may have been connected therewith, and to organize new parties upon such principles and with such views as the circumstances and exigencies of the nation may demand.

2. *Resolved,* That the times imperatively demand the reorganization of parties, and repudiating all previous party attachments, names and predilections, we unite ourselves together in defence of the liberty and constitution of the country, and will hereafter co-operate as the Republican party, pledged to the accomplishment of the following purposes: to bring the administration of the government back to the control of first principles; to restore Nebraska and Kansas to the position of free territories; that, as the constitution of the United States, vests in the States, and not in Congress, the power to legislate for the extradition of fugitives from labor, to repeal and entirely abrogate the fugitive slave law; to restrict slavery to those States in which it exists; to prohibit the admission of any more slave States into the Union; to abolish slavery in the District of Columbia; to exclude slavery from all the territories over which the general government has exclusive jurisdiction; and to resist the acquirements of any more territories unless the practice of slavery therein forever shall have been prohibited.

3. *Resolved,* That in furtherance of these principles we will use such constitutional and lawful means as shall seem best adapted to their accomplishment, and that we will support no man for office, under the general or State government, who is not positively and fully committed to the support of these principles, and whose personal character and conduct is not a guaranty that he is reliable, and who shall not have abjured old party allegiance and ties.

(The resolutions, as they were read, were cheered throughout.)

Now, gentlemen, your Black Republicans have cheered every one of those propositions, ("good and cheers,") and yet I venture to say that you cannot get Mr. Lincoln to come out and say that he is now in favor of each one of them. (Laughter and applause. "Hit him again.") That these propositions, one and all, constitute the platform of the Black

Republican party of this day, I have no doubt, ("good") and when you were not aware for what purpose I was reading them, your Black Republicans cheered them as good Black Republican doctrines. ("That's it," etc.) My object in reading these resolutions, was to put the question to Abraham Lincoln this day, whether he now stands and will stand by each article in that creed and carry it out. ("Good." "Hit him again.") I desire to know whether Mr. Lincoln to-day stands as he did in 1854, in favor of the unconditional repeal of the fugitive slave law. I desire him to answer whether he stands pledged to-day, as he did in 1854, against the admission of any more slave States into the Union, even if the people want them. I want to know whether he stands pledged against the admission of a new State into the Union with such a constitution as the people of that State may see fit to make. ("That's it;" "put it at him.") I want to know whether he stands to-day pledged to the abolition of slavery in the District of Columbia. I desire him to answer whether he stands pledged to the prohibition of the slave trade between the different States. ("He does.") I desire to know whether he stands pledged to prohibit slavery in all the territories of the United States, North as well as South of the Missouri Compromise line, ("Kansas too.") I desire him to answer whether he is opposed to the acquisition of any more territory unless slavery is first prohibited therein. I want his answer to these questions. Your affirmative cheers in favor of this Abolition platform is not satisfactory. I ask Abraham Lincoln to answer these questions, in order that when I trot him down to lower Egypt I may put the same questions to him. (Enthusiastic applause.) My principles are the same everywhere. (Cheers, and "hark.") I can proclaim them alike in the North, the South, the East, and the West. My principles will apply wherever the Constitution prevails and the American flag waves. ("Good," and applause.) I desire to know whether Mr. Lincoln's principles will bear transplanting from Ottawa to Jonesboro? I put these questions to him to-day distinctly, and ask an answer. I have a right to an answer ("that's so," "he can't dodge you," etc.), for I quote from the platform of the Republican party, made by himself and others at the time that party was formed, and the bargain made by Lincoln to dissolve and kill the old Whig

party, and transfer its members, bound hand and foot, to the
Abolition party, under the direction of Giddings and Fred
Douglass. (Cheers.) In the remarks I have made on this platform, and the position of Mr. Lincoln upon it, I mean nothing personally disrespectful or unkind to that gentleman. I
have known him for nearly twenty-five years. There were
many points of sympathy between us when we first got acquainted. We were both comparatively boys, and both struggling with poverty in a strange land. I was a school-teacher
in the town of Winchester, and he a flourishing grocery-
keeper in the town of Salem. (Applause and laughter.) He
was more successful in his occupation than I was in mine,
and hence more fortunate in this world's goods. Lincoln is
one of those peculiar men who perform with admirable skill
everything which they undertake. I made as good a school-
teacher as I could and when a cabinet maker I made a good
bedstead and tables, although my old boss said I succeeded
better with bureaus and secretaries than anything else;
(cheers,) but I believe that Lincoln was always more successful in business than I, for his business enabled him to get
into the Legislature. I met him there, however, and had a
sympathy with him, because of the up hill struggle we both
had in life. He was then just as good at telling an anecdote
as now. ("No doubt.") He could beat any of the boys wres-
tling, or running a foot race, in pitching quoits or tossing a
copper, could ruin more liquor than all the boys of the town
together, (uproarious laughter,) and the dignity and impartiality with which he presided at a horse race or fist fight,
excited the admiration and won the praise of everybody that
was present and participated. (Renewed laughter.) I sympathised with him, because he was struggling with difficulties and so was I. Mr. Lincoln served with me in the
Legislature in 1836, when we both retired, and he subsided,
or became submerged, and he was lost sight of as a public
man for some years. In 1846, when Wilmot introduced his
celebrated proviso, and the Abolition tornado swept over the
country, Lincoln again turned up as a member of Congress
from the Sangamon district. I was then in the Senate of the
United States, and was glad to welcome my old friend and
companion. Whilst in Congress, he distinguished himself by

his opposition to the Mexican war, taking the side of the common enemy against his own country; ("that's true,") and when he returned home he found that the indignation of the people followed him everywhere, and he was again submerged or obliged to retire into private life, forgotten by his former friends. ("And will be again.") He came up again in 1854, just in time to make this Abolition or Black Republican platform, in company with Giddings, Lovejoy, Chase, and Fred Douglass for the Republican party to stand upon. (Laughter, "Hit him again," &c.) Trumbull, too, was one of our own contemporaries. He was born and raised in old Connecticut, was bred a federalist, but removing to Georgia, turned nullifier when nullification was popular, and as soon as he disposed of his clocks and wound up his business, migrated to Illinois, (laughter,) turned politician and lawyer here, and made his appearance in 1841, as a member of the Legislature. He became noted as the author of the scheme to repudiate a large portion of the State debt of Illinois, which, if successful, would have brought infamy and disgrace upon the fair escutcheon of our glorious State. The odium attached to that measure consigned him to oblivion for a time. I helped to do it. I walked into a public meeting in the hall of the House of Representatives and replied to his repudiating speeches, and resolutions were carried over his head denouncing repudiation, and asserting the moral and legal obligation of Illinois to pay every dollar of the debt she owed and every bond that bore her seal. ("Good," and cheers.) Trumbull's malignity has followed me since I thus defeated his infamous scheme.

These two men having formed this combination to abolitionize the old Whig party and the old Democratic party, and put themselves into the Senate of the United States, in pursuance of their bargain, are now carrying out that arrangement. Matheny states that Trumbull broke faith; that the bargain was that Lincoln should be the Senator in Shields' place, and Trumbull was to wait for mine; (laughter and cheers,) and the story goes, that Trumbull cheated Lincoln, having control of four or five abolitionized Democrats who were holding over in the Senate; he would not let them vote for Lincoln, and which obliged the rest of the Abolitionists to support him in order to secure an Abolition Senator. There are a number of authorities for the truth of this besides Matheny, and I suppose that even Mr. Lincoln will not deny it. (Applause and laughter.)

Mr. Lincoln demands that he shall have the place intended for Trumbull, as Trumbull cheated him and got his, and Trumbull is stumping the State traducing me for the purpose of securing that position for Lincoln, in order to quiet him. ("Lincoln can never get it, &c.") It was in consequence of this arrangement that the Republican Convention was empanelled to instruct for Lincoln and nobody else, and it was on this account that they passed resolutions that he was their first, their last, and their only choice. Archy Williams was nowhere, Browning was nobody, Wentworth was not to be considered, they had no man in the Republican party for the place except Lincoln, for the reason that he demanded that they should carry out the arrangement. ("Hit him again.")

Having formed this new party for the benefit of deserters from Whiggery, and deserters from Democracy, and having laid down the Abolition platform which I have read, Lincoln now takes his stand and proclaims his Abolition doctrines. Let me read a part of them. In his speech at Springfield to the convention which nominated him for the Senate, he said:

In my opinion it will not cease until a crisis shall have been reached and passed. "A house divided against itself cannot stand." I believe this Government *cannot endure permanently half Slave and half Free.* I do not expect the Union to be dissolved—I do not expect the house to fall—*but I do expect it will cease to be divided.* It will become all one thing, or all the other. Either the opponents of Slavery *will arrest the further spread of it,* and place it where the public mind shall rest in the belief *that it is in the course of ultimate extinction*; or its advocates *will push it forward till it shall become alike lawful in all the States*—old as well as new, North as well as South.

("Good," "good," and cheers.)
I am delighted to hear you Black Republicans say "good." (Laughter and cheers.) I have no doubt that doctrine expresses your sentiments ("hit them again," "that's it,") and I will prove to you now, if you will listen to me, that it is revolutionary and destructive of the existence of this Gov-

ernment. ("Hurrah for Douglas," "good," and cheers.) Mr. Lincoln, in the extract from which I have read, says that this Government cannot endure permanently in the same condition in which it was made by its framers—divided into free and slave States. He says that it has existed for about seventy years thus divided, and yet he tells you that it cannot endure permanently on the same principles and in the same relative condition in which our fathers made it. ("Neither can it.") Why can it not exist divided into free and slave States? Washington, Jefferson, Franklin, Madison, Hamilton, Jay, and the great men of that day, made this Government divided into free States and slave States, and left each State perfectly free to do as it pleased on the subject of slavery. ("Right, right.") Why can it not exist on the same principles on which our fathers made it? ("It can.") They knew when they framed the Constitution that in a country as wide and broad as this, with such a variety of climate, production and interest, the people necessarily required different laws and institutions in different localities. They knew that the laws and regulations which would suit the granite hills of New Hampshire would be unsuited to the rice plantations of South Carolina, ("right, right,") and they, therefore, provided that each State should retain its own Legislature, and its own sovereignty with the full and complete power to do as it pleased within its own limits, in all that was local and not national. (Applause.) One of the reserved rights of the States, was the right to regulate the relations between Master and Servant, on the slavery question. At the time the Constitution was formed, there were thirteen States in the Union, twelve of which were slaveholding States and one a free State. Suppose this doctrine of uniformity preached by Mr. Lincoln, that the States should all be free or all be slave had prevailed and what would have been the result? Of course, the twelve slaveholding States would have overruled the one free State, and slavery would have been fastened by a Constitutional provision on every inch of the American Republic, instead of being left as our fathers wisely left it, to each State to decide for itself. ("Good, good," and three cheers for Douglas.) Here I assert that uniformity in the local laws and institutions of the different States is neither possible or desirable. If uniformity had been adopted when the government was established, it must inevitably have been the uniformity of slavery everywhere, or else the uniformity of negro citizenship and negro equality everywhere.

We are told by Lincoln that he is utterly opposed to the Dred Scott decision, and will not submit to it, for the reason that he says it deprives the negro of the rights and privileges of citizenship. (Laughter and applause.) That is the first and main reason which he assigns for his warfare on the Supreme Court of the United States and its decision. I ask you, are you in favor of conferring upon the negro the rights and privileges of citizenship? ("No, no.") Do you desire to strike out of our State Constitution that clause which keeps slaves and free negroes out of the State, and allow the free negroes to flow in, ("never,") and cover your prairies with black settlements? Do you desire to turn this beautiful State into a free negro colony, ("no, no,") in order that when Missouri abolishes slavery she can send one hundred thousand emancipated slaves into Illinois, to become citizens and voters, on an equality with yourselves? ("Never," "no.") If you desire negro citizenship, if you desire to allow them to come into the State and settle with the white man, if you desire them to vote on an equality with yourselves, and to make them eligible to office, to serve on juries, and to adjudge your rights, then support Mr. Lincoln and the Black Republican party, who are in favor of the citizenship of the negro. ("Never, never.") For one, I am opposed to negro citizenship in any and every form. (Cheers.) I believe this government was made on the white basis. ("Good.") I believe it was made by white men, for the benefit of white men and their posterity for ever, and I am in favor of confining citizenship to white men, men of European birth and descent, instead of conferring it upon negroes, Indians and other inferior races. ("Good for you." "Douglas forever.")

Mr. Lincoln, following the example and lead of all the little Abolition orators, who go around and lecture in the basements of schools and churches, reads from the Declaration of Independence, that all men were created equal, and then asks how can you deprive a negro of that equality which God and the Declaration of Independence awards to him. He and they maintain that negro equality is guarantied by the laws of God, and that it is asserted in the Declaration of Independence. If they think so, of course they have a right to say so, and so vote. I do not question Mr. Lincoln's conscientious belief that the negro was made his equal, and hence is his brother, (laughter,) but for my own part, I do not regard the negro as my equal, and positively deny that he is my brother or any kin to me whatever. ("Never." "Hit him again," and cheers.) Lincoln has evidently learned by heart Parson Lovejoy's catechism. (Laughter and applause.) He can repeat it as well as Farnsworth, and he is worthy of a medal from father Giddings and Fred Douglass for his Abolitionism. (Laughter.) He holds that the negro was born his equal and yours, and that he was endowed with equality by the Almighty, and that no human law can deprive him of these rights which were guarantied to him by the Supreme ruler of the Universe. Now, I do not believe that the Almighty ever intended the negro to be the equal of the white man. ("Never, never.") If he did, he has been a long time demonstrating the fact. (Cheers.) For thousands of years the negro has been a race upon the earth, and during all that time, in all latitudes and climates, wherever he has wandered or been taken, he has been inferior to the race which he has there met. He belongs to an inferior race, and must always occupy an inferior position. ("Good," "that's so," &c.) I do not hold that because the negro is our inferior that therefore he ought to be a slave. By no means can such a conclusion be drawn from what I have said. On the contrary, I hold that humanity and christianity both require that the negro shall have and enjoy every right, every privilege, and every immunity consistent with the safety of the society in which he lives. (That's so.) On that point, I presume, there can be no diversity of opinion. You and I are bound to extend to our inferior and dependent being every right, every privilege, every facility and immunity consistent with the public good. The question then arises what rights and privileges are consistent with the public good. This is a question which each State and each Territory must decide for itself— Illinois has decided it for herself. We have provided that the negro shall not be a slave, and we have also provided that he shall not be a citizen, but protect him in his civil rights, in his life, his person and his property, only depriving him of all political rights whatsoever, and refusing to put him on an equality with the white man. ("Good.") That policy of Illinois is satisfactory to the Democratic party and to me, and if it were to the Republicans, there would then be no question upon the subject; but the Republicans say that he ought to be made a citizen, and when he becomes a citizen he becomes your equal, with all your rights and privileges. ("He never shall.") They assert the Dred Scott decision to be monstrous because it denies that the negro is or can be a citizen under the Constitution. Now, I hold that Illinois had a right to abolish and prohibit slavery as she did, and I hold that Kentucky has the same right to continue and protect slavery that Illinois had to abolish it. I hold that New York had as much right to abolish slavery as Virginia has to continue it, and that each and every State of this Union is a sovereign power, with the right to do as it pleases upon this question of slavery, and upon all its domestic institutions. Slavery is not the only question which comes up in this controversy. There is a far more important one to you, and that is, what shall be done with the free negro? We have settled the slavery question as far as we are concerned; we have prohibited it in Illinois forever, and in doing so, I think we have done wisely, and there is no man in the State who would be more strenuous in his opposition to the introduction of slavery than I would; (cheers) but when we settled it for ourselves, we exhausted all our power over that subject. We have done our whole duty, and can do no more. We must leave each and every other State to decide for itself the same question. In relation to the policy to be pursued towards the free negroes, we have said that they shall not vote; whilst Maine, on the other hand, has said that they shall vote. Maine is a sovereign State, and has the power to regulate the qualifications of voters within her limits. I would never consent to confer the right of voting and of citizenship upon a negro, but still I am not going to quarrel with Maine for differing from me in opinion. Let Maine take care of her own negroes and fix the qualifications of her own voters to suit herself, without interfering with Illinois, and Illinois will not interfere with Maine. So with the State of New York. She allows the negro to vote provided he owns two hundred and fifty dollars' worth of property, but not otherwise. While I would not make any distinction whatever between a negro who held property and one who did not; yet if the sovereign State of New York chooses to make that distinction it is her business and not mine, and I will not quarrel with her for it. She can do as she pleases on this question if she minds her own business, and we will do the same thing. Now, my friends, if we will only act conscientiously and rigidly upon this great principle of popular sovereignty which guarantees to each State and Territory the right to do as it pleases on all things local and domestic instead of Congress interfering, we will continue at peace one with another. Why should Illinois be at war with Missouri, or Kentucky with Ohio, or Virginia with New York, merely because their institutions differ? Our fathers intended that our institutions should differ. They knew that the North and the South having different climates, productions and interests, required different institutions. This doctrine of Mr. Lincoln's of uniformity among the institutions of the different States is a new doctrine, never dreamed of by Washington, Madison, or the framers of this Government. Mr. Lincoln and the Republican party set themselves up as wiser than these men who made this government, which has flourished for seventy years under the principle of popular sovereignty, recognizing the right of each State to do as it pleased. Under that principle, we have grown from a nation of three or four millions to a nation of about thirty millions of people; we have crossed the Allegheny mountains and filled up the whole North West, turning the prairie into a garden, and building up churches and schools, thus spreading civilization and christianity where before there was nothing but savage-barbarism. Under that principle we have become from a feeble nation, the most powerful on the face of the earth, and if we only adhere to that principle, we can go forward increasing in territory, in power, in strength and in glory until the Republic of America shall be the North Star that shall guide the friends of freedom throughout the civilized world. ("Long may you live," and great applause.) And why can we not adhere to the great principle of self-government, upon which our institutions were originally based. ("We can.") I believe that this new doctrine preached by Mr. Lincoln and his party will dissolve the Union if it succeeds. They are trying to array all the Northern States in one body against the South, to excite a sectional war between the free States and the slave States, in order that the one or the other may be driven to the wall.

I am told that my time is out. Mr. Lincoln will now address you for an hour and a half, and I will then occupy a half hour in replying to him. (Three times three cheers were here given for Douglas.)

MR. LINCOLN'S REPLY.

Mr. Lincoln then came forward and was greeted with loud and protracted cheers from fully two-thirds of the audience. This was admitted by the Douglas men on the platform. It was some minutes before he could make himself heard, even by those on the stand. At last he said:

MY FELLOW-CITIZENS: When a man hears himself somewhat misrepresented, it provokes him—at least, I find it so with myself; but when the misrepresentation becomes very gross and palpable, it is more apt to amuse him. [Laughter.] The first thing I see fit to notice, is the fact that Judge Douglas alleges, after running through the history of the old Democratic and the old Whig parties, that Judge Trumbull and myself made an arrangement in 1854, by which I was to have the place of Gen. Shields in the United States Senate, and Judge Trumbull was to have the place of Judge Douglas. Now all I have to say upon that subject is, that I think no man—not even Judge Douglas—can prove it, *because it is not true*. [Cheers.] I have no doubt he is *"conscientious"* in saying it. [Laughter.] As to those resolutions that he took such a length of time to read, as being the platform of the Republican party in 1854, I say I never had anything to do with them, and I think Trumbull never had. [Renewed laughter.] Judge Douglas cannot show that either one of us ever did have any thing to do with them. I believe *this* is true about those resolutions: There was a call for a Convention to form a Republican party at Springfield, and I think that my friend Mr. Lovejoy, who is here upon this stand, had a hand in it. I think this is true, and I think if he will remember accurately, he will be able to recollect that he tried to get me into it, and I would not go in. [Cheers and laughter.] I believe it is also true, that I went away from Springfield when the Convention was in session, to attend court in Tazewell County. It is true they did place my name, though without authority, upon the Committee, and afterwards wrote me to attend the meeting of the Committee, but I refused to do so, and I never had anything to do with that organization. This is the plain truth about all that matter of the resolutions.

Now, about this story that Judge Douglas tells of Trumbull bargaining to sell out the old Democratic party, and Lincoln agreeing to sell out the old Whig party, I have the means of *knowing* about that; [laughter] Judge Douglas cannot have; and I know there is no substance to it whatever. [Applause.] Yet I have no doubt he is *"conscientious"* about it. [Laughter.] I know that after Mr. Lovejoy got into the Legislature that winter, he complained of me that I had told all the old Whigs in his district that the old Whig party was good enough for them, and some of them voted against him because I told them so. Now I have no means of totally disproving such charges as this which the Judge makes. A man cannot prove a negative, but he has a right to claim that when a man makes an affirmative charge, he must offer some proof to show the truth of what he says. I certainly cannot introduce testimony to show the negative about things, but I have a right to claim that if a man says he *knows* a thing, then he must show *how* he knows it. I always have a right to claim this, and it is not satisfactory to me that he may be "conscientious" on the subject. [Cheers and Laughter.]

Now gentlemen, I hate to waste my time on such things, but in regard to that general abolition tilt that Judge Douglas makes, when he says that I was engaged at that time in selling out and abolitionizing the old Whig party—I hope you will permit me to read a part of a printed speech that I made then at Peoria, which will show altogether a different view of the position I took in that contest of 1854.

VOICE—Put on your specs.

MR. LINCOLN—Yes, sir, I am obliged to do so. I am no longer a young man. [Laughter.]

This is the *repeal* of the Missouri Compromise. The foregoing history may not be precisely accurate in every particular; but I am sure it is sufficiently so, for all the uses I shall attempt to make of it, and in it, we have before us, the chief materials enabling us to correctly judge whether the repeal of the Missouri Compromise is right or wrong.

I think, and shall try to show, that it is wrong; wrong in its direct effect, letting slavery into Kansas and Nebraska—and wrong in its prospective principle, allowing it to spread to every other part of the wide world, where men can be found inclined to take it.

This *declared* indifference, but as I must think, covert *real* zeal for the spread of slavery, I can not but hate. I hate it because of the monstrous injustice of slavery itself. I hate it because it deprives our republican example of its just influence in the world—enables the enemies of free institutions, with plausibility, to taunt us as hypocrites—causes the real friends of freedom to doubt our sincerity, and especially because it forces so many really good men amongst ourselves into an open war with the very fundamental principles of civil liberty—criticising the Declaration of Independence, and insisting that there is no right principle of action but *self-interest*.

Before proceeding, let me say I think I have no prejudice against the Southern people. They are just what we would be in their situation. If slavery did not now exist amongst them, they would not introduce it. If it did now exist amongst us, we should not instantly give it up. This I believe of the masses north and south. Doubtless there are individuals, on both sides, who would not hold slaves under any circumstances; and others who would gladly introduce slavery anew, if it were out of existence. We know that some southern men do free their slaves, go north, and become tip-top abolitionists; while some northern ones go south, and become most cruel slave-masters.

When southern people tell us they are no more responsible for the origin of slavery, than we; I acknowledge the fact. When it is said that the institution exists, and that it is very difficult to get rid of it, in any satisfactory way, I can understand and appreciate the saying. I surely will not blame them for not doing what I should not know how to do myself. If all earthly power were given me, I should not know what to do, as to the existing institution. My first impulse would be to free all the slaves, and send them to Liberia,—to their own native land. But a moment's reflection would convince me, that whatever of high hope, (as I think there is) there may be in this, in the long run, its sudden execution is impossible. If they were all landed there in a day, they would all perish in the next ten days; and there are not surplus shipping and surplus money enough in the world to carry them there in many times ten days. What then? Free them all, and keep them among us as underlings? Is it quite certain that this betters their condition? I think I would not hold one in slavery, at any rate; yet the point is not clear enough to me to denounce people upon. What next? Free them, and make them politically and socially, our equals? My own feelings will not admit of this; and if mine would, we well know that those of the great mass of white people will not. Whether this feeling accords with justice and sound judgment, is not the sole question, if indeed, it is any part of it. A universal feeling, whether well or ill-founded, can not be safely disregarded. We can not, then, make them equals. It does seem to me that systems of gradual emancipation might be adopted; but for their tardiness in this, I will not undertake to judge our brethren of the south.

When they remind us of their constitutional rights, I acknowledge them, not grudgingly, but fully, and fairly; and I would give them any legislation for the reclaiming of their fugitives, which should not, in its stringency, be more likely to carry a free man into slavery, than our ordinary criminal laws are to hang an innocent one.

But all this; to my judgment, furnishes no more excuse for permitting slavery to go into our own free territory, than it would for reviving the African slave trade by law. The law which forbids the bringing of slaves *from* Africa; and that which has so long forbid the taking them *to* Nebraska, can hardly be distinguished on any moral principle; and the repeal of the former could find quite as plausible excuses as that of the latter.

I have reason to know that Judge Douglas *knows* that I said this. I think he has the answer here to one of the questions he put to me. I do not mean to allow him to catechise me unless he pays back for it in kind. I will not answer questions one after another unless he reciprocates, but as he made this inquiry and I have answered it before, he has got it without my getting anything in return. He has got my answer on the Fugitive Slave Law.

Now gentlemen, I don't want to read at any greater length, but this is the true complexion of all I have ever said in regard to the institution of slavery and the black race. This is the whole of it, and anything that argues me into his idea of perfect social and political equality with the negro, is but a specious and fantastic arrangement of words, by which a man can prove a horse chestnut to be a chestnut horse.

[Laughter.] I will say here, while upon this subject, that I have no purpose directly or indirectly to interfere with the institution of slavery in the States where it exists. I believe I have no lawful right to do so, and I have no inclination to do so. I have no purpose to introduce political and social equality between the white and the black races. There is a physical difference between the two, which in my judgment will probably forever forbid their living together upon the footing of perfect equality, and inasmuch as it becomes a necessity that there must be a difference, I, as well as Judge Douglas, am in favor of the race to which I belong, having the superior position. I have never said anything to the contrary, but I hold that notwithstanding all this, there is no reason in the world why the negro is not entitled to all the natural rights enumerated in the Declaration of Independence, the right to life, liberty and the pursuit of happiness. [Loud cheers.] I hold that he is as much entitled to these as the white man. I agree with Judge Douglas he is not my equal in many respects—certainly not in color, perhaps not in moral or intellectual endowment. But in the right to eat the bread, without leave of anybody else, which his own hand earns, *he is my equal and the equal of Judge Douglas, and the equal of every living man.* [Great applause.]

Now I pass on to consider one or two more of these little follies. The Judge is wofully at fault about his early friend Lincoln being a "grocery keeper." [Laughter.] I don't know as it would be a great sin, if I had been, but he is mistaken. Lincoln never kept a grocery anywhere in the world. [Laughter.] It is true that Lincoln did work the latter part of one winter in a small still house, up at the head of a hollow. [Roars of laughter.] And so I think my friend, the Judge, is equally at fault when he charges me at the time when I was in Congress of having opposed our soldiers who were fighting in the Mexican war. The Judge did not make his charge very distinctly but I can tell you what he can prove by referring to the record. You remember I was an old Whig, and whenever the Democratic party tried to get me to vote that the war had been righteously begun by the President, I would not do it. But whenever they asked for any money, or land warrants, or anything to pay the soldiers there, during all that time, I gave the same votes that Judge Douglas did. [Loud applause.] You can think as you please as to whether that was consistent. Such is the truth; and the Judge has the right to make all he can out of it. But when he, by a general charge, conveys the idea that I withheld supplies from the soldiers who were fighting in the Mexican war, or did anything else to hinder the soldiers, he is, to say the least, grossly and altogether mistaken, as a consultation of the records will prove to him.

As I have not used up so much of my time as I had supposed, I will dwell a little longer upon one or two of these minor topics upon which the Judge has spoken. He has read from my speech in Springfield, in which I say that "a house divided against itself cannot stand." Does the Judge say it *can* stand? [Laughter.] I don't know whether he does or not. The Judge does not seem to be attending to me just now, but I would like to know if it is his opinion that a house divided against itself *can stand*. If he does, then there is a question of veracity, not between him and me, but between the Judge and an authority of a somewhat higher character. [Laughter and applause.]

Now, my friends, I ask your attention to this matter for the purpose of saying something seriously. I know that the Judge may readily enough agree with me that the maxim which was put forth by the Saviour is true, but he may allege that I misapply it; and the Judge has a right to urge that, in my application, I do misapply it, and then I have a right to show that I do *not* misapply it. When he undertakes to say that because I think this nation, so far as the question of Slavery is concerned, will all become one thing or all the other, I am in favor of bringing about a dead uniformity in the various States, in all their institutions, he argues erroneously. The great variety of the local institutions in the States, springing from differences in the soil, differences in the face of the country, and in the climate, are bonds of Union. They do not make "a house divided against itself," but they make a house united. If they produce in one section of the country what is called for by the wants of another section, and this other section can supply the wants of the first, they are not matters of discord but bonds of union, true bonds of union. But can this question of slavery be considered as among *these* varieties in the institutions of the country? I leave it to you to say whether, in the history of our government, this institution of slavery has not always failed to be a bond of union, and, on the contrary, been an apple of discord and an element of division in the house. [Cries of "Yes, yes," and applause.] I ask you to consider whether, so long as the moral constitution of men's minds shall continue to be the same, after this generation and assemblage shall sink into the grave, and another race shall arise, with the same moral and intellectual development we have—whether, if that institution is standing in the same irritating position in which it now is, it will not continue an element of division? [Cries of "Yes, yes."] If so, then I have a right to say that in regard to this question, the Union is a house divided against itself, and when the Judge reminds me that I have often said to him that the institution of slavery has existed for eighty years in some States, and yet it does not exist in some others, I agree to the fact, and I account for it by looking at the position in which our fathers originally placed it—restricting it from the new Territories where it had not gone, and legislating to cut off its source by the abrogation of the slave trade, thus putting the seal of legislation *against its spread.* The public mind *did* rest in the belief that it was in the course of ultimate extinction. [Cries of "Yes, yes."] But lately, I think—and in this I charge nothing on the Judge's motives—lately, I think, that he, and those acting with him, have placed that institution on a new basis, which looks to the *perpetuity and nationalization of slavery.* [Loud cheers.] And while it is placed upon this new basis, I say, and I have said, that I believe we shall not have peace upon the question until the opponents of slavery arrest the further spread of it, and place it where the public mind shall rest in the belief that it is in the course of ultimate extinction; or, on the other hand, that its advocates will push it forward until it shall become alike lawful in all the States, old as well as new, North as well as South. Now, I believe if we could arrest the spread, and place it where Washington, and Jefferson, and Madison placed it, it *would be* in the course of ultimate extinction, and the public mind *would,* as for eighty years past, believe that it was in the course of ultimate extinction. The crisis would be past and the institution might be let alone for a hundred years, if it should live so long, in the States where it exists, yet it would be going out of existence in the way best for both the black and the white races. [Great cheering.]

A VOICE—Then do you repudiate Popular Sovereignty?

MR. LINCOLN—Well, then, let us talk about Popular Sovereignty! [Laughter.] What is Popular Sovereignty? [Cries of "A humbug," "a humbug."] Is it the right of the people to have Slavery or not have it, as they see fit, in the territories? I will state—and I have an able man to watch me—my understanding is that Popular Sovereignty, as now applied to the question of Slavery, does allow the people of a Territory to have Slavery if they want to, but does not allow them *not* to have it if they *do not* want it. [Applause and laughter.] I do not mean that if this vast concourse of people were in a Territory of the United States, any one of them would be obliged to have a slave if he did not want one; but I do say that, as I understand the Dred Scott decision, if any one man wants slaves, all the rest have no way of keeping that one man from holding them.

When I made my speech at Springfield, of which the Judge complains, and from which he quotes, I really was not thinking of the things which he ascribes to me at all. I had no thought in the world that I was doing anything to bring about a war between the free and slave States. I had no thought in the world that I was doing anything to bring about a political and social equality of the black and white races. It never occurred to me that I was doing anything or favoring anything to reduce to a dead uniformity all the local institutions of the various States. But I must say, in all fairness to him, if he thinks I am doing something which leads to these bad results, it is none the better that I did not mean it. It is just as fatal to the country, if I have any influence in producing it, whether I intend it or not. But can it be true, that placing this institution upon the original basis—the basis upon which our fathers placed it—can have any tendency to set the Northern and the Southern States at war with one another, or that it can have any tendency to make the people of Vermont raise sugar cane, because they raise it in Louisiana, or that it can compel the people of Illinois to cut pine logs on the Grand Prairie, where they will not grow, because they cut pine logs in Maine, where they do grow? [Laughter.] The Judge says this is a new principle started in regard to this question. Does the Judge claim that he is working on the plan of the founders of government? I think he says in some of his speeches—indeed I have one here now—that he saw evidence of a policy to allow slavery to be south of a certain line, while north of it should be excluded, and he saw an indisposition on the part of the country to stand upon that policy, and therefore he set about studying the subject upon *original principles*, and upon *original principles* he got up the Nebraska bill! I am fighting it upon these "original principles"—fighting it in the Jeffersonian, Washingtonian, and Madisonian fashion. [Laughter and applause.]

Now my friends I wish you to attend for a little while to one or two other things in that Springfield speech. My main object was to show, so far as my humble ability was capable of showing to the people of this country, what I believed was the truth—that there was a *tendency*, if not a conspiracy among those who have engineered this slavery question for the last four or five years, to make slavery perpetual and universal in this nation. Having made that speech principally for that object, after arranging the evidences that I thought tended to prove my proposition, I concluded with this bit of comment:

We cannot absolutely know that these exact adaptations are the result of pre-concert, but when we see a lot of framed timbers, different portions of which we know have been gotten out at different times and places, and by different workmen—Stephen, Franklin, Roger and James, for instance—and when we see these timbers joined together, and see they exactly make the frame of a house or a mill, all the tenons and mortices exactly fitting and all the lengths and proportions of the different pieces exactly adapted to their respective places and not a piece too many or too few—not omitting even the scaffolding—or if a single piece be lacking we see the place in the frame exactly fitted and prepared yet to bring such piece in—in such a case we feel it impossible not to believe that Stephen and Franklin, and Roger and James, all understood one another from the beginning, and all worked upon a common plan or draft drawn before the first blow was struck. [Great cheers.]

When my friend, Judge Douglas, came to Chicago, on the 9th of July, this speech having been delivered on the 16th of June, he made an harangue there, in which he took hold of this speech of mine, showing that he had carefully read it; and while he paid no attention to *this* matter at all, but complimented me as being a "kind, amiable, and intelligent gentleman," notwithstanding I had said this; he goes on and eliminates, or draws out, from my speech this tendency of mine to set the States at war with one another, to make all the institutions uniform, and set the niggers and white people to marrying together. [Laughter.] Then, as the Judge had complimented me with these pleasant titles, (I must confess to my weakness,) I was a little "taken," [laughter] for it came from a great man. I was not very much accustomed to flattery, and it came the sweeter to me. I was rather like the Hoosier, with the gingerbread, when he said he reckoned he loved it better than any other man, and got less of it. [Roars of laughter.] As the Judge had so flattered me, I could not make up my mind that he meant to deal unfairly with me; so I went to work to show him that he misunderstood the whole scope of my speech, and that I really never intended to set the people at war with one another. As an illustration, the next time I met him, which was at Springfield, I used this expression, that I claimed no right under the Constitution, nor had I any inclination, to enter into the Slave States and interfere with the institutions of slavery. He says upon that: Lincoln will not enter into the Slave States, but will go to the banks of the Ohio, on this side, and shoot over! [Laughter.] He runs on, step by step, in the horse-chestnut style of argument, until in the Springfield speech, he says, "Unless he shall be successful in firing his batteries until he shall have extinguished slavery in all the States, the Union shall be dissolved." Now I don't think that was exactly the way to treat a kind, amiable, intelligent gentleman. [Roars of laughter.] I know if I had asked the Judge to show when or where it was I had said that, if I didn't succeed in firing into the Slave States until slavery should be extinguished, the Union should be dissolved, he could not have shown it. I understand what he would do. He would say, "I don't mean to quote from you, but this was the *result* of what you say." But I have the right to ask, and I do ask now, Did you not put it in such a form that an ordinary reader or listener would take it as an expression *from me?* [Laughter.]

In a speech at Springfield, on the night of the 17th, I thought I might as well attend to my own business a little, and I recalled his attention as well as I could to this charge of conspiracy to nationalize Slavery. I called his attention to the fact that he had acknowledged, in my hearing twice, that he had carefully read the speech, and, in the language of the lawyers, as he had twice read the speech, and still had put in no plea or answer, I took a default on him. I insisted that I had a right then to renew that charge of conspiracy. Ten days afterwards, I met the Judge at Clinton—that is to say, I was on the ground, but not in the discussion—and heard him make a speech. Then he comes in with his plea to this charge, for the first time, and his plea when put in, as well as I can recollect it, amounted to this: that he never had any talk with Judge Taney or the President of the United States with regard to the Dred Scott decision before it was made. I (Lincoln) ought to know that the man who makes a charge without knowing it to be true, falsifies as much as he who knowingly tells a falsehood; and lastly, that he would pronounce the whole thing a falsehood; but he would make no personal application of the charge of falsehood, not because of any regard for the "kind, amiable, intelligent gentleman," but because of his own personal self-respect! [Roars of laughter.] I have understood since then, (but [turning to Judge Douglas] will not hold the Judge to it if he is not willing) that he has broken through the "self-respect," and has got to saying the thing *out*. The Judge nods to me that it is so. [Laughter.] It is fortunate for me that I can keep as good-humored as I do, when the Judge acknowledges that he has been trying to make a question of veracity with me. I know the Judge is a great man, while I am only a small man, but *I feel that I have got him*. [Tremendous cheering.] I demur to that plea. I waive all objections that it was not filed till after default was taken, and demur to it upon the merits. What if Judge Douglas never did talk with Chief Justice Taney and the President, before the Dred Scott decision was made, does it follow that he could not have had as perfect an understanding without talking, as with it? I am not disposed to stand upon my legal advantage. I am disposed to take his denial as being like an answer in chancery, that he neither had any knowledge, information or belief in the exis-

tence of such a conspiracy. I am disposed to take his answer
as being as broad as though he had put it in these words. And
now, I ask, even if he has done so, have not I a right to *prove
it on him*, and to offer the evidence of more than two witnesses, by whom to prove it; and if the evidence proves the
existence of the conspiracy, does his broad answer denying all
knowledge, information, or belief, disturb the fact? It can
only show that he was *used* by conspirators, and was not a
leader of them. [Vociferous cheering.]

Now in regard to his reminding me of the moral rule that
persons who tell what they do not know to be true, falsify as
much as those who knowingly tell falsehoods. I remember the
rule, and it must be borne in mind that in what I have read to
you, I do not say that I *know* such a conspiracy to exist. To
that, I reply *I believe it*. If the Judge says that I do *not* believe
it, then *he* says what *he* does not know, and falls within his
own rule, that he who asserts a thing which he does not know
to be true, falsifies as much as he who knowingly tells a falsehood. I want to call your attention to a little discussion on
that branch of the case, and the evidence which brought my
mind to the conclusion which I expressed as my *belief*. If, in
arraying that evidence, I had stated anything which was false
or erroneous, it needed but that Judge Douglas should point
it out, and I would have taken it back with all the kindness in
the world. I do not deal in that way. If I have brought forward anything not a fact, if he will point it out, it will not
even ruffle me to take it back. But if he will not point out
anything erroneous in the evidence, is it not rather for him to
show, by a comparison of the evidence that I have *reasoned*
falsely, than to call the "kind, amiable, intelligent gentleman,"
a liar? [Cheers and laughter.] If I have reasoned to a false
conclusion, it is the vocation of an able debater to show by
argument that I have wandered to an erroneous conclusion. I
want to ask your attention to a portion of the Nebraska Bill,
which Judge Douglas has quoted: "It being the true intent
and meaning of this act, not to legislate slavery into any Territory or State, nor to exclude it therefrom, but to leave the
people thereof perfectly free to form and regulate their domestic institutions in their own way, subject only to the Constitution of the United States." Thereupon Judge Douglas and

others began to argue in favor of "Popular Sovereignty"—the right of the people to have slaves if they wanted them, and to exclude slavery if they did not want them. "But," said, in substance, a Senator from Ohio, (Mr. Chase, I believe,) "we more than suspect that you do not mean to allow the people to exclude slavery if they wish to, and if you do mean it, accept an amendment which I propose expressly authorizing the people to exclude slavery." I believe I have the amendment here before me, which was offered, and under which the people of the Territory, through their proper representatives, might if they saw fit, prohibit the existence of slavery therein. And now I state it as a *fact*, to be taken back if there is any mistake about it, that Judge Douglas and those acting with him, *voted that amendment down.* [Tremendous applause.] I now think that those men who voted it down, had a *real reason* for doing so. They know what that reason was. It looks to us, since we have seen the Dred Scott decision pronounced holding that "under the Constitution" the people cannot exclude slavery—I say it looks to outsiders, poor, simple, "amiable, intelligent gentlemen," [great laughter,] as though the niche was left as a place to put that Dred Scott decision in—[laughter and cheers]—a niche which would have been spoiled by adopting the amendment. And now, I say again, if *this* was not the reason, it will avail the Judge much more to calmly and good-humoredly point out to these people what that *other* reason was for voting the amendment down, than, swelling himself up, to vociferate that he may be provoked to call somebody a liar. [Tremendous applause.]

Again: there is in that same quotation from the Nebraska bill this clause—"It being the true intent and meaning of this bill not to legislate slavery into any Territory or *State*." I have always been puzzled to know what business the word "State" had in that connection. Judge Douglas knows. *He put it there.* He knows what he put it there for. We outsiders cannot say what he put it there for. The law they were passing was not about States, and was not making provisions for States. What was it placed there for? After seeing the Dred Scott decision, which holds that the people cannot exclude slavery from a *Territory*, if another Dred Scott decision shall come, holding that they cannot exclude it from a *State*, we shall discover that when the word was originally put there, it was in view of something which was to come in due time, we shall see that it was the *other half* of something. [Applause.] I now say again, if there is any different reason for putting it there, Judge Douglas, in a good-humored way, without calling anybody a liar, *can tell what the reason was.* [Renewed cheers.]

When the Judge spoke at Clinton, he came very near making a charge of falsehood against me. He used, as I found it printed in a newspaper, which I remember was very nearly like the real speech, the following language:

> I did not answer the charge [of conspiracy] before, for the reason that I did not suppose there was a man in America with a heart so corrupt as to believe such a charge could be true. I have too much respect for Mr. Lincoln to suppose he is serious in making the charge.

I confess this is rather a curious view, that out of respect for me he should consider I was making what I deemed rather a grave charge in fun. [Laughter.] I confess it strikes me rather strangely. But I let it pass. As the Judge did not for a moment believe that there was a man in America whose heart was so "corrupt" as to make such a charge, and as he places me among the "men in America" who have hearts base enough to make such a charge, I hope he will excuse me if I hunt out another charge very like this; and if it should turn out that in hunting I should find that other, and it should turn out to be Judge Douglas himself who made it, I hope he will reconsider this question of the deep corruption of heart he has thought fit to ascribe to me. [Great applause and laughter.] In Judge Douglas' speech of March 22d, 1858, which I hold in my hand, he says:

> In this connection there is another topic to which I desire to allude. I seldom refer to the course of newspapers, or notice the articles which they publish in regard to myself; but the course of the Washington *Union* has been so extraordinary, for the last two or three months, that I think it well enough to make some allusion to it. It has read me out of the Democratic party every other day, at least for two or three months, and keeps reading me out, (laughter;) and, as if it had not succeeded still continues to read me out, using such terms as "traitor," "renegade," "deserter," and other kind and polite epithets of that nature. Sir, I have no vindication to make of my democracy against the Washington *Union*, or any other newspapers. I am willing to allow my history and action for the last twenty years to speak for themselves as to my political principles,

and my fidelity to political obligations. The Washington *Union* has a personal grievance. When its editor was nominated for Public Printer I declined to vote for him, and stated that at some time I might give my reasons for doing so. Since I declined to give that vote, this scurrilous abuse, these vindictive and constant attacks have been repeated almost daily on me. Will my friend from Michigan read the article to which I allude.

This is a part of the speech. You must excuse me from reading the entire article of the Washington *Union*, as Mr. Stuart read it for Mr. Douglas. The Judge goes on and sums up, as I think correctly:

Mr. President, you here find several distinct propositions advanced boldly by the Washington *Union* editorially and apparently *authoritatively*, and every man who questions any of them is denounced as an Abolitionist, a Free-Soiler, a fanatic. The propositions are, first, that the primary object of all government at its original institution is the protection of person and property; second, that the Constitution of the United States declares that the citizens of each State shall be entitled to all the privileges and immunities of citizens in the several States; and that, therefore, thirdly, all State laws, whether organic or otherwise, which prohibit the citizens of one State from settling in another with their slave property, and especially declaring it forfeited, are direct violations of the original intention of the Government and Constitution of the United States; and fourth, that the emancipation of the slaves of the northern States was a gross outrage on the rights of property, inasmuch as it was involuntarily done on the part of the owner.

Remember that this article was published in the *Union* on the 17th of November, and on the 18th appeared the first article giving the adhesion of the *Union* to the Lecompton constitution. It was in these words:

"KANSAS AND HER CONSTITUTION.—The vexed question is settled. The problem is solved. The dread point of danger is passed. All serious trouble to Kansas affairs is over and gone."

And a column, nearly of the same sort. Then, when you come to look into the Lecompton Constitution, you find the same doctrine incorporated in it which was put forth editorially in the *Union*. What is it?

"ARTICLE 7, *Section* 1. The right of property is before and higher than any constitutional sanction; and the right of the owner of a slave to such slave and its increase is the same and as inviolable as the right of the owner of any property whatever."

Then in the schedule is a provision that the Constitution may be amended after 1864 by a two-thirds vote.

"But no alteration shall be made to affect the right of property in the ownership of slaves."

It will be seen by these clauses in the Lecompton Constitution that they are identical in spirit with this *authoritative* article in the Washington *Union* of the day previous to its indorsement of this Constitution.

I pass over some portions of the speech, and I hope that any one who feels interested in this matter will read the entire section of the speech, and see whether I do the Judge injustice. He proceeds:

> When I saw that article in the *Union* of the 17th of November, followed by the glorification of the Lecompton Constitution on the 18th of November, and this clause in the Constitution asserting the doctrine that a State has no right to prohibit slavery within its limits, I saw that there was a *fatal blow* being struck at the sovereignty of the States of this Union.

I stop the quotation there, again requesting that it may all be read. I have read all of the portion I desire to comment upon. What is this charge that the Judge thinks I must have a very corrupt heart to make? It was a purpose on the part of certain high functionaries to make it impossible for the people of one State to prohibit the people of any other State from entering it with their "property," so called, and making it a slave State. In other words, it was a charge implying a design to make the institution of slavery national. And now I ask your attention to what Judge Douglas has himself done here. I know he made that part of the speech as a reason why he had refused to vote for a certain man for public printer, but when we get at it, the charge itself is the very one I made against him, that he thinks I am so corrupt for uttering. Now whom does he make that charge against? Does he make it against that newspaper editor merely? No; he says it is identical in spirit with the Lecompton Constitution, and so the framers of that Constitution are brought in with the editor of the newspaper in that "fatal blow being struck." He did not call it a "conspiracy." In his language it is a "fatal blow being struck." And if the words carry the meaning better when changed from a "conspiracy" into a "fatal blow being struck," I will change *my* expression and call it "fatal blow being struck." [Cheers and laughter.] We see the charge made not merely against the editor of the *Union* but all the framers of the Lecompton Constitution; and not only so, but the article was an *authoritative* article. By whose authority? Is there any question but he means it was by the authority of the President, and his Cabinet—the Administration?

Is there any sort of question but he means to make that charge? Then there are the editors of the *Union*, the framers of the Lecompton Constitution, the President of the United States and his Cabinet, and all the supporters of the Lecompton Constitution in Congress and out of Congress, who are all involved in this "fatal blow being struck." I commend to Judge Douglas' consideration the question of *how corrupt a man's heart must be to make such a charge!* [Vociferous cheering.]

Now my friends, I have but one branch of the subject, in the little time I have left, to which to call your attention, and as I shall come to a close at the end of that branch, it is probable that I shall not occupy quite all the time allotted to me. Although on these questions I would like to talk twice as long as I have, I could not enter upon another head and discuss it properly without running over my time. I ask the attention of the people here assembled and elsewhere, to the course that Judge Douglas is pursuing every day as bearing upon this question of making slavery national. Not going back to the records but taking the speeches he makes, the speeches he made yesterday and day before and makes constantly all over the country—I ask your attention to them. In the first place what is necessary to make the institution national? Not war. There is no danger that the people of Kentucky will shoulder their muskets and with a young nigger stuck on every bayonet march into Illinois and force them upon us. There is no danger of our going over there and making war upon them. Then what is necessary for the nationalization of slavery? It is simply the next Dred Scott decision. It is merely for the Supreme Court to decide that no *State* under the Constitution can exclude it, just as they have already decided that under the Constitution neither Congress nor the Territorial Legislature can do it. When that is decided and acquiesced in, the whole thing is done. This being true, and this being the way as I think that slavery is to be made national, let us consider what Judge Douglas is doing every day to that end. In the first place, let us see what influence he is exerting on public sentiment. In this and like communities, public sentiment is everything. With public sentiment, nothing can fail; without it nothing can succeed. Consequently he who moulds public sentiment, goes deeper than he who enacts statutes or pronounces decisions. He makes statutes and decisions possible or impossible to be executed. This must be borne in mind, as also the additional fact that Judge Douglas is a man of vast influence, so great that it is enough for many men to profess to believe anything, when they once find out that Judge Douglas professes to believe it. Consider also the attitude he occupies at the head of a large party—a party which he claims has a majority of all the voters in the country. This man sticks to a decision which forbids the people of a Territory from excluding slavery, and he does so not because he says it is right in itself—he does not give any opinion on that—but because it has been *decided by the court*, and being decided by the court, he is, and you are bound to take it in your political action as *law*—not that he judges at all of its merits, but because a decision of the court is to him a *"Thus saith the Lord."* [Applause.] He places it on that ground alone, and you will bear in mind that thus committing himself unreservedly to this decision, *commits him to the next one* just as firmly as to this. He did not commit himself on account of the merit or demerit of the decision, but it is a *Thus saith the Lord*. The next decision, as much as this, will be a *thus saith the Lord*. There is nothing that can divert or turn him away from this decision. It is nothing that I point out to him that his great prototype, Gen. Jackson, did not believe in the binding force of decisions. It is nothing to him that Jefferson did not so believe. I have said that I have often heard him approve of Jackson's course in disregarding the decision of the Supreme Court pronouncing a National Bank constitutional. He says, I did not hear him say so. He denies the accuracy of my recollection. I say he ought to know better than I, but I will make no question about this thing, though it still seems to me that I heard him say it twenty times. [Applause and laughter.] I will tell him though, that he now claims to stand on the Cincinnati platform, which affirms that Congress *cannot* charter a National Bank, in the teeth of that old standing decision that Congress *can* charter a bank. [Loud applause.] And I remind him of another piece of history on the question of respect for judicial decisions, and it is a piece of Illinois history, belonging to a time when the large party to which Judge Douglas belonged, were displeased with a decision of the Supreme Court of Illinois, because they had decided that a Governor could not remove a Secretary of State. You will find the whole story in Ford's History of Illinois, and I know that Judge Douglas will not deny that he was then in favor of overslaughing that decision by the mode of adding five new Judges, so as to vote down the four old ones. Not only so, but it ended in *the Judge's sitting down on that very bench as one of the five new Judges to break down the four old ones.* [Cheers and laughter.] It was in this way precisely that he got his title of Judge. Now, when the Judge tells me that men appointed conditionally to sit as members of a court, will have to be catechised beforehand upon some subject, I say "You know Judge; you have tried it." [Laughter.] When he says a court of this kind will lose the confidence of all men, will be prostituted and disgraced by such a proceeding, I say, "You know best, Judge; you have been through the mill." [Great laughter.] But I cannot shake Judge Douglas' teeth loose from the Dred Scott decision. Like some obstinate animal (I mean no disrespect,) that will hang on when he has once got his teeth fixed, you may cut off a leg, or you may tear away an arm, still he will not relax his hold. And so I may point out to the Judge, and say that he is bespattered all over, from the beginning of his political life to the present time, with attacks upon judicial decisions—I may cut off limb after limb of his public record, and strive to wrench him from a single dictum of the Court—yet I cannot divert him from it. He hangs to the last, to the Dred Scott decision. [Loud cheers.] These things show there is a purpose *strong as death and eternity* for which he adheres to this decision, and for which he will adhere to *all other decisions* of the same Court. [Vociferous applause.]

A HIBERNIAN.—Give us something besides Dred Scott.

MR. LINCOLN.—Yes; no doubt you want to hear something that don't hurt. [Laughter and applause.] Now, having spoken of the Dred Scott decision, one more word and I am done. Henry Clay, my beau ideal of a statesman, the man for whom I fought all my humble life—Henry Clay once said of a class of men who would repress all tendencies to liberty and ultimate emancipation, that they must, if they would do this, go back to the era of our Independence, and muzzle the cannon which thunders its annual joyous return; they must blow out the moral lights around us; they must penetrate the human soul, and eradicate there the love of liberty; and then and not till then, could they perpetuate slavery in this country! [Loud cheers.] To my thinking, Judge Douglas is, by his example and vast influence, doing that very thing in this community, [cheers,] when he says that the negro has nothing in the Declaration of Independence. Henry Clay plainly understood the contrary. Judge Douglas is going back to the era of our Revolution, and to the extent of his ability, muzzling the cannon which thunders its annual joyous return. When he invites any people willing to have slavery, to establish it, he is blowing out the moral lights around us. [Cheers.] When he says he "cares not whether slavery is voted down or voted up,"—that it is a sacred right of self government—he is in my judgment penetrating the human soul and eradicating the light of reason and the love of liberty in this American people. [Enthusiastic and continued applause.] And now I will only say that when, by all these means and appliances, Judge Douglas shall succeed in bringing public sentiment to an exact accordance with his own views—when these vast assemblages shall echo back all these sentiments—when they shall come to repeat his views and to avow his principles, and to say all that he says on these mighty questions—then it needs only the formality of the second Dred Scott decision, which he endorses in advance, to make Slavery alike lawful in all the States—old as well as new, North as well as South.

My friends, that ends the chapter. The Judge can take his half-hour.

MR. DOUGLAS' REPLY.

MR. DOUGLAS—Fellow citizens: I will now occupy the half hour allotted to me in replying to Mr. Lincoln. The first point

to which I will call your attention is, as to what I said about
the organization of the Republican party in 1854, and the platform that was formed on the 5th of October, of that year, and
I will then put the question to Mr. Lincoln whether or not he
approves of each article in that platform ("he answered that
already"), and ask for a specific answer. ("He has answered."
"You cannot make him answer," &c.) I did not charge him
with being a member of the committee which reported that
platform. ("Yes, you did.") I charged that that platform was
the platform of the Republican party adopted by them. The
fact that it was the platform of the Republican party is not
denied, but Mr. Lincoln now says, that although his name
was on the committee which reported it, that he does not
think he was there, but thinks he was in Tazewell, holding
court. ("He said he was there.") Gentlemen, I ask your silence, and no interruption. Now, I want to remind Mr. Lincoln that he was at Springfield, when that convention was
held, and those resolutions adopted. ("You can't do it." "He
wasn't there," &c.)

[MR. GLOVER, chairman of the Republican committee—I
hope no Republican will interrupt Mr. Douglas. The masses
listened to Mr. Lincoln attentively, and as respectable men we
ought now to hear Mr. Douglas, and without interruption.]
("Good.")

MR. DOUGLAS, resuming—The point I am going to remind
Mr. Lincoln of is this: that after I had made my speech in
1854, during the fair, he gave me notice that he was going to
reply to me the next day. I was sick at the time, but I staid
over in Springfield to hear his reply and to reply to him. On
that day this very convention, the resolutions adopted by
which I have read, was to meet in the Senate chamber. He
spoke in the hall of the House; and when he got through his
speech—my recollection is distinct, and I shall never forget
it—Mr. Codding walked in as I took the stand to reply, and
gave notice that the Republican State Convention would
meet instantly in the Senate chamber, and called upon the
Republicans to retire there and go into this very convention,
instead of remaining and listening to me. (Three cheers for
Douglas.)

MR. LINCOLN, interrupting, excitedly and angrily—Judge,

add that I went along with them. (This interruption was made in a pitiful, mean, sneaking way, as Lincoln floundered around the stand.)

MR. DOUGLAS—Gentlemen, Mr. Lincoln tells me to add that he went along with them to the Senate chamber. I will not add that, because I do not know whether he did or not.

MR. LINCOLN, again interrupting—I know he did not.

[Two of the Republican committee here seized Mr. Lincoln, and by a sudden jerk caused him to disappear from the front of the stand, one of them saying quite audibly, "What are you making such a fuss for. Douglas didn't interrupt you, and can't you see that the people don't like it."]

MR. DOUGLAS—I do not know whether he knows it or not, that is not the point, and I will yet bring him to on the question.

In the first place—Mr. Lincoln was selected by the very men who made the Republican organization, on that day to reply to me. He spoke for them and for that party, and he was the leader of the party; and on the very day he made his speech in reply to me preaching up this same doctrine of negro equality, under the Declaration of Independence, this Republican party met in Convention. (Three cheers for Douglas.) Another evidence that he was acting in concert with them is to be found in the fact that that convention waited an hour after its time of meeting to hear Lincoln's speech, and Codding, one of their leading men marched in the moment Lincoln got through, and gave notice that they did not want to hear me and would proceed with the business of the Convention. ("Strike him again,"—three cheers, etc.) Still another fact. I have here a newspaper printed at Springfield, Mr. Lincoln's own town, in October, 1854, a few days afterwards, publishing these resolutions, charging Mr. Lincoln with entertaining these sentiments, and trying to prove that they were also the sentiments of Mr. Yates, then candidate for Congress. This has been published on Mr. Lincoln over and over again, and never before has he denied it. (Three cheers.)

But my friends, this denial of his that he did not act on the committee is a miserable quibble to avoid the main issue, (applause.) ("That's so,") which is that this Republican platform declares in favor of the unconditional repeal of the Fugitive Slave Law. Has Lincoln answered whether he endorsed that or not? (No, no.) I called his attention to it when I first addressed you and asked him for an answer and I then predicted that he would not answer. (Bravo, glorious and cheers.) How does he answer. Why that he was not on the committee that wrote the resolutions. (Laughter.) I then repeated the next proposition contained in the resolutions, which was to restrict slavery in those states in which it exists and asked him whether he endorsed it. Does he answer yes, or no? He says in reply, "I was not on the committee at the time; I was up in Tazewell." The next question I put to him was, whether he was in favor of prohibiting the admission of any more slave States into the Union. I put the question to him distinctly, whether, if the people of the Territory, when they had sufficient population to make a State, should form their constitution recognizing slavery, he would vote for or against its admission. ("That's it.") He is a candidate for the United States Senate, and it is possible, if he should be elected, that he would have to vote directly on that question. ("He never will.") I asked him to answer me and you whether he would vote to admit a State into the Union, with slavery or without it, as its own people might choose. ("Hear him," "That's the doctrine," and applause.) He did not answer that question. ("He never will.") He dodges that question also, under the cover that he was not on the Committee at the time, that he was not present when the platform was made. I want to know if he should happen to be in the Senate when a State applied for admission, with a constitution acceptable to her own people, he would vote to admit that State, if slavery was one of its institutions. (That's the question.) He avoids the answer.

MR. LINCOLN—interrupting the third time excitedly, No, Judge—(Mr. Lincoln again disappeared suddenly aided by a pull from behind.)

MR. DOUGLAS. It is true he gives the abolitionists to understand by a hint that he would not vote to admit such a State. And why? He goes on to say that the man who would talk about giving each State the right to have slavery, or not, as it pleased, was akin to the man who would muzzle the guns

which thundered forth the annual joyous return of the day of
our independence. (Great laughter.) He says that that kind of
talk is casting a blight on the glory of this country. What is
the meaning of that? That he is not in favor of each State
having the right to do as it pleases on the slavery question?
("Stick it to him," "don't spare him," and applause.) I will put
the question to him again and again, and I intend to force it
out of him. (Immense applause.)

Then again, this platform which was made at Springfield
by his own party, when he was its acknowledged head, pro-
vides that Republicans will insist on the abolition of slavery
in the District of Columbia, and I asked Lincoln specifically
whether he agreed with them in that? Did you get an answer? ("No, no.") He is afraid to answer it. ("We will not
vote for him.") He knows I will trot him down to Egypt.
(Laughter and cheers.) I intend to make him answer there,
("that's right,") or I will show the people of Illinois that he
does not intend to answer these questions. ("Keep him to
the point," "give us more," etc.) The convention to which I
have been alluding goes a little further, and pledges itself to
exclude slavery from all the Territories over which the general government has exclusive jurisdiction north of 36 deg.
30 min., as well as South. Now I want to know whether he
approves that provision. (He'll never answer and cheers.) I
want him to answer, and when he does, I want to know his
opinion on another point, which is, whether he will redeem
the pledge of this platform and resist the acquirement of any
more territory unless slavery therein shall be forever prohibited. I want him to answer this last question. Each of the
questions I have put to him are practical questions, questions based upon the fundamental principles of the Black
Republican party, and I want to know whether he is the
first, last and only choice of a party with whom he does not
agree in principle. ("Great applause,") ("Rake him down.")
He does not deny but that that principle was unanimously
adopted by the Republican party; he does not deny that the
whole Republican party is pledged to it; he does not deny
that a man who is not faithful to it is faithless to the Republican party, and now I want to know whether that party is
unanimously in favor of a man who does not adopt that

creed and agree with them in their principles: I want to know whether the man who does not agree with them, and who is afraid to avow his differences and who dodges the issue, is the first, last and only choice of the Republican party. (Cheers.) A VOICE, how about the conspiracy?

MR. DOUGLAS, never mind, I will come to that soon enough. (Bravo, Judge, hurra, three cheers for Douglas.) But the platform which I have read to you not only lays down these principles but it adds:

Resolved, That in furtherance of these principles we will use such constitutional and lawful means as shall seem best adapted to their accomplishment, and that we will support no man for office, under the general or state government, who is not positively and fully committed to the support of these principles, and whose personal character and conduct is not a guarantee that he is reliable, and who shall not have abjured old party allegiance and ties.

("Good," "you have him," &c.)

The Black Republican party stands pledged that they will never support Lincoln until he has pledged himself to that platform, (tremendous applause, men throwing up their hats, and shouting, "you've got him,") but he cannot devise his answer; he has not made up his mind, whether he will or not. (Great laughter.) He talked about everything else he could think of to occupy his hour and a half, and when he could not think of anything more to say, without an excuse for refusing to answer these questions, he sat down long before his time was out. (Cheers.)

In relation to Mr. Lincoln's charge of conspiracy against me, I have a word to say. In his speech to-day he quotes a playful part of his speech at Springfield, about Stephen, and James, and Franklin, and Roger, and says that I did not take exception to it. I did not answer it, and he repeats it again. I did not take exception to this figure of his. He has a right to be as playful as he pleases in throwing his arguments together, and I will not object; but I did take objection to his second Springfield speech, in which he stated that he intended his first speech as a charge of corruption or conspiracy against the Supreme Court of the United States, President Pierce, President Buchanan, and myself. That gave the offensive character to the charge. He then said that when he made it he did not know whether it was true or not (laughter), but inasmuch as Judge Douglas had not denied it, although he had replied to the other parts of his speech three times, he repeated it as a charge of conspiracy against me, thus charging me with moral turpitude. When he put it in that form I did say that inasmuch as he repeated the charge simply because I had not denied it, I would deprive him of the opportunity of ever repeating it again, by declaring that it was in all its bearings an infamous lie. (Three cheers for Douglas.) He says he will repeat it until I answer his folly, and nonsense about Stephen, and Franklin, and Roger, and Bob, and James.

He studied that out, prepared that one sentence with the greatest care, committed it to memory, and put it in his first Springfield speech, and now he carries that speech around and reads that sentence to show how pretty it is. (Laughter.) His vanity is wounded because I will not go into that beautiful figure of his about the building of a house. (Renewed laughter.) All I have to say is, that I am not green enough to let him make a charge which he acknowledges he does not know to be true, and then take up my time in answering it, when I know it to be false and nobody else knows it to be true. (Cheers.)

I have not brought a charge of moral turpitude against him. When he, or any other man, brings one against me, instead of disproving it I will say that it is a lie, and let him prove it if he can. (Enthusiastic applause.)

I have lived twenty-five years in Illinois. I have served you with all the fidelity and ability which I possess, ("That's so," "good," and cheers,) and Mr. Lincoln is at liberty to attack my public action, my votes, and my conduct; but when he dares to attack my moral integrity, by a charge of conspiracy between myself, Chief Justice Taney, and the Supreme Court and two Presidents of the United States, I will repel it. ("Three cheers for Douglas.")

Mr. Lincoln has not character enough for integrity and truth merely on his own *ipse dixit* to arraign President Buchanan, President Pierce, and nine judges of the Supreme Court, not one of whom would be complimented by being put on an equality with him. ("Hit him again, three cheers" &c.) There is an unpardonable presumption in a man putting himself up before thousands of people, and pretending that his *ipse dixit*, without proof, without fact and without truth, is enough to bring down and destroy the purest and best of living men. ("Hear him," "Three cheers.")

Fellow-citizens, my time is fast expiring; I must pass on. Mr. Lincoln wants to know why I voted against Mr. Chase's amendment to the Nebraska Bill. I will tell him. In the first place, the bill already conferred all the power which Congress had, by giving the people the whole power over the subject. Chase offered a proviso that they might abolish slavery, which by implication would convey the idea that they could prohibit by not introducing that institution. Gen. Cass asked him to modify his amendment, so as to provide that the people might either prohibit or introduce slavery, and thus make it fair and equal. Chase refused to so modify his proviso, and then Gen. Cass and all the rest of us, voted it down. (Immense cheering.) These facts appear on the journals and debates of Congress, where Mr. Lincoln found the charge, and if he had told the whole truth, there would have been no necessity for me to occupy your time in explaining the matter. (Laughter and applause.)

Mr. Lincoln wants to know why the word "state," as well as "territory," was put into the Nebraska Bill! I will tell him. It was put there to meet just such false arguments as he has been adducing. (Laughter.) That first, not only the people of the territories should do as they pleased, but that when they come to be admitted as States, they should come into the Union with or without slavery, as the people determined. I meant to knock in the head this Abolition doctrine of Mr. Lincoln's, that there shall be no more slave States, even if the people want them. (Tremendous applause.) And it does not do for him to say, or for any other Black Republican to say, that there is nobody in favor of the doctrine of no more slave States, and that nobody wants to interfere with the right of the people to do as they please. What was the origin of the Missouri difficulty and the Missouri compromise? The people of Missouri formed a constitution as a slave State, and asked admission into the Union, but the Free Soil party of the North being in a majority, refused to admit her because she had slavery as one of her institutions. Hence this first slavery agitation arose upon a State and not upon a Territory, and yet Mr. Lincoln does not know why the word State was placed in the Kansas-Nebraska bill. (Great laughter and applause.) The whole Abolition agitation arose on that doctrine of prohibiting a State from coming in with slavery or not, as it pleased, and that same doctrine is here in this Republican platform of 1854; it has never been repealed; and every Black Republican stands pledged by that platform, never to vote for any man who is not in favor of it. Yet Mr. Lincoln does not know that there is a man in the world who is in favor of preventing a State from coming in as it pleases, notwithstanding. The Springfield platform says that they, the Republican party, will not allow a State to come in under such circumstances. He is an ignorant man. (Cheers.)

Now you see that upon these very points I am as far from bringing Mr. Lincoln up to the line as I ever was before. He does not want to avow his principles. I do want to avow mine, as clear as sunlight in mid-day. (Cheers and applause.) Democracy is founded upon the eternal principle of right. (That is the talk.) The plainer these principles are avowed before the people, the stronger will be the support which they will receive. I only wish I had the power to make them so clear that they would shine in the heavens for every man, woman, and child to read. (Loud cheering.) The first of those principles that I would proclaim would be in opposition to Mr. Lincoln's doctrine of uniformity between the different States, and I would declare instead the sovereign right of each State to decide the slavery question as well as all other domestic questions for themselves, without interference from any other State or power whatsoever. (Hurrah for Douglas.)

When that principle is recognized you will have peace and harmony and fraternal feeling between all the States of this Union; until you do recognize that doctrine there will be sectional warfare agitating and distracting the country. What does Mr. Lincoln propose? He says that the Union cannot exist divided into free and slave States. If it cannot endure thus divided, then he must strive to make them all free or all slave, which will inevitably bring about a dissolution of the Union. (Cries of "he can't do it.")

Gentlemen, I am told that my time is out and I am obliged to stop. (Three times three cheers were here given for Senator Douglas.)

To Joseph O. Cunningham

J. O. Cunningham, Esq   Ottawa,
My Dear Sir   Aug. 22. 1858

Yours of the 18th. signed as Secretary of the Rep. Club, is received. In the matter of making speeches I am a good pressed by invitations from almost all quarters; and while I hope to be at Urbana sometime during the canvass I cannot yet say when. Can you not see me at Monticello on the 6th. of Sept.?

Douglas and I, for the first time this canvass, crossed swords here yesterday; the fire flew some, and I am glad to know I am yet alive. There was a vast concourse of people— more than could near enough to hear. Yours as ever

To Ebenezer Peck

Hon: E. Peck   Henry, Aug: 23. 1858
My dear Sir

I have just written Judd that I wish him and you to meet me at Freeport next Friday to give me the benefit of a consultation with you. Douglas is propounding questions to me, which perhaps it is not quite safe to wholly disregard. I have my view of the means to dispose of them; but I also want yours and Judd's. I have written more at length to Judd, and would to you, but for lack of time. See Judd, you and he keep the matter to yourselves, and meet me at Freeport without fail.

Yours as ever

Second Lincoln-Douglas Debate, Freeport, Illinois

Second joint debate, August 27, 1858 at Freeport, Illinois.
Lincoln, as reported in the Press & Tribune. Douglas, as reported
in the Chicago Times.

MR. LINCOLN'S SPEECH.

Mr. Lincoln was introduced by Hon. Thomas J. Turner, and was greeted with loud cheers. When the applause had subsided, he said:

LADIES AND GENTLEMEN—On Saturday last, Judge Douglas and myself first met in public discussion. He spoke one hour, I an hour-and-a-half, and he replied for half an hour. The order is now reversed. I am to speak an hour, he an hour-and-a-half, and then I am to reply for half an hour. I propose to devote myself during the first hour to the scope of what was brought within the range of his half hour speech at Ottawa. Of course there was brought within the scope in that half hour's speech something of his own opening speech. In the course of that opening argument Judge Douglas proposed to me seven distinct interrogatories. In my speech of an hour and a half, I attended to some other parts of his speech, and incidentally, as I thought, answered one of the interrogatories then. I then distinctly intimated to him that I would answer the rest of his interrogatories on condition only that he should agree to answer as many for me. He made no intimation at the time of the proposition, nor did he in his reply allude at all to that suggestion of mine. I do him no injustice in saying that he occupied at least half of his reply in dealing with me as though I had *refused* to answer his interrogatories. I now propose that I will answer any of the interrogatories, upon condition that he will answer questions from me not exceeding the same number. I give him an opportunity to respond. The Judge remains silent. I now say to you that I will answer his interrogatories, whether he answers mine or not; [applause] and that after I have done so, I shall propound mine to him. [Applause.]

[Owing to the press of people against the platform, our reporter did not reach the stand until Mr. Lincoln had spoken to this point. The previous remarks were taken by a gentleman in Freeport, who has politely furnished them to us.]

I have supposed myself, since the organization of the Republican party at Bloomington, in May, 1856, bound as a party man by the platforms of the party, then and since. If in any interrogatories which I shall answer I go beyond the scope of what is within these platforms it will be perceived that no one is responsible but myself.

Having said thus much, I will take up the Judge's interrogatories as I find them printed in the Chicago *Times*, and answer them *seriatim*. In order that there may be no mistake about it, I have copied the interrogatories in writing, and also my answers to them. The first one of these interrogatories is in these words:

Question 1. "I desire to know whether Lincoln to-day stands, as he did in 1854, in favor of the unconditional repeal of the fugitive slave law?"

Answer. I do not now, nor ever did, stand in favor of the unconditional repeal of the fugitive slave law. [Cries of "Good," "Good."]

Q. 2. "I desire him to answer whether he stands pledged to-day, as he did in 1854, against the admission of any more slave States into the Union, even if the people want them?"

A. I do not now, nor ever did, stand pledged against the admission of any more slave States into the Union.

Q. 3. "I want to know whether he stands pledged against the admission of a new State into the Union with such a Constitution as the people of that State may see fit to make."

A. I do not stand pledged against the admission of a new State into the Union, with such a Constitution as the people of that State may see fit to make. [Cries of "good," "good."]

Q. 4. "I want to know whether he stands to-day pledged to the abolition of slavery in the District of Columbia?"

A. I do not stand to-day pledged to the abolition of slavery in the District of Columbia.

Q. 5. "I desire him to answer whether he stands pledged to the prohibition of the slave trade between the different States?"

A. I do not stand pledged to the prohibition of the slave trade between the different States.

Q. 6. "I desire to know whether he stands pledged to prohibit slavery in all the Territories of the United States, North as well as South of the Missouri Compromise line."

A. I am impliedly, if not expressly, pledged to a belief in the *right* and *duty* of Congress to prohibit slavery in all the United States Territories. [Great applause.]

Q. 7. "I desire him to answer whether he is opposed to the acquisition of any new territory unless slavery is first prohibited therein."

A. I am not generally opposed to honest acquisition of territory; and, in any given case, I would or would not oppose such acquisition, accordingly as I might think such acquisition would or would not agravate the slavery question among ourselves. [Cries of good, good.]

Now, my friends, it will be perceived upon an examination of these questions and answers, that so far I have only answered that I was not *pledged* to this, that or the other. The Judge has not framed his interrogatories to ask me anything more than this, and I have answered in strict accordance with the interrogatories, and have answered truly that I am not *pledged* at all upon any of the points to which I have answered. But I am not disposed to hang upon the exact form of his interrogatory. I am rather disposed to take up at least some of these questions, and state what I really think upon them.

As to the first one, in regard to the Fugitive Slave Law, I have never hesitated to say, and I do not now hesitate to say, that I think, under the Constitution of the United States, the people of the Southern States are entitled to a Congressional Fugitive Slave Law. Having said that, I have had nothing to say in regard to the existing Fugitive Slave Law further than that I think it should have been framed so as to be free from some of the objections that pertain to it, without lessening its efficiency. And inasmuch as we are not now in an agitation in regard to an alteration or modification of that law, I would not be the man to introduce it as a new subject of agitation upon the general question of slavery.

In regard to the other question of whether I am pledged to

the admission of any more slave States into the Union, I state to you very frankly that I would be exceedingly sorry ever to be put in a position of having to pass upon that question. I should be exceedingly glad to know that there would never be another slave State admitted into the Union; [applause]; but I must add, that if slavery shall be kept out of the Territories during the territorial existence of any one given Territory, and then the people shall, having a fair chance and a clear field, when they come to adopt the Constitution, do such an extraordinary thing as to adopt a Slave Constitution, uninfluenced by the actual presence of the institution among them, I see no alternative, if we own the country, but to admit them into the Union. [Applause.]

The third interrogatory is answered by the answer to the second, it being, as I conceive, the same as the second.

The fourth one is in regard to the abolition of slavery in the District of Columbia. In relation to that, I have my mind very distinctly made up. I should be exceedingly glad to see slavery abolished in the District of Columbia. [Cries of "good, good."] I believe that Congress possesses the constitutional power to abolish it. Yet as a member of Congress, I should not with my present views, be in favor of *endeavoring* to abolish slavery in the District of Columbia, unless it would be upon these conditions. *First*, that the abolition should be gradual. *Second*, that it should be on a vote of the majority of qualified voters in the District, and *third*, that compensation should be made to unwilling owners. With these three conditions, I confess I would be exceedingly glad to see Congress abolish slavery in the District of Columbia, and, in the language of Henry Clay, "sweep from our Capital that foul blot upon our nation." [Loud applause.]

In regard to the fifth interrogatory, I must say here, that as to the question of the abolition of the Slave Trade between the different States, I can truly answer, as I have, that I am *pledged* to nothing about it. It is a subject to which I have not given that mature consideration that would make me feel authorized to state a position so as to hold myself entirely bound by it. In other words, that question has never been prominently enough before me to induce me to investigate whether we really have the Constitutional power to do it. I could investigate it if I had sufficient time, to bring myself to a conclusion upon that subject, but I have not done so, and I say so frankly to you here, and to Judge Douglas. I must say, however, that if I should be of opinion that Congress does possess the Constitutional power to abolish the slave trade among the different States, I should still not be in favor of the exercise of that power unless upon some conservative principle as I conceive it, akin to what I have said in relation to the abolition of slavery in the District of Columbia.

My answer as to whether I desire that slavery should be prohibited in all the Territories of the United States is full and explicit within itself, and cannot be made clearer by any comments of mine. So I suppose in regard to the question whether I am opposed to the acquisition of any more territory unless slavery is first prohibited therein, my answer is such that I could add nothing by way of illustration, or making myself better understood, than the answer which I have placed in writing.

Now in all this, the Judge has me and he has me on the record. I suppose he had flattered himself that I was really entertaining one set of opinions for one place and another set for another place—that I was afraid to say at one place what I uttered at another. What I am saying here I suppose I say to a vast audience as strongly tending to Abolitionism as any audience in the State of Illinois, and I believe I am saying that which, if it would be offensive to any persons and render them enemies to myself, would be offensive to persons in this audience.

I now proceed to propound to the Judge the interrogatories, so far as I have framed them. I will bring forward a new installment when I get them ready. [Laughter.] I will bring them forward now, only reaching to number four.

The first one is—

Question 1. If the people of Kansas shall, by means entirely unobjectionable in all other respects, adopt a State Constitution, and ask admission into the Union under it, *before* they have the requisite number of inhabitants according to the English Bill—some ninety-three thousand—will you vote to admit them? [Applause.]

Q. 2. Can the people of a United States Territory, in any

lawful way, against the wish of any citizen of the United States, exclude slavery from its limits prior to the formation of a State Constitution? [Renewed applause.]

Q. 3. If the Supreme Court of the United States shall decide that States can not exclude slavery from their limits, are you in favor of acquiescing in, adopting and following such decision as a rule of political action? [Loud applause.]

Q. 4. Are you in favor of acquiring additional territory, in disregard of how such acquisition may affect the nation on the slavery question? [Cries of "good," "good."]

As introductory to these interrogatories which Judge Douglas propounded to me at Ottawa, he read a set of resolutions which he said Judge Trumbull and myself had participated in adopting, in the first Republican State Convention held at Springfield, in October, 1854. He insisted that I and Judge Trumbull, and perhaps, the entire Republican party were responsible for the doctrines contained in the set of resolutions which he read, and I understand that it was from that set of resolutions that he deduced the interrogatories which he propounded to me, using these resolutions as a sort of authority for propounding those questions to me. Now I say here today that I do not answer his interrogatories because of their springing at all from that set of resolutions which he read. I answered them because Judge Douglas thought fit to ask them. [Applause.] I do not now, nor never did recognize any responsibility upon myself in that set of resolutions. When I replied to him on that occasion, I assured him that I never had anything to do with them. I repeat here to-day, that I never in any possible form had anything to do with that set of resolutions. It turns out, I believe, that those resolutions were never passed in any Convention held in Springfield. [Cheers and Laughter.] It turns out that they were never passed at any Convention or any public meeting that I had any part in. I believe it turns out in addition to all this, that there was not, in the fall of 1854, any Convention holding a session in Springfield, calling itself a Republican State Convention; yet it is true there was a Convention, or assemblage of men calling themselves a Convention, at Springfield, that did pass *some* resolutions. But so little did I really know of the proceedings of that Convention, or what set of resolutions they had passed, though having a general knowledge that there had been such an assemblage of men there, that when Judge Douglas read the resolutions, I really did not know but they had been the resolutions passed then and there. I did not question that they were the resolutions adopted. For I could not bring myself to suppose that Judge Douglas could say what he did upon this subject without *knowing* that it was true. [Cheers and laughter.] I contented myself, on that occasion, with denying, as I truly could, all connection with them, not denying or affirming whether they were passed at Springfield. Now it turns out that he had got hold of some resolutions passed at some Convention or public meeting in Kane County. [Renewed laughter.] I wish to say here that I don't conceive that in any fair and just mind this discovery relieves me at all. I had just as much to do with the Convention in Kane County as that in Springfield. I am just as much responsible for the resolutions at Kane County as those at Springfield, the amount of the responsibility being exactly nothing in either case; no more than there would be in regard to a set of resolutions passed in the moon. [Laughter and loud cheers.]

I allude to this extraordinary matter in this canvass for some further purpose than anything yet advanced. Judge Douglas did not make his statement upon that occasion as matters that he believed to be true, but he stated them roundly as *being true*, in such form as to pledge his veracity for their truth. When the whole matter turns out as it does, and when we consider who Judge Douglas is—that he is a distinguished Senator of the United States—that he has served nearly twelve years as such—that his character is not at all limited as an ordinary Senator of the United States, but that his name has become of world-wide renown—it is *most extraordinary* that he should so far forget all the suggestions of justice to an adversary, or of prudence to himself, as to venture upon the assertion of that which the slightest investigation would have shown him to be wholly false. [Cheers.] I can only account for his having done so upon the supposition that that evil genius which has attended him through his life, giving to him an apparent astonishing prosperity, such as to lead very many good men to doubt there being any advantage in virtue over vice—[Cheers and laughter] I say I can only account for it on the supposition that that evil genius has at last made up its mind to forsake him. [Continued cheers and laughter.]

And I may add that another extraordinary feature of the Judge's conduct in this canvass—made more extraordinary by this incident—is that he is in the habit, in almost all the speeches he makes, of charging falsehood upon his adversaries—myself and others. I now ask whether he is able to find in anything that Judge Trumbull, for instance, has said, or in anything that I have said, a justification at all compared with what we have, in this instance, for that sort of vulgarity. [Cries of "good," "good," "good."]

I have been in the habit of charging as a matter of belief on my part, that, in the introduction of the Nebraska bill into Congress, there was a conspiracy to make slavery perpetual and national. I have arranged from time to time the evidence which establishes and proves the truth of this charge. I recurred to this charge at Ottawa. I shall not now have time to dwell upon it at very great length, but inasmuch as Judge Douglas in his reply of half an hour, made some points upon me in relation to it, I propose noticing a few of them.

The Judge insists that, in the first speech I made, in which I very distinctly made that charge, he thought for a good while I was in fun! that I was playful—that I was not sincere about it—and that he only grew angry and somewhat excited when he found that I insisted upon it as a matter of earnestness. He says he characterised it as a falsehood as far as I implicated his *moral character* in that transaction. Well, I did not know, till he presented that view that I had implicated his moral character. He is very much in the habit, when he argues me up into a position I never thought of occupying, of very cosily saying he has no doubt Lincoln is "conscientious" in saying so. He should remember that I did not know but what *he* was ALTOGETHER "CONSCIENTIOUS" in that matter. [Great Laughter.] I can conceive it possible for men to conspire to do a good thing, and I really find nothing in Judge Douglas' course or arguments that is contrary to or inconsistent with his belief of a conspiracy to nationalize and spread slavery as being a good and blessed thing, [Continued Laughter,] and so I hope he will understand that I do not at all question but that in all this matter he is entirely "conscientious." [More laughter and cheers.]

But to draw your attention to one of the points I made in this case, beginning at the beginning. When the Nebraska bill was introduced, or a short time afterwards, by an amendment I believe, it was provided that it must be considered "the true intent and meaning of this act not to legislate slavery into any State or Territory, or to exclude it therefrom, but to leave the people thereof perfectly free to form and regulate their own domestic institutions in their own way, subject only to the Constitution of the United States." I have called his attention to the fact that when he and some others began arguing that they were giving an increased degree of liberty to the people in the Territories over and above what they formerly had on the question of slavery, a question was raised whether the law was enacted to give such unconditional liberty to the people, and to test the sincerity of this mode of argument, Mr. Chase, of Ohio, introduced an amendment, in which he made the law—if the amendment were adopted—expressly declare that the people of the Territory should have the power to exclude slavery if they saw fit. I have asked attention also to the fact that Judge Douglas and those who acted with him, voted that amendment down, notwithstanding it expressed exactly the thing they said was the true intent and meaning of the law. I have called attention to the fact that in subsequent times, a decision of the Supreme Court has been made in which it has been declared that a Territorial Legislature has no constitutional right to exclude slavery. And I have argued and said that for men who did intend that the people of the territory should have the right to exclude slavery absolutely and unconditionally, the voting down of Chase's amendment is wholly inexplicable. It is a puzzle—a riddle. But I have said that with men who did look forward to such a decision, or who had it in contemplation, that such a decision of the Supreme Court would or might be made, the voting down of that amendment would be perfectly rational and intelligible. It would keep Congress from coming in collision with the decision when it was made. Anybody can conceive that if there was an intention or expectation that such a decision was to follow, it

would not be a very desirable party attitude to get into for the
Supreme Court—all or nearly all its members belonging to
the same party—to decide one way, when the party in Congress had decided the other way. Hence it would be very rational for men expecting such a decision, to keep the niche in
that law clear for it. After pointing this out, I tell Judge Douglas that it looks to me as though here was the reason why
Chase's amendment was voted down. I tell him that as he did
it, and knows why he did it, if it was done for a reason different from this, *he knows what that reason was, and can tell us
what it was.* I tell him, also, it will be vastly more satisfactory
to the country, for him to give some other plausible, intelligible reason *why* it was voted down than to stand upon his
dignity and call people liars. [Loud cheers.] Well, on Saturday
he did make his answer, and what do you think it was? He
says if I had only taken upon myself to tell the whole truth
about that amendment of Chase's no explanation would have
been necessary on his part—or words to that effect. Now, I
say here, that I am quite unconscious of having suppressed
anything material to the case, and I am very frank to admit if
there is any sound reason other than that which appeared to
me material, it is quite fair for him to present it. What reason
does he propose? That when Chase came forward with his
amendment expressly authorizing the people to exclude slavery from the limits of every Territory, Gen. Cass proposed to
Chase, if he (Chase) would add to his amendment that the
people should have the power to *introduce* or exclude, they
would let it go. (This is substantially all of his reply.) And
because Chase would not do that, they voted his amendment
down. Well, it turns out, I believe, upon examination, that
General Cass took some part in the little running debate upon
that amendment, and then ran away *and did not vote on it at
all.* [Laughter.] Is not that the fact? So confident, as I think,
was Gen. Cass, that there was a snake somewhere about, he
chose to run away from the whole thing. This is an inference
I draw from the fact that though he took part in the debate,
his name does not appear in the ayes and noes. But does
Judge Douglas' reply amount to a satisfactory answer? [Cries
of "yes," "yes," and "no," "no."] There is some little difference
of opinion here. [Laughter.] But I ask attention to a few more

views bearing on the question of whether it amounts to a satisfactory answer. The men, who were determined that that amendment should not get into the bill and spoil the place where the Dred Scott decision was to come in, sought an excuse to get rid of it somewhere. One of these ways—one of these excuses—was to ask Chase to add to his proposed amendment a provision that the people might *introduce* slavery if they wanted to. They very well knew Chase would do no such thing—that Mr. Chase was one of the men differing from them on the broad principle of his insisting that freedom was *better* than slavery—a man who would not consent to enact a law, penned with his own hand, by which he was made to recognize slavery on the one hand and liberty on the other as *precisely equal*; and when they insisted on his doing this, they very well knew they insisted on that which he would not for a moment think of doing, and that they were only bluffing him. I believe (I have not, since he made his answer, had a chance to examine the journals or *Congressional Globe*, and therefore speak from memory)—I believe the state of the bill at that time, according to parliamentary rules, was such that no member could propose an additional amendment to Chase's amendment. I rather think this is the truth—the Judge shakes his head. Very well. I would like to know, then, *if they wanted Chase's amendment fixed over, why somebody else could not have offered to do it?* If they wanted it amended, why did they not offer the amendment? Why did they stand there taunting and quibbling at Chase? [Laughter.] Why did they not *put it in themselves?* But to put it on the other ground; suppose that there was such an amendment offered, and Chase's was an amendment to an amendment; until one is disposed of by parliamentary law, you cannot pile another on. Then all these gentlemen had to do was to vote Chase's on, and then in the amended form in which the whole stood, add their own amendment to it if they wanted it put in that shape. This was all they were obliged to do, and the ayes and noes show that there were 36 who voted it down, against 10 who voted in favor of it. The 36 held entire sway and control. They could in some form or other have put that bill in the exact shape they wanted. If there was a rule preventing their amending it at the time, they could pass that, and then

Chase's amendment being merged, put it in the shape they wanted. They did not choose to do so, but they went into a quibble with Chase to get him to add what they knew he would not add, and because he would not, they stand upon that flimsy pretext for voting down what they argued was the meaning and intent of their own bill. They left room thereby for this Dred Scott decision, which goes very far to make slavery national throughout the United States.

I pass one or two points I have because my time will very soon expire, but I must be allowed to say that Judge Douglas recurs again, as he did upon one or two other occasions, to the enormity of Lincoln—an insignificant individual like Lincoln—upon his *ipse dixit* charging a conspiracy upon a large number of members of Congress, the Supreme Court and two Presidents, to nationalize slavery. I want to say that, in the first place, I have made no charge of this sort upon my *ipse dixit*. I have only arrayed the evidence tending to prove it, and presented it to the understanding of others, saying what I think it proves, but giving you the means of judging whether it proves it or not. This is precisely what I have done. I have not placed it upon my *ipse dixit* at all. On this occasion, I wish to recall his attention to a piece of evidence which I brought forward at Ottawa on Saturday, showing that he had made substantially the *same charge* against substantially the *same persons*, excluding his dear self from the category. I ask him to give some attention to the evidence which I brought forward, that he himself had discovered a "fatal blow being struck" against the right of the people to exclude slavery from their limits, which fatal blow he assumed as in evidence in an article in the Washington *Union*, published "by authority." I ask by whose authority? He discovers a similar or identical provision in the Lecompton Constitution. Made by whom? The framers of that Constitution. Advocated by whom? By all the members of the party in the nation, who advocated the introduction of Kansas into the Union under the Lecompton Constitution.

I have asked his attention to the evidence that he arrayed to prove that such a fatal blow was being struck, and to the facts which he brought forward in support of that charge—being identical with the one which he thinks so villainous in me.

He pointed it not at a newspaper editor merely, but at the President and his Cabinet and the members of Congress advocating the Lecompton Constitution and those framing that instrument. I must again be permitted to remind him, that although my *ipse dixit* may not be as great as his, yet it somewhat reduces the force of his calling my attention to the *enormity* of my making a like charge against him. [Loud applause.]

Go on, Judge Douglas.

MR. DOUGLAS' SPEECH.

Ladies and Gentlemen—The silence with which you have listened to Mr. Lincoln during his hour is creditable to this vast audience, composed of men of various political parties. Nothing is more honorable to any large mass of people assembled for the purpose of a fair discussion, than that kind and respectful attention that is yielded not only to your political friends, but to those who are opposed to you in politics.

I am glad that at last I have brought Mr. Lincoln to the conclusion that he had better define his position on certain political questions to which I called his attention at Ottawa. He there showed no disposition, no inclination to answer them. I did not present idle questions for him to answer merely for my gratification. I laid the foundation for those interrogatories by showing that they constituted the platform of the party whose nominee he is for the Senate. I did not presume that I had the right to catechise him as I saw proper, unless I showed that his party, or a majority of it, stood upon the platform and were in favor of the propositions upon which my questions were based. I desired simply to know, inasmuch as he had been nominated as the first, last, and only choice of his party, whether he concurred in the platform which that party had adopted for its government. In a few moments I will proceed to review the answers which he has given to these interrogatories; but in order to relieve his anxiety I will first respond to those which he has presented to me. Mark you, he has not presented interrogatories which have ever received the sanction of the party with which I am acting, and hence he has no other foundation for them than his own curiosity. ("That's a fact.")

First, he desires to know if the people of Kansas shall form a constitution by means entirely proper and unobjectionable and ask admission into the Union as a State, before they have the requisite population for a member of Congress, whether I will vote for that admission. Well, now, I regret exceedingly that he did not answer that interrogatory himself before he put it to me, in order that we might understand, and not be left to infer, on which side he is. (Good, good.) Mr. Trumbull, during the last session of Congress, voted from the beginning to the end against the admission of Oregon, although a free State, because she had not the requisite population for a member of Congress. (That's it.) Mr. Trumbull would not consent, under any circumstances, to let a State, free or slave, come into the Union until it had the requisite population. As Mr. Trumbull is in the field, fighting for Mr. Lincoln, I would like to have Mr. Lincoln answer his own question and tell me whether he is fighting Trumbull on that issue or not. (Good, put it to him, and cheers.) But I will answer his question. In reference to Kansas; it is my opinion, that as she has population enough to constitute a slave State, she has people enough for a free State. (Cheers.) I will not make Kansas an exceptional case to the other States of the Union. (Sound, and hear, hear.) I hold it to be a sound rule of universal application to require a territory to contain the requisite population for a member of Congress, before it is admitted as a State into the Union. I made that proposition in the Senate in 1856, and I renewed it during the last session, in a bill providing that no territory of the United States should form a constitution and apply for admission until it had the requisite population. On another occasion I proposed that neither Kansas, or any other territory, should be admitted until it had the requisite population. Congress did not adopt any of my propositions containing this general rule, but did make an exception of Kansas. I will not stand by that exception. (Cheers.) Either Kansas must come in as a free State, with whatever population she may have, or the rule must be applied to all the other territories alike. (Cheers.) I therefore answer at once, that it having been decided that Kansas has people enough for a slave State, I hold that she has enough for a free State. ("Good," and applause.) I hope Mr. Lincoln is satisfied with my answer; ("he ought to be," and cheers,) and now I would like to get his answer to his own interrogatory—whether or not he will vote to admit Kansas before she has the requisite population. ("Hit him again.") I want to know whether he will vote to admit Oregon before that Territory has the requisite population. Mr. Trumbull will not, and the same reason that commits Mr. Trumbull against the admission of Oregon, commits him against Kansas, even if she should apply for admission as a free State. ("You've got him," and cheers.) If there is any sincerity, any truth in the argument of Mr. Trumbull in the Senate against the admission of Oregon because she had not 93,420 people, although her population was larger than that of Kansas, he stands pledged against the admission of both Oregon and Kansas until they have 93,420 inhabitants. I would like Mr. Lincoln to answer this question. I would like him to take his own medicine. (Laughter.) If he differs with Mr. Trumbull, let him answer his argument against the admission of Oregon, instead of poking questions at me. ("Right, good, good," laughter and cheers.)

The next question propounded to me by Mr. Lincoln is, can the people of a territory in any lawful way against the wishes of any citizen of the United States; exclude slavery from their limits prior to the formation of a State Constitution? I answer emphatically, as Mr. Lincoln has heard me answer a hundred times from every stump in Illinois, that in my opinion the people of a territory can, by lawful means, exclude slavery from their limits prior to the formation of a State Constitution. (Enthusiastic Applause.) Mr. Lincoln knew that I had answered that question over and over again. He heard me argue the Nebraska bill on that principle all over the State in 1854, in 1855 and in 1856, and he has no excuse for pretending to be in doubt as to my position on that question. It matters not what way the Supreme Court may hereafter decide as to the abstract question whether slavery may or may not go into a territory under the constitution, the people have the lawful means to introduce it or exclude it as they please, for the reason that slavery cannot exist a day or an hour anywhere, unless it is supported by local police regulations. (Right, right.) Those police regulations can only be established by the local legislature, and if the people are opposed to slavery they will elect representatives to that body who will by unfriendly legislation effectually prevent the introduction of it into their midst. If, on the contrary, they are for it, their legislation will favor its extension. Hence, no matter what the decision of the Supreme Court may be on that abstract question, still the right of the people to make a slave territory or a free territory is perfect and complete under the Nebraska bill. I hope Mr. Lincoln deems my answer satisfactory on that point.

[Deacon Bross spoke.]

In this connection, I will notice the charge which he has introduced in relation to Mr. Chase's amendment. I thought that I had chased that amendment out of Mr. Lincoln's brain at Ottawa; (laughter) but it seems that it still haunts his imagination, and he is not yet satisfied. I had supposed that he would be ashamed to press that question further. He is a lawyer, and has been a Member of Congress, and has occupied his time and amused you by telling you about parliamentary proceedings. He ought to have known better than to try to palm off his miserable impositions upon this intelligent audience. ("Good," and cheers.) The Nebraska bill provided that the legislative power, and authority of the said Territory, should extend to all rightful subjects of legislation consistent with the organic act and the Constitution of the United States. It did not make any exception as to slavery, but gave all the power that it was possible for Congress to give, without violating the Constitution to the Territorial Legislature, with no exception or limitation on the subject of slavery at all. The language of that bill which I have quoted, gave the full power and the full authority over the subject of slavery, affirmatively and negatively, to introduce it or exclude it, so far as the Constitution of the United States would permit. What more could Mr. Chase give by his amendment? Nothing. He offered his amendment for the identical purpose for which Mr. Lincoln is using it, to enable demagogues in the country to try and deceive the people. ("Good, hit him again," and cheers.)

[Deacon Bross spoke.]

His amendment was to this effect. It provided that the Legislature should have the power to exclude slavery; and General Cass suggested, "why not give the power to introduce as well as exclude?" The answer was, they have the power already in the bill to do both. Chase was afraid his amendment would be adopted if he put the alternative proposition and so make it fair both ways, but would not yield. He offered it for the purpose of having it rejected. He offered it, as he has himself avowed over and over again, simply to make capital out of it for the stump. He expected that it would be capital for small politicians in the country, and that they would make an effort to deceive the people with it, and he was not mistaken, for Lincoln is carrying out the plan admirably. ("Good, good.") Lincoln knows that the Nebraska bill, without Chase's amendment, gave all the power which the Constitution would permit. Could Congress confer any more? ("No, no.") Could Congress go beyond the Constitution of the country? We gave all, a full grant, with no exception in regard to slavery one way or the other. We left that question as we left all others, to be decided by the people for themselves, just as they pleased. I will not occupy my time on this question. I have argued it before all over Illinois. I have argued it in this beautiful city of Freeport; I have argued it in the North, the South, the East and the West, avowing the same sentiments and the same principles. I have not been afraid to avow my sentiments up here for fear I would be trotted down into Egypt. (Cheers and laughter.)

The third question which Mr. Lincoln presented is, if the Supreme Court of the United States shall decide that a State of this Union cannot exclude slavery from its own limits will I submit to it? I am amazed that Lincoln should ask such a question. ("A school boy knows better.") Yes, a school boy does know better. Mr. Lincoln's object is to cast an imputation upon the Supreme Court. He knows that there never was but one man in America, claiming any degree of intelligence or decency, who ever for a moment pretended such a thing. It is true that the Washington *Union*, in an article published on the 17th of last December, did put forth that doctrine, and I denounced the article on the floor of the Senate, in a speech which Mr. Lincoln now pretends was against the President. The *Union* had claimed that slavery had a right to go into the free States, and that any provision in the Constitution or laws of the free States to the contrary were null and void. I denounced it in the Senate, as I said before, and I was the first man who did. Lincoln's friends, Trumbull, and Seward, and Hale, and Wilson, and the whole Black Republican side of the Senate were silent. They left it to me to denounce it. (Cheers.) And what was the reply made to me on that occasion? Mr. Toombs, of Georgia, got up and undertook to lecture me on the ground that I ought not to have deemed the article worthy of notice, and ought not to have replied to it; that there was not one man, woman or child south of the Potomac, in any slave State, who did not repudiate any such pretension. Mr. Lincoln knows that that reply was made on the spot, and yet now he asks this question. He might as well ask me, suppose Mr. Lincoln should steal a horse would I sanction it; (laughter,) and it would be as genteel in me to ask him, in the event he stole a horse, what ought to be done with him. He casts an imputation upon the Supreme Court of the United States by supposing that they would violate the Constitution of the United States. I tell him that such a thing is not possible. (Cheers.) It would be an act of moral treason that no man on the bench could ever descend to. Mr. Lincoln himself would never in his partizan feelings so far forget what was right as to be guilty of such an act. ("Good, good.")

The fourth question of Mr. Lincoln is, are you in favor of acquiring additional territory in disregard as to how such acquisition may effect the Union on the slavery questions. This question is very ingeniously and cunningly put.

[Deacon Bross here spoke, *sotto voce*,—the reporter understanding him to say, "Now we've got him."]

The Black Republican creed lays it down expressly, that under no circumstances shall we acquire any more territory unless slavery is first prohibited in the country. I ask Mr. Lincoln whether he is in favor of that proposition. Are you (addressing Mr. Lincoln) opposed to the acquisition of any more territory, under any circumstances, unless slavery is prohibited in it? That he does not like to answer. When I ask him whether he stands up to that article in the platform of his party, he turns, yankee-fashion, and without answering it, asks me whether I am in favor of acquiring territory without regard to how it may affect the Union on the slavery question. (Good.) I answer that whenever it becomes necessary, in our growth and progress to acquire more territory, that I am in favor of it, without reference to the question of slavery, and when we have acquired it, I will leave the people free to do as they please, either to make it slave or free territory, as they prefer. [Here Deacon Bross spoke, the reporter believes that he said, "That's bold." It was said solemnly.] It is idle to tell me or you that we have territory enough. Our fathers supposed that we had enough when our territory extended to the Mississippi river, but a few years' growth and expansion satisfied them that we needed more, and the Louisiana territory, from the West branch of the Mississippi, to the British possessions, was acquired. Then we acquired Oregon, then California and New Mexico. We have enough now for the present, but this is a young and a growing nation. It swarms as often as a hive of bees, and as new swarms are turned out each year, there must be hives in which they can gather and make their honey. (Good.) In less than fifteen years, if the same progress that has distinguished this country for the last fifteen years continues, every foot of vacant land between this and the Pacific ocean, owned by the United States, will be occupied. Will you not continue to increase at the end of fifteen years as well as now? I tell you, increase, and multiply, and expand, is the law of this nation's existence. (Good.) You cannot limit this great republic by mere boundary lines, saying, "thus far shalt thou go, and no further." Any one of you gentlemen might as well say to a son twelve years old that he is big enough, and must not grow any larger, and in order to prevent his growth put a hoop around him to keep him to his present size. What would be the result? Either the hoop must burst and be rent asunder, or the child must die. So it would be with this great nation. With our natural increase, growing with a rapidity unknown in any other part of the globe, with the tide of emigration that is fleeing from despotism in the old world to seek a refuge in our own, there is a constant torrent pouring into this country that requires more land, more territory upon which to settle, and just as fast as our interests and our destiny require additional territory in the north, in the south, or on the islands of the ocean, I am for it, and when we acquire it will leave the people, according to the Nebraska bill, free to do as they please on the subject of slavery and every other question. (Good, good, hurra for Douglas.)

I trust now that Mr. Lincoln will deem himself answered on his four points. He racked his brain so much in devising these four questions that he exhausted himself, and had not strength enough to invent the others. (Laughter.) As soon as he is able to hold a council with his advisers, Lovejoy, Farnsworth, and Fred. Douglass, he will frame and propound others. (Good, good, &c. Renewed laughter, in which Mr. Lincoln feebly joined, saying that he hoped with their aid to get seven questions, the number asked him by Judge Douglas, and so make *conclusions* even.) You Black Republicans who say good, I have no doubt think that they are all good men. (White, white.) I have reason to recollect that some people in this country think that Fred. Douglass is a very good man. The last time I came here to make a speech, while talking from the stand to you, people of Freeport, as I am doing to-day, I saw a carriage and a magnificent one it was, drive up and take a position on the outside of the crowd; a beautiful young lady was sitting on the box seat, whilst Fred. Douglass and her mother reclined inside, and the owner of the carriage acted as driver. (Laughter, cheers, cries of right, what have you to say against it, &c.) I saw this in your own town. ("What of it.") All I have to say of it is this, that if you, Black Republicans, think that the negro ought to be on a social equality with your wives and daughters, and ride in a carriage with your wife, whilst you drive the team, you have a perfect right to do so. (Good, good, and cheers, mingled with hooting and cries of white, white.) I am told that one of Fred. Douglass' kinsmen, another rich black negro, is now traveling in this part of the State making speeches for his friend Lincoln as the champion of black men. ("White men, white men," and "what have you got to say against it." That's right, &c.) All I have to say on that subject is that those of you who believe that the negro is your equal and ought to be on an equality with you socially, politically, and legally; have a right to entertain those opinions, and of course will vote for Mr. Lincoln. ("Down with the negro," no, no, &c.)

I have a word to say on Mr. Lincoln's answer to the interrogatories contained in my speech at Ottawa, and which he has pretended to reply to here to-day. Mr. Lincoln makes a great parade of the fact that I quoted a platform as having been adopted by the Black Republican party at Springfield in 1854, which, it turns out, was adopted at another place. Mr. Lincoln loses sight of the thing itself in his ecstasies over the mistake I made in stating the place where it was done. He thinks that that platform was not adopted on the right "spot."

When I put the direct questions to Mr. Lincoln to ascertain whether he now stands pledged to that creed—to the unconditional repeal of the fugitive slave law, a refusal to admit any more slave States into the Union even if the people want them, a determination to apply the Wilmot Proviso not only to all the territory, we now have, but all that we may hereafter acquire, he refused to answer, and his followers say, in excuse, that the resolutions upon which I based my interrogatories were not adopted at the *"right spot."* (Laughter and applause.) Lincoln and his political friends are great on *"spots."* (Renewed laughter.) In Congress, as a representative of this State, he declared the Mexican war to be unjust and infamous, and would not support it, or acknowledge his own country to be right in the contest, because he said that American blood was not shed on American soil in the *"right spot."* (Lay on to him.) And now he cannot answer the questions I put to him at Ottawa because the resolutions I read were not adopted at the *"right spot."* It may be possible that I was led into an error as to the *spot* on which the resolutions I then read were proclaimed, but I was not, and am not in error as to the fact of their forming the basis of the creed of the Republican party when that party was first organized. [Cheers.] I will state to you the evidence I had, and upon which I relied for my statement that the resolutions in question were adopted at Springfield on the 5th of October, 1854. Although I was aware that such resolutions had been passed in this district, and nearly all the northern Congressional districts and county conventions,

I had not noticed whether or not they had been adopted by any State convention. In 1856, a debate arose in Congress between Major Thomas L. Harris, of the Springfield district, and Mr. Norton, of the Joliet district, on political matters connected with our State, in the course of which Major Harris quoted those resolutions as having been passed by the first Republican State Convention that ever assembled in Illinois. I knew that Major Harris was remarkable for his accuracy, that he was a very conscientious and sincere man, and I also noticed that Norton did not question the accuracy of this statement. I therefore took it for granted that it was so, and the other day when I concluded to use the resolutions at Ottawa, I wrote to Charles H. Lanphier, editor of the State Register, at Springfield, calling his attention to them, telling him that I had been informed that Major Harris was lying sick at Springfield, and desiring him to call upon him and ascertain all the facts concerning the resolutions, the time and the place where they were adopted. In reply Mr. Lanphier sent me two copies of his paper, which I have here. The first is a copy of the State Register, published at Springfield, Mr. Lincoln's own town, on the 16th of October 1854, only eleven days after the adjournment of the convention, from which I desire to read the following:

During the late discussions in this city, Lincoln made a speech, to which Judge Douglas replied. In Lincoln's speech he took the broad ground that, according to the Declaration of Independence, the whites and blacks are equal. From this he drew the conclusion, which he several times repeated, that the white man had no right to pass laws for the government of the black man without the nigger's consent. This speech of Lincoln's was heard and applauded by all the Abolitionists assembled in Springfield. So soon as Mr. Lincoln was done speaking, Mr. Codding arose and requested all the delegates to the Black Republican convention to withdraw into the Senate chamber. They did so, and after long deliberation, they laid down the following abolition platform as the platform on which they stood. We call the particular attention of all our readers to it.

Then follows the identical platform, word for word, which I read at Ottawa. (Cheers.) Now, that was published in Mr. Lincoln's own town, eleven days after the convention was held, and it has remained on record up to this day never contradicted.

When I quoted the resolutions at Ottawa and questioned Mr. Lincoln in relation to them, he said that his name was on the committee that reported them, but he did not serve, nor did he think he served, because he was, or thought he was, in Tazewell county at the time the convention was in session. He did not deny that the resolutions were passed by the Springfield convention. He did not know better, and evidently thought that they were, but afterwards his friends declared that they had discovered that they varied in some respects from the resolutions passed by that convention. I have shown you that I had good evidence for believing that the resolutions had been passed at Springfield. Mr. Lincoln ought to have known better; but not a word is said about his ignorance on the subject, whilst I, notwithstanding the circumstances, am accused of forgery.

Now, I will show you that if I have made a mistake as to the place where these resolutions were adopted—and when I get down to Springfield I will investigate the matter and see whether or not I have—that the principles they enunciate were adopted as the Black Republican platform (white, white,) in the various counties and Congressional Districts throughout the north end of the State in 1854. This platform was adopted in nearly every county that gave a Black Republican majority for the Legislature in that year, and here is a man (pointing to Mr. Denio, who sat on the stand near Deacon Bross,) who knows as well as any living man that it was the creed of the Black Republican party at that time. I would be willing to call Denio as a witness, or any other honest man belonging to that party. I will now read the resolutions adopted at the Rockford Convention on the 30th of August, 1854, which nominated Washburne for Congress. You elected him on the following platform:

Resolved, That the continued and increasing aggressions of slavery in our country are destructive of the best rights of a free people, and that such aggressions cannot be successfully resisted without the united political action of all good men.

Resolved, That the citizens of the United States hold in their hands peaceful, constitutional, and efficient remedy against the encroachments of the slave power, the ballot box, and, if that remedy is boldly and wisely applied, the principles of liberty and eternal justice will be established.

Resolved, That we accept this issue forced upon us by the slave power, and, in defense of freedom, will co-operate and be known as Republicans, pledged to the accomplishment of the following purposes:

To bring the Administration of the Government back to the control of first principles; to restore Kansas and Nebraska to the position of free Territories; to repeal and entirely abrogate the fugitive slave law; to restrict slavery to those States in which it exists; to prohibit the admission of any more slave States into the Union; to exclude slavery from all the territories over which the general government has exclusive jurisdiction, and to resist the acquisition of any more territories unless the introduction of slavery therein forever shall have been prohibited.

Resolved, That in furtherance of these principles we will use such constitutional and lawful means as shall seem best adapted to their accomplishment, and that we will support no man for office under the General or State Government who is not positively committed to the support of these principles and whose personal character and conduct is not a guaranty that he is reliable and shall abjure all party allegiance and ties.

Resolved, That we cordially invite persons of all former political parties whatever in favor of the object expressed in the above resolutions to unite with us in carrying them into effect.

[Senator Douglas was frequently interrupted in reading these resolutions by loud cries of "Good, good," "that's the doctrine," and vociferous applause.]

Well, you think that is a very good platform, do you not? ("Yes, yes, all right," and cheers.) If you do, if you approve it now, and think it is all right, you will not join with those men who say that I libel you by calling these your principles, will you? ("Good, good, hit him again," and great laughter and cheers.) Now, Mr. Lincoln complains; Mr. Lincoln charges that I did you and him injustice by saying that this was the platform of your party. (Renewed laughter.) I am told that Washburne made a speech in Galena last night in which he abused me awfully for bringing to light this platform on which he was elected to Congress. He thought that you had forgotten it, as he and Mr. Lincoln desire to. (Laughter.) He did not deny but that you had adopted it, and that he had subscribed to and was pledged to it, but he did not think it was fair to call it up and remind the people that it was their platform.

[Here Deacon Bross spoke.]

But I am glad to find that you are more honest in your

abolitionism than your leaders, by avowing that it is your platform, and right in your opinion. (Laughter, "you have them, good, good.")

In the adoption of that platform, you not only declared that you would resist the admission of any more slave States, and work for the repeal of the Fugitive Slave law, but you pledged yourselves not to vote for any man for State or Federal offices who was not committed to these principles. ("Exactly so." Exactly so! Cheers.) You were thus committed. Similar resolutions to those were adopted in your county Convention here, and now with your admissions that they are your platform and embody your sentiments now as they did then, what do you think of Mr. Lincoln, your candidate for the U.S. Senate, who is attempting to dodge the responsibility of this platform, because it was not adopted in the right spot? (Shouts of laughter, hurra for Douglas, &c.) I thought that it was adopted in Springfield, but it turns out it was not, that it was adopted at Rockford and in the various counties which comprise this Congressional District. When I get into the next district, I will show that the same platform was adopted there, and so on through the State, until I nail the responsibility of it upon the back of the Black Republican party throughout the State. ("White, white," three cheers for Douglas.)

(A VOICE—Couldn't you modify and call it brown? Laughter.)

MR. DOUGLAS.—Not a bit. I thought that you were becoming a little brown when your members in Congress voted for the Crittenden-Montgomery bill, but since you have backed out from that position and gone back to Abolitionism, you are black, and not brown. (Shouts of laughter, and a voice, "Can't you ask him another question.")

Gentlemen, I have shown you what your platform was in 1854. You still adhere to it. The same platform was adopted by nearly all the counties where the Black Republican party had a majority in 1854. I wish now to call your attention to the action of your representatives in the Legislature when they assembled together at Springfield. In the first place you must remember that this was the organization of a new party. It is so declared in the resolutions themselves which say that you

are going to dissolve all old party ties and call the new party
Republican. The old Whig party was to have its throat cut
from ear to ear, and the Democratic party was to be annihilated and blotted out of existence, whilst in lieu of these parties the Black Republican party was to be organized on this
Abolition platform. You know who the chief leaders were in
breaking up and destroying these two great parties. Lincoln
on the one hand and Trumbull on the other, being disappointed politicians, (laughter,) and having retired or been
driven to obscurity by an outraged constituency because of
their political sins, formed a scheme to abolitionize the two
parties and lead the Old Line Whigs and Old Line Democrats
captive, bound hand and foot into the Abolition camp. Giddings, Chase, Fred. Douglass and Lovejoy were here to christen them whenever they were brought in. (Great laughter.)
Lincoln went to work to dissolve the Old Line Whig party.
Clay was dead, and although the sod was not yet green on his
grave, this man undertook to bring into disrepute those great
compromise measures of 1850, with which Clay and Webster
were identified. Up to 1854 the old Whig party and the Democratic party had stood on a common platform so far as this
slavery question was concerned. You Whigs and we Democrats differed about the bank, the tariff, distribution, the specie circular and the sub-treasury, but we agreed on this slavery
question and the true mode of preserving the peace and harmony of the Union. The compromise measures of 1850 were
introduced by Clay, were defended by Webster, and supported by Cass, and were approved by Fillmore, and sanctioned by the National men of both parties. They constituted
a common plank upon which both Whigs and Democrats
stood. In 1852 the Whig party in its last national convention at
Baltimore endorsed and approved these measures of Clay, and
so did the national convention of the Democratic party held
that same year. Thus the old line Whigs and the old line
Democrats stood pledged to the great principle of self-
government, which guarantees to the people of each Territory
the right to decide the slavery question for themselves. In 1854
after the death of Clay and Webster, Mr. Lincoln on the part
of the Whigs undertook to abolitionize the Whig party, by
dissolving it, transferring the members into the Abolition

camp and making them train under Giddings, Fred. Douglass, Lovejoy, Chase, Farnsworth, and other abolition leaders. Trumbull undertook to dissolve the Democratic party by taking old Democrats into the abolition camp. Mr. Lincoln was aided in his efforts by many leading Whigs throughout the State. Your member of Congress, Mr. Washburne, being one of the most active. (Good fellow.) Trumbull was aided by many renegades from the Democratic party, among whom were John Wentworth, (laughter,) Tom Turner and others with whom you are familiar.

MR. TURNER, who was one of the moderators, here interposed and said that he had drawn the resolutions which Senator Douglas had read.

MR. DOUGLAS—Yes, and Turner says that he drew these resolutions. ("Hurra for Turner." "Hurra for Douglas.") That is right, give Turner cheers for drawing the resolutions if you approve them. If he drew those resolutions he will not deny that they are the creed of the Black Republican party.

MR. TURNER.—They are our creed exactly. (Cheers.)

MR. DOUGLAS—And yet Lincoln denies that he stands on them. ("Good, good," and laughter.) Mr. Turner says that the creed of the Black Republican party is the admission of no more slave States, and yet Mr. Lincoln declares that he would not like to be placed in a position where he would have to vote for them. All I have to say to friend Lincoln is, that I do not think there is much danger of his being placed in such a position. (More laughter.) As Mr. Lincoln would be very sorry to be placed in such an embarrassing position as to be obliged to vote on the admission of any more slave States, I propose, out of mere kindness, to relieve him from any such necessity. (Renewed laughter and cheers.)

When the bargain between Lincoln and Trumbull was completed for abolitionizing the Whig and Democratic parties, they "spread" over the State, Lincoln still pretending to be an Old Line Whig in order to "rope in" the Whigs, and Trumbull pretending to be as good a Democrat as he ever was in order to coax the Democrats over into the Abolition ranks. ("That's exactly what we want.") They played the part that "decoy ducks" play down on the Potomac river. In that part of the country they make artificial ducks and put them on the water in places where the wild ducks are to be found for the purpose of decoying them. Well, Lincoln and Trumbull played the part of these "decoy ducks" and deceived enough Old Line Whigs and Old Line Democrats to elect a Black Republican Legislature. When that Legislature met, the first thing it did was to elect as Speaker of the House the very man who is now boasting that he wrote the Abolition platform on which Lincoln will not stand. ("Good;" "hit him again," and cheers.) I want to know of Mr. Turner whether or not, when he was elected he was a good embodiment of Republican principles?

MR. TURNER—I hope I was then and am now.

MR. DOUGLAS—He answers that he hopes he was then and is now. He wrote that Black Republican platform, and is satisfied with it now. ("Hurrah for Turner," "good," &c.) I admire and acknowledge Turner's honesty. Every man of you know that what he says about these resolutions being the platform of the Black Republican party is true, and you also know that each one of these men who are shuffling and trying to deny it are only trying to cheat the people out of their votes for the purpose of deceiving them still more after the election. ("Good," and cheers.) I propose to trace this thing a little further, in order that you can see what additional evidence there is to fasten this revolutionary platform upon the Black Republican party. When the Legislature assembled, there was an United States Senator to elect in the place of Gen. Shields, and before they proceeded to ballot, Lovejoy insisted on laying down certain principles by which to govern the party. It has been published to the world and satisfactorily proven that there was at the time the alliance was made between Trumbull and Lincoln to abolitionize the two parties, an agreement that Lincoln should take Shields' place in the United States Senate, and Trumbull should have mine so soon as they could conveniently get rid of me. When Lincoln was beaten for Shields' place in a manner I will refer to in a few minutes, he felt very sore and restive; his friends grumbled, and some of them came out and charged that the most infamous treachery had been practised against him; that the bargain was that Lincoln was to have had Shields' place, and Trumbull was to have waited for mine, but that Trumbull having the control of a few abolitionized Democrats, he prevented them from voting for Lincoln, thus keeping him within a few votes of an election until he succeeded in forcing the party to drop him and elect Trumbull. Well, Trumbull having cheated Lincoln, his friends made a fuss, and in order to keep them and Lincoln quiet, the party were obliged to come forward, in advance, at the last State election, and make a pledge that they would go for Lincoln and nobody else. Lincoln could not be silenced in any other way.

Now, there are a great many Black Republicans of you who do not know this thing was done. ("White, white," and great clamor.) I wish to remind you that while Mr. Lincoln was speaking there was not a Democrat vulgar and black-guard enough to interrupt him. (Great applause and cries of hurrah for Douglas.) But I know that the shoe is pinching you. I am clinching Lincoln now and you are scared to death for the result. (Cheers.) I have seen this thing before. I have seen men make appointments for joint discussions, and the moment their man has been heard, try to interrupt and prevent a fair hearing of the other side. I have seen your mobs before, and defy your wrath. (Tremendous applause.) My friends, do not cheer, for I need my whole time. The object of the opposition is to occupy my attention in order to prevent me from giving the whole evidence and nailing this double dealing on the Black Republican party. As I have before said, Lovejoy demanded a declaration of principles on the part of the Black Republicans of the Legislature before going into an election for United States Senator. He offered the following preamble and resolutions which I hold in my hand:

Whereas, human slavery is a violation of the principles of natural and revealed rights; and whereas, the fathers of the Revolution, fully imbued with the spirit of these principles, declared freedom to be the inalienable birthright of all men; and whereas, the preamble to the Constitution of the United States avers that that instrument was ordained to establish justice, and secure the blessings of liberty to ourselves and our posterity; and whereas, in furtherance of the above principles, slavery was forever prohibited in the old northwest territory, and more recently in all that territory lying west and north of the State of Missouri, by the act of the federal government; and whereas, the repeal of the prohibition, last referred to, was contrary to the wishes of the people of Illinois, a violation of an implied compact, long deemed and held sacred by the citizens of the United States, and a wide departure from the uniform action of the general government in relation to the extension of slavery; therefore,

Resolved, by the House of Representatives, the Senate concurring therein, That our Senators in Congress be instructed, and our Representatives requested, to introduce, if not otherwise introduced, and to vote for a bill to restore such prohibition to the aforesaid territories, and also to extend a similar prohibition to all territory which now belongs to the United States, or which may hereafter come under their jurisdiction.

Resolved, That our Senators in Congress be instructed, and our Representatives requested, to vote against the admission of any State into the Union, the constitution of which does not prohibit slavery, whether the territory out of which such State may have been formed shall have been acquired by conquest, treaty, purchase, or from original territory of the United States.

Resolved, That our Senators in Congress be instructed and our Representatives requested to introduce and vote for a bill to repeal an act entitled "an act respecting fugitives from justice and persons escaping from the service of their masters"; and, failing in that, for such a modification of it as shall secure the right of *habeas corpus* and trial by jury before the regularly-constituted authorities of the State, to all persons claimed as owing service or labor.

(Cries of "good," "good," and cheers.) Yes, you say "good," "good," and I have no doubt you think so. Those resolutions were introduced by Mr. Lovejoy immediately preceding the election of Senator. They declared first, that the Wilmot Proviso must be applied to all territory North of 36 deg., 30 min. Secondly, that it must be applied to all the territory South of 36 deg., 30 min. Thirdly, that it must be applied to all the territory now owned by the United States, and finally, that it must be applied to all territory hereafter to be acquired by the United States. The next resolution declares that no more slave States shall be admitted into this Union under any circumstances whatever, no matter whether they are formed out of territory now owned by us or that we may hereafter acquire, by treaty, by Congress, or in any manner whatever. (A VOICE, "That is right.") You say that is right. We will see in a moment. The next resolution demands the unconditional repeal of the fugitive slave law, although its unconditional repeal would leave no provision for carrying out that clause of the Constitution of the United States which guarantees the surrender of fugitives. If they could not get an unconditional repeal, they demanded that that law should be so modified as to make it as nearly useless as possible. Now I want to show you who voted for these resolutions. When the vote was taken on the first resolution it was decided in the affirmative—yeas 41, nays 32. You will find that this is a strict party vote, between the Democrats, on the one hand, and the Black Republicans, on the other. (Cries of white, white, and clamor.) I know your name, and always call things by their right name. The point I wish to call your attention to, is this: that these resolutions were adopted on the 7th day of February, and that on the 8th they went into an election for a U.S. Senator, and on that day every man who voted for these resolutions, with but two exceptions, voted for Lincoln for the U.S. Senate. (Cries of "good, good," and "give us their names.") I will read the names over to you if you want them, but I believe your object is to occupy my time. (Cries of "that is it.")

On the next resolution, the vote stood—yeas 33, nays 40, and on the third resolution—yeas 35, nays 47. I wish to impress it upon you, that every man who voted for those resolutions, with but two exceptions, voted on the next day for Lincoln, for U.S. Senator. Bear in mind that the members who thus voted for Lincoln were elected to the Legislature, pledged to vote for no man for office under the State or federal government who was not committed to this Black Republican platform. (Cries of "white, white," and "good for you.") They were all so pledged. Mr. Turner, who stands by me, and who then represented you, and who says that he wrote those resolutions, voted for Lincoln, when he was pledged not to do so unless Lincoln was committed in favor of those resolutions. I now ask Mr. Turner, (turning to Turner) did you violate your pledge in voting for Mr. Lincoln, or did he commit himself to your platform before you cast your vote for him? (Mr. Lincoln here started forward, and grasping Mr. Turner, shook him nervously, and said, "Don't answer, Turner, you have no right to answer.")

I could go through the whole list of names here and show you that all the Black Republicans in the Legislature, ("white, white,") who voted for Mr. Lincoln, had voted on the day previous for these resolutions. For instance, here are the names of Sargent and Little of Joe Daviess and Carroll;

Thomas J. Turner, of Stephenson; Lawrence, of Boone and McHenry; Swan, of Lake; Pinckney, of Ogle county, and Lyman, of Winnebago. Thus you see every member from your Congressional District voted for Mr. Lincoln, and they were pledged not to vote for him unless he was committed to the doctrine of no more slave States, the prohibition of slavery in the Territories, and the repeal of the Fugitive Slave law. Mr. Lincoln tells you to-day that he is not pledged to any such doctrine. Either Mr. Lincoln was then committed to those propositions, or Mr. Turner violated his pledges to you when he voted for him. Either Lincoln was pledged to each one of those propositions, or else every Black Republican—(cries of "white, white,")—representative from this Congressional District violated his pledge of honor to his constituents by voting for him. I ask you which horn of the dilemma will you take? Will you hold Lincoln up to the platform of his party, or will you accuse every representative you had in the Legislature of violating his pledge of honor to his constituents. (VOICES; "we go for Turner," "we go for Lincoln;" "hurrah for Douglas," "hurrah for Turner.") There is no escape for you. Either Mr. Lincoln was committed to those propositions, or your members violated their faith. Take either horn of the dilemma you choose. There is no dodging the question, I want Lincoln's answer. He says he was not pledged to repeal the fugitive slave law, that he does not quite like to do it; he will not introduce a law to repeal it, but thinks there ought to be some law; he does not tell what it ought to be; upon the whole, he is altogether undecided, and don't know what to think or to do. That is the substance of his answer upon the repeal of the fugitive slave law. I put the question to him distinctly, whether he endorsed that part of the Black Republican platform which calls for the entire abrogation and repeal of the fugitive slave law. He answers no! that he does not endorse that, but he does not tell what he is for, or what he will vote for. His answer is, in fact, no answer at all. Why cannot he speak out and say what he is for and what he will do? (Cries of "that's right.")

In regard to there being no more slave States, he is not pledged to that. He would not like, he says, to be put in a position where he would have to vote one way or another upon that question. I pray you do not put him in a position that would embarrass him so much. (Laughter.) Gentlemen, if he goes to the Senate, he may be put in that position, and then which way will he vote?

[A VOICE—How will you vote?]

MR. DOUGLAS—I will vote for the admission of just such a State as by the form of their Constitution the people show they want; if they want slavery, they shall have it; if they prohibit slavery, it shall be prohibited. They can form their institutions to please themselves, subject only to the Constitution; and I for one stand ready to receive them into the Union. ("Three cheers for Douglas.") Why cannot your Black Republican candidates talk out as plain as that when they are questioned? (Cries of "good, good.")

[Here Deacon Bross spoke.]

I do not want to cheat any man out of his vote. No man is deceived in regard to my principles if I have the power to express myself in terms explicit enough to convey my ideas.

Mr. Lincoln made a speech when he was nominated for the U.S. Senate which covers all these abolition platforms. He there lays down a proposition so broad in its abolitionism as to cover the whole ground.

In my opinion it (the slavery agitation) will not cease until a crisis shall have been reached and passed. "A house divided against itself cannot stand." I believe this Government cannot endure permanently half Slave and half Free. I do not expect the house to fall—but I do expect it will cease to be divided. It will become all one thing or all the other. Either the opponents of Slavery will arrest the further spread of it, and place it where the public mind shall rest in the belief that it is in the course of ultimate extinction, or its advocates will push it forward till it shall become alike lawful in all the States—old as well as new, North as well as South.

There you find that Mr. Lincoln lays down the doctrine that this Union cannot endure divided as our Fathers made it, with free and slave States. He says they must all become one thing, or all the other; that they must be all free or all slave, or else the Union cannot continue to exist. It being his opinion that to admit any more slave States, to continue to divide the Union into free and slave States, will dissolve it. I want to know of Mr. Lincoln whether he will vote for the admission of another Slave state. (Cries of "Bring him out.")

He tells you the Union cannot exist unless the States are all free or all slave; he tells you that he is opposed to making them all slave, and hence he is for making them all free, in order that the Union may exist; and yet he will not say that he will not vote against the admission of another slave State, knowing that the Union must be dissolved if he votes for it. (Great laughter.) I ask you if that is fair dealing? The true intent and inevitable conclusion to be drawn from his first Springfield speech is, that he is opposed to the admission of any more slave States under any circumstance. If he is so opposed why not say so? If he believes this Union cannot endure divided into free and slave States, that they must all become free in order to save the Union, he is bound, as an honest man, to vote against any more slave States. If he believes it he is bound to do it. Show me that it is my duty in order to save the Union to do a particular act, and I will do it if the constitution does not prohibit it. (Applause.) I am not for the dissolution of the Union under any circumstances. (Renewed applause.) I will pursue no course of conduct that will give just cause for the dissolution of the Union. The hope of the friends of freedom throughout the world rests upon the perpetuity of this Union. The down-trodden and oppressed people who are suffering under European despotism all look with hope and anxiety to the American Union as the only resting place and permanent home of freedom and self-government.

Mr. Lincoln says that he believes that this Union cannot continue to endure with slave States in it, and yet he will not tell you distinctly whether he will vote for or against the admission of any more slave States, but says he would not like to be put to the test. (Laughter.) I do not think he will be put to the test. (Renewed laughter.) I do not think that the people of Illinois desire a man to represent them who would not like to be put to the test on the performance of a high constitutional duty. (Cries of good.) I will retire in shame from the Senate of the United States when I am not willing to be put to the test in the performance of my duty. I have been put to severe tests. (That is so.) I have stood by my principles in fair weather and in foul, in the sunshine and in the rain. I have defended the great principles of self-government here among you when Northern sentiment ran in a torrent against me. (A VOICE,—that is so,) and I have defended that same great principle when Southern sentiment came down like an avalanche upon me. I was not afraid of any test they put to me. I knew I was right—I knew my principles were sound—I knew that the people would see in the end that I had done right, and I knew that the God of Heaven would smile upon me if I was faithful in the performance of my duty. (Cries of good, cheers and laughter.)

Mr. Lincoln makes a charge of corruption against the Supreme Court of the United States, and two Presidents of the United States, and attempts to bolster it up by saying that I did the same against the Washington *Union*. Suppose I did make that charge of corruption against the Washington *Union*, when it was true, does that justify him in making a false charge against me and others? That is the question I would put. He says that at the time the Nebraska bill was introduced, and before it was passed there was a conspiracy between the Judges of the Supreme Court, President Pierce, President Buchanan and myself by that bill, and the decision of the Court to break down the barrier and establish slavery all over the Union. Does he not know that that charge is historically false as against President Buchanan? He knows that Mr. Buchanan was at that time in England, representing this country with distinguished ability at the Court of St. James, that he was there for a long time before and did not return for a year or more after. He knows that to be true, and that fact proves his charge to be false as against Mr. Buchanan. (Cheers.) Then again, I wish to call his attention to the fact that at the time the Nebraska bill was passed the Dred Scott case was not before the Supreme Court at all; it was not upon the docket of the Supreme Court; it had not been brought there, and the Judges in all probability, knew nothing of it. Thus the history of the country proves the charge to be false as against them. As to President Pierce, his high character as a man of integrity and honor is enough to vindicate him from such a charge, (laughter and applause,) and as to myself, I pronounce the charge an infamous lie, whenever and wherever made, and by whomsoever made. I am willing that Mr.

Lincoln should go and rake up every public act of mine, every measure I have introduced, report I have made, speech delivered, and criticise them, but when he charges upon me a corrupt conspiracy for the purpose of perverting the institutions of the country, I brand it as it deserves. I say the history of the country proves it to be false, and that it could not have been possible at the time. But now he tries to protect himself in this charge, because I made a charge against the Washington *Union*. My speech in the Senate against the Washington *Union* was made because it advocated a revolutionary doctrine, by declaring that the free States had not the right to prohibit slavery within their own limits. Because I made that charge against the Washington *Union*, Mr. Lincoln says it was a charge against Mr. Buchanan. Suppose it was; is Mr. Lincoln the peculiar defender of Mr. Buchanan? Is he so interested in the federal administration, and so bound to it, that he must jump to the rescue and defend it from every attack that I may make against it? (Great laughter and cheers.) I understand the whole thing. The Washington *Union*, under that most corrupt of all men, Cornelius Wendell, is advocating Mr. Lincoln's claim to the Senate. Wendell was the printer of the last Black Republican House of Representatives; he was a candidate before the present Democratic House, but was ignominiously kicked out, and then he took the money which he had made out of the public printing by means of the Black Republicans, bought the Washington *Union*, and is now publishing it in the name of the Democratic party, and advocating Mr. Lincoln's election to the Senate. Mr. Lincoln therefore considers any attack upon Wendell and his corrupt gang as a personal attack upon him. (Immense cheering and laughter.) This only proves what I have charged, that there is an alliance between Lincoln and his supporters and the federal office-holders of this State, and Presidential aspirants out of it, to break me down at home.

[A VOICE.—That is impossible, and cheering.]

Mr. Lincoln feels bound to come in to the rescue of the Washington *Union*. In that speech which I delivered in answer to the Washington *Union*, I made it distinctly against the *Union*, and against the *Union* alone. I did not choose to go beyond that. If I have occasion to attack the President's conduct, I will do it in language that will not be misunderstood. When I differed with the President, I spoke out so that you all heard me. ("That you did," and cheers.) That question passed away; it resulted in the triumph of my principle by allowing the people to do as they please, and there is an end of the controversy. ("Hear, hear.") Whenever the great principle of self-government—the right of the people to make their own Constitution, and come into the Union with slavery, or without it, as they see proper—shall again arise, you will find me standing firm in defence of that principle, and fighting whoever fights it. ("Right, right." "Good, good," and cheers.) If Mr. Buchanan stands, as I doubt not he will, by the recommendation contained in his message, that hereafter all State constitutions ought to be submitted to the people before the admission of the State into the Union, he will find me standing by him firmly, shoulder to shoulder, in carrying it out. I know Mr. Lincoln's object, he wants to divide the Democratic party, in order that he may defeat me and get to the Senate.

Mr. Douglas' time here expired, and he stopped on the moment.

MR. LINCOLN'S REJOINDER.

As Mr. Lincoln arose he was greeted with vociferous cheers. He said:

My friends, it will readily occur to you that I cannot in half an hour notice all the things that so able a man as Judge Douglas can say in an hour and a half, and I hope, therefore, if there be anything that he has said upon which you would like to hear something from me, but which I omit to comment upon, you will bear in mind that it would be expecting an impossibility for me to go over his whole ground. I can but take up some of the points that he has dwelt upon, and employ my half-hour specially on them.

The first thing I have to say to you is a word in regard to Judge Douglas' declaration about the "vulgarity and blackguardism" in the audience—that no such thing, as he says, was shown by any Democrat while I was speaking. Now, I only wish, by way of reply on this subject, to say that while *I* was speaking *I* used no "vulgarity or blackguardism" towards any Democrat. [Great laughter and applause.]

Now, my friends, I come to all this long portion of the Judge's speech—perhaps half of it—which he has devoted to the various resolutions and platforms that have been adopted in the different counties in the different Congressional districts, and in the Illinois Legislature—which he supposes are at variance with the positions I have assumed before you today. It is true that many of these resolutions are at variance with the positions I have here assumed. All I have to ask is that we talk reasonably and rationally about it. I happen to know, the Judge's opinion to the contrary notwithstanding, that I have never tried to conceal my opinions, nor tried to deceive any one in reference to them. He may go and examine all the members who voted for me for United States Senator in 1855, after the election of 1854. They were pledged to certain things here at home, and were determined to have pledges from me, and if he will find any of these persons who will tell him anything inconsistent with what I say now, I will resign, or rather retire from the race, and give him no more trouble. [Applause.] The plain truth is this: At the introduction of the Nebraska policy, we believed there was a new era being introduced in the history of the Republic, which tended to the spread and perpetuation of slavery. But in our opposition to that measure we did not agree with one another in everything. The people in the north end of the State were for stronger measures of opposition than we of the central and southern portions of the State, but we were all opposed to the Nebraska doctrine. We had that one feeling and that one sentiment in common. You at the north end met in your Conventions and passed your resolutions. We in the middle of the State and further south did not hold such Conventions and pass the same resolutions, although we had in general a common view and a common sentiment. So that these meetings which the Judge has alluded to, and the resolutions he has read from were local and did not spread over the whole State. We at last met together in 1856 from all parts of the State, and we agreed upon a common platform. You, who held more extreme notions either yielded those notions, or if not wholly yielding them, agreed to yield them practically, for the sake of embodying the opposition to the measures which the opposite party were pushing forward at that time. We met you then, and if there was anything yielded, it was for practical purposes. We agreed then upon a platform for the party throughout the entire State of Illinois, and now we are all bound as a party, *to that platform*. And I say here to you, if any one expects of me—in the case of my election—that I will do anything not signified by our Republican platform and my answers here to-day, I tell you very frankly that person will be deceived. I do not ask for the vote of any one who supposes that I have secret purposes or pledges that I dare not speak out. Cannot the Judge be satisfied? If he fears, in the unfortunate case of my election, [Laughter] that my going to Washington will enable me to advocate sentiments contrary to those which I expressed when you voted for and elected me, I assure him that his fears are wholly needless and groundless. Is the Judge really afraid of any such thing? [Laughter.] I'll tell you what he is afraid of. *He is afraid we'll all pull together*. [Applause, and cries of "we will, we will."] This is what alarms him more than anything else. [Laughter.] For my part, I do hope that all of us, entertaining a common sentiment in opposition to what appears to us a design to nationalize and perpetuate slavery, will waive minor differences on questions which either belong to the dead past or the distant future, and all pull together in this struggle. What are your sentiments? ["We will, we will," and loud cheers.] If it be true, that on the ground which I occupy—ground which I occupy as frankly and boldly as Judge Douglas does his—my views, though partly coinciding with yours, are not as perfectly in accordance with your feelings as his are, I do say to you in all candor, Go for him and not for me. I hope to deal in all things fairly with Judge Douglas, and with the people of the State, in this contest. And if I should never be elected to any office, I trust I may go down with no stain of falsehood upon my reputation,— notwithstanding the hard opinions Judge Douglas chooses to entertain of me. [Laughter.]

The Judge has again addressed himself to the abolition tendencies of a speech of mine, made at Springfield in June last. I have so often tried to answer what he is always saying on that melancholy theme, that I almost turn with disgust from the discussion—from the repetition of an answer to it. I trust that nearly all of this intelligent audience have read that speech. ["We have; we have."] If you have, I may venture to leave it to you to inspect it closely, and see whether it contains any of those "bugaboos" which frighten Judge Douglas. [Laughter.]

The Judge complains that I did not fully answer his questions. If I have the sense to comprehend and answer those questions, I have done so fairly. If it can be pointed out to me how I can more fully and fairly answer him, I aver I have not the sense to see how it is to be done. He says I do not declare I would in any event vote for the admission of a slave State into the Union. If I have been fairly reported he will see that I did give an explicit answer to his interrogatories. I did not merely say that I would dislike to be put to the test; but I said clearly, if I were put to the test, and a Territory from which slavery had been excluded should present herself with a State Constitution sanctioning slavery—a most extraordinary thing and wholly unlikely ever to happen—I did not see how I could avoid voting for her admission. But he refuses to understand that I said so, and he wants this audience to understand that I did not say so. Yet it will be so reported in the printed speech that he cannot help seeing it.

He says if I should vote for the admission of a Slave State I would be voting for a dissolution of the Union, because I hold that the Union can not permanently exist half slave and half free. I repeat that I do not believe this Government *can* endure permanently half slave and half free, yet I do not admit, nor does it at all follow, that the admission of a single Slave State will permanently fix the character and establish this as a universal slave nation. The Judge is very happy indeed at working up these quibbles. [Laughter and cheers.] Before leaving the subject of answering questions I aver as my confident belief, when you come to see our speeches in print, that you will find every question which he has asked me more fairly and boldly and fully answered than he has answered those which I put to him. Is not that so? [Cries of yes, yes.] The two speeches may be placed side by side; and I will venture to leave it to impartial judges whether his questions have not been more directly and circumstantially answered than mine.

Judge Douglas says he made a charge upon the editor of the Washington *Union*, *alone*, of entertaining a purpose to rob the States of their power to exclude slavery from their limits. I undertake to say, and I make the direct issue, that he did *not* make his charge against the editor of the *Union* alone. [Applause.] I will undertake to prove by the record here, that he made that charge against more and higher dignitaries than the editor of the Washington *Union*. I am quite aware that he was shirking and dodging around the form in which he put it, but I can make it manifest that he leveled his "fatal blow" against more persons than this Washington editor. Will he dodge it now by alleging that I am trying to defend Mr. Buchanan against the charge? Not at all. Am I not making the same charge myself? [Laughter and applause.] I am trying to show that you, Judge Douglas, are a witness on my side. [Renewed Laughter.] I am not defending Buchanan, and I will tell Judge Douglas that in my opinion, when he made that charge, he had an eye farther North than he was to-day. He was then fighting against people who called *him* a Black Republican and an Abolitionist. It is mixed all through his speech, and it is tolerably manifest that his eye was a great deal farther North than it is to-day. [Cheers and laughter.] The Judge says that though he made this charge Toombs got up and declared there was not a man in the United States, except the editor of the *Union*, who was in favor of the doctrines put forth in that article. And thereupon, I understand that the Judge withdrew the charge. Although he had taken extracts from the newspaper, and then from the Lecompton Constitution, to show the existence of a conspiracy to bring about a "fatal blow," by which the States were to be deprived of the right of excluding slavery, it all went to pot as soon as Toombs got up and told him it was not true. [Laughter.] It reminds me of the story that John Phoenix, the California railroad surveyor, tells. He says they started out from the Plaza to the Mission of Dolores. They had two ways of determining distances. One was by a chain and pins taken over the ground. The other was by a "go-it-ometer"—an invention of his own—a three-legged instrument, with which he computed a series of triangles between the points. At night he turned to the chain-man to ascertain what distance they had come, and found that by some mistake he had merely dragged the chain over the ground without keeping any record. By the "go-it-ometer" he found he had made ten miles. Being skeptical about this, he asked a drayman who was passing how far it was to the plaza. The drayman replied it was just half a mile, and the surveyor put it down in his book—just as Judge Douglas says, after he had made his calculations and computations, he took Toombs' statement. [Great laughter.] I have no doubt that after Judge Douglas had made his charge, he was as easily satisfied about its truth as the surveyor was of the drayman's statement of the distance to the plaza. [Renewed laughter.] Yet it is a fact that the man who put forth all that matter which Douglas deemed a "fatal blow" at State sovereignty, was elected by the Democrats as public printer.

Now, gentlemen, you may take Judge Douglas' speech of March 22d, 1858, beginning about the middle of page 21, and reading to the bottom of page 24, and you will find the evidence on which I say that he did not make his charge against the editor of the *Union* alone. I cannot stop to read it, but I will give it to the reporters. Judge Douglas said:

Mr. President, you here find several distinct propositions advanced boldly by the Washington *Union* editorially and apparently *authoritatively*, and every man who questions any of them is denounced as an abolitionist, a Free-Soiler, a fanatic. The propositions are, first, that the primary object of all government at its original institution is the protection of persons and property; second, that the Constitution of the United States declares that the citizens of each State shall be entitled to all the privileges and immunities of citizens in the several States; and that, therefore, thirdly, all State laws, whether organic or otherwise, which prohibit the citizens of one State from settling in another with their slave property, and especially declaring it forfeited, are direct violations of the original intention of the Government and Constitution of the United States; and fourth, that the emancipation of the slaves of the Northern States was a gross outrage on the rights of property, inasmuch as it was involuntarily done on the part of the owner.

Remember that this article was published in the *Union* on the 17th of November, and on the 18th appeared the first article giving the adhesion of the *Union* to the Lecompton Constitution. It was in these words:

"KANSAS AND HER CONSTITUTION.—The vexed question is settled. The problem is solved. The dread point of danger is passed. All serious trouble to Kansas affairs is over and gone."

And a column, nearly, of the same sort. Then, when you come to look into the Lecompton Constitution, you find the same doctrine incorporated in it which was put forth editorially in the *Union*. What is it?

"ARTICLE 7. *Section* I. The right of property is before and higher than any constitutional sanction; and the right of the owner of a slave to such slave and its increase is the same and as inviolable as the right of the owner of any property whatever."

Then in the schedule is a provision that the Constitution may be amended after 1864 by a two-thirds vote.

"But no alteration shall be made to affect the right of property in the ownership of slaves."

It will be seen by these clauses in the Lecompton Constitution that they are identical in spirit with this *authoritative* article in the Washington *Union* of the day previous to its indorsement of this Constitution.

When I saw that article in the *Union* of the 17th of November, followed by the glorification of the Lecompton Constitution on the 18th of November, and this clause in the Constitution asserting the doctrine that a State has no right to prohibit slavery within its limits, I saw that there was a *fatal blow* being struck at the sovereignty of the States of this Union.

Here he says, "Mr. President, you here find several distinct propositions advanced boldly, and apparently *authoritatively*." By whose authority, Judge Douglas? [Great cheers and laughter.] Again, he says in another place, "It will be seen by these clauses in the Lecompton Constitution, that they are identical in spirit with this *authoritative* article." *By whose authority?* [Renewed cheers.] Who do you mean to say authorized the publication of these articles? He knows that the Washington *Union* is considered the organ of the Administration. *I* demand of Judge Douglas *by whose authority* he meant to say those articles were published, if not by the authority of the President of the United States and his Cabinet? I defy him to show whom he referred to, if not to these high functionaries in the Federal Government. More than this, he says the articles in that paper and the provisions of the Lecompton Constitution are "identical," and being identical, he argues that the authors are co-operating and conspiring together. He does not use the word "conspiring," but what other construction can you put upon it? He winds up with this:

When I saw that article in the *Union* of the 17th of November, followed by the glorification of the Lecompton Constitution on the 18th of November, and this clause in the Constitution asserting the doctrine that a State has no right to prohibit slavery within its limits, I saw that there was a *fatal blow* being struck at the sovereignty of the States of this Union.

I ask him if all this fuss was made over the editor of this newspaper. [Laughter.] It would be a terribly "*fatal* blow" indeed which a single man could strike, when no President, no Cabinet officer, no member of Congress, was giving strength and efficiency to the movement. Out of respect to Judge Douglas' good sense I must believe he didn't manufacture his idea of the "fatal" character of that blow out of such a miserable scapegrace as he represents that editor to be. But the Judge's eye is farther south now. [Laughter and cheers.] Then, it was very peculiarly and decidedly North. His hope rested on the idea of visiting the great "Black Republican" party, and making it the tail of his new kite. [Great laughter.] He knows he was then expecting from day to day to turn Republican and place himself at the head of our organization. He has found that these despised "Black Republicans" estimate him by a standard which he has taught them none too well. Hence he is crawling back into his old camp, and you will find him eventually installed in full fellowship among those whom he was then battling, and with whom he now pretends to be at such fearful variance. [Loud applause and cries of "go on, go on."] I cannot, gentlemen, my time has expired.

Portion of Speech at Edwardsville, Illinois

I have been requested to give a concise statement, as I understand it, of the difference between the Democratic and the Republican parties on the leading issues of this campaign. The question has just been put to me by a gentleman whom I do not know. I do not even know whether he is a friend of mine or a supporter of Judge Douglas in this contest; nor does that make any difference. His question is a pertinent one and, though it has not been asked me anywhere in the State before, I am very glad that my attention has been called to it to-day. Lest I should forget it, I will give you my answer before proceeding with the line of argument I had marked out for this discussion.

The difference between the Republican and the Democratic parties on the leading issue of this contest, as I understand it, is, that the former consider slavery a moral, social and political wrong, while the latter *do not* consider it either a moral, social or political wrong; and the action of each, as respects the growth of the country and the expansion of our population, is squared to meet these views. I will not allege that the Democratic party consider slavery morally, socially and politically *right*; though their tendency to that view has, in my opinion, been constant and unmistakable for the past five years. I prefer to take, as the accepted maxim of the party, the idea put forth by Judge Douglas, that he "don't care whether slavery is voted down or voted up." I am quite willing to believe that many Democrats would prefer that slavery be always voted down, and I am sure that some prefer that it be always "voted up"; but I have a right to insist that their action, especially if it be their *constant and unvarying* action, shall determine their ideas and preferences on the subject. Every measure of the Democratic party of late years, bearing directly or indirectly on the slavery question, has corresponded with this notion of utter indifference whether slavery or freedom shall outrun in the race of empire across the Pacific—every measure, I say, up to the Dred Scott decision, where, it seems to me, the idea is boldly suggested that slavery is *better* than freedom. The Republican party, on the contrary, hold that this government was instituted to secure the blessings of freedom, and that slavery is an unqualified evil to the negro, to the white man, to the soil, and to the State. Regarding it an evil, they will not molest it in the States where it exists; they will not overlook the constitutional guards which our forefathers have placed around it; they will do nothing which can give proper offence to those who hold slaves by legal sanction; but they will use every con-

stitutional method to prevent the evil from becoming larger
and involving more negroes, more white men, more soil, and
more States in its deplorable consequences. They will, if possible, place it where the public mind shall rest in the belief
that it is in course of ultimate peaceable extinction, in God's
own good time. And to this end they will, if possible, restore
the government to the policy of the fathers—the policy of
preserving the new territories from the baneful influence of
human bondage, as the Northwestern territories were sought
to be preserved by the ordinance of 1787 and the compromise
act of 1820. They will oppose, in all its length and breadth, the
modern Democratic idea that slavery is as good as freedom,
and ought to have room for expansion all over the continent,
if people can be found to carry it. All, or very nearly all, of
Judge Douglas' arguments about "Popular Sovereignty," as he
calls it, are logical if you admit that slavery is as good and as
right as freedom; and not one of them is worth a rush if you
deny it. This is the difference, as I understand it, between the
Republican and the Democratic parties; and I ask the gentleman, and all of you, whether his question is not satisfactorily
answered.—[Cries of "Yes, yes."]

OPINIONS OF HENRY CLAY.

In this connection let me read to you the opinions of our
old leader Henry Clay, on the question of whether slavery *is*
as good as freedom. The extract which I propose to read is
contained in a letter written by Mr. Clay in his old age, as late
as 1849. The circumstances which called it forth were these. A
convention had been called to form a new constitution for the
State of Kentucky. The old Constitution had been adopted in
the year 1799—half a century before, when Mr. Clay was a
young man just rising into public notice. As long ago as the
adoption of the old Constitution, Mr. Clay had been the earnest advocate of a system of gradual emancipation and colonization of the state of Kentucky. And again in his old age, in
the maturity of his great mind, we find the same wise project
still uppermost in his thoughts. Let me read a few passages
from his letter of 1849: "I know there are those who draw an
argument in favor of slavery from the alleged intellectual inferiority of the black race. Whether this argument is founded in

fact or not, I will not now stop to inquire, but merely say that if it proves anything at all, it proves too much. It proves that among the white races of the world any one might properly be enslaved by any other which had made greater advances in civilization. And, if this rule applies to nations there is no reason why it should not apply to individuals; and it might easily be proved that the wisest man in the world could rightfully reduce all other men and women to bondage," &c., &c. [Mr. Lincoln read at considerable length from Mr. Clay's letter—earnestly pressing the material advantages and moral considerations in favor of gradual emancipation in Kentucky.]

"POPULAR SOVEREIGNTY,"
WHAT DID DOUGLAS REALLY INVENT?

Let us inquire, what Douglas really invented, when he introduced, and drove through Congress, the Nebraska bill. He called it "Popular Sovereignty." What does Popular Sovereignty mean? Strictly and literally it means the sovereignty of the people over their own affairs—in other words, the right of the people of every nation and community to govern themselves. Did Mr. Douglas invent this? Not quite. The idea of Popular Sovereignty was floating about the world several ages before the author of the Nebraska bill saw daylight—indeed before Columbus set foot on the American continent. In the year 1776 it took tangible form in the noble words which you are all familiar with: "We hold these truths to be self-evident: That all men are created equal; That they are endowed by their Creator with certain inalienable rights; That among these are life, liberty and the pursuit of happiness; That to secure these rights governments are instituted among men, *deriving their just powers from the consent of the governed.*" Was not this the origin of Popular Sovereignty as applied to the American people? Here we are told that Governments are instituted among men to secure certain rights, and that they derive their just powers *from the consent of the governed.* If that is not Popular Sovereignty, then I have no conception of the meaning of words.

Then, if Mr. Douglas did not invent *this* kind of sovereignty, let us pursue the inquiry and find out what the invention really was. Was it the right of emigrants in Kansas and

Nebraska to govern themselves and a gang of niggers too, if they wanted them? Clearly this was no invention of his, because Gen. Cass put forth the same doctrine in 1848, in his so-called Nicholson letter—six whole years before Douglas thought of such a thing. Gen. Cass could have taken out a patent for the idea, if he had chosen to do so, and have prevented his Illinois rival from reaping a particle of benefit from it. Then what was it, I ask again, that this "Little Giant" invented? It never occurred to Gen. Cass to call his discovery by the odd name of "Popular Sovereignty." He had not the *impudence* to say that the *right of people to govern niggers* was the *right of people to govern themselves*. His notions of the fitness of things were not moulded to the brazen degree of calling the right to put a hundred niggers through under the lash in Nebraska, a *"sacred right of self-government."* And here, I submit to this intelligent audience and the whole world, was Judge Douglas' discovery, and the whole of it. He invented a *name* for Gen. Cass' old Nicholson letter dogma. He discovered that the right of the white man to breed and flog niggers in Nebraska was POPULAR SOVEREIGNTY!—[Great applause and laughter.]

WHAT MAY WE LOOK FOR
AFTER THE NEXT DRED SCOTT DECISION?

My friends, I have endeavored to show you the logical consequences of the Dred Scott decision, which holds that the people of a Territory cannot prevent the establishment of Slavery in their midst. I have stated what cannot be gainsayed—that the grounds upon which this decision is made are equally applicable to the Free States as to the Free Territories, and that the peculiar reasons put forth by Judge Douglas for endorsing this decision, commit him in advance to the next decision, and to all other decisions emanating from the same source. Now, when by all these means you have succeeded in dehumanizing the negro; when you have put him down, and made it forever impossible for him to be but as the beasts of the field; when you have extinguished his soul, and placed him where the ray of hope is blown out in darkness like that which broods over the spirits of the damned; are you quite sure the demon which you have roused *will not turn and rend you?* What constitutes the bulwark of our own liberty and independence? It is not our frowning battlements, our bristling sea coasts, the guns of our war steamers, or the strength of our gallant and disciplined army. These are not our reliance against a resumption of tyranny in our fair land. All of them may be turned against our liberties, without making us stronger or weaker for the struggle. Our reliance is in the *love of liberty* which God has planted in our bosoms. Our defense is in the preservation of the spirit which prizes liberty as the heritage of all men, in all lands, every where. Destroy this spirit, and you have planted the seeds of despotism around your own doors. Familiarize yourselves with the chains of bondage, and you are preparing your own limbs to wear them. Accustomed to trample on the rights of those around you, you have lost the genius of your own independence, and become the fit subjects of the first cunning tyrant who rises. And let me tell you, all these things are prepared for you with the logic of history, if the elections shall promise that the next Dred Scott decision and all future decisions will be quietly acquiesced in by the people. — [Loud applause.]

September 11, 1858

Third Lincoln-Douglas Debate, Jonesboro, Illinois

MR. DOUGLAS' SPEECH.

LADIES AND GENTLEMEN: I appear before you to-day in pursuance of a previous notice, and have made arrangements with Mr. Lincoln to divide time and discuss with him the leading political topics that now agitate the country.

Prior to 1854 this country was divided into two great political parties known as Whig and Democratic. These parties differed from each other on certain questions which were then deemed to be important to the best interests of the republic. Whigs and Democrats differed about a bank, the tariff, distribution, the specie circular and the sub-treasury. On those issues we went before the country and discussed the principles, objects and measures of the two great parties. Each of the parties could proclaim its principles in Louisiana as well as in Massachusetts, in Kentucky as well as in Illinois. Since that period, a great revolution has taken place in the formation of parties, by which they now seem to be divided by a geographical line, a large party in the North being arrayed under the abolition or republican banner in hostility to the Southern States, Southern people, and Southern institutions. It becomes important for us to inquire how this transformation of parties has occurred, made from those of national principles to geographical factions. You remember that in 1850, this country was agitated from its centre to its circumference about this slavery question, it became necessary for the leaders of the great Whig party and the leaders of the great Democratic party to postpone, for the time being, their particular disputes and unite first to save the Union before they should quarrel as to the mode in which it was to be governed. During the Congress of 1849, '50, Henry Clay was the leader of the Union men, supported by Cass and Webster and the leaders of the democracy and the leaders of the Whigs, in opposition to Northern abolitionists or Southern disunionists. That great contest of 1850 resulted in the establishment of the compromise measures of that year, which measures rested on the great principle that the people of each State and each territory of this Union ought to be permitted to regulate their own domestic institutions in their own way subject to no other limitation than that which the Federal Constitution imposes.

I now wish to ask you whether that principle was right or wrong which guaranteed to every State and every community the right to form and regulate their domestic institutions to suit themselves. These measures were adopted, as I have previously said, by the joint action of the Union Whigs and Union Democrats, in opposition to Northern Abolitionists and Southern Disunionists. In 1852, when the Whig party assembled at Baltimore, in national convention for the last time, they adopted the principle of the Compromise measures of 1850 as their rule of party action in the future. One month thereafter the Democrats assembled at the same place to nominate a candidate for the Presidency, and declared the same great principle as the rule of action by which the Democracy would be governed. The Presidential election of 1852 was fought on that basis. It is true that the Whigs claimed special merit for the adoption of those measures, because they asserted that their great Clay originated them, their God-like Webster defended them, and their Fillmore signed the bill making them the law of the land; but on the other hand the Democrats claimed special credit for the Democracy, upon the ground that we gave twice as many votes in both Houses of Congress for the passage of these measures as the Whig party.

Thus you see that in the Presidential election of 1852, the Whigs were pledged by their platform and their candidate to the principle of the Compromise measures of 1850, and the Democracy were likewise pledged by our principles, our platform, and our candidate to the same line of policy, to preserve peace and quiet between the different sections of this Union. Since that period the Whig party has been transformed into a sectional party, under the name of the Republican party, whilst the Democratic party continues the same national party it was at that day. All sectional men, all men of Abolition sentiments and principles, no matter whether they were old

Abolitionists or had been Whigs or Democrats, rally under the sectional Republican banner, and consequently all national men; all Union loving men, whether Whigs, Democrats, or by whatever name they have been known, ought to rally under the stars and stripes in defence of the Constitution, as our fathers made it, and of the Union as it has existed under the Constitution.

How has this departure from the faith of the Democracy and the faith of the Whig party been accomplished? In 1854, certain restless, ambitious, and disappointed politicians throughout the land took advantage of the temporary excitement created by the Nebraska bill to try and dissolve the old Whig party and the old Democratic party, to abolitionize their members and lead them, bound hand and foot, captives into the abolition camp. In the State of New York a convention was held by some of these men and a platform adopted, every plank of which was as black as night, each one relating to the negro, and not one referring to the interests of the white man. That example was followed throughout the Northern States, the effect being made to combine all the free States in hostile array against the slave States. The men who thus thought that they could build up a great sectional party, and through its organization control the political destinies of this country, based all their hopes on the single fact that the North was the stronger division of the nation, and hence, if the North could be combined against the South, a sure victory awaited their efforts. I am doing no more than justice to the truth of history when I say that in this State Abraham Lincoln, on behalf of the Whigs, and Lyman Trumbull, on behalf of the Democrats, were the leaders who undertook to perform this grand scheme of abolitionizing the two parties to which they belonged. They had a private arrangement as to what should be the political destiny of each of the contracting parties before they went into the operation. The arrangement was that Mr. Lincoln was to take the old line Whigs with him, claiming that he was still as good a Whig as ever, over to the Abolitionists, and Mr. Trumbull was to run for Congress in the Belleville district, and, claiming to be a good Democrat, coax the old Democrats into the Abolition camp, and when, by the joint efforts of the abolitionized Whigs, the abolitionized Democrats, and the old line Abolition and Free Soil party of this State, they should secure a majority in the legislature. Lincoln was then to be made United States Senator in Shields' place, Trumbull remaining in Congress until I should be accommodating enough to die or resign, and give him a chance to follow Lincoln. (Laughter, applause, and cries of "don't die.") That was a very nice little bargain so far as Lincoln and Trumbull were concerned, if it had been carried out in good faith, and friend Lincoln had attained to senatorial dignity according to the contract. They went into the contest in every part of the State, calling upon all disappointed politicians to join in the crusade against the Democracy, and appealed to the prevailing sentiments and prejudices in all the northern counties of the State. In three Congressional districts in the north end of the State they adopted, as the platform of this new party thus formed by Lincoln and Trumbull in the connection with the Abolitionists, all of those principles which aimed at a warfare on the part of the North against the South. They declared in that platform that the Wilmot proviso was to be applied to all the territories of the United States, North as well as South of 36 deg. 30 min., and not only to all the territory we then had, but all that we might hereafter acquire; that hereafter no more slave States should be admitted into this Union, even if the people of such State desired slavery; that the fugitive slave law should be absolutely and unconditionally repealed; that slavery should be abolished in the District of Columbia; that the slave trade should be abolished between the different States, and, in fact, every article in their creed related to this slavery question, and pointed to a Northern geographical party in hostility to the Southern States of this Union. Such were their principles in Northern Illinois. A little further south they became bleached and grew paler just in proportion as public sentiment moderated and changed in this direction. They were Republicans or Abolitionists in the north, anti-Nebraska men down about Springfield, and in this neighborhood they contented themselves with talking about the inexpediency of the repeal of the Missouri compromise. (Shouts of laughter.) In the extreme northern counties they brought out men to canvass the State whose complexion suited their political creed, and hence

Fred Douglass, the negro, was to be found there, following General Cass, and attempting to speak on behalf of Lincoln, Trumbull and abolitionism against that illustrious Senator. (Renewed laughter.) Why, they brought Fred Douglass to Freeport when I was addressing a meeting there in a carriage driven by the white owner, the negro sitting inside with the white lady and her daughter. (Shame.) When I got through canvassing the northern counties that year and progressed as far south as Springfield, I was met and opposed in discussion by Lincoln, Lovejoy, Trumbull, and Sidney Breese, who were on one side. (Laughter.) Father Giddings, the high priest of abolitionism, had just been there, and Chase came about the time I left. ("Why didn't you shoot him?") I did take a running shot at them, but as I was single-handed against the white, black and mixed drove, I had to use a short gun and fire into the crowd instead of taking them off singly with a rifle. (Great laughter and cheers.) Trumbull had for his lieutenants, in aiding him to abolitionize the democracy, such men as John Wentworth, of Chicago, Gov. Reynolds, of Belleville, Sidney Breese, of Carlisle, and John Dougherty, of Union, ("good," "good," "give it to them," &c.,) each of whom modified his opinions to suit the particular locality he was in. Dougherty, for instance, would not go much further than to talk about the inexpediency of the Nebraska bill, whilst his allies at Chicago, advocated negro citizenship and negro equality, putting the white man and the negro on the same basis under the law. (Never, never.) Now these men, four years ago, were engaged in a conspiracy to break down the democracy; to-day they are again acting together for the same purposes. They do not hoist the same flag; they do not own the same principles, or profess the same faith; but conceal their union for the sake of policy. In the northern counties, you find that all the conventions are called in the name of the Black Republican party; at Springfield, they dare not call a Republican Convention, but invite all the enemies of the democracy to unite, and when they get down into Egypt, Trumbull issues notices calling upon the *"free democracy"* to assemble and hear him speak. I have one of the handbills calling a Trumbull meeting at Waterloo the other day, which I received there, which is in the following language:

A meeting of the Free Democracy will take place in Waterloo, on Monday, Sept. 13th inst., whereat Hon. Lyman Trumbull, Hon. John Baker and others will address the people upon the different political topics of the day. Members of all parties are cordially invited to be present, and hear and determine for themselves.

THE MONROE FREE DEMOCRACY.

What is that name of "Free Democrats" put forth for unless to deceive the people, and make them believe that Trumbull and his followers are not the same party as that which raises the black flag of Abolitionism in the northern part of this State, and makes war upon the Democratic party throughout the State. When I put that question to them at Waterloo on Saturday last, one of them rose and stated that they had changed their name for political effect in order to get votes. There was a candid admission. Their object in changing their party organization and principles in different localities was avowed to be an attempt to cheat and deceive some portion of the people until after the election. Why cannot a political party that is conscious of the rectitude of its purposes and the soundness of its principles declare them every where alike. I would disdain to hold any political principles that I could not avow in the same terms in Kentucky that I declared in Illinois, in Charleston as well as in Chicago, in New Orleans as well as in New York. (Cheers.) So long as we live under a constitution common to all the States, our political faith ought to be as broad, as liberal, and just as that constitution itself, and should be proclaimed alike in every portion of the Union. (Hear, hear.) But it is apparent that our opponents find it necessary, for partizan effect, to change their colors in different counties in order to catch the popular breeze, and hope with these discordant materials combined together to secure a majority in the legislature for the purpose of putting down the Democratic party. This combination did succeed in 1854 so far as to elect a majority of their confederates to the legislature, and the first important act which they performed was to elect a Senator in the place of the eminent and gallant Senator Shields. His term expired in the United States Senate at that time, and he had to be crushed by the abolition coalition for the simple reason that he would not join in their conspiracy to wage war against one-half of the

Union. That was the only objection to Gen. Shields. He had served the people of the State with ability in the legislature, he had served you with fidelity and ability as auditor, he had performed his duties to the satisfaction of the whole country as head of the Land Department at Washington, he had covered the State and the Union with immortal glory on the bloody fields of Mexico in defence of the honor of our flag, and yet he had to be stricken down by this unholy combination. And for what cause? Merely because he would not join a combination of one-half of the States to make war upon the other half, after having poured out his heart's blood for all the States in the Union. Trumbull was put in his place by abolitionism. How did Trumbull get there? Before the Abolitionists would consent to go into an election for United States Senator they required all the members of this new combination to show their hands upon this question of abolitionism. Lovejoy, one of their high priests, brought in resolutions defining the abolition creed, and required them to commit themselves on it by their votes—yea or nay. In that creed, as laid down by Lovejoy, they declared first, that the Wilmot proviso must be put on all the territories of the United States north as well as south of 36 deg. 30 min., and that no more territory should ever be acquired unless slavery was at first prohibited therein; second, that no more States should ever be received into the Union unless slavery was first prohibited, by constitutional provision, in such States; third, that the fugitive slave law must be immediately repealed, or, failing in that, then such amendments were to be made to it as would render it useless and inefficient for the objects for which it was passed, &c. The next day after these resolutions were offered they were voted upon, part of them carried, and the others defeated, the same men who voted for them, with only two exceptions, voting soon after for Abraham Lincoln as their candidate for the United States Senate. He came within one or two votes of being elected, but he could not quite get the number required, for the simple reason that his friend Trumbull, who was a party to the bargain by which Lincoln was to take Shields' place, controlled a few abolitionized Democrats in the legislature, and would not allow them all to vote for him, thus wronging Lincoln by permitting him on each ballot to be almost elected, but not quite, until he forced them to drop Lincoln and elect him (Trumbull), in order to unite the party. (Immense laughter.) Thus you find, that although the legislature was carried that year by the bargain between Trumbull, Lincoln, and the Abolitionists, and the union of these discordant elements in one harmonious party; yet Trumbull violated his pledge, and played a yankee trick on Lincoln when they came to divide the spoils. (Laughter and cheers. Mr. Lincoln greatly agitated, his face buried in his hands.) Perhaps you would like a little evidence on this point. If you would, I will call Col. Jas. H. Matheny, of Springfield, to the stand, Mr. Lincoln's especial confidential friend for the last twenty years, and see what he will say upon the subject of this bargain. Matheny is now the Black Republican or Abolition candidate for Congress in the Springfield district against the gallant Col. Harris, and is making speeches all over that part of the State against me and in favor of Lincoln, in concert with Trumbull. He ought to be a good witness, and I will read an extract from a speech which he made in 1856, when he was mad because his friend Lincoln had been cheated. It is one of numerous speeches of the same tenor that were made about that time, exposing this bargain between Lincoln, Trumbull, and the Abolitionists. Matheny then said:

The Whigs, Abolitionists, Know Nothings, and renegade Democrats made a solemn compact for the purpose of carrying this State against the Democracy, on this plan: 1st. That they would all combine and elect Mr. Trumbull to Congress, and thereby carry his district for the legislature, in order to throw all the strength that could be obtained into that body against the Democrats. 2d. That when the legislature should meet, the officers of that body, such as speaker, clerks, door-keepers, &c., would be given to the Abolitionists; and 3d, That the Whigs were to have the United States Senator. That, accordingly, in good faith, Trumbull was elected to Congress, and his district carried for the legislature, and, when it convened, the Abolitionists got all the officers of that body, and thus far the "bond" was fairly executed. The Whigs, on their part, demanded the election of Abraham Lincoln to the United States Senate, that the bond might be fulfilled, the other parties to the contract having already secured to themselves all that was called for. But, in the most perfidious manner, they refused to elect Mr. Lincoln; and the mean, low-lived, sneaking Trumbull succeeded, by pledging all that was required by any party, in thrusting Lincoln aside and foisting himself, an excrescence from the rotten bowels of the Democracy, into the United States Senate:

and thus it has ever been, that an *honest* man makes a bad bargain when he conspires or contracts with rogues.

Matheny thought that his friend Lincoln made a bad bargain when he conspired and contracted with such rogues as Trumbull and his abolition associates in that campaign. (Great cheers and laughter; Lincoln looking very miserable.) Lincoln was shoved off the track, and he and his friends all at once began to mope, became sour and mad, (laughter,) and disposed to tell, but dare not; (shouts of laughter;) and this they stood for a long time until the Abolitionists coaxed and flattered him back by their assurances that he should certainly be a Senator in Douglas' place. (Roars of laughter, Lincoln looking as if he had not a friend on earth, although Herr Kriesman whispered "never mind" into his ear.) In that way the Abolitionists have been enabled to hold Lincoln to the alliance up to this time, and now they have brought him into a fight against me, and he is to see if he is again to be cheated by them. Lincoln this time though required more of them than a promise, and holds their bond, if not security, that Lovejoy shall not cheat him as Trumbull did. (Renewed shouts of laughter.)

When the Republican convention assembled at Springfield in June last for the purpose of nominating State officers only, the Abolitionists could not get Lincoln and his friends into it until they would pledge themselves that Lincoln should be their candidate for the Senate; and you will find, in proof of this, that that convention passed a resolution unanimously declaring that Abraham Lincoln was the "first, last and only choice" of the Republicans for United States Senator. He was not willing to have it understood that he was merely their first choice, or their last choice, but their *only* choice. The Black Republican party had nobody else. Browning was nowhere, Gov. Bissell was of no account, Archie Williams was not to be taken into consideration, John Wentworth was not worth mentioning, John M. Palmer was degraded, and their party presented the extraordinary spectacle of having but one—the first, last, and only choice for the Senate. (Laughter.) Suppose Lincoln should die, what a horrible condition the Republican party would be in. (A groan from Lincoln, and great laughter.) They would have nobody left. They have no other choice, and it was necessary for them to put themselves before the world in this ludicrous, ridiculous attitude of having no other choice in order to quiet Lincoln's suspicions, and assure him that he was not to be cheated by Lovejoy, and the trickery by which Trumbull out generalled him. Well, gentlemen, I think they will have a nice time of it before they get through. I do not intend to give them any chance to cheat Lincoln at all this time. (Cheers.) I intend to relieve him and them from all anxiety upon that subject, and spare them the mortification of more exposures of contracts violated, and the pledged honor of rogues forfeited. (Great applause.)

But I wish to invite your attention to the chief points at issue between Mr. Lincoln and myself in this discussion. Mr. Lincoln, knowing that he was to be the candidate of his party on account of the arrangement of which I have already spoken, knowing that he was to receive the nomination of the Convention for the United States Senate, had his speech, accepting that nomination, all written and committed to memory, ready to be delivered the moment the nomination was announced. Accordingly, when it was made he was in readiness, and delivered his speech, a portion of which I will read, in order that I may state his political principles fairly, by repeating them in his own language.

We are now far into the fifth year since a policy was instituted for the avowed object, and with the confident promise of putting an end to slavery agitation; under the operation of that policy, that agitation had only not ceased, but had constantly augmented. I believe it will not cease until a crisis shall have been reached and passed. A house divided against itself cannot stand. I believe this government cannot endure permanently half slave and half free. I do not expect the Union to be dissolved. I do not expect the house to fall, but I do expect it will cease to be divided. It will become all one thing or all the other. Either, the opponents of slavery will arrest the spread of it and place it where the public mind shall rest in the belief that it is in the course of ultimate extinction, or its advocates will push it forward until it shall become alike lawful in all the States North as well as South.

There you have Mr. Lincoln's first and main proposition, upon which he bases his claims, stated in his own language. He tells you that this Republic cannot endure permanently divided into slave and free States, as our fathers made it. He says that they must all become free or all become slave, that they must all be one thing or all be the other, or this government cannot last. Why can it not last if we will execute the government in the same spirit and upon the same principles upon which it is founded. Lincoln, by his proposition, says to the South, "If you desire to maintain your institutions as they are now, you must not be satisfied with minding your own business, but you must invade Illinois and all the other northern States, establish slavery in them and make it universal;" and in the same language he says to the north, "you must not be content with regulating your own affairs and minding your own business, but if you desire to maintain your freedom you must invade the Southern States, abolish slavery there and everywhere, in order to have the States all one thing or all the other." I say that this is the inevitable and irresistible result of Mr. Lincoln's argument inviting a warfare between the North and the South, to be carried on with ruthless vengeance, until the one section or the other shall be driven to the wall and become the victim of the rapacity of the other. What good would follow such a system of warfare? Suppose the North should succeed in conquering the South, how much would she be the gainer, or suppose the South should conquer the North, could the Union be preserved in that way? Is this sectional warfare to be waged between Northern States and Southern States until they all shall become uniform in their local and domestic institutions merely because Mr. Lincoln says that a house divided against itself cannot stand, and pretends that this scriptural quotation, this language of our Lord and Master, is applicable to the American Union and American constitution? Washington and his compeers in the convention that framed the constitution, made this government divided into free and slave States. It was composed then of thirteen sovereign and independent States, each having sovereign authority over its local and domestic institutions, and all bound together by the federal constitution. Mr. Lincoln likens that bond of the federal constitution joining free and slave States together to a house divided against itself, and says that it is contrary to the law of God and cannot stand. When did he learn, and by what authority does he proclaim, that this government is contrary to the law of God, and cannot stand? It has stood thus divided into free and slave States from its organization up to this day. During that period we have increased from four millions to thirty millions of people; we have extended our territory from the Mississippi to the Pacific ocean; we have acquired the Floridas and Texas and other territory sufficient to double our geographical extent; we have increased in population, in wealth, and in power beyond any example on earth; we have risen from a weak and feeble power to become the terror and admiration of the civilized world; and all this has been done under a constitution which Mr. Lincoln, in substance, says is in violation of the law of God, and under a union divided into free and slave States, which Mr. Lincoln thinks, because of such division, cannot stand. Surely, Mr. Lincoln is a wiser man than those who framed the government. Washington did not believe, nor did his compatriots, that the local laws and domestic institutions that were well adapted to the green mountains of Vermont were suited to the rice plantations of South Carolina; they did not believe at that day that in a republic so broad and expanded as this, containing such a variety of climate, soil and interest, that uniformity in the local laws and domestic institutions were either desirable or possible. They believed then as our experience has proved to us now, that each locality, having different interests, a different climate and different surroundings, required different local laws; local policy and local institutions adapted to the wants of that locality. Thus our government was formed on the principle of diversity in the local institutions and laws and not on that of uniformity.

As my time flies, I can only glance, at these points and not present them as fully as I would wish, because I desire to bring all the points in controversy between the two parties before you in order to have Mr. Lincoln's reply. He makes war on the decision of the Supreme Court in the case known as the Dred Scott case. I wish to say to you, fellow-citizens, that I have no war to make on that decision, or any other ever rendered by the Supreme Court. I am content to take that decision as it stands delivered by the highest judicial tribunal on earth, a tribunal established by the Constitution of the United States for that purpose, and hence that decision becomes the law of the land, binding on you, on me, and on every other good citizen, whether we like it or not. Hence I do not choose to go into an argument to prove, before this audience, whether or not Chief Justice Taney understood the law better than Abraham Lincoln. (Laughter.)

Mr. Lincoln objects to that decision, first and mainly because it deprives the negro of the rights of citizenship. I am as much opposed to his reason for that objection as I am to the objection itself. I hold that a negro is not and never ought to be a citizen of the United States. (Good, good, and tremendous cheers.) I hold that this government was made on the white basis, by white men, for the benefit of white men and their posterity forever, and should be administered by white men and none others. I do not believe that the Almighty made the negro capable of self-government. I am aware that all the abolition lecturers that you find traveling about through the country are in the habit of reading the Declaration of Independence to prove that all men were created equal and endowed by their Creator with certain inalienable rights, among which are life, liberty, and the pursuit of happiness. Mr. Lincoln is very much in the habit of following in the track of Lovejoy in this particular, by reading that part of the Declaration of Independence to prove that the negro was endowed by the Almighty with the inalienable right of equality with white men. Now, I say to you, my fellow-citizens, that in my opinion the signers of the Declaration had no reference to the negro whatever when they declared all men to be created equal. They desired to express by that phrase, white men, men of European birth and European descent, and had no reference either to the negro, the savage Indians, the Fejee, the Malay, or any other inferior and degraded race, when they spoke of the equality of men. One great evidence that such was their understanding, is to be found in the fact that at that time every one of the thirteen colonies was a slaveholding colony, every signer of the Declaration represented a slaveholding constituency, and we know that no one of them emancipated his slaves, much less offered citizenship to them when they signed the Declaration, and yet, if they had intended to declare that the negro was the equal of the white man, and entitled by divine right to an equality with him, they were bound, as honest men, that day and hour to have put their negroes on an equality with themselves. (Cheers.) Instead of doing so, with uplifted eyes to Heaven they implored the Divine blessing upon them, during the seven years' bloody war they had to fight to maintain that Declaration, never dreaming that they were violating divine law by still holding the negroes in bondage and depriving them of equality.

My friends, I am in favor of preserving this government as our fathers made it. It does not follow by any means that because a negro is not your equal or mine that hence he must necessarily be a slave. On the contrary, it does follow that we ought to extend to the negro every right, every privilege, every immunity which he is capable of enjoying consistent with the good of society. When you ask me what these rights are, what their nature and extent is, I tell you that that is a question which each State of this Union must decide for itself. Illinois has already decided the question. We have decided that the negro must not be a slave within our limits, but we have also decided that the negro shall not be a citizen within our limits; that he shall not vote, hold office, or exercise any political rights. I maintain that Illinois, as a sovereign State, has a right thus to fix her policy with reference to the relation between the white man and the negro; but while we had the right to decide the question for ourselves we must recognize the same right in Kentucky and in every other State to make the same decision, or a different one. Having decided our own policy with reference to the black race, we must leave Kentucky and Missouri and every other State perfectly free to make just such a decision as they see proper on that question.

Kentucky has decided that question for herself. She has said that within her limits a negro shall not exercise any political rights, and she has also said that a portion of the negroes under the laws of that State shall be slaves. She had as much right to adopt that as her policy as we had to adopt the contrary for our policy. New York has decided that in that State a negro may vote if he has $250 worth of property, and if he owns that much he may vote upon an equality with the white man. I, for one, am utterly opposed to negro suffrage anywhere and under any circumstances; yet, inasmuch as the

Supreme Court have decided in the celebrated Dred Scott case that a State has a right to confer the privilege of voting upon free negroes, I am not going to make war upon New York because she has adopted a policy repugnant to my feelings. (That's good.) But New York must mind her own business, and keep her negro suffrage to herself and not attempt to force it upon us. (Great applause.)

In the State of Maine they have decided that a negro may vote and hold office on an equality with a white man. I had occasion to say to the Senators from Maine in a discussion last session, that if they thought that the white people within the limits of their State were no better than negroes, I would not quarrel with them for it, but they must not say that my white constituents of Illinois were no better than negroes, or we would be sure to quarrel. (Cheers.)

The Dred Scott decision covers the whole question, and declares that each State has the right to settle this question of suffrage for itself, and all questions as to the relations between the white man and the negro. Judge Taney expressly lays down the doctrine. I receive it as law, and I say that while those States are adopting regulations on that subject disgusting and abhorrent, according to my views, I will not make war on them if they will mind their own business and let us alone. (Bravo, and cheers.)

I now come back to the question, why cannot this Union exist forever divided into free and slave States as our fathers made it? It can thus exist if each State will carry out the principles upon which our institutions were founded, to wit: the right of each State to do as it pleases, without meddling with its neighbors. Just act upon that great principle, and this Union will not only live forever, but it will extend and expand until it covers the whole continent, and make this confederacy one grand ocean-bound republic. We must bear in mind that we are yet a young nation growing with a rapidity unequalled in the history of the world, that our national increase is great, and that the emigration from the old world is increasing, requiring us to expand and acquire new territory from time to time in order to give our people land to live upon. If we live upon the principle of State rights and State sovereignty, each State regulating its own affairs and minding its own business, we can go on and extend indefinitely, just as fast and as far as we need the territory. The time may come, indeed has now come, when our interests would be advanced by the acquisition of the island of Cuba. (Terrific applause.) When we get Cuba we must take it as we find it, leaving the people to decide the question of slavery for themselves, without interference on the part of the federal government, or of any State of this Union. So, when it becomes necessary to acquire any portion of Mexico or Canada, or of this continent or the adjoining islands, we must take them as we find them, leaving the people free to do as they please, to have slavery or not, as they choose. I never have inquired and never will inquire whether a new State applying for admission has slavery or not for one of her institutions. If the constitution that is presented be the act and deed of the people and embodies their will, and they have the requisite population, I will admit them with slavery or without it just as the people shall determine. (That's good. That's right, and cheers.) My objection to the Lecompton constitution did not consist in the fact that it made Kansas a slave State. I would have been as much opposed to its admission under such a constitution as a free State as I was opposed to its admission under it as a slave State. I hold that that was a question which that people had a right to decide for themselves, and that no power on earth ought to have interfered with that decision. In my opinion, the Lecompton constitution was not the act and deed of the people of Kansas, and did not embody their will, and the recent election in that Territory, at which it was voted down by nearly ten to one, shows conclusively that I was right in saying when the constitution was presented, that it was not the act and deed of the people, and did not embody their will.

If we wish to preserve our institutions in their purity, and transmit them unimpaired to our latest posterity, we must preserve with religious good faith that great principle of self government which guarantees to each and every State, old and new, the right to make just such constitutions as they deserve, and come into the Union with their own constitution and not one palmed upon them. (Cheers.) Whenever you sanction the doctrine that Congress may crowd a constitution down the throats of an unwilling people against their consent, you will subvert the great fundamental principle upon which all our free institutions rest. In the future I have no fear that the attempt will ever be made. President Buchanan declared in his annual message, that hereafter the rule adopted in the Minnesota case, requiring a constitution to be submitted to the people, should be followed in all future cases, and if he stands by that recommendation there will be no division in the Democratic party on that principle in the future. Hence, the great mission of the Democracy is to unite the fraternal feeling of the whole country, restore peace and quiet by teaching each State to mind its own business, and regulate its own domestic affairs, and all to unite carrying out the constitution as our fathers made it, and thus to preserve the Union and render it perpetual in all time to come. Why should we not act as our fathers who made the government? There was no sectional strife in Washington's army. They were all brethren of a common confederacy, they fought under a common flag that they might bestow upon their posterity a common destiny, and to this end they poured out their blood in common streams and shared in some instances a common grave. (Three hearty cheers for Douglas.)

MR. LINCOLN'S REPLY.

Mr. Lincoln was then introduced to the audience by D. L. Phillips, Esq., and was greeted with three cheers, and then "three more;" after which he said:

LADIES AND GENTLEMEN: There is very much in the principles that Judge Douglas has here enunciated that I most cordially approve, and over which I shall have no controversy with him. In so far as he has insisted that all the States have the right to do exactly as they please about all their domestic relations, including that of slavery, I agree entirely with him. He places me wrong in spite of all I can tell him, though I repeat it again and again, insisting that I have no difference with him upon this subject. I have made a great many speeches, some of which have been printed, and it will be utterly impossible for him to find anything that I have ever put in print contrary to what I now say upon this subject. I hold myself under constitutional obligations to allow the people in all the States without interference, direct or indirect, to do exactly as they please, and I deny that I have any inclination to interfere with them, even if there were no such constitutional obligation. I can only say again that I am placed improperly—altogether improperly in spite of all I can say—when it is insisted that I entertain any other view or purposes in regard to that matter.

While I am upon this subject, I will make some answers briefly to certain propositions that Judge Douglas has put. He says, "Why can't this Union endure permanently, half slave and half free?" I have said that I supposed it could not, and I will try, before this new audience, to give briefly some of the reasons for entertaining that opinion. Another form of his question is, "Why can't we let it stand as our fathers placed it?" That is the exact difficulty between us. I say that Judge Douglas and his friends have changed them from the position in which our fathers originally placed it. I say in the way our fathers originally left the slavery question, the institution was in the course of ultimate extinction, and the public mind rested in the belief that it *was* in the course of ultimate extinction. I say when this government was first established it was the policy of its founders to prohibit the spread of slavery into the new Territories of the United States, where it had not existed. But Judge Douglas and his friends have broken up that policy and placed it upon a new basis by which it is to become national and perpetual. All I have asked or desired anywhere is that it should be placed back again upon the basis that the fathers of our government originally placed it upon. I have no doubt that it *would* become extinct, for all time to come, if we but re-adopted the policy of the fathers by restricting it to the limits it has already covered—restricting it from the new Territories.

I do not wish to dwell at great length on this branch of the subject at this time, but allow me to repeat one thing that I have stated before. Brooks, the man who assaulted Senator Sumner on the floor of the Senate, and who was complimented with dinners and silver pitchers, and gold-headed canes, and a good many other things for that feat, in one of his speeches declared that when this Government was originally established nobody expected that the institution of slavery would last until this day. That was but the opinion of one man, but it was such an opinion as we can never get from Judge Douglas or anybody in favor of slavery in the North at all. You *can* sometimes get it from a Southern man. He said at the same time that the framers of our Government did not have the knowledge that experience has taught us—that experience and the invention of the cotton-gin have taught us that the perpetuation of slavery is a necessity. He insisted, therefore, upon its being changed from the basis upon which the Fathers of the Government left it to the basis of its perpetuation and nationalization.

I insist that this is the difference between Judge Douglas and myself—that Judge Douglas is helping that change along. I insist upon this Government being placed where our fathers originally placed it.

I remember Judge Douglas once said that he saw the evidences on the statute books of Congress, of a policy in the origin of government to divide slavery and freedom by a geographical line—that he saw an indisposition to maintain that policy, and therefore he set about studying up a way to settle the institution on the right basis—the basis which he thought it ought to have been placed upon at first; and in that speech he confesses that he seeks to place it not upon the basis that the fathers placed it upon, but upon one gotten up on "original principles." When he asks me why we cannot get along with it in the attitude where our fathers placed it he had better clear up the evidences that he has himself changed it from that basis; that he has himself been chiefly instrumental in changing the policy of the fathers. [Applause.] Any one who will read his speech of the 22d of last March, will see that he there makes an open confession, showing that he set about fixing the institution upon an altogether different set of principles. I think I have fully answered him when he asks me why we cannot let it alone upon the basis where our fathers left it, by showing that he has himself changed the whole policy of the Government in that regard.

Now, fellow citizens, in regard to this matter about a contract that was made between Judge Trumbull and myself, and all that long portion of Judge Douglas' speech on this subject—I wish simply to say what I have said to him before, that he cannot know whether it is true or not, and I *do know* that there is not a word of truth in it. [Applause.] And I have told him so before. [Continued applause. "That's right." "Hit him again."] I don't want any harsh language indulged in, but I do not know how to deal with this persistent insisting on a story that I know to be utterly without truth. It used to be a fashion amongst men that when a charge was made some sort of proof was brought forward to establish it, and if no proof was found to exist, the charge was dropped. I don't know how to meet this kind of an argument. I don't want to have a fight with Judge Douglas, and I have no way of making an argument up into the consistency of a corn-cob and stopping his mouth with it. [Laughter and applause.] All I can do is, good-humoredly to say that from the beginning to the end of all that story about a bargain between Judge Trumbull and myself, *there is not a word of truth in it.* [Applause.] I can only ask him to show some sort of evidence of the truth of his story. He brings forward here and reads from what he contends is a speech by James H. Matheny charging such a bargain between Trumbull and myself. My own opinion is that Matheny did do some such immoral thing as to tell a story that he knew nothing about. I believe he did. I contradicted it instantly and it has been contradicted by Judge Trumbull, while nobody has produced any proof, because there is none. Now whether the speech which the Judge brings forward here is really the one Matheny made I do not know, and I hope the Judge will pardon me for doubting the genuineness of this document since his production of those Springfield Resolutions at Ottawa. [Laughter and cheers.] I do not wish to dwell at any great length upon this matter. I can say nothing when a long story like this is told except it is not true, and demand that he who insists upon it shall produce some proof. That is all any man can do, and I leave it in that way for I know of no other way of dealing with it.

The Judge has gone over a long account of the old Whig and Democratic parties, and it connects itself with this charge against Trumbull and myself. He says that they agreed upon a compromise in regard to the slavery question in 1850; that in a National Democratic Convention resolutions were passed to abide by that compromise as a finality upon the slavery question. He also says that the Whig party in National Convention agreed to abide by and regard as a finality, the compromise of 1850. I understand the Judge to be altogether right about that; I understand that part of the history of the country as stated by him to be correct. I recollect that I, as a member of that party, acquiesced in that compromise. I recollect in the Presidential election which followed, when we had General Scott up for the Presidency, Judge Douglas was around berating us Whigs as Abolitionists, precisely as he does to-day—not a bit of difference. I have often heard him. We could do nothing when the old Whig party was alive that was not Abolitionism, but it has got an extremely good name since it has passed away. [Laughter.]

When that compromise was made it did not repeal the old Missouri Compromise. It left a region of United States territory half as large as the present territory of the United States, North of the line of 36° 30′ in which slavery was prohibited by act of Congress. This compromise did not repeal that one. It did not affect or propose to repeal it. But at last it became Judge Douglas's duty, as he thought (and I find no fault with him) as Chairman of the Committee on Territories, to bring in a bill for the organization of a territorial government—first of one, then of two territories north of that line. When he did so it ended in his inserting a provision substantially repealing the Missouri Compromise. That was because the compromise of 1850 *had not* repealed it. And now I ask why he could not have let that compromise alone? We were quiet from the agitation of the slavery question. We were making no fuss about it. All had acquiesced in the compromise measures of 1850. We never had been seriously disturbed by any abolition agitation before that period. When he came to form governments for the territories North of the line of 36° 30′, why could he not have let that matter stand as it was standing? [Applause.] Was it necessary to the organization of a territory? Not at all. Iowa lay North of the line and had been organized as a territory and had come into the Union as a State without disturbing that Compromise. There was no sort of necessity for destroying it to organize these territories. But gentlemen, it would take up all my time to meet all the little quibbling arguments of Judge Douglas to show that the Missouri Compromise was repealed by the Compromise of 1850. My own opinion is that a careful investigation of all the arguments to sustain the position that that Compromise was virtually repealed by the Compromise of 1850 would show that they are the merest fallacies. I have the report that Judge Douglas first brought into Congress at the time of the introduction of the Nebraska bill, which in its original form *did not* repeal the Missouri Compromise, and he there expressly stated that he had forborne to do so *because it had not been done by the Compromise of 1850*. I close this part of the discussion on my part by asking him the question again "Why when we had peace under the Missouri Compromise could you not have let it alone?"

In complaining of what I said in my speech at Springfield in which he says I accepted my nomination for the Senatorship, (where by the way he is at fault, for if he will examine it he will find no acceptance in it;) he again quotes that portion in which I said that "a house divided against itself cannot stand." Let me say a word in regard to that matter.

He tries to persuade us that there must be a variety in the different institutions of the States of the Union; that that variety necessarily proceeds from the variety of soil, climate, of the face of the country and the difference in the natural features of the States. I agree to all that. Have these very matters ever produced any difficulty amongst us? Not at all. Have we ever had any quarrel over the fact that they have laws in Louisiana designed to regulate the commerce that springs from the production of sugar? Or because we have a different class relative to the production of flour in this State? Have they produced any differences? Not at all. They are the very cements of this Union. They don't make the house a house divided against itself. They are the props that hold up the house and sustain the Union.

But has it been so with this element of slavery? Have we not always had quarrels and difficulties over it? And when will we cease to have quarrels over it? Like causes produce like effects. It is worth while to observe that we have generally had comparative peace upon the slavery question and that there has been no cause for alarm until it was excited by the effort to spread it into new territory. Whenever it has been limited to its present bounds and there has been no effort to spread it, there has been peace. All the trouble and convulsion has proceeded from efforts to spread it over more territory. It was thus at the date of the Missouri Compromise. It was so again with the annexation of Texas; so with the territory acquired by the Mexican war, and it is so now. Whenever there has been an effort to spread it there has been agitation and resistance. Now I appeal to this audience, (very few of whom are my political friends,) as national men, whether we have reason to expect that the agitation in regard to this subject will cease while the causes that tend to reproduce agitation are actively at work? Will not the same cause that produced agitation in 1820 when the Missouri Compromise was formed—that which produced the agitation upon the annexation of Texas and at other times—work out the same results always? Do you think that the nature of man will be changed—that the same causes that produced agitation at one time will not have the same effect at another?

This has been the result so far as my observation of the Slavery question and my reading in history extends. What right have we then to hope that the trouble will cease—that the agitation will come to an end—until it shall either be placed back where it originally stood and where the fathers originally placed it, or on the other hand until it shall entirely master all opposition. This is the view I entertain, and this is the reason I entertained it, as Judge Douglas has read from my Springfield speech.

Now, my friends, there is one other thing that I feel myself under some sort of obligation to mention. Judge Douglas has here to-day—in a very rambling way, I was about saying—spoken of the platforms for which he seeks to hold me responsible. He says, "Why can't you come out and make an open avowal of principles in all places alike?" and he reads from an advertisement that he says was used to notify the people of a speech to be made by Judge Trumbull at Waterloo. In commenting on it he desires to know whether we cannot speak frankly and manfully as he and his friends do! How, I ask, do his friends speak out their own sentiments? A Convention of his party in this State met on the 21st of April, at Springfield, and passed a set of resolutions which they proclaim to the country as their platform. This does constitute their platform, and it is because Judge Douglas claims it is his platform—that these are his principles and purposes—that he has a right to declare he speaks his sentiments "frankly and manfully." On the 9th of June, Col. John Dougherty, Gov. Reynolds and others, calling themselves National Democrats, met in Springfield and adopted a set of resolutions which are as easily understood, as plain and as definite in stating to the country and to the world what they believed in and would stand upon, as Judge Douglas' platform. Now, what is the reason, that Judge Douglas is not willing that Col. Dougherty and Gov. Reynolds should stand upon their own written and printed platform as well as he upon his? Why must he look farther than their platform when he claims himself to stand by his platform?

Again, in reference to our platform; On the 16th of June the Republicans had their Convention and published their platform, which is as clear and distinct as Judge Douglas'. In it they spoke their principles as plainly and as definitely to the world. What is the reason that Judge Douglas is not willing I should stand upon that platform? Why must he go around hunting for some one who is supporting me, or has supported me at some time in his life, and who has said something at some time contrary to that platform? Does the Judge regard that rule as a good one? If it turn out that the rule is a good one for me—that I am responsible for any and every opinion that any man has expressed who is my friend—then it is a good rule for him. I ask, is it not as good a rule for him as it is for me? In my opinion, it is not a good rule for either of us. Do you think differently, Judge?

Mr. DOUGLAS—I do not.

Mr. LINCOLN—Judge Douglas says he does not think differently. I am glad of it. Then can he tell me why he is looking up resolutions of five or six years ago, and insisting that they were my platform, notwithstanding my protest that they are not, and never were my platform, and my pointing out the platform of the State Convention which he delights to say nominated me for the Senate? I cannot see what he means by parading these resolutions, if it is not to hold me responsible for them in some way. If he says to me here, that he does not hold the rule to be good, one way or the other, I do not comprehend how he could answer me more fully if he answered me at greater length. I will therefore put in as my answer to the resolutions that he has hunted up against me, what I, as a lawyer, would call a good plea to a bad declaration. [Laughter.] I understand that it is a maxim of law, that a poor plea may be a good plea to a bad declaration. I think that the opinions the Judge brings from those who support me, yet differ from me, is a bad declaration against me; but if I can bring the same things against him, I am putting in a good plea to that kind of declaration, and now I propose to try it.

At Freeport Judge Douglas occupied a large part of his time in producing resolutions and documents of various sorts, as I understood to make me somehow responsible for them; and I propose now doing a little of the same sort of thing for him. In 1850 a very clever gentleman by the name of Thompson Campbell, a personal friend of Judge Douglas and myself, a political friend of Judge Douglas and opponent of mine, was a candidate for Congress in the Galena District. He was interrogated as to his views on this same slavery question. I have here before me the interrogatories and Campbell's answers to them. I will read them:

INTERROGATORIES.

1st. Will you, if elected, vote for and cordially support a bill prohibiting slavery in the Territories of the United States?

2d. Will you vote for and support a bill abolishing slavery in the District of Columbia?

3d. Will you oppose the admission of any Slave States which may be formed out of Texas or the Territories?

4th. Will you vote for and advocate the repeal of the Fugitive Slave Law passed at the recent session of Congress?

5th. Will you advocate and vote for the election of a Speaker of the House of Representatives who shall be willing to organize the Committees of that House, so as to give the Free States their just influence in the business of legislation?

6th. What are your views not only as to the constitutional right of Congress to prohibit the slave trade between the States, but also as to the expediency of exercising that right immediately?

To the first and second interrogatories, I answer unequivocally in the affirmative.

To the third interrogatory I reply, that I am opposed to the admission of any more slave States into the Union, that may be formed out of Texan or any other Territory.

To the fourth and fifth interrogatories I unhesitatingly answer in the affirmative.

To the sixth interrogatory I reply, that so long as the slave States continue to treat slaves as articles of commerce, the Constitution confers power on Congress to pass laws regulating that peculiar COMMERCE, and that the protection of Human Rights imperatively demands the interposition of every constitutional means to prevent this most inhuman and iniquitous traffic.

T. CAMPBELL.

I want to say here that Thompson Campbell was elected to Congress on that platform as the Democratic candidate in the Galena District, against Martin P. Sweet.

JUDGE DOUGLAS.—Give me the date of the letter.

MR. LINCOLN.—The time Campbell ran was in 1850. I have not the exact date here. It was some time in 1850 that these interrogatories were put and the answer given. Campbell was elected to Congress, and served out his term. I think a second election came up before he served out his term and he was not re-elected. Whether defeated or not nominated, I do not know. [Mr. Campbell was nominated for re-election by the Democratic party, by acclamation.] At the end of his term his very good friend, Judge Douglas, got him a high office from President Pierce, and sent him off to California. Is not that the fact? Just at the end of his term in Congress it appears that our mutual friend Judge Douglas got our mutual friend Campbell a good office, and sent him to California upon it. And not only so, but on the 27th of last month when Judge Douglas and myself spoke at Freeport in joint discussion, there was his same friend Campbell, come all the way from California, to help the Judge beat me; and there was poor Martin P. Sweet standing on the platform, trying to help poor me to be elected. [Laughter.] That is true of one of Judge Douglas' friends.

So again, in that same race of 1850, there was a Congressional Convention assembled at Joliet, and it nominated R. S.

Molony, for Congress, and unanimously adopted the following resolutions:

Resolved, That we are uncompromisingly opposed to the extension of slavery; and while we would not make such opposition a ground of interference with the interests of the States where it exists, yet we moderately but firmly insist that it is the duty of Congress to oppose its extension into Territory now free, by all means compatible with the obligations of the Constitution, and with good faith to our sister States; that these principles were recognized by the Ordinance of 1787, which received the sanction of Thomas Jefferson, who is acknowledged by all to be the great oracle and expounder of our faith.

Subsequently the same interrogatories were propounded to Dr. Molony which had been addressed to Campbell, as above, with the exception of the 6th respecting the Inter-State slave trade, to which Dr. Molony, the Democratic nominee for Congress, replied as follows:

I received the written interrogatories this day, and as you will see by the LaSalle *Democrat* and Ottawa *Free Trader*, I took at Peru on the 5th and at Ottawa on the 7th the affirmative side of interrogatories 1st and 2d, and in relation to the admission of any more Slave States from Free Territory, my position taken at these meetings as correctly reported in said papers was *emphatically* and *distinctly* opposed to it. In relation to the admission of any more Slave States from Texas whether I shall go against it or not will depend upon the opinion that I may hereafter form of the true meaning and nature of the Resolutions of Annexation. If, by said resolutions, the honor and good faith of the nation is pledged to admit more Slave States from Texas when she (Texas) may apply for the admission of such State then I should, if in Congress, vote for their admission. But if not so PLEDGED and bound by sacred contract, then a bill for the admission of more Slave States from Texas would *never* receive my vote.

To your 4th interrogatory I answer *most decidedly* in the affirmative, and for reasons set forth in my reported remarks at Ottawa last Monday.

To your 5th interrogatory I also reply in the affirmative *most cordially*, and that I will use my utmost exertions to secure the nomination and election of a man who will accomplish the objects of said interrogatories. I most cordially approve of the resolutions adopted at the union meeting held at Princeton on the 27th September ult. Yours, &c.,

R. S. MOLONY.

All I have to say in regard to Dr. Molony, is that he was the regularly nominated Democratic candidate for Congress in his

District—was elected at that time, at the end of his term was appointed to a Land Office at Danville. (I never heard anything of Judge Douglas' instrumentality in this.) He held this office a considerable time, and when we were at Freeport the other day, there were hand bills scattered about notifying the public that after our debate was over, R. S. Molony would make a Democratic speech in favor of Judge Douglas. That is all I know of my own personal knowledge. It is added here to this resolution, and truly I believe that—

"Among those who participated in the Joliet Convention, and who supported its nominee, with his platform as laid down in the resolution of the Convention and in his reply as above given, we call at random the following names, all of which are recognized at this day as leading Democrats:"

"COOK COUNTY—E. B. Williams, Charles McDonell, Arno Voss, Thomas Hoyne, Isaac Cook."

I reckon we ought to except Cook. [Laughter.]

"F. C. Sherman."

"WILL—Joel A. Matteson, S. W. Bowen."

"KANE—B. F. Hall, G. W. Renwick, A. M. Herrington, Elijah Wilcox."

"McHENRY—W. M. Jackson, Enos W. Smith, Neil Donnelly."

"LASALLE—John Hise, William Reddick."

William Reddick! another one of Judge Douglas' friends that stood on the stand with him at Ottawa, at the time the Judge says my knees trembled so that I had to be carried away. [Laughter.] The names are all here:

"DUPAGE—Nathan Allen."

"DEKALB—Z. B. Mayo."

Here is another set of resolutions which I think are apposite to the matter in hand.

On the 28th of February of the same year, a Democratic District Convention was held at Naperville, to nominate a candidate for Circuit Judge. Among the delegates were Bowen and Kelly, of Will; Captain Naper, H. H. Cody, Nathan Allen, of DuPage; W. M. Jackson, J. M. Strode, P. W. Platt and Enos W. Smith, of McHenry; J. Horsman and others, of Winnebago. Col. Strode presided over the Convention. The following resolutions were unanimously adopted—the first on motion of P. W. Platt, the second on motion of William M. Jackson.

Resolved, That this Convention is in favor of the Wilmot Proviso, both in *Principle* and *Practice,* and that we know of no good reason why any *person* should oppose the largest latitude in *Free Soil, Free Territory* and *Free Speech.*

Resolved, That in the opinion of this Convention the time has arrived when *all men should be free,* whites as well as others.

JUDGE DOUGLAS—What is the date of those resolutions?

MR. LINCOLN—I understand it was in 1850, but I do not *know* it. I do not state a thing and say I know it, when I do not. But I have the highest belief that this is so. I know of no way to arrive at the conclusion that there is an error in it. I mean to put a case no stronger than the truth will allow. But what I *was* going to comment upon is an extract from a newspaper in DeKalb County, and it strikes me as being rather singular, I confess, under the circumstances. There is a Judge Mayo in that county, who is a candidate for the Legislature, for the purpose, if he secures his election, of helping to re-elect Judge Douglas. He is the editor of a newspaper [DeKalb County *Sentinel*], and in that paper I find the extract I am going to read. It is part of an editorial article in which he was electioneering as fiercely as he could for Judge Douglas and against me. It was a curious thing, I think, to be in such a paper. I will agree to that, and the Judge may make the most of it:

Our education has been such, that we have ever been rather *in favor of the equality of the blacks; that is, that they should enjoy all the privileges of the whites where they reside.* We are aware that this is not a very popular doctrine. We have had many a confab with some who are now strong "Republicans," we taking the broad ground of equality and they the opposite ground.

We were brought up in a State where blacks were voters, and we do not know of any inconvenience resulting from it, though perhaps it would not work as well where the blacks are more numerous. We have no doubt of the right of the whites to guard against such an evil, if it is one. Our opinion is that it would be best for all concerned to have the colored population in a State by themselves [In this I agree with him]; but if within the jurisdiction of the United States, *we say by all means they should have the right to have their Senators and Representatives in Congress, and to vote for President.* With us "worth makes the man, and want of it the fellow." We have seen many a "nigger" that we thought more of than some white men.

That is one of Judge Douglas' friends. Now I do not want to leave myself in an attitude where I can be misrepresented, so I will say I do not think the Judge is responsible for this article; but he is quite as responsible for it, as I would be if one of my friends had said it. I think that is fair enough. [Cheers.]

I have here also a set of resolutions placed by a Democratic State Convention in Judge Douglas' own good old State of Vermont, that I think ought to be good for him too:

> *Resolved,* That liberty is a right inherent and inalienable in man, and that herein *all men are equal.*
>
> *Resolved,* That we claim no authority in the Federal Government to abolish slavery in the several States, but we do claim for it constitutional power perpetually to prohibit the introduction of slavery into territory now free, and abolish it wherever, under the jurisdiction of Congress it exists.
>
> *Resolved,* That this power ought immediately to be exercised in prohibiting the introduction and existence of slavery in New Mexico and California, in abolishing slavery and the slave trade in the District of Columbia, on the high seas, and wherever else, under the Constitution, it can be reached.
>
> *Resolved,* That no more slave States should be admitted into the Federal Union.
>
> *Resolved,* That the Government ought to return to its ancient policy, not to extend, nationalize or encourage, but to limit, localize and discourage slavery.

At Freeport I answered several interrogatories that had been propounded to me by Judge Douglas at the Ottawa meeting. The Judge has yet not seen fit to find any fault with the position that I took in regard to those seven interrogatories, which were certainly broad enough, in all conscience, to cover the entire ground. In my answers, which have been printed, and all have had the opportunity of seeing, I take the ground that those who elect me must expect that I will do nothing which is not in accordance with those answers. I have some right to assert that Judge Douglas has no fault to find with them. But he chooses to still try to thrust me upon different ground without paying any attention to my answers, the obtaining of which from me cost him so much trouble and concern. At the same time, I propounded four interrogatories to him, claiming it as a right that he should answer as many interrogatories for me as I did for him, and I would reserve myself for a future installment when I got them ready. The Judge in answering me upon that occasion, put in what I suppose he intends as answers to all four of my interrogatories. The first one of these interrogatories I have before me, and it is in these words:

Question 1. If the people of Kansas shall, by means entirely unobjectionable in all other respects, adopt a State Constitution, and ask admission into the Union under it, *before* they have the requisite number of inhabitants according to the English Bill—some ninety-three thousand—will you vote to admit them?

As I read the Judge's answer in the newspaper, and as I remember it as pronounced at the time, he does not give any answer which is equivalent to yes or no—I will or I won't. He answers at very considerable length, rather quarreling with me for asking the question, and insisting that Judge Trumbull had done something that I ought to say something about; and finally getting out such statements as induce me to infer that he means to be understood he will, in that supposed case, vote for the admission of Kansas. I only bring this forward now for the purpose of saying that if he chooses to put a different construction upon his answer he may do it. But if he does not, I shall from this time forward assume that he will vote for the admission of Kansas in disregard of the English bill. He has the right to remove any misunderstanding I may have. I only mention it now that I may hereafter assume this to be the true construction of his answer, if he does not now choose to correct me.

The second interrogatory that I propounded to him, was this:

Q. 2. Can the people of a United States Territory, in any lawful way, against the wish of any citizen of the United States, exclude slavery from its limits prior to the formation of a State Constitution?

To this Judge Douglas answered that they can lawfully exclude slavery from the Territory prior to the formation of a constitution. He goes on to tell us how it can be done. As I understand him, he holds that it can be done by the Territorial Legislature refusing to make any enactments for the protection of slavery in the Territory, and especially by adopting unfriendly legislation to it. For the sake of clearness I state it again; that they can exclude slavery from the Territory, 1st, by withholding what he assumes to be an indispensable assistance to it in the way of legislation; and 2d, by unfriendly legislation. If I rightly understand him, I wish to ask your attention for a while to his position.

In the first place, the Supreme Court of the United States has decided that any Congressional prohibition of slavery in the Territories is unconstitutional—that they have reached this proposition as a conclusion from their former proposition that the Constitution of the United States expressly recognizes property in slaves, and from that other constitutional provision that no person shall be deprived of property without due process of law. Hence they reach the conclusion that as the Constitution of the United States expressly recognizes property in slaves, and prohibits any person from being deprived of property without due process of law, to pass an act of Congress by which a man who owned a slave on one side of a line would be deprived of him if he took him on the other side, is depriving him of that property without due process of law. That I understand to be the decision of the Supreme Court. I understand also that Judge Douglas adheres most firmly to that decision; and the difficulty is, how is it possible for any power to exclude slavery from the Territory unless in violation of that decision? That is the difficulty.

In the Senate of the United States, in 1856, Judge Trumbull in a speech, substantially if not directly, put the same interrogatory to Judge Douglas, as to whether the people of a Territory had the lawful power to exclude slavery prior to the formation of a constitution? Judge Douglas then answered at considerable length, and his answer will be found in the *Congressional Globe*, under date of June 9th, 1856. The Judge said that whether the people could exclude slavery prior to the formation of a constitution or not *was a question to be decided by the Supreme Court.* He put that proposition, as will be seen by the *Congressional Globe*, in a variety of forms, all running to the same thing in substance—that it was a question for the Supreme Court. I maintain that when he says, after the

Supreme Court have decided the question, that the people may yet exclude slavery by any means whatever, he does virtually say, that it is *not* a question for the Supreme Court [Applause]. He shifts his ground. I appeal to you whether he did not say it was a question for the Supreme Court. Has not the Supreme Court decided that question? When he now says the people *may* exclude slavery, does he not make it a question for the people? Does he not virtually shift his ground and say that it is *not* a question for the Court, but for the people? This is a very simple proposition—a very plain and naked one. It seems to me that there is no difficulty in deciding it. In a variety of ways he said that it was a question for the Supreme Court. He did not stop then to tell us that whatever the Supreme Court decides the people can by withholding necessary "police regulations" keep slavery out. He did not make any such answer. I submit to you now, whether the new state of the case has not induced the Judge to sheer away from his original ground. [Applause.] Would not this be the impression of every fair-minded man?

I hold that the proposition that slavery cannot enter a new country without police regulations is historically false. It is not true at all. I hold that the history of this country shows that the institution of slavery was originally planted upon this continent *without* these "police regulations" which the Judge now thinks necessary for the actual establishment of it. Not only so, but is there not another fact—how came this Dred Scott decision to be made? It was made upon the case of a negro being taken and actually held in slavery in Minnesota Territory, claiming his freedom because the act of Congress prohibited his being so held there. *Will the Judge pretend that Dred Scott was not held there without police regulations?* There is at least one matter of record as to his having been held in slavery in the Territory, not only without police regulations, but in the teeth of Congressional legislation supposed to be valid at the time. This shows that there is vigor enough in Slavery to plant itself in a new country even against unfriendly legislation. It takes not only law but the *enforcement* of law to keep it out. That is the history of this country upon the subject.

I wish to ask one other question. It being understood that

the Constitution of the United States guarantees property in slaves in the Territories, if there is any infringement of the right of that property, would not the United States Courts, organized for the government of the Territory, apply such remedy as might be necessary in that case? It is a maxim held by the Courts, that there is no wrong without its remedy; and the Courts have a remedy for whatever is acknowledged and treated as a wrong.

Again: I will ask you my friends, if you were elected members of the Legislature, what would be the first thing you would have to do before entering upon your duties? *Swear to support the Constitution of the United States.* Suppose you believe, as Judge Douglas does, that the Constitution of the United States guarantees to your neighbor the right to hold slaves in that Territory—that they are his property—how can you clear your oaths unless you give him such legislation as is necessary to enable him to enjoy that property? What do you understand by supporting the Constitution of a State or of the United States? Is it not to give such constitutional helps to the rights established by that Constitution as may be practically needed? Can you, if you swear to support the Constitution, and believe that the Constitution establishes a right, clear your oath, without giving it support? Do you support the Constitution if, knowing or believing there is a right established under it which needs specific legislation, you withhold that legislation? Do you not violate and disregard your oath? I can conceive of nothing plainer in the world. There can be nothing in the words "support the constitution," if you may run counter to it by refusing support to any right established under the constitution. And what I say here will hold with still more force against the Judge's doctrine of "unfriendly legislation." How could you, having sworn to support the Constitution, and believing it guaranteed the right to hold slaves in the Territories, assist in legislation *intended to defeat that right*? That would be violating your own view of the constitution. Not only so, but if you were to do so, how long would it take the courts to hold your votes unconstitutional and void? Not a moment.

Lastly I would ask—is not Congress, itself, under obligation to give legislative support to any right that is established

under the United States Constitution? I repeat the question—
is not Congress, itself, bound to give legislative support to
any right that is established in the United States Constitution?
A member of Congress swears to support the Constitution of
the United States, and if he sees a right established by that
Constitution which needs specific legislative protection, can
he clear his oath without giving that protection? Let me ask
you why many of us who are opposed to slavery upon principle give our acquiescence to a fugitive slave law? Why do we
hold ourselves under obligations to pass such a law, and abide
by it when it is passed? Because the Constitution makes provision that the owners of slaves shall have the right to reclaim
them. It gives the right to reclaim slaves, and that right is, as
Judge Douglas says, a barren right, unless there is legislation
that will enforce it.

The mere declaration "No person held to service or labor in
one State under the laws thereof, escaping into another, shall
in consequence of any law or regulation therein be discharged
from such service or labor, but shall be delivered up on claim
of the party to whom such service or labor may be due" is
powerless without specific legislation to enforce it. Now on
what ground would a member of Congress who is opposed to
slavery in the abstract vote for a fugitive law, as I would deem
it my duty to do? Because there is a Constitutional right
which needs legislation to enforce it. And although it is distasteful to me, I have sworn to support the Constitution, and
having so sworn I cannot conceive that I do support it if I
withheld from that right any necessary legislation to make it
practical. And if that is true in regard to a fugitive slave law, is
the right to have fugitive slaves reclaimed any better fixed in
the Constitution than the right to hold slaves in the Territories? For this decision is a just exposition of the Constitution
as Judge Douglas thinks. Is the one right any better than the
other? Is there any man who while a member of Congress
would give support to the one any more than the other? If I
wished to refuse to give legislative support to slave property
in the Territories, if a member of Congress, I could not do it
holding the view that the Constitution establishes that right.
If I did it at all, it would be because I deny that this decision
properly construes the Constitution. But if I acknowledge

with Judge Douglas that this decision properly construes the Constitution, I cannot conceive that I would be less than a perjured man if I should refuse in Congress to give such protection to that property as in its nature it needed.

At the end of what I have said here I propose to give the Judge my fifth interrogatory which he may take and answer at his leisure. My fifth interrogatory is this: If the slaveholding citizens of a United States Territory should need and demand Congressional legislation for the protection of their slave property in such territory, would you, as a member of Congress, vote for or against such legislation?

JUDGE DOUGLAS—Will you repeat that? I want to answer that question.

MR. LINCOLN—If the slaveholding citizens of a United States Territory should need and demand Congressional legislation for the protection of their slave property in such Territory, would you, as a member of Congress vote for or against such legislation?

I am aware that in some of the speeches Judge Douglas has made, he has spoken as if he did not know or think that the Supreme Court had decided that a territorial Legislature cannot exclude slavery. Precisely what the Judge would say upon the subject—whether he would say definitely that he does not understand they have so decided, or whether he would say he does understand that the Court have so decided, I do not know; but I know that in his speech at Springfield he spoke of it as a thing they had not decided yet; and in his answer to me at Freeport, he spoke of it so far again as I can comprehend it, as a thing that had not yet been decided. Now I hold that if the Judge does entertain that view I think he is not mistaken in so far as it can be said that the Court has not decided anything save the mere question of jurisdiction. I know the legal arguments that can be made—that after a court has decided that it cannot take jurisdiction of a case, it then has decided all that is before it, and that is the end of it. A plausible argument can be made in favor of that proposition, but I know that Judge Douglas has said in one of his speeches that the court went forward *like honest men as they were* and decided all the points in the case. If any points are really extrajudicially decided because not necessarily before them, then this one as to the power of the Territorial Legislature to exclude slavery is one of them, as also the one that the Missouri Compromise was null and void. They are both extra-judicial or neither is according as the Court held that they had no jurisdiction in the case between the parties, because of want of capacity of one party to maintain a suit in that Court. I want, if I have sufficient time, to show that the Court did *pass its opinion*, but that is the only thing actually done in the case. If they did not decide, they showed what they were ready to decide whenever the matter was before them. What is that opinion? After having argued that Congress had no power to pass a law excluding slavery from a United States Territory, they then used language to this effect: — that inasmuch as Congress itself could not exercise such a power, it followed as a matter of course that it could not authorize a territorial government to exercise it, for the Territorial Legislature can do no more than Congress could do. Thus it expressed its opinion emphatically against the power of a Territorial Legislature to exclude slavery, leaving us in just as little doubt on that point as upon any other point they really decided.

Now, my fellow citizens, I will detain you only a little while longer. My time is very nearly out. I find a report of a speech made by Judge Douglas at Joliet, since we last met at Freeport — published I believe in the *Missouri Republican* — on the 9th of this month, in which Judge Douglas says:

You know at Ottawa, I read this platform, and asked him if he concurred in each and all of the principles set forth in it. He would not answer these questions. At last I said frankly, I wish you to answer them, because when I get them up here where the color of your principles is a little darker than in Egypt, I intend to trot you down to Jonesboro. The very notice that I was going to take him down to Egypt made him tremble in the knees so that he had to be carried from the platform. He laid up seven days, and in the meantime held a consultation with his political physicians, they had Lovejoy and Farnsworth and all the leaders of the Abolition party, they consulted it all over, and at last Lincoln came to the conclusion that he would answer, so he came up to Freeport last Friday.

Now that statement altogether furnishes a subject for philosophical contemplation. [Laughter.] I have been treating it in that way, and I have really come to the conclusion that I can explain it in no other way than by believing the Judge is crazy. [Renewed laughter.] If he was in his right mind, I cannot conceive how he would have risked disgusting the four or five thousand of his own friends who stood there, and knew, as to my having been carried from the platform, that there was not a word of truth in it.

JUDGE DOUGLAS—Didn't they carry you off?

MR. LINCOLN—There; that question illustrates the character of this man Douglas, exactly. He smiles now and says, "Didn't they carry you off?" But he says then, *"He had to be carried off;"* and he said it to convince the country that he had so completely broken me down by his speech that I had to be carried away. Now he seeks to dodge it, and asks, "Didn't they carry you off?" Yes, they did. *But, Judge Douglas, why didn't you tell the truth?* [Great laughter and cheers.] I would like to know why you didn't tell the truth about it. [Continued laughter.] And then again, "He laid up seven days." He puts this in print for the people of the country to read as a serious document. I think if he had been in his sober senses he would not have risked that barefacedness in the presence of thousands of his own friends, who knew that I made speeches within six of the seven days at Henry, Marshall County; Augusta, Hancock County, and Macomb, McDonough County, including all the necessary travel to meet him again at Freeport at the end of the six days. Now, I say, there is no charitable way to look at that statement, except to conclude that he is actually crazy. [Laughter.] There is another thing in that statement that alarmed me very greatly as he states it, that he was going to "trot me down to Egypt." Thereby he would have you to infer that I would not come to Egypt unless he forced me—that I could not be got here, unless he, giant-like, had hauled me down here. [Laughter.] That statement he makes, too, in the teeth of the knowledge that I had made the stipulation to come down here, *and that he himself had been very reluctant to enter into the stipulation*. [Cheers and laughter.] More than all this, Judge Douglas, when he made that statement must have been crazy, and wholly out of his sober senses, or else he would have known that when he got me down here—that promise—that windy promise—of his powers to annihilate me, wouldn't amount to anything. Now, how little do I look like being carried away trembling? Let the Judge go on, and after he is done with his half hour, I want you all, if I can't go home myself, to let me stay and rot here; and if anything happens to the Judge, if I cannot carry him to the hotel and put him to bed, let me stay here and rot. [Great laughter.] I say, then, there is something *extraordinary* in this statement. I ask you if you know any other living man who would make such a statement? [Cries of "No," "no." "Yes," "yes."] I will ask my friend Casey, over there, if he would do such a thing? [Casey dropped his head and said nothing.] Would he send that out and have his men take it as the truth? Did the Judge talk of trotting me down to Egypt to scare me to death? Why, I know this people better than he does. I was raised just a little east of here. I am a part of this people. But the Judge was raised further north, and perhaps he has some horrid idea of what this people might be induced to do. [Roars of laughter and cheers.] But really I have talked about this matter perhaps longer than I ought, for it is no great thing, and yet the smallest are often the most difficult things to deal with. The Judge has set about seriously trying to make the impression that when we meet at different places I am literally in his clutches—that I am a poor, helpless, decrepit mouse, and that I can do nothing at all. This is one of the ways he has taken to create that impression. I don't know any other way to meet it, except this. I don't want to quarrel with him—to call him a liar—but when I come square up to him I don't know what else to call him, if I must tell the truth out. [Cheers and laughter.] I want to be at peace, and reserve all my fighting powers for necessary occasions. My time, now, is very nearly out, and I give up the trifle that is left to the Judge to let him set my knees trembling again, if he can.

MR. DOUGLAS' REPLY.

Mr. Douglas on again taking the stand was greeted with thundering applause. He said:

My friends, while I am very grateful to you for the enthusiasm which you show for me, I will say in all candor, that your quietness will be much more agreeable than your applause, inasmuch as you deprive me of some part of my time whenever you cheer. (All right, go ahead, we won't interrupt, &c.)

I will commence where Mr. Lincoln left off, and make a remark upon this serious complaint of his about my speech at Joliet. I did say there in a playful manner that when I put these questions to Mr. Lincoln at Ottawa he failed to answer, and that he trembled and had to be carried off the stand, and required seven days to get up his reply. (Laughter.) That he did not walk off from that stand he will not deny. That when the crowd went away from the stand with me, a few persons carried him home on their shoulders and laid him down, he will admit. (Shouts of laughter.) I wish to say to you that whenever I degrade my friends and myself by allowing them to carry me on their backs along through the public streets when I am able to walk I am willing to be deemed crazy. ("All right, Douglas," laughter and applause. Lincoln chewing his nails in a rage in a back corner.) I did not say whether I beat him or he beat me in the argument. It is true I put these questions to him, and I put them not as mere idle questions, but showed that I based them upon the creed of the Black Republican party as declared by their conventions in that portion of the State which he depends upon to elect him, and desired to know whether he endorsed that creed. He would not answer. When I reminded him that I intended bringing him into Egypt and renewing my questions if he refused to answer, he then consulted and did get up his answers one week after,—answers which I may refer to in a few minutes and show you how equivocal they are. My object was to make him avow whether or not he stood by the platform of his party; the resolutions I then read, and upon which I based my questions, had been adopted by his party in the Galena Congressional district, and the Chicago and Bloomington Congressional districts, composing a large majority of the counties in this State that give Republican or Abolition majorities. Mr. Lincoln cannot and will not deny that the doctrines laid down in these resolutions were in substance put forth in Lovejoy's resolutions which were voted for by a majority of his party, some of them, if not all, receiving the support of every man of his party. Hence, I laid a foundation for my questions to him before I asked him whether that was or was not the platform of his party. He says that he answered my questions. One of them was whether he would vote to admit any more slave States into the Union. The creed of the Republican party as set forth in the resolutions of their various conventions was that they would under no circumstances vote to admit another slave State. It was put forth in the Lovejoy resolutions in the legislature, it was put forth and passed in a majority of all the counties of this State which give Abolition or Republican majorities, or elect members to the legislature of that school of politics. I had a right to know whether he would vote for or against the admission of another slave State in the event the people wanted it. He first answered that he was not pledged on the subject, and then said, "In regard to the other question of whether I am pledged to the admission of any more slave States into the Union, I state to you very frankly that I would be exceedingly sorry ever to be put in the position of having to pass on that question. ("No doubt," and laughter. Mr. Lincoln looks savagely into the crowd for the man who said "no doubt.") I should be exceedingly glad to know that there would never be another slave State admitted into the Union; but I must add that if slavery shall be kept out of the territories during the territorial existence of any one given territory, and then the people, having a fair chance and clean field when they come to adopt a constitution, do such an extraordinary thing as adopt a slave constitution, uninfluenced by the actual presence of the institution among them, I see no alternative, if we own the country, but to admit them into the Union."

Now analyze that answer. In the first place he says he would be exceedingly sorry to be put in a position where he would have to vote on the question of the admission of a slave State. Why is he a candidate for the Senate if he would be sorry to be put in that position? I trust the people of Illinois will not put him in a position which he would be so sorry to occupy. ("There's no danger," &c.) The next position he takes is that he would be glad to know that there would never be another slave State, yet, in certain contingencies, he might have to vote for one. What is that contingency? "If Congress keeps slavery out by law while it is a territory, and then the people should have a fair chance and should adopt slavery, uninfluenced by the presence of the institution," he supposes he would have to admit the State. Suppose Congress should not keep slavery out during their territorial existence, then how would he vote when the people applied for admission into the Union with a slave constitution? That he does not answer, and that is the condition of every territory we have now got. Slavery is not kept out of Kansas by act of Congress, and when I put the question to Mr. Lincoln whether he will vote for the admission with or without slavery, as her people may desire, he will not answer, and you have not got an answer from him. In Nebraska slavery is not prohibited by act of Congress, but the people are allowed, under the Nebraska bill, to do as they please on the subject; and when I ask him whether he will vote to admit Nebraska with a slave constitution if her people desire it, he will not answer. So with New Mexico, Washington territory, Arizona, and the four new States to be admitted from Texas. You cannot get an answer from him to these questions. His answer only applies to a given case, to a condition—things which he knows do not exist in any one territory in the Union. He tries to give you to understand that he would allow the people to do as they please, and yet he dodges the question as to every territory in the Union. I now ask why cannot Mr. Lincoln answer to each of these territories? He has not done it, and he will not do it. The Abolitionists up North understand that this answer is made with a view of not committing himself on any one territory now in existence. It is so understood there, and you cannot expect an answer from him on a case that applies to any one territory, or applies to the new States which by compact we are pledged to admit out of Texas, when they have the requisite population and desire admission. I submit to you whether he has made a frank answer, so that you can tell how he would vote in any one of these cases. "He would be sorry to be put in the position." Why would he be sorry to be put in this position if his duty required him to give the vote? If the people of a territory ought to be permitted to come into the Union as a State, with slavery or without it, as they pleased, why not give the vote admitting them cheerfully? If in his opinion they ought not to come in with slavery, even if they wanted to, why not say that he would cheerfully vote against their admission? His intimation is that conscience would not let him vote "No," and he would be sorry to do that which his conscience would compel him to do as an honest man. (Laughter and cheers.)

In regard to the contract or bargain between Trumbull, the Abolitionists and him, which he denies, I wish to say that the charge can be proved by notorious historical facts. Trumbull, Lovejoy, Giddings, Fred Douglass, Hale, and Banks, were traveling the State at that time making speeches on the same side and in the same cause with him. He contents himself with the simple denial that no such thing occurred. Does he deny that he, and Trumbull, and Breese, and Giddings, and Chase, and Fred Douglass, and Lovejoy, and all those Abolitionists and deserters from the Democratic party, did make speeches all over this State in the same common cause? Does he deny that Jim Matheny was then and is now his confidential friend, and does he deny that Matheny made the charge of the bargain and fraud in his own language, as I have read it from his printed speech. Matheny spoke of his own personal knowledge of that bargain existing between Lincoln, Trumbull, and the Abolitionists. He still remains Lincoln's confidential friend, and is now a candidate for Congress, and is canvassing the Springfield district for Lincoln. I assert that I can prove the charge to be true in detail if I can ever get it where I can summon and compel the attendance of witnesses. I have the statement of another man to the same effect as that made by Matheny, which I am not permitted to use yet, but Jim Matheny is a good witness on that point, and the history of the country is conclusive upon it. That Lincoln up to that time had been a Whig, and then undertook to Abolitionize the Whigs and bring them into the Abolition camp, is beyond denial; that Trumbull up to that time had been a Democrat, and deserted, and undertook to Abolitionize the Democracy, and take them into the Abolition camp, is beyond denial; that they are both now active, leading, distinguished members of this Abolition Republican party, in full communion, is a fact that cannot be questioned or denied.

But Lincoln is not willing to be responsible for the creed of his party. He complains because I hold him responsible, and in order to avoid the issue, he attempts to show that individuals in the Democratic party, many years ago, expressed abolition sentiments. It is true that Tom Campbell, when a candidate for Congress in 1850, published the letter which Lincoln read. When I asked Lincoln for the date of that letter he could not give it. The date of the letter has been suppressed by other speakers who have used it, though I take it for granted that Lincoln did not know the date. If he will take the trouble to examine, he will find that the letter was published only two days before the election, and was never seen until after it, except in one county. Tom Campbell would have been beat to death by the Democratic party if that letter had been made public in his district. As to Molony, it is true he uttered sentiments of the kind referred to by Mr. Lincoln, and the best democrats would not vote for him for that reason. I returned from Washington after the passage of the Compromise measures in 1850, and when I found Molony running under John Wentworth's tutelage, and on his platform, I denounced him, and declared that he was no democrat. In my speech at Chicago, just before the election that year, I went before the infuriated people of that city and vindicated the Compromise measures of 1850. Remember the city council had passed resolutions nullifying acts of Congress and instructing the police to withhold their assistance from the execution of the laws, and as I was the only man in the city of Chicago who was responsible for the passage of the Compromise measures, I went before the crowd, justified each and every one of those measures, and let it be said to the eternal honor of the people of Chicago, that when they were convinced by my exposition of those measures that they were right and they had done wrong in opposing them, they repealed their nullifying resolutions and declared that they would acquiesce in and support the laws of the land. These facts are well known, and Mr. Lincoln can only get up individual instances, dating back to 1849, '50, which are contradicted by the whole tenor of the democratic creed.

But Mr. Lincoln does not want to be held responsible for the Black Republican doctrine of no more slave States. Farnsworth is the candidate of his party to-day in the Chicago district, and he made a speech in the last Congress in which he called upon God to palsy his right arm if he ever voted for the admission of another slave State, whether the people wanted it or not. Lovejoy is making speeches all over the State for Lincoln now, and taking ground against any more slave States. Washburne, the Black Republican candidate for Congress in the Galena district, is making speeches in favor of this same abolition platform declaring no more slave States. Why are men running for Congress in the northern districts, and taking that abolition platform for their guide, when Mr. Lincoln does not want to be held to it down here in Egypt and in the centre of the State, and objects to it so as to get votes here. (He can't get any.) Let me tell Mr. Lincoln that his party in the northern part of the State hold to that abolition platform, and that if they do not in the south and in the centre they present the extraordinary spectacle of a house divided against itself, and hence cannot stand. (Hurra.) I now bring down upon him the vengeance of his own scriptural quotation, and give it a more appropriate application than he did, when I say to him that his party, abolition in one end of the State and opposed to it in the other, is a house divided against itself, and cannot stand, and ought not to stand, for it attempts to cheat the American people out of their votes by disguising its sentiments. (Cheers.)

Mr. Lincoln attempts to cover up and get over his abolitionism by telling you that he was raised a little east of you, (laughter,) beyond the Wabash in Indiana, and he thinks that makes a mighty sound and good man of him on all these questions. I do not know that the place where a man is born or raised has much to do with his political principles. The worst Abolitionists I have ever known in Illinois have been men who have sold their slaves in Alabama and Kentucky, and have come here and turned Abolitionists whilst spending the money got for the negroes they sold, (that's so, and laughter,) and I do not know that an Abolitionist from

Indiana or Kentucky ought to have any more credit because he was born and raised among slaveholders. (Not a bit, not as much, &c.) I do not know that a native of Kentucky is more excusable because raised among slaves, his father and mother having owned slaves, he comes to Illinois, turns Abolitionist, and slanders the graves of his father and mother, and breathes curses upon the institutions under which he was born, and his father and mother bred. True, I was not born out west here. I was born away down in Yankee land, (good,) I was born in a valley in Vermont (all right,) with the high mountains around me. I love the old green mountains and valleys of Vermont, where I was born, and where I played in my childhood. I went up to visit them some seven or eight years ago, for the first time for twenty odd years. When I got there they treated me very kindly. They invited me to the commencement of their college, placed me on the seats with their distinguished guests, and conferred upon me the degree of L.L.D. in latin, (doctor of laws,) the same as they did on old Hickory, at Cambridge, many years ago, and I give you my word and honor I understood just as much of the latin as he did. (Laughter.) When they got through conferring the honorary degree, they called upon me for a speech, and I got up with my heart full and swelling with gratitude for their kindness, and I said to them, "My friends, Vermont is the most glorious spot on the face of this globe for a man to be born in, *provided* he emigrates when he is very young." (Uproarious shouts of laughter.)

I emigrated when I was very young. I came out here when I was a boy, and I found my mind liberalized, and my opinions enlarged when I got on these broad prairies, with only the Heavens to bound my vision, instead of having them circumscribed by the little narrow ridges that surrounded the valley where I was born. But, I discard all flings of the land where a man was born. I wish to be judged by my principles, by those great public measures and constitutional principles upon which the peace, the happiness and the perpetuity of this republic now rest.

Mr. Lincoln has framed another question, propounded it to me, and desired my answer. As I have said before, I did not put a question to him that I did not first lay a foundation for by showing that it was a part of the platform of the party whose votes he is now seeking, adopted in a majority of the counties where he now hopes to get a majority, and supported by the candidates of his party now running in those counties. But I will answer his question. It is as follows: "If the slaveholding citizens of a United States territory should need and demand congressional legislation for the protection of their slave property in such territory, would you, as a member of Congress, vote for or against such legislation?" I answer him that it is a fundamental article in the Democratic creed that there should be non-interference and non-intervention by Congress with slavery in the States or territories. (Immense cheering.) Mr. Lincoln could have found an answer to his question in the Cincinnati platform, if he had desired it. (Renewed applause.) The Democratic party have always stood by that great principle of non-interference and non-intervention by Congress with slavery in the States and territories alike, and I stand on that platform now. (Cheer after cheer was here given for Douglas.)

Now I desire to call your attention to the fact that Lincoln did not define his own position in his own question. ("He can't, it's too far South," and laughter.) How does he stand on that question? He put the question to me at Freeport whether or not I would vote to admit Kansas into the Union before she had 93,420 inhabitants. I answered him at once that it having been decided that Kansas had now population enough for a slave State, she had population enough for a free State. ("Good; that's it," and cheers.)

I answered the question unequivocally, and then I asked him whether he would vote for or against the admission of Kansas before she had 93,420 inhabitants, and he would not answer me. To-day he has called attention to the fact that in his opinion my answer on that question was not quite plain enough, and yet he has not answered it himself. (Great Laughter.) He now puts a question in relation to Congressional interference in the territories to me. I answer him direct, and yet he has not answered the question himself. I ask you whether a man has any right, in common decency, to put questions in these public discussions, to his opponent, which he will not answer himself, when they are pressed home to him. I have asked him three times, whether he would vote to admit Kansas whenever the people applied with a constitution of their own making and their own adoption, under circumstances that were fair, just and unexceptionable, but I cannot get an answer from him. Nor will he answer the question which he put to me, and which I have just answered in relation to Congressional interference in the territories, by making a slave code there.

It is time that he goes on to answer the question by arguing that under the decision of the Supreme Court it is the duty of a man to vote for a slave code in the territories. He says that it is his duty, under the decision that the court has made, and if he believes in that decision he would be a perjured man if he did not give the vote. I want to know whether he is not bound to a decision which is contrary to his opinions just as much as to one in accordance with his opinions. (Certainly.) If the decision of the Supreme Court, the tribunal created by the constitution to decide the question, is final and binding, is he not bound by it just as strongly as if he was for it instead of against it originally. Is every man in this land allowed to resist decisions he does not like, and only support those that meet his approval? What are important courts worth unless their decisions are binding on all good citizens? It is the fundamental principles of the judiciary that its decisions are final. It is created for that purpose so that when you cannot agree among yourselves on a disputed point you appeal to the judicial tribunal which steps in and decides for you, and that decision is then binding on every good citizen. It is the law of the land just as much with Mr. Lincoln against it as for it. And yet he says that if that decision is binding he is a perjured man if he does not vote for a slave code in the different territories of this Union. Well, if you (turning to Mr. Lincoln) are not going to resist the decision, if you obey it, and do not intend to array mob law against the constituted authorities, then, according to your own statement, you will be a perjured man if you do not vote to establish slavery in these territories. My doctrine is, that even taking Mr. Lincoln's view that the decision recognizes the right of a man to carry his slaves into the territories of the United States, if he pleases, yet after he gets there he needs affirmative law to make that right of any value. The same doctrine not only applies to slave property, but all other kinds of property. Chief Justice Taney places it upon the ground that slave property is on an equal footing with other property. Suppose one of your merchants should move to Kansas and open a liquor store; he has a right to take groceries and liquors there, but the mode of selling them, and the circumstances under which they shall be sold, and all the remedies must be prescribed by local legislation, and if that is unfriendly it will drive him out just as effectually as if there was a constitutional provision against the sale of liquor. So the absence of local legislation to encourage and support slave property in a territory excludes it practically just as effectually as if there was a positive constitutional provision against it. Hence, I assert that under the Dred Scott decision you cannot maintain slavery a day in a territory where there is an unwilling people and unfriendly legislation. If the people are opposed to it, our right is a barren, worthless, useless right, and if they are for it, they will support and encourage it. We come right back, therefore, to the practical question, if the people of a territory want slavery they will have it, and if they do not want it you cannot force it on them. And this is the practical question, the great principle upon which our institutions rest. ("That's the doctrine.") I am willing to take the decision of the Supreme Court as it was pronounced by that august tribunal without stopping to inquire whether I would have decided that way or not. I have had many a decision made against me on questions of law which I did not like, but I was bound by them just as much as if I had had a hand in making them, and approved them. Did you ever see a lawyer or a client lose his case that he approved the decision of the court. They always think the decision unjust when it is given against them. In a government of laws like ours we must sustain the constitution as our fathers made it, and maintain the rights of the States as they are guaranteed under the constitution, and then we will have peace and harmony between the different States and sections of this glorious Union. (Prolonged cheering.)

September 15, 1858

To Martin P. Sweet

Hon: M. P. Sweet   Centralia,
My dear Sir   Sept. 16 1858

Yesterday Douglas and I met at Jonesboro. A very trifling thing occurred which gives me a little uneasiness. I was, at the suggestion of friends, putting in, some resolutions and the like of abolition caste, passed by Douglas friends, some time ago, as a Set-off to his attempts of a like character against me. Among others I put the questions to T. Campbell and his answers to them, in 1850 when you and he ran for Congress. As my attention was divided, half lingering upon that case, and half advancing to the next one, I mentioned your name, as Campbell's opponent, in a confused sentence, which, when I heard it myself, struck me as having something disparaging to you in it. I instantly corrected it, and asked the reporters to suppress it; but my fear now is that those villainous reporters Douglas has with him will try to make something out of it. I do not myself exactly remember what it was, so little connection had it with any distinct thought in my mind, and I really hope no more may be heared of it; but if there should, I write this to assure you that nothing can be farther from me than to *feel*, much less, intentionally *say* anything disrespectful to you.

I sincerely hope you may hear nothing of it except what I have written. Yours very truly,

To Elihu B. Washburne

Hon: E. B. Washburne   Centralia,
Dear Sir   Sept. 16, 1858—

Yesterday at Jonesborough, Douglas, by way of placing you and me on different ground, alledged that you were every where, pledging yourself unconditionally against the admission of any more Slave States. If his allegation be true, burn this without answering it. If it be untrue, write me such a letter as I may make public with which to contradict him. Yours truly

Address to Springfield.

Fourth Lincoln-Douglas Debate, Charleston, Illinois

Fourth joint debate September 18. 1858. Lincoln, as reported in the Press & Tribune. Douglas, as reported in the Chicago Times.

MR. LINCOLN'S SPEECH.

Mr. Lincoln took the stand at a quarter before three, and was greeted with vociferous and protracted applause; after which, he said:

LADIES AND GENTLEMEN: It will be very difficult for an audience so large as this to hear distinctly what a speaker says, and consequently it is important that as profound silence be preserved as possible.

While I was at the hotel to-day an elderly gentleman called upon me to know whether I was really in favor of producing a perfect equality between the negroes and white people. [Great laughter.] While I had not proposed to myself on this occasion to say much on that subject, yet as the question was asked me I thought I would occupy perhaps five minutes in saying something in regard to it. I will say then that I am not, nor ever have been in favor of bringing about in any way the social and political equality of the white and black races, [applause]—that I am not nor ever have been in favor of making voters or jurors of negroes, nor of qualifying them to hold office, nor to intermarry with white people; and I will say in addition to this that there is a physical difference between the white and black races which I believe will for ever forbid the two races living together on terms of social and political equality. And inasmuch as they cannot so live, while they do remain together there must be the position of superior and inferior, and I as much as any other man am in favor of having the superior position assigned to the white race. I say upon this occasion I do not perceive that because the white man is to have the superior position the negro should be denied everything. I do not understand that because I do not want a negro woman for a slave I must necessarily want her for a wife. [Cheers and laughter.]

My understanding is that I can just let her alone. I am now in my fiftieth year, and I certainly never have had a black woman for either a slave or a wife. So it seems to me quite possible for us to get along without making either slaves or wives of negroes. I will add to this that I have never seen to my knowledge a man, woman or child who was in favor of producing a perfect equality, social and political, between negroes and white men. I recollect of but one distinguished instance that I ever heard of so frequently as to be entirely satisfied of its correctness—and that is the case of Judge Douglas' old friend Col. Richard M. Johnson. [Laughter.] I will also add to the remarks I have made, (for I am not going to enter at large upon this subject,) that I have never had the least apprehension that I or my friends would marry negroes if there was no law to keep them from it, [laughter] but as Judge Douglas and his friends seem to be in great apprehension that they might, if there were no law to keep them from it, [roars of laughter] I give him the most solemn pledge that I will to the very last stand by the law of this State, which forbids the marrying of white people with negroes. [Continued laughter and applause.] I will add one further word, which is this, that I do not understand there is any place where an alteration of the social and political relations of the negro and the white man can be made except in the State Legislature—not in the Congress of the United States—and as I do not really apprehend the approach of any such thing myself, and as Judge Douglas seems to be in constant horror that some such danger is rapidly approaching, I propose as the best means to prevent it that the Judge be kept at home and placed in the State Legislature to fight the measure. [Uproarious laughter and applause.] I do not propose dwelling longer at this time on this subject.

When Judge Trumbull, our other Senator in Congress, returned to Illinois in the month of August, he made a speech at Chicago in which he made what may be called *a charge* against Judge Douglas, which I understand proved to be very offensive to him. The Judge was at that time out upon one of his speaking tours through the country, and when the news of it reached him, as I am informed, he denounced Judge Trumbull in rather harsh terms for having said what he did in regard to that matter. I was traveling at that time and speaking at the same places with Judge Douglas on subsequent days, and when I heard of what Judge Trumbull had said of Douglas and what Douglas had said back again, I felt that I was in a position where I could not remain entirely silent in regard to the matter. Consequently upon two or three occasions I alluded to it, and alluded to it in no other wise than to say that in regard to the charge brought by Trumbull against Douglas, I *personally* knew nothing and sought to say nothing about it—that I did personally know Judge Trumbull—that I believed him to be a man of veracity—that I believed him to be a man of capacity sufficient to know very well whether an assertion he was making as a conclusion drawn from a set of facts, was true or false; and as a conclusion of my own from that, I stated it as my belief, if Trumbull should ever be called upon he would prove everything he had said. I said this upon two or three occasions. Upon a subsequent occasion, Judge Trumbull spoke again before an audience at Alton, and upon that occasion not only repeated his charge against Douglas, but arrayed the evidence he relied upon to substantiate it. This speech was published at length; and subsequently at Jacksonville Judge Douglas alluded to the matter. In the course of his speech, and near the close of it, he stated in regard to myself what I will now read: "Judge Douglas proceeded to remark that he should not hereafter occupy his time in refuting such charges made by Trumbull, but that Lincoln having indorsed the character of Trumbull for veracity, he should hold him (Lincoln) responsible for the slanders." I have done simply what I have told you, to subject me to this invitation to notice the charge. I now wish to say that it had not originally been my purpose to discuss that matter at all. But inasmuch as it seems to be the wish of Judge Douglas to hold me responsible for it, then for once in my life I will play General Jackson and to the just extent I take the responsibility. [Great applause and cries of "good, good," "hurrah for Lincoln," etc.]

I wish to say at the beginning that I will hand to the reporters that portion of Judge Trumbull's Alton speech which was devoted to this matter, and also that portion of Judge Douglas' speech made at Jacksonville in answer to it. I shall thereby furnish the readers of this debate with the complete discussion between Trumbull and Douglas. I cannot now read them, for the reason that it would take half of my first hour to do so. I can only make some comments upon them. Trumbull's charge is in the following words: "Now, the charge is, that there was a plot entered into to have a constitution formed for Kansas and put in force without giving the people an opportunity to vote upon it, and that Mr. Douglas was in the plot." I will state, without quoting further, for all will have an opportunity of reading it hereafter, that Judge Trumbull brings forward what he regards as sufficient evidence to substantiate this charge.

[The extracts handed to our reporter by Mr. Lincoln are quite too lengthy to appear in this number of the Press and Tribune. Judge Trumbull's speech at Alton has already had a place in our columns, and Senator Douglas' remarks at Jacksonville are faithfully repeated in his portion of this (Charleston) debate.]

It will be perceived Judge Trumbull shows that Senator Bigler, upon the floor of the Senate, had declared there had been a conference among the Senators, in which conference it was determined to have an Enabling Act passed for the people of Kansas to form a Constitution under, and in this conference it was agreed among them that it was best not to have a provision for submitting the Constitution to a vote of the people after it should be formed. He then brings forward to show, and showing, as he deemed, that Judge Douglas reported the bill back to the Senate with that clause stricken out. He then shows that there was a new clause inserted into the bill, which would in its nature *prevent* a reference of the Constitution back for a vote of the people—if, indeed, upon a mere silence in the law, it could be assumed that they had the right to vote upon it. These are the general statements that he has made.

I propose to examine the points in Judge Douglas' speech, in which he attempts to answer that speech of Judge Trumbull's. When you come to examine Judge Douglas' speech, you will find that the first point he makes is—"Suppose it were true that there was such a change in the bill, and that I struck it out—is that a proof of a plot to force a Constitution upon them against their will?" His striking out such a provision, if there was such a one in the bill, he argues does not establish the proof that it was stricken out for the purpose of robbing the people of that right. I would say, in the first place, that that would be a *most manifest* reason for it. It is true, as Judge Douglas states, that many Territorial bills have passed without having such a provision in them. I believe it is true, though I am not certain, that in some instances, Constitutions framed, under such bills have been submitted to a vote of the people, with the law silent upon the subject, but it does not appear that they once had their Enabling Acts framed with an express provision *for* submitting the Constitution to be framed, to a vote of the people, and then that they were stricken out when Congress did not mean to alter the effect of the law. That there have been bills which never had the provision in, I do not question; but when was that provision taken out of one that it was in? More especially does this evidence tend to prove the proposition that Trumbull advanced, when we remember that the provision was stricken out of the bill almost simultaneously with the time that Bigler says there was a conference among certain Senators, and in which it was agreed that a bill should be passed leaving that out. Judge Douglas, in answering Trumbull, omits to attend to the testimony of Bigler, that there was a meeting in which it was agreed they should so frame the bill that there should be no submission of the Constitution to a vote of the people. The Judge does not notice this part of it. If you take this as one piece of evidence, and then ascertain that simultaneously Judge Douglas struck out a provision that did require it to be submitted, and put the two together, I think it will make a pretty fair show of proof that Judge Douglas did, as Trumbull says, enter into a plot to put in force a Constitution for Kansas without giving the people any opportunity of voting upon it.

But I must hurry on. The next proposition that Judge Douglas puts is this: "But upon examination it turns out that the Toombs bill never did contain a clause requiring the Constitution to be submitted." This is a mere question of fact, and can be determined by evidence. I only want to ask this question—Why did not Judge Douglas say that these words

were not stricken out of the Toombs bill, or this bill from
which it is alleged the provision was stricken out—a bill
which goes by the name of Toombs, because he originally
brought it forward? I ask why, if the Judge wanted to make a
direct issue with Trumbull, did he not take the exact proposition Trumbull made in his speech, and say it was not stricken
out? Trumbull has given the exact words that he says were in
the Toombs bill, and he alleges that when the bill came back,
they were stricken out. Judge Douglas does not say that the
words which Trumbull says were stricken out, were not so
stricken out, but he says there was no provision in the
Toombs bill to submit the Constitution to a vote of the people. We see at once that he is merely making an issue upon the
meaning of the words. He has not undertaken to say that
Trumbull tells a lie about these words being stricken out; but
he is really, when pushed up to it, only taking an issue upon
the meaning of the words. Now, then, if there be any issue
upon the meaning of the words, or if there be upon the question of fact as to whether these words were stricken out, I
have before me what I suppose to be a genuine copy of the
Toombs bill, in which it can be shown that the words Trumbull says were in it, were, in fact, originally there. If there be
any dispute upon the fact, I have got the documents here
to show they were there. If there be any controversy upon
the sense of the words—whether these words which were
stricken out really constituted a provision for submitting the
matter to a vote of the people, as that is a matter of argument,
I think I may as well use Trumbull's own argument. He says
that the proposition is in these words:

That the following propositions be and the same are hereby offered to
the said convention of the people of Kansas when formed, for their free
acceptance or rejection; which, if accepted by the convention *and ratified
by the people at the election for the adoption of the Constitution*, shall be
obligatory upon the United States and the said State of Kansas.

Now, Trumbull alleges that these last words were stricken
out of the bill when it came back, and he says this was a
provision for submitting the Constitution to a vote of the
people, and his argument is this: "Would it have been possible to ratify the land propositions at the election for the

adoption of the Constitution, unless such an election was to be held?" [Applause and laughter.] That is Trumbull's argument. Now Judge Douglas does not meet the charge at all, but he stands up and says there was no such proposition in that bill for submitting the Constitution to be framed to a vote of the people. Trumbull admits that the language is not a direct provision for submitting it, but it is a provision necessarily implied from another provision. He asks you how it is possible to ratify the land proposition at the election for the adoption of the Constitution, if there was no election to be held for the adoption of the Constitution. And he goes on to show that it is not any less a law because the provision is put in that indirect shape than it would be if it was put directly. But I presume I have said enough to draw attention to this point, and I pass it by also.

Another one of the points that Judge Douglas makes upon Trumbull, and at very great length, is, that Trumbull, while the bill was pending, said in a speech in the Senate that he supposed the Constitution to be made would have to be submitted to the people. He asks, if Trumbull thought so then, what ground is there for anybody thinking otherwise now? Fellow citizens, this much may be said in reply: That bill had been in the hands of a party to which Trumbull did not belong. It had been in the hands of the Committee at the head of which Judge Douglas stood. Trumbull perhaps had a printed copy of the original Toombs bill. I have not the evidence on that point, except a sort of inference I draw from the general course of business there. What alterations, or what provisions in the way of altering, were going on in committee, Trumbull had no means of knowing, until the altered bill was reported back. Soon afterwards, when it was reported back, there was a discussion over it, and perhaps Trumbull in reading it hastily in the altered form did not perceive all the bearings of the alterations. He was hastily borne into the debate, and it does not follow that because there was something in it Trumbull did not perceive, that something did not exist. More than this, is it true that what Trumbull did can have any effect on what Douglas did? [Applause.] Suppose Trumbull had been in the plot with these other men, would that let Douglas out of it? [Applause and laughter.] Would it exonerate Douglas that Trumbull didn't then perceive he was in the plot? He also asks the question: Why didn't Trumbull propose to amend the bill if he thought it needed any amendment? Why, I believe that everything Judge Trumbull had proposed, particularly in connection with this question of Kansas and Nebraska, since he had been on the floor of the Senate, had been promptly voted down by Judge Douglas and his friends. He had no promise that an amendment offered by him to anything on this subject would receive the slightest consideration. Judge Trumbull did bring to the notice of the Senate at that time the fact that there was no provision for submitting the Constitution about to be made for the people of Kansas, to a vote of the people. I believe I may venture to say that Judge Douglas made some reply to this speech of Judge Trumbull's, *but he never noticed that part of it at all*. And so the thing passed by. I think, then, the fact that Judge Trumbull offered no amendment, does not throw much blame upon him; and if it did, it does not reach the question of fact *as to what Judge Douglas was doing*. [Applause.] I repeat that if Trumbull had himself been in the plot, it would not at all relieve the others who were in it from blame. If I should be indicted for murder, and upon the trial it should be discovered that I had been implicated in that murder, but that the prosecuting witness was guilty too, that would not at all touch the question of my crime. It would be no relief to my neck that they discovered this other man who charged the crime upon me to be guilty too.

Another one of the points Judge Douglas makes upon Judge Trumbull is, that when he spoke in Chicago he made his charge to rest upon the fact that the bill had the provision in it for submitting the Constitution to a vote of the people, when it went into his (Judge Douglas') hands, that it was missing when he reported it to the Senate, and that in a public speech he had subsequently said the alteration in the bill was made while it was in committee, and that they were made in consultation between him (Judge Douglas) and Toombs. And Judge Douglas goes on to comment upon the fact of Trumbull's adducing in his Alton speech the proposition that the bill not only came back with that proposition stricken out, but with another clause and another provision in it, saying that "until the complete execution of this act there shall be no election in said Territory,"—which Trumbull argued was not only taking the provision for submitting to a vote of the people out of the bill, but was adding an affirmative one, in that it prevented the people from exercising the right under a bill that was merely silent on the question. Now in regard to what he says, that Trumbull shifts the issue—that he shifts his ground—and I believe he uses the term, that "it being proven false, he has changed ground"—I call upon all of you, when you come to examine that portion of Trumbull's speech, (for it will make a part of mine,) to examine whether Trumbull has shifted his ground or not. I say he did not shift his ground, but that he brought forward his original charge and the evidence to sustain it yet more fully, but precisely as he originally made it. Then, in addition thereto, he brought in a new piece of evidence. He shifted no ground. He brought no new piece of evidence inconsistent with his former testimony, but he brought a new piece, tending, as he thought, and as I think, to prove his proposition. To illustrate: A man brings an accusation against another, and on trial the man making the charge introduces A and B to prove the accusation. At a second trial he introduces the same witnesses, who tell the same story as before, and a third witness, who tells the same thing, and in addition, gives further testimony corroborative of the charge. So with Trumbull. There was no shifting of ground, nor inconsistency of testimony between the new piece of evidence and what he originally introduced.

But Judge Douglas says that he himself moved to strike out that last provision of the bill, and that on his motion it was stricken out and a substitute inserted. That I presume is the truth. I presume it is true that that last proposition was stricken out by Judge Douglas. Trumbull has not said it was not. Trumbull has himself said that it was so stricken out. He says: "I am speaking of the bill as Judge Douglas reported it back. It was amended somewhat in the Senate before it passed, but I am speaking of it as he brought it back." Now when Judge Douglas parades the fact that the provision was stricken out of the bill when it came back, he asserts nothing contrary to what Trumbull alleges. Trumbull has only said that he originally put it in—not that he did not strike it out. Trumbull says it was not in the bill when it went to the committee. When it came back it was in, and Judge Douglas said the alterations were made by him in consultation with Toombs. Trumbull alleges therefore as his conclusion that Judge Douglas put it in. Then if Douglas wants to contradict Trumbull and call him a liar, let him say he did not put it in, and not that he didn't take it out again. It is said that a bear is sometimes hard enough pushed to drop a cub, and so I presume it was in this case. [Loud applause.] I presume the truth is that Douglas put it in and afterwards took it out. [Laughter and cheers.] That I take it is the truth about it. Judge Trumbull says one thing; Douglas says another thing, and the two don't contradict one another at all. The question is, what did he put it in for? In the first place what did he take the other provision out of the bill for?—the provision which Trumbull argued was necessary for submitting the Constitution to a vote of the people? What did he take that out for, and having taken it out, what did he put this in for? I say that in the run of things it is not unlikely forces conspire, to render it vastly expedient for Judge Douglas to take that latter clause out again. The question that Trumbull has made is that Judge Douglas put it in, and he don't meet Trumbull at all unless he denies that.

In the clause of Judge Douglas' speech upon this subject he uses this language towards Judge Trumbull. He says: "He forges his evidence from beginning to end, and by falsifying the record he endeavors to bolster up his false charge." Well, that is a pretty serious statement. Trumbull forges his evidence from beginning to end. Now upon my own authority I say that it is not true. [Great cheers and laughter.] What is a forgery? Consider the evidence that Trumbull has brought forward. When you come to read the speech, as you will be able to, examine whether the evidence is a forgery from beginning to end. He had the bill or document in his hand like that [holding up a paper]. He says that is a copy of the Toombs bill—the amendment offered by Toombs. He says that is a copy of the bill as it was introduced and went into Judge Douglas' hands. Now, does Judge Douglas say that is a forgery? That is one thing Trumbull brought forward.

Judge Douglas says he forged it from beginning to end! That is the "beginning," we will say. Does Douglas say that is a forgery? Let him say it to-day and we will have a subsequent examination upon this subject. [Loud applause.] Trumbull then holds up another document like this and says that is an exact copy of the bill as it came back in the amended form out of Judge Douglas' hands. Does Judge Douglas say that is a forgery? Does he say it in his general sweeping charge? Does he say so now? If he does not, then take this Toombs bill and the bill in the amended form and it only needs to compare them to see that the provision is in the one and not in the other; it leaves the inference inevitable that it was taken out. [Applause.]

But while I am dealing with this question let us see what Trumbull's other evidence is. One other piece of evidence I will read. Trumbull says there are in this original Toombs bill these words: "That the following propositions be, and the same are hereby offered to the said convention of the people of Kansas, when formed, for their free acceptance or rejection; which, if accepted by the convention and ratified by the people at the election for the adoption of the constitution, shall be obligatory upon the United States and the said State of Kansas." Now, if it is said that this is a forgery, we will open the paper here and see whether it is or not. Again, Trumbull says as he goes along, that Mr. Bigler made the following statement in his place in the Senate, December 9, 1857.

I was present when that subject was discussed by Senators before the bill was introduced, and the question was raised and discussed, whether the constitution, when formed, should be submitted to a vote of the people. It was held by those most intelligent on the subject, that in view of all the difficulties surrounding that Territory, the danger of any experiment at that time of a popular vote, it would be better there should be no such provision in the Toombs bill; and it was my understanding, in all the intercourse I had, that the Convention would make a constitution, and send it here without submitting it to the popular vote.

Then Trumbull follows on: "In speaking of this meeting again on the 21st December, 1857, (*Congressional Globe*, same vol., page 113,) Senator Bigler said:

Nothing was further from my mind than to allude to any social or confidential interview. The meeting was not of that character. Indeed, it was semi-official and called to promote the public good. My recollection was clear that I left the conference under the impression that it had been deemed best to adopt measures to admit Kansas as a State through the agency of one popular election, and that for delegates to this Convention. This impression was stronger because I thought the spirit of the bill infringed upon the doctrine of non-intervention, to which I had great aversion; but with the hope of accomplishing a great good, and as no movement had been made in that direction in the Territory, I waived this objection, and concluded to support the measure. I have a few items of testimony as to the correctness of these impressions, and with their submission I shall be content. I have before me the bill reported by the Senator from Illinois on the 7th of March, 1856, providing for the admission of Kansas as a State, the third section of which reads as follows:

"That the following propositions be, and the same are hereby offered to the said Convention of the people of Kansas, when formed, for their free acceptance or rejection; which if accepted by the Convention and ratified by the people at the election for the adoption of the Constitution, shall be obligatory upon the United States and the said State of Kansas."

The bill read in his place by the Senator from Georgia, on the 25th of June, and referred to Committee on Territories, contained the same section, word for word. Both these bills were under consideration at the conference referred to; but, Sir, when the Senator from Illinois reported the Toombs bill to the Senate with amendments, the next morning it did not contain that portion of the third section which indicated to the Convention that the Constitution should be approved by the people. The words "AND RATIFIED BY THE PEOPLE AT THE ELECTION FOR THE ADOPTION OF THE CONSTITUTION," had been stricken out.

Now these things Trumbull says were stated by Bigler upon the floor of the Senate on certain days, and that they are recorded in the "Congressional Globe" on certain pages. Does Judge Douglas say this is a forgery? Does he say there is no such thing in the "Congressional Globe?" What does he mean when he says Judge Trumbull forges his evidence from beginning to end? So again he says in another place, that Judge Douglas, in his speech Dec. 9, 1857, ("Congressional Globe," part 1, page 15) stated:

That during the last session of Congress I [Mr. Douglas] reported a bill from the Committee on Territories, to authorize the people of

Kansas to assemble and form a Constitution for themselves. Subsequently the Senator from Georgia [Mr. Toombs] brought forward a substitute for my bill, which, *after having been modified by him and myself in consultation*, was passed by the Senate.

Now Trumbull says this is a quotation from a speech of Douglas, and is recorded in the "Congressional Globe." Is *it* a forgery? Is it there or not? It may not be there, but I want the Judge to take these pieces of evidence, and distinctly say they are forgeries if he dare do it. [Great applause.]

A VOICE—"He will."

MR. LINCOLN—Well, sir, you had better not commit him. [Cheers and laughter.] He gives other quotations—another from Judge Douglas. He says:

I will ask the Senator to show me an intimation, from any one member of the Senate, in the whole debate on the Toombs bill, and in the Union, from any quarter, that the Constitution was not to be submitted to the people. I will venture to say that on all sides of the chamber it was so understood at the time. If the opponents of the bill had understood it was not, they would have made the point on it; and if they had made it, we should certainly have yielded to it; and put in the clause. That is a discovery made since the President found out that it was not safe to take it for granted that that would be done, which ought in fairness to have been done.

Judge Trumbull says Douglas made that speech and it is recorded. Does Judge Douglas say it is a forgery and was not true? Trumbull says somewhere, and I propose to skip it, but it will be found by any one who will read this debate, that he did distinctly bring it to the notice of those who were engineering the bill, that it lacked that provision, and then he goes on to give another quotation from Judge Douglas, where Judge Trumbull uses this language:

Judge Douglas, however, on the same day and in the same debate, probably recollecting or being reminded of the fact that I had objected to the Toombs bill when pending that it did not provide for a submission of the Constitution to the people, made another statement, which is to be found in the same volume of the *Globe*, page 22, in which he says:

"That the bill was silent on this subject was true, and my attention was called to that about the time it was passed; and I took the fair construction to be, that powers not delegated were reserved, and that of course the Constitution would be submitted to the people."

Whether this statement is consistent with the statement just before made, that had the point been made it would have been yielded to, or that it was a new discovery, you will determine.

So I say, I do not know whether Judge Douglas will dispute this, and yet maintain his position that Trumbull's evidence "was forged from beginning to end." I will remark that I have not got these Congressional Globes with me. They are large books and difficult to carry about, and if Judge Douglas shall say that on these points where Trumbull has quoted from them, there are no such passages there, I shall not be able to prove they are there upon this occasion, but I will have another chance. Whenever he points out the forgery and says, "I declare that this particular thing which Trumbull has uttered is not to be found where he says it is," then my attention will be drawn to that, and I will arm myself for the contest—stating now that I have not the slightest doubt on earth that I will find every quotation just where Trumbull says it is. Then the question is, how can Douglas call that a forgery? How can he make out that it is a forgery? What is a forgery? It is the bringing forward something in writing or in print purporting to be of certain effect when it is altogether untrue. If you come forward with my note for one hundred dollars when I have never given such a note, there is a forgery. If you come forward with a letter purporting to be written by me which I never wrote, there is another forgery. If you produce anything in writing or print saying it is so and so, the document not being genuine, a forgery has been committed. How do you make this a forgery when every piece of the evidence is genuine? If Judge Douglas does say these documents and quotations are false and forged he has a full right to do so, but until he does it specifically we don't know how to get at him. If he does say they are false and forged, I will then look further into it, and I presume I can procure the certificates of the proper officers that they are genuine copies. I have no doubt each of these extracts will be found exactly where Trumbull says it is. Then I leave it to you if Judge Douglas, in making his sweeping charge that Judge Trumbull's evidence is forged from beginning to end, at all meets the case—if that is the way to get at the facts. I repeat again, if he will point out which one is a forgery, I will carefully examine it, and if it proves that any one of them is really a forgery it will not be me who will hold to it any longer. I have always wanted to deal with every one I meet candidly and honestly. If I have made any assertion not warranted by facts, and it is pointed out to me, I will withdraw it cheerfully. But I do not choose to see Judge Trumbull calumniated, and the evidence he has brought forward branded in general terms, "a forgery from beginning to end." This is not the legal way of meeting a charge, and I submit to all intelligent persons, both friends of Judge Douglas and of myself, whether it is.

Now coming back—how much time have I left?

THE MODERATOR—Three minutes.

MR. LINCOLN—The point upon Judge Douglas is this. The bill that went into his hands had the provision in it for a submission of the constitution to the people; and I say its language amounts to an express provision for a submission, and that he took the provision out. He says it was known that the bill was silent in this particular; *but I say, Judge Douglas, it was not silent when you got it.* [Great applause.] It was vocal with the declaration when you got it, for a submission of the constitution to the people. And now, my direct question to Judge Douglas is, to answer why, if he deemed the bill silent on this point, he found it necessary to strike out those particular harmless words. If he had found the bill silent and without this provision, he might say what he does now. If he supposed it was implied that the constitution would be submitted to a vote of the people, how could these two lines so encumber the statute as to make it necessary to strike them out? How could he infer that a submission was still implied, after its express provision had been stricken from the bill? I find the bill vocal with the provision, while he silenced it. He took it out, and although he took out the other provision preventing a submission to a vote of the people, I ask, *why did you first put it in?* I ask him whether he took the original provision out, which Trumbull alleges was in the bill? If he admits that he did take it, *I ask him what he did it for?* It looks to us as if he had altered the bill. If it looks differently to him—if he has a different reason for his action from the one we assign him— he can tell it. I insist upon knowing why he made the bill silent upon that point when it was vocal before he put his hands upon it.

I was told, before my last paragraph, that my time was within three minutes of being out. I presume it is expired now. I therefore close. [Three tremendous cheers were given as Mr. Lincoln retired.]

SENATOR DOUGLAS' SPEECH.

LADIES AND GENTLEMEN:—I had supposed that we assembled here to-day for the purpose of a joint discussion between Mr. Lincoln and myself upon the political questions that now agitate the whole country. The rule of such discussions is, that the opening speaker shall touch upon all the points he intends to discuss in order that his opponent, in reply, shall have the opportunity of answering them. Let me ask you what questions of public policy relating to the welfare of this State or the Union, has Mr. Lincoln discussed before you? (None, none, and great applause.) Gentlemen, allow me to suggest that silence is the best compliment you can pay me. I need my whole time, and your cheering only occupies it. Mr. Lincoln simply contented himself at the outset by saying, that he was not in favor of social and political equality between the white man and the negro, and did not desire the law so changed as to make the latter voters or eligible to office. I am glad that I have at last succeeded in getting an answer out of him upon this question of negro citizenship and eligibility to office, for I have been trying to bring him to the point on it ever since this canvass commenced.

I will now call your attention to the question which Mr. Lincoln has occupied his entire time in discussing. He spent his whole hour in retailing a charge made by Senator Trumbull against me. The circumstances out of which that charge was manufactured, occurred prior to the last Presidential election, over two years ago. If the charge was true, why did not Trumbull make it in 1856, when I was discussing the questions of that day all over this State with Lincoln and him, and when it was pertinent to the then issue. He was then as silent as the grave on the subject. If that charge was true, the time to have brought it forward was the canvass of 1856, the year when the Toombs bill passed the Senate. When the facts were fresh in the public mind, when the Kansas question was the paramount question of the day, and when such a charge would have had a material bearing on the election. Why did he and Lincoln remain silent then, knowing that such a charge could be made and proven if true? Were they not false to you and false to the country in going through that entire campaign, concealing their knowledge of this enormous conspiracy which, Mr. Trumbull says, he then knew and would not tell? (Laughter.) Mr. Lincoln intimates in his speech, a good reason why Mr. Trumbull would not tell, for, he says, that it might be true, as I proved that it was at Jacksonville, that Trumbull was also in the plot, yet that the fact of Trumbull's being in the plot would not in any way relieve me. He illustrates this argument by supposing himself on trial for murder, and says that it would be no extenuating circumstance if, on his trial, another man was found to be a party to his crime. Well, if Trumbull was in the plot, and concealed it in order to escape the odium which would have fallen upon himself, I ask you whether you can believe him now when he turns State's evidence, and avows his own infamy in order to implicate me. (He is a liar, and a traitor. We couldn't believe Lyman Trumbull under oath, &c.) I am amazed that Mr. Lincoln should now come forward and endorse that charge, occupying his whole hour in reading Mr. Trumbull's speech in support of it. Why, I ask, does not Mr. Lincoln make a speech of his own instead of taking up his time reading Trumbull's speech at Alton? (Cheers.) I supposed that Mr. Lincoln was capable of making a public speech on his own account, or I should not have accepted the banter from him for a joint discussion. (Cheers, and voices: "How about the charges?") Do not trouble yourselves, I am going to make my speech in my own way, and I trust as the Democrats listened patiently and respectfully to Mr. Lincoln, that his friends will not interrupt me when I am answering him. When Mr. Trumbull returned from the East, the first thing he did when he landed at Chicago was to make a speech wholly devoted to assaults upon my public character and public action. Up to that time I had never alluded to his course in Congress, or to him directly or indirectly, and hence his assaults upon me were entirely without provocation and without excuse. Since then he has been traveling from one end of the State to the other repeating his vile charge. I propose now to read it in his own language:

Now, fellow citizens, I make the distinct charge, that there was a pre-concerted arrangement and plot entered into by the very men who now claim credit for opposing a constitution formed and put in force without giving the people any opportunity to pass upon it. This, my friends, is a serious charge, but I charge it to-night that the very men who traverse the country under banners proclaiming popular sovereignty, by design concocted a bill on purpose to force a constitution upon that people.

In answer to some one in the crowd, who asked him a question, Trumbull said:

And you want to satisfy yourself that he was in the plot to force a constitution upon that people? I will satisfy you. I will cram the truth down any honest man's throat until he cannot deny it. And to the man who does deny it, I will cram the lie down his throat till he shall cry enough. (Voices, "shameful," "that's decency for you," &c.)

It is preposterous—it is the most damnable effrontery that man ever put on, to conceal a scheme to defraud and cheat the people out of their rights and then claim credit for it.

That is the polite language Senator Trumbull applied to me, his colleague, when I was two hundred miles off. (That's like him.) Why did he not speak out as boldly in the Senate of the United States, and cram the lie down my throat when I denied the charge, first made by Bigler, and made him take it back. You all recollect how Bigler assaulted me when I was engaged in a hand to hand fight, resisting a scheme to force a constitution on the people of Kansas against their will. He then attacked me with this charge; but I proved its utter falsity; nailed the slander to the counter, and made him take the back track. There is not an honest man in America who read that debate who will pretend that the charge is true. (Hurra for Douglas.) Trumbull was then present in the Senate, face to face with me, and why did he not then rise and repeat the charge, and say he would cram the lie down my throat. (He was afraid.) I tell you that

Trumbull then knew it was a lie. He knew that Toombs denied that there ever was a clause in the bill he brought forward calling for and requiring a submission of the Kansas constitution to the people. I will tell you what the facts of the case were. I introduced a bill to authorize the people of Kansas to form a constitution, and come into the Union as a State whenever they should have the requisite population for a member of Congress, and Mr. Toombs proposed a substitute, authorizing the people of Kansas, with their then population of only 25,000, to form a constitution, and come in at once. The question at issue was, whether we would admit Kansas with a population of 25,000, or, make her wait until she had the ratio entitling her to a representative in Congress, which was 93,420. That was the point of dispute in the Committee of Territories, to which both my bill and Mr. Toombs' substitute had been referred. I was overruled by a majority of the committee, my proposition rejected, and Mr. Toombs' proposition to admit Kansas then, with her population of 25,000, adopted. Accordingly, a bill to carry out his idea of immediate admission was reported as a substitute for mine—the only points at issue being, as I have already said, the question of population, and the adoption of safeguards against frauds at the election. Trumbull knew this—the whole Senate knew it—and hence he was silent at that time. He waited until I became engaged in this canvass, and finding that I was showing up Lincoln's Abolitionism and negro equality doctrines (cheers), that I was driving Lincoln to the wall, and white men would not support his rank Abolitionism, he came back from the East and trumped up a system of charges against me, hoping that I would be compelled to occupy my entire time in defending myself, so that I would not be able to show up the enormity of the principles of the Abolitionists. Now, the only reason, and the true reason, why Mr. Lincoln has occupied the whole of his first hour in this issue between Trumbull and myself is, to conceal from this vast audience the real questions which divide the two great parties. (That's it; and cheers.)

I am not going to allow them to waste much of my time with these personal matters. I have lived in this State twenty-five years, most of that time have been in public life, and my record is open to you all. If that record is not enough to vindicate me from these petty, malicious assaults, I despise ever to be elected to office by slandering my opponents and traducing other men. (Cheers.) Mr. Lincoln asks you to elect him to the United States Senate to-day solely because he and Trumbull can slander me. Has he given any other reason? (No, no.) Has he avowed what he was desirous to do in Congress on any one question? (No, no.) He desires to ride into office not upon his own merits, not upon the merits and soundness of his principles, but upon his success in fastening a stale old slander upon me. ("That's the truth." "Hear, hear.")

I wish you to bear in mind that up to the time of the introduction of the Toombs bill, and after its introduction, there had never been an act of Congress for the admission of a new State which contained a clause requiring its constitution to be submitted to the people. The general rule made the law silent on the subject, taking it for granted that the people would demand and compel a popular vote on the ratification of their constitution. Such was the general rule under Washington, Jefferson, Madison, Jackson and Polk, under the Whig Presidents and the Democratic Presidents from the beginning of the government down, and nobody dreamed that an effort would ever be made to abuse the power thus confided to the people of a territory. For this reason our attention was not called to the fact of whether there was or was not a clause in the Toombs bill compelling submission, but it was taken for granted that the constitution would be submitted to the people whether the law compelled it or not.

Now, I will read from the report made by me as Chairman of the Committee on Territories at the time I reported back the Toombs substitution to the Senate. It contained several things which I had voted against in committee, but had been overruled by a majority of the members, and it was my duty as chairman of the committee to report the bill back as it was agreed upon by them. The main point upon which I had been overruled was the question of population. In my report accompanying the Toombs bill, I said:

In the opinion of your committee, whenever a constitution shall be formed in any territory, preparatory to its admission into the Union as a

State, justice, the genius of our institutions, the whole theory of our republican system imperatively demand that the voice of the people shall be fairly expressed, and their will embodied in that fundamental law, without fraud, or violence, or intimidation, or any other improper or unlawful influence, and subject to no other restrictions than those imposed by the Constitution of the United States. (Cheers.)

There you find that we took it for granted that the constitution was to be submitted to the people whether the bill was silent on the subject or not. Suppose I had reported it so, following the example of Washington, Adams, Jefferson, Madison, Monroe, Adams, Jackson, Van Buren, Harrison, Tyler, Polk, Taylor, Fillmore, and Pierce, would that fact have been evidence of a conspiracy to force a constitution upon the people of Kansas against their will? (A unanimous "No!") If the charge which Mr. Lincoln makes be true against me, it is true against Zachary Taylor, Millard Fillmore, and every Whig President as well as every Democratic President, and against Henry Clay, who, in the Senate or the House, for forty years advocated bills similar to the one I reported, no one of them containing a clause compelling the submission of the constitution to the people. Are Mr. Lincoln and Mr. Trumbull prepared to charge upon all those eminent men from the beginning of the government down to the present day, that the absence of a provision compelling submission, in the various bills passed by them authorizing the people of territories to form State constitutions, is evidence of a corrupt design on their part to force a constitution upon an unwilling people? ("We'll skin them if they dare to.")

I ask you to reflect on these things, for I tell you that there is a conspiracy to carry this election for the Black Republicans by slander, and not by fair means. Mr. Lincoln's speech this day is conclusive evidence of the fact. He has devoted his entire time to an issue between Mr. Trumbull and myself, and has not uttered a word about the politics of the day. Are you going to elect Mr. Trumbull's colleague upon an issue between Mr. Trumbull and me? (Laughter, and "No, no!") I thought I was running against Abraham Lincoln, that he claimed to be my opponent, had challenged me to a discussion of the public questions of the day with him, and was discussing these questions with me; but it turns out that his only hope is to ride into office on Trumbull's back, who will carry him by falsehood. (Cheers.)

Permit me to pursue this subject a little further. An examination of the record proves that Trumbull's charge—that the Toombs bill originally contained a clause requiring the constitution to be submitted to the people—*is false*. The printed copy of the bill which Mr. Lincoln held up before you, and which he pretends contains such a clause, merely contains a clause requiring a submission of the land grant, and *there is no clause in it requiring a submission of the constitution*. Mr. Lincoln can not find such a clause in it. My report shows that we took it for granted that the people would require a submission of the constitution, and secure it for themselves. There never was a clause in the Toombs bill requiring the constitution to be submitted; Trumbull knew it at the time, and his speech made on the night of its passage discloses the fact that he knew it was silent on the subject; Lincoln pretends, and tells you that Trumbull has not changed his evidence in support of his charge since he made his speech in Chicago. Let us see. The Chicago TIMES took up Trumbull's Chicago speech, compared it with the official records of Congress, and proved that speech to be false in its charge that the original Toombs bill required a submission of the constitution to the people. Trumbull then saw that he was caught—and his falsehood exposed—and he went to Alton, and, under the very walls of the penitentiary, (laughter,) made a new speech, in which he predicated his assault upon me in the allegation that I had caused to be voted into the Toombs bill a clause which prohibited the convention from submitting the constitution to the people, and quoted what he pretended was the clause. Now, has not Mr. Trumbull entirely changed the evidence on which he bases his charge? ("Yes, yes!" "Lincoln's as big a liar as Trumbull," &c.) The clause which he quoted in his Alton speech (which he has published and circulated broadcast over the State) as having been put into the Toombs bill by me is in the following words:

And until the complete execution of this act, no other election shall be held in said territory.

Trumbull says that the object of that amendment was to

prevent the convention from submitting the constitution to a vote of the people.

Now, I will show you that when Trumbull made that statement at Alton he knew it to be untrue. I read from Trumbull's speech in the Senate on the Toombs bill on the night of its passage. He then said:

> There is nothing said in this bill, so far as I have discovered, about submitting the constitution which is to be formed, to the people for their sanction or rejection. Perhaps the convention will have the right to submit it, if it should think proper, but it is certainly not compelled to do so according to the provisions of the bill.

Thus you see that Trumbull, when the bill was on its passage in the Senate, said that it was silent on the subject of submission, and that there was nothing in the bill one way or the other on it. In his Alton speech he says that there was a clause in the bill preventing its submission to the people, and that I had it voted in as an amendment. Thus I convict him of falsehood and slander by quoting from him on the passage of the Toombs' bill in the Senate of the United States, his own speech, made on the night of July 2, 1856, and reported in the *Congressional Globe* for the 1st session 34th Congress, Vol. 33. What will you think of a man who makes a false charge and falsifies the records to prove it? I will now show you that the clause which Trumbull says was put in the bill on my motion, was never put in at all by me, but was stricken out on my motion and another substituted in its place. I call your attention to the same volume of the *Congressional Globe* to which I have already referred, page 795, where you will find the following in the report of the proceedings of the Senate:

> MR. DOUGLAS—I have an amendment to offer from the committee on territories. On page 8, section 11, strike out the words "until the complete execution of this act no other election shall be held in said territory," and insert the amendment which I hold in my hand.

You see from this that I moved to strike out the very words that Trumbull says I put in. The committee on territories overruled me in committee and put the clause in, but as soon as I got the bill back into the Senate I moved to strike it out and put another clause in its place. On the same page you will find that my amendment was agreed to *unanimously*. I then offered another amendment, recognizing the right of the people of Kansas under the Toombs bill, to order just such elections as they saw proper. You can find it on page 796 of the same volume. I will read it.

MR. DOUGLAS—I have another amendment to offer from the committee, to follow the amendment which has been adopted. The bill reads now, "And until the complete execution of this act, no other election shall be held in said territory." It has been suggested that it should be modified in this way, "And to avoid conflict in the complete execution of this act, all other elections in said territory are hereby postponed until such time as said convention shall appoint," so that they can appoint the day in the event that there should be a failure to come into the Union.

The amendment was *unanimously* agreed to—clearly and distinctly recognizing the right of the convention to order just as many elections as they saw proper in the execution of the act. Trumbull concealed in his Alton speech the fact that the clause he quoted had been stricken out in my motion, and the other fact that this other clause was put in the bill on my motion, and made the false charge that I incorporated into the bill a clause preventing submission, in the face of the fact, that on my motion, the bill was so amended before it passed as to recognize in express words the right and duty of submission.

On this record that I have produced before you, I repeat my charge that Trumbull did falsify the public records of the country, in order to make his charge against me, ("it's plain," and tremendous applause,) and I tell Mr. Abraham Lincoln that if he will examine these records, he will then know that what I state is true. Mr. Lincoln has this day endorsed Mr. Trumbull's veracity after he had my word for it that that veracity was proved to be violated and forfeited by the public records. It will not do for Mr. Lincoln in parading his calumnies against me to put Mr. Trumbull between him and the odium and responsibility which justly attaches to such calumnies. I tell him that I am as ready to persecute the endorser as the maker of a forged note. (Cheers.) I regret the necessity of occupying my time with these petty personal matters. It is unbecoming the dignity of a canvass for an office of the character for which we are candidates. When I commenced the canvass at Chicago, I spoke of Mr. Lincoln in terms of kindness as an old friend—I said that he was a good citizen, of unblemished character, against whom I had nothing to say. I repeated these complimentary remarks about him in my successive speeches, until he became the endorser for these and other slanders against me. If there is anything personally disagreeable, uncourteous or disreputable in these personalities, the sole responsibility rests on Mr. Lincoln, Mr. Trumbull, and their backers.

I will show you another charge made by Mr. Lincoln against me, as an offset to his determination of willingness to take back anything that is incorrect, and to correct any false statement he may have made. He has several times charged that the Supreme Court, President Pierce, President Buchanan and myself, at the time I introduced the Nebraska bill in January, 1854, at Washington, entered into a conspiracy to establish slavery all over this country. I branded this charge as a falsehood, and then he repeated it, asked me to analyze its truth and answer it. I told him, "Mr. Lincoln, I know what you are after—you want to occupy my time in personal matters, to prevent me from showing up the revolutionary principles which the Abolition party—whose candidate you are—have proclaimed to the world." But he asked me to analyze his proof, and I did so. I called his attention to the fact that at the time the Nebraska bill was introduced, there was no such case as the Dred Scott case pending in the Supreme Court, nor was it brought there for years afterwards, and hence that it was impossible there could have been any such conspiracy between the Judges of the Supreme Court and the other parties involved. I proved by the record that the charge was false, and what did he answer? Did he take it back like an honest man and say that he had been mistaken? No, he repeated the charge, and said, that although there was no such case pending that year, that there was an understanding between the Democratic owners of Dred Scott and the Judges of the Supreme Court and other parties involved that the case should be brought up. I then demanded to know who these Democratic owners of Dred Scott were. He could not or would not tell; he did not know. In truth, there were no Democratic owners of Dred

Scott on the face of the land. (Laughter.) Dred Scott was owned at that time by the Rev. Dr. Chaffee, an Abolition member of Congress from Springfield, Massachusetts, and his wife, (immense laughter and applause,) and Mr. Lincoln ought to have known that Dred Scott was so owned, for the reason that as soon as the decision was announced by the court, Dr. Chaffee and his wife executed a deed emancipating him, and put that deed on record. (Cheers.) It was a matter of public record, therefore, that at the time the case was taken to the Supreme Court, Dred Scott was owned by an Abolition member of Congress, a friend of Lincoln's, and a leading man of his party, while the defence was conducted by Abolition lawyers—and thus the Abolitionists managed both sides of the case. I have exposed these facts to Mr. Lincoln, and yet he will not withdraw his charge of conspiracy. I now submit to you whether you can place any confidence in a man who continues to make a charge when its utter falsity is proven by the public records. I will state another fact to show how utterly reckless and unscrupulous this charge against the Supreme Court, President Pierce, President Buchanan and myself is. Lincoln says that President Buchanan was in the conspiracy at Washington in the winter of 1854, when the Nebraska bill was introduced. The history of this country shows that James Buchanan was at that time representing this country at the court of St. James, Great Britain, with distinguished ability and usefulness, that he had not been in the United States for nearly a year previous, and that he did not return until about three years after. (Cheers.) Yet Mr. Lincoln keeps repeating this charge of conspiracy against Mr. Buchanan, when the public records prove it to be untrue. Having proved it to be false as far as the Supreme Court and President Buchanan are concerned, I drop it, leaving the public to say whether I, by myself, without their concurrence, could have gone into a conspiracy with them. (Laughter and cheers.) My friends, you see that the object clearly is to conduct the canvass on personal matters, and hunt me down with charges that are proven to be false by the public records of the country. I am willing to throw open my whole public and private life to the inspection of any man, or all men who desire to investigate it. Having resided among you twenty-five years, during nearly the whole of which time a public man, exposed to more assaults, perhaps more abuse than any man living of my age, or who ever did live, and having survived it all and still commanded your confidence, I am willing to trust to your knowledge of me and my public conduct without making any more defence against these assaults. (Great cheering.)

Fellow-citizens, I came here for the purpose of discussing the leading political topics which now agitate the country. I have no charges to make against Mr. Lincoln, none against Mr. Trumbull, and none against any man who is a candidate, except in repelling their assaults upon me. If Mr. Lincoln is a man of bad character, I leave you to find it out; if his votes in the past are not satisfactory, I leave others to ascertain the fact; if his course on the Mexican war was not in accordance with your notions of patriotism and fidelity to our own country as against a public enemy, I leave you to ascertain the fact. I have no assaults to make upon him except to trace his course on the questions that now divide the country and engross so much of the people's attention.

You know that prior to 1854 this country was divided into two great political parties, one the Whig, the other the Democratic. I, as a Democrat for twenty years prior to that time, had been in public discussions in this State as an advocate of Democratic principles, and I can appeal with confidence to every old line Whig within the hearing of my voice to bear testimony that during all that period I fought you Whigs like a man on every question that separated the two parties. I had the highest respect for Henry Clay as a gallant party leader, as an eminent statesman, and as one of the bright ornaments of this country; but I conscientiously believed that the Democratic party was right on the questions which separated the Democrats from the Whigs. The man does not live who can say that I ever personally assailed Henry Clay or Daniel Webster, or any one of the leaders of that great party, whilst I combatted with all my energy the measures they advocated. What did we differ about in those days? Did Whigs and Democrats differ about this slavery question. On the contrary, did we not, in 1850, unite to a man in favor of that system of compromise measures which Mr. Clay introduced, Webster defended, Cass supported, and Fillmore approved and made the law of the land by his signature. While we agreed on those compromise measures we differed about a bank, the tariff, distribution, the specie circular, the sub-treasury, and other questions of that description. Now let me ask you which one of those questions on which Whigs and Democrats then differed now remains to divide two great parties. Every one of those questions which divide Whigs and Democrats has passed away, the country has out-grown them, they have passed into history. Hence it is immaterial whether you were right or I was right on the bank, the sub-treasury, and other questions, because they no longer continue living issues. What then has taken the place of those questions about which we once differed? The slavery question has now become the leading and controlling issue; that question on which you and I agreed, on which the Whigs and Democrats united, has now become the leading issue between the national Democracy on the one side, and the Republican or Abolition party on the other.

Just recollect for a moment the memorable contest of 1850, when this country was agitated from its centre to its circumference by the slavery agitation. All eyes in this nation were then turned to the three great lights that survived the days of the revolution. They looked to Clay, then in retirement at Ashland, and to Webster and Cass in the United States Senate. Clay had retired to Ashland, having, as he supposed, performed his mission on earth, and was preparing himself for a better sphere of existence in another world. In that retirement he heard the discordant, harsh and grating sounds of sectional strife and disunion, and he aroused and came forth and resumed his seat in the Senate, that great theatre of his great deeds. From the moment that Clay arrived among us he became the leader of all the Union men whether whigs or democrats. For nine months we each assembled, each day, in the council chamber, Clay in the chair, with Cass upon his right hand and Webster upon his left, and the democrats and whigs gathered around, forgetting differences, and only animated by one common, patriotic sentiment to devise means and measures by which we could defeat the mad and revolutionary scheme of the northern abolitionists and southern disunionists. (Cheers.) We did devise those means. Clay brought them forward, Cass advocated them, the Union democrats and Union whigs voted for them, Fillmore signed them, and they gave peace and quiet to the country. Those Compromise measures of 1850 were founded upon the great fundamental principle that the people of each State and each territory ought to be left free to form and regulate their own domestic institutions in their own way subject only to the Federal Constitution. (Cheers. Hear, hear.) I will ask every old line Democrat and every old line Whig within the hearing of my voice, if I have not truly stated the issues as they then presented themselves to the country. You recollect that the abolitionists raised a howl of indignation and cried for vengeance and the destruction of Democrats and Whigs both, who supported those Compromise measures of 1850. When I returned home to Chicago, I found the citizens inflamed and infuriated against the authors of those great measures. Being the only man in that city who was held responsible for affirmative votes on all those measures, I came forward and addressed the assembled inhabitants, defended each and every one of Clay's Compromise measures as they passed the Senate and the House and were approved by President Fillmore. Previous to that time, the city council had passed resolutions nullifying the act of Congress and instructing the police to withhold all assistance from its execution; but the people of Chicago listened to my defense, and like candid, frank, conscientious men, when they became convinced that they had done an injustice to Clay, Webster, Cass, and all of us who had supported those measures, they repealed their nullifying resolutions and declared that the laws should be executed and the supremacy of the constitution maintained. Let it always be recorded in history to the immortal honor of the people of Chicago, that they returned to their duty when they found that they were wrong, and did justice to those whom they had blamed and abused unjustly. When the legislature of this State assembled that year, they proceeded to pass resolutions approving the Compromise measures of 1850. When the Whig party assembled in 1852 at Baltimore in National Convention for the last time, to nominate Scott for the Presidency, they adopted as a part of their platform the Compromise measures of 1850 as the cardinal plank upon which every Whig would stand and by which he would regulate his future conduct. When the democratic party assembled at the same place one month after to nominate General Pierce, we adopted the same platform so far as those Compromise measures were concerned, agreeing that we would stand by those glorious measures as a cardinal article in the democratic faith. Thus you see that in 1852 all the old Whigs and all the old Democrats stood on a common plank so far as this slavery question was concerned, differing on other questions.

Now, let me ask how is it, that since that time so many of you Whigs have wandered from the true path marked out by Clay and carried out broad and wide by the great Webster? How is it that so many old line Democrats have abandoned the old faith of their party and joined with Abolitionism and Freesoilism to overturn the platform of the old Democrats, and the platform of the old Whigs? You cannot deny that since 1854, there has been a great revolution on this one question. How has it been brought about? I answer, that no sooner was the sod grown green over the grave of the immortal Clay, no sooner was the rose planted on the tomb of the Godlike Webster, than many of the leaders of the Whig party, such as Seward, of New York and his followers, led off and attempted to abolitionize the Whig party, and transfer all your old Whigs bound hand and foot into the abolition camp. Seizing hold of the temporary excitement produced in this country by the introduction of the Nebraska bill, the disappointed politicians in the Democratic party, united with the disappointed politicians in the Whig party, and endeavored to form a new party composed of all the abolitionists, of abolitionized Democrats and abolitionized Whigs, banded together in an abolition platform.

And who led that crusade against National principles in this State? I answer, Abraham Lincoln on behalf of the Whigs, and Lyman Trumbull on behalf of the Democrats, formed a scheme by which they would abolitionize the two great parties in this State on condition that Lincoln should be sent to the United States Senate in place of Gen. Shields, and that Trumbull should go to Congress from the Belleville district, until I would be accommodating enough either to die or resign for his benefit, and then he was to go to the Senate in my place. You all remember that during the year 1854 these two worthy gentlemen, Mr. Lincoln and Mr. Trumbull, one an Old Line Whig and the other an Old Line Democrat, were hunting in partnership to elect a legislature against the Democratic party. I canvassed the State that year from the time I returned home until the election came off, and spoke in every county that I could reach during that period. In the northern part of the State I found Lincoln's ally, in the person of FRED. DOUGLASS, THE NEGRO, preaching abolition doctrines, while Lincoln was discussing the same principles down here, and Trumbull, a little farther down, was advocating the election of members to the legislature who would act in concert with Lincoln's and Fred. Douglass' friends. I witnessed an effort made at Chicago by Lincoln's then associates, and now supporters, to put Fred. Douglass, the negro, on the stand at a Democratic meeting to reply to the illustrious Gen. Cass when he was addressing the people there. (Shame on them.) They had the same negro hunting me down, and they now have a negro traversing the northern counties of the State, and speaking in behalf of Lincoln. (Hit him again; he's a disgrace to the white people, &c.) Lincoln knows that when we were at Freeport in joint discussion, there was a distinguished colored friend of his there then who was on the stump for him, (shouts of laughter,) and who made a speech there the night before we spoke, and another the night after, a short distance from Freeport, in favor of Lincoln, and in order to show how much interest the colored brethren felt in the success of their brother Abe. (Renewed laughter.) I have with me here, and would read if it would not occupy too much of my time, a speech made by Fred. Douglass in Poughkeepsie, N.Y., a short time since to a large convention, in which he conjures all the friends of negro equality and negro citizenship to rally as one man around Abraham Lincoln, the perfect embodiment of their principles, and by all means to defeat Stephen A. Douglas. (It can't be done, &c.) Thus you find that this Republican party in the northern part of the State had colored gentlemen for their advocates in 1854, in company with Lincoln and Trumbull, as they have now. When in October, 1854, I went down to Springfield to attend the State fair, I found the leaders of this party all assembled together under the title of an Anti-Nebraska meeting. It was Black Republicans up north, and Anti-Nebraska at Springfield. I found Lovejoy, a high priest of Abolitionism, and Lincoln one of the leaders who was towing the old line Whigs into the abolition camp, and Trumbull, Sidney Breese, and Gov. Reynolds, all making speeches against the Democratic party and myself, at the same place and in the same cause. (They're all birds of a feather, shun them.) The same men who are now fighting the Democratic party and the regular Democratic nominees in this State were fighting us then. They did not then acknowledge that they had become abolitionists, and many of them deny it now. Breese, Dougherty, and Reynolds were then fighting the Democracy under the title of Anti-Nebraska men, and now they are fighting the Democracy under the pretence that they are *simon pure* Democrats. (Laughter.) Saying that they are authorized to have every office-holder in Illinois beheaded who prefers the election of Douglas to that of Lincoln, or the success of the Democratic ticket in preference to the Abolition ticket for members of Congress, State officers, members of the Legislature, or any office in the State. They canvassed the State against us in 1854, as they are doing now, owning different names and different principles in different localities, but having a common object in view, viz: the defeat of all men holding national principles in opposition to this sectional Abolition party. They carried the legislature in 1854, and when it assembled in Springfield they proceeded to elect a United States Senator, all voting for Lincoln with one or two exceptions, which exceptions prevented them from quite electing him. And why should they not elect him? Had not Trumbull agreed that Lincoln should have Shields' place? Had not the abolitionists agreed to it? Was it not the solemn compact, the condition on which Lincoln agreed to abolitionize the old Whigs that he should be Senator? Still, Trumbull having control of a few abolitionized Democrats, would not allow them all to vote for Lincoln on any one ballot, and thus kept him for some time within one or two votes of an election until he worried out Lincoln's friends, and compelled them to drop him and elect Trumbull in violation of the bargain. (Cheers.) I desire to read you a piece of testimony in confirmation of the notoriously public facts which I have stated to you. Col. Jas. H. Matheny, of Springfield, is and for twenty years has been the confidential personal and political friend and manager of Mr. Lincoln. Matheny is this very day the candidate of the Republican or Abolition party for Congress against the gallant Major Thos. L. Harris, in the Springfield district, and is making speeches for Lincoln and against me. I will read you the testimony of Matheny about this bargain between Lincoln and Trumbull when they undertook to abolitionize Whigs and Democrats only four years ago. Matheny being mad at Trumbull for having played a Yankee trick on Lincoln, exposed the bargain in a public speech two years ago, and I will read the published report of that speech, the correctness of which Mr. Lincoln will not deny:

The Whigs, Abolitionists, Know Nothings, and renegade Democrats, made a solemn compact for the purpose of carrying this State against the Democracy on this plan: 1st, That they would all combine and elect Mr. Trumbull to Congress, and thereby carry his district for the legislature, in order to throw all the strength that could be obtained into that body against the Democrats. 2d, That when the legislature should meet, the officers of that body, such as speaker, clerks, door-keepers, &c, would be given to the Abolitionists; and 3d, That the Whigs were to have the United States Senator. Thus, accordingly, in good faith, Trumbull was elected to Congress, and his district carried for the Legislature, and when it convened the Abolitionists got all the officers of that body, and thus far the "bond" was fairly executed. The Whigs, on their part, demanded the election of Abraham Lincoln to the United States Senate, that the bond might be fulfilled, the other parties to the contract having already secured to themselves all that was called for. But, in the most perfidious manner, they refused to elect Mr. Lincoln; and the mean, low-lived, sneaking Trumbull succeeded by pleading all that was required by any party, in thrusting Lincoln aside and foisting himself, an excrescence from the rotten bowels of the Democracy into the United States Senate: and thus it has ever been, that an *honest* man makes a bad bargain when he conspires or contracts with rogues.

Lincoln's confidential friend, Matheny, thought that Lincoln made a bad bargain when he conspired with such rogues as Trumbull and the Abolitionists. (Great laughter.) I would like to know whether Lincoln had as high an opinion of Trumbull's veracity when the latter agreed to support him for the Senate, and then cheated him as he does now, (renewed laughter,) when Trumbull comes forward and makes charges against me. You could not then prove Trumbull an honest man either by Lincoln, by Matheny, or by any of Lincoln's friends. They charged everywhere that Trumbull had cheated them out of the bargain, and Lincoln found sure enough that it was a *bad bargain* to contract and conspire with rogues. (Laughter.)

And now I will explain to you what has been a mystery all over the State and Union, the reason why Lincoln was nominated for the United States Senate by the Black Republican convention. You know it has never been usual for any party, or any convention to nominate a candidate for United States Senator. Probably this was the first time that such a thing was ever done. The Black Republican convention had not been called for that purpose, but to nominate a State ticket, and every man was surprised and many disgusted when Lincoln was nominated. Archie Williams thought he was entitled to it. Browning knew that he deserved it, Wentworth was certain that he would get it, Peck had hopes, Judd felt sure that he was the man, and Palmer had claims and had made arrangements to secure it; but to their utter amazement, Lincoln was nominated by the convention, (laughter,) and not only that, but he received the nomination unanimously, by a resolution declaring that Abraham Lincoln was "the first, last, and only choice" of the Republican party. How did this occur? Why, because they could not get Lincoln's friends to make another bargain with "rogues," (laughter,) unless the whole party would come up as one man and pledge their honor that they would stand by Lincoln first, last and all the time, and that he should not be cheated by Lovejoy this time, as he was by Trumbull before. Thus, by passing this resolution, the Abolitionists are all for him, Lovejoy and Farnsworth are canvassing for him, Giddings is ready to come here in his behalf, and the negro speakers are already on the stump for him, and he is sure not to be cheated this time. He would not go into the arrangement until he got their bond for it, and Trumbull is compelled now to take the stump, get up false charges against me, and travel all over the State to try and elect

Lincoln, in order to keep Lincoln's friends quiet about the bargain in which Trumbull cheated them four years ago. You see, now, why it is that Lincoln and Trumbull are so mighty fond of each other. (Tremendous laughter.) They have entered into a conspiracy to break me down by these assaults on my public character, in order to draw my attention from a fair exposure of the mode in which they attempted to abolitionize the old Whig and the old Democratic parties and lead them captive into the Abolition camp. (That's so, and hear, hear.) Do you not all remember that Lincoln went around here four years ago making speeches to you, and telling you that you should all go for the Abolition ticket, and swearing that he was as good a Whig as he ever was; (laughter;) and that Trumbull went all over the State making pledges to the old Democrats, and trying to coax them into the Abolition camp, swearing by his Maker, with the uplifted hand, that he was still a Democrat, always intended to be, and that never would he desert the Democratic party. (Laughter.) He got your votes to elect an Abolition legislature, which passed Abolition resolutions, attempted to pass Abolition laws, and sustained Abolitionists for office, State and national. Now, the same game is attempted to be played over again. Then Lincoln and Trumbull made captives of the old Whigs and old Democrats and carried them into the Abolition camp where Father Giddings, the high priest of Abolitionism, received and christened them in the dark cause just as fast as they were brought in. (Hear, hear.) Giddings found the converts so numerous that he had to have assistance, and he sent for John P. Hale, N. P. Banks, Chase, and other Abolitionists, and they came on, and with Lovejoy and Fred. Douglass, the negro, helped to baptize these new converts as Lincoln, Trumbull, Breese, Reynolds, and Dougherty could capture them and bring them within the Abolition clutch. Gentlemen, they are now around making the same kind of speeches. Trumbull was down in Monroe county the other day assailing me and making a speech in favor of Lincoln, and I will show you under what notice his meeting was called. You see these people are Black Republicans or Abolitionists up North, while at Springfield to-day, they dare not call their convention "Republican," but are obliged to say "a convention of all men opposed to the Democratic party," and in Monroe county and lower Egypt Trumbull advertises their meetings as follows:

A meeting of the Free Democracy will take place at Waterloo, on Monday, September 12th inst., whereat Hon. Lyman Trumbull, Hon. John Baker, and others, will address the people upon the different political topics of the day. Members of all parties are cordially invited to be present, and hear and determine for themselves.

September 9, 1858.   THE FREE DEMOCRACY.

Did you ever before hear of this new party called the "Free Democracy?"

What object have these Black Republicans in changing their name in every county? (To cheat people.) They have one name in the North, another in the centre, and another in the South. When I used to practice law before my distinguished judicial friend, whom I recognize in the crowd before me, if a man was charged with horse stealing and the proof showed that he went by one name in Stephenson county, another in Sangamon, a third in Monroe, and a fourth in Randolph, we thought that the fact of his changing his name so often to avoid detection, was pretty strong evidence of his guilt. I would like to know why it is that this great free soil abolition party is not willing to avow the same name in all parts of the State? (They dare not.) If this party believes that its course is just, why does it not avow the same principle in the North, and in the South, in the East and in the West, wherever the American flag waves over American soil. (Cheers.)

A VOICE—The party does not call itself Black Republican in the North.

MR. DOUGLAS—Sir, if you will get a copy of the paper published at Waukegan, fifty miles from Chicago, which advocates the election of Mr. Lincoln, and has his name flying at its mast-head, you will find that it declares that "this paper is devoted to the cause of *Black Republicanism*." (Good, hit him again, and cheers.) I had a copy of it and intended to bring it down here into Egypt to let you see what name the party rallied under up in the Northern part of the State, and to convince you that their principles are as different in the two sections of the State as is their name. I am sorry that I have mislaid it and have not got it here. Their principles in the North are jet black, (laughter,) in the centre they are in color a decent mulatto, (renewed laughter,) and in lower Egypt they are almost white. (Shouts of laughter.) Why, I admired many of the white sentiments contained in Lincoln's speech at Jonesboro, and could not help but contrast them with the speeches of the same distinguished orator made in the Northern part of the State. Down here he denies that the Black Republican party is opposed to the admission of any more slave States, under any circumstances, and says that they are willing to allow the people of each State when it wants to come into the Union, to do just as it pleases on the question of slavery. In the North, you find Lovejoy, their candidate for Congress in the Bloomington district, Farnsworth, their candidate in the Chicago district, and Washburne, their candidate in the Galena district, all declaring that never will they consent, under any circumstances, to admit another slave State, even if the people want it. (That's so.) Thus, while they avow one set of principles up there, they avow another and entirely different set down here. And here let me recall to Mr. Lincoln the scriptural quotation which he has applied to the federal government, that a house divided against itself cannot stand, and ask him how does he expect this Abolition party to stand when in one-half of the State it advocates a set of principles which it has repudiated in the other half. (Laughter and applause.)

I am told that I have but eight minutes more. I would like to talk to you an hour and a half longer, but I will make the best use I can of the remaining eight minutes. Mr. Lincoln said in his first remarks that he was not in favor of the social and political equality of the negro with the white man. Everywhere up north he has declared that he was not in favor of the social and political equality of the negro, but he would not say whether or not he was opposed to negroes voting and negro citizenship. I want to know whether he is for or against negro citizenship? He declared his utter opposition to the Dred Scott decision, and advanced as a reason that the court had decided that it was not possible for a negro to be a citizen under the constitution of the United States. If he is opposed to the Dred Scott decision for that reason he must be in favor of conferring the right and privilege of citizenship upon the negro! I have been trying to get an answer from him on that point, but have never yet obtained one, and I will show you why. In every speech he made in the north he quoted the Declaration of Independence to prove that all men were created equal, and insisted that the phrase "all men," included the negro as well as the white man, and that the equality rested upon Divine law. Here is what he said on that point:

> I should like to know if, taking this old declaration of independence, which declares that all men are equal upon principle, and making exceptions to it where will it stop. If one man says it does not mean a negro, why may not another say it does not mean some other man? If that declaration is not the truth let us get the statute book in which we find it and tear it out!

Lincoln maintains there that the Declaration of Independence asserts that the negro is equal to the white man, and that under Divine law, and if he believes so it was rational for him to advocate negro citizenship, which, when allowed, puts the negro on an equality under the law. (No negro equality for us; down with Lincoln.) I say to you in all frankness, gentlemen, that in my opinion a negro is not a citizen, cannot be, and ought not to be, under the constitution of the United States. (That's the doctrine.) I will not even qualify my opinion to meet the declaration of one of the Judges of the Supreme Court in the Dred Scott case, "that a negro descended from African parents, who was imported into this country as a slave, is not a citizen, and cannot be." I say that this government was established on the white basis. It was made by white men, for the benefit of white men and their posterity forever, and never should be administered by any except white men. (Cheers.) I declare that a negro ought not to be a citizen, whether his parents were imported into this country as slaves or not, or whether or not he was born here. It does not depend upon the place a negro's parents were born, or whether they were slaves or not, but upon the fact that he is a negro, belonging to a race incapable of self government, and for that reason ought not to be on an equality with white men. (Immense applause.)

My friends, I am sorry that I have not time to pursue this

argument further, as I might have done but for the fact that Mr. Lincoln compelled me to occupy a portion of my time in repelling those gross slanders and falsehoods that Trumbull has invented against me and put in circulation. In conclusion, let me ask you why should this government be divided by a geographical line—arraying all men North in one great hostile party against all men South? Mr. Lincoln tells you, in his speech at Springfield, "that a house divided against itself cannot stand; that this government, divided into free and slave States, cannot endure permanently; that they must either be all free or all slave; all one thing or all the other." Why cannot this government endure divided into free and slave States, as our fathers made it? When this government was established by Washington, Jefferson, Madison, Jay, Hamilton, Franklin, and the other sages and patriots of that day, it was composed of free States and slave States, bound together by one common constitution. We have existed and prospered from that day to this thus divided, and have increased with a rapidity never before equalled in wealth, the extension of territory, and all the elements of power and greatness, until we have become the first nation on the face of the globe. Why can we not thus continue to prosper? We can if we will live up to and execute the government upon those principles upon which our fathers established it. During the whole period of our existence Divine Providence has smiled upon us, and showered upon our nation richer and more abundant blessings than have ever been conferred upon any other.

Senator Douglas' time here expired, and he stopped on the minute, amidst deafening applause.

MR. LINCOLN'S REJOINDER.

As Mr. Lincoln stepped forward, the crowd sent up three rousing cheers.

MR. LINCOLN said:

Fellow Citizens—It follows as a matter of course that a half-hour answer to a speech of an hour-and-a-half can be but a very hurried one. I shall only be able to touch upon a few of the points suggested by Judge Douglas, and give them a brief attention, while I shall have to totally omit others for the want of time.

Judge Douglas has said to you that he has not been able to get from me an answer to the question whether I am in favor of negro-citizenship. So far as I know, the Judge never asked me the question before. [Applause.] He shall have no occasion to ever ask it again, for I tell him very frankly that I am not in favor of negro citizenship. [Renewed applause.] This furnishes me an occasion for saying a few words upon the subject. I mentioned in a certain speech of mine which has been printed, that the Supreme Court had decided that a negro could not possibly be made a citizen, and without saying what was my ground of complaint in regard to that, or whether I had any ground of complaint, Judge Douglas has from that thing manufactured nearly every thing that he ever says about my disposition to produce an equality between the negroes and the white people. [Laughter and applause.] If any one will read my speech, he will find I mentioned that as one of the points decided in the course of the Supreme Court opinions, but I did not state what objection I had to it. But Judge Douglas tells the people what my objection was when I did not tell them myself. [Loud applause and laughter.] Now my opinion is that the different States have the power to make a negro a citizen under the Constitution of the United States if they choose. The Dred Scott decision decides that they have not that power. If the State of Illinois had that power I should be opposed to the exercise of it. [Cries of "good," "good," and applause.] That is all I have to say about it.

Judge Douglas has told me that he heard my speeches north and my speeches south—that he had heard me at Ottawa and at Freeport in the north, and recently at Jonesboro in the south, and there was a very different cast of sentiment in the speeches made at the different points. I will not charge upon Judge Douglas that he wilfully misrepresents me, but I call upon every fair-minded man to take these speeches and read them, *and I dare him to point out any difference between my printed speeches north and south*. [Great cheering.] While I am here perhaps I ought to say a word, if I have the time, in regard to the latter portion of the Judge's speech, which was a sort of declamation in reference to my having said I entertained the belief that this government would not endure, half slave and half free. I have said so and I did not say it without what seemed to me to be good reasons. It perhaps would require more time than I have now to set forth these reasons in detail; but let me ask you a few questions. Have we ever had any peace on this slavery question? [No, no.] When are we to have peace upon it if it is kept in the position it now occupies? [Never.] How are we ever to have peace upon it? That is an important question. To be sure if we will all stop and allow Judge Douglas and his friends to march on in their present career until they plant the institution all over the nation, here and wherever else our flag waves, and we acquiesce in it, there will be peace. But let me ask Judge Douglas how he is going to get the people to do that? [Applause.] They have been wrangling over this question for at least forty years. This was the cause of the agitation resulting in the Missouri Compromise—this produced the troubles at the annexation of Texas, in the acquisition of the territory acquired in the Mexican war. Again, this was the trouble which was quieted by the Compromise of 1850, when it was settled *"forever,"* as both the great political parties declared in their National Conventions. That "forever" turned out to be just four years, [laughter] *when Judge Douglas himself re-opened it.* [Immense applause, cries of "hit him again," &c.] When is it likely to come to an end? He introduced the Nebraska bill in 1854 to put *another end* to the slavery agitation. He promised that it would finish it all up immediately, and he has never made a speech since until he got into a quarrel with the President about the Lecompton Constitution, in which he has not declared that we are *just at the end* of the slavery agitation. But in one speech, I think last winter, he did say that he didn't quite see when the end of the slavery agitation would come. [Laughter and cheers.] Now he tells us again that it is all over, and the people of Kansas have voted down the Lecompton Constitution. How is it over? That was only one of the attempts at putting an end to the slavery agitation—one of these "final settlements." [Renewed laughter.] Is Kansas in the Union? Has she formed a Constitution that she is likely to come in under? Is not the slavery agitation still an open question in that Territory? Has the voting down of that Constitution put an end to all the trouble? Is that more likely to settle it than every one of these previous attempts to settle the slavery agitation. [Cries of "No," "No."] Now, at this day in the history of the world we can no more foretell where the end of this slavery agitation will be than we can see the end of the world itself. The Nebraska-Kansas bill was introduced four years and a half ago, and if the agitation is ever to come to an end, we may say we are four years and a half nearer the end. So, too, we can say we are four years and a half nearer the end of the world; and we can just as clearly see the end of the world as we can see the end of this agitation. [Applause.] The Kansas settlement did not conclude it. If Kansas should sink to-day, and leave a great vacant space in the earth's surface, this vexed question would still be among us. I say, then, there is no way of putting an end to the slavery agitation amongst us but to put it back upon the basis where our fathers placed it, [applause] no way but to keep it out of our new Territories [renewed applause]—to restrict it forever to the old States where it now exists. [Tremendous and prolonged cheering; cries of "That's the doctrine," "Good," "Good," &c.] Then the public mind *will* rest in the belief that it is in the course of ultimate extinction. That is one way of putting an end to the slavery agitation. [Applause.]

The other way is for us to surrender and let Judge Douglas and his friends have their way and plant slavery over all the States—cease speaking of it as in any way a wrong—regard slavery as one of the common matters of property, and speak of negroes as we do of our horses and cattle. But while it drives on in its state of progress as it is now driving, and as it has driven for the last five years, I have ventured the opinion, and I say to-day, that we will have no end to the slavery agitation until it takes one turn or the other. [Applause.] I do not mean that when it takes a turn towards ultimate extinction it will be in a day, nor in a year, nor in two years. I do not suppose that in the most peaceful way ultimate extinction would occur in less than a hundred years at the least; but that it will occur in the best way for both races in God's own good time, I have no doubt. [Applause.] But, my friends, I have used up more of my time than I intended on this point.

Now, in regard to this matter about Trumbull and myself having made a bargain to sell out the entire Whig and Democratic parties in 1854 — Judge Douglas brings forward no evidence to sustain his charge, except the speech Matheny is said to have made in 1856, in which he told a cock-and-bull story of that sort, upon the same moral principles that Judge Douglas tells it here to-day. [Loud applause.] This is the simple truth. I do not care greatly for the story, but this is the truth of it, and I have twice told Judge Douglas to his face, that from beginning to end there is not one word of truth in it. [Thunders of applause.] I have called upon him for the proof, and he does not at all meet me as Trumbull met him upon that of which we were just talking, by producing the record. He didn't bring the record, because there was no record for him to bring. [Cheers and laughter.] When he asks if I am ready to indorse Trumbull's veracity after he has broken a bargain with me, I reply that if Trumbull *had* broken a bargain with me, I would not be likely to indorse his veracity [laughter and applause]; but I am ready to indorse his veracity because *neither in that thing, nor in any other, in all the years that I have known Lyman Trumbull, have I known him to fail of his word or tell a falsehood, large or small.* [Great cheering.] It is for that reason that I indorse Lyman Trumbull.

MR. JAMES BROWN — (*Douglas Post Master*). —What does Ford's history say about him?

MR. LINCOLN — Some gentleman asks me what Ford's History says about him. My own recollection is, that Ford speaks of Trumbull in very disrespectful terms in several portions of his book, *and that he talks a great deal worse of Judge Douglas.* [Roars of laughter and applause.] I refer you, sir, to the history for examination. [Cheers.]

Judge Douglas complains, at considerable length, about a disposition on the part of Trumbull and myself to attack him personally. I want to attend to that suggestion a moment. I don't want to be unjustly accused of dealing illiberally or unfairly with an adversary, either in court, or in a political canvass, or anywhere else. I would despise myself if I supposed myself ready to deal less liberally with an adversary than I was willing to be treated myself. Judge Douglas, in a general way, without putting it in a direct shape, revives the old charge against me, in reference to the Mexican War. He does not take the responsibility of putting it in a very definite form, but makes a general reference to it. That charge is more than ten years old. He complains of Trumbull and myself, because he says we bring charges against him one or two years old. He knows, too, that in regard to the Mexican War story, the more respectable papers of his own party throughout the State have been compelled to take it back and acknowledge that it was a lie. [Continued and vociferous applause.]

Here Mr. Lincoln turned to the crowd on the platform, and selecting Hon. Orlando B. Ficklin, led him forward and said:

I do not mean to do anything with Mr. Ficklin except to present his face and tell you that *he personally knows it to be a lie!* He was a member of Congress at the only time I was in Congress, and he (Ficklin) knows that whenever there was an attempt to procure a vote of mine which would indorse the origin and justice of the war, I refused to give such indorsement, and voted against it; but I never voted against the supplies for the army, and he knows, as well as Judge Douglas, that whenever a dollar was asked by way of compensation or otherwise, for the benefit of the soldiers, *I gave all the votes that Ficklin or Douglas did, and perhaps more.* [Loud applause.]

MR. FICKLIN—My friends, I wish to say this in reference to the matter. Mr. Lincoln and myself are just as good personal friends as Judge Douglas and myself. In reference to this Mexican war, my recollection is that when Ashmun's resolution (amendment) was offered by Mr. Ashmun of Massachusetts, in which he declared that the Mexican war was unnecessarily and unconstitutionally commenced by the President—my recollection is that Mr. Lincoln voted for that resolution.

MR. LINCOLN—That is the truth. Now you all remember that was a resolution censuring the President for the manner in which the war was *begun.* You know they have charged that I voted against the supplies, by which I starved the

soldiers who were out fighting the battles of their country.
I say that Ficklin knows it is false. When that charge was
brought forward by the Chicago *Times*, the Springfield *Register* (Douglas organ) reminded the *Times* that the charge
really applied to John Henry; and I do know that John Henry
is now making speeches and fiercely battling for Judge Douglas.
[Loud applause.] If the Judge now says that he offers this as
a sort of a set-off to what I said to-day in reference to Trumbull's charge, then I remind him that he made this charge
before I said a word about Trumbull's. He brought this forward at Ottawa, the first time we met face to face; and in
the opening speech that Judge Douglas made, he attacked
me in regard to a matter ten years old. Isn't he a pretty man
to be whining about people making charges against him
only *two* years old. [Cheers.]

The Judge thinks it is altogether wrong that I should have
dwelt upon this charge of Trumbull's at all. I gave the apology for doing so in my opening speech. Perhaps it didn't fix
your attention. I said that when Judge Douglas was speaking
at places where I spoke on the succeeding day, he used very
harsh language about this charge. Two or three times afterwards I said I had confidence in Judge Trumbull's veracity
and intelligence; and my own opinion was, from what I
knew of the character of Judge Trumbull, that he would vindicate his position, and prove whatever he had stated to be
true. This I repeated two or three times; and then I dropped
it, without saying anything more on the subject for weeks—
perhaps a month. I passed it by without noticing it at all till
I found at Jacksonville, Judge Douglas, in the plenitude of
his power, is not willing to answer Trumbull and let me
alone; but he comes out there and uses this language: "He
should not hereafter occupy his time in refuting such charges
made by Trumbull, but that Lincoln, having indorsed the
character of Trumbull for veracity, he should hold him
(Lincoln) responsible for the slanders." What was Lincoln to
do? [Laughter.] Did he not do right, when he had the fit
opportunity of meeting Judge Douglas here, to tell him he
was ready for the responsibility? [Enthusiastic cheering,
"good, good. Hurrah for Lincoln!"] I ask a candid audience
whether in doing thus Judge Douglas was not the assailant

rather than I? ["Yes, yes, Hit him again!"] Here I meet him face to face and say I am ready to take the responsibility so far as it rests upon me.

Having done so, I ask the attention of this audience to the question whether I have succeeded in sustaining the charge ["yes," "yes"], and whether Judge Douglas has at all succeeded in rebutting it? [Loud cries of "no, no."] You all heard me call upon him to say *which of these pieces of evidence was a forgery?* Does he say that what I present here as a copy of the original Toombs bill is a forgery? ["No," "no."] Does he say that what I present as a copy of the bill reported by himself is a forgery? ["No," "no," "no."] Or what is presented as a transcript from the *Globe*, of the quotations from Bigler's speech is a forgery? [No, no, no.] Does he say the quotations from his own speech are forgeries? ["No," "no," "no."] Does he say this transcript from Trumbull's speech is a forgery? [Loud cries of "no, no." "He didn't deny one of them."] *I would then like to know how it comes about, that when each piece of a story is true, the whole story turns out false?* [Great cheers and laughter.] I take it these people have some sense; they see plainly that Judge Douglas is playing cuttlefish, [Laughter] a small species of fish that has no mode of defending itself when pursued except by throwing out a black fluid, which makes the water so dark the enemy cannot see it and thus it escapes. [Roars of laughter.] Ain't the Judge playing the cuttlefish? ["Yes, yes," and cheers.]

Now I would ask very special attention to the consideration of Judge Douglas' speech at Jacksonville; and when you shall read his speech of to-day, I ask you to watch closely and see which of these pieces of testimony, every one of which he says is a forgery, he has shown to be such. *Not one of them has he shown to be a forgery.* Then I ask the original question, if each of the pieces of testimony is true, *how is it possible that the whole is a falsehood?* [Loud and continued cheers.]

In regard to Trumbull's charge that he (Douglas) inserted a provision into the bill to prevent the Constitution being submitted to the people, what was his answer? He comes here and reads from the *Congressional Globe* to show that on his motion that provision was struck out of the bill. Why, Trumbull has not said it was not stricken out, but Trumbull says he

(Douglas) put it in, and it is no answer to the charge to say he afterwards took it out. Both are perhaps true. It was in regard to that thing precisely that I told him he had dropped the cub. [Roars of laughter.] Trumbull shows you that by his introducing the bill it was his cub. [Laughter.] It is no answer to that assertion to call Trumbull a liar merely because he did not specially say Douglas struck it out. Suppose that were the case, does it answer Trumbull? [No, no.] I assert that you (pointing to an individual,) are here to-day, and you undertake to prove me a liar by showing that you were in Mattoon yesterday. [Laughter.] I say that you took your hat off your head, and you prove me a liar by putting it on your head. [Roars of laughter.] That is the whole force of Douglas' argument.

Now, I want to come back to my original question. Trumbull says that Judge Douglas had a bill with a provision in it for submitting a Constitution to be made to a vote of the people of Kansas. Does Judge Douglas deny that fact? [Cries of "no, no."] Does he deny that the provision which Trumbull reads was put in that bill? ["No, no."] Then Trumbull says he struck it out. Does he dare to deny that? ["No, no, no."] He does not, and I have the right to repeat the question—*why, Judge Douglas took it out?* [Immense applause.] Bigler has said there was a combination of certain Senators, among whom he did not include Judge Douglas, by which it was agreed that the Kansas bill should have a clause in it not to have the Constitution formed under it submitted to a vote of the people. He did not say that Douglas was among them, but we prove by another source that about the same time Douglas comes into the Senate *with that provision stricken out of the bill.* Although Bigler cannot say they were all working in concert, yet it looks very much as if the thing was agreed upon and done with a mutual understanding after the conference; and while we do not know that it was absolutely so, yet it looks so probable that we have a right to call upon the man who knows the true reason why it was done, *to tell what the true reason was.* [Great cheers.] When he will not tell what the true reason was, he stands in the attitude of an accused thief who has stolen goods in his possession, and when called to account, refuses to tell where he got them. [Immense applause.] Not only is this the evidence, but when he comes in with the bill having the provision stricken out, he tells us in a speech, not then but since, that these alterations and modifications in the bill *had been made by* HIM, *in consultation with Toombs, the originator of the bill.* He tells us the same to-day. He says there were certain modifications made in the bill in committee that he did not vote for. I ask you to remember while certain amendments were made which he disapproved of, but which a majority of the committee voted in, he has himself told us that in this particular *the alterations and modifications were made by him upon consultation with Toombs.* [Enthusiastic cheering.] We have his own word that these alterations were made *by him* and not by the committee. ["That's so," "good, good."] Now, I ask what is the reason Judge Douglas is so chary about coming to the exact question? What is the reason he will not tell you anything about HOW it was made, BY WHOM it was made, or that he remembers it being made at all? Why does he stand playing upon the meaning of words, and quibbling around the edges of the evidence? If he can explain all this, but leaves it unexplained, I have a right to infer that Judge Douglas understood it was the purpose of his party, in engineering that bill through, to make a Constitution and have Kansas come into the Union with that Constitution, *without its being submitted to a vote of the people.* ["That's it."] If he will explain his action on this question, by giving a *better reason* for the facts that happened, than he has done, it will be satisfactory. But until he does that—until he gives a better or more plausible reason than he has offered against the evidence in the case—*I suggest to him it will not avail him at all that he swells himself up, takes on dignity, and calls people liars.* [Great applause and laughter.] Why, sir, there is not a word in Trumbull's speech that depends on Trumbull's veracity at all. He has only arrayed the evidence and told you what follows as a matter of reasoning. There is not a statement in the whole speech that depends on Trumbull's word. If you have ever studied geometry, you remember that by a course of reasoning Euclid proves that all the angles in a triangle are equal to two right angles. Euclid has shown you how to work it out. Now, if you undertake to disprove that proposition, and to show that it is erroneous, would you prove it to be false by calling Euclid a liar? [Roars of laughter and enthusiastic cheers.] They tell me that my time is out, and therefore I close.

To Norman B. Judd

Hon. N. B. Judd: Danville, Ill., Sept. 23, 1858.

My Dear Sir: We had a fine and altogether satisfactory meeting here yesterday. Our friends here wish a German speaker, before the election. Can't you send one? Address Dr. W. Fithian, and set a time sufficiently distant to give full notice. I am behind in general news; and this is a bad point to get any. Still I believe we have got the gentleman, unless they overcome us by fraudulent voting. We must be especially prepared for this. It must be taken into anxious consideration at once. How can it be done? Men imported from other states and men not naturalized can be fought out; but if they should string out the qualified Irish voters of Chicago (for instance) into a doubtful district, having them to swear to an actual residence when they offer to vote, how can we prevent it? Is "Long John" at hand? His genius should be employed on this question. Tell him so for me. I do not mean by this that the rest of us are to dismiss the question. It is a great danger, and we must all attend to it. Yours as ever,

Verses to Rosa Haggard

To Rosa—

You are young, and I am older;
  You are hopeful, I am not—
Enjoy life, ere it grow colder—
  Pluck the roses ere they rot.

Teach your beau to heed the lay—
  That sunshine soon is lost in shade—
That *now's* as good as any day—
  To take thee, Rosa, ere she fade.

Winchester, Sep. 28. 1858.

Verse to Linnie Haggard

To Linnie—
> A sweet plaintive song did I hear,
>   And I fancied that she was the singer—
> May emotions as pure, as that song set a-stir
>   Be the worst that the future shall bring her.

Winchester Sep. 30— 1858—

On Pro-slavery Theology

Suppose it is true, that the negro is inferior to the white, in the gifts of nature; is it not the exact reverse justice that the white should, for that reason, take from the negro, any part of the little which has been given him? "*Give* to him that is needy" is the christian rule of charity; but "Take from him that is needy" is the rule of slavery.

PRO-SLAVERY THEOLOGY.

The sum of pro-slavery theology seems to be this: "Slavery is not universally *right*, nor yet universally *wrong*; it is better for *some* people to be slaves; and, in such cases, it is the Will of God that they be such."

Certainly there is no contending against the Will of God; but still there is some difficulty in ascertaining, and applying it, to particular cases. For instance we will suppose the Rev. Dr. Ross has a slave named Sambo, and the question is "Is it the Will of God that Sambo shall remain a slave, or be set free?" The Almighty gives no audable answer to the question, and his revelation—the Bible—gives none—or, at most, none but such as admits of a squabble, as to it's meaning. No one thinks of asking Sambo's opinion on it. So, at last, it comes to this, that *Dr. Ross* is to decide the question. And while he considers it, he sits in the shade, with gloves on his hands, and subsists on the bread that Sambo is earning in the burning sun. If he decides that God Wills Sambo to continue a slave, he thereby retains his own comfortable position; but if he decides that God will's Sambo to be free, he thereby has to walk out of the shade, throw off his gloves, and delve for his own bread. Will Dr. Ross be actuated by that perfect impartiality, which has ever been considered most favorable to correct decisions?

But, slavery is good for some people!!! As a *good* thing, slavery is strikingly peculiar, in this, that it is the only good thing which no man ever seeks the good of, *for himself.*

Nonsense! Wolves devouring lambs, not because it is good for their own greedy maws, but because it is good for the lambs!!!

1858?

Fifth Lincoln-Douglas Debate, Galesburg, Illinois

Fifth joint debate October 7. 1858, at Galesburg, Illinois Douglas, as reported in the Chicago Times. Lincoln, as reported in the Press & Tribune.

MR. DOUGLAS' SPEECH.

When Senator Douglas appeared on the stand he was greeted with three tremendous cheers. He said:

Ladies and Gentlemen: Four years ago I appeared before the people of Knox county for the purpose of defending my political action upon the compromise measures of 1850 and the passage of the Kansas-Nebraska bill. Those of you before me, who were present then, will remember that I vindicated myself for supporting those two measures by the fact that they rested upon the great fundamental principle that the people of each State and each territory of this Union have the right, and ought to be permitted to exercise the right of regulating their own domestic concerns in their own way, subject to no other limitation or restriction than that which the Constitution of the United States imposes upon them. I then called upon the people of Illinois to decide whether that principle of self-government was right or wrong. If it was, and is right, then the compromise measures of 1850 were right, and, consequently, the Kansas and Nebraska bill, based upon the same principle, must necessarily have been right. (That's so, and cheers.)

The Kansas and Nebraska bill declared, in so many words, that it was the true intent and meaning of the act not to legislate slavery into any State or territory, nor to exclude it therefrom, but to leave the people thereof perfectly free to form and regulate their domestic institutions in their own way, subject only to the Constitution of the United States. For the last four years I have devoted all my energies, in private and public, to commend that principle to the American people. Whatever else may be said in condemnation or support of my political course, I apprehend that no honest man will doubt the fidelity with which, under all circumstances, I have stood by it.

During the last year a question arose in the Congress of the United States whether or not that principle would be violated by the admission of Kansas into the Union under the Lecompton constitution. In my opinion, the attempt to force Kansas in under that constitution was a gross violation of the principle enunciated in the compromise measures of 1850, and Kansas and Nebraska bill of 1854, and therefore I led off in the fight against the Lecompton constitution and conducted it until the effort to carry that constitution through Congress was abandoned. And I can appeal to all men, friends and foes, Democrats and Republicans, Northern men, Southern men, that during the whole of that fight I carried the banner of Popular Sovereignty aloft, and never allowed it to trail in the dust, or lowered my flag until victory perched upon our arms. (Cheers!) When the Lecompton constitution was defeated, the question arose in the minds of those who had advocated it what they should next resort to in order to carry out their views. They devised a measure known as the English bill, and granted a general amnesty and political pardon to all men who had fought against the Lecompton constitution, provided they would support that bill. I for one did not choose to accept the pardon or to avail myself of the amnesty granted on that condition. The fact that the supporters of Lecompton were willing to forgive all differences of opinion at that time in the event those who opposed it favored the English bill, was an admission that they did not think that opposition to Lecompton impaired a man's standing in the Democratic party. Now the question arises, what was that English bill which certain men are now attempting to make a test of political orthodoxy in this country? It provided, in substance, that the Lecompton constitution should be sent back to the people of Kansas for their adoption or rejection, at an election which was held in August last, and in case they refused admission under it that Kansas should be kept out of the Union until she had 93,420 inhabitants. I was in favor of sending the constitution back in order to enable the people to say whether or not it was their act and deed, and embodied their will; but the other proposition, that if they refused to come into the Union under it, they should be kept out until they had double or treble the population they then had, I never would sanction by my vote. The reason why I could not sanction it is to be found in the fact that by the English bill, if the people of Kansas had only agreed to become a slaveholding State under the Lecompton constitution, they could have done so with 35,000 people, but if they insisted on being a free State, as they had a right to do, then they were to be punished by being kept out of the Union until they had nearly three times that population. I then said in my place in the Senate, as I now say to you, that whenever Kansas has population enough for a slave State she has population enough for a free State. (That's it, and cheers.) I have never yet given a vote, and I never intend to record one making an odious and unjust distinction between the different States of this Union. (Applause.) I hold it to be a fundamental principle in our republican form of government that all the States of this Union, old and new, free and slave, stand on an exact equality. Equality among the different States is a cardinal principle on which all our institutions rest. Wherever, therefore, you make a discrimination, saying to a slave State that it shall be admitted with 35,000 inhabitants, and to a free State that it shall not be admitted until it has 93,000 or 100,000 inhabitants, you are throwing the whole weight of the federal government into the scale in favor of one class of States against the other. Nor would I on the other hand any sooner sanction the doctrine that a free State could be admitted into the Union with 35,000 people, while a slave State was kept out until it had 93,000. I have always declared in the Senate my willingness, and I am willing now to adopt the rule, that no territory shall ever become a State until it has the requisite population for a member of Congress, according to the then existing ratio. But while I have always been, and am now willing to adopt that general rule, I was not willing and would not consent to make an exception of Kansas, as a punishment for her obstinacy, in demanding the right to do as she pleased in the formation of her constitution. It is proper that I should remark here, that my opposition to the Lecompton constitution did not rest upon the peculiar position taken by Kansas on the subject of slavery. I held then, and hold now, that if the people of Kansas want a slave State, it is their right to make one and be received into the Union under it; if, on the contrary, they want a free State, it is their right to have it, and no man should ever oppose their admission because they ask it under the one or the other. I hold to that great principle of self-government which asserts the right of every people to decide for themselves the nature and character of the domestic institutions and fundamental law under which they are to live.

The effort has been and is now being made in this State by certain postmasters and other federal office holders, to make a test of faith on the support of the English bill. These men are now making speeches all over the State against me and in favor of Lincoln, either directly or indirectly, because I would not sanction a discrimination between slave and free States by voting for the English bill. But while that bill is made a test in Illinois for the purpose of breaking up the Democratic organization in this State, how is it in the other States? Go to Indiana, and there you find English himself, the author of the English bill, who is a candidate for re-election to Congress, has been forced by public opinion to abandon his own darling project, and to give a promise that he will vote for the admission of Kansas at once, whenever she forms a constitution in pursuance of law, and ratifies it by a majority vote of her people. Not only is this the case with English himself, but I am informed that every Democratic candidate for Congress in Indiana takes that same ground. Pass to Ohio, and there you find that Groesbeck, and Pendleton, and Cox, and all the other anti-Lecompton men who stood shoulder to shoulder with me against the Lecompton constitution, but voted for the English bill, now repudiate it and take the same ground that I do on that question. So it is with the Joneses and others of Pennsylvania, and so it is with every other Lecompton Democrat in the free States. They now abandon even the English bill, and come back to the true platform which I proclaimed at the time in the Senate, and upon which the Democracy of Illinois now stand. And yet, notwithstanding the fact, that every Lecompton and anti-Lecompton Democrat in the free States has abandoned the English bill, you are told that it is to be made a test upon me, while the power and patronage of the government are all exerted to elect men to Congress in the other States who occupy the same position with reference to it that I do. It seems that my political offence consists in the fact that I first did not vote for the English bill, and thus pledge myself to keep Kansas out of the Union until she has a population of 93,420, and then return home, violate that pledge, repudiate the bill, and take the opposite ground. If I had done this, perhaps the administration would now be advocating my re-election, as it is that of the others who have pursued this course. I did not choose to give that pledge, for the reason that I did not intend to carry out that principle. I never will consent, for the sake of conciliating the frowns of power, to pledge myself to do that which I do not intend to perform. I now submit the question to you as my constituency, whether I was not right, first, in resisting the adoption of the Lecompton constitution; and secondly, in resisting the English bill. (An universal "Yes," from the crowd.) I repeat, that I opposed the Lecompton constitution because it was not the act and deed of the people of Kansas, and did not embody their will. I denied the right of any power on earth under our system of government to force a constitution on an unwilling people. (Hear, hear; that's the doctrine and cheers.) There was a time when some men could pretend to believe that the Lecompton constitution embodied the will of the people of Kansas, but that time has passed. The question was referred to the people of Kansas under the English bill last August, and then, at a fair election, they rejected the Lecompton constitution by a vote of from eight to ten against it to one in its favor. Since it has been voted down by so overwhelming a majority, no man can pretend that it was the act and deed of that people. (That's so; and cheers.) I submit the question to you whether or not if it had not been for me that constitution would have been crammed down the throats of the people of Kansas against their consent. (It would, it would. Hurra for Douglas; three cheers for Douglas, &c.) While at least ninety-nine out of every hundred people here present agree that I was right in defeating that project, yet my enemies use the fact that I did defeat it by doing right, to break me down and put another man in the U.S. Senate in my place. (No, no, you'll be returned; three cheers, &c.) The very men who acknowledge that I was right in defeating Lecompton, now form an alliance with federal office holders, professed Lecompton men, to defeat me, because I did right. (It can't be done.) My political opponent, Mr. Lincoln, has no hope on earth, and has never dreamed that he had a chance of success, were it not for the aid he is receiving from federal office holders, who are using their influence and the patronage of the government against me in revenge for my having defeated the Lecompton constitution. (Hear him; and applause.) What do you Republicans think of a political organization that will try to make an unholy and unnatural combination with its professed foes to beat a man merely because he has done right? (Shame on it.) You know such is the fact with regard to your own party. You know that the axe of decapitation is suspended over every man in office in Illinois, and the terror of proscription is threatened every Democrat by the present administration unless he supports the Republican ticket in preference to my Democratic associates and myself. (The people are with you. Let them threaten, &c.) I could find an instance in the postmaster of the city of Galesburg, and in every other postmaster in this vicinity, all of whom have been stricken down simply because they discharged the duties of their offices honestly, and supported the regular Democratic ticket in this State in the right. The Republican party is availing itself of every unworthy means in the present contest to carry the election, because its leaders know that if they let this chance slip they will never have another, and their hopes of making this a Republican State will be blasted forever.

Now, let me ask you whether the country has any interest in sustaining this organization known as the Republican party? That party is unlike all other political organizations in this country. All other parties have been national in their character—have avowed their principles alike in the slave and the free States, in Kentucky as well as in Illinois, in Louisiana as well as in Massachusetts. Such was the case with the old Whig party, and such was and is the case with the Democratic party. Whigs and Democrats could proclaim their principles boldly and fearlessly in the north and in the south, in the east and in the west, wherever the constitution ruled and the American flag waved over American soil.

But now you have a sectional organization, a party which appeals to the northern section of the Union against the southern, a party which appeals to northern passion, northern pride, northern ambition, and northern prejudices, against southern people, the southern States and southern institutions. The leaders of that party hope that they will be able to unite the northern States in one great sectional party, and inasmuch as the North is the strongest section, that they will thus be enabled to out vote, conquer, govern, and control the South. Hence you find that they now make speeches advocating principles and measures which cannot be defended in any slaveholding State of this Union. Is there a Republican residing in Galesburg who can travel into Kentucky and carry his principles with him across the Ohio? (No.) What Republican from Massachusetts can visit the Old Dominion without leaving his principles behind him when he crosses Mason and Dixon's line? Permit me to say to you in perfect good humor, but in all sincerity, that no political creed is sound which cannot be proclaimed fearlessly in every State of this Union where the Federal Constitution is the supreme law of the land. ("That's so," and cheers.) Not only is this Republican party unable to proclaim its principles alike in the North and in the South, in the free States and in the slave States, but it cannot even proclaim them in the same forms and give them the same strength and meaning in all parts of the same State. My friend Lincoln finds its extremely difficult to manage a debate in the centre part of the State, where there is a mixture of men from the North and the South. In the extreme northern part of Illinois he can proclaim as bold and radical abolitionism as ever Giddings, Lovejoy, or Garrison enunciated, but when he gets down a little further South he claims that he is an old line Whig, (great laughter,) a disciple of Henry Clay, ("Singleton says he defeated Clay's nomination for the Presidency," and cries of "that's so,") and declares that he still adheres to the old line Whig creed, and has nothing whatever to do with Abolitionism, or negro equality, or negro citizenship. ("Hurrah for Douglas.") I once before hinted this of

Mr. Lincoln in a public speech, and at Charleston he defied me to show that there was any difference between his speeches in the North and in the South, and that they were not in strict harmony. I will now call your attention to two of them, and you can then say whether you would be apt to believe that the same man ever uttered both. (Laughter and cheers.) In a speech in reply to me at Chicago in July last, Mr. Lincoln, in speaking of the equality of the negro with the white man used the following language:

I should like to know, if taking this old Declaration of Independence, which declares that all men are equal upon principle, and making exceptions to it, where will it stop? If one man says it does not mean a negro, why may not another man say it does not mean another man? (Laughter.) If the Declaration is not the truth, let us get the statute book in which we find it and tear it out. Who is so bold as to do it? If it is not true, let us tear it out.

You find that Mr. Lincoln there proposed that if the doctrine of the Declaration of Independence, declaring all men to be born equal, did not include the negro and put him on an equality with the white man, that we should take the statute book and tear it out. (Laughter and cheers.) He there took the ground that the negro race is included in the Declaration of Independence as the equal of the white race, and that there could be no such thing as a distinction in the races, making one superior and the other inferior. I read now from the same speech:

My friends, [he says,] I have detained you about as long as I desire to do, and I have only to say let us discard all this quibbling about this man and the other man—this race and that race, and the other race being inferior and therefore they must be placed in an inferior position, discarding our standard that we have left us. Let us discard all these things, and unite as one people throughout this land, until we shall once more stand up declaring that all men are created equal.

("That's right," &c.)

Yes, I have no doubt that you think it is right, but the Lincoln men down in Coles, Tazewell and Sangamon counties *do not* think it is right. (Immense applause and laughter. Hit him again, &c.) In the conclusion of the same speech, talking to the Chicago Abolitionists, he said: "I leave you, hoping that the lamp of liberty will burn in your bosoms until there shall no longer be a doubt that all men are created free and equal." (Good, good, shame, &c.) Well, you say good to that, and you are going to vote for Lincoln because he holds that doctrine. ("That's so.") I will not blame you for supporting him on that ground, but I will show you in immediate contrast with that doctrine, what Mr. Lincoln said down in Egypt in order to get votes in that locality where they do not hold to such a doctrine. In a joint discussion between Mr. Lincoln and myself, at Charleston, I think, on the 18th of last month, Mr. Lincoln referring to this subject used the following language:

> I will say then, that I am not nor never have been in favor of bringing about in any way, the social and political equality of the white and black races; that I am not nor never have been in favor of making voters of the free negroes, or jurors, or qualifying them to hold office, or having them to marry with white people. I will say in addition, that there is a physical difference between the white and black races, which, I suppose, will forever forbid the two races living together upon terms of social and political equality, and inasmuch as they cannot so live, that while they do remain together, there must be the position of superior and inferior, that I as much as any other white man am in favor of the superior position being assigned to the white man.

(Good for Lincoln.)

Fellow-citizens, here you find men hurrahing for Lincoln and saying that he did right, when in one part of the State he stood up for negro equality, and in another part for political effect, discarded the doctrine and declared that there always must be a superior and inferior race. (They're not men. Put them out, &c.) Abolitionists up north are expected and required to vote for Lincoln because he goes for the equality of the races, holding that by the Declaration of Independence the white man and the negro were created equal and endowed by the Divine law with that equality, and down south he tells the old Whigs, the Kentuckians, Virginians, and Tennesseeans, that there is a physical difference in the races, making one superior and the other inferior, and that he is in favor of maintaining the superiority of the white race over the negro. Now, how can you reconcile those two positions of Mr. Lincoln? He is to be voted for in the south as a pro-slavery man, and he is to be voted for in the north as an Abolitionist.

("Give it to him." "Hit him again.") Up here he thinks it is all nonsense to talk about a difference between the races, and says that we must "discard all quibbling about this race and that race and the other race being inferior, and therefore they must be placed in an inferior position." Down south he makes this "quibble" about this race and that race and the other race being inferior as the creed of his party, and declares that the negro can never be elevated to the position of the white man. You find that his political meetings are called by different names in different counties in the State. Here they are called Republican meetings, but in old Tazewell, where Lincoln made a speech last Tuesday, he did not address a *Republican* meeting, but "a grand rally of the *Lincoln men.*" (Great laughter.) There are very few Republicans there, because Tazewell county is filled with old Virginians and Kentuckians, all of whom are Whigs or Democrats, and if Mr. Lincoln had called an Abolition or Republican meeting there, he would not get many votes. (Laughter.) Go down into Egypt and you find that he and his party are operating under an alias there, which his friend Trumbull has given them, in order that they may cheat the people. When I was down in Monroe county a few weeks ago addressing the people, I saw handbills posted announcing that Mr. Trumbull was going to speak in behalf of Lincoln, and what do you think the name of his party was there? Why the *"Free Democracy."* (Great laughter.) Mr. Trumbull and Mr. Jehu Baker were announced to address the Free Democracy of Monroe county, and the bill was signed "Many Free Democrats." The reason that Lincoln and his party adopted the name of "Free Democracy" down there was because Monroe county has always been an old fashioned Democratic county, and hence it was necessary to make the people believe that they were Democrats, sympathized with them, and were fighting for Lincoln as Democrats. (That's it, &c.) Come up to Springfield, where Lincoln now lives and always has lived, and you find that the convention of his party which assembled to nominate candidates for legislature, who are expected to vote for him if elected, dare not adopt the name of Republican, but assembled under the title of "all opposed to the Democracy." (Laughter and cheers.) Thus you find that Mr. Lincoln's creed cannot travel through even one half of the counties of this State, but that it changes its hues and becomes lighter and lighter, as it travels from the extreme North, until it is nearly white, when it reaches the extreme south end of the State. (That's so, it's true, etc.) I ask you, my friends, why cannot Republicans avow their principles alike everywhere? I would despise myself if I thought that I was procuring your votes by concealing my opinions, and by avowing one set of principles in one part of the State, and a different set in another part. If I do not truly and honorably represent your feelings and principles, then I ought not to be your Senator; and I will never conceal my opinions, or modify or change them a hair's breadth in order to get votes. I tell you that this Chicago doctrine of Lincoln's—declaring that the negro and the white man are made equal by the Declaration of Independence and by Divine Providence—is a monstrous heresy. (That's so, and terrific applause.) The signers of the Declaration of Independence never dreamed of the negro when they were writing that document. They referred to white men, to men of European birth and European descent, when they declared the equality of all men. I see a gentleman there in the crowd shaking his head. Let me remind him that when Thomas Jefferson wrote that document he was the owner, and so continued until his death, of a large number of slaves. Did he intend to say in that Declaration that his negro slaves, which he held and treated as property, were created his equals by Divine law, and that he was violating the law of God every day of his life by holding them as slaves? ("No, no.") It must be borne in mind that when that Declaration was put forth every one of the thirteen colonies were slaveholding colonies, and every man who signed that instrument represented a slaveholding constituency. Recollect, also, that no one of them emancipated his slaves, much less put them on an equality with himself, after he signed the Declaration. On the contrary, they all continued to hold their negroes as slaves during the revolutionary war. Now, do you believe—are you willing to have it said—that every man who signed the Declaration of Independence declared the negro his equal, and then was hypocrite enough to continue to hold him as a slave, in violation of what he believed to be the divine law? ("No, no.") And yet when you say that the Declaration of Independence includes the negro, you charge the signers of it with hypocrisy.

I say to you, frankly, that in my opinion this government was made by our fathers on the white basis. It was made by white men for the benefit of white men and their posterity forever, and was intended to be administered by white men in all time to come. (That's so, and cheers.) But while I hold that under our constitution and political system the negro is not a citizen, cannot be a citizen, and ought not to be a citizen, it does not follow by any means that he should be a slave. On the contrary it does follow that the negro, as an inferior race, ought to possess every right, every privilege, every immunity which he can safely exercise consistent with the safety of the society in which he lives. (That's so, and cheers.) Humanity requires, and Christianity commands that you shall extend to every inferior being, and every dependent being, all the privileges, immunities and advantages which can be granted to them consistent with the safety of society. If you ask me the nature and extent of these privileges, I answer that that is a question which the people of each State must decide for themselves. (That's it.) Illinois has decided that question for herself. We have said that in this State the negro shall not be a slave, nor shall he be a citizen. Kentucky holds a different doctrine. New York holds one different from either, and Maine one different from all. Virginia, in her policy on this question, differs in many respects from the others, and so on, until there is hardly two States whose policy is exactly alike in regard to the relation of the white man and the negro. Nor can you reconcile them and make them alike. Each State must do as it pleases. Illinois had as much right to adopt the policy which we have on that subject as Kentucky had to adopt a different policy. The great principle of this government is that each State has the right to do as it pleases on all these questions, and no other State, or power on earth has the right to interfere with us, or complain of us merely because our system differs from theirs. In the compromise measures of 1850, Mr. Clay declared that this great principle ought to exist in the territories as well as in the States, and I reasserted his doctrine in the Kansas and Nebraska bill in 1854.

But Mr. Lincoln cannot be made to understand, and those

who are determined to vote for him, no matter whether he is a pro-slavery man in the south and a negro equality advocate in the north, cannot be made to understand how it is that in a territory the people can do as they please on the slavery question under the Dred Scott decision. Let us see whether I cannot explain it to the satisfaction of all impartial men. Chief Justice Taney has said in his opinion in the Dred Scott case, that a negro slave being property, stands on an equal footing with other property, and that the owner may carry them into United States territory the same as he does other property. (That's so.) Suppose any two of you, neighbors, should conclude to go to Kansas, one carrying $100,000 worth of negro slaves and the other $100,000 worth of mixed merchandise, including quantities of liquors. You both agree that under that decision you may carry your property to Kansas, but when you get it there, the merchant who is possessed of the liquors is met by the Maine liquor law, which prohibits the sale or use of his property, and the owner of the slaves is met by equally unfriendly legislation, which makes his property worthless after he gets it there. What is the right to carry your property into the territory worth to either, when unfriendly legislation in the territory renders it worthless after you get it there? The slaveholder when he gets his slaves there finds that there is no local law to protect him in holding them, no slave code, no police regulation maintaining and supporting him in his right, and he discovers at once that the absence of such friendly legislation excludes his property from the territory, just as irresistibly as if there was a positive constitutional prohibition excluding it. Thus you find it is with any kind of property in a territory, it depends for its protection on the local and municipal law. If the people of a territory want slavery, they make friendly legislation to introduce it, but if they do not want it, they withhold all protection from it, and then it cannot exist there. Such was the view taken on the subject by different Southern men when the Nebraska bill passed. See the speech of Mr. Orr, of South Carolina, the present Speaker of the House of Representatives of Congress made at that time, and there you will find this whole doctrine argued out at full length. Read the speeches of other southern congressmen, Senators and Representatives, made in 1854, and

you will find that they took the same view of the subject as
Mr. Orr—that slavery could never be forced on a people who
did not want it. I hold that in this country there is no power
on the face of the globe that can force any institution on an
unwilling people. The great fundamental principle of our
government is that the people of each State and each territory
shall be left perfectly free to decide for themselves what shall
be the nature and character of their institutions. When this
government was made, it was based on that principle. At the
time of its formation there were twelve slaveholding States
and one free State in this Union. Suppose this doctrine of Mr.
Lincoln and the Republicans, of uniformity of the laws of all
the States on the subject of slavery, had prevailed; suppose
Mr. Lincoln himself had been a member of the convention
which framed the constitution, and that he had risen in that
august body, and addressing the father of his country, had
said as he did at Springfield:

> A house divided against itself cannot stand. I believe this government
> cannot endure permanently half slave and half free. I do not expect the
> Union to be dissolved—I do not expect the house to fall, but I do ex-
> pect it will cease to be divided. It will become all one thing or all one
> other.

What do you think would have been the result? (Hurrah for
Douglas.) Suppose he had made that convention believe that
doctrine and they had acted upon it, what do you think
would have been the result? Do you believe that the one free
State would have outvoted the twelve slaveholding States,
and thus abolished slavery? (No! no! and cheers.) On the contrary, would not the twelve slaveholding States have outvoted
the one free State, and under his doctrine have fastened
slavery by an irrevocable constitutional provision upon every
inch of the American Republic? Thus you see that the doctrine he now advocates, if proclaimed at the beginning of
the government, would have established slavery everywhere
throughout the American continent, and are you willing, now
that we have the majority section, to exercise a power which
we never would have submitted to when we were in the minority? ("No, no," and great applause.) If the Southern States
had attempted to control our institutions, and make the

States all slave when they had the power, I ask would you have submitted to it? If you would not, are you willing now that we have become the strongest under that great principle of self-government that allows each State to do as it pleases— to attempt to control the Southern institutions? ("No, no.") Then, my friends, I say to you that there is but one path of peace in this republic, and that is to administer this government as our fathers made it, divided into free and slave States, allowing each State to decide for itself whether it wants slavery or not. If Illinois will settle the slavery question for herself, mind her own business and let her neighbors alone, we will be at peace with Kentucky, and every other Southern State. If every other State in the Union will do the same there will be peace between the North and the South, and in the whole Union.

I am told that my time has expired. (Nine cheers for Douglas.)

MR. LINCOLN'S REPLY.

Mr. Lincoln was received as he came forward with three enthusiastic cheers, coming from every part of the vast assembly. After silence was restored, Mr. Lincoln said:

MY FELLOW CITIZENS—A very large portion of the speech which Judge Douglas has addressed to you has previously been delivered and put in print. [Laughter.] I do not mean that for a hit upon the Judge at all. [Renewed laughter.] If I had not been interrupted, I was going to say that such an answer as I was able to make to a very large portion of it, had already been more than once made and published. There has been an opportunity afforded to the public to see our respective views upon the topics discussed in a large portion of the speech which he has just delivered. I make these remarks for the purpose of excusing myself for not passing over the entire ground that the Judge has traversed. I however desire to take up some of the points that he has attended to, and ask your attention to them, and I shall follow him backwards upon some notes which I have taken, reversing the order by beginning where he concluded.

The Judge has alluded to the Declaration of Independence, and insisted that negroes are not included in that Declaration; and that it is a slander upon the framers of that instrument, to suppose that negroes were meant therein; and he asks you: Is it possible to believe that Mr. Jefferson, who penned the immortal paper, could have supposed himself applying the language of that instrument to the negro race, and yet held a portion of that race in slavery? Would he not at once have freed them? I only have to remark upon this part of the Judge's speech, (and that, too, very briefly, for I shall not detain myself, or you, upon that point for any great length of time,) that I believe the entire records of the world, from the date of the Declaration of Independence up to within three years ago, may be searched in vain for one single affirmation, from one single man, that the negro was not included in the Declaration of Independence. I think I may defy Judge Douglas to show that he ever said so, that Washington ever said so, that any President ever said so, that any member of Congress ever said so, or that any living man upon the whole earth ever said so, until the necessities of the present policy of the Democratic party, in regard to slavery, had to invent that affirmation. [Tremendous applause.] And I will remind Judge Douglas and this audience, that while Mr. Jefferson was the owner of slaves, as undoubtedly he was, in speaking upon this very subject, he used the strong language that "he trembled for his country when he remembered that God was just;" and I will offer the highest premium in my power to Judge Douglas if he will show that he, in all his life, ever uttered a sentiment at all akin to that of Jefferson. [Great applause and cries of "Hit him again," "good," "good."]

The next thing to which I will ask your attention is the Judge's comments upon the fact, as he assumes it to be, that we cannot call our public meetings as Republican meetings; and he instances Tazewell county as one of the places where the friends of Lincoln have called a public meeting and have not dared to name it a Republican meeting. He instances Monroe county as another where Judge Trumbull and Jehu Baker addressed the persons whom the Judge assumes to be the friends of Lincoln, calling them the "Free Democracy." I have the honor to inform Judge Douglas that he spoke in that very county of Tazewell last Saturday, and I was there on Tuesday last, and when he spoke there he spoke under a call not venturing to use the word "Democrat." [Cheers and laughter.] (Turning to Judge Douglas.) What do you think of this? [Immense applause and roars of laughter.]

So again, there is another thing to which I would ask the Judge's attention upon this subject. In the contest of 1856 his party delighted to call themselves together as the "National Democracy," but now, if there should be a notice put up anywhere for a meeting of the "National Democracy," Judge Douglas and his friends would not come. [Laughter.] They would not suppose themselves invited. [Renewed laughter and cheers.] They would understand that it was a call for those hateful Postmasters whom he talks about. [Uproarious laughter.]

Now a few words in regard to these extracts from speeches of mine, which Judge Douglas has read to you, and which he supposes are in very great contrast to each other. Those speeches have been before the public for a considerable time, and if they have any inconsistency in them, if there is any conflict in them the public have been able to detect it. When the Judge says, in speaking on this subject, that I make speeches of one sort for the people of the Northern end of the State, and of a different sort for the Southern people, he assumes that I do not understand that my speeches will be put in print and read North and South. I knew all the while that the speech that I made at Chicago and the one I made at Jonesboro and the one at Charleston, would all be put in print and all the reading and intelligent men in the community would see them and know all about my opinions. And I have not supposed, and do not now suppose, that there is any conflict whatever between them. ["They are all good speeches!" "Hurrah for Lincoln!"] But the Judge will have it that if we do not confess that there is a sort of inequality between the white and black races, which justifies us in making them slaves, we must, then, insist that there is a degree of equality that requires us to make them our wives. [Loud applause, and cries, "Give it to him;" "Hit him again."] Now, I have all the while taken a broad distinction in regard to that matter; and that is all there is in these different speeches which he arrays here, and the entire reading of either of the speeches will show that that distinction was made. Perhaps by taking two parts of the same speech, he could have got up as much of a conflict as the one he has found. I have all the while maintained, that in so far as it should be insisted that there was an equality between the white and black races that should produce a perfect social and political equality, it was an impossibility. This you have seen in my printed speeches, and with it I have said, that in their right to "life, liberty and the pursuit of happiness," as proclaimed in that old Declaration, the inferior races are our equals. [Long-continued cheering.] And these declarations I have constantly made in reference to the abstract moral question, to contemplate and consider when we are legislating about any new country which is not already cursed with the actual presence of the evil—slavery. I have never manifested any impatience with the necessities that spring from the actual presence of black people amongst us, and the actual existence of slavery amongst us where it does already exist; but I have insisted that, in legislating for new countries, where it does not exist, there is no just rule other than that of moral and abstract right! With reference to those new countries, those maxims as to the right of a people to "life, liberty and the pursuit of happiness," were the just rules to be constantly referred to. There is no misunderstanding this, except by men interested to misunderstand it. [Applause.] I take it that I have to address an intelligent and reading community, who will peruse what I say, weigh it, and then judge whether I advance improper or unsound views, or whether I advance hypocritical, and deceptive, and contrary views in different portions of the country. I believe myself to be guilty of no such thing as the latter, though, of course, I cannot claim that I am entirely free from all error in the opinions I advance.

The Judge has also detained us a while in regard to the distinction between his party and our party. His he assumes to be a national party—ours, a sectional one. He does this in asking the question whether this country has any interest in the maintenance of the Republican party? He assumes that our party is altogether sectional—that the party to which he adheres is national; and the argument is, that no party can be a rightful party—can be based upon rightful principles—unless it can announce its principles everywhere. I presume that Judge Douglas could not go into Russia and announce the doctrine of our national democracy; he could not denounce the doctrine of kings, and emperors, and monarchies, in Russia; and it may be true of this country, that in some places we may not be able to proclaim a doctrine as clearly true as the truth of democracy, because there is a section so directly opposed to it that they will not tolerate us in doing so. Is it the true test of the soundness of a doctrine, that in some places people won't let you proclaim it? [No, no, no.] Is that the way to test the truth of any doctrine? [No, no, no.] Why, I understood that at one time the people of Chicago would not let Judge Douglas preach a certain favorite doctrine of his. [Laughter and cheers.] I commend to his consideration the question, whether he takes that as a test of the unsoundness of what he wanted to preach. [Loud cheers.]

There is another thing to which I wish to ask attention for a little while on this occasion. What has always been the evidence brought forward to prove that the Republican party is a sectional party? The main one was that in the southern portion of the Union the people did not let the Republicans proclaim their doctrine amongst them. That has been the main evidence brought forward—that they had no supporters, or substantially none, in the Slave States. The South have not taken hold of our principles as we announce them; nor does Judge Douglas now grapple with those principles. We have a Republican State Platform, laid down in Springfield in June last, stating our position all the way through the questions before the country. We are now far advanced in this canvass. Judge Douglas and I have made perhaps forty speeches apiece, and we have now for the fifth time met face to face in debate, and up to this day I have not found either Judge Douglas or any friend of his taking hold of the Republican platform or laying his finger upon anything in it that is wrong. [Cheers.] I ask you all to recollect that. Judge Douglas turns away from the platform of principles to the fact that he can find people somewhere who will not allow us to announce those principles. [Applause.] If he had great confidence that our principles were wrong, he would take hold of them and demonstrate them to be wrong. But he does not do so. The only evidence he has of their being wrong is in the fact that there are people who won't allow us to preach them. I ask again, is that the way to test the soundness of a doctrine? [Cries of "No," "No."]

I ask his attention also to the fact that by the rule of nationality he is himself fast becoming sectional. [Great cheers and laughter.] I ask his attention to the fact that his speeches would not go as current now south of the Ohio River as they have formerly gone there. [Loud cheers.] I ask his attention to the fact that he felicitates himself to-day that all the Democrats of the Free States are agreeing with him, [applause,] while he omits to tell us that the Democrats of any Slave State agree with him. If he has not thought of this, I commend to his consideration the evidence in his own declaration, on this day, of his becoming sectional too. [Immense cheering.] I see it rapidly approaching. Whatever may be the result of this ephemeral contest between Judge Douglas and myself, I see the day rapidly approaching when his pill of sectionalism, which he has been thrusting down the throats of Republicans for years past, will be crowded down his own throat. [Tremendous applause.]

Now in regard to what Judge Douglas said (in the beginning of his speech) about the Compromise of 1850, containing the principle of the Nebraska bill, although I have often presented my views upon that subject, yet as I have not done so in this canvass, I will, if you please, detain you a little with them. I have always maintained, so far as I was able, that there was nothing of the principle of the Nebraska bill in the compromise of 1850 at all—nothing whatever. Where can you find the principle of the Nebraska bill in that compromise? If anywhere, in the two pieces of the compromise organizing the Territories of New Mexico and Utah. It was expressly provided in these two acts, that, when they came to be admitted into the Union, they should be admitted with or without slavery, as they should choose, by their own constitutions. Nothing was said in either of those acts as to what was to be done in relation to slavery during the territorial existence of

those territories, while Henry Clay constantly made the declaration, (Judge Douglas recognizing him as a leader) that, in
his opinion, the old Mexican laws would control that question during the territorial existence, and that these old Mexican laws excluded slavery. How can that be used as a principle
for declaring that during the territorial existence as well as at
the time of framing the constitution, the people, if you please,
might have slaves if they wanted them? I am not discussing
the question whether it is right or wrong; but how are the
New Mexican and Utah laws patterns for the Nebraska bill? I
maintain that the organization of Utah and New Mexico *did
not* establish a general principle at all. It had no feature of
establishing a general principle. The acts to which I have referred were a part of a general system of Compromises. They
did not lay down what was proposed as a regular policy for
the Territories; only an agreement in this particular case to do
in that way, because other things were done that were to be a
compensation for it. They were allowed to come in in that
shape, because in another way it was paid for—considering
that as a part of that system of measures called the Compromise of 1850, which finally included half a dozen acts. It included the admission of California as a free State, which was
kept out of the Union for half a year because it had formed a
free Constitution. It included the settlement of the boundary
of Texas, which had been undefined before, which was in itself a slavery question; for, if you pushed the line farther west,
you made Texas larger, and made more slave territory; while,
if you drew the line towards the east, you narrowed the
boundary and diminished the domain of slavery, and by so
much increased free territory. It included the abolition of the
slave trade in the District of Columbia. It included the passage of a new Fugitive Slave Law. All these things were put
together, and though passed in separate acts, were nevertheless in legislation, (as the speeches at the time will show,)
made to depend upon each other. Each got votes, with the
understanding that the other measures were to pass, and by
this system of compromise, in that series of measures, those
two bills—the New Mexico and Utah bills—were passed;
and I say for that reason they could not be taken as models,
framed upon their own intrinsic principle, for all future Terri-

tories. And I have the evidence of this in the fact that Judge Douglas, a year afterwards, or more than a year afterwards, perhaps, when he first introduced bills for the purpose of framing new Territories, did not attempt to follow these bills of New Mexico and Utah; and even when he introduced this Nebraska bill, I think you will discover that he did not exactly follow them. But I do not wish to dwell at great length upon this branch of the discussion. My own opinion is, that a thorough investigation will show most plainly that the New Mexico and Utah bills were part of a system of compromise, and not designed as patterns for future territorial legislation; and that this Nebraska bill did not follow them as a pattern at all.

The Judge tells, in proceeding, that he is opposed to making any odious distinctions between Free and Slave States. I am altogether unaware that the Republicans are in favor of making any odious distinctions between the Free and Slave States. But there still is a difference, I think, between Judge Douglas and the Republicans in this. I suppose that the real difference between Judge Douglas and his friends, and the Republicans on the contrary, is that the Judge is not in favor of making any difference between Slavery and Liberty—that he is in favor of eradicating, of pressing out of view, the questions of preference in this country for Free over Slave institutions; and consequently every sentiment he utters discards the idea that there is any wrong in Slavery. Everything that emanates from him or his coadjutors in their course of policy, carefully excludes the thought that there is anything wrong in Slavery. All their arguments, if you will consider them, will be seen to exclude the thought that there is anything whatever wrong in Slavery. If you will take the Judge's speeches, and select the short and pointed sentences expressed by him—as his declaration that he "don't care whether Slavery is voted up or down"—you will see at once that this is perfectly logical, if you do not admit that Slavery is wrong. If you do admit that it is wrong, Judge Douglas cannot logically say that he don't care whether a wrong is voted up or voted down. Judge Douglas declares that if any community want Slavery they have a right to have it. He can say that logically, if he says that there is no wrong in Slavery; but if you admit that there is a wrong in it, he cannot logically say that anybody has a right to do wrong. He insists that, upon the score of equality, the owners of slaves and owners of property—of horses and every other sort of property—should be alike and hold them alike in a new Territory. That is perfectly logical, if the two species of property are alike and are equally founded in right. But if you admit that one of them is wrong, you cannot institute any equality between right and wrong. And from this difference of sentiment—the belief on the part of one that the institution is wrong, and a policy springing from that belief which looks to the arrest of the enlargement of that wrong; and this other sentiment, that it is no wrong, and a policy sprung from that sentiment which will tolerate no idea of preventing that wrong from growing larger, and looks to there never being an end of it through all the existence of things,—arises the real difference between Judge Douglas and his friends, on the one hand, and the Republicans on the other. Now, I confess myself as belonging to that class in the country who contemplate slavery as a moral, social and political evil, having due regard for its actual existence amongst us and the difficulties of getting rid of it in any satisfactory way, and to all the constitutional obligations which have been thrown about it; but, nevertheless, desire a policy that looks to the prevention of it as a wrong, and looks hopefully to the time when as a wrong it may come to an end. [Great applause.]

Judge Douglas has again, for, I believe, the fifth time, if not the seventh, in my presence, reiterated his charge of a conspiracy or combination between the National Democrats and Republicans. What evidence Judge Douglas has upon this subject I know not, inasmuch as he never favors us with any. [Laughter and cheers.] I have said upon a former occasion, and I do not choose to suppress it now, that I have no objection to the division in the Judge's party. [Cheers.] He got it up himself. It was all his and their work. He had, I think, a great deal more to do with the steps that led to the Lecompton Constitution than Mr. Buchanan had [applause]; though at last, when they reached it, they quarrelled over it, and their friends divided upon it. [Applause.] I am very free to confess to Judge Douglas that I have no objection to the division, [loud applause and laughter]; but I defy the Judge to show any evidence that I have in any way promoted that division, unless he insists on being a witness himself in merely saying so. [Laughter.] I can give all fair friends of Judge Douglas here to understand exactly the view that Republicans take in regard to that division. Don't you remember how two years ago the opponents of the Democratic party were divided between Fremont and Fillmore? I guess you do. ["Yes, sir, we remember it mighty well."] Any Democrat who remembers that division, will remember also that he was at the time very glad of it, [laughter,] and then he will be able to see all there is between the National Democrats and the Republicans. What we now think of the two divisions of Democrats, you then thought of the Fremont and Fillmore divisions. [Great cheers.] That is all there is of it.

But, if the Judge continues to put forward the declaration that there is an unholy and unnatural alliance between the Republicans and the National Democrats, I now want to enter my protest against receiving him as an entirely competent witness upon that subject. [Loud cheers.] I want to call to the Judge's attention an attack he made upon me in the first one of these debates, at Ottawa, on the 21st of August. In order to fix extreme Abolitionism upon me, Judge Douglas read a set of resolutions which he declared had been passed by a Republican State Convention, in Oct., 1854, at Springfield, Illinois, and he declared I had taken part in that Convention. It turned out that although a few men calling themselves an Anti-Nebraska State Convention had sat at Springfield about that time, yet neither did I take any part in it, nor did it pass the resolutions or any such resolutions as Judge Douglas read. [Great applause.] So apparent had it become that the resolutions which he read had not been passed at Springfield at all, nor by a State Convention in which I had taken part, that seven days afterwards, at Freeport, Judge Douglas declared that he had been misled by Charles H. Lanphier, editor of the *State Register*, and Thomas L. Harris, member of Congress in that District, and he promised in that speech that when he went to Springfield he would investigate the matter. Since then Judge Douglas has been to Springfield, and I presume has made the investigation; but a month has passed since he has been there, and so far as I know, he has made no report of the result of his investigation. [Great applause.] I have waited as I think sufficient time for the report of that investigation, and I have some curiosity to see and hear it. [Applause.] A fraud—an absolute forgery was committed, and the perpetration of it was traced to the three—Lanphier, Harris and Douglas. [Applause and laughter.] Whether it can be narrowed in any way so as to exonerate any one of them, is what Judge Douglas' report would probably show. [Applause and laughter.]

It is true that the set of resolutions read by Judge Douglas were published in the Illinois *State Register* on the 16th Oct., 1854, as being the resolutions of an Anti-Nebraska Convention, which had sat in that same month of October, at Springfield. But it is also true that the publication in the *Register* was a forgery then, [cheers], and the question is still behind, which of the three, if not all of them, committed that forgery? [Great applause.] The idea that it was done by mistake, is absurd. The article in the Illinois *State Register* contains part of the real proceedings of that Springfield Convention, showing that the writer of the article had the real proceedings before him, and purposely threw out the genuine resolutions passed by the Convention, and fraudulently substituted the others. Lanphier then, as now, was the editor of the *Register*, so that there seems to be but little room for his escape. But then it is to be borne in mind that Lanphier had less interest in the object of that forgery than either of the other two. [Cheers.] The main object of that forgery at that time was to beat Yates and elect Harris to Congress, and that object was known to be exceedingly dear to Judge Douglas at that time. [Laughter.] Harris and Douglas were both in Springfield when the Convention was in session, and although they both left before the fraud appeared in the *Register*, subsequent events show that they have both had their eyes fixed upon that Convention.

The fraud having been apparently successful upon the occasion, both Harris and Douglas have more than once since then been attempting to put it to new uses. As the fisherman's wife, whose drowned husband was brought home with his body full of eels, said when she was asked, "What was to be done with him?" *"Take the eels out and set him again."* [great laughter;] so Harris and Douglas have shown a disposition to

take the eels out of that stale fraud by which they gained
Harris' election, and set the fraud again more than once. [Tre-
mendous cheering and laughter.] On the 9th of July, 1856,
Douglas attempted a repetition of it upon Trumbull on the
floor of the Senate of the United States, as will appear from
the appendix of the *Congressional Globe* of that date.

On the 9th of August Harris attempted it again upon
Norton in the House of Representatives, as will appear by the
same documents—the appendix to the *Congressional Globe* of
that date. On the 21st of August last all three—Lanphier,
Douglas and Harris—re-attempted it upon me at Ottawa.
[Tremendous applause.] It has been clung to and played out
again and again as an exceedingly high trump by this blessed
trio. [Roars of laughter and tumultuous applause, "Give it to
him," &c.] And now that it has been discovered publicly to be
a fraud, we find that Judge Douglas manifests no surprise at it
at all. [Laughter, "That's it," "Hit him again."] He makes no
complaint of Lanphier who must have known it to be a fraud
from the beginning. He, Lanphier and Harris are just as cozy
now, and just as active in the concoction of new schemes as
they were before the general discovery of this fraud. Now all
this is very natural if they are all alike guilty in that fraud,
[laughter and cheers,] and it is very unnatural if any one of
them is innocent. [Great laughter, "Hit him again," "Hurrah
for Lincoln."] Lanphier perhaps insists that the rule of honor
among thieves does not quite require him to take all upon
himself, [laughter,] and consequently my friend Judge Douglas finds it difficult to make a satisfactory report upon his
investigation. [Laughter and applause.] But meanwhile the
three are agreed that each is *"a most honorable man."* [Cheers
and explosions of laughter.]

Judge Douglas requires an indorsement of his truth and
honor by a re-election to the United States Senate, and he
makes and reports against me and against Judge Trumbull
day after day charges which we know to be utterly untrue,
without for a moment seeming to think that this one unexplained fraud, which he promised to investigate, will be the
least drawback to his claim to belief. Harris ditto. He asks a
re-election to the lower House of Congress without seeming
to remember at all that he is involved in this dishonorable

fraud! The Illinois *State Register*, edited by Lanphier, then, as now, the central organ of both Harris and Douglas, continues to din the public ear with this assertion without seeming to suspect that these assertions are at all lacking in title to belief.

After all, the question still recurs upon us, how did that fraud originally get into the *State Register?* Lanphier then as now was the editor of that paper. Lanphier knows. Lanphier cannot be ignorant of how and by whom it was originally concocted. Can he be induced to tell, or if he has told, can Judge Douglas be induced to tell how it originally was concocted? It may be true that Lanphier insists that the two men for whose benefit it was originally devised, shall at least bear their share of it! How that is, I do not know, and while it remains unexplained I hope to be pardoned if I insist that the mere fact of Judge Douglas making charges against Trumbull and myself is not quite sufficient evidence to establish them! [Great cheering. "Hit him again." "Give it to him," &c.]

While we were at Freeport, in one of these joint discussions, I answered certain interrogatories which Judge Douglas had propounded to me, and there in turn propounded some to him, which he in a sort of way answered. The third one of these interrogatories I have with me and wish now to make some comments upon it. It was in these words: "If the Supreme Court of the United States shall decide that the States cannot exclude slavery from their limits, are you in favor of acquiescing in, adhering to and following such decision, as a rule of political action?"

To this interrogatory Judge Douglas made no answer in any just sense of the word. He contented himself with sneering at the thought that it was possible for the Supreme Court ever to make such a decision. He sneered at me for propounding the interrogatory. I had not propounded it without some reflection, and I wish now to address to this audience some remarks upon it.

In the second clause of the sixth article, I believe it is of the Constitution of the United States, we find the following language: "This Constitution and the laws of the United States which shall be made in pursuance thereof; and all treaties made or which shall be made under the authority of the

United States, shall be the supreme law of the land; and the judges in every State shall be bound thereby anything in the Constitution or laws of any State to the contrary notwithstanding."

The essence of the Dred Scott case is compressed into the sentence which I will now read: "Now, as we have already said in an earlier part of this opinion, upon a different point, the right of property in a slave is distinctly and expressly affirmed in the Constitution." I repeat it, *"The right of property in a slave is distinctly and expressly affirmed in the Constitution!"* What is it to be *"affirmed"* in the Constitution? Made firm in the Constitution—so made that it cannot be separated from the Constitution without breaking the Constitution—durable as the Constitution, and part of the Constitution. Now, remembering the provision of the Constitution which I have read, affirming that that instrument is the supreme law of the land; that the Judges of every State shall be bound by it, any law or Constitution of any State to the contrary notwithstanding; that the right of property in a slave is affirmed in that Constitution, is made, formed into and cannot be separated from it without breaking it; durable as the instrument; part of the instrument;—what follows as a short and even syllogistic argument from it? I think it follows, and I submit to the consideration of men capable of arguing, whether as I state it in syllogistic form the argument has any fault in it:

Nothing in the Constitution or laws of any State can destroy a right distinctly and expressly affirmed in the Constitution of the United States.

The right of property in a slave is distinctly and expressly affirmed in the Constitution of the United States;

Therefore, nothing in the Constitution or laws of any State can destroy the right of property in a slave.

I believe that no fault can be pointed out in that argument; assuming the truth of the premises, the conclusion, so far as I have capacity at all to understand it, follows inevitably. There is a fault in it as I think, but the fault is not in the reasoning; but the falsehood in fact is a fault of the premises. I believe that the right of property in a slave *is not* distinctly and expressly affirmed in the Constitution, and Judge Douglas thinks it *is*. I believe that the Supreme Court and the advocates of that decision may search in vain for the place in the Constitution where the right of property in a slave is distinctly and expressly affirmed. I say, therefore, that I think one of the premises is not true in fact. But it is true with Judge Douglas. It is true with the Supreme Court who pronounced it. They are estopped from denying it, and being estopped from denying it, the conclusion follows that the Constitution of the United States being the supreme law, no constitution or law can interfere with it. It being affirmed in the decision that the right of property in a slave is distinctly and expressly affirmed in the Constitution, the conclusion inevitably follows that no State law or constitution can destroy that right. I then say to Judge Douglas and to all others, that I think it will take a better answer than a sneer to show that those who have said that the right of property in a slave is distinctly and expressly affirmed in the Constitution, are not prepared to show that no constitution or law can destroy that right. I say I believe it will take a far better argument than a mere sneer to show to the minds of intelligent men that whoever has so said, is not prepared, whenever public sentiment is so far advanced as to justify it, to say the other. ["That's so."] This is but an opinion, and the opinion of one very humble man; but it is my opinion that the Dred Scott decision, as it is, never would have been made in its present form if the party that made it had not been sustained previously by the elections. My own opinion is, that the new Dred Scott decision, deciding against the right of the people of the States to exclude slavery, will never be made, if that party is not sustained by the elections. [Cries of "Yes, yes."] I believe, further, that it is just as sure to be made as to-morrow is to come, if that party shall be sustained. ["We won't sustain it, never, never."] I have said, upon a former occasion, and I repeat it now, that the course of argument that Judge Douglas makes use of upon this subject, (I charge not his motives in this), is preparing the public mind for that new Dred Scott decision. I have asked him again to point out to me the reasons for his firm adherence to the Dred Scott decision as it is. I have turned his attention to the fact that General Jackson differed with him in regard to the political obligation of a Supreme Court decision. I have asked his attention to the fact

that Jefferson differed with him in regard to the political obligation of a Supreme Court decision. Jefferson said, that
"Judges are as honest as other men, and not more so." And he
said, substantially, that "whenever a free people should give
up in absolute submission to any department of government,
retaining for themselves no appeal from it, their liberties were
gone." I have asked his attention to the fact that the Cincinnati platform, upon which he says he stands, disregards a
time-honored decision of the Supreme Court, in denying the
power of Congress to establish a National Bank. I have asked
his attention to the fact that he himself was one of the most
active instruments at one time in breaking down the Supreme
Court of the State of Illinois, because it had made a decision
distasteful to him—a struggle ending in the remarkable circumstance of his sitting down as one of the new Judges who
were to overslaugh that decision—[loud applause]—getting
his title of Judge in that very way. [Tremendous applause and
laughter.]

So far in this controversy I can get no answer at all from
Judge Douglas upon these subjects. Not one can I get from
him, except that he swells himself up and says, "All of us who
stand by the decision of the Supreme Court are the friends of
the Constitution; all you fellows that dare question it in any
way, are the enemies of the Constitution." [Continued laughter and cheers.] Now, in this very devoted adherence to this
decision, in opposition to all the great political leaders whom
he has recognized as leaders—in opposition to his former self
and history, there is something very marked. And the manner
in which he adheres to it—not as being right upon the merits, as he conceives (because he did not discuss that at all), but
as being absolutely obligatory upon every one simply because
of the source from whence it comes—as that which no man
can gainsay, whatever it may be,—this is another marked feature of his adherence to that decision. It marks it in this respect, that it commits him to the next decision, whenever it
comes, as being as obligatory as this one, since he does not
investigate it, and won't inquire whether this opinion is right
or wrong. So he takes the next one without inquiring
whether *it* is right or wrong. [Applause.] He teaches men this
doctrine, and in so doing prepares the public mind to take the

next decision when it comes, without any inquiry. In this I think I argue fairly (without questioning motives at all) that Judge Douglas is most ingeniously and powerfully preparing the public mind to take that decision when it comes; and not only so, but he is doing it in various other ways. In these general maxims about liberty—in his assertions that he "don't care whether Slavery is voted up or voted down;" that "whoever wants Slavery has a right to have it;" that "upon principles of equality it should be allowed to go everywhere;" that "there is no inconsistency between free and slave institutions." In this he is also preparing (whether purposely or not), the way for making the institution of Slavery national! [Cries of "Yes," "Yes," "That's so."] I repeat again, for I wish no misunderstanding, that I do not charge that he means it so; but I call upon your minds to inquire, if you were going to get the best instrument you could, and then set it to work in the most ingenious way, to prepare the public mind for this movement, operating in the free States, where there is now an abhorrence of the institution of Slavery, could you find an instrument so capable of doing it as Judge Douglas? or one employed in so apt a way to do it? [Great cheering. Cries of "Hit him again," "That's the doctrine."]

I have said once before, and I will repeat it now, that Mr. Clay, when he was once answering an objection to the Colonization Society, that it had a tendency to the ultimate emancipation of the slaves, said that "those who would repress all tendencies to liberty and ultimate emancipation must do more than put down the benevolent efforts of the Colonization Society—they must go back to the era of our liberty and independence, and muzzle the cannon that thunders its annual joyous return—they must blot out the moral lights around us—they must penetrate the human soul, and eradicate the light of reason and the love of liberty!" And I do think—I repeat, though I said it on a former occasion—that Judge Douglas, and whoever like him teaches that the negro has no share, humble though it may be, in the Declaration of Independence, is going back to the era of our liberty and independence, and, so far as in him lies, muzzling the cannon that thunders its annual joyous return; ["That's so."] that he is blowing out the moral lights around us, when he contends that whoever wants slaves has a right to hold them; that he is penetrating, so far as lies in his power, the human soul, and eradicating the light of reason and the love of liberty, when he is in every possible way preparing the public mind, by his vast influence, for making the institution of slavery perpetual and national. [Great applause, and cries of "Hurrah for Lincoln," "That's the true doctrine."]

There is, my friends, only one other point to which I will call your attention for the remaining time that I have left me, and perhaps I shall not occupy the entire time that I have, as that one point may not take me clear through it.

Among the interrogatories that Judge Douglas propounded to me at Freeport, there was one in about this language: "Are you opposed to the acquisition of any further territory to the United States, unless slavery shall first be prohibited therein?" I answered as I thought, in this way, that I am not generally opposed to the acquisition of additional territory, and that I would support a proposition for the acquisition of additional territory, according as my supporting it was or was not calculated to aggravate this slavery question amongst us. I then proposed to Judge Douglas another interrogatory, which was correlative to that: "Are you in favor of acquiring additional territory in disregard of how it may affect us upon the slavery question?" Judge Douglas answered, that is, in his own way he answered it. [Laughter.] I believe that, although he took a good many words to answer it, it was a little more fully answered than any other. The substance of his answer was, that this country would continue to expand—that it would need additional territory—that it was as absurd to suppose that we could continue upon our present territory, enlarging in population as we are, as it would be to hoop a boy twelve years of age, and expect him to grow to man's size without bursting the hoops. [Laughter.] I believe it was something like that. Consequently he was in favor of the acquisition of further territory, as fast as we might need it, in disregard of how it might affect the slavery question. I do not say this as giving his exact language, but he said so substantially, and he would leave the question of slavery where the territory was acquired, to be settled by the people of the acquired territory. ["That's the doctrine."] May be it is; let us consider that for a while.

This will probably, in the run of things, become one of the concrete manifestations of this slavery question. If Judge Douglas' policy upon this question succeeds, and gets fairly settled down, until all opposition is crushed out, the next thing will be a grab for the territory of poor Mexico, an invasion of the rich lands of South America, then the adjoining islands will follow, each one of which promises additional slave fields. And this question is to be left to the people of those countries for settlement. When we shall get Mexico, I don't know whether the Judge will be in favor of the Mexican people that we get with it settling that question for themselves and all others; because we know the Judge has a great horror for mongrels, [laughter,] and I understand that the people of Mexico are most decidedly a race of mongrels. [Renewed laughter.] I understand that there is not more than one person there out of eight who is pure white, and I suppose from the Judge's previous declaration that when we get Mexico or any considerable portion of it, that he will be in favor of these mongrels settling the question, which would bring him somewhat into collision with his horror of an inferior race.

It is to be remembered, though, that this power of acquiring additional territory is a power confided to the President and Senate of the United States. It is a power not under the control of the Representatives of the people any further than they, the President and the Senate can be considered the representatives of the people. Let me illustrate that by a case we have in our history. When we acquired the territory from Mexico in the Mexican war, the House of Representatives, composed of the immediate representatives of the people all the time insisted that the territory thus to be acquired should be brought in upon condition that slavery should be forever prohibited therein, upon the terms and in the language that slavery had been prohibited from coming into this country. That was insisted upon constantly, and never failed to call forth an assurance that any territory thus acquired should have that prohibition in it, so far as the House of Representatives was concerned. But at last the President and Senate acquired the territory without asking the House of Representatives anything about it, and took it without that prohibition. They have the power of acquiring territory without the immediate representatives of the people being called upon to say anything about it, and thus furnishing a very apt and powerful means of bringing new territory into the Union, and when it is once brought into the country, involving us anew in this slavery agitation. It is, therefore, as I think, a very important question for the consideration of the American people, whether the policy of bringing in additional territory, without considering at all how it will operate upon the safety of the Union in reference to this one great disturbing element in our national politics, shall be adopted as the policy of the country. You will bear in mind that it is to be acquired, according to the Judge's view, as fast as it is needed, and the indefinite part of this proposition is that we have only Judge Douglas and his class of men to decide how fast it is needed. We have no clear and certain way of determining or demonstrating how fast territory is needed by the necessities of the country. Whoever wants to go out filibustering, then, thinks that more territory is needed. Whoever wants wider slave fields, feels sure that some additional territory is needed as slave territory. Then it is as easy to show the necessity of additional slave territory as it is to assert anything that is incapable of absolute demonstration. Whatever motive a man or a set of men may have for making annexation of property or territory, it is very easy to assert, but much less easy to disprove, that it is necessary for the wants of the country.

And now it only remains for me to say that I think it is a very grave question for the people of this Union to consider whether, in view of the fact that this Slavery question has been the only one that has ever endangered our republican institutions—the only one that has ever threatened or menaced a dissolution of the Union—that has ever disturbed us in such a way as to make us fear for the perpetuity of our liberty—in view of these facts, I think it is an exceedingly interesting and important question for this people to consider, whether we shall engage in the policy of acquiring additional territory, discarding altogether from our consideration, while obtaining new territory, the question how it may affect us in regard to this the only endangering element to our liberties and national greatness. The Judge's view has been expressed. I, in my answer to his question, have expressed mine. I think it will become an important and practical question. Our views are before the public. I am willing and anxious that they should consider them fully—that they should turn it about and consider the importance of the question, and arrive at a just conclusion as to whether it is or is not wise in the people of this Union, in the acquisition of new territory, to consider whether it will add to the disturbance that is existing amongst us—whether it will add to the one only danger that has ever threatened the perpetuity of the Union or our own liberties. I think it is extremely important that they shall decide, and rightly decide that question before entering upon that policy.

And now, my friends, having said the little I wish to say upon this head, whether I have occupied the whole of the remnant of my time or not, I believe I could not enter upon any new topic so as to treat it fully without transcending my time, which I would not for a moment think of doing. I give way to Judge Douglas.

Three tremendous cheers for Lincoln from the whole vast audience were given with great enthusiasm, as their favorite retired.

MR. DOUGLAS' REPLY.

When Senator Douglas rose to reply to Mr. Lincoln, six cheers were called for in the crowd, and given with great spirit. He said, quieting the applause:

Gentlemen—The highest compliment you can pay me during the brief half hour that I have to conclude is by observing a strict silence. I desire to be heard rather than to be applauded. (Good.)

The first criticism that Mr. Lincoln makes on my speech was that it was in substance what I have said everywhere else in the State where I have addressed the people. I wish I could say the same of his speech. (Good; you have him, and applause.) Why, the reason I complain of him is because he makes one speech north and another south. (That's so.) Because he has one set of sentiments for the abolition counties and another set for the counties opposed to abolitionism. (Hit him over the knuckles.) My point of complaint against him is that I cannot induce him to hold up the same standard, to carry the same flag in all parts of the State. He does not pretend, and no other man will, that I have one set of principles for Galesburg and another for Charleston. (No, no.) He does not pretend that I hold to one doctrine in Chicago and to an opposite one in Jonesboro. I have proved that he has a different set of principles for each of these localities. All I asked of him was that he should deliver the speech that he has made here to-day in Coles county instead of in old Knox. It would have settled the question between us in that doubtful county. Here I understand him to reaffirm the doctrine of negro equality, and to assert that by the Declaration of Independence the negro is declared equal to the white man. He tells you to-day that the negro was included in the Declaration of Independence when it asserted that all men were created equal. ("We believe it.") Very well. (Here an uproar arose, persons in various parts of the crowd indulging in cat calls, groans, cheers, and other noises, preventing the speaker from proceeding.)

MR. DOUGLAS—Gentlemen, I ask you to remember that Mr. Lincoln was listened to respectfully, and I have the right to insist that I shall not be interrupted during my reply.

MR. LINCOLN—I hope that silence will be preserved.

MR. DOUGLAS—Mr. Lincoln asserts to-day as he did at Chicago, that the negro was included in that clause of the Declaration of Independence which says that all men were created equal and endowed by the Creator with certain inalienable rights, among which are life, liberty and the pursuit of happiness. (Ain't that so?) If the negro was made his equal and mine, if that equality was established by Divine law, and was the negro's inalienable right, how came he to say at Charleston to the Kentuckians residing in that section of our State, that the negro was physically inferior to the white man, belonged to an inferior race, and he was for keeping him always in that inferior condition? (Good.) I wish you to bear these things in mind. At Charleston he said that the negro belonged to an inferior race, and that he was for keeping him in that inferior condition. There he gave the people to understand that there was no moral question involved, because the inferiority being established, it was only a question of degree and not a question of right; here, to-day, instead of making it a question of degree, he makes it a moral question, says that it is a great crime to hold the negro in that inferior condition. (He's right.) Is he right now or was he right in Charleston? (Both.) He is right then, sir, in your estimation, not because he is consistent, but because he can trim his principles any way in any section, so as to secure votes. All I desire of him is that he will declare the same principles in the South that he does in the North.

But did you notice how he answered my position that a man should hold the same doctrines throughout the length and breadth of this republic? He said, "Would Judge Douglas go to Russia and proclaim the same principles he does here?" I would remind him that Russia is not under the American constitution. ("Good," and laughter.) If Russia was a part of the American republic, under our federal constitution, and I was sworn to support that constitution, I would maintain the same doctrine in Russia that I do in Illinois. (Cheers.) The slaveholding States are governed by the same federal constitution as ourselves, and hence a man's principles, in order to be in harmony with the constitution, must be the same in the South as they are in the North, the same in the free States as they are in the slave States. Whenever a man advocates one set of principles in one section, and another set in another section, his opinions are in violation of the spirit of the constitution which he has sworn to support. ("That's so.") When Mr. Lincoln went to Congress in 1847, and laying his hand upon the holy evangelists, made a solemn vow in the presence of high Heaven that he would be faithful to the constitution,— what did he mean? the constitution as he expounds it in Galesburg, or the constitution as he expounds it in Charleston? (Cheers.)

Mr. Lincoln has devoted considerable time to the circumstance that at Ottawa I read a series of resolutions as having been adopted at Springfield, in this State, on the 4th or 5th of October, 1854, which happened not to have been adopted there. He has used hard names; has dared to talk about fraud, (laughter), about forgery, and has insinuated that there was a conspiracy between Mr. Lanphier, Mr. Harris, and myself to perpetrate a forgery. (Renewed laughter.) Now, bear in mind that he does not deny that these resolutions were adopted in a majority of all the Republican counties of this State in that year; he does not deny that they were declared to be the platform of this Republican party in the first Congressional district, in the second, in the third, and in many counties of the fourth, and that they thus became the platform of his party in a majority of the counties upon which he now relies for support; he does not deny the truthfulness of the resolutions, but takes exception to the *spot* on which they were adopted. He takes to himself great merit because he thinks they were not adopted on the right spot for me to use them against him, just as he was very severe in Congress upon the government of his country when he thought that he had discovered that the Mexican war was not begun in the right *spot*, and was therefore unjust. (Renewed laughter.) He tries very hard to make out that there is something very extraordinary in the place where the thing was done, and not in the thing itself. I never believed before that Abraham Lincoln would be guilty of what he has done this day in regard to those resolutions. In the first place, the moment it was intimated to me that they had been adopted at Aurora and Rockford instead of Springfield, I did not wait for him to call my attention to the fact, but led off and explained in my first meeting after the Ottawa debate, what the mistake was, and how it had been made. (That's so.) I supposed that for an honest man, conscious of his own rectitude, that explanation would be sufficient. I did not wait for him, after the mistake was made, to call my attention to it, but frankly explained it at once as an honest man would. (Cheers.) I also gave the authority on which I had stated that these resolutions were adopted by the Springfield Republican convention. That I had seen them quoted by Major Harris in a debate in Congress, as having been adopted by the first Republican State convention in Illinois, and that I had written to him and asked him for the authority as to the time and place of their adoption; that Major Harris being extremely ill, Charles H. Lanphier had written to me for him, that they were adopted at Springfield, on the 5th of October, 1854, and had sent me a copy of the Springfield paper containing them. I read them from the newspaper just as Mr. Lincoln reads the proceedings of meetings held years ago from the newspapers. After giving that explanation, I did not think there was an honest man in the State of Illinois who doubted that I had been led into the error, if it was such, innocently, in the way I detailed; and I will now say that I do not now believe that there is an honest man on the face of the globe who will not regard with abhorrence and disgust Mr. Lincoln's insinuations of my complicity in that forgery, if it was a forgery. (Cheers.) Does Mr. Lincoln wish to push these things to the point of personal difficulties here? I commenced this contest by treating him courteously and kindly; I always spoke of him in words of respect, and in return he has sought, and is now seeking, to divert public attention from the enormity of his revolutionary principles by impeaching men's sincerity and integrity, and inviting personal quarrels. (Give it to him, and cheers.)

I desired to conduct this contest with him like a gentleman, but I spurn the insinuation of complicity and fraud made upon the simple circumstance of an editor of a newspaper having made a mistake as to the place where a thing was done, but not as to the thing itself. These resolutions were the platform of this Republican party of Mr. Lincoln's of that year. They were adopted in a majority of the Republican counties in the State; and when I asked him at Ottawa whether they formed the platform upon which he stood, he did not answer, and I could not get an answer out of him. He then thought, as I thought, that those resolutions were adopted at the Springfield convention, but excused himself by saying that he was not there when they were adopted, but had gone to Tazewell court in order to avoid being present at the convention. He saw them published as having been adopted at Springfield, and so did I, and he knew that if there was a mistake in regard to them, that I had nothing under heaven to do with it. Besides, you find that in all these northern counties where the Republican candidates are running pledged to him, that the conventions which nominated them adopted that identical platform. One cardinal point in that platform which he shrinks from is this—that there shall be no more slave States admitted into the Union, even if the people want them. Lovejoy stands pledged against the admission of any more slave States. (Right, so do we.) So do you, you say. Farnsworth stands pledged against the admission of any more slave States. (Most right.) Washburne stands pledged the same way. (Good, good.) The candidate for the legislature who is running on Lincoln's ticket in Henderson and Warren, stands committed by his vote in the legislature to the same thing, and I am informed, but do not know of the fact, that your candidate here is also so pledged. (Hurrah for him, good.) Now, you Republicans all hurrah for him, and for the doctrine of "no more slave States," and yet Lincoln tells you that his conscience will not permit him to sanction that doctrine. (Immense applause.) And complains because the resolutions I read at Ottawa made him as a member of the party, responsible for sanctioning the doctrine of no more slave States. You are one way, you confess, and he is or pretends to be the other, and yet you are both governed by *principle* in supporting one another. If it be true, as I have shown it is, that the whole Republican party in the northern part of the State stands committed to the doctrine of no more slave States, and that this same doctrine is repudiated by the Republicans in the other part of the State, I wonder whether Mr. Lincoln and his party do not present the case which he cited from the Scriptures, of a house divided against itself which cannot stand! (Tremendous shouts of applause.) I desire to know what are Mr. Lincoln's principles and the principles of his party? I hold, and the party with which I am identified hold, that the people of each State, old and new, have the right to decide the slavery question for themselves, ("That's it," "Right," and immense applause,) and when I used the remark that I did not care whether slavery was voted up or down, I used it in the connection that I was for allowing Kansas to do just as she pleased on the slavery question. I said that I did not care whether they voted slavery up or down, because they had the right to do as they pleased on the question, and therefore my action would not be controlled by any such consideration. (That's the doctrine.) Why cannot Abraham Lincoln, and the party with which he acts, speak out their principles so that they may be understood? Why do they claim to be one thing in one part of the State and another in the other part? Whenever I allude to the abolition doctrines, which he considers a slander to be charged with being in favor of, you all endorse them, and hurrah for them, not knowing that your candidate is ashamed to acknowledge them. (You have them; and cheers.)

I have a few words to say upon the Dred Scott decision, which has troubled the brain of Mr. Lincoln so much. (Laughter.) He insists that that decision would carry slavery into the free States, notwithstanding that the decision says directly the opposite; and goes into a long argument to make you believe that I am in favor of, and would sanction the doctrine that would allow slaves to be brought here and held as slaves contrary to our constitution and laws. Mr. Lincoln knew better when he asserted this; he knew that one newspaper, and so far as is within my knowledge, but one ever asserted that doctrine, and that I was the first man in either House of Congress that read that article in debate, and denounced it on the floor of the Senate as revolutionary. When the Washington *Union*, on the 17th of last November published an article to that effect, I branded it at once, and denounced it, and hence the *Union* has been pursuing me ever since. Mr. Toombs, of Georgia, replied to me, and said that there was not a man in any of the slave States south of the Potomac river that held any such doctrine. Mr. Lincoln knows that there is not a member of the Supreme Court who holds that doctrine; he knows that every one of them, as shown by their opinions, holds the reverse. Why this attempt, then, to bring the Supreme Court into disrepute among the people? It looks as if there was an effort being made to destroy public confidence in the highest judicial tribunal on earth. Suppose he succeeds in destroying public confidence in the court, so that the people will not respect its decisions, but will feel at liberty to disregard them, and resist the laws of the land, what will he have gained? He will have changed the government from one of laws into that of a mob, in which the strong arm of violence will be substituted for the decisions of the courts of justice. ("That's so.") He complains because I did not go into an argument reviewing Chief Justice Taney's opinion, and the other opinions of the different judges, to determine whether their reasoning is right or wrong on the questions of law. What use would that be? He wants to take an appeal from the Supreme Court to this meeting to determine whether the questions of law were decided properly. He is going to appeal from the Supreme Court of the United States to every town meeting in the hope that he can excite a prejudice against that court, and on the wave of that prejudice ride into the Senate of the United States, when he could not get there on his own principles, or his own merits. (Laughter and cheers; "hit him again.") Suppose he should succeed in getting into the Senate of the United States, what then will he have to do with the decision of the Supreme Court in the Dred Scott case? Can he reverse that decision when he gets there? Can he act upon it? Has the Senate any right to reverse it or revise it? He will not pretend that it has. Then why drag the matter into this contest, unless for the purpose of making a false issue, by which he can direct public attention from the real issue?

He has cited General Jackson in justification of the war he is making on the decision of the court. Mr. Lincoln misunderstands the history of the country, if he believes there is any parallel in the two cases. It is true that the Supreme Court once decided that if a bank of the United States was a necessary fiscal agent of the government, it was constitutional, and if not, that it was unconstitutional, and also, that whether or not it was necessary for that purpose, was a political question for Congress and not a judicial one for the courts to determine. Hence the court would not determine the bank unconstitutional. Jackson respected the decision, obeyed the law, executed it and carried it into effect during its existence; (that's so,) but after the charter of the bank expired and a proposition was made to create a new bank, General Jackson said, "It is unnecessary, and improper, and therefore, I am against it on constitutional grounds as well as those of expediency." Is Congress bound to pass every act that is constitutional? Why, there are a thousand things that are constitutional, but yet are inexpedient and unnecessary, and you surely would not vote for them merely because you had the right to? And because General Jackson would not do a thing which he had a right to do, but did not deem expedient or proper, Mr. Lincoln is going to justify himself in doing that which he has no right to do. (Laughter.) I ask him, whether he is not bound to respect and obey the decisions of the Supreme Court as well as me? The Constitution has created that Court to decide all constitutional questions in the last resort, and when such decisions have been made, they become the law of the land, (that's so,) and you, and he, and myself, and every other good citizen are bound by them. Yet, he argues that I am bound by their decisions and he is not. He says that their decisions are binding on Democrats, but not on Republicans. (Laughter and applause.) Are not Republicans bound by the laws of the land, as well as Democrats? And when the court has fixed the construction of the constitution on the validity of a given law, is not their decision binding upon Republicans as well as upon Democrats? (It ought to be.) Is it possible that you Republicans have the right to raise your mobs and oppose the laws of the land and the constituted authorities, and yet hold us Democrats bound to obey them? My time is within half a minute of expiring, and all I have to say is, that I stand by the laws of the land. (That's it; hurrah for Douglas.) I stand by the constitution as our fathers made it, by the laws as they are enacted, and by the decisions of the court upon all points within their jurisdiction as they are pronounced by the highest tribunal on earth; and any man who resists these must resort to mob law and violence to overturn the government of laws.

Sixth Lincoln-Douglas Debate, Quincy, Illinois

Sixth joint debate. October 13. 1858 at Quincy, Illinois.
Lincoln as reported in the Press & Tribune   Douglas as
reported in the Chicago Times.

MR. LINCOLN'S SPEECH.

At precisely half past two o'clock Mr. Lincoln was introduced to the audience, and having been received with three cheers, he proceeded:

LADIES AND GENTLEMEN:—I have had no immediate conference with Judge Douglas, but I will venture to say he and I will perfectly agree that your entire silence both when I speak and when he speaks will be most agreeable to us.

In the month of May, 1856, the elements in the State of Illinois, which have since been consolidated into the Republican party, assembled together in a State Convention at Bloomington. They adopted at that time what, in political language, is called a platform. In June of the same year, the elements of the Republican party in the nation assembled together in a National Convention at Philadelphia. They adopted what is called the National Platform. In June, 1858—the present year—the Republicans of Illinois re-assembled at Springfield, in State Convention, and adopted again their platform, as I suppose not differing in any essential particular from either of the former ones, but perhaps adding something in relation to the new developments of political progress in the country.

The Convention that assembled in June last did me the honor, if it be one, and I esteem it such, to nominate me as their candidate for the United States Senate. I have supposed that in entering upon this canvass I stood generally upon these platforms. We are now met together on the 13th of October of the same year, only four months from the adoption of the last platform, and I am unaware that in this canvass, from the beginning until to-day, any one of our adversaries has taken hold of our platforms or laid his finger upon anything that he calls wrong in them.

In the very first one of these joint discussions between Senator Douglas and myself, Senator Douglas, without alluding at all to these platforms, or any one of them, of which I have spoken, attempted to hold me responsible for a set of resolutions passed long before the meeting of either one of these Conventions of which I have spoken. And as a ground for holding me responsible for these resolutions, he assumed that they had been passed at a State Convention of the Republican party, and that I took part in that Convention. It was discovered afterwards that this was erroneous, that the resolutions which he endeavored to hold me responsible for, had not been passed by any State Convention anywhere—had not been passed at Springfield, where he supposed they had, or assumed that they had, and that they had been passed in no Convention in which I had taken part. The Judge, nevertheless, was not willing to give up the point that he was endeavoring to make upon me, and he therefore thought to still hold me to the point that he was endeavoring to make, by showing that the resolutions that he read, had been passed at a local Convention in the northern part of the State, although it was not a local Convention that embraced my residence at all, nor one that reached, as I suppose, nearer than 150 or 200 miles of where I was when it met, nor one in which I took any part at all. He also introduced other resolutions passed at other meetings, and by combining the whole, although they were all antecedent to the two State Conventions, and the one National Convention I have mentioned, still he insisted and now insists, as I understand, that I am in some way responsible for them.

At Jonesboro, on our third meeting, I insisted to the Judge that I was in no way rightfully held responsible for the proceedings of this local meeting or convention in which I had taken no part, and in which I was in no way embraced; but I insisted to him that if he thought I was responsible for every man or every set of men everywhere, who happen to be my friends, the rule ought to work both ways, and he ought to be responsible for the acts and resolutions of all men or sets of men who were or are now his supporters and friends, [good, good,] and gave him a pretty long string of resolutions, passed by men who are now his friends, and announcing doctrines for which he does not desire to be held responsible.

This still does not satisfy Judge Douglas. He still adheres to his proposition, that I am responsible for what some of my friends in different parts of the State have done; but that he is not responsible for what his have done. At least so I understand him. But in addition to that, the Judge at our meeting in Galesburg, last week, undertakes to establish that I am guilty of a species of double-dealing with the public—that I make speeches of a certain sort in the North, among the Abolitionists, which I would not make in the South, and that I make speeches of a certain sort in the South which I would not make in the North. I apprehend in the course I have marked out for myself that I shall not have to dwell at very great length upon this subject.

As this was done in the Judge's opening speech at Galesburg, I had an opportunity, as I had the middle speech then, of saying something in answer to it. He brought forward a quotation or two from a speech of mine delivered at Chicago, and then to contrast with it he brought forward an extract from a speech of mine at Charleston, in which he insisted that I was greatly inconsistent, and insisted that his conclusion followed that I was playing a double part, and speaking in one region one way and in another region another way. I have not time now to dwell on this as long as I would like, and I wish only now to re-quote that portion of my speech at Charleston which the Judge quoted, and then make some comments upon it. This he quotes from me as being delivered at Charleston, and I believe correctly: "I will say, then, that I am not, nor ever have been, in favor of bringing about in any way the social and political equality of the white and black races—that I am not nor ever have been in favor of making voters or jurors of negroes, nor of qualifying them to hold office, nor to intermarry with white people; and I will say in addition to this that there is a physical difference between the white and black races which will ever forbid the two races living together on terms of social and political equality. And inasmuch as they cannot so live, while they do remain together, there must be the position of superior & inferior. I am as much as any other man in favor of having the superior position assigned to the white race." ["Good," "Good," and loud cheers.] This, I believe, is the entire quotation from the Charleston speech as the Judge made it. His comments are as follows:

> Yes, here you find men who hurrah for Lincoln, and say he is right when he discards all distinction between races, or when he declares that he discards the doctrine that there is such a thing as a superior and inferior race; and Abolitionists are required and expected to vote for Mr. Lincoln because he goes for the equality of the races, holding that in the Declaration of Independence the white man and the negro were declared equal, and endowed by Divine law with equality. And down South with the Old Line Whigs, with the Kentuckians, the Virginians, and the Tennesseeans, he tells you that there is a physical difference between the races, making the one superior, the other inferior, and he is in favor of maintaining the superiority of the white race over the negro.

Those are the Judge's comments. Now I wish to show you, that a month, or only lacking three days of a month, before I made the speech at Charleston, which the Judge quotes from, he had himself heard me say substantially the same thing. It was in our first meeting, at Ottawa—and I will say a word about where it was and the atmosphere it was in, after a while—but, at our first meeting, at Ottawa, I read an extract from an old speech of mine, made nearly four years ago, not merely to show my sentiments, but to show that my sentiments were long entertained and openly expressed; in which extract I expressly declared that my own feelings would not admit a social and political equality between the white and black races, and that even if my own feelings would admit of it, I still knew that the public sentiment of the country would not, and that such a thing was an utter impossibility, or substantially that. That extract from my old speech the reporters, by some sort of accident, passed over, and it was not reported. I lay no blame upon anybody. I suppose they thought that I would hand it over to them, and dropped reporting while I was reading it, but afterwards went away without getting it from me. At the end of that quotation from my old speech, which I read at Ottawa, I made the comments which were reported at that time, and which I will now read, and ask you to notice how very nearly they are the same as Judge Douglas says were delivered by me down in Egypt. After reading I added these words: "Now, gentlemen, I don't want to read at any great length, but this is the true complexion of all I have ever said in regard to the institution of slavery or the black race, and this is the whole of it; and anything that argues me into his idea of perfect social and political equality with the negro is but a specious and fantastical arrangement of words by which a man can prove a horse-chestnut to be a chestnut horse. I will say here, while upon this subject, that I have no purpose directly or indirectly to interfere with the institution in the States where it exists. I believe I have no right to do so. I have no inclination to do so. I have no purpose to introduce political and social equality between the white and black races. There is a physical difference between the two, which, in my judgment, will probably forever forbid their living together on the footing of perfect equality, and inasmuch as it becomes a necessity that there must be a difference, I as well as Judge Douglas am in favor of the race to which I belong having the superior position." [Cheers, "That's the doctrine."] "I have never said anything to the contrary, but I hold that, notwithstanding all this, there is no reason in the world why the negro is not entitled to all the rights enumerated in the Declaration of Independence—the right of life, liberty and the pursuit of happiness. I hold that he is as much entitled to these as the white man. I agree with Judge Douglas that he is not my equal in many respects, certainly not in color—perhaps not in intellectual and moral endowments; but in the right to eat the bread without leave of anybody else which his own hand earns, he is my equal and the equal of Judge Douglas, and the equal of every other man." [Loud cheers.]

I have chiefly introduced this for the purpose of meeting the Judge's charge that the quotation he took from my Charleston speech was what I would say down south among the Kentuckians, the Virginians, &c., but would not say in the regions in which was supposed to be more of the Abolition element. I now make this comment: That speech from which I have now read the quotation, and which is there given correctly, perhaps too much so for good taste, was made away up north in the Abolition district of this State *par excellence*—in the Lovejoy District—in the personal presence of Lovejoy, for he was on the stand with us when I made it. It had been made and put in print in that region only three days less than a month before the speech made at Charleston, the like of which Judge Douglas thinks I would not make where there was any abolition element. I only refer to this matter to say that I am altogether unconscious of having attempted any double dealing anywhere—that upon one occasion I may say one thing and leave other things unsaid, and *vice versa*; but that I have said anything on one occasion that is inconsistent with what I have said elsewhere, I deny—at least I deny it so far as the intention is concerned. I find that I have devoted to this topic a larger portion of my time than I had intended. I wished to show, but I will pass it upon this occasion, that in the sentiment I have occasionally advanced upon the Declaration of Independence, I am entirely borne out by the sentiments advanced by our old Whig leader, Henry Clay, and I have the book here to show it from; but because I have already occupied more time than I intended to do on that topic, I pass over it.

At Galesburg, I tried to show that by the Dred Scott Decision, pushed to its legitimate consequences, slavery would be established in all the States as well as in the Territories. I did this because, upon a former occasion, I had asked Judge Douglas whether, if the Supreme Court should make a decision declaring that the States had not the power to exclude slavery from their limits, he would adopt and follow that decision as a rule of political action; and because he had not directly answered that question, but had merely contented himself with sneering at it, I again introduced it, and tried to show that the conclusion that I stated followed inevitably and logically from the proposition already decided by the court. Judge Douglas had the privilege of replying to me at Galesburg, and again he gave me no direct answer as to whether he would or would not sustain such a decision if made. I give him this third chance to say yes or no. He is not obliged to do either— probably he will not do either—[laughter] but I give him the third chance. I tried to show then that this result—this conclusion inevitably followed from the point already decided by the court. The Judge, in his reply, again sneers at the thought of the court making any such decision, and in the course of his remarks upon this subject, uses the language which I will now read. Speaking of me, the Judge says:

"He goes on and insists that the Dred Scott Decision would carry slavery into the Free States, notwithstanding the decision itself says the contrary." And he adds: "Mr. Lincoln knows that there is no member of the Supreme Court that holds that doctrine. He knows that every one of them in their opinions held the reverse."

I especially introduce this subject again for the purpose of saying that I have the Dred Scott Decision here, and I will thank Judge Douglas to lay his finger upon the place in the entire opinions of the court where any one of them "says the contrary." It is very hard to affirm a negative with entire confidence. I say, however, that I have examined that decision with a good deal of care, as a lawyer examines a decision, and so far as I have been able to do so, the Court has no where in its opinions said that the States have the power to exclude slavery, nor have they used other language substantially that. I also say, so far as I can find, not one of the concurring Judges has said that the States can exclude slavery, nor said anything that was substantially that. The nearest approach that any one of them has made to it, so far as I can find, was by Judge Nelson, and the approach he made to it was exactly, in substance, the Nebraska Bill—that the States had the exclusive power over the question of slavery, so far as they are not limited by the Constitution of the United States. I asked the question, therefore, if the non-concurring Judges, McLean or Curtis, had asked to get an express declaration that the States could absolutely exclude slavery from their limits, what reason have we to believe that it would not have been voted down by the majority of the Judges, just as Chase's amendment was voted down by Judge Douglas and his compeers when it was offered to the Nebraska Bill. [Cheers.]

Also at Galesburg, I said something in regard to those Springfield Resolutions that Judge Douglas had attempted to use upon me at Ottawa, and commented at some length upon the fact that they were, as presented, not genuine. Judge Douglas in his reply to me seemed to be somewhat exasperated. He said he would never have believed that Abraham Lincoln, as he kindly called me, would have attempted such a thing as

I had attempted upon that occasion; and among other expressions which he used toward me, was that I dared to say forgery—that I had *dared* to say forgery [turning to Judge Douglas]. Yes, Judge, I did dare to say forgery. [Loud applause.] But in this political canvass, the Judge ought to remember that I was not the first who *dared* to say forgery. At Jacksonville Judge Douglas made a speech in answer to something said by Judge Trumbull, and at the close of what he said upon that subject, he *dared* to say that Trumbull had forged his evidence. He said, too, that he should not concern himself with Trumbull any more, but thereafter he should hold Lincoln responsible for the slanders upon him. [Laughter.] When I met him at Charleston after that, although I think that I should not have noticed the subject if he had not said he would hold me responsible for it, I spread out before him the statements of the evidence that Judge Trumbull had used, and I asked Judge Douglas, piece by piece, to put his finger upon one piece of all that evidence that he would say was a forgery! When I went through with each and every piece, Judge Douglas did not *dare* then to say that any piece of it was a forgery. [Laughter, and cries of "good, good."] So it seems that there are some things that Judge Douglas dares to do, and some that he dares not to do. [Great applause and laughter.]

A VOICE—It's the same thing with you.

MR. LINCOLN—Yes, sir, it's the same thing with me. I do dare to say forgery, when it's true, and I don't dare to say forgery when it's false. [Thunders of applause. Cries of "Hit him again," "Give it to him, Lincoln."] Now, I will say here to this audience and to Judge Douglas, I have not dared to say he committed a forgery, and I never shall until I know it; but I did dare to say—just to suggest to the Judge—that a forgery had been committed, which by his own showing had been traced to him and two of his friends. [Roars of laughter and loud cheers.] I dared to suggest to him that he had expressly promised in one of his public speeches to investigate that matter, and I dared to suggest to him that there was an implied promise that when he investigated it he would make known the result. I dared to suggest to the Judge that he could not expect to be quite clear of suspicion of that fraud, for since the time that promise was made he had been with

those friends, and had not kept his promise in regard to the
investigation and the report upon it. [Loud laughter. Cries of
"Good, good," "Hit him hard."] I am not a very daring man,
[laughter] but I dared that much, Judge, and I am not much
scared about it yet. [Uproarious laughter and applause.]
When the Judge says he wouldn't have believed of Abraham
Lincoln that he would have made such an attempt as that, he
reminds me of the fact that he entered upon this canvass with
the purpose to treat me courteously; that touched me somewhat. [Great laughter.] It sets me to thinking. I was aware,
when it was first agreed that Judge Douglas and I were to
have these seven joint discussions, that they were the successive acts of a drama—perhaps I should say, to be enacted not
merely in the face of audiences like this, but in the face of the
nation, and to some extent, by my relation to him, and not
from anything in myself, in the face of the world; and I am
anxious that they should be conducted with dignity and in the
good temper which would be befitting the vast audience before which it was conducted. But when Judge Douglas got
home from Washington and made his first speech in Chicago,
the evening afterwards I made some sort of a reply to it. His
second speech was made at Bloomington, in which, he commented upon my speech at Chicago, and said that I had used
language ingeniously contrived to conceal my intentions, or
words to that effect. Now, I understand that this is an imputation upon my veracity and my candor. I do not know what
the Judge understood by it; but in our first discussion at
Ottawa, he led off by charging a bargain, somewhat corrupt
in its character, upon Trumbull and myself—that we had
entered into a bargain, one of the terms of which was that
Trumbull was to abolitionize the old Democratic party, and I
(Lincoln) was to abolitionize the old Whig party—I pretending to be as good an Old Line Whig as ever. Judge Douglas
may not understand that he implicated my truthfulness and
my honor, when he said I was doing one thing and pretending another; and I misunderstood him if he thought he was
treating me in a dignified way, as a man of honor and truth,
as he now claims he was disposed to treat me. Even after that
time, at Galesburg, when he brings forward an extract from a
speech made at Chicago, and an extract from a speech made

at Charleston, to prove that I was trying to play a double part—that I was trying to cheat the public, and get votes upon one set of principles at one place and upon another set of principles at another place—I do not understand but what he impeaches my honor, my veracity and my candor, and because *he* does this, I do not understand that I am bound, if I see a truthful ground for it, to keep my hands off of him. As soon as I learned that Judge Douglas was disposed to treat me in this way, I signified in one of my speeches that I should be driven to draw upon whatever of humble resources I might have—to adopt a new course with him. I was not entirely sure that I should be able to hold my own with him, but I at least had the purpose made to do as well as I could upon him; and now I say that I will not be the first to cry "hold." I think it originated with the Judge, and when he quits, I probably will. [Roars of laughter.] But I shall not ask any favors at all. He asks me, or he asks the audience, if I wish to push this matter to the point of personal difficulty. I tell him, no. He did not make a mistake, in one of his early speeches, when he called me an "amiable" man, though perhaps he did when he called me an "intelligent" man. [Laughter.] It really hurts me very much to suppose that I have wronged anybody on earth. I again tell him, no! I very much prefer, when this canvass shall be over, however it may result, that we at least part without any bitter recollections of personal difficulties.

The Judge, in his concluding speech at Galesburg, says that I was pushing this matter to a personal difficulty, to avoid the responsibility for the enormity of my principles. I say to the Judge and to this audience now, that I will again state our principles as well as I hastily can in all their enormity, and if the Judge hereafter chooses to confine himself to a war upon these principles, he will probably not find me departing from the same course.

We have in this nation this element of domestic slavery. It is a matter of absolute certainty that it is a disturbing element. It is the opinion of all the great men who have expressed an opinion upon it, that it is a dangerous element. We keep up a controversy in regard to it. That controversy necessarily springs from difference of opinion, and if we can learn exactly—can reduce to the lowest elements—what that difference of opinion is, we perhaps shall be better prepared for discussing the different systems of policy that we would propose in regard to that disturbing element. I suggest that the difference of opinion, reduced to its lowest terms, is no other than the difference between the men who think slavery a wrong and those who do not think it wrong. The Republican party think it wrong—we think it is a moral, a social and a political wrong. We think it is a wrong not confining itself merely to the persons or the States where it exists, but that it is a wrong in its tendency, to say the least, that extends itself to the existence of the whole nation. Because we think it wrong, we propose a course of policy that shall deal with it as a wrong. We deal with it as with any other wrong, in so far as we can prevent its growing any larger, and so deal with it that in the run of time there may be some promise of an end to it. We have a due regard to the actual presence of it amongst us and the difficulties of getting rid of it in any satisfactory way, and all the constitutional obligations thrown about it. I suppose that in reference both to its actual existence in the nation, and to our constitutional obligations, we have no right at all to disturb it in the States where it exists, and we profess that we have no more inclination to disturb it than we have the right to do it. We go further than that; we don't propose to disturb it where, in one instance, we think the Constitution would permit us. We think the Constitution would permit us to disturb it in the District of Columbia. Still we do not propose to do that, unless it should be in terms which I don't suppose the nation is very likely soon to agree to—the terms of making the emancipation gradual and compensating the unwilling owners. Where we suppose we have the constitutional right, we restrain ourselves in reference to the actual existence of the institution and the difficulties thrown about it. We also oppose it as an evil so far as it seeks to spread itself. We insist on the policy that shall restrict it to its present limits. We don't suppose that in doing this we violate anything due to the actual presence of the institution, or anything due to the constitutional guarantees thrown around it.

We oppose the Dred Scott decision in a certain way, upon which I ought perhaps to address you a few words. We do not propose that when Dred Scott has been decided to be a slave by the court, we, as a mob, will decide him to be free. We do not propose that, when any other one, or one thousand, shall be decided by that court to be slaves, we will in any violent way disturb the rights of property thus settled; but we nevertheless do oppose that decision as a political rule which shall be binding on the voter, to vote for nobody who thinks it wrong, which shall be binding on the members of Congress or the President to favor no measure that does not actually concur with the principles of that decision. We do not propose to be bound by it as a political rule in that way, because we think it lays the foundation not merely of enlarging and spreading out what we consider an evil, but it lays the foundation for spreading that evil into the States themselves. We propose so resisting it as to have it reversed if we can, and a new judicial rule established upon this subject.

I will add this, that if there be any man who does not believe that slavery is wrong in the three aspects which I have mentioned, or in any one of them, that man is misplaced, and ought to leave us. While, on the other hand, if there be any man in the Republican party who is impatient over the necessity springing from its actual presence, and is impatient of the constitutional guarantees thrown around it, and would act in disregard of these, he too is misplaced standing with us. He will find his place somewhere else; for we have a due regard, so far as we are capable of understanding them, for all these things. This, gentlemen, as well as I can give it, is a plain statement of our principles in all their enormity.

I will say now that there is a sentiment in the country contrary to me—a sentiment which holds that slavery is not wrong, and therefore it goes for policy that does not propose dealing with it as a wrong. That policy is the Democratic policy, and that sentiment is the Democratic sentiment. If there be a doubt in the mind of any one of this vast audience that this is really the central idea of the Democratic party, in relation to this subject, I ask him to bear with me while I state a few things tending, as I think, to prove that proposition. In the first place, the leading man—I think I may do my friend Judge Douglas the honor of calling him such—advocating the present Democratic policy, never himself says it is wrong. He has the high distinction, so far as I know, of never having

said slavery is either right or wrong. [Laughter.] Almost everybody else says one or the other, but the Judge never does.
If there be a man in the Democratic party who thinks it is
wrong, and yet clings to that party, I suggest to him in the
first place that his leader don't talk as he does, for he never
says that it is wrong. In the second place, I suggest to him
that if he will examine the policy proposed to be carried forward, he will find that he carefully excludes the idea that there
is anything wrong in it. If you will examine the arguments
that are made on it, you will find that every one carefully
excludes the idea that there is anything wrong in slavery. Perhaps that Democrat who says he is as much opposed to
slavery as I am, will tell me that I am wrong about this. I wish
him to examine his own course in regard to this matter a
moment, and then see if his opinion will not be changed a
little. You say it is wrong; but don't you constantly object to
anybody else saying so? Do you not constantly argue that this
is not the right place to oppose it? You say it must not be
opposed in the free States, because slavery is not here; it must
not be opposed in the slave States, because it is there; it must
not be opposed in politics, because that will make a fuss; it
must not be opposed in the pulpit, because it is not religion.
[Loud cheers.] Then where is the place to oppose it? There is
no suitable place to oppose it. There is no place in the country to oppose this evil overspreading the continent, which you
say yourself is coming. Frank Blair and Gratz Brown tried to
get up a system of gradual emancipation in Missouri, had an
election in August and got beat, and you, Mr. Democrat,
threw up your hat, and halloed "hurrah for Democracy." [En-
thusiastic cheers.] So I say again that in regard to the arguments that are made, when Judge Douglas says he "don't care
whether slavery is voted up or voted down," whether he
means that as an individual expression of sentiment, or only
as a sort of statement of his views on national policy, it is alike
true to say that he can thus argue logically if he don't see
anything wrong in it; but he cannot say so logically if he
admits that slavery is wrong. He cannot say that he would as
soon see a wrong voted up as voted down. When Judge Douglas says that whoever, or whatever community, wants slaves,
they have a right to have them, he is perfectly logical if there

is nothing wrong in the institution; but if you admit that it is wrong, he cannot logically say that anybody has a right to do wrong. When he says that slave property and horse and hog property are alike to be allowed to go into the Territories, upon the principles of equality, he is reasoning truly, if there is no difference between them as property; but if the one is property, held rightfully, and the other is wrong, then there is no equality between the right and wrong; so that, turn it in any way you can, in all the arguments sustaining the Democratic policy, and in that policy itself, there is a careful, studied exclusion of the idea that there is anything wrong in slavery. Let us understand this. I am not, just here, trying to prove that we are right and they are wrong. I have been stating where we and they stand, and trying to show what is the real difference between us; and I now say that whenever we can get the question distinctly stated—can get all these men who believe that slavery is in some of these respects wrong, to stand and act with us in treating it as a wrong—then, and not till then, I think we will in some way come to an end of this slavery agitation. [Prolonged cheers.]

SENATOR DOUGLAS' REPLY.

Senator Douglas, in taking the stand, was greeted with tremendous applause. He said:

Ladies and Gentlemen:—Permit me to say that unless silence is observed it will be impossible for me to be heard by this immense crowd, and my friends can confer no higher favor upon me than by omitting all expressions of applause or approbation. (We cannot help it, Douglas, &c.) I desire to be heard rather than to be applauded. I wish to address myself to your reason, your judgment, your sense of justice, and not to your passions.

I regret that Mr. Lincoln should have deemed it proper for him to again indulge in gross personalities and base insinuations in regard to the Springfield resolutions. It has imposed upon me the necessity of using some portion of my time for the purpose of calling your attention to the facts of the case, and it will then be for you to say what you think of a man who can predicate such a charge upon the circumstances he has this. I had seen the platform adopted by a Republican Congressional convention held in Aurora, the second Congressional district, in September, 1854, published as purporting to be the platform of the Republican party. That platform declared that the Republican party was pledged never to admit another slave State into the Union, and also that it pledged to prohibit slavery in all the territories of the United States, not only all that we then had, but all that we should thereafter acquire, and to repeal unconditionally the fugitive slave law, abolish slavery in the District of Columbia, and prohibit the slave trade between the different States. These and other articles against slavery were contained in this platform, and unanimously adopted by the Republican Congressional convention in that district. I had also seen that the Republican Congressional conventions at Rockford, in the first district, and at Bloomington, in the third, had adopted the same platform that year, nearly word for word, and had declared it to be the platform of the Republican party. I had noticed that Major Thomas L. Harris, a member of Congress from the Springfield district, had referred to that platform in a speech in Congress as having been adopted by the first Republican State Convention which assembled in Illinois. When I had occasion to use the fact in this canvass, I wrote to Major Harris to know on what day that convention was held, and to ask him to send me its proceedings. He being sick, Charles H. Lanphier answered my letter by sending me the published proceedings of the convention held at Springfield on the 5th of October, 1854, as they appeared in the report of the *State Register*. I read those resolutions from that newspaper the same as any of you would refer back and quote any fact from the files of a newspaper which had published it. Mr. Lincoln pretends that after I had so quoted those resolutions he discovered that they had never been adopted at Springfield. He does not deny their adoption by the Republican party at Aurora, at Bloomington, and at Rockford, and by nearly all the Republican county conventions in northern Illinois where his party is in a majority, but merely because they were not

adopted on the *"spot"* on which I said they were, he chooses
to quibble about the place rather than meet and discuss the
merits of the resolutions themselves. I stated when I quoted
them that I did so from the *State Register*. I gave my authority. Lincoln believed at the time, as he has since admitted,
that they had been adopted at Springfield, as published. Does
he believe now, that I did not tell the truth when I quoted
those resolutions? He knows, in his heart, that I quoted them
in good faith, believing, at the time, that they had been
adopted at Springfield. I would consider myself an infamous
wretch, if, under such circumstances, I could charge any man
with being a party to a trick or a fraud. (Great applause.) And
I will tell him, too, that it will not do to charge a forgery on
Charles H. Lanphier or Thomas L. Harris. No man on earth,
who knows them, and knows Lincoln, would take his oath
against their word. (Cheers.) There are not two men in the
State of Illinois, who have higher characters for truth, for
integrity, for moral character, and for elevation of tone, as
gentlemen, than Mr. Lanphier and Mr. Harris. Any man who
attempts to make such charges as Mr. Lincoln has indulged in
against them, only proclaims himself a slanderer. (Vociferous
applause.)

I will now show you that I stated with entire fairness, as
soon as it was made known to me, that there was a mistake
about the spot where the resolutions had been adopted, although their truthfulness, as a declaration of the principles of
the Republican party, had not, and could not be questioned. I
did not wait for Lincoln to point out the mistake; but the
moment I discovered it, I made a speech, and published it to
the world, correcting the error. I corrected it myself, as a gentleman, and an honest man, and as I always feel proud to do
when I have made a mistake. I wish Mr. Lincoln could show
that he has acted with equal fairness, and truthfulness, when I
have convinced him that he has been mistaken. (Hit him
again, and cheers.) I will give you an illustration to show you
how he acts in a similar case: In a speech at Springfield, he
charged Chief Justice Taney, and his associates, President
Pierce, President Buchanan, and myself, with having entered
into a conspiracy at the time the Nebraska bill was introduced, by which the Dred Scott decision was to be made by

the Supreme Court, in order to carry slavery everywhere under the constitution. I called his attention to the fact, that at the time alluded to, to wit: the introduction of the Nebraska bill, it was not possible that such a conspiracy could have been entered into, for the reason that the Dred Scott case had never been taken before the Supreme Court, and was not taken before it for a year after; and I asked him to take back that charge. Did he do it? (No.) I showed him that it was impossible that the charge could be true, I proved it by the record, and I then called upon him to retract his false charge. What was his answer? Instead of coming out like an honest man and doing so, he reiterated the charge, and said that if the case had not gone up to the Supreme Court from the courts of Missouri at the time he charged that the Judges of the Supreme Court entered into the conspiracy, yet, that there was an understanding with the Democratic owners of Dred Scott, that they would take it up. I have since asked him who the Democratic owners of Dred Scott were, but he could not tell, and why? Because there were no such Democratic owners in existence. Dred Scott at the time was owned by the Rev. Dr. Chaffee, an Abolition member of Congress, of Springfield, Massachusetts, in right of his wife. He was owned by one of Lincoln's friends, and not by Democrats at all; (immense cheers, "give it to him," &c.) his case was conducted in court by Abolition lawyers, so that both the prosecution and the defense were in the hands of the Abolition political friends of Mr. Lincoln. (Renewed cheering.) Notwithstanding I thus proved by the record that his charge against the Supreme Court was false, instead of taking it back, he resorted to another false charge to sustain the infamy of it. (Cheers.) He also charged President Buchanan with having been a party to the conspiracy. I directed his attention to the fact that the charge could not possibly be true, for the reason that at the time specified, Mr. Buchanan was not in America, but was three thousand miles off, representing the United States at the Court of St. James, and had been there for a year previous, and did not return until three years afterwards. Yet, I never could get Mr. Lincoln to take back his false charge, although I have called upon him over and over again. He refuses to do it, and either remains silent, or, resorts to other tricks to try and palm his slander off on the country. (Cheers.) Therein you will find the difference between Mr. Lincoln and myself. When I make a mistake, as an honest man, I correct it without being asked to do so, but when he makes a false charge he sticks to it, and never corrects it. ("Don't spare him," and cheers.) One word more in regard to these resolutions: I quoted them at Ottawa merely to ask Mr. Lincoln whether he stood on that platform. That was the purpose for which I quoted them. I did not think that I had a right to put idle questions to him, and I first laid a foundation for my questions by showing that the principles which I wished him either to affirm or deny had been adopted by some portion of his friends, at least, as their creed. Hence I read the resolutions, and put the questions to him, and he then refused to answer them. (Laughter, "he was afraid," &c.) Subsequently, one week afterwards, he did answer a part of them, but the others he has not answered up to this day. ("No, and never will," "never can," and cheers.) My friends, if you are my friends, you will be silent, instead of interrupting me by your applause. ("We can't help it.")

Now, let me call your attention for a moment to the answers which Mr. Lincoln made at Freeport to the questions which I propounded him at Ottawa, based upon the platform adopted by a majority of the Abolition counties of the State, which now as then supported him. In answer to my question whether he endorsed the Black Republican principle of "no more slave States," he answered that he was not pledged against the admission of any more slave States, but that he would be very sorry if he should ever be placed in a position where he would have to vote on the question; that he would rejoice to know that no more slave States would be admitted into the Union; "but," he added, "if slavery shall be kept out of the territories during the territorial existence of any one given territory, and then the people shall, having a fair chance and a clear field when they come to adopt the constitution, do such an extraordinary thing as to adopt a slave constitution, uninfluenced by the actual presence of the institution among them, I see no alternative, if we own the country, but to admit them into the Union." The point I wish him to answer is this: Suppose Congress should not prohibit slavery in the territory, and it applied for admission with a constitution recognizing slavery, then how would he vote? His answer at Freeport does not apply to any territory in America. I ask you, (turning to Lincoln,) will you vote to admit Kansas into the Union, with just such a constitution as her people want, with slavery or without as they shall determine? He will not answer. (He's afraid, and cheers.) I have put that question to him time and time again, and have not been able to get an answer out of him. I ask you again, Lincoln, will you vote to admit New Mexico when she has the requisite population with such a constitution as her people adopt, either recognizing slavery or not as they shall determine? He will not answer. I put the same question to him in reference to Oregon and the new States to be carved out of Texas, in pursuance of the contract between Texas and the United States, and he will not answer. He will not answer these questions in reference to any territory now in existence; but says, that if Congress should prohibit slavery in a territory, and when its people asked for admission as a State, they should adopt slavery as one of their institutions, that he supposes he would have to let it come in. (Laughter.) I submit to you whether that answer of his to my question does not justify me in saying that he has a fertile genius in devising language to conceal his thoughts. (Good for you, hurrah for Douglas, &c.) I ask you whether there is an intelligent man in America who does not believe, that that answer was made for the purpose of concealing what he intended to do. (No, no, and cheers.) He wished to make the old line Whigs believe that he would stand by the compromise measures of 1850, which declared that the States might come into the Union with slavery, or without as they pleased, while Lovejoy and his abolition allies up North, explained to the abolitionists, that in taking this ground he preached good abolition doctrine, because his proviso would not apply to any territory in America, and therefore there was no chance of his being governed by it. It would have been quite easy for him to have said, that he would let the people of a State do just as they pleased, if he desired to convey such an idea. Why did he not do it? (He was afraid to.) He would not answer my question directly, because up North, the abolition creed declares that there shall be no more slave States,

while down south, in Adams county, in Coles, and in Sangamon, he and his friends are afraid to advance that doctrine.
Therefore, he gives an evasive and equivocal answer, to be
construed one way in the south and another way in the north,
which, when analyzed, it is apparent is not an answer at all
with reference to any territory now in existence. ("Hit him on
the woolly side," "Hurrah for Douglas," &c.)

Mr. Lincoln complains that, in my speech the other day at
Galesburg, I read an extract from a speech delivered by him at
Chicago, and then another from his speech at Charleston, and
compared them, thus showing the people that he had one set
of principles in one part of the State and another in the other
part. And how does he answer that charge? Why, he quotes
from his Charleston speech as I quoted from it, and then
quotes another extract from a speech which he made at another place, which he says is the same as the extract from his
speech at Charleston; but he does not quote the extract from
his Chicago speech, upon which I convicted him of double
dealing. (Cheers.) I quoted from his Chicago speech to prove
that he held one set of principles up north among the abolitionists, and from his Charleston speech to prove that he held
another set down at Charleston and in southern Illinois. In
his answer to this charge, he ignores entirely his Chicago
speech, and merely argues that he said the same thing which
he said at Charleston at another place. If he did, it follows
that he has twice, instead of once, held one creed in one part
of the State and a different creed in another part. (He can't
get out of it, and cheers.) Up at Chicago, in the opening of
the campaign, he reviewed my reception speech, and undertook to answer my argument attacking his favorite doctrine of
negro equality. I had shown that it was a falsification of the
Declaration of Independence to pretend that that instrument
applied to and included negroes in the clause declaring that all
men were created equal. What was Lincoln's reply? I will read
from his Chicago speech, and the one which he did not
quote, and dare not quote, in this part of the State. ("Good,"
"hear, hear," &c.) He said:

I should like to know, if taking this old Declaration of Independence,
which declares that all men are equal upon principle, and making exceptions to it, where will it stop? If one man says it does not mean a negro,

why may not another man say it does not mean another man? If that declaration is not the truth, let us get the statute book in which we find it and tear it out!

There you find that Mr. Lincoln told the abolitionists of Chicago that if the Declaration of Independence did not declare that the negro was created by the Almighty the equal of the white man, that you ought to take that instrument and tear out the clause which says that all men were created equal. ("Hurrah for Douglas.") But let me call your attention to another part of the same speech. You know that in his Charleston speech, an extract from which he has read, he declared that the negro belongs to an inferior race; is physically inferior to the white man, and should always be kept in an inferior position. I will now read to you what he said at Chicago on that point. In concluding his speech at that place, he remarked:

My friends, I have detained you about as long as I desire to do, and I have only to say let us discard all this quibbling about this man and the other man—this race and that race and the other race being inferior, and therefore they must be placed in an inferior position, discarding our standard that we have left us. Let us discard all these things, and unite as one people throughout this land until we shall once more stand up declaring that all men are created equal.

Thus you see, that when addressing the Chicago abolitionists he declared that all distinctions of race must be discarded and blotted out, because the negro stood on an equal footing with the white man; that if one man said the Declaration of Independence did not mean a negro when it declared all men are created equal, that another man would say that it did not mean another man; and hence we ought to discard all differences between the negro race and all other races, and declare them all created equal. Did old Giddings, when he came down among you four years ago, preach more radical abolitionism than that? ("No, never.") Did Lovejoy, or Lloyd Garrison, or Wendell Phillips, or Fred. Douglass, ever take higher abolition grounds than that? Lincoln told you that I had charged him with getting up these personal attacks to conceal the enormity of his principles, and then commenced talking about something else, omitting to quote this part of his Chicago speech which contained the enormity of his principles to which I alluded. He knew that I alluded to his negro-equality doctrines when I spoke of the enormity of his principles, yet he did not find it convenient to answer on that point. Having shown you what he said in his Chicago speech in reference to negroes being created equal to white men, and about discarding all distinctions between the two races, I will again read to you what he said at Charleston:

I will say then, that I am not nor ever have been in favor of bringing about in any way, the social and political equality of the white and black races; that I am not nor ever have been in favor of making voters of the free negroes, or jurors, or qualifying them to hold office, or having them to marry with white people. I will say in addition, that there is a physical difference between the white and black races, which, I suppose, will forever forbid the two races living together upon terms of social and political equality, and inasmuch as they cannot so live, that while they do remain together, there must be the position of superior and inferior, that I as much as any other man am in favor of the superior position being assigned to the white man.

A VOICE—That's the doctrine.

MR. DOUGLAS—Yes, sir, that is good doctrine, but Mr. Lincoln is afraid to advocate it in the latitude of Chicago, where he hopes to get his votes. (Cheers.) It is good doctrine in the anti-abolition counties for him, and his Chicago speech is good doctrine in the abolition counties. I assert, on the authority of these two speeches of Mr. Lincoln, that he holds one set of principles in the abolition counties, and a different and contradictory set in the other counties. ("That's so," and cheers.) I do not question that he said at Ottawa what he quoted, but that only convicts him further, by proving that he has twice contradicted himself instead of once. ("Good," and applause.) Let me ask him why he cannot avow his principles the same in the North as in the South—the same in every county, if he has a conviction that they are just? But I forgot—he would not be a Republican if his principles would apply alike to every part of the country. The party to which he belongs is bounded and limited by geographical lines. With their principles they cannot even cross the Mississippi river on your ferry boats. (Immense applause.) They cannot cross over the Ohio into Kentucky. Lincoln himself cannot visit the land of his fathers, the scenes of his childhood, the graves of his ancestors, and carry his abolition principles, as he declared them at Chicago, with him. ("Hit him again," and cheers.)

This Republican organization appeals to the North against the South; it appeals to northern passion, northern prejudice, and northern ambition, against southern people, southern States, and southern institutions, and its only hope of success is by that appeal. Mr. Lincoln goes on to justify himself in making a war upon slavery, upon the ground that Frank Blair and Gratz Brown did not succeed in their warfare upon the institution in Missouri. (Laughter.) Frank Blair was elected to Congress in 1856, from the State of Missouri as a Buchanan Democrat, and he turned Fremonter after the people elected him, thus belonging to one party before his election, and another afterwards. (Treachery never succeeds.) What right then had he to expect, after having thus cheated his constituency, that they would support him at another election? ("None." "Hurrah for Douglas," &c.) Mr. Lincoln thinks that it is his duty to preach a crusade in the free States, against slavery, because it is a crime, as he believes, and ought to be extinguished; and because the people of the slave States will never abolish it. How is he going to abolish it? Down in the southern part of the State he takes the ground openly that he will not interfere with slavery where it exists, and says that he is not now and never was in favor of interfering with slavery where it exists in the States. Well, if he is not in favor of that, how does he expect to bring slavery in a course of ultimate extinction? ("Hit him again.") How can he extinguish it in Kentucky, in Virginia, in all the slave States by his policy, if he will not pursue a policy which will interfere with it in the States where it exists? ("That's so.") In his speech at Springfield before the Abolition or Republican convention, he declared his hostility to any more slave States in this language:

Under the operation of that policy the agitation has not only not ceased, but has constantly augmented. In my opinion it will not cease until a crisis shall have been reached and passed. "A house divided against itself cannot stand." I believe this Government cannot endure permanently half slave and half free. I do not expect the Union to be dissolved—I do not expect the house to fall—but I do expect it will cease to be divided. It will become all one thing or all the other. Either the opponents of slavery will arrest the further spread of it, and place it where the public mind shall rest in the belief that it is in the course of ultimate extinction; or, its advocates will push it forward until it shall become alike lawful in all the States—old as well as new, North as well as South.

Mr. Lincoln there told his Abolition friends that this government could not endure permanently, divided into free and slave States as our fathers made it, and that it must become all free or all slave, otherwise, that the government could not exist. How then does Lincoln propose to save the Union, unless by compelling all the States to become free, so that the house shall not be divided against itself? He intends making them all free; he will preserve the Union in that way, and yet, he is not going to interfere with slavery anywhere it now exists. How is he going to bring it about? Why, he will agitate, he will induce the North to agitate until the South shall be worried out, and forced to abolish slavery. Let us examine the policy by which that is to be done. He first tells you that he would prohibit slavery everywhere in the territories. He would thus confine slavery within its present limits. When he thus gets it confined, and surrounded, so that it cannot spread, the natural laws of increase will go on until the negroes will be so plenty that they cannot live on the soil. He will hem them in until starvation seizes them, and by starving them to death, he will put slavery in the course of ultimate extinction. If he is not going to interfere with slavery in the States, but intends to interfere and prohibit it in the territories, and thus smother slavery out, it naturally follows, that he can extinguish it only by extinguishing the negro race, for his policy would drive them to starvation. This is the humane and Christian remedy that he proposes for the great crime of slavery.

He tells you that I will not argue the question whether slavery is right or wrong. I tell you why I will not do it. I hold that under the Constitution of the United States, each State of this Union has a right to do as it pleases on the subject of slavery. In Illinois we have exercised that sovereign right by prohibiting slavery within our own limits. I approve of that line of policy. We have performed our whole duty in Illinois. We have gone as far as we have a right to go under the constitution of our common country. It is none of our business whether slavery exists in Missouri or not. Missouri is a sovereign State of this Union, and has the same right to decide the slavery question for herself that Illinois has to decide it for herself. (Good.) Hence I do not choose to occupy the time allotted to me in discussing a question that we have no right to act upon. (Right.) I thought that you desired to hear us upon those questions coming within our constitutional power of action. Lincoln will not discuss these. What one question has he discussed that comes within the power or calls for the action or interference of an United States Senator? He is going to discuss the rightfulness of slavery when Congress cannot act upon it either way. He wishes to discuss the merits of the Dred Scott decision when under the constitution, a Senator has no right to interfere with the decision of judicial tribunals. He wants your exclusive attention to two questions that he has no power to act upon; to two questions that he could not vote upon if he was in Congress, to two questions that are not practical, in order to conceal your attention from other questions which he might be required to vote upon should he ever become a member of Congress. He tells you that he does not like the Dred Scott decision. Suppose he does not, how is he going to help himself? He says that he will reverse it. How will he reverse it? I know of but one mode of reversing judicial decisions, and that is by appealing from the inferior to the superior court. But I have never yet learned how or where an appeal could be taken from the Supreme Court of the United States! The Dred Scott decision was pronounced by the highest tribunal on earth. From that decision there is no appeal this side of Heaven. Yet, Mr. Lincoln says he is going to reverse that decision. By what tribunal will he reverse it? Will he appeal to a mob? Does he intend to appeal to violence, to Lynch law? Will he stir up strife and rebellion in the land and overthrow the court by violence? He does not deign to tell you how he will reverse the Dred Scott decision, but keeps appealing each day from the Supreme Court of the United States to political meetings in the country. (Laughter.) He wants me to argue with you the merits of each point of that decision before this political meeting. I say to you, with all due respect, that I choose to

abide by the decisions of the Supreme Court as they are pronounced. It is not for me to inquire after a decision is made
whether I like it in all the points or not. When I used to
practice law with Lincoln, I never knew him to be beat in a
case that he did not get mad at the judge and talk about appealing; (laughter,) and when I got beat I generally thought
the court was wrong, but I never dreamed of going out of the
court house and making a stump speech to the people against
the judge, merely because I had found out that I did not
know the law as well as he did. (Great laughter.) If the decision did not suit me, I appealed until I got to the Supreme
Court, and then if that court, the highest tribunal in the
world, decided against me, I was satisfied, because it is the
duty of every law-abiding man to obey the constitutions,
the laws, and the constituted authorities. He who attempts to
stir up odium and rebellion in the country against the constituted authorities, is stimulating the passions of men to resort
to violence and to mobs instead of to the law. Hence, I tell
you that I take the decisions of the Supreme Court as the law
of the land, and I intend to obey them as such.

But, Mr. Lincoln says that I will not answer his question as
to what I would do in the event of the court making so ridiculous a decision as he imagines they would by deciding that
the free State of Illinois could not prohibit slavery within her
own limits. I told him at Freeport why I would not answer
such a question. I told him that there was not a man possessing any brains in America, lawyer or not, who ever dreamed
that such a thing could be done. (Right.) I told him then, as I
say now, that by all the principles set forth in the Dred Scott
decision, it is impossible. I told him then, as I do now, that it
is an insult to men's understanding, and a gross calumny on
the court, to presume in advance that it was going to degrade
itself so low as to make a decision known to be in direct violation of the constitution.

A Voice.—The same thing was said about the Dred Scott
decision before it passed.

Mr. Douglas—Perhaps you think that the Court did the
same thing in reference to the Dred Scott decision: I have
heard a man talk that way before. The principles contained
in the Dred Scott decision had been affirmed previously in

various other decisions. What court or judge ever held that a negro was a citizen? (Laughter.) The State courts had decided that question over and over again, and the Dred Scott decision on that point only affirmed what every court in the land knew to be the law.

But, I will not be drawn off into an argument upon the merits of the Dred Scott decision. It is enough for me to know that the Constitution of the United States created the Supreme Court for the purpose of deciding all disputed questions touching the true construction of that instrument, and when such decisions are pronounced, they are the law of the land, binding on every good citizen. Mr. Lincoln has a very convenient mode of arguing upon the subject. He holds that because he is a Republican that he is not bound by the decisions of the Court, but that I being a Democrat am so bound. (Laughter and cheers.) It may be that Republicans do not hold themselves bound by the laws of the land and the Constitution of the country as expounded by the courts; it may be an article in the Republican creed that men who do not like a decision, have a right to rebel against it; but when Mr. Lincoln preaches that doctrine, I think he will find some honest Republican—some law-abiding man in that party—who will repudiate such a monstrous doctrine. The decision in the Dred Scott case is binding on every American citizen alike; and yet Mr. Lincoln argues that the Republicans are not bound by it, because they are opposed to it, (laughter,) whilst Democrats are bound by it, because we will not resist it. A Democrat cannot resist the constituted authorities of this country. (Good.) A Democrat is a law-abiding man, a Democrat stands by the Constitution and the laws, and relies upon liberty as protected by law, and not upon mob or political violence.

I have never yet been able to make Mr. Lincoln understand, or can I make any man who is determined to support him, right or wrong, understand how it is that under the Dred Scott decision the people of a Territory, as well as a State, can have slavery or not, just as they please. I believe that I can explain that proposition to all constitution-loving, law-abiding men in a way that they cannot fail to understand it. Chief Justice Taney, in his opinion in the Dred Scott case, said that slaves being property, the owner of them has a right to take them into a territory the same as he would any other property; in other words, that slave property, so far as the right to enter a territory is concerned, stands on the same footing with other property. Suppose we grant that proposition. Then any man has a right to go to Kansas and take his property with him, but when he gets there he must rely upon the local law to protect his property, whatever it may be. (That's so.) In order to illustrate this, imagine that three of you conclude to go to Kansas. One takes $10,000 worth of slaves, another $10,000 worth of liquors, and the third $10,000 worth of dry goods. When the man who owns the dry goods arrives out there and commences selling them, he finds that he is stopped and prohibited from selling until he gets a license, which will destroy all the profits he can make on his goods to pay for. When the man with the liquors gets there and tries to sell he finds a Maine liquor law in force which prevents him. Now, of what use is his right to go there with his property unless he is protected in the enjoyment of that right after he gets there? (That's it.) The man who goes there with his slaves finds that there is no law to protect him when he arrives there. He has no remedy if his slaves run away to another country: there is no slave code or police regulations, and the absence of them excludes his slaves from the territory just as effectually and as positively as a constitutional prohibition could.

Such was the understanding when the Kansas and Nebraska bill was pending in Congress. Read the speech of Speaker Orr, of South Carolina, in the House of Representatives, in 1856, on the Kansas question, and you will find that he takes the ground that while the owner of a slave has a right to go into a territory, and carry his slaves with him, that he cannot hold them one day or hour unless there is a slave code to protect him. He tells you that slavery would not exist a day in South Carolina, or any other State, unless there was a friendly people and friendly legislation. Read the speeches of that giant in intellect, Alexander H. Stephens, of Georgia, and you will find them to the same effect. Read the speeches of Sam Smith, of Tennessee, and of all Southern men, and you will find that they all understood this doctrine then as we understand it now. Mr. Lincoln cannot be made to understand it, however. Down at Jonesboro, he went on to argue that if it be the law that a man has a right to take his slaves into territory of the United States under the constitution, that then a member of Congress was perjured if he did not vote for a slave code. I ask him whether the decision of the Supreme Court is not binding upon him as well as on me? If so, and he holds that he would be perjured if he did not vote for a slave code under it, I ask him whether, if elected to Congress, he will so vote? I have a right to his answer, and I will tell you why. He put that question to me down in Egypt, and did it with an air of triumph. This was about the form of it: "In the event of a slaveholding citizen of one of the territories should need and demand a slave code to protect his slaves, will you vote for it?" I answered him that a fundamental article in the Democratic creed, as put forth in the Nebraska bill and the Cincinnati platform, was non-intervention by Congress with slavery in the States and territories, ("Good," "That's the doctrine," and cheers,) and hence, that I would not vote in Congress for any code of laws either for or against slavery in any territory. I will leave the people perfectly free to decide that question for themselves. (Cheers.)

Mr. Lincoln and the Washington *Union* both think this a monstrous bad doctrine. Neither Mr. Lincoln or the Washington *Union* like my Freeport speech on that subject. The *Union*, in a late number, has been reading me out of the Democratic party because I hold that the people of a territory, like those of a State, have the right to have slavery or not, as they please. It has devoted three and a half columns to prove certain propositions, one of which I will read. It says:

We propose to show that Judge Douglas' action in 1850 and 1854 was taken with especial reference to the announcement of doctrine and programme which was made at Freeport. The declaration at Freeport was, that "in his opinion the people can, by lawful means, exclude slavery from a territory before it comes in as a State;" and he declared that his competitor had "heard him argue the Nebraska bill on that principle all over Illinois in 1854, 1855, and 1856, and had no excuse to pretend to have any doubt upon that subject."

The Washington *Union* there charges me with the monstrous crime of now proclaiming on the stump the same doctrine that I carried out in 1850, by supporting Clay's compromise measures. The *Union* also charges that I am now proclaiming the same doctrine that I did in 1854 in support of the Kansas and Nebraska bill. It is shocked that I should now stand where I stood in 1850, when I was supported by Clay, Webster, Cass and the great men of that day, and where I stood in 1854, and in 1856, when Mr. Buchanan was elected President. It goes on to prove and succeeds in proving from my speeches in Congress on Clay's compromise measures, that I held the same doctrines at that time that I do now, and then proves that by the Kansas and Nebraska bill I advanced the same doctrine that I now advance. It remarks:

So much for the course taken by Judge Douglas on the compromises of 1850. The record shows, beyond the possibility of cavil or dispute, that he expressly intended in those bills to give the territorial legislatures power to exclude slavery. How stands his record in the memorable session of 1854 with reference to the Kansas-Nebraska bill itself? We shall not overhaul the votes that were given on that notable measure. Our space will not afford it. We have his own words, however, delivered in his speech closing the great debate on that bill on the night of March 3, 1854, to show that *he meant* to do in 1854 precisely what *he had meant* to do in 1850. The Kansas-Nebraska bill being upon its passage, he said:

It then quotes my remarks upon the passage of the bill as follows:

The principle which we propose to carry into effect by this bill is this: That Congress shall neither legislate slavery into any Territory or State nor out of the same; but the people shall be left free to regulate their domestic concerns in their own way, subject only to the Constitution of the United States. In order to carry this principle into practical operation, it becomes necessary to remove whatever legal obstacles might be found in the way of its free exercise. It is only for the purpose of carrying out this great fundamental principle of self-government that the bill renders the eighth section of the Missouri act inoperative and void.

Now, let me ask, will those Senators who have arraigned me, or any one of them, have the assurance to rise in his place and declare that this great principle was never thought of or advocated as applicable to territorial bills, in 1850; that, from that session until the present, nobody ever thought of incorporating this principle in all new territorial organizations, &c., &c. I will begin with the compromises of 1850. Any Senator who will take the trouble to examine our journals will find that on the 25th of March of that year I reported from the committee on territories two bills, including the following measures: the admission of California, a territorial government for Utah, a territorial government for New Mexico and the adjustment of the Texas boundary. These bills proposed to leave the people of Utah and New Mexico free to decide the slavery question for themselves, *in the precise language of the Nebraska bill* now under discussion. A few weeks afterwards the committee of thirteen took those bills and put a wafer between them and reported them back to the Senate as one bill, with some slight amendments. *One of these amendments was, that the territorial legislatures should not legislate upon the subject of African slavery. I objected to this provision,* upon the ground that it subverted the great principle of self-government, *upon which the bill had been originally framed by the territorial committee.* On the first trial the Senate refused to strike it out, but subsequently did so, upon full debate, in order to establish that principle as the rule of action in territorial organizations.

The *Union* comments thus upon my speech on that occasion:

Thus it is seen that, in framing the Nebraska-Kansas bill, Judge Douglas framed it in the terms and upon the model of those of Utah and New Mexico, and that in the debate he took pains expressly to revive the recollection of the voting which had taken place upon amendments affecting the powers of the territorial legislatures over the subject of slavery in the bills of 1850, in order to give the same meaning, force, and effect to the Nebraska-Kansas bill on this subject as had been given to those of Utah and New Mexico.

The *Union* proves the following propositions: First, that I sustained Clay's compromise measures on the ground that they established the principle of self-government in the territories. Secondly, that I brought in the Kansas and Nebraska bill founded upon the same principles as Clay's compromise measures of 1850; and thirdly, that my Freeport speech is in exact accordance with those principles. And what do you think is the imputation that the *Union* casts upon me for all this? It says that my Freeport speech is not Democratic, and that I was not a Democrat in 1854 or in 1850! Now, is not that funny? (Great laughter and cheers.) Think that the author of the Kansas and Nebraska bill was not a Democrat when he introduced it. The *Union* says I was not a sound Democrat in 1850, nor in 1854, nor in 1856, nor am I in 1858 because I have always taken and now occupy the ground that the people of a territory, like those of a State, have the right to decide for themselves whether slavery shall or shall not exist in a territory. I wish to cite for the benefit of the Washington *Union* and the followers of that sheet, one authority on that point, and I hope the authority will be deemed satisfactory to that class of politicians. I will read from Mr. Buchanan's letter accepting the nomination of the Democratic Convention for the Presidency. You know that Mr. Buchanan, after he was nominated, declared to the Keystone Club, in a public speech, that he was no longer James Buchanan, but the embodiment of the Democratic platform. In his letter to the committee which informed him of his nomination, accepting it he defined the meaning of the Kansas and Nebraska bill and the Cincinnati platform in these words:

> The recent legislation of Congress respecting domestic slavery, derived as it has been from the original and pure fountain of legitimate political power, the will of the majority, promises ere long to allay the dangerous excitement. This legislation is founded upon principles as ancient as free government itself, and in accordance with them has simply declared that the people of a territory like those of a State shall decide for themselves whether slavery shall or shall not exist within their limits.

Thus you see that James Buchanan accepted the nomination at Cincinnati, on the condition that the people of a territory, like those of a State, should be left to decide for themselves whether slavery should, or should not exist within their limits. I sustained James Buchanan for the Presidency on that platform, as adopted at Cincinnati, and expounded by himself. He was elected President on that platform, and now we are told by the Washington *Union* that no man is a true Democrat who stands on the platform on which Mr. Buchanan was nominated, and which he has explained and expounded himself. (Laughter.) We are told that a man is not a Democrat who stands by Clay, Webster, and Cass, and the Compromise measures of 1850, and the Kansas and Nebraska bill of 1854. Whether a man be a Democrat or not on that platform, I intend to stand there as long as I have life. (Stick to it, and cheers.) I intend to cling firmly to that great principle which declares the right of each State and each territory to settle the question of slavery, and every other domestic question for themselves. I hold that if they want a slave State they have a right under the Constitution of the United States to make it so, and if they want a free State, it is their right to have it. But the *Union*, in advocating the claims of Lincoln over me to the Senate, lays down two unpardonable heresies which it says I advocate. The first, is the right of the people of a territory, the same as a State, to decide for themselves the question whether slavery shall exist within their limits, in the language of Mr. Buchanan; and the second is, that a constitution shall be submitted to the people of a territory for its adoption or rejection before their admission as a State under it. It so happens that Mr. Buchanan is pledged to both these heresies, for supporting which the Washington *Union* has read me out of the Democratic church. In his annual message he said that he trusted that the example of the Minnesota case would be followed in all future cases, requiring a submission of the constitution; and in his letter of acceptance, he said that the people of a territory, the same as a State, had the right to decide for themselves whether slavery should exist within their limits. Thus you find that this little corrupt gang who control the *Union*, and wish to elect Lincoln in preference to me—because, as they say, of these two heresies which I support—denounce President Buchanan when they denounce me, if he stands now by the principles upon which he was elected. Will they pretend that he does not now stand by the principles on which he was elected? Do they hold that he has abandoned the Kansas-Nebraska bill, the Cincinnati platform, and his own letter accepting his nomination, all of which declare the right of the people of a territory, the same as a State, to decide the slavery question for themselves? I will not believe that he has betrayed or intends to betray the platform which elected him ("good"); but if he does, I will not follow him. ("Good again.") I will stand by that great principle, no matter who may desert it. I intend to stand by it for the purpose of preserving peace between the North and the South, the free and the slave States. ("Hurrah for Douglas.") If each State will only agree to mind its own business, and let its neighbors alone, there will be peace forever between us. We in Illinois tried slavery when a territory, and found it was not good for us in this climate and with our surroundings, and hence we abolished it. We then adopted a free State constitution, as we had a right to do. In this State we have declared that a negro shall not be a citizen ("all right"), and we have also declared that he shall not be a slave. We had a right to adopt that policy. Missouri has just as good a right to adopt the other policy. (That's it.) I am now speaking of rights under the constitution, and not of moral or religious rights. I do not discuss the morals of the people of Missouri, but let them settle that matter for themselves. I hold that the people of the slaveholding States are civilized men as well as ourselves, that they bear consciences as well as we, and that they are accountable to God and their posterity and not to us. It is for them to decide therefore the moral and religious right of the slavery question for themselves within their own limits. I assert that they had as much right under the constitution to adopt the system of policy which they have as we had to adopt ours. So it is with every other State in this Union. Let each State stand firmly by that great constitutional right, let each State mind its own business and let its neighbors alone, and there will be no trouble on this question. If we will stand by that principle, then Mr. Lincoln will find that this republic can exist forever divided into free and slave States, as our fathers made it and the people of each State have decided. Stand by that great principle and we can go on as we have done, increasing in wealth, in population, in power, and in all the elements of greatness, until we shall be the admiration and terror of the world. We can go on and enlarge as our population increases, and we require more room, until we make this continent one ocean-bound republic. Under that principle the United States can perform that great mission, that destiny which Providence has marked out for us. Under that principle we can receive with entire safety that stream of intelligence which is constantly flowing from the Old World to the New, filling up our prairies, clearing our wildernesses and building cities, towns, railroads and other internal improvements, and thus make this the asylum of the oppressed of the whole earth. We have this great mission to perform, and it can only be performed by adhering faithfully to that principle of self-government on which our institutions were all established. I repeat that the principle is the right of each State, each territory, to decide this slavery question for itself, to have slavery or not, as it chooses, and it does not become Mr. Lincoln, or anybody else, to tell the people of Kentucky that they have no consciences, that they are living in a state of iniquity, and that they are cherishing an institution to their bosoms in violation of the law of God. Better for him to adopt the doctrine of "judge not lest ye be judged." (Good, and applause.) Let him perform his own duty at home, and he will have a better fate in the future. I think there are objects of charity enough in the free States to excite the sympathies and open the pockets of all the benevolence we have amongst us, without going abroad in search of negroes, of whose condition we know nothing. We have enough objects of charity at home, and it is our duty to take care of our own poor, and our own suffering, before we go abroad to intermeddle with other people's business.

My friends, I am told that my time is within two minutes of expiring. I have omitted many topics that I would like to have discussed before you at length. There were many points touched by Mr. Lincoln that I have not been able to take up for the want of time. I have hurried over each subject that I have discussed as rapidly as possible so as to omit but few, but one hour and a half is not time sufficient for a man to discuss at length one half of the great questions which are now dividing the public mind.

In conclusion, I desire to return to you my grateful acknowledgements for the kindness and the courtesy with which you have listened to me. It is something remarkable that in an audience as vast as this, composed of men of opposite politics and views, with their passions highly excited, there should be so much courtesy, kindness and respect exhibited not only towards one another, but towards the speakers, and I feel that it is due to you that I should thus express my gratitude for the kindness with which you have treated me. (Nine cheers were here given for Douglas.)

MR. LINCOLN'S REJOINDER.

On taking the stand, Mr. Lincoln was received with a tremendous cheer. He said:

MY FRIENDS: — Since Judge Douglas has said to you in his conclusion that he had not time in an hour and a half to answer all I had said in an hour, it follows of course that I will not be able to answer in half an hour all that he said in an hour and a half. [Cheers and laughter.]

I wish to return Judge Douglas my profound thanks for his public annunciation here to-day, to be put on record, that his system of policy in regard to the institution of slavery *contemplates that it shall last forever*. [Great cheers, and cries of "Hit him again."] We are getting a little nearer the true issue of this controversy, and I am profoundly grateful for this one sentence. Judge Douglas asks you "why cannot the institution of slavery, or rather, why cannot the nation, part slave and part free, continue as our fathers made it *forever*?" In the first place, I insist that our fathers *did not* make this nation half slave and half free, or part slave and part free. [Applause, and "That's so."] I insist that they found the institution of slavery existing here. They did not make it so, but they left it so because they knew of no way to get rid of it at that time. ["Good," "Good," "That's true."] When Judge Douglas undertakes to say that as a matter of choice the fathers of the government made this nation part slave and part free, *he assumes what is historically a falsehood*. [Long continued applause.] More than that; when the fathers of the government cut off the source of slavery by the abolition of the slave trade, and adopted a system of restricting it from the new Territories where it had not existed, I maintain that they placed it where they understood, and all sensible men understood, it was in the course of ultimate extinction ["that's so"]; and when Judge Douglas asks me why it cannot continue as our fathers made it, I ask him why he and his friends could not let it remain as our fathers made it? [Tremendous cheering.]

It is precisely all I ask of him in relation to the institution of slavery, that it shall be placed upon the basis that our fathers placed it upon. Mr. Brooks, of South Carolina, once said, and truly said, that when this government was established, no one expected the institution of slavery to last until this day; and that the men who formed this government were wiser and better men than the men of these days; but the men of these days had experience which the fathers had not, and that experience had taught them the invention of the cotton gin, and this had made the perpetuation of the institution of slavery a necessity in this country. Judge Douglas could not let it stand upon the basis upon which our fathers placed it, but removed it and *put it upon the cotton gin basis.* [Roars of laughter and enthusiastic applause.] It is a question, therefore, for him and his friends to answer—why they could not let it remain where the fathers of the Government originally placed it. [Cheers, and cries of "Hurrah for Lincoln!" "Good!" "Good!"]

I hope nobody has understood me as trying to sustain the doctrine that we have a right to quarrel with Kentucky, or Virginia, or any of the slave States, about the institution of slavery—thus giving the Judge an opportunity to make himself eloquent and valiant against us in fighting for their rights. I expressly declared in my opening speech, that I had neither the inclination to exercise, nor the belief in the existence of the right to interfere with the States of Kentucky or Virginia in doing as they pleased with slavery or any other existing institution. [Loud applause.] Then what becomes of all his eloquence in behalf of the rights of States, which are assailed by no living man? [Applause. "He knows it's all humbuggery."]

But I have to hurry on, for I have but a half hour. The Judge has informed me, or informed this audience, that the Washington *Union* is laboring for my election to the United States Senate. [Cheers and laughter.] That is news to me— not very ungrateful news either. [Turning to Mr. W. H. Carlin, who was on the stand]—I hope that Carlin will be elected to the State Senate and will vote for me. [Mr. Carlin shook his head.] Carlin don't fall in, I perceive, and I suppose he will not do much for me [laughter], but I am glad of all the support I can get anywhere, if I can get it without practicing any deception to obtain it. In respect to this large portion of Judge Douglas' speech, in which he tries to show that in the controversy between himself and the Administration party he is in the right, I do not feel myself at all competent or inclined to answer him. I say to him, "Give it to them [laughter]— give it to them just all you can" [renewed laughter and cheers]—and, on the other hand, I say to Carlin, and Jake

Davis, and to this man Wagley up here in Hancock, "Give it to Douglas [roars of laughter]—just pour it into him." [Cheers and laughter—"Good for you," "Hurrah for Lincoln!"]

Now in regard to this matter of the Dred Scott decision, I wish to say a word or two. After all, the Judge will not say whether, if a decision is made holding that the people of the *States* cannot exclude slavery, he will support it or not. He obstinately refuses to say what he will do in that case. The Judges of the Supreme Court as obstinately refused to say what they would do on this subject. Before this I reminded him that at Galesburg he had said the Judges had expressly declared the contrary, and you remember that in my opening speech I told him I had the book containing that decision here, and I would thank him to lay his finger on the place where any such thing was said. He has occupied his hour and a half, and he has not ventured to try to sustain his assertion. [Loud cheers.] *He never will.* [Renewed cheers.] But he is desirous of knowing how we are going to reverse the Dred Scott decision. Judge Douglas ought to know how. Did not he and his political friends find a way to reverse the decision of that same Court in favor of the constitutionality of the National Bank? [Cheers and laughter.] Didn't they find a way to do it so effectually that they have reversed it as completely as any decision ever was reversed—so far as its practical operation is concerned? [Cheers, and cries of "good," "good."] And let me ask you, didn't Judge Douglas find a way to reverse the decision of our Supreme Court, when it decided that Carlin's father—old Governor Carlin— had not the constitutional power to remove a Secretary of State? [Great cheering and laughter.] Did he not appeal to the "MOBS" as he calls them? Did he not make speeches in the lobby to show how villainous that decision was, and how it ought to be overthrown? Did he not succeed too in getting an act passed by the Legislature to have it overthrown? And didn't he himself sit down on that bench as one of the five added judges, who were to overslaugh the four old ones—getting his name of "Judge" in that way and no other? [Thundering cheers and laughter.] If there is a villainy in using disrespect or making opposition to Supreme

Court decisions, I commend it to Judge Douglas' earnest consideration. [Cheers and laughter.] I know of no man in the State of Illinois who ought to know so well about *how much* villainy it takes to oppose a decision of the Supreme Court, as our honorable friend, Stephen A. Douglas. [Long continued applause.]

Judge Douglas also makes the declaration that I say the Democrats are bound by the Dred Scott decision while the Republicans are not. In the sense in which he argues, I never said it; but I will tell you what I have said and what I do not hesitate to repeat to-day. I have said that as the Democrats believe that decision to be correct and that the extension of slavery is affirmed in the National Constitution, they are bound to support it as such; and I will tell you here that General Jackson once said each man was bound to support the Constitution "as he understood it." Now, Judge Douglas understands the Constitution according to the Dred Scott decision, and he is bound to support it as he understands it. [Cheers.] I understand it another way, and therefore I am bound to support it in the way in which I understand it. [Prolonged applause.] And as Judge Douglas believes that decision to be correct, I will remake that argument if I have time to do so. Let me talk to some gentleman down there among you who looks me in the face. We will say you are a member of the Territorial Legislature, and like Judge Douglas, you believe that the right to take and hold slaves there is a constitutional right. The first thing you do is to *swear you will support the Constitution* and all rights guaranteed therein; that you will, whenever your neighbor needs your legislation to support his constitutional rights, not withhold that legislation. If you withhold that necessary legislation for the support of the Constitution and constitutional rights, do you not commit perjury? [Cries of "Yes."] I ask every sensible man, if that is not so? ["Yes, yes"—"That's a fact."] That is undoubtedly just so, say what you please. Now that is precisely what Judge Douglas says, that this is a constitutional right. Does the Judge mean to say that the Territorial Legislature in legislating may by withholding necessary laws, or by passing unfriendly laws, *nullify that constitutional right*? Does he mean to say that? Does he mean to ignore the proposition so long known and well established in the law, that what you cannot do directly, you cannot do indirectly? Does he mean that? The truth about the matter is this: Judge Douglas has sung paeans to his "Popular Sovereignty" doctrine until his Supreme Court cooperating with him has *squatted* his Squatter Sovereignty out. [Uproarious laughter and applause.] But he will keep up this species of humbuggery about Squatter Sovereignty. He has at last invented this sort of *do nothing Sovereignty*— [renewed laughter]—that the people may exclude slavery by a sort of "Sovereignty" that is exercised by doing nothing at all. [Continued laughter.] Is not that running his Popular Sovereignty down awfully? [Laughter.] Has it not got down as thin as the homoeopathic soup that was made by boiling the shadow of a pigeon that had starved to death? [Roars of laughter and cheering.] But at last, when it is brought to the test of close reasoning, there is not even that thin decoction of it left. It is a presumption impossible in the domain of thought. It is precisely no other than the putting of that most unphilosophical proposition, that two bodies may occupy the same space at the same time. The Dred Scott decision covers the whole ground, and while it occupies it, there is no room even for the shadow of a starved pigeon to occupy the same ground. [Great cheering and laughter.]

A VOICE, on the platform—"Your time is almost out." [Loud cries of "Go on, go on"—"We'll listen all day."]

Well, I'll talk to you a little longer. Judge Douglas, in reply to what I have said about having upon a previous occasion made the speech at Ottawa as the one he took an extract from, at Charleston, says it only shows that I practiced the deception twice. Now, my friends, are any of you obtuse enough to swallow that? ["No, no, we're not such fools."] Judge Douglas had said I had made a speech at Charleston that I would not make up north, and I turned around and answered him by showing I *had* made that same speech up north—had made it at Ottawa—made it in his hearing— made it in *the* Abolition District—in Lovejoy's District—in the personal presence of Lovejoy himself—in the same atmosphere exactly in which I had made my Chicago speech of which he complains so much.

Now, in relation to my not having said anything about the quotation from the Chicago speech: He thinks that is a terrible subject for me to handle. Why, gentlemen, I can show you that the substance of the Chicago speech I delivered two years ago in "Egypt," as he calls it. It was down at Springfield. That speech is here in this book, and I could turn to it and read it to you but for the lack of time. I have not now the time to read it. ["Read it, read it, read it."] No, gentlemen, I am obliged to use discretion in disposing most advantageously of my brief time. The Judge has taken great exception to my adopting the heretical statement in the Declaration of Independence, that "all men are created equal," and he has a great deal to say about negro equality. I want to say that in sometimes alluding to the Declaration of Independence, I have only uttered the sentiments that Henry Clay used to hold. Allow me to occupy your time a moment with what he said. Mr. Clay was at one time called upon in Indiana, and in a way that I suppose was very insulting, to liberate his slaves, and he made a written reply to that application, and one portion of it is in these words:

What is the *foundation* of this appeal to me in Indiana, to liberate the slaves under my care in Kentucky? It is a general declaration in the act announcing to the world the independence of the thirteen American colonies, that *"men are created equal."* Now, as an abstract principle, *there is no doubt of the truth of that declaration*, and it is desirable in the *original construction* of society, and in organized societies, to keep it in view as a great fundamental principle.

[Loud cheers. "Hurrah for Clay."] When I sometimes, in relation to the organization of new societies in new countries, where the soil is clean and clear, insisted that we should keep that principle in view, Judge Douglas will have it that I want a negro wife. [Great laughter.] He never can be brought to understand that there is any middle ground on this subject. I have lived until my fiftieth year, and have never had a negro woman either for a slave or a wife, [cheers] and I think I can live fifty centuries, for that matter, without having had one for either. [Cheers and laughter.] I maintain that you may take Judge Douglas' quotations from my Chicago speech, and from my Charleston speech, and the Galesburg speech, —in his speech of to-day, and compare them over, and I am willing to trust them with you upon his proposition that they show rascality or double dealing. I deny that they do. [Great applause.]

The Judge does not seem at all disposed to have peace, but I find he is disposed to have a personal warfare with me. He says that my oath would not be taken against the bare word of Charles H. Lanphier or Thomas L. Harris. Well, that is altogether a matter of opinion. [Laughter.] It is certainly not for me to vaunt my word against oaths of these gentlemen, but I will tell Judge Douglas again the facts upon which I *"dared"* to say they proved a forgery. I pointed out at Galesburg that the publication of these resolutions in the Illinois *State Register* could not have been the result of accident, as the proceedings of that meeting bore unmistakable evidence of being done by a man who *knew* it was a forgery; that it was a publication partly taken from the real proceedings of the convention, and partly from the proceedings of a convention at another place; which showed that he had the real proceedings before him, and taking one part of the resolutions, he threw out another part and substituted false and fraudulent ones in their stead. I pointed that out to him, and also that his friend Lanphier, who was editor of the *Register* at that time and now is, must have known how it was done. Now whether *he* did it or got some friend to do it for him, I could not tell, but he certainly knew all about it. I pointed out to Judge Douglas that in his Freeport speech he had promised to *investigate* that matter. Does he now say he did not make that promise? ["No," "No."] I have a right to ask *why he did not keep it?* [Tremendous applause.] I call upon him to tell here to-day why he did not keep that promise. That fraud has been traced up so that it lies between him, Harris and Lanphier. There is little room for escape for Lanphier. [Laughter.] Lanphier is doing the Judge good service, and Douglas desires his word to be taken for the truth. He desires Lanphier to be taken as authority in what he states in his newspaper. He desires Harris to be taken as a man of vast credibility, and when this thing lies among them, they will not press it to show where the guilt really belongs. Now, as he has said that he would investigate it, and implied that he would tell us the result of his investigation, I demand of him to tell why he did not investigate it, if he did not; and if he did, *why he won't tell the result.* [Great cheers.] I call upon him for that.

This is the third time that Judge Douglas has assumed that he learned about these resolutions by Harris' attempting to use them against Norton on the floor of Congress. I tell Judge Douglas the public records of the country show that *he* himself attempted it upon Trumbull a month before Harris tried them on Norton [great applause]—that Harris had the opportunity of *learning it from him,* rather than he from Harris. I now ask his attention to that part of the record on the case. My friends, I am not disposed to detain you longer in regard to that matter.

I am told that I still have five minutes left. There is another matter I wish to call attention to. He says, when he discovered there was a mistake in that case, he came forward magnanimously, without my calling his attention to it, and explained it. I will tell you how he became so magnanimous. When the newspapers of our side had discovered and published it, and put it beyond his power to deny it, then he came forward and made a virtue of necessity by acknowledging it. [Great applause.] Now he argues that all the point there was in those resolutions, although never passed at Springfield, is retained by their being passed at other localities. Is that true? He said I had a hand in passing them, in his opening speech—that I was in the Convention and helped to pass them. Do the resolutions touch me at all? It strikes me there is some difference between holding a man responsible for an act which he *has not* done, and holding him responsible for an act that he *has* done. You will judge whether there is any difference in the *"spots."* [Laughter and cheers.] And he has taken credit for great magnanimity in coming forward and acknowledging what is proved on him beyond even the capacity of Judge Douglas to deny, and he has more capacity in that way than any other living man. [Laughter and cheers.]

Then he wants to know why I won't withdraw the charge in regard to a conspiracy to make slavery national, as he has withdrawn the one he made. May it please his worship, I will withdraw it *when it is proven false on me as that was proved false on him.* [Shouts of applause and laughter.] I will add a little more than that. I will withdraw it whenever a reasonable man shall be brought to believe that the charge is not true. [Renewed applause.] I have asked Judge Douglas' attention to certain matters of fact tending to prove the charge of a conspiracy to nationalize slavery, and he says he convinces me that this is all untrue because Buchanan was not in the country at that time, and because the Dred Scott case had not then got into the Supreme Court; and he says that I say the *Democratic* owners of Dred Scott got up the case. I never did say that. [Applause.] I defy Judge Douglas to show that I ever said so *for I never uttered it*. [One of Mr. Douglas' reporters gesticulated affirmatively at Mr. Lincoln.] I don't care if your hireling does say I did, I tell you myself that *I never said the "Democratic" owners of Dred Scott got up the case*. [Tremendous enthusiasm.] I have never pretended to know whether Dred Scott's owners were Democrats or Abolitionists, or Free Soilers or Border Ruffians. I have said that there is evidence about the case tending to show that it was a made up case, for the purpose of getting that decision. I have said that that evidence was very strong in the fact that when Dred Scott was declared to be a slave, the owner of him made him free, showing that he had had the case tried and the question settled for such use as could be made of that decision; he cared nothing about the property thus declared to be his by that decision. [Enthusiastic applause.] But my time is out and I can say no more.

Seventh Lincoln-Douglas Debate, Alton, Illinois

Seventh, and last joint debate. October 15. 1858. Douglas as reported in the Chicago Times. Lincoln as reported in the Press & Tribune.

SENATOR DOUGLAS' SPEECH.

Long and loud bursts of applause greeted Senator Douglas when he appeared on the stand. As he was about to commence speaking, he was interrupted by Dr. Hope, one of the Danite faction.

DR. HOPE.—Judge, before you commence speaking, allow me to ask you a question.

SENATOR DOUGLAS.—If you will not occupy too much of my time.

DR. HOPE.—Only an instant.

SENATOR DOUGLAS.—What is your question?

DR. HOPE.—Do you believe that the Territorial legislatures ought to pass laws to protect slavery in the territories?

SENATOR DOUGLAS.—You will get an answer in the course of my remarks. (Applause.)

LADIES AND GENTLEMEN: It is now nearly four months since the canvass between Mr. Lincoln and myself commenced. On the 16th of June the Republican Convention assembled at Springfield and nominated Mr. Lincoln as their candidate for the U.S. Senate, and he, on that occasion, delivered a speech in which he laid down what he understood to be the Republican creed and the platform on which he proposed to stand during the contest. The principal points in that speech of Mr. Lincoln's were: First, that this government could not endure permanently divided into free and slave States, as our fathers made it; that they must all become free or all become slave; all become one thing or all become the other, otherwise this Union could not continue to exist. I give you his opinions almost in the identical language he used. His second proposition was a crusade against the Supreme Court of the United States because of the Dred Scott decision;

urging as an especial reason for his opposition to that decision that it deprived the negroes of the rights and benefits of that clause in the Constitution of the United States which guarantees to the citizens of each State, all the rights, privileges, and immunities of the citizens of the several States. On the 10th of July I returned home, and delivered a speech to the people of Chicago, in which I announced it to be my purpose to appeal to the people of Illinois to sustain the course I had pursued in Congress. In that speech I joined issue with Mr. Lincoln on the points which he had presented. Thus there was an issue clear and distinct made up between us on these two propositions laid down in the speech of Mr. Lincoln at Springfield, and controverted by me in my reply to him at Chicago. On the next day, the 11th of July, Mr. Lincoln replied to me at Chicago, explaining at some length, and re-affirming the positions which he had taken in his Springfield speech. In that Chicago speech he even went further than he had before, and uttered sentiments in regard to the negro being on an equality with the white man. (That's so.) He adopted in support of this position the argument which Lovejoy and Codding, and other Abolition lecturers had made familiar in the northern and central portions of the State, to wit: that the Declaration of Independence having declared all men free and equal, by Divine law, also that negro equality was an inalienable right, of which they could not be deprived. He insisted, in that speech, that the Declaration of Independence included the negro in the clause asserting that all men were created equal, and went so far as to say that if one man was allowed to take the position, that it did not include the negro, others might take the position that it did not include other men. He said that all these distinctions between this man and that man, this race and the other race, must be discarded, and we must all stand by the Declaration of Independence, declaring that all men were created equal.

The issue thus being made up between Mr. Lincoln and myself on three points, we went before the people of the State. During the following seven weeks, between the Chicago speeches and our first meeting at Ottawa, he and I addressed large assemblages of the people in many of the central counties. In my speeches I confined myself closely to those three positions which he had taken controverting his proposition that this Union could not exist as our fathers made it, divided into free and slave States, controverting his proposition of a crusade against the Supreme Court because of the Dred Scott decision, and controverting his proposition that the Declaration of Independence included and meant the negroes as well as the white men, when it declared all men to be created equal. (Cheers for Douglas.) I supposed at that time that these propositions constituted a distinct issue between us, and that the opposite positions we had taken upon them we would be willing to be held to in every part of the State. I never intended to waver one hair's breadth from that issue either in the north or the south, or wherever I should address the people of Illinois. I hold that when the time arrives that I cannot proclaim my political creed in the same terms not only in the northern but the southern part of Illinois, not only in the northern but the southern States, and wherever the American flag waves over American soil, that then there must be something wrong in that creed. ("Good, good," and cheers.) So long as we live under a common constitution, so long as we live in a confederacy of sovereign and equal States, joined together as one for certain purposes, that any political creed is radically wrong which cannot be proclaimed in every State, and every section of that Union alike. I took up Mr. Lincoln's three propositions in my several speeches, analyzed them, and pointed out what I believed to be the radical errors contained in them. First, in regard to his doctrine that this government was in violation of the law of God which says, that a house divided against itself cannot stand, I repudiated it as a slander upon the immortal framers of our constitution. I then said, have often repeated, and now again assert, that in my opinion this government can endure forever, (good) divided into free and slave States as our fathers made it,—each State having the right to prohibit, abolish or sustain slavery just as it pleases. ("Good," "right," and cheers.) This government was made upon the great basis of the sovereignty of the States, the right of each State to regulate its own domestic institutions to suit itself, and that right was conferred with understanding and expectation that inasmuch as each locality had separate interests, each locality must have different and distinct local and domestic institutions, corresponding to its wants and interests. Our fathers knew when they made the government, that the laws and institutions which were well adapted to the green mountains of Vermont, were unsuited to the rice plantations of South Carolina. They knew then, as well as we know now, that the laws and institutions which would be well adapted to the beautiful prairies of Illinois would not be suited to the mining regions of California. They knew that in a Republic as broad as this, having such a variety of soil, climate and interest, there must necessarily be a corresponding variety of local laws—the policy and institutions of each State adapted to its condition and wants. For this reason this Union was established on the right of each State to do as it pleased on the question of slavery, and every other question; and the various States were not allowed to complain of, much less interfere, with the policy of their neighbors. ("That's good doctrine," "that's the doctrine," and cheers.)

Suppose the doctrine advocated by Mr. Lincoln and the abolitionists of this day had prevailed when the Constitution was made, what would have been the result? Imagine for a moment that Mr. Lincoln had been a member of the convention that framed the Constitution of the United States, and that when its members were about to sign that wonderful document, he had arisen in that convention as he did at Springfield this summer, and addressing himself to the President, had said "a house divided against itself cannot stand; (laughter) this government divided into free and slave States cannot endure, they must all be free or all be slave, they must all be one thing or all be the other, otherwise, it is a violation of the law of God, and cannot continue to exist;"—suppose Mr. Lincoln had convinced that body of sages, that that doctrine was sound, what would have been the result? Remember that the Union was then composed of thirteen States, twelve of which were slaveholding and one free. Do you think that the one free State would have outvoted the twelve slaveholding States, and thus have secured the abolition of slavery? (No, no.) On the other hand, would not the twelve slaveholding States have outvoted the one free State, and thus have fastened slavery, by a Constitutional provision, on every foot of the American Republic forever? You see that if this abolition doctrine of Mr. Lincoln had prevailed when the government was made, it would have established slavery as a permanent institution, in all the States whether they wanted it or not, and the question for us to determine in Illinois now as one of the free States is, whether or not we are willing, having become the majority section, to enforce a doctrine on the minority, which we would have resisted with our heart's blood had it been attempted on us when we were in a minority. ("We never will," "good, good," and cheers.) How has the South lost her power as the majority section in this Union, and how have the free States gained it, except under the operation of that principle which declares the right of the people of each State and each territory to form and regulate their domestic institutions in their own way. It was under that principle that slavery was abolished in New Hampshire, Rhode Island, Connecticut, New York, New Jersey, and Pennsylvania; it was under that principle that one half of the slave-holding States became free; it was under that principle that the number of free States increased until from being one out of twelve States, we have grown to be the majority of States of the whole Union, with the power to control the House of Representatives and Senate, and the power, consequently, to elect a President by Northern votes without the aid of a Southern State. Having obtained this power under the operation of that great principle, are you now prepared to abandon the principle and declare that merely because we have the power you will wage a war against the Southern States and their institutions until you force them to abolish slavery everywhere. (No, never, and great applause.)

After having pressed these arguments home on Mr. Lincoln for seven weeks, publishing a number of my speeches, we met at Ottawa in joint discussion, and he then began to crawfish a little, and let himself down. (Immense applause.) I there propounded certain questions to him. Amongst others, I asked him whether he would vote for the admission of any more slave States in the event the people wanted them. He would not answer. (Applause and laughter.) I then told him that if he did not answer the question there I would renew it at Freeport, and would then trot him down into Egypt and again put it to him. (Cheers.) Well, at Freeport, knowing that the next joint discussion took place in Egypt, and being in dread of it, he did answer my question in regard to no more slave States in a mode which he hoped would be satisfactory to me, and accomplish the object he had in view. I will show you what his answer was. After saying that he was not pledged to the Republican doctrine of "no more slave States," he declared

> I state to you freely, frankly, that I should be exceedingly sorry to ever be put in the position of having to pass upon that question. I should be exceedingly glad to know that there never would be another slave State admitted into this Union.

Here, permit me to remark, that I do not think the people will ever force him into a position against his will. (Great laughter and applause.) He went on to say:

> But I must add in regard to this, that if slavery shall be kept out of the territory during the territorial existence of any one given territory and then the people should, having a fair chance and clear field when they come to adopt a constitution, if they should do the extraordinary thing of adopting a slave constitution, uninfluenced by the actual presence of the institution among them, I see no alternative if we own the country, but we must admit it into the Union.

That answer Mr. Lincoln supposed would satisfy the old-line Whigs, composed of Kentuckians and Virginians, down in the southern part of the State. Now, what does it amount to? I desired to know whether he would vote to allow Kansas to come into the Union with slavery or not as her people desired. He would not answer; but in a round about way said that if slavery should be kept out of a territory during the whole of its territorial existence, and then the people, when they adopted a State constitution, asked admission as a slave State, he supposed he would have to let the State come in. The case I put to him was an entirely different one. I desired to know whether he would vote to admit a State if Congress had not prohibited slavery in it during its territorial existence, as Congress never pretended to do under Clay's compromise measures of 1850. He would not answer, and I have not yet been able to get an answer from him. (Laughter, "he'll answer this time," "he's afraid to answer," etc.) I have asked him whether he would vote to admit Nebraska if her people asked to come in as a State with a constitution recognizing slavery, and he refused to answer. ("Put him through," "give it to him," and cheers.) I have put the question to him with reference to New Mexico, and he has not uttered a word in answer. I have enumerated the territories, one after another, putting the same question to him with reference to each, and he has not said, and will not say, whether, if elected to Congress, he will vote to admit any territory now in existence with such a constitution as her people may adopt. He invents a case which does not exist, and cannot exist under this government, and answers it; but he will not answer the question I put to him in connection with any of the territories now in existence. ("Hurrah for Douglas," "three cheers for Douglas.") The contract we entered into with Texas when she entered the Union obliges us to allow four States to be formed out of the old State, and admitted with or without slavery as the respective inhabitants of each may determine. I have asked Mr. Lincoln three times in our joint discussions whether he would vote to redeem that pledge, and he has never yet answered. He is as silent as the grave on the subject. (Laughter, "Lincoln must answer," "he will," &c.) He would rather answer as to a state of the case which will never arise than commit himself by telling what he would do in a case which would come up for his action soon after his election to Congress. ("He'll never have to act on any question," and laughter.) Why can he not say whether he is willing to allow the people of each State to have slavery or not as they please, and to come into the Union when they have the requisite population as a slave or a free State as they decide? I have no trouble in answering the question. I have said everywhere, and now repeat it to you, that if the people of Kansas want a slave State they have a right, under the constitution of the United States, to form such a State, and I will let them come into the Union with slavery or without, as they determine. ("That's right," "good," "hurrah for Douglas all the time," and cheers.) If the people of any other territory desire slavery let them have it. If they do not want it let them prohibit it. It is their business not mine. ("That's the doctrine.") It is none of your business in Missouri whether Kansas shall adopt slavery or reject it. It is the business of her people and none of yours. The people of Kansas has as much right to decide that question for themselves as you have in Missouri to decide it for yourselves, or we in Illinois to decide it for ourselves. ("That's what we believe," "We stand by that," and cheers.)

And here I may repeat what I have said in every speech I have made in Illinois, that I fought the Lecompton constitution to its death, not because of the slavery clause in it, but because it was not the act and deed of the people of Kansas. I said then in Congress, and I say now, that if the people of Kansas want a slave State, they have a right to have it. If they wanted the Lecompton constitution, they had a right to have it. I was opposed to that constitution because I did not believe that it was the act and deed of the people, but on the contrary, the act of a small, pitiful minority acting in the name of the majority. When at last it was determined to send that constitution back to the people, and accordingly, in August last, the question of admission under it was submitted to a popular vote, the citizens rejected it by nearly ten to one, thus showing conclusively, that I was right when I said that the Lecompton constitution was not the act and deed of the people of Kansas, and did not embody their will. (Cheers.)

I hold that there is no power on earth, under our system of government, which has the right to force a constitution upon an unwilling people. (That's so.) Suppose there had been a majority of ten to one in favor of slavery in Kansas, and suppose there had been an abolition President, and an abolition administration, and by some means the abolitionists succeeded in forcing an abolition constitution on those slaveholding people, would the people of the South have submitted to that act for one instant. (No, no.) Well, if you of the South would not have submitted to it a day, how can you, as fair, honorable and honest men insist on putting a slave constitution on a people who desire a free State. ("That's so," and cheers.) Your safety and ours depend upon both of us acting in good faith, and living up to that great principle which asserts the right of every people to form and regulate their domestic institutions to suit themselves, subject only to the Constitution of the United States. ("That's the doctrine," and immense applause.)

Most of the men who denounced my course on the Lecompton question, objected to it not because I was not right, but because they thought it expedient at that time, for the sake of keeping the party together, to do wrong. (Cheers.) I never knew the Democratic party to violate any one of its principles out of policy or expediency, that it did not pay the debt with sorrow. There is no safety or success for our party unless we always do right, and trust the consequences to God and the people. I chose not to depart from principle for the sake of expediency in the Lecompton question, and I never intend to do it on that or any other question. (Good.)

But I am told that I would have been all right if I had only voted for the English bill after Lecompton was killed. (Laughter and cheers.) You know a general pardon was granted to all political offenders on the Lecompton question, provided they would only vote for the English bill. I did not accept the benefits of that pardon, for the reason that I had been right in the course I had pursued, and hence did not require any forgiveness. Let us see how the result has been worked out. English brought in his bill referring the Lecompton Constitution back to the people, with the provision that if it was rejected Kansas should be kept out of the Union until she had the full ratio of population required for a member of Congress, thus in effect declaring that if the people of Kansas would only consent to come into the Union under the Lecompton Constitution, and have a slave State when they did not want it, they should be admitted with a population of 35,000, but that if they were so obstinate as to insist upon having just such a constitution as they thought best, and to desire admission as a free State, then they should be kept out until they had 93,420 inhabitants. I then said, and I now repeat to you, that whenever Kansas has people enough for a slave State she has people enough for a free State. ("That's the doctrine all over," "Hurrah for Douglas.") I was and am willing to adopt the rule that no State shall ever come into the Union until she has the full ratio of population for a member of Congress, provided that rule is made uniform. I made that proposition in the Senate last winter, but a majority of the Senators would not agree to it; and I then said to them if you will not adopt the general rule I will not consent to make an exception of Kansas.

I hold that it is a violation of the fundamental principles of this government to throw the weight of federal power into the scale, either in favor of the free or the slave States. Equality among all the States of this Union is a fundamental principle in our political system. We have no more right to throw the weight of the federal government into the scale in favor of the slaveholding than the free States, and last of all should our friends in the South consent for a moment that Congress should withhold its powers either way when they know that there is a majority against them in both Houses of Congress.

Fellow citizens, how have the supporters of the English bill stood up to their pledges not to admit Kansas until she obtained a population of 93,420 in the event she rejected the Lecompton constitution? How? The newspapers inform us that English himself, whilst conducting his canvass for re-election, and in order to secure it, pledged himself to his constituents that if returned he would disregard his own bill and vote to admit Kansas into the Union with such population as she might have when she made application. (Laughter and applause.) We are informed that every Democratic candidate for Congress in all the States where elections have recently been held, was pledged against the English bill, with perhaps one or two exceptions. Now, if I had only done as these Anti-Lecompton men who voted for the English bill in Congress, pledging themselves to refuse to admit Kansas if she refused to become a slave State until she had a population of 93,420, and then returned to their people, forfeited their pledge, and made a new pledge to admit Kansas at any time she applied, without regard to population, I would have had no trouble. You saw the whole power and patronage of the federal government wielded in Indiana, Ohio, and Pennsylvania to re-elect Anti-Lecompton men to Congress who voted against Lecompton, then voted for the English bill, and then denounced the English bill, and pledged themselves to their people to disregard it. (Good.) My sin consists in not having given a pledge, and then in not having afterwards forfeited it. For that reason, in this State, every postmaster, every route agent, every collector of the ports, and every federal office holder, forfeits his head the moment he expresses a preference

for the Democratic candidates against Lincoln and his abolition associates. (That's so, and cheers.) A Democratic Administration which we helped to bring into power, deems it
consistent with its fidelity to principle and its regard to duty,
to wield its power in this State in behalf of the Republican
abolition candidates in every county and every Congressional
district against the Democratic party. All I have to say in reference to the matter is, that if that administration have not
regard enough for principle, if they are not sufficiently attached to the creed of the Democratic party to bury forever
their personal hostilities in order to succeed in carrying out
our glorious principles, I have. (Good, good, and cheers.) I
have no personal difficulties with Mr. Buchanan or his cabinet. He chose to make certain recommendations to Congress
as he had a right to do on the Lecompton question. I could
not vote in favor of them. I had as much right to judge for
myself how I should vote as he had how he should recommend. He undertook to say to me, if you do not vote as I tell
you, I will take off the heads of your friends. (Laughter.) I
replied to him, "you did not elect me, I represent Illinois and
I am accountable to Illinois, as my constituency, and to God,
but not to the President or to any other power on earth."
(Good, good, and vociferous applause.)

   And now this warfare is made on me because I would not
surrender my connections of duty, because I would not abandon my constituency, and receive the orders of the executive
authorities how I should vote in the Senate of the United
States. ("Never do it," "three cheers," &c.) I hold that an attempt to control the Senate on the part of the Executive is
subversive of the principles of our constitution. ("That's
right.") The Executive department is independent of the Senate, and the Senate is independent of the President. In matters
of legislation the President has a veto on the action of the
Senate, and in appointments and treaties the Senate has a veto
on the President. He has no more right to tell me how I shall
vote on his appointments than I have to tell him whether he
shall veto or approve a bill that the Senate has passed. Whenever you recognize the right of the Executive to say to a Senator, "do this, or I will take off the heads of your friends,"
you convert this government from a republic into a des-

potism. (Hear, hear, and cheers.) Whenever you recognize the right of a President to say to a member of Congress, "vote as I tell you, or I will bring a power to bear against you at home which will crush you," you destroy the independence of the representative, and convert him into a tool of Executive power. ("That's so," and applause.) I resisted this invasion of the constitutional rights of a Senator, and I intend to resist it as long as I have a voice to speak, or a vote to give. Yet, Mr. Buchanan cannot provoke me to abandon one iota of Democratic principles out of revenge or hostility to his course. ("Good, good, three cheers for Douglas.") I stand by the platform of the Democratic party, and by its organization, and support its nominees. If there are any who choose to bolt, the fact only shows that they are not as good Democrats as I am. ("That's so," "good," and applause.)

My friends, there never was a time when it was as important for the Democratic party, for all national men, to rally and stand together as it is to-day. We find all sectional men giving up past differences and continuing the one question of slavery, and when we find sectional men thus uniting, we should unite to resist them and their treasonable designs. Such was the case in 1850, when Clay left the quiet and peace of his home, and again entered upon public life to quell agitation and restore peace to a distracted Union. Then we Democrats, with Cass at our head, welcomed Henry Clay, whom the whole nation regarded as having been preserved by God for the times. He became our leader in that great fight, and we rallied around him the same as the Whigs rallied around old Hickory in 1832, to put down nullification. (Cheers.) Thus you see that whilst Whigs and Democrats fought fearlessly in old times about banks, the tariff, distribution, the specie circular, and the sub-treasury, all united as a band of brothers when the peace, harmony, or integrity of the Union was imperiled. (Tremendous applause.) It was so in 1850, when abolitionism had even so far divided this country, North and South, as to endanger the peace of the Union; Whigs and Democrats united in establishing the compromise measures of that year, and restoring tranquillity and good feeling. These measures passed on the joint action of the two parties. They rested on the great principle that the people of each State and each territory should be left perfectly free to form and regulate their domestic institutions to suit themselves. You Whigs and we Democrats justified them in that principle. In 1854, when it became necessary to organize the territories of Kansas and Nebraska, I brought forward the bill on the same principle. In the Kansas-Nebraska bill you find it declared to be the true intent and meaning of the act not to legislate slavery into any State or territory, nor to exclude it therefrom, but to leave the people thereof perfectly free to form and regulate their domestic institutions in their own way. ("That's so," and cheers.) I stand on that same platform in 1858 that I did in 1850, 1854, and 1856. The Washington *Union*, pretending to be the organ of the Administration, in the number of the 5th of this month, devotes three columns and a half to establish these propositions: First, that Douglas, in his Freeport speech, held the same doctrine that he did in his Nebraska bill in 1854; second, that in 1854 Douglas justified the Nebraska bill upon the ground that it was based upon the same principle as Clay's compromise measures of 1850. The *Union* thus proved that Douglas was the same in 1858 that he was in 1856, 1854, and 1850, and consequently argued that he was never a Democrat. (Great laughter.) Is it not funny that I was never a Democrat? (Renewed laughter.) There is no pretence that I have changed a hair's breadth. The *Union* proves by my speeches that I explained the compromise measures of 1850 just as I do now, and that I explained the Kansas and Nebraska bill in 1854 just as I did in my Freeport speech, and yet says that I am not a Democrat, and cannot be trusted, because I have not changed during the whole of that time. It has occurred to me that in 1854 the author of the Kansas and Nebraska bill was considered a pretty good Democrat. (Cheers.) It has occurred to me that in 1856, when I was exerting every nerve and every energy for James Buchanan, standing on the same platform then that I do now, that I was a pretty good Democrat. (Renewed applause.) They now tell me that I am not a Democrat, because I assert that the people of a territory, as well as those of a State, have the right to decide for themselves whether slavery can or can not exist in such territory. Let me read what James Buchanan said on that point when he accepted the Democratic nomination for the Presidency in 1856. In his letter of acceptance, he used the following language:

The recent legislation of Congress respecting domestic slavery, derived as it has been from the original and pure fountain of legitimate political power, the will of the majority, promises ere long to allay the dangerous excitement. This legislation is founded upon principles as ancient as free government itself, and in accordance with them has simply declared that the people of a territory like those of a state, shall decide for themselves WHETHER SLAVERY SHALL OR SHALL NOT EXIST WITHIN THEIR LIMITS.

Dr. Hope will there find my answer to the question he propounded to me before I commenced speaking. (Vociferous shouts of applause.) Of course no man will consider it an answer, who is outside of the Democratic organization, bolts Democratic nominations, and indirectly aids to put abolitionists into power over Democrats. But whether Dr. Hope considers it an answer or not, every fair minded man will see that James Buchanan has answered the question, and has asserted that the people of a territory, like those of a State, shall decide for themselves whether slavery shall or shall not exist within their limits. I answer specifically if you want a further answer, and say that while under the decision of the Supreme Court, as recorded in the opinion of Chief Justice Taney, slaves are property like all other property and can be carried into territory of the United States the same as any other description of property, yet when you get them there they are subject to the local law of the territory just like all other property. You will find in a recent speech delivered by that able and eloquent statesman, Hon. Jefferson Davis, at Bangor, Maine, that he took the same view of this subject that I did in my Freeport speech. He there said:

If the inhabitants of any territory should refuse to enact such laws and police regulations as would give security to their property or to his, it would be rendered more or less valueless in proportion to the difficulties of holding it without such protection. In the case of property in the labor of man, or what is usually called slave property, the insecurity would be so great that the owner could not ordinarily retain it. Therefore, though the right would remain, the remedy being withheld, it would follow that the owner would be practically debarred, by the circumstances of the case, from taking slave property into a territory where the sense of the inhabitants was opposed to its introduction. So much for the oft repeated fallacy of forcing slavery upon any community.

You will also find that the distinguished Speaker of the present House of Representatives, Hon. Jas. L. Orr, construed the Kansas and Nebraska bill in this same way in 1856, and also that great intellect of the South, Alex. H. Stephens, put the same construction upon it in Congress that I did in my Freeport speech. The whole South are rallying to the support of the doctrine that if the people of a Territory want slavery they have a right to have it, and if they do not want it that no power on earth can force it upon them. I hold that there is no principle on earth more sacred to all the friends of freedom than that which says that no institution, no law, no constitution, should be forced on an unwilling people contrary to their wishes; and I assert that the Kansas and Nebraska bill contains that principle. It is the great principle contained in that bill. It is the principle on which James Buchanan was made President. Without that principle he never would have been made President of the United States. I will never violate or abandon that doctrine if I have to stand alone. (Hurrah for Douglas.) I have resisted the blandishments and threats of power on the one side, and seduction on the other, and have stood immovably for that principle, fighting for it when assailed by Northern mobs, or threatened by Southern hostility. ("That's the truth," and cheers.) I have defended it against the North and the South, and I will defend it against whoever assails it, and I will follow it wherever its logical conclusions lead me. ("So will we all," "hurrah for Douglas.") I say to you that there is but one hope, one safety for this country, and that is to stand immovably by that principle which declares the right of each State and each territory to decide these questions for themselves. (Hear him, hear him.) This government was founded on that principle, and must be administered in the same sense in which it was founded.

But the Abolition party really think that under the Declaration of Independence the negro is equal to the white man, and that negro equality is an inalienable right conferred by the Almighty, and hence, that all human laws in violation of it are null and void. With such men it is no use for me to argue. I hold that the signers of the Declaration of Independence had no reference to negroes at all when they declared all men to be created equal. They did not mean negro, nor the savage Indians, nor the Fejee Islanders, nor any other barbarous race. They were speaking of white men. ("It's so," "it's so," and cheers.) They alluded to men of European birth and European descent—to white men, and to none others, when they declared that doctrine. ("That's the truth.") I hold that this government was established on the white basis. It was established by white men for the benefit of white men and their posterity forever, and should be administered by white men, and none others. But it does not follow, by any means, that merely because the negro is not a citizen, and merely because he is not our equal, that, therefore, he should be a slave. On the contrary, it does follow, that we ought to extend to the negro race, and to all other dependent races all the rights, all the privileges, and all the immunities which they can exercise consistently with the safety of society. Humanity requires that we should give them all these privileges; christianity commands that we should extend those privileges to them. The question then arises what are those privileges, and what is the nature and extent of them. My answer is that that is a question which each State must answer for itself. We in Illinois have decided it for ourselves. We tried slavery, kept it up for twelve years, and finding that it was not profitable we abolished it for that reason, and became a free State. We adopted in its stead the policy that a negro in this State shall not be a slave and shall not be a citizen. We have a right to adopt that policy. For my part I think it is a wise and sound policy for us. You in Missouri must judge for yourselves whether it is a wise policy for you. If you choose to follow our example, very good; if you reject it, still well, it is your business, not ours. So with Kentucky. Let Kentucky adopt a policy to suit herself. If we do not like it we will keep away from it, and if she does not like ours let her stay at home, mind her own business and let us alone. If the people of all the States will act on that great principle, and each State mind its own business, attend to its own affairs, take care of its own negroes and not meddle with its neighbors, then there will be peace between the North and the South, the East and the West, throughout the whole Union. (Cheers.) Why can we not thus have peace? Why should we thus allow a sectional party to agitate this country, to array the North against the South, and convert us into enemies instead of friends, merely that a few ambitious men may ride into power on a sectional hobby? How long is it since these ambitious Northern men wished for a sectional organization? Did any one of them dream of a sectional party as long as the North was the weaker section and the South the stronger? Then all were opposed to sectional parties; but the moment the North obtained the majority in the House and Senate by the admission of California, and could elect a President without the aid of Southern votes, that moment ambitious Northern men formed a scheme to excite the North against the South, and make the people be governed in their votes by geographical lines, thinking that the North, being the stronger section, would outvote the South, and consequently they, the leaders, would ride into office on a sectional hobby. I am told that my hour is out. It was very short.

MR. LINCOLN'S REPLY.

On being introduced to the audience, after the cheering had subsided Mr. Lincoln said:

LADIES AND GENTLEMEN:—I have been somewhat, in my own mind, complimented by a large portion of Judge Douglas' speech—I mean that portion which he devotes to the controversy between himself and the present Administration. [Cheers and laughter.] This is the seventh time Judge Douglas and myself have met in these joint discussions, and he has been gradually improving in regard to his war with the Administration. [Laughter, "That's so."] At Quincy, day before yesterday, he was a little more severe upon the Administration than I had heard him upon any former occasion, and I took pains to compliment him for it. I then told him to "Give it to them with all the power he had;" and as some of them were present I told them I would be very much obliged if they would *give it to him* in about the same way. [Uproarious laughter and cheers.] I take it he has now vastly improved upon the attack he made then upon the Administration. I flatter myself he has really taken my advice on this subject. All I can say now is to recommend to him and to them what I then commended—to prosecute the war against one another in the most vigorous manner. I say to them again—"Go it, husband!—Go it, bear!" [Great laughter.]

There is one other thing I will mention before I leave this branch of the discussion—although I do not consider it much of my business, any way. I refer to that part of the Judge's remarks where he undertakes to involve Mr. Buchanan in an inconsistency. He reads something from Mr. Buchanan, from which he undertakes to involve him in an inconsistency; and he gets something of a cheer for having done so. I would only remind the Judge that while he is very valiantly fighting for the Nebraska bill and the repeal of the Missouri Compromise, it has been but a little while since he was the *valiant advocate of* the Missouri Compromise. [Cheers.] I want to know if Buchanan has not as much right to be inconsistent as Douglas has? [Loud applause and laughter; "Good, good!" "Hurrah for Lincoln!"] Has Douglas the *exclusive right*, in this country, of being *on all sides of all questions*? Is nobody allowed that high privilege but himself? Is he to have an entire *monopoly* on that subject? [Great laughter.]

So far as Judge Douglas addressed his speech to me, or so far as it was about me, it is my business to pay some attention to it. I have heard the Judge state two or three times what he has stated to day—that in a speech which I made at Springfield, Illinois, I had in a very especial manner, complained that the Supreme Court in the Dred Scott case had decided that a negro could never be a citizen of the United States. I have omitted by some accident heretofore to analyze this statement, and it is required of me to notice it now. In point of fact it is *untrue.* I never have complained *especially* of the Dred Scott decision because it held that a negro could not be a citizen, and the Judge is always wrong when he says I ever did so complain of it. I have the speech here, and I will thank him or any of his friends to show where I said that a negro should be a citizen, and complained especially of the Dred Scott decision because it declared he could not be one. I have done no such thing, and Judge Douglas' so persistently insisting that I have done so, has strongly impressed me with the belief of a pre-determination on his part to misrepresent me. He could not get his foundation for insisting that I was in favor of this negro equality anywhere else as well as he could by assuming that untrue proposition. Let me tell this audience what is true in regard to that matter; and the means by which they may correct me if I do not tell them truly is by a recurrence to the speech itself. I spoke of the Dred Scott decision in my Springfield speech, and I was then endeavoring to prove that the Dred Scott decision was a portion of a system or scheme to make slavery national in this country. I pointed out what things had been decided by the court. I mentioned as a fact that they had decided that a negro could not be a citizen—that they had done so, as I supposed, to deprive the negro, under all circumstances, of the remotest possibility of ever becoming a citizen and claiming the rights of a citizen of the United States under a certain clause of the Constitution. I stated that, without making any complaint of it at all. I then went on and stated the other points decided in the case, namely: that the bringing of a negro into the State of Illinois and holding him in slavery for two years here was a matter in regard to which they would not decide whether it made him free or not; that they decided the further point that taking him into a United States Territory where slavery was prohibited by act of Congress, did not make him free because that act of Congress as they held was unconstitutional. I mentioned these three things as making up the points decided in that case. I mentioned them in a lump taken in connection with the introduction of the Nebraska bill, and the amendment of Chase, offered at the time, declaratory of the right of the people of the Territories to *exclude slavery*, which was voted down by the friends of the bill. I mentioned all these things together, as evidence tending to prove a combination and conspiracy to make the institution of slavery national. In that connection and in that way I mentioned the decision on the point that a negro could not be a citizen, and in no other connection.

Out of this, Judge Douglas builds up his beautiful fabrication—of my purpose to introduce a perfect, social, and political equality between the white and black races. His assertion that I made an "especial objection" (that is his exact language) to the decision on this account, is untrue in point of fact.

Now, while I am upon this subject, and as Henry Clay has been alluded to, I desire to place myself, in connection with Mr. Clay, as nearly right before this people as may be. I am quite aware what the Judge's object is here by all these allusions. He knows that we are before an audience, having strong sympathies southward by relationship, place of birth, and so on. He desires to place me in an extremely Abolition attitude. He read upon a former occasion, and alludes without reading to-day, to a portion of a speech which I delivered in Chicago. In his quotations from that speech as he has made them upon former occasions, the extracts were taken in such a way, as I suppose, brings them within the definition of what is called *garbling*—taking portions of a speech which, when taken by themselves, do not present the entire sense of the speaker as expressed at the time. I propose, therefore, out of that same speech, to show how one portion of it which he skipped over (taking an extract before and an extract after) will give a different idea and the true idea I intended to convey. It will take me some little time to read it, but I believe I will occupy the time in that way.

You have heard him frequently allude to my controversy with him in regard to the Declaration of Independence. I confess that I have had a struggle with Judge Douglas on that matter, and I will try briefly to place myself right in regard to it on this occasion. I said—and it is between the extracts Judge Douglas has taken from this speech, and put in his published speeches—:

It may be argued that there are certain conditions that make necessities and impose them upon us, and to the extent that a necessity is imposed upon a man he must submit to it. I think that was the condition in which we found ourselves when we established this government. We had slaves among us, we could not get our Constitution unless we permitted them to remain in slavery, we could not secure the good we did secure if we grasped for more; and having by necessity submitted to that much, it does not destroy the principle that is the charter of our liberties. Let that charter remain as our standard.

Now I have upon all occasions declared as strongly as Judge Douglas against the disposition to interfere with the existing institution of slavery. You hear me read it from the same speech from which he takes garbled extracts for the purpose of proving upon me a disposition to interfere with the institution of slavery, and establish a perfect social and political equality between negroes and white people.

Allow me while upon this subject briefly to present one other extract from a speech of mine, more than a year ago, at Springfield, in discussing this very same question, soon after Judge Douglas took his ground that negroes were not included in the Declaration of Independence:

I think the authors of that notable instrument intended to include *all* men, but they did not mean to declare all men equal *in all respects*. They did not mean to say all men were equal in color, size, intellect, moral development or social capacity. They defined with tolerable distinctness in what they did consider all men created equal—equal in certain inalienable rights, among which are life, liberty and the pursuit of happiness. This they said, and this they meant. They did not mean to assert the obvious untruth, that all were then actually enjoying that equality, nor yet, that they were about to confer it immediately upon them. In fact they had no power to confer such a boon. They meant simply to declare the *right* so that the *enforcement* of it might follow as fast as circumstances should permit.

They meant to set up a standard maxim for free society which should be familiar to all: constantly looked to, constantly labored for, and even though never perfectly attained, constantly approximated and thereby constantly spreading and deepening its influence and augmenting the happiness and value of life to all people, of all colors, everywhere.

There again are the sentiments I have expressed in regard to the Declaration of Independence upon a former occasion—sentiments which have been put in print and read wherever anybody cared to know what so humble an individual as myself chose to say in regard to it.

At Galesburg the other day, I said in answer to Judge Douglas, that three years ago there never had been a man, so far as I knew or believed, in the whole world, who had said that the Declaration of Independence did not include negroes in the term "all men." I re-assert it to-day. I assert that Judge Douglas and all his friends may search the whole records of the country, and it will be a matter of great astonishment to me if they shall be able to find that one human being three years ago had ever uttered the astounding sentiment that the term "all men" in the Declaration did not include the negro. Do not let me be misunderstood. I know that more than three years ago there were men who, finding this assertion constantly in the way of their schemes to bring about the ascendancy and perpetuation of slavery, *denied the truth of it*. I know that Mr. Calhoun and all the politicians of his school denied the truth of the Declaration. I know that it ran along in the mouths of some Southern men for a period of years, ending at last in that shameful though rather forcible declaration of Pettit of Indiana, upon the floor of the United States Senate, that the Declaration of Independence was in that respect "a self-evident lie," rather than a self-evident truth. But I say, with a perfect knowledge of all this hawking at the Declaration without directly attacking it, that three years ago there never had lived a man who had ventured to assail it in the sneaking way of pretending to believe it and then asserting it did not include the negro. [Cheers.] I believe the first man who ever said it was Chief Justice Taney in the Dred Scott case, and the next to him was our friend Stephen A. Douglas. [Cheers and laughter.] And now it has become the catch-word of the entire party. I would like to call upon his friends everywhere to consider how they have come in so short a time to view this matter in a way so entirely different from their former belief? to ask whether they are not being borne along by an irresistible current—whither, they know not? [Great applause.]

In answer to my proposition at Galesburg last week, I see that some man in Chicago has got up a letter addressed to the Chicago *Times*, to show as he professes that somebody *had* said so before; and he signs himself "An Old Line Whig," if I remember correctly. In the first place I would say he *was not* an Old Line Whig. I am somewhat acquainted with Old Line Whigs. I was with the Old Line Whigs from the origin to the end of that party; I became pretty well acquainted with them, and I know they always had some sense, whatever else you could ascribe to them. [Great laughter.] I know there never was one who had not more sense than to try to show by the evidence he produces that some man had, prior to the time I named, said that negroes were not included in the term "all men" in the Declaration of Independence. What is the evidence he produces? I will bring forward *his* evidence and let you see what *he* offers by way of showing that somebody more than three years ago had said negroes were not included in the Declaration. He brings forward part of a speech from Henry Clay—*the* part of *the* speech of Henry Clay which I used to bring forward to prove precisely the contrary. [Laughter.] I guess we are surrounded to some extent to-day, by the old friends of Mr. Clay, and they will be glad to hear anything from that authority. While he was in Indiana a man presented him a petition to liberate his negroes, and he, (Mr. Clay) made a speech in answer to it, which I suppose he carefully wrote out himself and caused to be published. I have before me an extract from that speech which constitutes the evidence this pretended "Old Line Whig" at Chicago brought forward to show that Mr. Clay didn't suppose the negro was included in the Declaration of Independence. Hear what Mr. Clay said:

And what is the foundation of this appeal to me in Indiana, to liberate the slaves under my care in Kentucky? It is a general declaration in the act announcing to the world the independence of the thirteen American colonies, that all men are created equal. Now, as an abstract principle, *there is no doubt of the truth of that declaration*; and it is desirable *in the original construction of society, and in organized societies*, to keep it in view as a great fundamental principle. But, then, I apprehend that in no society that ever did exist, or ever shall be formed, was or can the equality asserted among the members of the human race be practically enforced and carried out. There are portions, large portions, women, minors, insane, culprits, transient sojourners, that will always probably remain subject to the government of another portion of the community.

That declaration whatever may be the extent of its import, was made by the delegations of the thirteen States. In most of them slavery existed, and had long existed, and was established by law. It was introduced and forced upon the colonies by the paramount law of England. Do you believe, that in making that Declaration the States that concurred in it intended that it should be tortured into a virtual emancipation of all the slaves within their respective limits? Would Virginia and other Southern States have ever united in a declaration which was to be interpreted into an abolition of slavery among them? Did any one of the thirteen colonies entertain such a design or expectation? To impute such a secret and unavowed purpose would be to charge a political fraud upon the noblest band of patriots that ever assembled in council; a fraud upon the confederacy of the Revolution; a fraud upon the union of those States whose constitution not only recognized the law-fulness of slavery, but permitted the importation of slaves from Africa until the year 1808.

This is the entire quotation brought forward to prove that somebody previous to three years ago had said the negro was not included in the term "all men" in the Declaration. How does it do so? In what way has it a tendency to prove that? Mr. Clay says *it is true as an abstract principle* that all men are created equal, but that we cannot practically apply it in all cases. He illustrates this by bringing forward the cases of females, minors and insane persons with whom it cannot be enforced; but he says it is true as an abstract principle in the organization of society as well as in organized society, and it should be kept in view as a fundamental principle. Let me read a few words more before I add some comments of my own. Mr. Clay says a little further on:

> I desire no concealment of my opinions in regard to the institution of slavery. I look upon it as a great evil; and deeply lament that we have derived it from the parental government; and from our ancestors. But here they are and the question is, how can they be best dealt with? If a state of nature existed and we were about to lay the foundations of soci-ety, *no man would be more strongly opposed than I should be, to incorporating the institution of slavery among its elements.*

Now here in this same book—in this same speech—is this same extract brought forward to prove that Mr. Clay held that the negro was not included in the Declaration of Inde-pendence—no such statement on his part, but the declaration *that it is a great fundamental truth*, which should be con-stantly kept in view in the organization of society and in soci-eties already organized. But if I say a word about it—if I attempt, as Mr. Clay said all good men ought to do, to keep it in view—if, in this "organized society," I ask to have the public eye turned upon it—if I ask, in relation to the organi-zation of new Territories that the public eye should be turned upon it—forthwith I am villified as you hear me to-day. What have I done, that I have not the license of Henry Clay's illustrious example here in doing? Have I done aught that I have not his authority for, while maintaining that in organiz-ing new Territories and societies this fundamental principle should be regarded, and in organized society holding it up to the public view and recognizing what *he* recognized as the great principle of free government? [Great applause, and cries of "Hurrah for Lincoln."]

And when this new principle—this new proposition that no human being ever thought of three years ago,—is brought forward, *I combat it* as having an evil tendency, if not an evil design; I combat it as having a tendency to dehumanize the negro—to take away from him the right of ever striving to be a man. I combat it as being one of the thousand things constantly done in these days to prepare the public mind to make property, and nothing but property of the *negro in all the States of this Union.* [Tremendous applause. "Hurrah for Lincoln." "Hurrah for Trumbull."]

But there is a point that I wish before leaving this part of the discussion to ask attention to. I have read, and I repeat the words of Henry Clay:

> I desire no concealment of my opinions in regard to the institution of slavery. I look upon it as a great evil and deeply lament that we have derived it from the parental government, and from our ancestors. I wish every slave in the United States was in the country of his ancestors. But here they are; the question is how they can best be dealt with? If a state of nature existed and we were about to lay the foundation of society, no man would be more strongly opposed than I should be to incorporate the institution of slavery among its elements.

The principle upon which I have insisted in this canvass, is in relation to laying the foundations of new societies. I have never sought to apply these principles to the old States for the purpose of abolishing slavery in those States. It is nothing but a miserable perversion of what I *have* said, to assume that I have declared Missouri, or any other slave State shall emancipate her slaves. I have proposed no such thing. But when Mr. Clay says that in laying the foundations of societies in our Territories where it does not exist he would be opposed to the introduction of slavery as an element, I insist that we have *his warrant*—his license for insisting upon the exclusion of that element, which he declared in such strong and emphatic language *was most hateful to him.* [Loud applause.]

Judge Douglas has again referred to a Springfield speech in which I said "a house divided against itself cannot stand." The

Judge has so often made the entire quotation from that speech that I can make it from memory. I used this language:

We are now far into the fifth year since a policy was initiated with the avowed object and confident promise of putting an end to the slavery agitation. Under the operation of this policy, that agitation has not only not ceased but has constantly augmented. In my opinion it will not cease until a crisis shall have been reached and passed. "A house divided against itself cannot stand." I believe this government cannot endure permanently half Slave and half Free. I do not expect the house to fall — but I do expect it will cease to be divided. It will become all one thing, or all the other. Either the opponents of Slavery will arrest the further spread of it, and place it where the public mind shall rest in the belief that it is in the course of ultimate extinction, or its advocates will push it forward till it shall become alike lawful in all the States — old as well as new, North as well as South.

That extract and the sentiments expressed in it, have been extremely offensive to Judge Douglas. He has warred upon them as Satan does upon the Bible. [Laughter.] His perversions upon it are endless. Here now are my views upon it in brief.

I said we were now far into the fifth year since a policy was initiated with the avowed object and confident promise of putting an end to the slavery agitation. Is it not so? When that Nebraska bill was brought forward four years ago last January, was it not for the "avowed object" of putting an end to the slavery agitation? We were to have no more agitation in Congress; it was all to be banished to the Territories. By the way, I will remark here that, as Judge Douglas is very fond of complimenting Mr. Crittenden in these days, Mr. Crittenden has said there was a falsehood in that whole business, for there was *no slavery agitation at that time to allay*. We were for a little while *quiet* on the troublesome thing and that very allaying plaster of Judge Douglas', stirred it up again. [Applause and laughter.] But was it not understood or intimated with the "confident promise" of putting an end to the slavery agitation. Surely it was. In every speech you heard Judge Douglas make, until he got into this "imbroglio," as they call it, with the Administration about the Lecompton Constitution, every speech on that Nebraska bill was full of his felicitations that we were *just at the end* of the slavery agitation.

The last tip of the last joint of the old serpent's tail was just drawing out of view. [Cheers and laughter.] But has it proved so? I have asserted that under that policy that agitation "has not only not ceased, but has constantly augmented." When was there ever a greater agitation in Congress than last winter? When was it as great in the country as to-day?

There was a collateral object in the introduction of that Nebraska policy which was to clothe the people of the Territories with a superior degree of self-government, beyond what they had ever had before. The first object and the main one of conferring upon the people a higher degree of "self government," is a question of fact to be determined by you in answer to a single question. Have you ever heard or known of a people any where on earth who had as little to do, as, in the first instance of its use, the people of Kansas had with this same right of "self-government"? [Loud applause.] In its main policy, and in its collateral object, *it has been nothing but a living, creeping lie from the time of its introduction, till to-day.* [Loud cheers.]

I have intimated that I thought the agitation would not cease until a crisis should have been reached and passed. I have stated in what way I thought it would be reached and passed. I have said that it might go one way or the other. We might, by arresting the further spread of it and placing it where the fathers originally placed it, put it where the public mind should rest in the belief that it was in the course of ultimate extinction. Thus the agitation may cease. It may be pushed forward until it shall become alike lawful in all the States, old as well as new, North as well as South. I have said, and I repeat, my wish is that the further spread of it may be arrested, and that it may be placed where the public mind shall rest in the belief that it is in the course of ultimate extinction. [Great applause.] I have expressed that as my wish. I entertain the opinion upon evidence sufficient to my mind, that the fathers of this Government placed that institution where the public mind *did* rest in the belief that it was in the course of ultimate extinction. Let me ask why they made provision that the source of slavery—the African slave trade— should be cut off at the end of twenty years? Why did they make provision that in all the new territory we owned at that time slavery should be forever inhibited? Why stop its spread in one direction and cut off its source in another, if they did not look to its being placed in the course of ultimate extinction?

Again; the institution of slavery is only mentioned in the Constitution of the United States two or three times, and in neither of these cases does the word "slavery" or "negro race" occur; but covert language is used each time, and for a purpose full of significance. What is the language in regard to the prohibition of the African slave trade? It runs in about this way: "The migration or importation of such persons as any of the States now existing shall think proper to admit, shall not be prohibited by the Congress prior to the year one thousand eight hundred and eight."

The next allusion in the Constitution to the question of slavery and the black race, is on the subject of the basis of representation, and there the language used is, "Representatives and direct taxes shall be apportioned among the several States which may be included within this Union, according to their respective numbers, which shall be determined by adding to the whole number of free persons, including those bound to service for a term of years, and excluding Indians not taxed—three-fifths of all other persons."

It says "persons," not slaves, not negroes; but this "three-fifths" can be applied to no other class among us than the negroes.

Lastly, in the provision for the reclamation of fugitive slaves it is said: "No person held to service or labor in one State under the laws thereof escaping into another, shall in consequence of any law or regulation therein, be discharged from such service or labor, but shall be delivered up, on claim of the party to whom such service or labor may be due." There again there is no mention of the word "negro" or of slavery. In all three of these places, being the only allusions to slavery in the instrument, covert language is used. Language is used not suggesting that slavery existed or that the black race were among us. And I understand the contemporaneous history of those times to be that covert language was used with a purpose, and that purpose was that in our Constitution, which it was hoped and is still hoped will endure for-

ever—when it should be read by intelligent and patriotic
men, after the institution of slavery had passed from among
us—there should be nothing on the face of the great charter
of liberty suggesting that such a thing as negro slavery had
ever existed among us. [Enthusiastic applause.] This is part of
the evidence that the fathers of the Government expected and
intended the institution of slavery to come to an end. They
expected and intended that it should be in the course of ultimate extinction. And when I say that I desire to see the further spread of it arrested I only say I desire to see that done
which the fathers have first done. When I say I desire to see it
placed where the public mind will rest in the belief that it is in
the course of ultimate extinction, I only say I desire to see it
placed where they placed it. It is not true that our fathers, as
Judge Douglas assumes, made this government part slave and
part free. Understand the sense in which he puts it. He assumes that slavery is a rightful thing within itself,—was introduced by the framers of the Constitution. The exact truth
is, that they found the institution existing among us, and they
left it as they found it. But in making the government they
left this institution with many clear marks of disapprobation
upon it. They found slavery among them and they left it
among them because of the difficulty—the absolute impossibility of its immediate removal. And when Judge Douglas asks
me why we cannot let it remain part slave and part free as the
fathers of the government made, he asks a question based
upon an assumption which is itself a falsehood; and I turn
upon him and ask him the question, when the policy that the
fathers of the government had adopted in relation to this element among us was the best policy in the world—the only
wise policy—the only policy that we can ever safely continue
upon—that will ever give us peace unless this dangerous element masters us all and becomes a national institution—*I
turn upon him and ask him why he could not let it alone?* [Great
and prolonged cheering.] I turn and ask him why he was
driven to the necessity of introducing a *new policy* in regard to
it? He has himself said he introduced a new policy. He said so
in his speech on the 22d of March of the present year, 1858. I
ask him why he could not let it remain where our fathers
placed it? I ask too of Judge Douglas and his friends why we

shall not again place this institution upon the basis on which the fathers left it? I ask you when he infers that I am in favor of setting the free and slave States at war, when the institution was placed in that attitude by those who made the constitution, *did they make any war?* ["No;" "no;" and cheers.] If we had no war out of it when thus placed, wherein is the ground of belief that we shall have war out of it if we return to that policy? Have we had any peace upon this matter springing from any other basis? ["No, no."] I maintain that we have not. I have proposed nothing more than a return to the policy of the fathers.

I confess, when I propose a certain measure of policy, it is not enough for me that I do not intend anything evil in the result, but it is incumbent on me to show that it has not a *tendency* to that result. I have met Judge Douglas in that point of view. I have not only made the declaration that I do not *mean* to produce a conflict between the States, but I have tried to show by fair reasoning, and I think I have shown to the minds of fair men, that I propose nothing but what has a most peaceful tendency. The quotation that I happened to make in that Springfield speech, that "a house divided against itself cannot stand," and which has proved so offensive to the Judge, was part and parcel of the same thing. He tries to show that variety in the domestic institutions of the different States is necessary and indispensable. I do not dispute it. I have no controversy with Judge Douglas about that. I shall very readily agree with him that it would be foolish for us to insist upon having a cranberry law here, in Illinois, where we have no cranberries, because they have a cranberry law in Indiana, where they have cranberries. [Laughter, "good, good."] I should insist that it would be exceedingly wrong in us to deny to Virginia the right to enact oyster laws where they have oysters, because we want no such laws here. [Renewed laughter.] I understand, I hope, quite as well as Judge Douglas or anybody else, that the variety in the soil and climate and face of the country, and consequent variety in the industrial pursuits and productions of a country, require systems of law conforming to this variety in the natural features of the country. I understand quite as well as Judge Douglas, that if we here raise a barrel of flour more than we want, and the Louisianians raise a barrel of sugar more than they want, it is of mutual advantage to exchange. That produces commerce, brings us together, and makes us better friends. We like one another the more for it. And I understand as well as Judge Douglas, or anybody else, that these mutual accommodations are the cements which bind together the different parts of this Union—that instead of being a thing to "divide the house"—figuratively expressing the Union,—they tend to sustain it; they are the props of the house tending always to hold it up.

But when I have admitted all this, I ask if there is any parallel between these things and this institution of slavery? I do not see that there is any parallel at all between them. Consider it. When have we had any difficulty or quarrel amongst ourselves about the cranberry laws of Indiana, or the oyster laws of Virginia, or the pine lumber laws of Maine, or the fact that Louisiana produces sugar, and Illinois flour? When have we had any quarrels over these things? When have we had perfect peace in regard to this thing which I say is an element of discord in this Union? We have sometimes had peace, but when was it? It was when the institution of slavery remained quiet where it was. We have had difficulty and turmoil whenever it has made a struggle to spread itself where it was not. I ask then, if experience does not speak in thunder tones, telling us that the policy which has given peace to the country heretofore, being returned to, gives the greatest promise of peace again. ["Yes;" "yes;" "yes."] You may say and Judge Douglas has intimated the same thing, that all this difficulty in regard to the institution of slavery is the mere agitation of office seekers and ambitious Northern politicians. He thinks we want to get "his place," I suppose. [Cheers and laughter.] I agree that there are office seekers amongst us. The Bible says somewhere that we are desperately selfish. I think we would have discovered that fact without the Bible. I do not claim that I am any less so than the average of men, but I do claim that I am not more selfish than Judge Douglas. [Roars of laughter and applause.]

But is it true that all the difficulty and agitation we have in regard to this institution of slavery springs from office seeking—from the mere ambition of politicians? Is that the truth?

How many times have we had danger from this question? Go back to the day of the Missouri Compromise. Go back to the Nullification question, at the bottom of which lay this same slavery question. Go back to the time of the Annexation of Texas. Go back to the troubles that led to the Compromise of 1850. You will find that every time, with the single exception of the Nullification question, they sprung from an endeavor to spread this institution. There never was a party in the history of this country, and there probably never will be of sufficient strength to disturb the general peace of the country. Parties themselves may be divided and quarrel on minor questions, yet it extends not beyond the parties themselves. But does *not* this question make a disturbance outside of political circles? Does it not enter into the churches and rend them asunder? What divided the great Methodist Church into two parts, North and South? What has raised this constant disturbance in every Presbyterian General Assembly that meets? What disturbed the Unitarian Church in this very city two years ago? What has jarred and shaken the great American Tract Society recently, not yet splitting it, but sure to divide it in the end. Is it not this same mighty, deep seated power that somehow operates on the minds of men, exciting and stirring them up in every avenue of society—in politics, in religion, in literature, in morals, in all the manifold relations of life? [Applause.] Is this the work of politicians? Is that irresistible power which for fifty years has shaken the government and agitated the people to be stilled and subdued by pretending that it is an exceedingly simple thing, and we ought not to talk about it? [Great cheers and laughter.] If you will get everybody else to stop talking about it, I assure I will quit before they have half done so. [Renewed laughter.] But where is the philosophy or statesmanship which assumes that you can quiet that disturbing element in our society which has disturbed us for more than half a century, which has been the only serious danger that has threatened our institutions—I say, where is the philosophy or the statesmanship based on the assumption that we are to quit talking about it [applause], and that the public mind is all at once to cease being agitated by it? Yet this is the policy here in the North that Douglas is advocating—that we are to care nothing about it! I ask you if it is not a false philosophy? Is it not a false statesmanship that undertakes to build up a system of policy upon the basis of caring nothing about *the very thing that every body does care the most about*? ["Yes, yes," and applause]—a thing which all experience has shown we care a very great deal about? [Laughter and applause.]

The Judge alludes very often in the course of his remarks to the exclusive right which the States have to decide the whole thing for themselves. I agree with him very readily that the different States have that right. He is but fighting a man of straw when he assumes that I am contending against the right of the States to do as they please about it. Our controversy with him is in regard to the new Territories. We agree that when the States come in as States they have the right and the power to do as they please. We have no power as citizens of the free States or in our federal capacity as members of the Federal Union through the general government, to disturb slavery in the States where it exists. We profess constantly that we have no more inclination than belief in the power of the Government to disturb it; yet we are driven constantly to defend ourselves from the assumption that we are warring upon the rights of the *States*. What I insist upon is, that the new Territories shall be kept free from it while in the Territorial condition. Judge Douglas assumes that we have no interest in them—that we have no right whatever to interfere. I think we have some interest. I think that as white men we have. Do we not wish for an outlet for our surplus population, if I may so express myself? Do we not feel an interest in getting to that outlet with such institutions as we would like to have prevail there? If *you* go to the Territory opposed to slavery and another man comes upon the same ground with his slave, upon the assumption that the things are equal, it turns out that he has the equal right all his way and you have no part of it your way. If he goes in and makes it a slave Territory, and by consequence a slave State, is it not time that those who desire to have it a free State were on equal ground. Let me suggest it in a different way. How many Democrats are there about here ["a thousand"] who have left slave States and come into the free State of Illinois to get rid of the institution of slavery. [Another voice—"a thousand and one."] I reckon there are a thousand and one. [Laughter.] I will ask you, if the policy you are now advocating had prevailed when this country was in a Territorial condition, where would you have gone to get rid of it? [Applause.] Where would you have found your free State or Territory to go to? And when hereafter, for any cause, the people in this place shall desire to find new homes, if they wish to be rid of the institution, where will they find the place to go to? [Loud cheers.]

Now irrespective of the moral aspect of this question as to whether there is a right or wrong in enslaving a negro, I am still in favor of our new Territories being in such a condition that white men may find a home—may find some spot where they can better their condition—where they can settle upon new soil and better their condition in life. [Great and continued cheering.] I am in favor of this not merely, (I must say it here as I have elsewhere,) for our own people who are born amongst us, but as an outlet for *free white people everywhere*, the world over—in which Hans and Baptiste and Patrick, and all other men from all the world, may find new homes and better their conditions in life. [Loud and long continued applause.]

I have stated upon former occasions, and I may as well state again, what I understand to be the real issue in this controversy between Judge Douglas and myself. On the point of my wanting to make war between the free and the slave States, there has been no issue between us. So, too, when he assumes that I am in favor of introducing a perfect social and political equality between the white and black races. These are false issues, upon which Judge Douglas has tried to force the controversy. There is no foundation in truth for the charge that I maintain either of these propositions. The real issue in this controversy—the one pressing upon every mind—is the sentiment on the part of one class that looks upon the institution of slavery *as a wrong*, and of another class that *does not* look upon it as a wrong. The sentiment that contemplates the institution of slavery in this country as a wrong is the sentiment of the Republican party. It is the sentiment around which all their actions—all their arguments circle—from which all their propositions radiate. They look upon it as being a moral, social and political wrong; and while they contemplate it as such, they nevertheless have due regard for its actual existence among us, and the difficulties of getting rid of it in any satisfactory way and to all the constitutional obligations thrown about it. Yet having a due regard for these, they desire a policy in regard to it that looks to its not creating any more danger. They insist that it should as far as may be, *be treated* as a wrong, and one of the methods of treating it as a wrong is to *make provision that it shall grow no larger*. [Loud applause.] They also desire a policy that looks to a peaceful end of slavery at sometime, as being wrong. These are the views they entertain in regard to it as I understand them; and all their sentiments—all their arguments and propositions are brought within this range. I have said and I repeat it here, that if there be a man amongst us who does not think that the institution of slavery is wrong in any one of the aspects of which I have spoken, he is misplaced and ought not to be with us. And if there be a man amongst us who is so impatient of it as a wrong as to disregard its actual presence among us and the difficulty of getting rid of it suddenly in a satisfactory way, and to disregard the constitutional obligations thrown about it, that man is misplaced if he is on our platform. We disclaim sympathy with him in practical action. He is not placed properly with us.

On this subject of treating it as a wrong, and limiting its spread, let me say a word. Has any thing ever threatened the existence of this Union save and except this very institution of Slavery? What is it that we hold most dear amongst us? Our own liberty and prosperity. What has ever threatened our liberty and prosperity save and except this institution of Slavery? If this is true, how do you propose to improve the condition of things by enlarging Slavery—by spreading it out and making it bigger? You may have a wen or a cancer upon your person and not be able to cut it out lest you bleed to death; but surely it is no way to cure it, to engraft it and spread it over your whole body. That is no proper way of treating what you regard a wrong. You see this peaceful way of dealing with it as a wrong—restricting the spread of it, and not allowing it to go into new countries where it has not already existed. That is the peaceful way, the old-fashioned way, the way in which the fathers themselves set us the example.

On the other hand, I have said there is a sentiment which treats it as *not* being wrong. That is the Democratic sentiment of this day. I do not mean to say that every man who stands within that range positively asserts that it is right. That class will include all who positively assert that it is right, and all who like Judge Douglas treat it as indifferent and do not say it is either right or wrong. These two classes of men fall within the general class of those who do not look upon it as a wrong. And if there be among you anybody who supposes that he as a Democrat, can consider himself "as much opposed to slavery as anybody," I would like to reason with him. You never treat it as a wrong. What other thing that you consider as a wrong, do you deal with as you deal with that? Perhaps you *say* it is wrong, *but your leader never does, and you quarrel with anybody who says it is wrong*. Although you pretend to say so yourself you can find no fit place to deal with it as a wrong. You must not say anything about it in the free States, *because it is not here*. You must not say anything about it in the slave States, *because it is there*. You must not say anything about it in the pulpit, because that is religion and has nothing to do with it. You must not say anything about it in politics, *because that will disturb the security of "my place."* [Shouts of laughter and cheers.] There is no place to talk about it as being a wrong, although you say yourself it *is* a wrong. But finally you will screw yourself up to the belief that if the people of the slave States should adopt a system of gradual emancipation on the slavery question, you would be in favor of it. You would be in favor of it. You say that is getting it in the right place, and you would be glad to see it succeed. But you are deceiving yourself. You all know that Frank Blair and Gratz Brown, down there in St. Louis, undertook to introduce that system in Missouri. They fought as valiantly as they could for the system of gradual emancipation which you pretend you would be glad to see succeed. Now I will bring you to the test. After a hard fight they were beaten, and when the news came over here you threw up your hats and *hurrahed for Democracy*. [Great applause and laughter.] More than that, take all the argument made in favor of the system you have proposed, and it carefully excludes the idea that there is anything wrong in the institution of slavery. The arguments to sustain that policy carefully excluded it. Even here to-day you heard Judge Douglas quarrel with me because I uttered a wish that it might sometime come to an end. Although Henry Clay could say he wished every slave in the United States was in the country of his ancestors, I am denounced by those pretending to respect Henry Clay for uttering a wish that it might sometime, in some peaceful way, come to an end. The Democratic policy in regard to that institution will not tolerate the merest breath, the slightest hint, of the least degree of wrong about it. Try it by some of Judge Douglas' arguments. He says he "don't care whether it is voted up or voted down" in the Territories. I do not care myself in dealing with that expression, whether it is intended to be expressive of his individual sentiments on the subject, or only of the national policy he desires to have established. It is alike valuable for my purpose. Any man can say that who does not see anything wrong in slavery, but no man can logically say it who does see a wrong in it; because no man can logically say he don't care whether a wrong is voted up or voted down. He may say he don't care whether an indifferent thing is voted up or down, but he must logically have a choice between a right thing and a wrong thing. He contends that whatever community wants slaves has a right to have them. So they have if it is not a wrong. But if it is a wrong, he cannot say people have a right to do wrong. He says that upon the score of equality, slaves should be allowed to go in a new Territory, like other property. This is strictly logical if there is no difference between it and other property. If it and other property are equal, his argument is entirely logical. But if you insist that one is wrong and the other right, there is no use to institute a comparison between right and wrong. You may turn over everything in the Democratic policy from beginning to end, whether in the shape it takes on the statute book, in the shape it takes in the Dred Scott decision, in the shape it takes in conversation or the shape it takes in short maxim-like arguments—it everywhere carefully excludes the idea that there is anything wrong in it.

That is the real issue. That is the issue that will continue in this country when these poor tongues of Judge Douglas and myself shall be silent. It is the eternal struggle between these two principles—right and wrong—throughout the world. They are the two principles that have stood face to face from the beginning of time; and will ever continue to struggle. The one is the common right of humanity and the other the divine right of kings. It is the same principle in whatever shape it develops itself. It is the same spirit that says, "You work and toil and earn bread, and I'll eat it." [Loud applause.] No matter in what shape it comes, whether from the mouth of a king who seeks to bestride the people of his own nation and live by the fruit of their labor, or from one race of men as an apology for enslaving another race, it is the same tyrannical principle. I was glad to express my gratitude at Quincy, and I re-express it here to Judge Douglas—*that he looks to no end of the institution of slavery.* That will help the people to see where the struggle really is. It will hereafter place with us all men who really do wish the wrong may have an end. And whenever we can get rid of the fog which obscures the real question—when we can get Judge Douglas and his friends to avow a policy looking to its perpetuation—we can get out from among them that class of men and bring them to the side of those who treat it as a wrong. Then there will soon be an end of it, and that end will be its "ultimate extinction." Whenever the issue can be distinctly made, and all extraneous matter thrown out so that men can fairly see the real difference between the parties, this controversy will soon be settled, and it will be done peaceably too. There will be no war, no violence. It will be placed again where the wisest and best men of the world, placed it. Brooks of South Carolina once declared that when this Constitution was framed, its framers did not look to the institution existing until this day. When he said this, I think he stated a fact that is fully borne out by the history of the times. But he also said they were better and wiser men than the men of these days; yet the men of these days had experience which they had not, and by the invention of the cotton gin it became a necessity in this country that slavery should be perpetual. I now say that willingly or unwillingly, purposely or without purpose, Judge Douglas has been the most prominent instrument in changing the position of the institution of slavery which the fathers of the government expected to come to an end ere this—*and putting it upon Brooks' cotton gin basis,* [Great applause,]—placing it where he openly confesses he has no desire there shall ever be an end of it. [Renewed applause.]

I understand I have ten minutes yet. I will employ it in saying something about this argument Judge Douglas uses, while he sustains the Dred Scot decision, that the people of the Territories can still somehow exclude slavery. The first thing I ask attention to is the fact that Judge Douglas constantly said, before the decision, that whether they could or not, *was a question for the Supreme Court.* [Cheers.] But after the Court has made the decision he virtually says it is *not* a question for the Supreme Court, but for the people. [Renewed applause.] And how is it he tells us they can exclude it? He says it needs "police regulations," and that admits of "unfriendly legislation." Although it is a right established by the constitution of the United States to take a slave into a Territory of the United States and hold him as property, yet unless the Territorial Legislature will give friendly legislation, and, more especially, if they adopt unfriendly legislation, they can practically exclude him. Now, without meeting this proposition as a matter of fact, I pass to consider the real constitutional obligation. Let me take the gentleman who looks me in the face before me, and let us suppose that he is a member of the Territorial Legislature. The first thing he will do will be to swear that he will support the Constitution of the United States. His neighbor by his side in the Territory has slaves and needs Territorial legislation to enable him to enjoy that constitutional right. Can he withhold the legislation which his neighbor needs for the enjoyment of a right which is fixed in his favor in the Constitution of the United States which he has sworn to support? Can he withhold it without violating his oath? And more especially, can he pass unfriendly legislation to violate his oath? Why this is a *monstrous* sort of talk about the Constitution of the United States! [Great applause.] *There has never been as outlandish or lawless a doctrine from the mouth of any respectable man on earth.* [Tremendous cheers.] I do not believe it is a constitutional right to hold slaves in a Territory of the United States. I believe the decision was improperly made and I go for reversing it. Judge Douglas is furious against those who go for reversing a decision. But he is for legislating it out of all force while the law itself stands. I repeat that there has never been so monstrous a doctrine uttered from the mouth of a respectable man. [Loud cheers.]

I suppose most of us, (I know it of myself,) believe that the people of the Southern States are entitled to a Congressional fugitive slave law—that it is a right fixed in the Constitution. But it cannot be made available to them without Congressional legislation. In the Judge's language, it is a "barren right" which needs legislation before it can become efficient and valuable to the persons to whom it is guaranteed. And as the right is constitutional I agree that the legislation shall be granted to it—and that not that we like the institution of slavery. We profess to have no taste for running and catching niggers—at least I profess no taste for that job at all. Why then do I yield support to a fugitive slave law? Because I do not understand that the Constitution, which guarantees that right, can be supported without it. And if I believed that the right to hold a slave in a Territory was equally fixed in the Constitution with the right to reclaim fugitives, I should be bound to give it the legislation necessary to support it. I say that no man can deny his obligation to give the necessary legislation to support slavery in a Territory, who believes it is a constitutional right to have it there. No man can, who does not give the Abolitionist an argument to deny the obligation enjoined by the constitution to enact a fugitive slave law. Try it now. It is the strongest abolition argument ever made. I say if that Dred Scott decision is correct then the right to hold slaves in a Territory is equally a constitutional right with the right of a slaveholder to have his runaway returned. No one can show the distinction between them. The one is express, so that we cannot deny it. The other is construed to be in the constitution, so that he who believes the decision to be correct believes in the right. And the man who argues that by unfriendly legislation, in spite of that constitutional right, slavery may be driven from the Territories, cannot avoid furnishing an argument by which Abolitionists may deny the obligation to return fugitives, and claim the power to pass laws unfriendly to the right of the slaveholder to reclaim his fugitive. I do not know how such an argument may strike a popular assembly like this, but I defy anybody to go before a body of men whose minds are educated to estimating evidence and reasoning, and show that there is an iota of difference between the constitutional right to reclaim a fugitive, and the constitutional right to hold a slave, in a Territory, provided this Dred Scott decision is correct. [Cheers.] I defy any man to make an argument that will justify unfriendly legislation to deprive a slaveholder of his right to hold his slave in a Territory, that will not equally, in all its length, breadth and thickness furnish an argument for nullifying the fugitive slave law. Why there is not such an Abolitionist in the nation as Douglas, after all. [Loud and enthusiastic applause.]

MR. DOUGLAS' REPLY.

Mr. Lincoln has concluded his remarks by saying that there is not such an Abolitionist as I am in all America. (Laughter.) If he could make the Abolitionists of Illinois believe that, he would not have much show for the Senate. (Great laughter and applause.) Let him make the Abolitionists believe the truth of that statement and his political back is broken. (Renewed laughter.)

His first criticism upon me is the expression of his hope that the war of the administration will be prosecuted against me and the Democratic party of his State with vigor. He wants that war prosecuted with vigor; I have no doubt of it. His hopes of success, and the hopes of his party depend solely upon it. They have no chance of destroying the Democracy of this State except by the aid of federal patronage. ("That's a fact," "good," and cheers.) He has all the federal office-holders here as his allies, ("That's so,") running separate tickets against the Democracy to divide the party although the leaders all intend to vote directly the Abolition ticket, and only leave the green-horns to vote this separate ticket who refuse to go into the Abolition camp. (Laughter and cheers.) There is something really refreshing in the thought that Mr. Lincoln is in favor of prosecuting one war vigorously. (Roars of laughter.) It is the first war I ever knew him to be in favor of prosecuting. (Renewed laughter.) It is the first war that I ever knew him to believe to be just or constitutional. (Laughter and cheers.) When the Mexican war was being waged, and the American army was surrounded by the enemy in Mexico, he thought that war was unconstitutional, unnecessary and unjust. ("That's so," "you've got him," "he voted against it," &c.) He thought it was not commenced on the right *spot*. (Laughter.)

When I made an incidental allusion of that kind in the joint discussion over at Charleston some weeks ago, Lincoln, in replying, said that I, Douglas, had charged him with voting against supplies for the Mexican war, and then he reared up, full length, and swore that he never voted against the supplies—that it was a slander—and caught hold of Ficklin, who sat on the stand, and said, "Here, Ficklin, tell the people that it is a lie." (Laughter and cheers.) Well, Ficklin, who had served in Congress with him, stood up and told them all that he recollected about it. It was that when George Ashmun, of Massachusetts, brought forward a resolution declaring the war unconstitutional, unnecessary, and unjust, that Lincoln had voted for it. "Yes," said Lincoln, "I did." Thus he confessed that he voted that the war was wrong, that our country was in the wrong, and consequently that the Mexicans were in the right; but charged that I had slandered him by saying that he voted against the supplies. I never charged him with voting against the supplies in my life, because I knew that he was not in Congress when they were voted. (Tremendous shouts of laughter.) The war was commenced on the 13th day of May, 1846, and on that day we appropriated in Congress ten millions of dollars and fifty thousand men to prosecute it. During the same session we voted more men and more money, and at the next session we voted more men and more money, so that by the time Mr. Lincoln entered Congress we had enough men and enough money to carry on the war, and had no occasion to vote any more. (Laughter and cheers.) When he got into the House, being opposed to the war, and not being able to stop the supplies, because they had all gone forward, all he could do was to follow the lead of Corwin, and prove that the war was not begun on the right spot, and that it was unconstitutional, unnecessary, and wrong. Remember, too, that this he did after the war had been begun. It is one thing to be opposed to the declaration of a war, another and very different thing to take sides with the enemy against your own country after the war has been commenced. ("Good," and cheers.) Our army was in Mexico at the time, many battles had been fought; our citizens, who were defending the honor of their country's flag, were surrounded by the daggers, the guns and the poison of the enemy. Then it was that Corwin made his speech in which he declared that the American soldiers ought to be welcomed by the Mexicans with bloody hands and hospitable graves; then it was that Ashmun and Lincoln voted in the House of Representatives that the war was unconstitutional and unjust; and Ashmun's resolution, Corwin's speech, and Lincoln's vote were sent to Mexico and read at the head of the Mexican army, to prove to them that there was a Mexican party in the Congress of the United States who were doing all in their power to aid them. ("That's the truth," "Lincoln's a traitor," etc.) That a man who takes sides with the common enemy against his own country in time of war should rejoice in a war being made on me now, is very natural. (Immense applause.) And in my opinion, no other kind of a man would rejoice in it. ("That's true," "hurrah for Douglas," and cheers.)

Mr. Lincoln has told you a great deal to-day about his being an old line Clay Whig. ("He never was.") Bear in mind that there are a great many old Clay Whigs down in this region. It is more agreeable, therefore, for him to talk about the old Clay Whig party than it is for him to talk Abolitionism. We did not hear much about the old Clay Whig party up in the Abolition districts. How much of an old line Henry Clay Whig was he? Have you read Gen. Singleton's speech at Jacksonville? (Yes, yes, and cheers.) You know that Gen. Singleton was, for twenty-five years, the confidential friend of Henry Clay in Illinois, and he testified that in 1847, when the constitutional convention of this State was in session, the Whig members were invited to a Whig caucus at the house of Mr. Lincoln's brother-in-law, where Mr. Lincoln proposed to throw Henry Clay overboard and take up Gen. Taylor in his place, giving, as his reason, that if the Whigs did not take up Gen. Taylor the Democrats would. (Cheers and laughter.)

Singleton testifies that Lincoln, in that speech, urged, as another reason for throwing Henry Clay overboard, that the Whigs had fought long enough for principle and ought to begin to fight for success. Singleton also testifies that Lincoln's speech did have the effect of cutting Clay's throat, and that he, Singleton, and others withdrew from the caucus in indignation. He further states that when they got to Philadelphia to attend the national convention of the Whig party, that Lincoln was there, the bitter and deadly enemy of Clay, and that he tried to keep him (Singleton) out of the convention because he insisted on voting for Clay, and Lincoln was determined to have Taylor. (Laughter and applause.) Singleton says that Lincoln rejoiced with very great joy when he found the mangled remains of the murdered Whig statesman lying cold before him. Now, Mr. Lincoln tells you that he is an old line Clay Whig! (Laughter and cheers.) Gen. Singleton testifies to the facts I have narrated in a public speech which has been printed and circulated broadcast over the State for weeks, yet not a lisp have we heard from Mr. Lincoln on the subject, except that he is an old Clay Whig.

What part of Henry Clay's policy did Lincoln ever advocate? He was in Congress in 1848−9 when the Wilmot proviso warfare disturbed the peace and harmony of the country until it shook the foundation of the republic from its centre to its circumference. It was that agitation that brought Clay forth from his retirement at Ashland again to occupy his seat in the Senate of the United States, to see if he could not, by his great wisdom and experience, and the renown of his name, do something to restore peace and quiet to a disturbed country. Who got up that sectional strife that Clay had to be called upon to quell? I have heard Lincoln boast that he voted forty-two times for the Wilmot proviso, and that he would have voted as many times more if he could. (Laughter.) Lincoln is the man, in connection with Seward, Chase, Giddings, and other Abolitionists, who got up that strife that I helped Clay to put down. (Tremendous applause.) Henry Clay came back to the Senate in 1849, and saw that he must do something to restore peace to the country. The Union Whigs and the Union Democrats welcomed him the moment he arrived, as the man for the occasion. We believed that he, of all men on earth, had been preserved by Divine Providence to guide us out of our difficulties, and we Democrats rallied under Clay then, as you Whigs in nullification time rallied under the banner of old Jackson, forgetting party when the country was in danger, in order that we might have a country first, and parties afterwards. ("Three cheers for Douglas.")

And this reminds me that Mr. Lincoln told you that the slavery question was the only thing that ever disturbed the peace and harmony of the Union. Did not nullification once raise its head and disturb the peace of this Union in 1832? Was that the slavery question, Mr. Lincoln? Did not disunion raise its monster head during the last war with Great Britain? Was that the slavery question, Mr. Lincoln? The peace of this country has been disturbed three times, once during the war with Great Britain, once on the tariff question, and once on the slavery question. ("Three cheers for Douglas.") His argument, therefore, that slavery is the only question that has ever created dissension in the Union falls to the ground. It is true that agitators are enabled now to use this slavery question for the purpose of sectional strife. ("That's so.") He admits that in regard to all things else, the principle that I advocate, making each State and territory free to decide for itself ought to prevail. He instances the cranberry laws, and the oyster laws, and he might have gone through the whole list with the same effect. I say that all these laws are local and domestic, and that local and domestic concerns should be left to each State and each territory to manage for itself. If agitators would acquiesce in that principle, there never would be any danger to the peace and harmony of this Union. ("That's so," and cheers.)

Mr. Lincoln tries to avoid the main issue by attacking the truth of my proposition, that our fathers made this government divided into free and slave States, recognizing the right of each to decide all its local questions for itself. Did they not thus make it? It is true that they did not establish slavery in any of the States, or abolish it in any of them; but finding thirteen States twelve of which were slave and one free, they agreed to form a government uniting them together, as they stood divided into free and slave States, and to guarantee forever to each State the right to do as it pleased on the slavery question. (Cheers.) Having thus made the government, and conferred this right upon each State forever, I assert that this government can exist as they made it, divided into free and slave States, if any one State chooses to retain slavery. (Cheers.) He says that he looks forward to a time when slavery shall be abolished everywhere. I look forward to a time when each State shall be allowed to do as it pleases. If it chooses to keep slavery forever, it is not my business, but its own; if it chooses to abolish slavery, it is its own business —not mine. I care more for the great principle of self-government, the right of the people to rule, than I do for all the negroes in Christendom. (Cheers.) I would not endanger the perpetuity of this Union. I would not blot out the great inalienable rights of the white men for all the negroes that ever existed. (Renewed applause.) Hence, I say, let us maintain this government on the principles that our fathers made it, recognizing the right of each State to keep slavery as long as its people determine, or to abolish it when they please. (Cheers.) But Mr. Lincoln says that when our fathers made this government they did not look forward to the state of things now existing; and therefore he thinks the doctrine was wrong; and he quotes Brooks, of South Carolina, to prove that our fathers then thought that probably slavery would be abolished, by each State acting for itself before this time. Suppose they did; suppose they did not foresee what has occurred,—does that change the principles of our government? They did not probably foresee the telegraph that transmits intelligence by lightning, nor did they foresee the railroads that now form the bonds of union between the different States, or the thousand mechanical inventions that have elevated mankind. But do these things change the principles of the government? Our fathers, I say, made this government on the principle of the right of each State to do as it pleases in its own domestic affairs, subject to the constitution, and allowed the people of each to apply to every new change of circumstance such remedy as they may see fit to improve their condition. This right they have for all time to come. (Cheers.)

Mr. Lincoln went on to tell you that he does not at all desire to interfere with slavery in the States where it exists, nor does his party. I expected him to say that down here. (Laughter.) Let me ask him then how he is going to put slavery in the course of ultimate extinction everywhere, if he does not intend to interfere with it in the States where it exists? (Renewed laughter.) He says that he will prohibit it in all territories, and the inference is then that unless they make free States out of them he will keep them out of the Union; for, mark you, he did not say whether or not he would vote to admit Kansas with slavery or not, as her people might apply; (he forgot that as usual, &c;) he did not say whether or not he was in favor of bringing the territories now in existence into the Union on the principle of Clay's compromise measures on the slavery question. I told you that he would not. (Give it to him, he deserves it, &c.) His idea is that he will prohibit slavery in all the territories, and thus force them all to become free States, surrounding the slave States with a cordon of free States, and hemming them in, keeping the slaves confined to their present limits whilst they go on multiplying until the soil on which they live will no longer feed them, and he will thus be able to put slavery in a course of ultimate extinction by starvation. (Cheers.) He will extinguish slavery in the Southern States as the French general exterminated the Algerines when he smoked them out. He is going to extinguish slavery by surrounding the slave States, hemming in the slaves, and starving them out of existence as you smoke a fox out of his hole. And he intends to do that in the name of humanity and Christianity, in order that we may get rid of the terrible crime and sin entailed upon our fathers of holding slaves. (Laughter and cheers.) Mr. Lincoln makes out that line of policy, and appeals to the moral sense of justice, and to the Christian feeling of the community to sustain him. He says that any man who holds to the contrary doctrine is in the position of the king who claimed to govern by divine right. Let us examine for a moment and see what principle it was that overthrew the divine right of George the Third to govern us. Did not these colonies rebel because the British parliament had no right to pass laws concerning our property and domestic and private institutions without our consent? We demanded that the British government should not pass such laws unless they gave us representation in the body passing them,—and this the British government insisting on doing,—we went to war, on the principle that the home government should not control and govern distant colonies without giving them a representation. Now, Mr. Lincoln proposes to govern the territories without giving the people a representation, and calls on Congress to pass laws controlling their property and domestic concerns without their consent and against their will. Thus, he asserts for his party the identical principle asserted by George III. and the tories of the Revolution. (Cheers.)

I ask you to look into these things, and then to tell me whether the democracy or the abolitionists are right. I hold that the people of a territory, like those of a State, (I use the language of Mr. Buchanan in his letter of acceptance,) have the right to decide for themselves whether slavery shall or shall not exist within their limits. ("That's the idea," "Hurrah for Douglas.") The point upon which Chief Justice Taney expresses his opinion is simply this, that slaves being property, stand on an equal footing with other property, and consequently that the owner has the same right to carry that property into a territory that he has any other, subject to the same conditions. Suppose that one of your merchants was to take fifty or one hundred thousand dollars worth of liquors to Kansas. He has a right to go there under that decision, but when he gets there he finds the Maine liquor law in force, and what can he do with his property after he gets it there? He cannot sell it, he cannot use it, it is subject to the local law, and that law is against him, and the best thing he can do with it is to bring it back into Missouri or Illinois and sell it. If you take negroes to Kansas, as Col. Jeff. Davis said in his Bangor speech, from which I have quoted to-day, you must take them there subject to the local law. If the people want the institution of slavery they will protect and encourage it; but if they do not want it they will withhold that protection, and the absence of local legislation protecting slavery excludes it as completely as a positive prohibition. ("That's so," and cheers.) You slaveholders of Missouri might as well understand what you know practically, that you cannot carry slavery where the people do not want it. ("That's so.") All you have a right to ask is that the people shall do as they please; if they want slavery let them have it; if they do not want it, allow them to refuse to encourage it.

My friends, if, as I have said before, we will only live up to this great fundamental principle there will be peace between the North and the South. Mr. Lincoln admits that under the constitution on all domestic questions, except slavery, we ought not to interfere with the people of each State. What right have we to interfere with slavery any more than we have to interfere with any other question. He says that this slavery question is now the bone of contention. Why? Simply because agitators have combined in all the free States to make war upon it. Suppose the agitators in the States should combine in one-half of the Union to make war upon the railroad system of the other half? They would thus be driven to the same sectional strife. Suppose one section makes war upon any other peculiar institution of the opposite section, and the same strife is produced. The only remedy and safety is that we shall stand by the constitution as our fathers made it, obey the laws as they are passed, while they stand the proper test and sustain the decisions of the Supreme Court and the constituted authorities.

To James N. Brown

Hon. J. N. Brown   Springfield,
My dear Sir   Oct. 18. 1858

I do not perceive how I can express myself, more plainly, than I have done in the foregoing extracts. In four of them I have expressly disclaimed all intention to bring about social and political equality between the white and black races, and, in all the rest, I have done the same thing by clear implication.

I have made it equally plain that I think the negro is included in the word "men" used in the Declaration of Independence.

I believe the declaration that "all men are created equal" is the great fundamental principle upon which our free institutions rest; that negro slavery is violative of that principle; but that, by our frame of government, that principle has not been made one of legal obligation; that by our frame of government, the States which have slavery are to retain it, or surrender it at their own pleasure; and that all others—individuals, free-states and national government—are constitutionally bound to leave them alone about it.

I believe our government was thus framed because of the *necessity* springing from the actual presence of slavery, when it was framed.

That such necessity does not exist in the teritories, where slavery is not present.

In his Mendenhall speech Mr. Clay says

"Now, as an abstract principle, there is no doubt of the truth of that declaration (all men created equal) and it is desireable, in the original construction of society, and in organized societies, to keep it in view, as a great fundamental principle"

Again, in the same speech Mr. Clay says:

"If a state of nature existed, and we were about to lay the foundations of society, no man would be more strongly opposed than I should to incorporate the institution of slavery among it's elements;"

Exactly so. In our new free teritories, a state of nature *does* exist. In them Congress lays the foundations of society; and, in laying those foundations, I say, with Mr. Clay, it is desireable that the declaration of the equality of all men shall be kept in view, as a great fundamental principle; and that Congress, which lays the foundations of society, should, like Mr. Clay, be strongly opposed to the incorporation of slavery among it's elements.

But it does not follow that social and political equality between whites and blacks, *must* be incorporated, because slavery must *not*. The declaration does not so require. Yours as ever

To Norman B. Judd

Hon. N. B. Judd   Rushville, Oct. 20, 1858

My dear Sir: I now have a high degree of confidence that we shall succeed, if we are not over-run with fraudulent votes to a greater extent than usual. On alighting from the cars and walking three squares at Naples on Monday, I met about fifteen Celtic gentlemen, with black carpet-sacks in their hands.

I learned that they had crossed over from the Rail-road in Brown county, but where they were going no one could tell. They dropped in about the doggeries, and were still hanging about when I left. At Brown County yesterday I was told that about four hundred of the same sort were to be brought into Schuyler, before the election, to work on some new Railroad; but on reaching here I find Bagby thinks that is not so.

What I most dread is that they will introduce into the doubtful districts numbers of men who are legal voters in all respects except *residence* and who will swear to residence and thus put it beyond our power to exclude them. They can & I fear will swear falsely on that point, because they know it is next to impossible to convict them of Perjury upon it.

Now the great remaining part of the campaign, is finding a way to head this thing off. Can it be done at all?

I have a bare suggestion. When there is a known body of these voters, could not a true man, of the *"detective"* class, be introduced among them in disguise, who could, at the nick of time, control their votes? Think this over. It would be a great thing, when this trick is attempted upon us, to have the saddle come up on the other horse.

I have talked, more fully than I can write, to Mr. Scripps, and he will talk to you.

If we can head off the fraudulent votes we shall carry the day. Yours as ever

Portion of Speech at Carthage, Illinois

At Carthage, Hancock County, Oct. 22, Mr. Lincoln discussed the following topics, not included in any of the joint debates with Judge Douglas:

On the 4th of October, at Woodford County, I learned that Judge Douglas had been imputing to me and my friends a purpose to release the Central Railroad Company from paying into the State Treasury the seven per cent, upon their gross earnings, which, by law, they are now bound to do. I learn he repeated the same imputation at Pekin, Oquawka, Monmouth and this place, though he has never mentioned it at any of our joint meetings, or elsewhere in my presence. I mention it now to correct any false impression that may have been made. I understand the Judge states, among other things, that I once received a fee of $5,000 from that Company. My partner and I did receive such fee under the following circumstances: By their charter, the Company are bound to make periodical payments into the State Treasury, in exemption of all other taxes. This exempts them from county and city taxes. The Legislature intended, as I understand, in consideration of the large land grant, to make the Company pay about as much as they could bear; and to make them pay it into the State Treasury, so that the *whole* people could share the benefit, instead of paying any to the counties through which the road passes, to the exclusion of those through which it does not pass. This was a fair way of dealing with the whole people, as was thought. The county of McLean, one of the counties through which the road passes, claimed that the exemption was unconstitutional, and that the Company was bound to pay county taxes on their property within the limits of the county; and the parties went to Court to try the question. The Railroad Company employed me as one of their lawyers in the case, the county having declined to employ me. I was not upon a salary, and no agreement was made as to the amount of fee. The Railroad Company finally gained the case. The decision, I thought, and still think, was worth half a million dollars to them. I wanted them to pay me $5,000, and they wanted to pay me about $500. I sued them and got the $5,000. This is the whole truth about the fee; and what tendency it has to prove that I received any of the people's money, or that I am on very cozy terms with the Railroad Company, I do not comprehend.

It is a matter of interest to you that the Company shall not be released from their obligations to pay money into the State Treasury. Every dollar they so pay relieves the whole people of just so much in the way of taxation. I am a candidate for no office wherein I could release them, if elected. The State Legislature alone can release them. Therefore, all you need to do is to know your candidates for the Legislature, how they will vote on the question of release, if elected. I doubt not every candidate who is a friend of mine is ready to show his hand; and perhaps it would be well to have Judge Douglas' friends show their hands also. See to your members of the Legislature, and you are beyond the power of all others as to releasing the Central Railroad from its obligations. This is your perfect security.

To Edward Lusk

Edward Lusk, Esq   Springfield,
Dear Sir   Oct. 30, 1858
    I understand the story is still being told, and insisted upon, that I have been a Know-Nothing. I repeat, what I stated in a public speech at Meredosia, that I am not, nor ever have been, connected with the party called the Know-Nothing party, or party calling themselves the American party. *Certainly* no man of truth, and I *believe*, no man of good character for truth can be found to say on his own knowledge that I ever was connected with that party. Yours very truly

Portion of Last Speech in Campaign of 1858, Springfield, Illinois

My friends, to-day closes the discussions of this canvass. The planting and the culture are over; and there remains but the preparation, and the harvest.
    I stand here surrounded by friends—some *political, all personal* friends, I trust. May I be indulged, in this closing scene, to say a few words of myself. I have borne a laborious, and, in some respects to myself, a painful part in the contest. Through all, I have neither assailed, nor wrestled with any part of the constitution. The legal right of the Southern people to reclaim their fugitives I have constantly admitted. The legal right of Congress to interfere with their institution in the states, I have constantly denied. In resisting the spread of

slavery to new teritory, and with that, what appears to me to be a tendency to subvert the first principle of free government itself my whole effort has consisted. To the best of my judgment I have labored *for*, and not *against* the Union. As I have not felt, so I have not expressed any harsh sentiment towards our Southern bretheren. I have constantly declared, as I really believed, the only difference between them and us, is the difference of circumstances.

I have meant to assail the motives of no party, or individual; and if I have, in any instance (of which I am not conscious) departed from my purpose, I regret it.

I have said that in some respects the contest has been painful to me. Myself, and those with whom I act have been constantly accused of a purpose to destroy the union; and bespattered with every imaginable odious epithet; and some who were friends, as it were but yesterday have made themselves most active in this. I have cultivated patience, and made no attempt at a retort.

Ambition has been ascribed to me. God knows how sincerely I prayed from the first that this field of ambition might not be opened. I claim no insensibility to political honors; but today could the Missouri restriction be restored, and the whole slavery question replaced on the old ground of "toleration by *necessity*" where it exists, with unyielding hostility to the spread of it, on principle, I would, in consideration, gladly agree, that Judge Douglas should never be *out*, and I never *in*, an office, so long as we both or either, live.

October 30, 1858

To John J. Crittenden

Hon: J. J. Crittenden   Springfield, Novr. 4– 1858

My dear Sir   Yours of the 27th. ult. was taken from the Post-Office by my law-partner, and, in the confusion consequent upon the recent election, was handed to me only this moment. I am sorry the allusion made in the Mo. Republican, to the private correspondence between yourself and me, has given you any pain. It gave me scarcely a thought, perhaps for the reason that, being away from home, I did not see it till only two days before the election. It never occurred to me to cast any blame upon you. I have been told that the correspondence has been alluded to in the Mo. Rep. several times, but I only saw one, of the allusions, and in which it was stated, as I remember that a gentleman of St. Louis had seen a copy of your letter to me. As I had given no copy, nor ever showed the original, of course I infered he had seen it in your hands, but it did not occur to me to blame you for showing what you had written yourself. It was not said that the gentleman had seen a copy or the original of my letter to you.

The emotions of defeat, at the close of a struggle in which I felt more than a merely selfish interest, and to which defeat the use of your name contributed largely, are fresh upon me; but, even in this mood, I can not for a moment suspect you of anything dishonorable. Your Obt. Servt.

To Norman B. Judd

Hon N. B. Judd   Springfield, Nov. 15. 1858.
My dear Sir

I have the pleasure to enform you that I am convalescent, and hoping these lines may find you in the same improving state of health. Doubtless you have suspected for some time that I entertained a personal wish for a term in the U.S. Senate; and had the suspicion taken the shape of a direct charge, I think I could not have truthfully denied it. But let the past as nothing be. For the future my view is that the fight must go on. The returns here are not yet complete; but it is believed that Daugherty's vote will be slightly greater than Millers majority over Fondey. We have some hundred and twenty thousand clear Republican votes. That *"pile"* is worth keeping together. It will elect a State ticket two years hence. In that day I shall fight in the ranks, but shall be in no ones' way for any of the places. I am especially for Trumbull's re-election; and, by the way, this brings me to the principal object of this letter. Can you not take your draft of an apportionment law, and carefully revise it till it shall be strictly and obviously just in all particulars, and then by an early and persistent effort, get enough of the enemies' men to enable you to pass it? I believe if you and Peck make a job of it, begin early, and work earnestly and quietly, you can succeed in it. Unless something be done Trumbull is inevitably beaten two years hence. Take this into serious consideration.

Yours as ever

To Norman B. Judd

Hon: N. B. Judd   Springfield, Nov. 16. 1858

My dear Sir   Yours of the 15th. is just received. I wrote *you* the same day. As to the pecuniary matter, I am willing to pay according to my ability; but I am the poorest hand living to get others to pay. I have been on expences so long without earning any thing that I am absolutely without money now for even household purposes. Still, if you can put in two hundred and fifty dollars for me towards discharging the debt of the Committee, I will allow it when you and I settle the private matter between us. This, with what I have already paid, and with an outstanding note of mine, will exceed my subscription of five hundred dollars. This too, is exclusive of my ordinary expences during the campaign, all which being added to my loss of time and business, bears pretty heavily upon one no better off in world's goods than I; but as I had the post of honor, it is not for me to be over-nice.

You are feeling badly. *"And this too shall pass away."* Never fear. Yours as ever

To Samuel C. Davis and Company

Messrs S. C. Davis & Co   Springfield,
Gentlemen   Novr. 17. 1858

You perhaps need not to be reminded how I have been personally engaged the last three or four months. Your letter to Lincoln & Herndon, of Oct. 1st. complaining that the lands of those against whom we obtained judgments last winter for you, have not been sold on execution has just been handed to me to-day. I will try to "explain how our" (your) "interests have been so much neglected" as you choose to express it. After these judgments were obtained we wrote you that under our law, the selling of land on execution is a delicate and dangerous, matter; that it could not be done safely, without a careful examination of titles; and also of the *value* of the property. Our letters to you will show this. To do this would require a canvass of half the State. We were puzzled, & you sent no definite instructions. At length we employed a young man to visit all the localities, and make as accurate a report on titles and values as he could. He did this, expending three or four weeks time, and as he said, over a hundred dollars of his own money in doing so. When this was done we wrote you, asking if we should sell and bid in for you in accordance with this information. This letter you never answered.

My mind is made up. I will have no more to do with this class of business. I can do business in Court, but I can not, and will not follow executions all over the world. The young man who collected the information for us is an active young lawyer living at Carrollton, Greene County I think. We promised him a share of the compensation we should ultimately receive. He must be somehow paid; and I believe you would do well to turn the whole business over to him. I believe we have had, of legal fees, which you are to recover back from the defendants, one hundred dollars. I would not go through the same labor and vexation again for five hundred; still, if you will clear us of Mr. William Fishback (such is his name) we will be most happy to surrender to him, or to any other person you may name. Yours &c

To Henry Asbury

Henry Asbury, Esq
My dear Sir

Springfield,
Novr. 19, 1858

Yours of the 13th. was received some days ago. The fight must go on. The cause of civil liberty must not be surrendered at the end of *one*, or even, one *hundred* defeats. Douglas had the ingenuity to be supported in the late contest both as the best means to *break down*, and to *uphold* the Slave interest. No ingenuity can keep those antagonistic elements in harmony long. Another explosion will soon come. Yours truly

To Anson G. Henry

Dr. A. G. Henry   Springfield, Ills. Nov: 19, 1858

My dear Sir   Yours of the 27th. of Sept. was received two days ago. I was at Oquawka, Henderson county, on the 9th. of October; and I may then have seen Majr. A. N. Armstrong; but having nothing then to fix my attention, I do not remember such a man. I have concluded, as the best way of serving you, to inclose your letter to E. A. Paine, Esq, of Monmouth, Ills, a reliable lawyer, asking him to do what you ask of me. If a suit is to be brought, he will correspond directly with you.

You doubtless have seen, ere this, the result of the election here. Of course I *wished*, but I did not much *expect* a better result. The popular vote of the State is with us; so that the seat in the [   ] whole canvass. On the contrary, John and George Weber, and several such old democrats were furiously for me. As a general rule, out of Sangamon, as well as in it, much of the plain old democracy is with us, while nearly all the old exclusive silk-stocking whiggery is against us. I do not mean nearly all the old whig party; but nearly all of the nice exclusive sort. And why not? There has been nothing in politics since the Revolution so congenial to their nature, as the present position of the great democratic party.

I am glad I made the late race. It gave me a hearing on the great and durable question of the age, which I could have had in no other way; and though I now sink out of view, and shall be forgotten, I believe I have made some marks which will tell for the cause of civil liberty long after I am gone.

Mary joins me in sending our best wishes to Mrs. Henry and others of your family; [   ]

To Charles H. Ray

Dr. C. H. Ray   Springfield,
My dear Sir   Novr. 20, 1858

I wish to preserve a Set of the late debates (if they may be called so) between Douglas and myself. To enable me to do so, please get two copies of each number of your paper containing the whole, and send them to me by Express; and I will pay you for the papers & for your trouble. I wish the two sets, in order to lay one away in the raw, and to put the other in a Scrap-book. Remember, if part of any debate is on *both* sides of one sheet, it will take two sets to make one scrapbook.

I believe, according to a letter of yours to Hatch you are "feeling like h—ll yet." Quit that. You will soon feel better. Another "blow-up" is coming; and we shall have fun again. Douglas managed to be supported both as the best instrument to *put down* and to *uphold* the slave power; but no ingenuity can long keep these antagonisms in harmony. Yours as ever

To Lyman Trumbull

Hon. L. Trumbull: Springfield,
My dear Sir   Decr. 11. 1858

Your letter of the 7th. inclosing one from Mr. Underwood, is received. I have not the slightest thought of being a candidate for Congress in this District. I am not spoken of in that connection; and I can scarcely conceive what has misled Mr. Underwood in regard to the matter.

As to what we shall do, the Republicans are a little divided. The Danites say if we will stand out of the way, they will run a man, and divide the democratic forces with the Douglasites; and some of our friends are in favor of this course. Others think such a course would demoralize us, and hurt us in the future; and they, of course, are in favor of running a man of our own at all events. This latter view will probably prevail.

Since you left, Douglas has gone South, making characteristic speeches, and seeking to re-instate himself in that section.

The majority of the democratic politicians of the nation mean to kill him; but I doubt whether they will adopt the aptest way to do it. Their true way is to present him with no new test, let him into the Charleston Convention, and then outvote him, and nominate another. In that case, he will have no pretext for bolting the nomination, and will be as powerless as they can wish. On the other hand, if they push a Slave code upon him, as a test, he will bolt at once, turn upon us, as in the case of Lecompton, and claim that all Northern men shall make common cause in electing him President as the best means of breaking down the Slave power. In that case, the democratic party go into a minority inevitably; and the struggle in the whole North will be, as it was in Illinois last summer and fall, whether the Republican party can maintain it's identity, or be broken up to form the tail of Douglas' new kite. Some of our great Republican doctors will then have a splendid chance to swallow the pills they so eagerly prescribed for us last Spring. Still I hope they will not swallow them; and although I do not feel that I owe the said doctors much, I will help them, to the best of my ability, to reject the said pills. The truth is, the Republican principle can, in no wise live with Douglas; and it is arrant folly now, as it was last Spring, to waste time, and scatter labor already performed, in dallying with him. Your friend as ever

Chronology

town, Kentucky. (Father and stepmother knew each other when Lincolns lived in Hardin County.)

1820   Attends school briefly with sister Sarah.

1822   Attends school for several months.

1824   Helps with plowing and planting and works for neighbors for hire. Attends school in fall and winter. Reads family Bible, and borrows books whenever possible (reading will include Mason Locke Weems's *The Life and Memorable Actions of George Washington*, Daniel Defoe's *Robinson Crusoe*, Aesop's *Fables*, John Bunyan's *Pilgrim's Progress*, William Grimshaw's *History of the United States*, and Thomas Dilworth's *A New Guide to the English Tongue*).

1827   Works as boatman and farmhand at junction of Anderson Creek and the Ohio River, near Troy, Indiana.

1828   Sister Sarah, now married to Aaron Grigsby, dies in childbirth on January 20. In April, Lincoln and Allen Gentry leave Rockport, Indiana, on flatboat trip to New Orleans with cargo of farm produce. While trading in coastal Louisiana sugar-growing regions, they fight off seven black men trying to rob them. Returns home by steamboat. Watches trials at county courthouses.

1830   In March, moves with family to Illinois, where they settle on uncleared land ten miles southwest of Decatur in Macon County. Makes first known political speech, in favor of improving navigation on Sangamon River, at campaign meeting in Decatur.

1831   Builds flatboat with stepbrother John D. Johnston and cousin John Hanks in spring and makes second trip to New Orleans, carrying corn, live hogs, and barreled pork. Returns to Illinois in summer and moves to village of New Salem, twenty miles northwest of Springfield in Sangamon County (family has moved to Coles County, Illinois). Clerks in general store, where he sleeps in the back, helps run mill, and does odd jobs. Accepts challenge to wrestle Jack Armstrong, leader of the "Clary's Grove boys," local group of rowdy young men, and stands his ground when they rush him to prevent Armstrong's defeat. Match is agreed to be a draw, and Lincoln gains respect and friendship of group. Becomes friends with tavernkeeper James Rutledge, his daughter Ann, and schoolmaster Mentor Graham. Learns basic mathematics, reads Shakespeare and Robert Burns, and participates in local debating society.

1832   Borrows and studies Samuel Kirkham's *English Grammar*. Announces candidacy for House of Representatives, lower chamber of Illinois General Assembly, in March. Volunteers for Illinois militia at outbreak of Black Hawk Indian War in early April and is elected company captain. Reenlists as private when his company is mustered out in late May and serves until July 10 in Rock River country of northern Illinois, covering much ground but seeing no action. Loses election on August 6, running eighth in field of thirteen candidates seeking four seats. Becomes partner in New Salem general store with William F. Berry.

1833   Store fails and leaves Lincoln deeply in debt. Works as hired hand and begins to write deeds and mortgage papers for neighbors. Boards with different families, moving every few months. Appointed postmaster of New Salem in May (serves until office is moved to nearby Petersburg in 1836); regularly reads newspapers in the mail. Studies surveying with Mentor Graham's help after being appointed deputy surveyor of Sangamon County.

1834   Makes first known survey in January and first town survey on site of New Boston, Illinois, in September (works as surveyor for three years). Elected as a Whig on August 4 to Illinois House of Representatives, running second in field of thirteen seeking four Sangamon County seats. Begins to study law, reading Blackstone's *Commentaries* and Joseph Chitty's *Precedents in Pleading* and borrowing other lawbooks from attorney John T. Stuart. Takes his seat on December 1 at capital in Vandalia. Rooms with Stuart, who is elected floor leader by Whig minority in House. Meets Stephen A. Douglas, 21-year-old lawyer active in Democratic party politics.

1835   Serves on twelve special committees and helps draft bills and resolutions for other Whigs. Votes with the majority to charter state bank and to build canal linking the Illinois River and Lake Michigan. Death of former store partner William Berry in January increases Lincoln's debt to approximately $1,100, which he repays over several years. Returns to New Salem after legislature adjourns on February 13. Ann Rutledge dies on August 25 from fever at age twenty-two. Attends special legislative session in December, called to speed up work on Illinois and Michigan Canal and other internal improvements. Votes for bill pledging credit of state to payment of canal loan.

1836   Returns to New Salem after legislature adjourns on January 18. Wins reelection on August 1, running first in field of seventeen candidates contesting seven Sangamon County seats in lower chamber. Receives license to practice law on September 9. Begins halfhearted courtship of Mary Owens, 28-year-old Kentucky woman visiting her sister in New Salem. Has episode of severe depression ("hypochondria") soon after returning to Vandalia in early December for new legislative session.

1837   Lincoln and other members of nine-man Whig delegation from Sangamon County (known as the "Long Nine" because they average over six feet in height) lead successful campaign to move state capital from Vandalia to Springfield, a shift that reflects population growth in central and northern counties. Supports ambitious internal improvements program. With fellow Whig representative Dan Stone, enters protest against anti-abolitionist resolutions adopted in their chamber. Legislature adjourns on March 6. Moves to Springfield on April 15, rooming with storeowner Joshua F. Speed, who becomes a close friend. Becomes law partner of John T. Stuart and begins extensive and varied civil and criminal practice. (Lincoln occasionally acts as prosecutor, but appears for the defense in almost all of his criminal cases throughout his career.) At special legislative session in July, votes with majority to continue internal improvements despite national financial panic. Mary Owens rejects his proposal of marriage, and courtship is broken off in August.

1838   Delivers address on "The Perpetuation of Our Political Institutions" to the Springfield Young Men's Lyceum on

January 27. Helps defend Henry Truett in widely publicized murder case, delivering final argument to jury; Truett is acquitted. In May, debates Douglas, who is running for Congress against Stuart. Reelected to the legislature, August 6, running first of seven successful candidates in field of seventeen. Nominated for speaker by Whig caucus when legislature convenes on December 3, but is defeated by Democrat W.L.D. Ewing. Serves as Whig floor leader.

1839   Legislature adjourns on March 4. Lincoln makes first extensive trip on Illinois Eighth Judicial Circuit, attending court sessions held successively in nine counties in central and eastern Illinois. Chosen presidential elector in October by first Whig state convention. Debates Douglas in Springfield on issue of national bank. Assumes greater share of legal partnership when Stuart leaves for Congress in November. Admitted to practice in United States Circuit Court on December 3. Legislature convenes in special session, December 9, meeting at Springfield for the first time. Becomes acquainted with Mary Todd, 21-year-old daughter of prominent Kentucky Whig banker, sister-in-law of Illinois Whig legislator Ninian W. Edwards, and cousin of John T. Stuart.

1840   Votes in minority against repeal of internal improvements law of 1837, which has caused financial crisis (state defaults on its debt in July 1841). Legislature adjourns on February 3. Campaigns for Whig presidential candidate, William Henry Harrison, debating Douglas and other Democratic speakers. Argues his first case before Illinois Supreme Court in June (Lincoln will appear before it in over 240 cases). Reelected to the legislature, August 3, polling lowest vote of five candidates elected from Sangamon County. Becomes engaged to Mary Todd in fall. Legislature meets in special session on November 23. Lincoln is again defeated by Ewing in voting for speaker. In parliamentary maneuver to protect failing state bank, Whigs attempt to block adjournment of special session by preventing quorum. When plan fails on December 5, Lincoln and two other Whigs jump out of ground-floor window in unsuccessful attempt not to be counted as present; incident causes widespread derision in the Democratic press.

1841   Breaks engagement with Mary Todd on January 1. Is severely depressed for weeks and absent from legislature for several days. Legislature adjourns, March 1. Dissolves partnership with Stuart, who is often absent on political business, and forms new partnership with Stephen T. Logan, prominent Illinois Whig known for methodical legal work. Wins appeal before Illinois Supreme Court in case of *Bailey* v. *Cromwell*, successfully arguing that unpaid promissory note written by his client, David Bailey, for purchase of slave was legally void in Illinois due to the prohibitions against slavery in the Ordinance of 1787 and the state constitution. Visits Speed at his family home near Lexington, Kentucky, in August and September. On return trip by steamboat, sees twelve slaves chained together "like so many fish upon a trot-line."

1842   Delivers address to local temperance society on February 22. Does not seek reelection to legislature. Resumes courtship of Mary Todd during summer. In September, accepts challenge from Democratic state auditor James Shields, who is angered by four published pseudonymous letters ridiculing him (one was written by Mary Todd and a friend, another by Lincoln). Lincoln chooses broadswords as weapons, but duel is averted on September 22 when Shields accepts Lincoln's explanation that the letters were purely political in nature and not intended to impugn Shields's personal honor. Marries Mary Todd on November 4 in parlor of her sister's Springfield mansion, then moves with her into room in the Globe Tavern.

1843   Unsuccessfully seeks Whig nomination for Congress, then tries to establish arrangement with John J. Hardin and Edward D. Baker for each of them to be nominated in turn to serve for one term. Son Robert Todd Lincoln born August 1. Lincolns move into rented cottage.

1844   Lincolns move in May into house, bought for $1,500, at Eighth and Jackson streets in Springfield (their home until 1861). Campaigns as Whig elector for Henry Clay in the presidential election. Visits former Indiana home in fall. Partnership with Logan is dissolved in December so that Logan can take his son as new partner; Lincoln establishes his own practice and takes 26-year-old William H. Herndon as junior partner.

1845   Works to assure himself Whig congressional nomination when Hardin refuses to abide by principle of rotation. Income from law practice is approximately $1,500 a year.

1846   Second son, Edward Baker Lincoln, born March 10. Wins congressional nomination at Whig district convention held on May 1. Speaks on May 30 at mass meeting in Springfield that calls for united support of recently declared war against Mexico. Helps prosecute manslaughter charge in June; jury deadlocks and case is never retried. Elected to U.S. House of Representatives on August 3, defeating Democrat Peter Cartwright, a Methodist preacher, by 6,340 to 4,829 votes.

1847   Makes first visit to Chicago in early July to attend convention protesting President James K. Polk's veto of bill for river and harbor improvements. In October, represents slave-owner Robert Matson at habeas corpus hearing in Coles County. Lincoln argues that Bryants, slave family Matson had brought from Kentucky to do seasonal farmwork on his Illinois land, were not state residents and thus were not freed by antislavery provisions of Illinois law. Court rules against Matson and frees Bryants. After visit with wife's family in Lexington, Kentucky, travels with wife and sons to Washington, D.C., and moves into boarding house near the Capitol. Takes seat in the House of Representatives when Thirtieth Congress convenes on December 6. Presents resolutions on December 22 requesting President Polk to inform the House whether the "spot" where hostilities with Mexico began was or was not on Mexican soil.

1848   Serves on Expenditures in the War Department and Post Office and Post Roads committees. Attacks Polk's war policy in speech on floor of the House, January 22 (almost all fighting had ended with the American capture of Mexico City in September 1847, but peace treaty had yet to be signed). Ridiculed as "spotty Lincoln" by Illinois Democratic press. Wife and children leave Washington to stay with her family in Kentucky. Attends national Whig convention at Philadelphia in early June as supporter of General Zachary Taylor, who is nominated for president. Abides by his own rule of rotation and does not seek second term in Congress. Rejoined by family in late July. House adjourns on August 14. Campaigns for Taylor in Maryland and Massachusetts; meets former New York governor William H. Seward at Whig rally in Boston on September 22. Visits Niagara Falls before taking steamer to Chicago. Campaigns in Illinois until election. Returns to Washington, December 7, for second session of Thirtieth Congress. Supports the principle of the Wilmot Proviso by voting to prohibit slavery in the territory acquired from Mexico.

1849   Votes to exclude slavery from federal territories and abolish slave trade in the District of Columbia, but does not speak in congressional debates on slavery. Congress adjourns on March 4. Makes only appearance before United States Supreme Court, March 7–8, unsuccessfully appealing U.S. circuit court ruling concerning application of Illinois statute of limitations on nonresidents' suits. Applies for patent (later granted) on device for reducing draft of steamboats in shallow water. Returns to Springfield on March 31. Visits father and stepmother in Coles County in late May. Goes to Washington in June in pursuit of position as commissioner of the General Land Office, but fails to receive appointment from the new Taylor administration. Resumes law practice in Illinois. Declines appointment as secretary and then as governor of Oregon Territory.

1850   Son Edward dies on February 1 after illness of nearly two months. Lincoln returns to Eighth Judicial Circuit (now covering fourteen counties), making 400-mile, 12-week trip in spring and fall. Becomes a closer friend of David Davis, who had practiced law with Lincoln on the circuit before becoming its judge in 1848. Delivers eulogy of Zachary Taylor at Chicago memorial meeting in July. Studies Euclidean geometry. Third son, William Wallace (Willie), born December 21.

1851   Learns that father is seriously ill in Coles County. Writes to stepbrother John D. Johnston that he cannot visit because of wife's health. Father dies on January 17.

1852   Wife joins First Presbyterian Church in Springfield. Lincoln rents a pew and attends at times but never himself becomes a member of any church. Delivers eulogy of Henry Clay at Springfield memorial meeting in July. Serves as Whig elector and makes several speeches in support of Winfield Scott during presidential campaign.

1853   Fourth son, Thomas (Tad), born April 4. In May, Lincoln serves as court-appointed prosecutor in child-rape case and wins conviction (defendant is sentenced to eighteen years in prison). Accepts retainer from Illinois Central Railroad in October in suit to prevent taxation by McLean County, a case crucial to railroad's claim that it could be taxed only by the state government.

1854   Helps argue McLean County case in Illinois Supreme Court, February 28; court orders that it be re-argued. Lincoln's declining interest in politics is revived when Congress passes the Kansas-Nebraska Act on May 22, repealing antislavery restriction in the Missouri Compromise. Completion of direct railroad link increases Lincoln's practice in U.S. district and circuit courts in Chicago. Runs for Illinois House of Representatives to help campaign of Richard Yates, a congressman who opposed the Kansas-Nebraska Act. Speaks against the act at Bloomington, September 26, Springfield, October 4, and Peoria, October 16, appearing before or after Senator Stephen A. Douglas, its principal author. Elected to legislature, but declines seat to become eligible for election to the United States Senate.

1855   Legislature meets to elect United States senator, February 8. Lincoln leads on first ballot, but eventually throws dwindling support to anti-Nebraska Democrat Lyman Trumbull, who is elected on tenth ballot. Goes to Cincinnati in September to appear for defense in *McCormick* v. *Manny*, federal patent infringement suit originally scheduled to be tried in Illinois. Is excluded from case by other defense attorneys, including Edwin Stanton of Pittsburgh, and does not participate in trial, but stays to watch arguments. Lincoln's earnings now total about $5,000 a year.

1856   Re-argues McLean County tax case before Illinois Supreme Court, January 16–17 (court later rules in railroad's favor, but Lincoln is forced to sue railroad for payment of his fee). Attends meeting of anti-Nebraska newspaper editors, held in Decatur on February 22, that calls for convention to organize new free-soil political party. Joins in founding Republican Party of Illinois at convention in Bloomington, May 29, and inspires delegates with address that goes unrecorded (later known as the "Lost Speech"). Receives 110 votes from eleven delegations on first ballot for vice-presidential nomination at the first Republican national convention, held in Philadelphia, June 19. Makes more than fifty speeches throughout Illinois as presidential elector for Republican candidate John C. Frémont.

1857   Helps prosecute murder case in which defendant is acquitted for reasons of insanity. Wins suit against Illinois Central Railroad over his fee in the McLean County tax case on June 23 (receives $4,800 in August as balance of $5,000 billed, his largest legal fee, and continues to represent Illinois Central in important litigation). Delivers major speech against Dred Scott decision in Springfield on June 26. Visits New York City, Niagara Falls, and Canada with wife in late July. In September defends Rock Island Railroad in the *Effie Afton* case, involving steamboat destroyed by fire after striking the first railroad bridge across the Mississippi River. Trial ends when jury deadlocks 9–3 in railroad's favor, a significant setback to riverboat interests in their efforts to block railroad expansion.

1858   In May, wins acquittal for William (Duff) Armstrong, son of New Salem friends Jack and Hannah Armstrong, by using almanac to discredit testimony of key prosecution witness as to height of the moon at time of alleged murder, and by suggesting that deceased had died because of a drunken fall from his horse. Charges no fee for defense. Accepts endorsement on June 16 by the Republican state convention at Springfield as its "first and only choice" for Senate seat held by Douglas and delivers "House-Divided" speech. Attends speech by Douglas in Chicago, July 9, and replies the following day. Begins following Douglas through state, occasionally riding as ordinary passenger on the same train that carried Douglas in his private car. On July 24, invites Douglas to "divide time" on the same platform for remainder of campaign. Douglas declines, but agrees to seven debates, which are held on August 21, 27, September 15, 18, and October 7, 13, 15. Audiences at debates probably number between 10,000 and 15,000, except for about 1,200 at Jonesboro on September 15 and perhaps as many as 20,000 at Galesburg on October 7. Both candidates also deliver scores of speeches throughout state, concentrating on counties of central Illinois. Republicans win a plurality in the election on November 2, but they do not gain control of the legislature because of Democratic holdovers and an unfavorable apportionment of seats. In December, Lincoln assembles newspaper clippings of debates and major campaign speeches in scrapbook.

1859   Legislature reelects Douglas to the Senate on January 5 by vote of 54 to 46. Lincoln begins negotiations in March for publication of debates. Son Robert fails Harvard College entrance exams and enrolls at Phillips Exeter Academy in New Hampshire. From August to October Lincoln makes speeches for Republican candidates in Iowa, Ohio, and Wisconsin. Begins to be mentioned as possible presidential candidate. In fall makes last trip through Eighth Circuit (reduced to five counties in 1857). Speaks in Kansas before its territorial elections in early December.

1860   Delivers address on slavery and the framers of the Constitution to audience of 1,500 at Cooper Union in New York City on February 27. Visits Robert at Exeter and speaks to enthusiastic crowds in Rhode Island, New Hampshire, and Connecticut before returning to Springfield. *Political Debates between Hon. Abraham Lincoln and Hon. Stephen A. Douglas in the Celebrated Campaign of 1858, in Illinois*, printed from Lincoln's scrapbook, published in March by Follett, Foster & Co. in Columbus, Ohio. Republican state convention, meeting at Decatur on May 10, instructs Illinois delegation to vote for Lincoln at national convention. Lincoln remains in Springfield while team of supporters, led by Judge David Davis and Norman B. Judd, chairman of the Illinois Republican state central committee, canvasses delegates at Republican national convention in Chicago. Wins nomination for president on the third ballot, May 18, defeating main rival Senator William H. Seward of New York as well as Senator Simon Cameron of Pennsylvania, Senator Salmon P. Chase of Ohio, and Edward Bates of Missouri. Learns of his victory and of nomination of Senator Hannibal Hamlin of Maine for vice-president at office of *Illinois State Journal*. Studies platform, which opposes the extension of slavery, vaguely endorses a protective tariff policy, and calls for homestead legislation, internal improvements, and a transcontinental railroad. Following established practice, Lincoln does not campaign and makes no formal speeches, but corresponds extensively with Republican leaders. Makes one of his last court appearances on June 20 in a federal patent case. (At conclusion of legal career has net worth of approximately $15,000.) Hires 28-year-old John G. Nicolay and 22-year-old John Hay as personal secretaries. Son Robert is admitted to Harvard College. Follows election returns in Springfield telegraph office, November 6. Defeats Stephen A. Douglas (Northern Democratic), John C. Breckinridge of Kentucky (Southern Democratic), and John Bell of Tennessee (Constitutional Union) to become first Republican president. Receives 180 of the 303 electoral votes while winning plurality of 40 percent of the popular vote. Meets with Republican leaders in Springfield, considers Cabinet appointments, and is beset by office-seekers. South Carolina secedes from the Union on December 20 (Mississippi, Florida, Alabama, Georgia, Louisiana, and Texas follow within two months).

1861   Works on inaugural address. Sees stepmother for the last time at her home in Coles County, January 31–February 1. Leaves Springfield by train on February 11, making brief speeches and appearances in Indiana, Ohio, Pennsylvania, New York, and New Jersey. Warned in Philadelphia that he might be assassinated in Baltimore, travels secretly to Washington on night of February 22–23; trip is ridiculed by opposition press. Finishes selecting Cabinet that includes the other major contenders for the Republican presidential nomination: William H. Seward (secretary of state), Salmon P. Chase (secretary of the treasury), Simon Cameron (secretary of war), and Edward Bates (attorney general), as well as Gideon Welles (secretary of the navy), Montgomery Blair (postmaster general), and Caleb B. Smith (secretary of the interior). Inaugurated on March 4. Decides, after much discussion with Cabinet, to send naval expedition to resupply Fort Sumter in Charleston harbor. Confederates open fire on the fort, April 12, and its garrison surrenders two days later. On April 15, Lincoln calls forth 75,000 militia and summons Congress to meet on July 4 in special session. Meets with Douglas, who supports Lincoln's efforts to preserve the Union and advises calling for 200,000 troops. Virginia secedes on April 17 and is followed within five weeks by North Carolina, Tennessee, and Arkansas, forming eleven-state Confederacy. On April 19, Lincoln proclaims blockade of Southern ports, and on April 27 he authorizes the military to suspend the writ of habeas corpus along the Philadelphia–Washington railroad line. Issues proclamation on May 3 directing expansion of the regular army and navy. Consults with various members of Congress, including Massachusetts senator Charles Sumner, beginning a personal friendship. Suffers first sense of personal loss in the war at the news of the death on May 24 of his young friend Colonel Elmer Ellsworth, shot while removing a Confederate flag from a building in Alexandria. Disregards *Ex parte Merryman* opinion of Chief Justice Roger B. Taney, finding his suspension of habeas corpus unconstitutional (Taney had sought unsuccessfully to enforce a writ issued by himself, not the full Court, which did not hear the case). Has White House draped in mourning after Douglas dies in Illinois on June 3 while rallying support for the Union. Follows progress of battle and Union defeat at Bull Run, July 21, from War Department telegraph office (will receive news and send orders from there for remainder of war). Appoints George B. McClellan commander of the Department (later Army) of the Potomac on July 27. Sees visitors, including Cabinet members, senators, congressmen, military officers, office-seekers, and ordinary citizens, for several hours each weekday. Often takes carriage rides in the afternoon. Writes letters and signs commissions in the evening. Enjoys attending theater, opera, and concerts. Reads Shakespeare, the Bible, and humorous writings of Artemus Ward, Orpheus C. Kerr, and Petroleum V. Nasby. On September 11, revokes General John C. Frémont's proclamation of emancipation in Missouri, bitterly disappointing many antislavery advocates. Saddened by death on October 21 of friend and former Illinois Whig colleague Edward D. Baker in skirmish at Ball's Bluff, Virginia. On October 24, signs order relieving Frémont of his command. Replaces him with General David Hunter. On November 1, appoints McClellan commander of the Union army after Winfield Scott retires. In message to Congress, December 3, recommends program of emancipation and colonization for slaves confiscated from Confederate owners. After Cabinet meetings on December 25 and 26, agrees to the release of two Confederate envoys seized from British ship *Trent* in November, resolving serious Anglo-American crisis.

1862 Reads General Henry Halleck's *Elements of Military Art and Science*. Meets with congressional Committee on the Conduct of the War and rejects demand of its chairman, Ohio Republican senator Benjamin Wade, that McClellan be dismissed for inaction. On January 13, replaces Simon Cameron with Democrat Edwin Stanton amid charges of widespread corruption and incompetence in the War Department. Nominates Noah Swayne of Ohio to the Supreme Court. Issues General War Order No. 1 on January 27, calling for a simultaneous Union advance on several fronts beginning February 22. Is frustrated by McClellan's unwillingness to take offensive action in Virginia. Recommends promotion of Ulysses S. Grant to major general after capture of Fort Donelson in Tennessee by Grant's army on February 16. Son Willie falls ill in early February (probably with typhoid fever) and dies on February 20. Wife is overcome with grief and never recovers emotionally. Lincoln relieves McClellan as general-in-chief on March 11 and assumes direct command of the Union armies (retains McClellan as commander of the Army of the Potomac). Appoints Halleck as commander of western armies. Reluctantly agrees to McClellan's plan for an advance on Richmond by way of the peninsula between the York and James rivers and is frustrated by its slow progress. Signs act on April 16 abolishing slavery in the District of Columbia. Refuses to dismiss Grant, who is widely blamed for heavy Union losses at battle of Shiloh. Visits Peninsula, May 5–12, and directs successful Union attack on Norfolk, Virginia. On May 15, approves legislation establishing the Department of Agriculture, and signs the Homestead Act on May 20. Visits General Irvin McDowell's corps at Fredericksburg, May 22–23. On May 24, concerned about safety of Washington, cancels planned movement of McDowell's troops to join McClellan's army near Richmond and orders that McDowell launch an attack on Thomas (Stonewall) Jackson's command in the Shenandoah Valley. To escape the heat, moves with family in early June to cottage at Soldiers' Home on hill four miles northwest of White House (will live there each summer). On June 19, approves legislation prohibiting slavery in the territories. Issues order on June 26 that consolidates Union forces in the Shenandoah Valley and northern Virginia as the Army of Virginia, under General John Pope. Signs Pacific Railroad Act and bill providing land grants for agricultural colleges on July 2. Visits Peninsula, July 7–10, conferring with McClellan and his corps commanders in aftermath of the Seven Days' battles. Returns to Washington and appoints Halleck general-in-chief on July 11 (does not name new overall western commander to replace Halleck). Nominates Iowa Republican Samuel Miller to Supreme Court. On July 17, signs Second Confiscation Act, authorizing seizure of slaves and other property of persons found by federal courts to be supporting the rebellion, after Congress appends resolution satisfying most of his reservations. Reads draft of preliminary Emancipation Proclamation to Cabinet on July 22, but delays issuing it, apparently agreeing with Seward that it should follow a Union military victory to avoid being seen as an act of desperation. Agrees with Halleck's decision to abandon Peninsula campaign and withdraw Army of the Potomac (order is issued on August 3); move is widely criticized, with campaign's failure attributed to Lincoln's withholding of troops for defense of Washington. Relieves Pope after his defeat at the second battle of Bull Run, August 29–30, and places his army under McClellan's command, despite distrust of McClellan in the Cabinet and Congress. Union victory at Antietam on September 17 ends Lee's invasion of Maryland. Lincoln issues preliminary Emancipation Proclamation on September 22, to take effect January 1, 1863, in all territory still in rebellion against the national government. Worried by significant Democratic gains in fall congressional and state elections. Nominates his friend David Davis to the Supreme Court. Removes Don Carlos Buell from command of the Army of the Ohio, October 23, and replaces him on October 30 with William Rosecrans (command becomes Army of the Cumberland). Replaces McClellan with Ambrose Burn-

side as commander of the Army of the Potomac on November 5, and confers with Burnside at Aquia Creek, Virginia, on November 27. In annual message to Congress,
December 1, recommends constitutional amendment authorizing gradual, compensated emancipation. Extends
clemency to 265 of 303 Sioux Indians condemned to death
after summer uprising in Minnesota. Army of the Potomac
suffers costly defeat at Fredericksburg on December 13.
Lincoln holds lengthy meeting on December 19 with Cabinet (excluding Seward) and nine senators from Republican caucus seeking Seward's dismissal and greater Cabinet
role in running government. Meeting results in submission of resignation by Chase, Seward's chief Cabinet
critic; Lincoln rejects it, along with previously submitted
resignation of Seward, thereby resolving crisis. Signs bill
on December 31 admitting West Virginia to the Union.

1863   On January 1, issues the Emancipation Proclamation freeing all slaves in Confederate-held territory. Responding
to protests, on January 4 revokes Grant's order of December 17, 1862, that expelled all Jews from the Department
of Tennessee. John P. Usher succeeds Caleb B. Smith as
secretary of the interior. Appoints Joseph Hooker to succeed Burnside on January 25. Approves bill on February 25
creating a national banking system, and signs act on
March 3 introducing military conscription. Nominates
California judge Stephen J. Field to the Supreme Court.
Concerned by allegations that Grant is incompetent and
frequently drunk, is reassured by reports of Charles A.
Dana, Stanton's special emissary at Grant's headquarters.
April 4–10, visits Army of the Potomac at its winter quar-
ters in Falmouth, Virginia, and views Fredericksburg bat-
tlefield from Union front line. Battle of Chancellorsville,
May 1–4, ends in Union defeat, and Lincoln returns to
Falmouth on May 7 to confer with Hooker. Replaces
Hooker with George G. Meade, June 28, during Lee's invasion of Pennsylvania. Greatly encouraged by Lee's defeat
at Gettysburg on July 3 and by capture of Vicksburg, last
major Confederate stronghold on the Mississippi, by
Grant's army on July 4. Discusses recruitment and treatment of Negro troops with abolitionist Frederick Douglass at White House on August 10; Douglass is impressed
by seriousness with which Lincoln receives him. Encouraged by victories of administration supporters in Ohio

and Pennsylvania state elections. With Chattanooga under Confederate siege after the Union defeat at Chickamauga, September 19–20, appoints Grant to command of all operations in the western theater and authorizes him to replace Rosecrans with George H. Thomas as commander of the Army of the Cumberland. Delivers dedicatory address at the Gettysburg Cemetery on November 19 to audience of 15,000–20,000, following two-hour oration by Edward Everett. Ill with varioloid (mild form of smallpox) for three weeks after return to Washington. Issues proclamation of amnesty and reconstruction, a program for restoration of the Union, on December 8. Retains Chase in Cabinet despite Chase's willingness to challenge him for the Republican nomination.

1864 "Pomeroy Circular," a letter produced by radicals supporting Chase's candidacy and distributed to influential Republicans, is published in late February. It embarrasses Chase and rallies support for Lincoln. He receives endorsement for second term from Republican caucus in Ohio, Chase's home state, and in early March Chase withdraws from campaign. On March 12, appoints Grant general-in-chief of the armies, Halleck chief of staff, and William T. Sherman as Grant's successor commanding in the West. Grant makes his headquarters with the Army of the Potomac while retaining Meade as its commander. Responding to a recommendation from Lincoln and Stanton, Congress repeals provision in conscription law that allows payment of $300 in lieu of service. Signed by Lincoln on July 4, the act retains the provision that permits hiring a substitute. Nominated for president June 8 on first ballot by nearly unanimous vote of the National Union Convention, a coalition of Republicans and War Democrats. Convention nominates Democrat Andrew Johnson, military governor of Tennessee, for vice-president and endorses proposed constitutional amendment abolishing slavery. Lincoln accepts Chase's resignation on June 30 and names Republican senator William P. Fessenden of Maine as his successor. Pocket-vetoes the Wade-Davis bill, congressional reconstruction plan he considers too severe, on July 4. Observes fighting on outskirts of Washington from parapet of Fort Stevens during unsuccessful Confederate attack, July 11–12, and comes under fire. Writes private memorandum on August 23, acknowledging that he probably will not be reelected. Feels less pessimistic about his election prospects after capture of Atlanta by Sherman's army on September 2 and General Philip H. Sheridan's decisive victory in the Shenandoah Valley at Cedar Creek on October 19. Appeases Republican radicals by replacing conservative Montgomery Blair as postmaster general with William Dennison on September 23. On Grant's advice, approves Sherman's planned march from Atlanta to the sea. Follows election returns at War Department telegraph office on November 8. Defeats Democratic nominee, General George B. McClellan, winning 55 percent of popular vote and 212 of 233 electoral votes. Appoints James Speed (brother of friend Joshua F. Speed) as attorney general to replace retiring Edward Bates. Nominates Salmon P. Chase as chief justice of the Supreme Court on December 6.

1865   Uses influence to gain some Democratic support in House of Representatives for resolution proposing submission of Thirteenth Amendment, abolishing slavery, to states for ratification (Senate had approved amendment in April 1864). House passes resolution by three-vote margin on January 31. Meets with Confederate representatives in unsuccessful peace conference at Hampton Roads, Virginia, on February 3. Signs bill on March 3 creating bureau for relief of freedmen and refugees. Inaugurated for second term on March 4. Names Comptroller of the Currency Hugh McCullough as secretary of the treasury when Fessenden returns to Senate. Leaves for City Point, Virginia, on March 23 and confers with Grant, Sherman, and Admiral David D. Porter on military and political situation, March 27–28. Visits Richmond on April 4 after its evacuation by the Confederate army. Returns to Washington on April 9, the day of Lee's surrender to Grant at Appomattox Court House. Makes last public speech on April 11, devoting it mainly to problems of reconstruction. Shot in the head by well-known actor John Wilkes Booth while watching performance of comedy *Our American Cousin* at Ford's Theatre shortly after 10 P.M., April 14. Dies in nearby house without regaining consciousness at 7:22 A.M., April 15. After funeral service in the White House on April 19, casket is viewed by millions as it is carried by special train to Illinois before burial in Oak Ridge Cemetery, outside Springfield, on May 4.

Note on the Texts

This volume presents the texts of 240 letters, speeches, poems, drafts, and fragments written or delivered by Abraham Lincoln from March 9, 1832, to December 11, 1858. Almost all of the texts included here are from the first three volumes of the Abraham Lincoln Association's *The Collected Works of Abraham Lincoln* (eight volumes and an index, 1953–55), edited by Roy P. Basler, with the assistance of Marion Dolores Pratt and Lloyd A. Dunlap. Eleven items are from *The Collected Works of Abraham Lincoln: Supplement 1832–1865* (1974), edited by Roy P. Basler, and four letters are from "Lincoln's Published Writings: A History and Supplement," by Thomas F. Schwartz, in the *Journal of the Abraham Lincoln Association* (1987).

Many of the items in this volume existed only as autograph manuscript during Lincoln's lifetime. His speeches, however, were often printed in newspapers, based on reporters' shorthand transcriptions and notes or set from manuscripts provided by Lincoln. Some pieces were written by him specifically for newspaper publication and a few of his speeches were printed in pamphlet form. Lincoln prepared a scrapbook of his campaign in 1858 against Stephen A. Douglas for the U.S. Senate, which included newspaper clippings of separate speeches by the candidates as well as the debates between them. He made a few corrections of his own words (but none of Douglas's) and deleted reports of the audience's reactions. The scrapbook text was published, with Lincoln's cooperation, as *Political Debates* in 1860.

The first major collection of Lincoln's writings was the *Complete Works of Abraham Lincoln*, edited by John G. Nicolay and John Hay, published first in two volumes in 1894 and later expanded to twelve volumes in 1905. Nicolay and Hay had served as secretaries to Lincoln during his presidency, and they prepared the *Complete Works* with the cooperation of Lincoln's son, Robert Todd Lincoln, who gave them access to a large archive of papers under his control. Their edition continues to be valuable because it is the only source for some items of which the originals have since been lost or destroyed.

However, Nicolay and Hay frequently made changes in Lincoln's spelling, diction, punctuation, sentence structure, and paragraphing. Subsequent collections of Lincoln's writings, which were published as new material was found in the decades following the Nicolay and Hay edition, also adopted editorial policies that allowed great freedom with the original documents.

In contrast, Roy P. Basler, as editor of *The Collected Works* (1953–55), and its *Supplement* (1974), restricted the emendation of previously printed pieces to the correction of typographical errors, and he transcribed and printed manuscripts without alterations, except in a few instances: a single period after abbreviations and initials replaces the double period Lincoln often used, and periods are substituted for the dashes Lincoln used to close his sentences. Basler began his editorial work for the Abraham Lincoln Association in 1947, using its large collection of Lincoln materials, as well as the recently opened Robert Todd Lincoln Collection in the Library of Congress, which contained material that previously had been available only to Nicolay and Hay. If an item still existed in manuscript and was not later revised by Lincoln, he used that version, showing variants in printed versions either in brackets or in footnotes. If an item existed in manuscript but was subsequently revised by Lincoln, Basler usually used the revised version, and printed the earlier readings in footnotes. Where no manuscript source was available, the editors of *The Collected Works* chose the best alternative source as their copy, usually the newspaper version that most fully reported Lincoln's words. If a second newspaper version provided significant variants, Basler showed these either in brackets or in footnotes. For the Lincoln-Douglas debates, *The Collected Works* used Lincoln's scrapbook copy, incorporating Lincoln's handwritten corrections and restoring the crowd reactions that Lincoln had deleted. In a few cases, when the original source for an item could not be found or was no longer available for publication, Basler took the text from a later printed version, most often from the Nicolay-Hay edition.

Because *The Collected Works* (1953–55), and its *Supplement* (1974), best preserves Lincoln's own usage, the texts from that edition are printed here. The following are the eleven items in this volume taken from the *Supplement*: To Andrew McCormick, c. December 1840–January 1841 (dated January 1841? in the *Supplement*); To Benjamin F. James, December 6, 1845; To David Davis, February 12, 1849; Notes on the Practice of Law, 1850?; To Richard J. Oglesby, September 8, 1854; To Jonathan Y. Scammon, November 10, 1854; To Richard Yates, January 14, 1855; To David Davis, July 7, 1856; To Ozias M. Hatch, March 24, 1858; To Ebenezer Peck, August 23, 1858; To Norman B. Judd, November 15, 1858. Since that edition appeared a few more letters have been found. The following are the four letters in this volume taken from "Lincoln's Published Writings: A History and Supplement" by Thomas F. Schwartz in the *Journal of the Abraham Lincoln Association* (1987): To Thomas Ewing, June 22, 1849; To Thomas Ewing, October 13, 1849; To Lyman Trumbull, June 27, 1856; To Newton Deming and George P. Strong, May 25, 1857.

In the present volume bracketed conjectural readings provided by Basler in cases where the original manuscript text was damaged or difficult to read are accepted without brackets when that reading seems the only possible one; otherwise the missing words are indicated by a bracketed space, i.e., [   ]. Errors made by Lincoln in manuscript were most often omissions or repetitions of words and letters. A similar rule is followed in these cases. If Lincoln's omission could be filled by any of several words, Basler's bracketed conjectural reading is not accepted and the sentence is printed as Lincoln wrote it. The present volume eliminates the editorial *sic* and makes the correction in the one instance where Lincoln included an extra letter (at 749.34, "selected" rather than "seclected [*sic*]") and in the eighteen instances where Lincoln repeated words (for example at 72.30, "other" rather than "other other [*sic*]"). In addition, three of Lincoln's slips of the pen are corrected in the present volume even though the words were not followed by "[*sic*]" or corrected with brackets in Basler: at 355.11, "every" is changed to "ever"; at 370.12, "Fremomont" is changed to "Fremont"; and at 373.39, "Buchan" is changed to "Buchanan."

Where there were apparent errors in the printed text, the editors of *The Collected Works* printed the error and bracketed the conjectural correction next to it; for example at 319.4, the newspaper version read "Missouri" instead of "Mexican." The editors showed this by "Missouri [Mexican?]." (A few other examples of this kind of correction occur at 322.9, "acquaintances [acquisitions?]"; 335.26, "agrees [aggresses?]"; 337.22, "few [free?]".) If the conjectural reading is clearly correct, this volume removes the brackets and accepts the editorial emendation. In those cases where bracketed words were inserted by Basler to show variant readings among two or more printed sources, the present volume removes the bracketed word (some of these variants can be found in the notes to this volume). A few errors in the originals not corrected in *The Collected Works* are corrected here: at 53.18, "officers?" is changed to "officer"; at 406.38, "found" is changed to "bound"; at 550.39, "I will stand" is changed to "I will not stand"; at 587.13, "In 1858" is changed to "In 1852"; at 597.35, "case," is changed to "case."; at 624.8, "statement?" is changed to "statement."; and at 693.23, "is not" is changed to "is."

This volume presents the texts of the editions chosen for inclusion here but does not attempt to reproduce features of their typographic design. Some headings have been changed, and Abraham Lincoln's name at the end of letters (which he almost invariably signed "A. Lincoln") has been omitted. The texts are printed without alteration except for the changes previously discussed and for the correction of typographical errors. Spelling, punctuation, and capitalization are often expressive features, and they are not altered, even when inconsistent or irregular.

The following is a list of typographical errors corrected, cited by page and line number: 7.18, petion; 24.3, anwers; 71.33, than; 103.21, Your; 104.9, new—; 124.15, clcaims; 168.12, envasion; 175.28, hmiself; 180.30, Indiana.; 185.14, *aggression*"; 223.28, space; 237.25, friend; 237.31, paper; 238.3, in the; 243.19, right. ¶What; 301.18, misdemesnor; 355.10, 5?.; 358.37, Your; 367.7, electe; 367.14, spoke the; 367.19, speakes; 388.7, that first; 388.11, plaintiffs; 388.16, Libellants; 388.20, cases; 395.8, in part;; 427.22, *not exclude*; 481.11, appology; 513.11, upon with; 564.8, stand; 603.18, us; 614.32, around.; 618.4,

[Applause.]; 626.6, answered by; 628.7, vote.; 651.33–34, did Trumbull; 668.21, 2d.; 671.34, *Republicanism.*; 753.34, wrong; 774.17, MR.; 823.20, elements; 827.23–24, "toleration ["] by necessity. Error corrected fifth printing: 101.15, Geod. Error corrected ninth printing: 808.11, undertand.

Notes

In the notes that follow, the reference numbers denote page and line of this volume (the line count includes item headings). No note is made for material included in a standard desk-reference book. Correspondents and names mentioned by Lincoln are identified only when they are essential to an understanding of the text. Prefatory and end notes within the text are Lincoln's own. For more detailed notes and references to other studies, see *The Collected Works of Abraham Lincoln*, 8 volumes plus index (New Brunswick: Rutgers University Press, 1953–55), edited by Roy P. Basler, Marion Dolores Pratt, and Lloyd A. Dunlap; *The Collected Works of Abraham Lincoln: Supplement 1832–1865* (Westport, Connecticut: Greenwood Press, 1974), edited by Roy P. Basler; *Lincoln Day by Day: A Chronology*, 3 volumes (Washington, D.C.: Lincoln Sesquicentennial Commission, 1960), edited by Earl Schenck Miers, William E. Baringer, and C. Percy Powell; and Mark E. Neely, Jr., *The Abraham Lincoln Encyclopedia* (New York: McGraw-Hill, 1982).

7.1   *Mary S. Owens*] Owens (1808–77), the only woman besides Mary Todd whom Lincoln is known to have courted, came to New Salem from Kentucky in 1836 for an extended visit with her sister, Elizabeth Owens Abell.

9.5   Mr. Linder] Usher F. Linder (1809–76), an attorney and Democratic legislator. In 1838 Linder became a Whig, but his hatred of abolitionism caused him to return to the Democrats in the 1850s. He appeared with and against Lincoln in many law cases.

18.4   Resolutions] The resolutions passed by the legislature were more emphatically anti-abolitionist than the Stone-Lincoln statement.

19.31   hypo] Hypochondria, hypochondriasm; at this time it meant a general depression of spirits.

21.1   *Second Reply*] In one of Lincoln's first law cases, he sought to recover for the heirs of Joseph Anderson a ten-acre parcel of land that had passed into the hands of Anderson's one-time attorney, James Adams. Lincoln charged that Adams, a man of dubious character but considerable local popularity, had forged the assignment on which his claim to the land rested. According to Lincoln, the spurious document had been discovered by Benjamin Talbott, the county recorder, when he was examining Adams's title to the property. The controversy between the two men was carried on not only in court but in handbills distributed to the public and in letters to the Springfield newspapers. The case never came to trial and was abated when Adams died in 1843.

21.15   *the election*] In the election of Sangamon County probate justice of the peace on August 5, 1837, Adams, a Democrat, defeated Whig candidate Dr. Anson G. Henry, Lincoln's friend and sometime physician.

23.33   Miller's deposition] Joseph Miller, who Adams claimed had lawfully deeded the land to him.

26.20–21   Burns . . . tryin,"] "Address to the Deil" (1786).

31.39–40   throw . . . editors] Lincoln's only reference to the recent lynching of abolitionist Elijah P. Lovejoy in nearby Alton, Illinois, on November 7, 1837. His printing press had been the target of previous attacks.

36.35   "the gates . . . it."] Matthew 16:18.

37.1   *Mrs. Orville H. Browning*] Née Eliza Caldwell, the wife of a Whig state senator from Quincy. The Brownings were personal friends of Lincoln's for the remainder of his life.

37.13   sister] Mary Owens.

40.1   *William Butler*] Butler was clerk of the Sangamon County circuit court.

41.27   Mr. Baker] Edward D. Baker (1811–61), a Whig state representative, 1837–40, state senator, 1840–44, congressman, 1845–47, 1849–51, and a Republican senator from Oregon, 1860–61. He was killed at the battle of Ball's Bluff on October 21, 1861.

44.20   Mr. Douglass] Stephen A. Douglas.

44.21   Locos] Democrats. A shorter form of "Locofoco," a name first derisively given to a dissident faction of New York Democrats. The term was later used for Democrats in general.

67.14   to beat Douglass] Stuart, Lincoln's first law partner, had been elected to Congress in 1838, defeating Stephen A. Douglas.

67.28   voting for Walters] William Walters, editor of the Democratic *Illinois State Register*, was a candidate for reelection as public printer by the state legislature.

68.16–18   I have . . . hypochondriaism] Lincoln was severely depressed for weeks after the breakup on January 1, 1841, of his engagement to Mary Todd.

69.2–3   General Ticket system] Election of congressmen at large throughout the state rather than in individual districts. The system was not adopted.

69.32   Judge Logan] Stephen T. Logan (1800–80), who became Lincoln's second law partner in the spring of 1841.

69.34   *Joshua F. Speed*] Speed (1814–82), Lincoln's closest friend, had left Springfield and returned to Kentucky early in 1841.

70.5–6   Archibald . . . murdered]   Nearly five years later, Lincoln wrote a longer account of this affair for newspaper publication. See "Remarkable Case of Arrest for Murder," pp. 130–37 in this volume.

70.40   *nolens volens*]   Willy-nilly.

73.34   *Mary Speed*]   Half-sister of Joshua F. Speed. Lincoln visited Farmington, the Speed family home near Louisville, in the late summer of 1841, and Speed then returned with him to Springfield for an extended visit.

75.1–2   "God . . . lamb,"]   From a French proverb, popularized in its English form by Laurence Sterne in *A Sentimental Journey through France and Italy* (1768).

75.17   Miss Fanny Henning]   The future wife of Joshua F. Speed.

76.4   the enterprize . . . in]   Speed's approaching marriage to Fanny Henning.

86.20–21   "While . . . return."]   Isaac Watts (1674–1748), *Hymns and Spiritual Songs* (1707), Book I, Hymn 88.

89.6–7   "these . . . army"]   Cf. Ezekiel 37:10.

89.7–9   "Come . . . live."]   Ezekiel 37:9.

93.13   fatal . . . Jany. '41.]   See note 68.16–18

95.29   "Stand . . . Lord"]   Exodus 14:13; 2 Chronicles 20:17.

96.16   *"Rebecca" Letter*]   Lincoln's contribution to a series of satirical attacks on Democratic state officials, especially James Shields, the state auditor.

98.13   Ford]   Thomas Ford (1800–50), governor-elect of Illinois.

98.14   Carpenter]   State treasurer Milton Carpenter.

99.9   Carlin]   Governor Thomas Carlin (1786–1852).

103.21   my duel with Shields]   The duel was called off when friends of Lincoln and Shields arranged a settlement of their quarrel, based on Lincoln's written explanation. See p. 102.20–30 of this volume.

105.32   Friend Richard: . . .]   The editors of the *Collected Works* were unable to find the original of this letter and used the text provided in *Uncollected Letters of Abraham Lincoln*, edited by Gilbert A. Tracy. This ellipsis is almost certainly Tracy's, indicating either his abridgment of the text, or an illegible portion of the original.

106.24   *To Martin S. Morris*]   The text of this letter is taken from a copy made by Morris, a Menard County Whig.

107.32   Hardin]   John J. Hardin (1810–47), a Whig, served in the Illinois House of Representatives, 1836–42, and was elected to Congress in 1843. He was killed at the battle of Buena Vista on February 23, 1847.

110.28–29   "coming events"]   Robert Todd Lincoln was born August 1, 1843.

113.1   *Benjamin F. James*]   Editor of the *Tazewell Whig*, published at Tremont.

113.19   Before Baker left]   Edward D. Baker had been elected to Congress in 1844 as John J. Hardin's successor.

114.34   Francis]   Simeon Francis (1796–1872), editor of the *Sangamo Journal* (later the *Illinois State Journal*), Springfield's Whig newspaper.

117.34   new plan]   John J. Hardin proposed to replace the convention system, which was itself a recent innovation, with what amounted to a primary election among Whig voters in the congressional district. Thirty-three electoral votes were to be apportioned among the eleven counties according to their representation in the lower house of the legislature, and the winner in each county was to receive its entire electoral vote.

120.1   *My Childhood-Home*]   This manuscript was apparently written early in 1846, though it may have been begun before then. In his letter to Andrew Johnston of February 24, 1846, Lincoln said that the piece was "almost done." A revised version of these verses was later published in the Quincy *Whig*. See Lincoln to Johnston, April 18, 1846, pp. 137–39; September 6, 1846, pp. 141–43; February 25, 1847, pp. 145–46, in this volume.

126.39   resolution . . . Pekin]   After Hardin's nomination for Congress in 1843, Lincoln had secured passage of a resolution declaring that the members of the convention recommended "E. D. Baker as a suitable person to be voted for by the whigs of this district, for Representative to Congress, at the election in 1844."

130.14   *Andrew Johnston*]   Johnston was an attorney practicing in Quincy, Illinois.

130.16–18   I have . . . enclosed.]   Lincoln sent Johnston a copy of "Mortality," by Scottish poet William Knox (1789–1825), better known by its first line: "O, why should the spirit of mortal be proud?" and first published in Knox's *The Songs of Israel* (1824). See Lincoln's comments on the poem in his letter to Johnston, April 18, 1846, p. 137.21–29 in this volume. Lincoln quotes six verses from the poem on pp. 254–55 in this volume.

130.27   *Remarkable Case*]   This version of a story previously recounted to Joshua F. Speed in a letter of June 19, 1841, (see pp. 69–73 in this volume) was written for publication and appeared first in the Quincy *Whig*.

138.5   four . . . cantos]   The available evidence indicates that Lincoln completed only three cantos.

140.12   *Allen N. Ford*]   Editor of the *Illinois Gazette*, published at Lacon.

140.19   Cartwright]   Peter Cartwright (1785–1872), a noted Methodist

circuit rider and Lincoln's unsuccessful Democratic opponent in the congressional election held on August 3, 1846.

145.20   another boy] Edward Baker Lincoln.

146.1   proposal to publish] The first two cantos (see pp. 138–39 and pp.
142–43 in this volume) appeared anonymously in the Quincy *Whig* of May 5,
1847. They were given the title "The Return" and subtitled "Part I — Reflection" and "Part II — The Maniac."

146.3   third canto] Probably "The Bear Hunt," as promised by Lincoln
in his letter of September 6, 1846. The third canto was not published.

153.21–22   "In . . . bread"] Genesis 3:19.

158.7–8   (The foregoing . . . Dec. 1847)] This parenthetical note was
written by Lincoln, probably in the summer of 1860.

161.1–2   *Speech . . . Mexico*] The text follows Lincoln's handwritten draft.
The version published in the *Congressional Globe* contains several emenda-
tions, presumably inserted by Lincoln in printer's proof. They are indicated
in succeeding notes.

164.4   equally incomprehensible.] After these words in the *Congressional
Globe* version, Lincoln inserted the following sentence: "The outrage upon
common *right*, of seizing as our own what we have once sold, merely because
it *was* ours *before* we sold it, is only equalled by the outrage on common *sense*
of any attempt to justify it."

166.33–35   This strange . . . design.] In the *Congressional Globe* version,
Lincoln revised this sentence to read: "In this strange omission chiefly consists the deception of the President's evidence — an omission which, it does
seem to me, could scarcely have occurred but by design."

166.39   point . . . case] In the *Congressional Globe* version, Lincoln
changed these words to "position pressed upon him by the prosecution."

168.28–29   Heaven against him] After these words in the *Congressional
Globe* version, Lincoln inserted the following clause: "; that he ordered General Taylor into the midst of a peaceful Mexican settlement, purposely to
bring on a war;".

171.11   *Jonathan R. Diller*] Postmaster in Springfield.

172.14   Mr. Ashmun's amendment] To a resolution praising General
Zachary Taylor, George Ashmun, Massachusetts Whig, offered an amendment condemning President James K. Polk. It was approved by a party-line
vote of 82 to 81.

174.3–5   Mr. Stephens . . . speech] Alexander H. Stephens (1812–83)
served in Congress, 1843–59, and was vice-president of the Confederacy,
1861–65. His speech denounced Polk's Mexican policy.

176.22   *Thomas S. Flournoy*]   Flournoy (1811–83) was a Whig congressman from Virginia, 1847–49.

177.20   *Solomon Lincoln*]   Solomon Lincoln lived in Hingham, Massachussetts.

184.6   desert . . . Nueces]   The area between the Nueces and Rio Grande rivers.

184.10   overthrow . . . Paredes]   Mexican president José Joaquín Herrera was forcibly ousted in late December 1845 by the more militant Mariano Paredes y Arrillaga, who became president in early January 1846.

185.18–19   "Whatsoever . . . them"]   Matthew 7:12.

185.32–33   Barnburners, Native Americans,]   Barnburners, the liberal wing of the New York State Democratic party, opposed the expansion of slavery and broke away to help form the Free Soil party in 1848. Native Americans (precursors of the Americans or Know-Nothings of the 1850s) were organized opponents of immigrant and Catholic influence in American public life.

186.4   the . . . Haman]   Cf. Esther, chapters 5–7.

193.12–13   "Bears . . . over."]   Cf. John Trumbull (1750–1831), *M'Fingal* (1775–76), Canto I.

197.24–25   Attempt . . . out.]   Robert Herrick (1591–1674), "Seek and Find," in *Hesperides* (1648).

197.31   Chicago convention]   The River and Harbor Convention that met in Chicago, July 5–7, 1847, in support of internal improvements legislation. Lincoln attended it as a delegate from Sangamon County.

199.32   hollow]   Variant of "hollo," to urge on by shouting.

206.28–29   None . . . variation.]   Instead of this sentence, Lincoln had earlier written and then crossed out in his manuscript: "They are more alike than the accounts of the crucifixion, as given by any two of the evangelists—more alike, or at least as much alike, as any two accounts of the inscription, written and erected by Pilate at that time."

207.3   Wilmot Proviso]   The proposal, first made in August 1846, that slavery be prohibited in any territory acquired from Mexico. It passed the House but not the Senate.

214.5   the broken sword]   Cass broke his sword rather than surrender it to the British following General Hull's capitulation at Detroit in 1812.

214.26   black . . . federalism]   The black cockade became a symbol of the Federalist party in 1798. Lincoln was presumably referring to the common Democratic charge that Whigs were latter-day Federalists.

220.3   one fell]   Hardin. See note 107.32.

221.34   *William Schouler*]   Editor of the Boston *Daily Atlas*, a Whig paper.

222.8   the Reserve]   The Western Reserve, a tract of land in the northeast corner of Ohio reserved by Connecticut when that state ceded the rest of its western land claim to the United States in 1786. Connecticut transferred jurisdiction over the reserve to the federal government in 1800, and it became part of the newly created Ohio Territory.

222.13–14   how Logan was defeated]   The defeat of his former law partner, Stephen T. Logan, by Democrat Thomas L. Harris in the race for the congressional seat held by Lincoln was attributed in some quarters to Lincoln's critical attitude toward the Mexican War.

222.30   *Fragment on Niagara Falls*]   Lincoln visited Niagara Falls in late September 1848, while returning to Illinois by way of the Great Lakes.

224.6   *John D. Johnston*]   The youngest son of Lincoln's stepmother, Sarah Bush Lincoln, by her first husband.

226.15   he should have *something*]   Davis was eventually appointed receiver of public monies in Springfield.

227.11   vote . . . resolution]   The House of Representatives had earlier passed a resolution calling for legislation prohibiting the slave trade in the District of Columbia. A motion to reconsider that action was pending when Lincoln read his proposed bill. The House did vote reconsideration later that same day, but Lincoln made no further effort to advance his proposal.

229.36   Land-office]   The position of commissioner of the General Land Office.

232.31   *William B. Preston*]   Preston (1805–62) was a Whig congressman from Virginia, 1847–49, and secretary of the navy in the Taylor administration, 1849–50.

233.27   *Josiah M. Lucas*]   A clerk at the Land Office in Washington and former publisher of a Whig newspaper, the *Illinoisan*, in Jacksonville, Illinois.

233.32–33   Butterfield]   Justin Butterfield, a leading Chicago attorney.

236.29   *Elisha Embree*]   An Indiana attorney, Embree (1801–63) was a Whig congressman, 1847–49.

237.13   *To Josiah B. Herrick*]   Herrick was an anatomy instructor at Rush Medical College in Chicago. Lincoln wrote similar letters to a number of men.

242.11   *John Addison*]   A clerk in the Interior Department.

243.32   withhold a recommendation]   On May 7, 1849, Lincoln had refused to recommend Rives for a position in Minnesota Territory, saying that he had already made one recommendation for a Minnesota appointment and did not want to weaken it by adding another.

247.3 Nov. 2nd,] Taylor was born on November 24.

254.23–24 "he . . . exalted."] Luke 14:11; 18:14.

254.35–255.20 "Oh, . . . proud!] From "Mortality," by William Knox. See Lincoln's comments on the poem, p. 137.21–29 in this volume.

255.24–25 Harriett] Harriett Hanks Chapman, daughter of Lincoln's stepsister, Elizabeth Johnston Hanks.

256.6 case of baby-sickness] The Lincolns' third son, William Wallace, was born on December 21, 1850.

256.10–11 He notes . . . heads;] Cf. Matthew 10:29–30; Luke 12:6–7.

256.23–24 Galatin & Saline . . . case] On July 3, 1851, the Illinois Supreme Court ruled that the legislature had unconstitutionally merged Gallatin and Saline counties.

257.14 Eastern forty acres] Ten years earlier, in order to relieve his father's financial distress, Lincoln had bought this land from him for $200, allowing both Thomas and Sarah Bush Lincoln to retain lifelong possession.

257.17 other two forties] These eighty acres, inherited from his father in 1851, Lincoln had deeded to Johnston for the sum of one dollar, subject to his stepmother's dower right of one-third use for life.

257.26 Chapman] Augustus H. Chapman, husband of Sarah Bush Lincoln's granddaughter, Harriett.

258.3 Abram] Johnston's son, age thirteen.

261.12–13 'One . . . die,'] Fitz-Greene Halleck, "Marco Bozzaris" (1825).

267.9 Mr. Jefferson . . . wrote:] In a letter to John Holmes, April 22, 1820.

273.27–28 "a fainting General;"] Pierce had fainted on August 19, 1847, after his horse fell on him and wrenched his knee during the advance on Churubusco. He fainted again the following day when he reinjured his knee while leading his men under fire. Both incidents had given rise to accusations of cowardice.

279.12–13 "And Enoch . . . him."] Genesis 5:24.

279.18 African church] The First African Baptist Church, a black congregation under a white minister, formed in 1841 when the First Baptist Church was divided along racial lines. Its building was frequently used for public meetings and entertainments.

282.6–7 The man . . . died.] Oliver Goldsmith (?1730–74), "Elegy on the Death of a Mad Dog."

285.17–18 burning . . . Caroline] On the night of December 29, 1837,

Canadian forces crossed to the American side of the Niagara River and burned the steamer *Caroline*, which had been carrying supplies to Canadian rebels led by William Lyon McKenzie.

287.12   a biographical sketch] *Life and Services of Gen. Pierce, Respectfully Dedicated to Gen'l Lewis Cass*, an anonymous pamphlet printed in Concord, Massachusetts. Allegedly published by the Democrats, it was probably the work of Whigs seeking to ridicule Pierce.

287.29–30   letter . . . Shields] Written on August 5, 1852, it appeared in the *Illinois State Register* on August 23.

295.34   His supposed . . . law"] On March 11, 1850, Seward made a speech in the Senate opposing Henry Clay's compromise measures. He argued that the prohibition of slavery in the federal territories was permitted by the Constitution and that slavery was unjust under "a higher law than the Constitution."

297.11   hunkerism] Hunkers were the conservative faction of the Democratic party in New York.

297.27   "Billy the Barber"] William Florville, a black resident of Springfield.

298.10   allowed . . . try.] Contrary to Lincoln's expectation, Turley found two witnesses who supported his claim, with the result that he was relieved of paying about fourteen years' interest on the note. In September 1853 Lincoln did obtain a judgment of $116.90 against Turley for his client, Lewis M. Hays.

298.11   *Thompson R. Webber*] Clerk of the Champaign County circuit court.

299.1   *Mason Brayman*] An attorney for the Illinois Central Railroad.

299.10   *James F. Joy*] Joy (1810–96) was general counsel for the Illinois Central Railroad.

303.22   *John M. Palmer*] Palmer (1817–1900) was a Democratic state senator from Macoupin County who joined the Illinois Republican party when it was formed in 1856. Later governor of Illinois (1869–73) and United States senator (1891–97), he was the presidential nominee of the "Gold" Democrats in 1896.

304.9   Major Harris] Thomas L. Harris, Democratic candidate for Congress in the Springfield district.

304.26   Yates' re-election] Richard Yates, Whig congressman, was defeated by Harris in the November election.

306.6   John Calhoun] Calhoun (1806–59) was an Illinois Democrat with whom Lincoln had debated two days earlier. He later served as president of the constitutional convention held at Lecompton, Kansas, in 1857 (see note 412.18).

307.1–2   *Speech . . . Peoria, Illinois*] Lincoln had already given much the same speech at Springfield on October 4 and had developed it in earlier speeches denouncing the Kansas-Nebraska Act.

309.9–10   prohibition . . . deed] In letters to John L. Scripps, June 16, 1860, and James O. Putnam, September 13, 1860, Lincoln acknowledged that this statement was erroneous.

322.8–9   "sufficient . . . thereof."] Matthew 6:34.

327.25–26   some . . . tread."] Alexander Pope, *An Essay on Criticism* (1711), line 625.

328.35   PRO TANTO] For so much; to that extent.

333.16   "It hath . . . it."] Cf. *Hamlet*, III, iii, 92.

339.10   Pettit] John Pettit (1807–77) was a Democratic congressman from Indiana, 1843–49, and served in the Senate, 1853–55.

346.4   Phillips] British orator Charles Phillips, author of *The Character of Napoleon* (1817).

349.16   decline . . . Representative] Lincoln had agreed to be a candidate for the General Assembly for the purpose of furthering the anti-Nebraska cause and helping Yates win reelection to Congress. He seems to have become only belatedly aware that the Illinois constitution prohibited the legislature from electing one of its own members to the U.S. Senate.

350.3–4   Republican party] This small group of antislavery militants had no organizational connection with the Republican party that Lincoln helped organize two years later in Illinois.

352.7   Wentworth] John Wentworth (1815–88), an antislavery Democrat who represented Chicago in Congress, 1843–51 and 1853–55, later the Republican mayor of Chicago, 1857–58 and 1860–61.

354.3   Bissell] William H. Bissell (1811–60), Democratic congressman who in 1856 became the first Republican to be elected governor of Illinois.

354.33   Govr. Matteson] Joel A. Matteson (1808–73), the incumbent governor of Illinois, a Democrat.

354.34   Koerner] Gustave P. Koerner (1809–96), the incumbent lieutenant-governor, an antislavery Democrat.

359.4   The volume] Robertson (1790–1874), a prominent Kentucky lawyer and judge, served in Congress, 1817–21, and taught law at Transylvania College in Lexington, 1834–57. His *Scrap Book on Law and Politics, Men and Times* was published in 1855.

359.8   exact question]   The effort in 1819 to prohibit slavery in Arkansas Territory, which Robertson, then a member of Congress, had opposed.

361.33   Reeder]   Andrew H. Reeder (1807–64), first governor of Kansas Territory (1854–55), who had recently been dismissed by President Franklin Pierce for supporting the free-soil settlers there.

363.11   Stringfellow]   Benjamin F. Stringfellow, leader of an armed pro-slavery group in Kansas.

364.28   "chalked hat"]   A railroad pass. Morgan was an official of the Chicago and Alton Railroad.

365.7   the job]   Lincoln had drawn up papers for Floyd in connection with the leasing of a Quincy, Illinois, hotel.

365.10   *Speech at Bloomington, Illinois*]   This brief newspaper report is the only contemporary record of Lincoln's famous "Lost Speech," said to be one of the greatest of his life in its effect upon his audience. It was delivered to the state convention of the newly organized Republican party. A "reconstruction" of the speech by Henry C. Whitney is considered highly unreliable.

365.18–19   "Liberty . . . inseparable."]   The final sentence of Daniel Webster's second reply to Robert Hayne of South Carolina, delivered on January 26, 1830, as part of their extensive debate in the U.S. Senate.

367.1   *To Lyman Trumbull*]   Parts of several lines are missing from the original, cut away along with Lincoln's signature on the reverse side.

367.5   had . . . McLean]   John C. Frémont had been nominated by the new Republican party as its first candidate for president, running against James Buchanan, Democrat, and Millard Fillmore, the candidate of the American or Know-Nothing party. Lincoln would have preferred the Republican choice to have been John McLean, associate justice of the U.S. Supreme Court.

367.25   Swett . . . Lovejoy]   Lincoln's friend Leonard Swett, seeking the Republican nomination for Congress, had been defeated by Owen Lovejoy, an abolitionist and the brother of Elijah P. Lovejoy (see note 31.39–40).

368.32   Judd and Peck]   Norman B. Judd, Chicago lawyer and politician, chairman of the Republican state central committee, 1856–60; Ebenezer Peck, a prominent Chicago Republican.

370.1   *On Sectionalism*]   This material was probably used in one or more of Lincoln's many speeches supporting John C. Frémont for president.

384.4   *Julian M. Sturtevant*]   President of Illinois College at Jacksonville, known for his antislavery views.

384.21   Twenty-two years ago]   This comment in Lincoln's handwriting can be approximately dated by his penciled note in a copy of an 1860 campaign biography that he first saw Douglas in December 1834.

385.25–26   "He's . . . cod."] Cf. *King Lear*, I, iv, 200.

387.1   *Notes for Speech*] Taken from two autograph pages, only the first of which is unquestionably part of Lincoln's speech at Chicago.

387.21   We were . . . history] Here begins the second page of the manuscript.

388.21   benefit . . . "nigger"] This is Lincoln's first recorded reference to the Dred Scott decision.

388.27   *On the Dred Scott Case*] Although the phrasing seems to date this fragment before the announcement of the Dred Scott decision on March 6, 1857, the argument is a comment on Democratic criticism of the Republican response to the decision. See especially the quotation from Douglas's Springfield speech of June 12, 1857, in Lincoln's own speech of June 26, 1857 (p. 393.26–39 in this volume).

394.6   veto message] Jackson vetoed the re-charter on July 10, 1832. The message was actually written by a group of his advisers, chiefly Amos Kendall and Roger B. Taney.

404.1–2   *Rock Island Bridge Case*] On May 6, 1856, the steamer *Effie Afton* crashed into one of the piers of the bridge, the first ever built across the Mississippi.

405.11   Judge Wead] Hezekiah M. Wead, counsel for the plaintiff and a former circuit judge.

406.34   Judge McLean] John McLean, associate justice of the U.S. Supreme Court, presided at the trial, which was held in U.S. circuit court.

412.2   a year ago] Referring to the campaign and election of 1856, this phrase indicates that the fragment was written sometime in the latter part of 1857.

412.18   Kansas constitution] The Lecompton constitution, adopted by a proslavery convention on November 7, 1857, was supported by Buchanan and opposed by Douglas.

412.27   *Draft of a Speech*] Only the last two paragraphs are known to be extant in Lincoln's handwriting. John G. Nicolay and John Hay, who presumably had the entire manuscript before them, dated it October 1, 1858, in their *Complete Works of Abraham Lincoln*; the editors of the *Collected Works* proposed May 18, 1858, as a likelier date; but the subject matter indicates that the manuscript (or most of it, at least) was written in late December 1857.

412.33   speech . . . Senate] Douglas spoke out against the Lecompton constitution on December 9, 1857, the day after Buchanan endorsed it in his annual message to Congress.

414.18–19   resolution . . . September] This resolution, endorsing the

Dred Scott decision and denouncing Negro equality, was allegedly dropped by Douglas in the Jacksonville, Illinois, railway station during a visit on September 9, 1857. It was printed in a local newspaper and subsequently adopted by the Morgan County Democratic convention.

414.20–21   Chicago . . . church"]   According to a report in the Chicago *Daily Democratic Press*, a hostile Republican newspaper, Douglas told an audience on November 11, 1857, that the Republicans would allow blacks to *"stink us out of our places of worship . . ."*

414.28   Cuffy]   A colloquial expression for Negroes, derived from *kofi*, a Gold Coast word for a boy born on Friday.

416.39   Silliman letter]   Written by Buchanan on August 15, 1857, in response to a protest against administration policy in Kansas signed by forty Connecticut educators and clergymen.

417.14   *A house . . . stand.*]   Cf. Matthew 12:25; Mark 3:25.

417.16   expressed . . . ago]   This statement seems to support the recollection of Lincoln's friend T. Lyle Dickey that Lincoln used the house-divided analogy in a speech at Bloomington on September 12, 1856. It is possible, however, that this part of the manuscript was written in 1859 and mistakenly included here by Nicolay and Hay.

418.29   "the sum . . . villanies"]   Cf. John Wesley (1703–91), *Journal*, February 12, 1772: "That execrable sum of all villainies, commonly called the Slave Trade."

420.1   *Ozias M. Hatch*]   Hatch (1814–93), a Republican, was elected secretary of state of Illinois in 1856 and reelected in 1860.

420.18–19   two . . . conventions]   The Lecompton controvery had split the Illinois Democratic party into Buchanan and Douglas factions, both of which held conventions in Springfield on April 21, 1858.

421.8   Charley Wilson]   Charles L. Wilson, editor of the Chicago *Journal*.

421.9   Dr. Ray]   Charles H. Ray, joint editor of the Chicago *Tribune*.

424.32   Buc. men]   Democrats who supported Buchanan rather than Douglas.

426.1   *"House Divided" Speech*]   There are two contemporary texts of this address. One was published in the *Illinois State Journal* from Lincoln's original manuscript (itself not preserved). The other was published in the Chicago *Tribune* from a shorthand transcript of the speech as delivered. Lincoln included the *Tribune* version in the scrapbook of the debates with Douglas that he assembled after the 1858 campaign, making some corrections and adding a prefatory note. The scrapbook text was then used in the publication of the debates as a book, *Political Debates between Hon. Abraham Lincoln and Hon. Stephen A. Douglas in the Celebrated Campaign of 1858, in Illinois* (1860). The editors of the *Collected Works* collated the two sources but inadvertently incorporated an error made in the *State Journal* version (see note 427.8–10).

427.8–10   But, so far . . . more.]   In the *Illinois State Journal* version this paragraph is erroneously located before the three preceding paragraphs, an error that is repeated in the *Collected Works*.

431.7   Stephen . . . James]   Stephen A. Douglas, Franklin Pierce, Roger B. Taney, and James Buchanan.

431.38   McLean or Curtis]   John McLean and Benjamin R. Curtis were the two dissenting justices in the Dred Scott decision.

432.6   Judge Nelson]   In the Dred Scott case, Justice Samuel Nelson had written a separate opinion, originally intended to be the opinion of the Court, ruling against Scott on narrower grounds than those given in Chief Justice Taney's opinion.

433.8–9   "a *living* . . . *lion.*"]   Ecclesiastes 9:4.

434.23   *John L. Scripps*]   Scripps (1818–66) had co-founded the Chicago *Daily Democratic Press* with William Bross in 1852. On July 1, 1858, it merged with the Chicago *Tribune* to form the *Press and Tribune*, and Scripps became an editor of the new paper.

436.2   croaking about Wentworth]   Some Democratic newspapers had been suggesting that John Wentworth, who had just completed a term as mayor of Chicago, would be the Republican candidate for the Senate.

436.14   The Times]   The Chicago *Times*, a Douglas organ.

438.19   my natural life.]   A version published in *Abraham Lincoln: A New Portrait* by Emanuel Hertz (1931) adds the following two sentences, which, because they do not appear in the existing facsimile of the autograph draft, have not been included here: "But I can not doubt either that it will come in due time. Even in this view, I am proud, in my passing speck of time, to contribute an humble mite to that glorious consummation, which my own poor eyes may not last to see."

439.1   *Speech at Chicago*]   The text follows that of the Chicago *Democrat*, as emended by Lincoln in the debates scrapbook. Some variations in the Chicago *Press and Tribune* version that seem more likely to be correct are indicated in following notes.

439.2–4   *The succeeding . . . present.*]   Prefatory statement written by Lincoln in the debates scrapbook. Douglas had spoken the day before, with Lincoln in the audience.

443.13   now]   In the *Press and Tribune*, "new."

443.21   John Calhoun]   See note 306.6

447.2   great]   In the *Press and Tribune*, "next."

450.17   those]   In the *Press and Tribune*, "those things."

453.21–22   Cincinnati platform]   Adopted by the Democratic national convention that nominated Buchanan for president in June 1856.

454.16   its ultimate extinction]   In the *Press and Tribune* this is followed by "— who will believe, if it ceases to spread, that it is in course of ultimate extinction."

455.33   understood]   In the *Press and Tribune*, "understand."

457.13   Turn in]   In the *Press and Tribune*, "Turn it."

457.23–24   why not]   In the *Press and Tribune*, "may not."

458.3–4   "As . . . perfect."]   Cf. Matthew 5:48.

460.1   *Speech at Springfield*]   The text follows the pamphlet reprint that Lincoln used in the debates scrapbook. Some variations in the *Illinois State Journal* version that seem more likely to be correct are indicated below.

460.2–3   *Delivered . . . present.*]   Prefatory statement written by Lincoln in the debates scrapbook. Douglas had spoken earlier the same day.

460.27   already taken]   At this point, according to the *State Journal*, a rocket went up outside a window, and Lincoln said: "I expect that we shall have as much of that as we can conveniently get along with. I was saying that . . ."

463.16   the matter]   In the *State Journal*, "this matter."

465.30   specially]   In the *State Journal*, "specifically."

466.24–26   Lecompton . . . bill]   In March 1858 the Senate voted to admit Kansas as a state under the proslavery Lecompton constitution, but the House of Representatives refused to do so, passing instead the Crittenden-Montgomery resolution, which called for resubmitting the constitution to the voters of Kansas. Both the House and the Senate then passed the compromise English bill, which resubmitted the Lecompton constitution under the guise of a land-grant referendum. It was overwhelmingly rejected on August 2, 1858.

466.37   parable . . . sheep]   Cf. Matthew 18:12–13; Luke 15:4–7.

469.20   reconstruct]   In the *State Journal*, "reconsider."

475.5   when he likes]   In the *State Journal*, "when he likes them."

475.12   nor opposed to any]   In the *State Journal*, "nor I opposed to any."

476.18   Americans]   Members of the American party, also known as the Know-Nothing party.

480.8   Americans]   Gillespie had for a time been associated with the American party.

481.9   Yours . . . 24th.]   Douglas, replying to Lincoln's letter of July 24, rejected the proposal that they canvass the state together and then made the following counterproposal: "I will, in order to accommodate you as far as it is in my power to do so, take the responsibility of making an arrangement with you for a discussion between us at one prominent point in each congressional district in the state, excepting the second and sixth districts, where we have both spoken and in each of which cases you had the concluding speech. If agreeable to you I will indicate the following places as those most suitable in the several congressional districts at which we should speak, to wit, Freeport, Ottawa, Galesburg, Quincy, Alton, Jonesboro and Charleston."

485.19   slave . . . Texas]   By the terms of annexation in 1845, Texas, with its own consent, could be divided into as many as five states.

487.18   *Draft of a Speech*]   The text follows that provided by Nicolay and Hay in their *Complete Works*. Only two manuscript pages of this document are known to be extant.

493.15   In this age]   From here on, the manuscript is extant.

495.1   *First Lincoln-Douglas Debate*]   The text of the debates includes various corrections and insertions written by Lincoln into the debates scrapbook.

495.3–5   *First . . . Tribune*]   This is Lincoln's prefatory note in the debates scrapbook, as are the notes at pp. 537.3–5, 636.3–4, 687.3–5, 730.3–5, and 774.3–5 in this volume.

499.28   Egypt]   A colloquial name for the southern, or the southernmost, part of Illinois.

500.10–11   grocery-keeper]   In frontier Illinois, a grocery was an establishment licensed to sell liquor by the drink. See Lincoln's reply, p. 512.24–29 in this volume.

528.20–24   MR. GLOVER . . . Good.")]   This interruption does not appear in the *Press and Tribune* account and was deleted by Lincoln from his debates scrapbook.

528.40–529.15   MR. LINCOLN . . . question.]   In the debates scrapbook, Lincoln deleted the pro-Douglas *Times* account of his interruption, which therefore went unmentioned in the 1860 edition of the debates. The incident was reported in the *Press and Tribune* as follows:

MR. LINCOLN—Let the Judge add that Lincoln went along with them.

JUDGE DOUGLAS.—Mr. Lincoln says let him add that he went along with them to the Senate Chamber. I will not add that for I do not know it.

MR. LINCOLN.—I do know it.

JUDGE DOUGLAS.—But whether he knows or not my point is this, and I will yet bring him to his milk on this point.

530.33–35   MR. LINCOLN . . . behind.)]   This paragraph was deleted from the debates scrapbook. The *Press and Tribune* did not report this interruption.

552.15   Deacon Bross] William Bross, one of the editors of the Chicago *Press and Tribune*, who sat on the speakers' platform. In the debates scrapbook, Lincoln deleted this and subsequent references to Bross's speaking, none of which appeared in the *Press and Tribune* account.

556.15–18   (Good, . . . even.)] This response, as well as the one at p. 567.33–35 in this volume, was not reported by the *Press and Tribune*. Lincoln deleted both of these passages from the debates scrapbook.

561.29   Crittenden-Montgomery bill] See note 466.24–26.

594.5–6   (Great . . . miserable.)] Lincoln deleted from the debates scrapbook this account of his reaction, as well as the ones at pp. 594.12–14, 594.39–40, 625.20–21, and 626.21–23 in this volume. None of them appeared in the *Press and Tribune* version.

613.17   I reckon . . . Cook] Isaac Cook (1810–86), Chicago postmaster and onetime Douglas supporter. He had helped found the Chicago *Times* in 1854 but was now siding with the Buchanan administration in its battle with Douglas.

635.15–18   I instantly . . . it.] The Chicago *Times* reported Lincoln as having said about Sweet (the name appears as "Swett" in their account): ". . . and there was Martin P. Swett 'sneaking about'—take back that ugly word (to the reporters), you must not put that in—doing all he could to help me along." Cf. the *Press and Tribune* account, p. 611.36–38 in this volume.

637.10–11   case . . . Johnson] Johnson, a Kentucky Democrat who was vice-president in the Van Buren administration, was widely known to have had a mulatto mistress.

639.18–19   Senator Bigler] William Bigler (1814–80) was a Democratic senator from Pennsylvania, 1856–61.

640.37   Toombs bill] A bill introduced by Senator Robert Toombs of Georgia that called for a new registration of Kansas voters by federal commissioners and the election of delegates to a convention for drawing up a state constitution. It passed the Senate in July 1856, but was not approved by the House.

678.28   Ford's history] *History of Illinois from its Commencement as a State in 1818 to 1847*, by Thomas Ford, published posthumously in 1854. See note 98.13.

684.19   "Long John"] John Wentworth, who was six feet six inches tall.

684.23–685.7   *Verses . . . 1858–*] Written in the autograph albums of the daughters of the proprietor of the Winchester, Illinois, hotel where Lincoln was staying.

685.22–23   Rev. Dr. Ross]   Probably a reference to the Reverend Frederick A. Ross (1796–1883), a Presbyterian minister in Huntsville, Alabama, author of *Slavery Ordained by God* (1857).

702.27–28   "he trembled . . . just;"]   Cf. *Notes on the State of Virginia* (1785), Query XVIII, "Manners."

764.4   "judge . . . judged."]   Cf. Matthew 7:1; Luke 6:37.

770.17–19   Mr. Clay . . . application,]   Henry Clay responded in a speech given at Richmond, Indiana, on October 1, 1842, to an emancipation petition presented by Mr. Mendenhall, a member of the Society of Friends.

774.10   Danite faction]   Buchanan Democrats.

822.24   foregoing extracts.]   This letter was written in a notebook sent to Brown, a former Whig state assemblyman. It contained seven newspaper clippings from Lincoln's speeches. In a prefatory note Lincoln wrote, "I believe they contain the substance of all I have ever said about 'negro equality.' " The first three extracts were from Lincoln's speech at Peoria on October 16, 1854 (pp. 315.14–317.11, pp. 328.16–329.9, and p. 346.8–27); the fourth, from his speech at Springfield on June 26, 1857 (pp. 398.19–399.11); the fifth, from his speech at Chicago on July 10, 1858 (pp. 454.33–458.35); the sixth, from his reply to Douglas in the first debate, held at Ottawa on August 21, 1858 (pp. 511.37–512.23); and the seventh, from his opening speech in the fourth debate, held at Charleston on September 18, 1858 (pp. 636.13–637.32; all page numbers refer to this volume).

824.34   Central Railroad Company]   For Lincoln's association with the Illinois Central, see his letters to Thompson R. Webber, September 12, 1853, and Mason Brayman, October 3, 1853, pp. 298–99 in this volume.

826.19   *Portion . . . Speech*]   This is printed from the two manuscript pages of the speech that are known to be extant.

827.29   *John J. Crittenden*]   Crittenden (1787–1863), a Kentucky Whig, was Henry Clay's successor in the U.S. Senate and a leading advocate of sectional compromise. Lincoln had written to him on July 7, 1858, about rumors that he intended to endorse Douglas in the Illinois senatorial contest. "I do not believe the story," Lincoln declared, "but still it gives me some uneasiness . . . You have no warmer friends than here in Illinois, and I assure you nine tenths—I believe ninety-nine hundredths—of them would be mortified exceedingly by anything of the sort from you." Crittenden replied on July 29 that he had been gratified by Douglas's opposition to the Lecompton constitution for Kansas and favored his reelection to the Senate as a rebuke to the Buchanan administration. Although the correspondence was not published during the campaign, a report of its existence appeared in the *Missouri Republican* of St. Louis (a Democratic newspaper). Crittenden accordingly wrote to Lincoln on October 27, disclaiming responsibility for the breach of confidentiality.

828.28–29   Millers majority] James Miller, the Republican candidate for state treasurer, received 125,430 votes, defeating William B. Fondey, the candidate of the Douglas Democrats, who received 121,609, and John Dougherty, a Buchanan Democrat, who received 5,071.

829.26   *Samuel C. Davis and Company*] Wholesale merchants in St. Louis, Missouri.

830.28   William Fishback] By this time, Fishback had moved to Arkansas. On December 19, 1858, Lincoln sent him $100 received from the Davis company and urged him to return to Illinois. "With the general chances of a young man, and additional business of the same sort we could . . . put in your hands," Lincoln wrote, "I feel confident you could make a living." Fishback chose to remain in Arkansas. In 1864 he was elected to the Senate by the state's new pro-Union legislature, but was prevented from taking his seat by the opposition of radical Republicans in Congress. He was elected governor of Arkansas in 1892.

831.5   *To Anson G. Henry*] The lower portion of the original of this letter has been cut away.

832.24–25   a candidate . . . District] Thomas L. Harris, the Democratic incumbent, had died on November 24. The special election to fill his seat was won by John A. McClernand, a Democrat.

Index

Cataloging Information

Lincoln, Abraham, 1809–1865.
  Speeches and Writings 1832–1858:
  Speeches, Letters, and Miscellaneous Writings;
  The Lincoln-Douglas Debates.
  Edited by Don E. Fehrenbacher

  (The Library of America ; 45)
  Includes index.
  1. Illinois—Politics and government—To 1865.
2. United States—Politics and government—1849–1861.
3. Lincoln, Abraham, 1809–1865—Political career
before 1861. I. Title. II. Series.
E457.92   1989   973.5   89–2362
ISBN 0–940450–43–7   (alk. paper)

For a list of titles in The Library of America, write:
The Library of America
14 East 60th Street
New York, New York 10022

THE LIBRARY OF AMERICA SERIES

The Library of America fosters appreciation and pride in America's literary heritage by publishing, and keeping permanently in print, authoritative editions of America's best and most significant writing. An independent nonprofit organization, it was founded in 1979 with seed money from the National Endowment for the Humanities and the Ford Foundation.

This book is set in 10 point Linotron Galliard,
a face designed for photocomposition by Matthew Carter
and based on the sixteenth-century face Granjon. The paper
is acid-free lightweight opaque and meets the requirements
for permanence of the American National Standards Institute.
The binding material is Brillianta, a woven rayon cloth made
by Van Heek-Scholco Textielfabrieken, Holland. Com-
position by The Clarinda Company. Printing by
Malloy Incorporated. Binding by Dekker Book-
binding. Designed by Bruce Campbell.

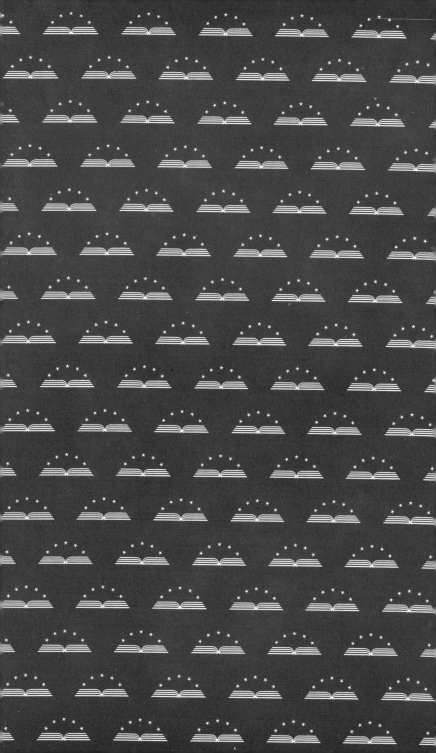